Springer Series on Comparative Treatments for Psychological Disorders

Arthur Freeman, EdD, ABPP, Series Editor

Mark A. Reinecke, Ph.D., is Associate Professor of Child and Adolescent Psychiatry and Director of the Center for Cognitive Therapy at the University of Chicago School of Medicine. He also serves on the faculty of the School of Social Service Administration and is Director of the Program in Mental Health Research at the University of Chicago. His research and clinical interests include childhood depression and suicide, cognitive and social vulnerability for depression, anxiety disorders, and cognitive mediation of adjustment to chronic illness. He has lectured internationally and served as a Visiting Assistant Professor at National Chengchi University, Taipei, Taiwan. Widely published, he is coauthor (with Arthur Freeman) of *Cognitive therapy of suicidal behavior* and coeditor (with Arthur Freeman and Frank Dattilio) of *Cognitive therapy with children and adolescents.* He is a diplomate of the American Board of Professional Psychology and is a Founding Fellow of the Academy of Cognitive Therapy.

Michael R. Davison, Psy.D., is on the core doctoral faculty at the Adler School of Professional Psychology. Dr. Davison teaches courses in psychological assessment, psychotherapy, psychopathology and Adlerian psychology. He is also a licensed clinical psychologist, and is in private practice in Arlington Heights and Crystal Lake, IL. His clinical and research interests include Cognitive and Adlerian treatment approaches of substance use disorders, sexual deviance, domestic violence and mood disorders. He has conducted professional workshops and seminars on various treatment, as well as on the assessment, prediction and treatment of physical and sexual violence. His previous publications have been in the area of the treatment of depression and brief therapy.

Comparative Treatments of Depression

Mark A. Reinecke, PhD
Michael R. Davison, PsyD
Editors

**Springer Series on
Comparative Treatments for
Psychological Disorders**

Springer Publishing Company, Inc.
536 Broadway
New York, NY 10012-3955

Acquisitions Editor: Sheri W. Sussman
Production Editor: Janice Stangel
Cover design by Joanne Honigman

02 03 04 05 06 / 5 4 3 2 1

Library of Congress Cataloging-in-Publication Data

Comparative treatments of depression / Mark A. Reinecke, Michael R. Davison, editors.
    p. cm. — (Springer series on comparative treatments for psychological disorders)
  Includes bibliographical references and index.
  ISBN 0-8261-4681-3
  1. Depression, Mental—Treatment. I. Reinecke, Mark A.
II. Davison, Michael R. III. Series.
RC537.C644 2002
616.85'2706—dc21   2002017007
                                                      CIP

Printed in the United States of America by Maple-Vail

Contents

Contributors

Larry E. Beutler, Ph.D.
Department of Education
University of California-Santa
   Barbara
Santa Barbara, California

Roslyn Caldwell, Ph.D.
Department of Education
University of California-Santa
   Barbara
Santa Barbara, California

Bertram Cohler, Ph.D.
Committee on Human
   Development
Department of Psychiatry
University of Chicago
Chicago, Illinois

Paul Crits-Christoph, Ph.D.
Department of Psychiatry
University of Pennsylvania School
   of Medicine
Philadelphia, Pennsylvania

Matthew J. Davis
Department of Psychology
University of Utah
Salt Lake City, Utah

Raymond DiGiuseppe, Ph.D.
Department of Psychology
St. John's University
New York, New York

E. Thomas Dowd, Ph.D.
Department of Psychology
Kent State University
Kent, Ohio

Kristene Doyle, Ph.D.
Department of Psychology
St. John's University
New York, New York

Norman Epstein, Ph.D.
Department of Family Studies
University of Maryland
College Park, Maryland

Robert M. Galatzer-Levy, M.D.
Department of Psychiatry
University of Chicago School of
   Medicine
Chicago, Illinois

Mary Beth Connolly Gibbons, Ph.D.
Department of Psychiatry
University of Pennsylvania School of Medicine
Philadelphia, Pennsylvania

Ilpo T. Kaariainen, M.D.
Department of Psychiatry
University of Chicago School of Medicine
Chicago, Illinois

Aaron Kaplan, Ph.D
Department of Psychology
University of Hawaii
Honolulu, Hawaii

Michael J. Lambert, Ph.D.
Department of Psychology
Brigham Young University
Provo, Utah

David Mark, Ph.D.
Department of Psychiatry
University of Pennsylvania School of Medicine
Philadelphia, Pennsylvania

Anthony J. Marsella, Ph.D.
Department of Psychology
University of Hawaii
Honolulu, Hawaii

Daniel E. Mattila, M.Div., MSW
Cognitive Therapy Center of New York
New York, New York

John C. Norcross, Ph.D.
Department of Psychology
University of Scranton
Scranton, Pennsylvania

Michael W. O'Hara, Ph.D.
Department of Psychology
University of Iowa
Iowa City, Iowa

Raphael D. Rose, Ph.D.
Department of Psychiatry
Dartmouth University Medical School
Hanover, New Hampshire

Mark H. Stone, Ph.D.
Adler School of Professional Psychology
Chicago, Illinois

Scott Stuart, M.D.
Department of Psychiatry
University of Iowa
Iowa City, Iowa

Edward Suarez, Ph.D.
Department of Psychology
University of Hawaii
Honolulu, Hawaii

Frank Summers, Ph.D.
Division of Psychology
Department of Psychiatry & Behavioral Sciences
Northwestern University Medical School
Chicago, Illinois

Jeffrey E. Young, Ph.D.
Department of Psychiatry
Columbia University
Director; Cognitive Therapy Centers of New York and Connecticut
New York, New York

Foreword

Major Depression is one of the major health problems around the world for people of all socioeconomic and educational levels. Depressive illnesses are devastating in terms of their morbidity and mortality. Absenteeism from work, diminished productivity, disrupted interpersonal relationships, loss of pleasure in one's activities, alcohol or other substance abuse, increased incidence of a variety of general medical illnesses, decreased cognitive functioning, and suicide are but a few of the hallmarks of this set of illnesses. Furthermore, the natural course is chronic and recurrent. Single episodes are not the norm.

This book is about comparative treatments with an emphasis on nonpharmacological models and treatments. However, before understanding how to best organize treatment programs for our patients, a fundamental understanding of depressive illness is necessary and, as many of the authors in this book say, a reconsideration and reevaluation of theoretical models is necessary, particularly implications of the different models for treatment planning. Depression is a complicated, multifactorial illness; indeed a set of illnesses. Clinical depressions are not all the same. Broadly speaking, when discussing treatments one could talk about comparative treatments for Major Recurrent Depressive Disorder, Bipolar Disorder, and Dysthymic Disorder as well as many subsets of the above. However, before going too far down this road, some understanding of the nature of the disorders is important. As in the case of most medical illnesses they are complex and some framework for understanding the multiple variables is necessary.

Several publications (Akiskal & McKinney, 1973; Akiskal & McKinney, 1975; Whybrow, 1984; Whybrow & Parlatore, 1973) in the 1970s and 80s for the first time proposed an integrated framework for understanding depression which related some of the individual models to each other and thereby provided a basis for combined treatments. There have been and continue to be many individual models for depression, e.g., aggression turned inward, object loss, loss of self esteem, cognitive, learned helplessness, loss of reinforcement, biogenic amine or neurotransmitter theories, genetic, and neurophysiological. The above publications proposed a final common pathway hypothesis which conceptualizes the depressive syndrome as the behavioral manifestation of a new psychobiological state, the outcome of a final common pathway of various interlocking processes at the neurophysiological, biochemical, experiential, and behavioral levels. "We suggest that the biological disturbance concomitant with the behavioral changes, in the language of neurophysiology, exists as a reversible regulatory impairment, both interoceptive and exteroceptive, of the limbic-diencephalic brain centers serving psychomotor activity, mood, reward, and arousal. In this new state the individual loses many of the characteristics of adaptive health and becomes locked into a cycle of behavior which shows remarkable autonomy, self reinforcement, pathological periodicity, and resistance to perturbation" (Akiskal & McKinney, 1973). This theoretical model of the illness is an interactive one and considers the individual (both biologically and intrapsychically) together with the larger social environment as a general system. For example, serious depressive episodes can sometimes be precipitated by environmental stressors, which we now know, from both human clinical studies as well as extensive work in animal models, can induce major neurobiological disturbances, but this is clearly not equivalent to suggesting that the illness is environmentally determined. It is preposterous, for example, to think that in the case of the person who has a heart attack while snow shoveling that the snow shoveling caused the heart disease. Environmental and personal challenges contribute to the onset of many diseases, including depression, but not all who are challenged become ill. This model has major implications for organizing treatment programs for depression and especially for carefully thinking through the place and organization of combined treatments which are discussed in this book, e.g., pharmacotherapy with various forms of psychotherapy.

Yes, these are illnesses with major genetic vulnerability, but many other factors are involved in determining how and whether this vulnerability becomes phenotypically expressed. Genetic markers have assumed central importance in contemporary psychiatry especially with the rapid advances in molecular neurobiology and with genomic research. However, genetic markers represent indices of risk and by themselves are unlikely to be sufficient to lead to the phenotypic expression of the disease. For example, genetic vulnerability to affective illness can be compounded by loss during childhood through parental illness, suicide, separation, divorce, or more subtle forms of affective deprivation secondary to disturbed interaction between parents. A central part of the final common pathway hypothesis is that the "permission" for serious disturbance likely builds over many years and is determined by a variety of factors, e.g., developmental events such as childhood separation or loss, major trauma, assaults on self esteem, physical illness, aging, etc. For most individuals it is a weaving together of biological, social, and psychological factors that determines the outcome. These include genetic vulnerability, predisposing temperament (reflecting inherited subclinical factors enhancing vulnerability) and character traits, age and gender, physical illness and its treatment, and developmental events. In organizing treatment programs, careful assessment of individuals is critical to maximize the likelihood of a successful outcome. It stands to reason that pharmacotherapy alone will unlikely be sufficient if there are major environmental stressors, or if the person has such low self esteem and this is not dealt with by appropriate psychotherapies. On the other hand, predisposing parameters alone are likely to be sufficient to lead to expression of the illness in the absence of vulnerability though the nature of the event if traumatic enough could potentially overcome the adaptive capacities of even people with minimal vulnerability. Many of the above domains, which can heavily influence phenotypical expression of genetic vulnerability, are properly the subject of psychotherapeutic intervention and of combined therapies. Indeed an emerging body of evidence, which is covered in this book, supports the use of combined therapies to enhance outcomes. The largely unanswered question is which therapies for which individuals and how best to combine them with the pharmacotherapies and other somatic therapies.

Thus, the concept of a final common pathway involves the feedback interaction of diverse events leading to certain neurobiological changes and the resultant shared clinical features found in a heterogeneous group of depressive disorders. Given the multiple systems that need to interact, the issue of temporal sequencing and varied parameters upon which the precipitating factors impinge, it is not surprising that there is phenomenological heterogeneity.

The treatment of depressed patients is complex. One is dealing with a severe chronic, recurrent illness that is the result of many variables and unless all of these contributing variables are carefully considered in designing individualized treatment programs, the outcome will not be optimal. For example, medications alone in most people are unlikely to be sufficient to induce full remission. While there is a wide range of antidepressants with established efficacy the response rate to the first recommended antidepressant is somewhere around 50%. This does not mean remission but response. If remission is accepted as the outcome criterion then this rate decrease considerably. There are virtually no empirical data to guide decision making about what to do next. Efficacy studies in most clinical trials, which result in a drug being approved for clinical use, are typically short term and little attention is paid to functional outcome measures. There is an increasing tendency to go from descriptive diagnosis based on DSM IV phenomenology to prescription without sufficient attention to other factors that may be related to the onset of the current episode and which may merit psychotherapeutic attention. Managed care pressures compound this unitary approach, but part of the problem is also a training issue. Unfortunately, many programs are training residents to think that they understand depression when they have made a descriptive diagnosis. Prescriptions are often written based on this limited perspective. The concept of a formulation that provides an integrative perspective rather than a narrower one based on a particular theory of psychopathology is critical as a prelude to the successful treatment of patients with depressive disorders. This book provides the reader a scholarly treatment of the different approaches to such treatment and assumes an integrated perspective of mood disorders.

Whybrow (Whybrow, 1997, p.233) summarizes this perspective. "When it comes to understanding emotional behavior and abnormal mood states, no single scientific discipline can serve. Many levels of interdependent discourse . . . must be considered if progress is to be made. This is especially so when we are advancing our scientific knowledge, but it is also true when considering the appropriate treatment for each individual patient. . . . After all, the disciplines of molecular genetics, anatomy, neurochemistry, physiology, psychology, pharmacology, and so forth are arbitrary divisions of our own manufacture. . . . Fragments of information obtained from the technical investigation of biology are presumed to say something fundamental about the development of the illness and its management." In the same section of the book Whybrow quotes a patient: (Whybrow, 1997, pp. 233–234)

> I have no really satisfactory explanation for our blind faith in technology. Perhaps knowledge derived through a complex machine . . . has greater credibility than that gained through careful personal observation. I also think that

physicians, and especially some psychiatrists, are prone to confuse information with cause when it comes to the biological investigation of the brain, rather than recognizing it as another part of the puzzle. The biological perspective is a welcome shift from a few years ago, when many psychiatrists considered Freud's dynamic theories of intrapsychic life to be a complete explanation, but I wonder whether the swing has gone too far. . . . From the patient's standpoint, biology is only part of the story. . . . We know, for example, that I have a special vulnerability to manic depression. And I also know from reading that if the distribution of the blood flow in my brain had been measured by a PET scan during one of my depressions probably it would have differed from what is going on in my skull at this moment. Now I find such studies genuinely exciting, but unusual patterns of blood flow do not explain madness, nor do they guide me in what I can do about it. Blood-flow studies are not a sufficient explanation of cause. The manias and depressions I suffered were usually precipitated by grief. Certainly, that's what triggered the first episode—trying to cope with the death of my father, and especially that he had committed suicide.

So if we are looking for an explanation of the *origins* of my illness, a combination of that dreadful social situation plus my family's genes is to me the most reasonable, rather than a change in blood flow in my brain. Measuring blood flow represents an important level of biological inquiry and may tell researchers something about where to look for abnormal brain activity once the depression has been triggered, but it tells us little about what pulled the trigger in the first place. And that's what the patient wants to know. Then there is a hope of gaining greater control, and perhaps a chance for prevention.

Thus the need for a book like this, reviewing the various therapies with a focus on models, psychotherapies and integrated approaches. But the same patient goes on in a discussion of taking lithium for manic depression:

It makes it too easy for patients to take themselves off the hook of personal responsibility and to behave like victims, which is not healthy in the long run. I see it as similar to taking insulin for diabetes and then ignoring the need for an appropriate diet.

And the same holds true in reverse. . . . Psychotherapy by itself is not the answer. You can't think your way out of mania. . . . The secret to successful self-care is a combination of pharmacology and self knowledge.

We clearly need to move away from arbitrary division of treatments into biological and psychological and tailor combinations of treatments to the needs of individual patients recognizing that how these are combined will need to vary across time with individual patients as well as between patients. Treatment strategies need to be related to models of the disease and, in so far as possible, be evidence based. Continuing research into combined treatments is critical given the multifactorial nature of depressive illness.

REFERENCES

Akiskal, H. S., & McKinney, W. T. (1973). Depressive disorders: Toward a unified hypothesis. *Science, 182,* 20–29.

Akiskal, H. S., & McKinney, W. T. (1975). Overview of Recent Research in depression: Integration of Ten Conceptual Models Into a Comprehensive Clinical Frame. *Archives of General Psychiatry, 32,* 285–305.

Whybrow, Peter C. (1997). *A mood apart: Depression, mania, and other afflictions of the self.* Basic Books: New York.

Whybrow, P. C., Akiskal, H. S., & McKinney, W. T. (1984). *Mood disorders: Toward a new psychobiology.* Plenum: New York.

Whybrow, P., & Parlatore, A. (1973). Melancholia, a model in madness: A discussion of recent psychobiologic research into depressive illness. *International Journal of Psychiatry in Medicine, 4,* 351–378.

WILLIAM T. MCKINNEY, MD
Director, Asher Depression Research Center
Helen & Norman Asher Professor,
Department of Psychiatry & Behavioral Sciences
Northwestern University School of Medicine

Acknowledgments

Sadness, bereavement, grief and loss play a central part of our lives. One cannot be human without experiencing these emotions, these troubles of the soul. Our understanding of depression and its treatment has expanded exponentially over the past 15 years. During this time we have had the pleasure and privilege of working with many scholars and clinicians who have dedicated themselves to understanding the basic nature of this disorder and to developing effective treatments. Although there are too many to name, we owe them a debt of gratitude.

This book would not be possible without the contributions of a number of individuals. We would like to express our sincere appreciation to each. Our series editor, Art Freeman, has provided encouragement, judicious feedback, and valuable comments on the contents of the book. One could not ask for more from an editor, a colleague, or a friend. Our editor, Sheri Sussman, and the staff at Springer Publishing have skillfully edited the manuscript and expertly shepherded it through the production process. Their support, patience and steady editorial guidance have proven invaluable. We wish to thank our contributors, whose broad experience and sensitive insights have made for a useful and thought provoking volume. Finally we wish to acknowledge our families—MAR would like to thank his wife, Marsha, and daughter, Gracie; MRD wishes to acknowledge his wife, Lisa, his son, Jon, and his daughter, Jenna. We truly appreciate their ongoing emotional support and patience.

We are grateful to them all.

MAR
Geneva, IL

MRD
Cary, IL

1

Alternative Treatments of Depression: Points of Convergence and Divergence

Mark A. Reinecke

Depression stands as a central part of human experience. Loss, isolation, hopelessness, emptiness, and anomie have been recurrent themes in philosophy and literature for centuries. Depression is inescapable and, in many ways, insurmountable. But is clinical depression, the abyss of the human spirit, entirely unyielding? Although our attempts to understand and treat clinical depression are of relatively recent origin, recent findings have been promising (DeRubeis & Crits-Christoph, 1998; Dobson, 1989; Elkin et al., 1989; Frank, Kupfer, Perel, Cornes, & Jarrett, 1990). Moreover, an emerging body of work suggests that forms of depression may be preventable, at least in some situations (Gillham, Reivich, Jaycox, & Seligman, 1995; Hollon, DeRubeis, & Seligman, 1992; Munoz, Ying, Perez-Stable, & Miranda, 1993; Munoz, Mrazek, & Haggerty, 1996).

The recent proliferation of books, chapters, and articles on depression points both to its importance as a feature of modern society, and to the effectiveness of biological and psychosocial approaches for treating it. Moreover, recent developments, including the identification of empirically-supported treatments (Chambless et al., 1996; Kazdin, 1996), the increased use of treatment manuals (Chambless & Hollon, 1998), and an emphasis on objectively assessing treatment outcomes (Eisen & Dickey, 1996; Lambert & Brown, 1996) are reshaping graduate education, residency training, and clinical practice (Calhoun, Moras, Pilkonis, & Rehm, 1998). Given this, it seems timely to consider the relationships between alternative models of depression and the major forms of treatment that are derived from them. The fundamental questions we wish to address are, on the surface, quite simple: What are the most effective treatments for clinical depression and how do they work? The purpose of this book is to compare and contrast alternative models of clinical depression. In this chapter we will propose an outline for accomplishing this—we will discuss dimensions along which alternative models of depression and forms of treatment can be compared in an attempt to identify points of commonality and divergence between them. This will be followed by brief discussions of a number of related issues, including mechanisms of change, the need to critically evaluate the adequacy of our conceptual models, the importance of attending to both points of contact and divergence between approaches, and the relationship of theory to clinical practice.

DIMENSIONS OF COMPARISON

Research and clinical experience indicate that a number of forms of treatment, including psychotherapy, can be effective in alleviating depression. But just what is psychotherapy and how does it differ from other forms of social discourse? At its most basic level, psychotherapy may be defined as a trusting interpersonal relationship in which developmental, social, and intrapsychic factors associated with personal distress are examined. Positive outcomes are seen as stemming from the additive effects of common or nonspecific factors and theory-specific interventions. Beyond this, however, there is relatively little agreement. Alternative forms of psychotherapy differ dramatically both in the ways in which they conceptualize depression and in the proposed technologies of change. These conceptual, strategic, and technical differences between alternative forms of treatment are a central focus of this book.

For the sake of discussion we would suggest that alternative forms of treatment can be compared and contrasted on two levels—the conceptual and the technical. The first refers to the assumptions of the models and their philosophical foundations. This includes assumptions about the nature of psychopathology and the processes of human development and change. These are assumptions that we implicitly accept when we offer a specific form of treatment. The second dimension refers to practical matters. Technical differences between models include assessment strategies, the role of case formulation, clinical goals and strategies, the use of specific techniques, and approaches to understanding the therapeutic relationship. Technical differences, as such, center upon what the treatment looks like in practice. Not surprisingly, conceptual and technical factors often overlap and influence one another. That is to say, how one thinks about depression and human change often influences one's clinical approach. The selection of a specific intervention for a specific patient should, however, challenge us to consider the assumptions we are making about the origins of their distress and the mechanisms of clinical improvement.

As the following chapters will show, there are important conceptual and technical differences between alternative treatment approaches. In an attempt to organize this material, we would suggest that these approaches may usefully be compared along a number of dimensions. These dimensions are presented in Table 1.1.

MECHANISMS OF CHANGE IN PSYCHOTHERAPY AND PHARMACOTHERAPY

As noted, outcome studies indicate that both pharmacological and psychosocial treatments can be effective in alleviating clinical depression. Alternative approaches to treatment tend, however, to postulate different mechanisms of therapeutic change. How can we account for the fact that various forms of psychotherapy and various classes of medication can be effective in alleviating clinical depression? One possibility, of course, is that there are alternative pathways to change. Inasmuch as clinical depression is characterized by affective, behavioral, social, cognitive, neurochemical, and physiological changes, it is plausible to assume that interventions directed toward changing any one of these systems may facilitate clinical improvement. The possibility also exists, however, that alternative treatment approaches share a common functional substrate. As several authors have noted, effective forms of psychotherapy share a number of characteristics or features (Arkowitz &

TABLE 1.1   Conceptual and Technical Dimensions for Comparing Alternative Treatments of Depression

Conceptual:
  (1) Etiology of depression
  (2) Maintaining factors
  (3) Mechanisms of clinical change
      i) Role of insight
      ii) Role of language and cognition vs. experiential interventions
      iii) Nature and role of the therapeutic alliance
  (4) Emphasis upon here-and-now vs. developmental or historical factors
  (5) Emphasis on environment vs. internal processes
  (6) Emphasis placed on genetic or biological vulnerability

Technical:
  (7) Importance of identifying and pursuing specific treatment goals
  (8) Importance of objective diagnosis and assessment of symptom severity
  (9) Importance of obtaining specific information from patients and family members
 (10) Identification of patient characteristics that are predictive of clinical improvement
 (11) Role of case formulation in guiding selection of specific interventions
 (12) The relative emphasis placed on therapeutic structure, maintaining a problem-focus, and directive intervention vs. an unstructured and nondirective therapeutic stance
 (13) The relative emphasis placed on insight vs. skill development
 (14) Importance of specific strategies, interventions and techniques

Hannah, 1989). Effective treatments tend, as a group, to be active, focused, and problem-oriented. Moreover, each has a clear rationale that is shared with the patient, providing the therapist and patient with a common language for understanding the origins of their distress and the actions that must be taken to remediate it. Effective therapies tend to be structured, and encourage active attempts by the patient to address difficulties as they arise. They tend, as well, to encourage patients to monitor their progress, and to examine the relationship of their feelings of depression to thoughts, behavior, environmental events, and interpersonal styles. Patients are encouraged to actively change conditions associated with their negative mood.

But how can we account for the equivalent effectiveness of medications and psychotherapy? The possibility exists that both medications and psychotherapy function by altering specific neurochemical systems in the brain. Although a common biological pathway for clinical improvement among depressed patients has not been identified, this possibility is consistent with recent research on the treatment of anxiety. Studies of patients with obsessive-compulsive disorder, for example, indicate that both medications and cognitive-behavioral psychotherapy are associated with normalization of brain metabolism in regions implicated in the maintenance of compulsive behaviors (Baxter et al., 1992; Schwartz, Stoessel, Baxter, Martin, & Phelps, 1996). In a similar manner, it has been observed that psychodynamic psychotherapy may be associated with changes in serotonin metabolism (Viinamaki, Kuikka, Tiihonen, & Lehtonen, 1998). It is possible, as such, that both psychosocial and pharmacological interventions exert their effect by normalizing the function of specific neurochemical systems that regulate mood. Although the specific mechanisms by which this occurs are not well understood, the possibility exists that it may involve functioning of the prefrontal cortex—an area of the brain implicated in planning, problem-solving, and executive regulation of mood and behavior (Baxter, 1991; Baxter et al., 1989; Maeda, Keenan, & Pascual-Leone, 2000). It appears that interactions between the brain and the environment are dynamic, and that the brain responds to environmental influence through the regulation of gene expression (Gottlieb, 2000). If psychotherapy is viewed as a learning experience—albeit one accompanied by strong affect—then it is reasonable to assume that these experiences affect cerebral function, most likely through the modulation of gene transcription (Kandel, 1998). The possibility that psychotherapy and medications may function through shared mechanisms may not, then, be so very far-fetched. It is a possibility with important implications for our understanding of both human adaptation and clinical practice, and is worthy of careful consideration.

CONCEPTUAL ADEQUACY OF ALTERNATIVE MODELS

A difficulty with synthetic, "big-picture" scholarship is that it often attempts to impose a pattern on too much information. This is true in both the humanities and the social sciences. In comparing and contrasting alternative theories of depression, it is important to keep the specific goals and objectives of each model in mind. Put another way, what is the range or scope of each model? Were they, for example, developed as models of clinical depression, of psychopathology more generally, of psychotherapy, or of normative human development? Can the models successfully account for the phenomena they were designed to describe and predict? What are the limits or bounds of what they attempt to describe and predict?

As Elster (1990) observed, there are two ways in which conceptual models can fail—through indeterminacy and through inadequacy. As he noted, a theory is indeterminant to the extent that it fails to yield specific predictions, and is inadequate to the extent that its predictions are disconfirmed. Of these, the latter is the more serious concern. A theory may have a relatively narrow range of convenience, and yet have some explanatory power and clinical utility if it excludes at least some possible alternatives and serves as an effective guide for intervention. A model can be weak, but not useless. It is a more serious problem if the model makes predictions that are falsified by research—that is, if it makes predictions that are not supported by observation. It is worse, in short, for a theory to predict wrongly, than to predict weakly but truthfully. As regards our models of depression, it is worth asking, what *specifically* does each model predict? Are its predictions supported by empirical research and by clinical observation? Are its concepts and predictions made in such a way that we can distinguish it from other, alternative models? Do the clinical strategies and interventions logically follow from the proposed model of psychopathology? Are there ways in which the concepts employed by the model should be modified, clarified, or supplemented? It is a sign of intellectual honesty when we are able to modify or discard concepts and "interpretive keys" when they are not supported by observation or evidence, and when they no longer serve our purposes as guides for effective treatment. Our first challenge, then, is to determine the conceptual adequacy of each model in the light of evidence and observation.

This is particularly important given the heterogeneity of clinical depression. It is possible that some models may be more effective for understanding specific subtypes of depression or for guiding the treatment of specific groups of patients than are others. Abramson, Metalsky, and Alloy (1989), for example, proposed that feelings of hopelessness may serve as a proximal, sufficient cause of depression in a subset of patients. Theirs is not, then, a general model of depression. Rather, it is a descriptive and predictive model for a subset of depressed patients. With this in mind, a number of additional questions arise: Has the scope and range of convenience of each of the models been clearly defined? Have their limits been described and have populations for which they are not appropriate been identified? As we consider evidence in support of the models we may ask, how good is the fit between the specific theory of depression and the test? That is, does the methodology of the study allow for an adequate examination of the central tenets of the model?

SYNTHESIS AND DIVERGENCE

As a number of pundits have noted, there are two types of people in the world, lumpers and splitters. Lumpers are those who look for convergence and overlap. They seek to integrate findings and attempt to discern emerging patterns. From this perspective, we attempt to identify points of similarity and contact between alternative treatment approaches, and to identify shared mechanisms of change. Splitters, in contrast, are those who attempt to identify points of departure or divergence. From this perspective, alternative models may be seen as distinct and are viewed as inextricably tied to their historical and cultural contexts. In understanding the literature on the treatment of depression, we would suggest that both approaches have merit. There are, to be sure, points of technical contact between alternative models of psychotherapy of depression. These center on three issues: the nature of an optimal therapeutic relationship, an emerging acknowledgement of the central role of the self as an organizing construct, and the recognition that alternative treatment approaches may share a common pathway to change—the provision of new experiences which, when accompanied by strong affect, result in the disconfirmation and change of expectancies and interpersonal patterns that mediate the maintenance of the depressive episode (Arkowitz & Hannah, 1989). There are, as well, important points of difference between the alternative approaches to treatment. Experienced therapists do, in fact, appear to engage in different behaviors in therapy and studies suggest that predictors of change may vary systematically between one form of psychotherapy and another (DeRubeis, Hollon, Evans, & Bemis, 1982; Luborsky, Woody, Lellan, O'Brien, & Rosenzweig, 1982). In practice, then, all forms of therapy are not created equal.

There also are conceptual similarities between several of the psychosocial theories to be discussed. Many, for example, postulate that intrapsychic systems play a central role in human adaptation. Cognitive therapy (CT) and schema-focused psychotherapy, for example, propose that dysfunctional schema play a causal role in the etiology and maintenance of depressive episodes. Schema are typically viewed as stable core beliefs and patterns of thinking. They may be defined as tacit information processing templates which serve as "cognitive blueprints" for the perception, encoding, organizing, construal, retrieval, and management of information. Schema are similar, in many ways, to Alfred Adler's concept of "life style" and to notions of the self found in Object Relations theories. The ways in which the concepts of "schema," "life style," and self are similar or different from one another, however, are rarely examined. In the same way, Beck's (1976) concept of "sociotropy" is similar, in some respects, to the psychodynamic concept of "dependency" (Arieti & Bemporad, 1980; Blatt & Bers, 1993). The relationships between these concepts, however, have not been fully explored.

To be sure, many of the concepts to be discussed in this book are, at least on the surface, similar. A caveat, however, is needed. Our contributors were encouraged to clearly articulate both the assumptions of their models and to describe the treatment strategies derived from them. The possibility remains, however, that readers may misunderstand these different approaches. There is a natural tendency to attempt to understand alternative models by applying concepts and terms one is more familiar with. We assimilate the unfamiliar by reframing it in terms of what we know. While we might think of sociotropy and dependency, for example, as essentially the same (i.e., they both describe the importance of human needs for affiliation and closeness, they both suggest that this need for affiliation may play a role in vulnerability for depression, and they both address this issue therapeutically), it is worth keeping in mind that they are derived from fundamentally different models of human adaptation—an information-processing paradigm and a drive-dynamic model. Viewing them as essentially equivalent— different names for the same concept—does not do justice to either the richness of the models or the important differences between them. In a similar manner, one might conceptualize psychodynamic interpretations as "mild behavioral punishments"—inducing patients to cease and desist in making specific depressive statements. This is an interesting notion, but one that does not acknowledge the depth or breadth of the underlying dynamic model. In sum, although reframing of concepts can be useful in identifying points of contact between models, it can be problematic in that it can obscure essential points of difference between the approaches.

Technical similarities exist between many forms of psychotherapy. Strategic, brief forms of psychotherapy have become increasingly popular and evidence indicates that they can be useful in treating clinical depression. As noted, many contemporary forms of psychotherapy are active and problem-focused. Many tend, as well, to emphasize the importance of maintaining an empathic, warm, supportive, and responsive therapeutic relationship. The question, then, arises—is there a relationship between these shared technical factors and therapeutic improvement? Only comparative outcome and process studies can answer this question. Our impression is that clinical improvement is predicted by both nonspecific factors (such as the development of a trusting therapeutic rapport) and theory-specific technical features. Effective forms of psychotherapy tend to efficiently and directly provide the patient with a parsimonious rationale for their difficulties, develop a shared understanding of the origins of the patient's difficulties and the steps that must be taken to address them, encourage activity, generate feelings of hope and an expectation that change is possible, and develop personal feelings of efficacy, control, and worth.

Although clinicians tend, based on their experience and training, to assert that specific forms of medication or psychotherapy may be beneficial for specific patients, it is worth acknowledging that a consensus has not yet emerged as to the most effective approach for treating clinical depression. With this in mind, a balanced, critical, and open-minded understanding of the broader literature is recommended.

FOUR FACTORS IMPLICATED IN THE ETIOLOGY OF DEPRESSION

There is an emerging consensus among researchers that depression results from the interaction of causal factors, and that there may be multiple etiological pathways. Distal and proximal causes of depression fall into four categories: biological and genetic factors, interpersonal and environmental factors, developmental history, and social-cognitive variables. Models of depression differ in the relative emphasis placed on these factors and in the manner in which they are believed to interact. In reviewing the literature on alternative models of depression, it may be useful to ask how they account for each of these factors and how this is reflected in the treatment process.

A range of biological factors have been associated with major depression (Thase & Howland, 1995), and there is evidence from twin, adoption, and linkage studies of genetic heritability in risk for major affective disorders (Cadoret, 1978; Gershon et al., 1975). These findings serve as a conceptual foundation for pharmacological treatments of depression. It is worth keeping in mind, however, that the identification of replicable physiological and neurochemical abnormalities among patients with major depression does not prove that these disturbances play a causal role in the etiology of the disorder, and that research with monozygotic twin indicates that environmental and social factors play a critical role in the etiology of depression (Kendler & Gardner, 2001).

In a similar manner, interpersonal loss and maladaptive social interaction patterns associated with depression serve as a basis for both interpersonal psychotherapy (IPT) and social skills training approaches. Environmental losses and decreased social reinforcement have been found to accompany depression, and serve as a basis for behavioral and self-reinforcement therapies. Work in the field of child development indicates that early losses and disruptions in the social environment can influence later emotional and social development and can place youth at risk for behavioral and emotional difficulties. These findings serve as a foundation for psychodynamic and attachment-focused interventions, developmentally-focused cognitive therapies, and for treatments which attempt to develop affect regulation skills. Finally, individuals with depression manifest a range of deficits in cognition and information processing (Engel & DeRubeis, 1993; Ingram, Miranda, & Segal, 1998). This pattern of cognitive distortions and deficiencies serves as foundation for a family of cognitive-behavioral therapies for depression, including CT, schema-focused psychotherapy, and social problem-solving therapies.

Given the range of factors associated with risk of depression, it seems sensible to suggest that models of depression should clearly identify causal relationships among each of the variables believed to play a central role in the depressive episode. Variables implicated in the development and maintenance of a depressive episode should be clearly defined, and their relationship to related constructs should be discussed. Moreover, models should clearly identify which factors are associated with vulnerability for depression, and these should be distinguished from those associated with severity, relapse, recurrence, and response to treatment. Clarification of a theoretical model is essential if its validity is to be put to the test. This is, to be sure, a high standard. It is, in fact, a standard that few models have met.

As Marsella (this volume, chapter 3) cogently argues, we should be cautious as we review our models of depression. There is a risk that we may be implicitly accepting a shared set of assumptions about the nature of human experience, depression, and human change. These assumptions, based in Western conceptions of human nature and science, are not universally accepted. Cultural differences appear to exist, for example, between Western and Asian systems of thought. It has been suggested that traditional Asian cultures adopt a holistic stance, and rely less on formal logic and categorization of objects; whereas Westerners tend to employ reductionism and analytic logic to understand human adaptation. These approaches to understanding behavior and emotions are based in different tacit epistemologies which, in turn, may be related to different social systems. The possibility that different cultures employ different naïve metaphysical systems for understanding behavior and emotions brings into question commonly accepted assumptions about mood, cognition, development, and the processes underlying human change and adaptation. It also brings into question the validity of commonly accepted scientific methods for testing alternative models and treatments. In the spirit of encouraging a pluralistic understanding of human suffering and its treatment, we would do well to keep in mind that our assumptions of empiricism, objectivity, and reductionism are simply that, assumptions.

This is not, however, to say that disinterested inquiry is impossible or that concepts of objectivity, evidence, and validity should play no role in the development of our models and interventions. A number of psychologists, sociologists, and philosophers have suggested that intellectual inquiry is neither desirable nor possible because concepts of evidence and validity are culturally and historically based. There is, from this perspective, no support for notions of objectivity or truth. Richard Rorty (1991) noted, for example, that he has not much "use for notions like . . . objective truth." As he stated, to call a statement true "is just to give it a rhetorical pat on the back." Rules of evidence, empirical inquiry, and attempts to objectively evaluate data as a means of validating models are dismissed, then, as cultural artifacts of a hegemonistic Western science. This perspective has, however, been challenged as reflecting a misunderstanding of scientific process (Haack, 1998). In the spirit of a pluralistic evaluation of our models, a moderate stance is recommended—neither reifying empirical findings nor adopting an attitude of ascientific relativism. To be sure, metaphors, models, and theories can be useful. They organize our ways of thinking about our patients and their distress, and serve as guides for our clinical practice. Scientific evidence and systematic inquiry can and should be brought to bear in their evaluation. We should, however, be attentive to the cultural foundations of our models, the cultural heritage of the individuals we endeavor to help, and the very real limits of our knowledge.

THE RELATIONSHIP OF THEORY, RESEARCH, AND PRACTICE

Although it is something of a truism, clinical practice with depressed patients is both an art and a science. Effective treatment, regardless of one's therapeutic orientation, requires the development of a case formulation to guide treatment and creative, flexible therapeutic tactics. Clinical practices, however, are often based as much on personal preference and early training as on an understanding of the recent literature. This lack of contact between research and clinical practice has been widely discussed and remains an important problem. Although an impressive body of empirical evidence has accumulated in support of the efficacy of several forms of treatment, a consensus has not emerged as to the most effective treatment for depression among adults. Moreover, evidence for the effectiveness of specific forms of treatment cannot be taken as evidence in support of the underlying model of psychopathology and behavioral change. Although, for example, there is consistent evidence in support of cognitive therapy for treating depression among adults (Dobson, 1989; Solomon & Haaga, in press), evidence for the underlying model of psychopathology and behavior change is far more modest (Clark & Beck, 1999). Similar considerations apply to our understanding of pharmacological, psychodynamic, and interpersonal models of depression. With this in mind, it is sensible to view current models of depression as provisional.

It is often suggested that alternative forms of therapy are equally effective and that, as a consequence, clinical improvement stems from nonspecific factors, including empathy, rapport, acceptance, unconditional regard, warmth, and support. We would suggest, however, that these two statements are incorrect, and that they misrepresent recent findings. Reviews of controlled outcome studies indicate that not all forms of psychotherapy are equally effective. Several forms of psychotherapy, including CT and IPT, appear to be reasonably effective in treating clinically depressed adults. Their utility has been described as empirically "well-established" and "probably efficacious" (Chambless et al., 1998). Moreover, a range of patient, therapist, and interpersonal factors appear to be predictive of therapeutic improvement. Patient factors (including symptom severity and the presence or absence of a personality disorder), therapist factors (including therapeutic competence and therapeutic rapport), and technical variables (including therapeutic compliance, use of active interventions, insight, and therapeutic expressiveness) have all been found to be predictive of clinical improvement. Disparate approaches have been found effective in treating depression among adults, and other approaches are promising but have not yet received empirical scrutiny. Taken together, these findings suggest that there may be alternative mechanisms for initiating therapeutic change. There may, in short, be many ways to do right by our patients.

In the best of worlds, our interventions should follow directly from our theories of psychopathology and treatment. In practice, however, this is not always the case. Treatment with any given patient may bear little relationship to a specific therapeutic model. It is not uncommon, for example, to encounter clinicians who state that they "just do what works" (an atheoretical eclecticism), that it "looks like a biological depression, but it's mild so psychotherapy may do some good," or that they "conceptualize dynamically, but treat cognitively." An eclectic stance may, on the one hand, bode well in that it reflects clinical and conceptual flexibility. In the absence of empirical support for the effectiveness of therapeutic eclecticism, however, this may as easily be seen as evidence of clinical confusion.

It is important to keep in mind that the usefulness of any clinical intervention is tied to the context in which it is applied. It can be challenging, as a consequence, to discriminate the effectiveness of a specific form of therapy from the therapeutic context in which interventions are made. A number of years ago, for example, a depressed and dependent young woman began softly crying during our therapy session. When I asked what she had been feeling, she remarked that she felt I truly cared for her. She had observed that I had been writing down her comments and that I had read my notes from a prior session. As she stated, "You're the first person who has ever really taken what I had to say seriously." This was for her an important therapeutic moment and counteracted her belief that others were essentially uncaring toward her. Thinking I had come across a useful intervention, I began actively taking notes during sessions with other patients. A patient later that same week reacted to my pad and pen, however, in a rather different manner. As he tartly remarked, "Why don't you just put down the damn paper and *listen* to what I have to say?" Same intervention, different response. The clinical lesson had been learned—the effectiveness of any given technique depends on the context and on the skill with which it is introduced. On closer examination, however, this vignette raises an important methodological question—can we separate technique or intervention from the quality of the therapeutic relationship? Does my failure with the second patient reflect the misguided use of a specific intervention (a technical misstep), or might it more usefully be seen as a breakdown in the therapeutic rapport (a nonspecific factor)? In fact, does this reflect a breakdown or failure at all? That is, might this have occurred regardless of what I'd done with my notes? Might our discussion of his anger and frustration later in the session have offered an important opportunity for therapeutic growth? Effective psychotherapy, then, is more than an empathic and supportive relationship, and more that an assemblage of theory-driven techniques. With this in mind, future research should focus not only on efficacy and effectiveness of different treatment approaches, but on describing the processes of change for individual clients over the course of individual therapy sessions. Clinically useful research should attend to the complexities that our clients present in day-to-day practice.

SUMMARY AND RECOMMENDATIONS

As our understanding of the nature of depression and its treatment increases, many of our assumptions, models and practices will be modified, adapted, and replaced. Existing models do not adequately address a range of issues, including vulnerability, relapse, recurrence, comorbidity, and prediction of treatment response. With this in mind, we will need to develop models that are at the same time broader and more specific. This next generation of models will go a long way toward alleviating severe and recurrent depression, and toward reducing its social costs. To accomplish this, we will need to carefully and critically evaluate our current assumptions, models, and practices. Our models should be open to empirical test and our interventions should be based on the most recent evidence.

Although a large body of research indicates that medications and psychotherapy can be effective for treating depression, recurrent depression remains an intractable problem. Moreover, many individuals do not make use of treatments that are available. As Andrews and

Henderson (2000) noted, only 20–50% of individuals who meet diagnostic criteria for a mental illness actually receive treatment. Although this is due, at least in part, to cost and availability, many individuals decline to seek treatment due to stigma, the perception that it will not be effective, or a tendency to minimize the severity of their distress. We need, then, to both improve our treatments and to make them more available and acceptable to a broader range of individuals. We need, in short, to attend to the complex world of community practice and community health. It is one thing to demonstrate that an intervention can be effective when applied conscientiously with a homogenous, well-defined research sample. It is quite another to know that these treatments work in community settings, when applied by an average clinician with an average patient. These issues—availability, acceptability, treatment integrity, treatment compliance, moderators and mediators of change, effectiveness, and prediction of treatment response—have received relatively little study, but will become increasingly important over the years ahead. We will be able to improve the quality of the care we provide for patients with depression by encouraging research and training that addresses these real-world clinical problems.

To summarize, there are a number of dimensions along which alternate models of depression can be compared and contrasted. With this in mind, it may useful to take the broad view and consider the full range of conceptual and technical points of contact between them. In accomplishing this we recommend attempting to simultaneously look for points of convergence and divergence and suggest resisting the natural temptation to reframe models in terms borrowed from other orientations that we may be more familiar with. The questions we ask of our theories are simple. Are the models well-articulated? Do they make specific predictions and are these predictions consistent with both the empirical literature and clinical observation? Are the models stated in terms that are falsifiable, and are they, at a minimum, discriminable from other models of depression? What is the range of convenience of the model? Do recommended treatments follow logically from the model? Finally, it is worth noting that our assumptions are simply that, assumptions. Many are culturally based and should be carefully examined.

As the title indicates, this is a book about the treatment of depression. We have adopted a broad view, and have focused upon forms of treatment that serve as the foundation of the field. Among these are older forms of psychotherapy that have endured for decades. Examples include individual, object relations, self-psychological, and behavioral approaches to psychotherapy. These are refined and sophisticated models which continue to influence contemporary training and clinical practice. In addition, we have included several forms of treatment that have emerged only recently. These approaches—including CT, IPT, schema-focused psychotherapy, and integrative psychotherapy—have attracted a great deal of empirical interest and will likely influence our ways of thinking about depression and its treatment for some time to come.

To facilitate the comparison of the models, our contributors were provided with specific guidelines and questions to address in their chapters. We wished to provide a structure to make it simpler for our readers to compare alternative approaches for understanding depression, while allowing our authors the latitude to describe the nuances of their clinical approaches. We asked our contributors to first describe the essential features of their models and to discuss how they would approach the treatment of a specific patient. Each of the contributors then provided an overview of their model, a review of its historical development, and a description of its basic concepts. They were asked to discuss factors associated with the etiology and maintenance of the depression, as well as the mechanisms of change postulated by the model. Each contributor briefly reviewed empirical evidence for both the model and the treatments derived from it. So that the reader may have a clearer sense of how these approaches look and feel in practice, each of the contributors includes a conceptual formulation and a discussion of treatment goals for the patient. This is followed by a more formal discussion of recommended treatment strategies and interventions. Particular attention is paid to how the therapeutic relationship is understood and how it can be used to facilitate clinical improvement. Specific assessment instruments are reviewed, and the structure and goals of individual treatment sessions are discussed. The discussion of the case example concludes with a discussion of termination issues, relapse prevention, and recommendations for follow-up care. Finally, our contributors were asked to provide suggestions for additional reading to supplement their chapters. These include case studies, empirical articles and reviews, and "key" books or standard references.

We end, then, with the simple question with which we began: What are the most effective treatments for clinical depression and how do they work? On closer inspection we see that these questions are complex and that the answers may depend as much on our assumptions and goals as on the outcome literature. Although flexibility, compassion, and creativity are essential components of effective clinical practice, psychiatry and clinical psychology are, at their core, sciences. This is worth reiterating for at least two reasons. First, because a critical understanding of the contemporary literature is essential if we are to develop more sophisticated models of affective disorders and treatment; and second because, as concerned clinicians, we must draw upon our knowledge of the literature and use it as a guide for our practice. Before we can do this, however, we must hold these models up to scrutiny. To paraphrase William James, we should clearly describe our assumptions and clinical practices and make them give good account of themselves before we let them pass. We hope that *Comparative Treatments of Depression* facilitates this process and that it will be a useful aid for both students and skilled clinicians.

REFERENCES

Abramson, L., Metalsky, G., & Alloy, L. (1989). Hopelessness depression: A theory-based subtype of depression. *Psychological Review, 96*, 358–372.

Andrews, G., & Henderson, S. (Eds.) (2000). *Unmet need in psychiatry.* Cambridge, England: Cambridge University Press.

Arieti, S., & Bemporad, J. (1980). The psychological organization of depression. *American Journal of Psychiatry, 137*, 1360–1365.

Arkowitz, H., & Hannah, M. (1989). Cognitive, behavioral, and psychodynamic therapies: Converging or diverging pathways to change? In A. Freeman, K. Simon, L. Beutler, & H. Arkowitz (Eds.), *Comprehensive handbook of cognitive therapy* (pp. 143–168). New York: Plenum Press.

Baxter, L. (1991). PET studies of cerebral function in major depression and obsessive-compulsive disorder: The emerging prefrontal cortex consensus. *Annals of Clinical Psychiatry, 3*, 103–109.

Baxter, L., Schwartz, J., Phelps, M., et al. (1989). Reduction of prefrontal cortex glucose metabolism common to three types of depression. *Archives of General Psychiatry, 46*, 243–250.

Baxter, L., Schwartz, J., Bergman, K., Szuba, M., Guze, B., Mazziotta, J., Alazraki, A., Selin, C., Ferng, H., Munford, P., & Phelps, M. (1992). Caudate glucose metabolic rate changes with both drug and behavior therapy for obsessive-compulsive disorder. *Archives of General Psychiatry, 49*(9), 681–689.

Beck, A. (1976). *Cognitive therapy of the emotional disorders.* New York: New American Library.

Blatt, S., & Bers, S. (1993). The sense of self in depression: A psychodynamic perspective. In Z. Segal & S. Blatt (Eds.), *The self in emotional distress: Cognitive and psychodynamic perspectives*. New York: Guilford Press.

Cadoret, R. (1978). Evidence for genetic inheritance of primary affective disorders in adoptees. *American Journal of Psychiatry, 134,* 463–466.

Calhoun, K., Moras, K., Pilkonis, P., & Rehm, L. (1998). Empirically supported treatments: Implications for training. *Journal of Consulting and Clinical Psychology, 66,* 151–162.

Chambless, D., Sanderson, W., Shoham, V., Johnson, S., Pope, K., Crits-Christoph, P., Baker, M., Johnson, B., Woody, S., Sue, S., Beutler, L., Williams, D., & McCurry, S. (1996). Update on empirically-validated therapies. *The Clinical Psychologist, 49,* 5–18.

Chambless, D., Baker, M., Baucom, D., Beutler, L., Calhoun, K., Crits-Christoph, P., Daiuto, A., DeRubeis, R., Detweiler, J., Haaga, D., Johnson, S., McCurry, S., Mueser, K., Pope, K., Sanderson, W., Shoham, V., Stickle, T., Williams, D., & Woody, S. (1998). Update on empirically-validated therapies: II. *The Clinical Psychologist, 51,* 3–16.

Chambless, D., & Hollon, S. (1998). Defining empirically-supported therapies. *Journal of Consulting and Clinical Psychology, 66,* 7–18.

Clark, D., & Beck, A. (1999). *Scientific foundations of cognitive theory and therapy of depression.* New York: John Wiley.

DeRubeis, R., Hollon, S., Evans, M., & Bemis, K. (1982). Can psychotherapies for depression be discriminated? A systematic investigation of cognitive therapy and interpersonal therapy. *Journal of Consulting and Clinical Psychology, 50,* 744–756.

DeRubeis, R., & Crits-Christoph, P. (1998). Empirically-supported individual and group psychological treatments for adult mental disorders. *Journal of Consulting and Clinical Psychology, 60,* 904–908.

Dobson, K. (1989). A meta-analysis of the efficacy of cognitive therapy for depression. *Journal of Consulting and Clinical Psychology, 57,* 414–419.

Eisen, S., & Dickey, B. (1996). Mental health outcome assessment: The new agenda. *Psychotherapy, 33,* 181–189.

Elkin, I., Shea, M., Watkins, J., Imber, S., Sotsky, S., Collins, J., Glass, D., Pilkonis, D., Leber, W., Docherty, J., Feister, S., & Parloff, M. (1989). National Institute of Mental Health treatment of depression collaborative research program: General effectiveness of treatment. *Archives of General Psychiatry, 46,* 971–983.

Elster, J. (1990). When rationality fails. In K. Cook & M. Levi (Eds.), *The limits of rationality*. Chicago, IL: University of Chicago Press.

Engel, R., & DeRubeis, R. (1993). The role of cognition in depression. In K. Dobson & P. Kendall (Eds.), *Psychopathology and cognition.* San Diego: Academic Press.

Frank, E., Kupfer, D., Perel, J., Cornes, C., & Jarrett, B. (1990). Three-year outcomes for maintenance therapies in recurrent depression. *Archives of General Psychiatry, 47,* 1093–1099.

Gershon, E., Mark, A., Cohen, N., Belizon, N., Baron, M., & Knobe, K. (1975). Transmitted factors in the morbid risk of affective disorders: A controlled study. *Journal of Psychiatry Research, 12,* 283–299.

Gillham, J., Reivich, K., Jaycox, L., & Seligman, M. (1995). Prevention of depressive symptoms in schoolchildren: A two year follow-up. *Psychological Science, 6,* 343–351.

Gottlieb, G. (2000). Environmental and behavioral influences on gene activity. *Current Directions in Psychological Science, 9*(3), 93–97.

Haack, S. (1998). *Manifesto of a passionate moderate.* Chicago: University of Chicago Press.

Hollon, S., DeRubeis, R., & Seligman, M. (1992). Cognitive therapy and the prevention of depression. *Applied and Preventive Psychology, 1,* 89–95.

Ingram, R., Miranda, J., & Segal, Z. (1998). *Cognitive vulnerability to depression.* New York: Guilford Press.

Kandel, E. (1998). A new intellectual framework for psychiatry. *American Journal of Psychiatry, 155,* 457–469.

Kazdin, A. (1996). Validated treatments: Multiple perspectives and issues: Introduction to the series. *Clinical Psychology: Science and Practice, 3,* 216–217.

Kendler, K., & Gardner, C. (2001). Monozygotic twins discordant for major depression: A preliminary exploration of the role of environmental experiences in the aetiology and course of illness. *Psychological Medicine, 31,* 411–423.

Lambert, M., & Brown, G. (1996). Data-based management for tracking outcome in private practice. *Clinical Psychology: Science and Practice, 3,* 172–178.

Luborsky, L., Woody, G., Lellan, A., O'Brien, C., & Rosenzweig, J. (1982). Can independent judges recognize independent psychotherapies? *Journal of Consulting and Clinical Psychology, 50,* 49–62.

Maeda, F., Keenan, J., & Pascual-Leone, A. (2000). Interhemispheric asymmetry of motor cortical excitability in major depression as measured by transcranial magnetic stimulation. *British Journal of Psychiatry, 177,* 169–173.

Munoz, R., Ying, Y., Perez-Stable, E., & Miranda, J. (1993). *The prevention of depression: Research and practice.* Baltimore: Johns Hopkins University Press.

Munoz, R., Mrazek, P., & Haggerty, R. (1996). Institute of Medicine report on prevention of mental disorders: Summary and commentary. *American Psychologist, 51,* 1116–1122.

Rorty, R. (1991). *Essays on Heidegger and others.* Cambridge, England: Cambridge University Press.

Schwartz, J., Stoessel, P., Baxter, L., Martin, K., & Phelps, M. (1996). Systematic changes in cerebral glucose metabolic rate after successful behavior modification treatment of obsessive-compulsive disorder. *Archives of General Psychiatry, 53*(2), 109–113.

Solomon & Haaga, D. (in press). Cognitive theory and therapy of depression. In M. Reinecke & D. Clark (Eds.), *Cognitive therapy across the lifespan.* Cambridge, England: Cambridge University Press.

Thase, M., & Howland, R. (1995). Biological processes in depression: An updated review and integration. In E. Beckham & W. Leber (Eds.), *Handbook of depression* (2nd ed.). New York: Guilford Press.

Viinamaki, H., Kuikka, J., Tiihonen, J., & Lehtonen, J. (1998). Changes in monoamine transporter density related to clinical recovery: A case-control study. *Nordic Journal of Psychiatry, 52,* 39–44.

2

Treatment for Depression: What the Research Says

Michael J. Lambert and Matthew J. Davis

In 1952, H. J. Eysenck wrote a seminal paper on psychotherapy research which claimed that untreated emotional disorders were as likely to go into remission as disorders in treated patients. This paper spawned a flurry of research that, for the next several decades, attempted to demonstrate empirically that Eysenck's findings were wrong. This endeavor, for the most part, has been successful. In study after study, psychotherapy has been shown to alleviate painful and debilitating mental disorders with thousands of patients throughout the Western world. The results have repeatedly shown that, contrary to Eysenck's claims, psychotherapy produces beneficial effects above those that occur in the natural healing process alone (Lambert & Bergin, 1994).

Over the past decade, psychotherapy researchers have turned their attention to more specific challenges including research on how therapy works, with what type of patients, and for which disorders. Recently, much of this research has been driven increasingly by third party payors who demand to understand both what they are paying for and why they are paying for it.

No mental health disorder has received more attention from psychotherapy researchers than depression. Depressive disorders have been characterized as the common cold of mental health problems. Research has shown, however, that unlike the common cold, depressive symptoms can be alleviated and not merely masked. This chapter will review the current state of research on the effectiveness of psychotherapy in ameliorating depressive disorders. The variables contributing to treatment outcome can be divided into three major sources: treatment, therapist, and client. Our review will look at what the current outcome research shows us concerning each of these three factors and their relationship to effective treatment of depression. The knowledge gained from outcome research cannot be summarized easily in one chapter. For this reason, we have chosen to concentrate on only the most important conclusions in studies examining major depression in adult outpatients.

DEPRESSION DEFINED

The Diagnostic and Statistical Manual of Mental Disorders-Fourth Edition (DSM-IV) defines a major depressive disorder (MDD) as comprised of one or more depressive episodes in the absence of any manic episodes (American Psychiatric Association, 1994). A depressive episode is further defined by a depressed mood or loss of interest in almost all usual activities. Roth and Fonagy (1996) describe the accompanying symptoms as they are widely accepted in the field. They include disturbances in appetite, weight, and sleep; decreased energy; difficulty concentrating or thinking; feelings of worthlessness or guilt; hopelessness and thoughts of death or suicide or suicidal attempts. The DSM-IV requires that five of nine specific symptoms must be present nearly every day for at least two weeks in order to qualify for a diagnosis of MDD. Additionally, these symptoms must cause significant distress in social, occupational, or other important areas of functioning (Roth & Fonagy, 1996).

NATURAL HISTORY OF DEPRESSION

Major depression is the most common mental health disorder (Bland, 1997). The National Institute of Mental Health Epidemiologic Catchment Area Study (ECA) in 1991 sampled 15,000 adults at five sites (Robins & Regier, 1991). This study, using DSM-III criteria, reported 6% of the sample having a diagnosable affective disorder during a six-month period. Among this percentage, MDD accounted for approximately 3%. The National Comorbidity Survey estimated the lifetime prevalence of MDD at 17.1% (Blazer, Kessler, McGonagle, & Swartz, 1994). Prevalence of MDD in the ECA and National Comorbidity studies was nearly twice as high in women as in men and greater in young adults. Women are reported to have a higher rate of depression than men in part because men are less likely to recall a depressive episode (Ernst & Angst, 1991; Romanski et al., 1992). Others have attributed differential gender rates to the effects of environmental inequities, gender role, and gender bias (McGrath, Keita, Strickland, & Russo, 1990; Mirowsky, 1996; Sprock & Yoder, 1997).

Burke, Burke, Rae, and Regier (1991) have presented evidence that MDD within young adults is increasing (see also Bland, 1997). The ECA study reported the mean age of onset at 27 years. It has also been reported that onset of depression is occurring earlier for both sexes (Cross National Collaborative Group, 1992). The lifetime prevalence for adolescents has been estimated at 15% to 20%, or comparable to that of adults (Harrington, Rutter, & Fombonne, 1996). MDD appears to occur twice as often in adolescent females, or similar to the percentages in adults (Fleming & Offord, 1990; Lewinsohn, Clark, Seeley, & Rohde, 1994).

The natural history of a depressive disorder suggests it reoccurs throughout the lifespan of the patient. Research on treatments for depression must be viewed with this knowledge in mind. Furthermore, studies that examine methods of reducing relapse are therefore as important as those that treat the initial episode.

The economic costs associated with depression are also quite substantial. Costs due to losses in productivity take not only a heavy personal toll but affect society as a whole. The annual cost of depressive disorders in the United States has been estimated at $43 billion, the majority of which are due specifically to MDD (Bland, 1997).

Depressive disorders also have high comorbidity rates with other serious mental disorders, including substance abuse, anxiety disorders, and schizophrenia (Weissman et al., 1996). It has been reported, however, that the presence of additional psychiatric disorders is not higher in persons with only a single episode of depression when compared to those with no history of depression.

The mortality rate among those with symptoms of depression has been reported at almost twice that of the general population (Bland, 1997). At a 16-year follow-up one study found that among subjects who had shown signs of depression, 92% had a chronic or recurring physical illness or suffered premature death (Bland, 1997). Spitzer, Koenke, and Linzer (1995) state that mood disorders account for more of the decrease in quality of life due to health problems than other common medical disorders. Major depression has also been reported as the fourth leading cause of the disease burden worldwide (Murray & Lopez, 1997). Mortality rates among people suffering MDD, in contrast to prevalence rates, are higher in men than in women. Recent research reiterates that suicide is a leading cause of death among adolescents and adults (Cicchetti & Toth, 1998). Persons afflicted with MDD carry a high risk of suicide, with research reporting between 13% and 30% of afflicted persons eventually committing suicide.

TREATMENT

It should be stated at the outset, that despite a substantial body of research on psychotherapeutic techniques for depression, the link between a specific treatment and improvement continues to evade the best of efforts. Luborsky, Singer, and Luborsky's (1975) position that "everyone has won and all must have prizes" (p. 995) remains true. Research on the ameliorative effects of psychotherapy for major depression can be divided into two broad categories according to the methodological approach used; studies employing either a naturalistic design or a randomized controlled trial. As will be seen, each design yields different insights due to the methodological strengths and weaknesses inherent in the approach. When results of both approaches are taken together, however, a comprehensive picture emerges which shows psychotherapy provides substantial relief for persons suffering from depression.

Most major studies and reviews have examined different combinations of brief cognitive, behavioral, and interpersonal therapies. Because of this fact our discussion of effective treatments will focus on these approaches. However, less studied or longer term therapies should not be equated with ineffective therapies, and for this reason after looking at the most researched approaches, we will present several others treatments that have been shown to be effective including experiential, analytic, marital, and bibliotherapy. Finally, we will conclude our section on treatments by looking at the efficacy of pharmacological treatments in relation to psychotherapy.

NATURALISTIC STUDIES

An exploration of the research on treatments for depression begins with a look at naturalistic studies, those that have examined depression *in vivo,* or as it occurs in the general population. While these studies are scientifically less rigorous than studies in a randomized controlled trial (RCT), it has been argued that they might generalize better to psychotherapy as it is actually practiced than studies using the RCT. Patients in RCTs are carefully selected according to strict criteria in an attempt to limit patient variability to an adequately narrow scope so that the effect of a particular treatment is not lost in a sea of confounds. The front line clinician, of course, cannot afford this luxury. Psychotherapy as practiced involves many patients whose problems are complex, frequently crossing disorder boundaries rather than presenting in tidy syndromal packages. As stated above, this picture is especially true with MDD due to a high comorbidity rate with other mental health problems. Therefore naturalistic studies are important because they can generalize to treatments as actually practiced. Additionally, these studies have importance because they include long-term follow-up of treated patients, a necessary requirement given the high relapse rate associated with the disorder.

Successful outcomes in these studies are usually defined as a reduced score or score below a certain predetermined level on a rating scale that measures depressive symptomatology. The Hamilton Depression Rating Scale (HDRS) is the most frequently used instrument among naturalistic designs (Bland, 1997). The degree of change the studies required in order to qualify a subject as recovered vary widely, from a score of 5 to 15. This variance limits the generalizability of results across studies because a score that would qualify a case as recovered in one study might not qualify it in another study.

Studies from the National Institute of Mental Health's Collaborative Study on the Psychobiology of Depression report that approximately 50% of patients had recovered from an MDD episode by one year from initial onset, with a full 77% recovering within four years. Further analysis showed the most improvement taking place early on with 63% of patients recovered at four months and only an additional 11% recovering during the remaining eight months of the first year. Acute onset of symptomatology predicted a better prognosis, whereas underlying chronic depression of two years or longer was associated with poorer outcomes. The generalizability of this study is limited because it included only treated subjects after they had sought treatment.

Piccinelli and Wilkinson (1994) reviewed more studies reporting on the outcome of MDD in clinical settings. Three of the studies, using a follow-up of ten years or more, found that 24% of treated clients had a full recovery, 76% had one or more recurrences, and 12% showed chronic depressive symptomatology (Surtees & Barklay, 1994). In the ECA report, the one-year remission rate for MDD was 45% with men having a slightly higher rate than women. On the whole, naturalistic studies have shown that for patients treated with psychotherapy, the majority will gain a substantial degree of lasting relief and achieve better functioning.

RANDOMIZED CONTROLLED STUDIES

While studies that employ naturalistic designs have illuminated the positive benefits of psychotherapy for depressed patients, they are of limited use when attempting to understand the differential effectiveness of *specific* treatments. Without a control group against which results can be measured, it can never be known whether change is the result of the treatment or some other factor such as time alone. Additionally, when the question is narrowed to which competing treatment is most effective, only studies employing Randomized Controlled Trials can demonstrate what the active variable is when a patient achieves remission. Among the research that has utilized RCTs, four studies are of particular importance because they are scientifically rigorous and methodologically strict.

THE NIMH TREATMENT OF DEPRESSION STUDY

The largest study to date is the National Institute of Mental Health Treatment of Depression Collaborative Research Program (TDCRP), completed in 1989. This study had two major goals: to test the practicality of a large collaborative multi-site clinical trial model and to examine the differential effectiveness of two brief psychotherapies, cognitive behavioral therapy (CBT) and interpersonal therapy (IPT), in treating depression (Elkin, 1994). The two psychotherapies were compared with a treatment of established efficacy, the antidepressant drug imipramine hydrochloride (IMI-CM). While the inclusion of a medication condition has led some to believe that this study was meant as a head-to-head comparison between psychotherapy and pharmacotherapy, this is not the case. A treatment which has been shown to be efficacious in ameliorating MDD was included to ensure that patient change was not due to a common variable outside or among the psychotherapies.

Additionally, the TDCRP study employed a control condition which comprised a placebo pill plus clinical management (PLA-CM). The placebo condition insured that the imipramine group was in actuality an adequate standard reference treatment in this *particular* study. Clinical management was also included in the imipramine and placebo conditions to control for general factors in the psychotherapies that might lead to patient improvement such as receiving attention or talking about one's problems. Guidelines for the clinical management component allowed for managing medication or placebo, monitoring side effects, and providing general support and encouragement only.

The TDCRP study included such state-of-the-art strategies as studying pure form therapy by using procedural manuals that specified in detail how each treatment was to be carried out and employed competency ratings to ensure that the manuals were implemented accurately in the therapeutic situation. Treatment was provided by experienced therapists who were carefully selected to meet high competency standards and who received further training in the treatment approaches. The therapists were subjected to ongoing supervision for the entire study period. The subjects were restricted to nonbipolar, nonpsychotic, depressed outpatients, similar to the kind of patient for which CBT and IPT have been reported effective in past studies. In addition to measuring general depressive symptomatology, measures were included that examined each area specifically targeted by a particular treatment. For IPT, measures of social adjustment were included, dysfunctional attitude measures were used with CBT, and endogenous symptoms were measured in the IMI-CM condition.

The general effectiveness of the treatments was evaluated with four different measures. The Beck Depression Inventory (BDI) and the Hopkins Symptom Checklist-90 (HSCL-90) gave the rating perspective of the patient, while the Hamilton Rating Scale for Depression (HRSD) and the Global Assessment Scale (GAS) were used to measure the rating perspective of the clinician. Within the IMI-CM condition, the general direction of the results was similar on all measures, at all sites. Patients within this condition were the least symptomatic at the termination of treatment. In contrast, PLA-CM patients were the most symptomatic, with IPT and CBT subjects falling somewhat below the medication condition. Among the patients who had improved enough to be classified as recovered, using a criteria score of six or less on the HRSD and 9 or less on the BDI, IPT and IMI-CM had a significantly higher percentage of positive results than PLA-CM. From the general findings, it is evident that the IMI-CM condition was relevant in this study as a standard reference treatment. More importantly, no evidence of major significant differences between IPT and CBT in reducing depressive symptomatology was found. In terms of which therapy produced patient change first, the IMI-CM condition had consistently more rapid effects as measured by the HRSD and BDI.

In the areas specifically targeted by the individual treatments, three measures were used to examine change. The Social Adjustment Scale (SAS) was employed for IPT, the Dysfunctional Attitudes Scale (DAS) for CBT, and the Endogenous Scale of the SADS-C for IMI-CM. From the results on these measures, Imber et al. (1990) concluded that support for the superiority of either therapy in specific domains appeared quite limited. As they stated, "None of the therapies produced consistent effects on measures related to its theoretical origins." Elkin also noted that a previous study of IPT found differential effectiveness in the area of social adjustment only at follow-up.

In examining whether particular patient characteristics were related to the effectiveness of a specific treatment, several conclusions were reached. Three variables, cognitive dysfunction, social dysfunction, and work dysfunction, demonstrated differential treatment effects. Patients with low social dysfunction had lowered depression severity scores posttreatment when treated with IPT. CBT produced lower severity scores in patients who were high on cognitive functioning. IMI-CM appeared to be more effective in patients with high work dysfunction. Sotsky et al. (1991) explains these results as possibly originating in the specific learning techniques each psychotherapy employs. Patients with adequate capacity in an area emphasized by theory are in a better position to make good use of that approach. If this is true, depressed patients with significant impairment in the learning area that their particular psychotherapy focuses on may require longer treatment or alternative treatments (Elkin, 1994).

Several patient variables were related to better outcomes across all treatment conditions. Patients displaying low cognitive dysfunction and higher expectations of improvement had better outcomes. Patients who had depressive episodes that were short and who were younger in age also appeared to do better. Significantly fewer patients with personality disorders were classified as recovered at termination. Patients diagnosed as having double depression, i.e., an MDD episode overlying a chronic, mild to moderate depression, had worse outcomes.

Elkin (1994) sums the findings to date as supporting no major differences in efficacy between cognitive behavioral therapy and interpersonal therapy. Further, the only significant difference between the psychotherapies and the imipramine-clinical management was found in the medication condition patients' more rapid improvement and better results among those with higher initial severity. Follow-up findings have continued to demonstrate no significant difference between the psychotherapies in terms of relapse percentages (Shea et al., 1992). This information has also shown that a relatively small percentage of successful patients were relapse-free throughout an 18 month follow-up period. In light of these findings, Elkin has raised the possibility of whether or not short-term treatments are sufficient to achieve lasting remission.

THE SECOND SHEFFIELD PSYCHOTHERAPY STUDY

The Second Sheffield Psychotherapy Project (1990) was a head-to-head comparison of two psychotherapies to CBT and IPT. The study was designed to answer questions concerning three main issues: therapist allegiance, initial symptom severity, and differential response rates between therapies over time. While several studies, in contrast to the TDCRP study, have claimed differential effectiveness between CBT and IPT, these results disappeared when investigator allegiance to a particular therapy was controlled for statistically (Robinson, Berman, & Neimeyer, 1990). The Sheffield Project researchers claimed equal allegiance to both CBT and IPT. As stated above, the TDCRP study found that severely depressed patients were harder to treat with psychotherapy (Elkin, 1999). The Sheffield Project attempted to explore this question further by including measures of initial severity in the study design. Previous research by Howard, Krause, and Orlinsky (1986) reported that most treatment gains are made within the first 8 to 16 sessions. Subjects in the Sheffield study, therefore, were offered therapy courses consisting of either 8 or 16 sessions in order to examine the dose-response relationship of each psychotherapy.

Of 169 patients admitted to the study with a diagnosis of MDD, using DSM-IIIR criteria and the present state examination (PSE) to determine diagnosis, 117 completed the study. Patients were assigned to groups according to initial symptom severity, e.g., low, medium, or high. They were then randomized to receive one of the two psychotherapies and further randomized for a treatment length of either 8 or 16 weeks. Results were measured using the BDI. Both CBT and IPT were once again found to lack differential effectiveness and, furthermore, appeared to lack differential rates of response. In addition, all three levels of initial symptom severity appeared to have equivalent results. Treatment length, however, was found to interact with initial symptom severity. Patients exhibiting low or medium depressive symptomatology had equal outcomes with either 8 or 16 sessions. Subjects with more severe depression, however, showed significantly better outcomes in the group receiving 16 weeks of therapy.

Shapiro et al. (1995) followed up the Sheffield subjects at one year to examine relapse rates. Of the subjects classified as treatment responders, 57% were found to have maintained their functioning level, 32% had partially maintained this level, and 11% were classified as relapsed or having a recurrence. Equal response rates between the two therapies continued to be present at the one year follow-up. There was, however, an interaction between the type of psychotherapy received and length of treatment. Patients who had eight sessions of IPT appeared to fare less well than those receiving eight sessions of CBT. There also appeared to be somewhat better maintenance gains for patients who had 16 sessions of CBT.

In summary, the Sheffield Project lends further support to the TDCRP study in finding CBT and IPT equally effective. It further suggests that eight sessions of IPT are too little a dose to maintain treatment gains for an extended period of time and that there is limited evidence for a prophylactic effect of CBT. The Sheffield study has been criticized as having limited generalizability to clinical samples because the majority of patients were self-referred or referred through their employment and therefore might not represent a typical clinical population (Roth & Fonagy, 1996).

UNIVERSITY OF MINNESOTA STUDY OF COGNITIVE THERAPY AND PHARMACOTHERAPY

The University of Minnesota Study of Cognitive Therapy and Pharmacotherapy is another scientifically rigorous study. It was a comparison of CBT versus medication. One hundred and seven moderately to severely depressed patients were randomized among four treatment conditions. The first three conditions, consisting of imipramine plus clinical management (IMI-CM), cognitive behavioral therapy (CBT), and cognitive behavioral therapy plus imipramine (CBT-IMI) were 12 weeks in length. The fourth condition consisted of imipramine prescribed for the initial 12-week period with clinical management (IMI-CM). Patients in this condition continued on imipramine for one year.

As in the TDCRP study, therapists in this study were experienced with the treatments offered. Treatment, however, was more intensive, consisting of 20 sessions in the 12-week period. The clinical management component was similar in structure to the TDCRP study. It is important to note that, unlike the past two studies reported, attrition rate in the University of Minnesota study was quite high, with only 64 patients completing all treatments. Patient change was measured using the Beck Depression Inventory (BDI).

Results of the study once again showed neither of the two therapies to be superior. Unlike the TDCRP study, no interaction between initial symptom severity and treatment outcome was found. After two years, however, 44 of the 64 subjects who completed treatment were examined and clear differences between treatment conditions existed. Patients who received IMI-CM for only 12 weeks showed a relapse rate of 50%, most of which occurred within the first four months after termination. The relapse rate of patients receiving CBT alone or CBT-IMI was much lower, at 18%. When relapse did occur for these patients, it occurred at a mean of 17.4 months, significantly longer after treatment when contrasted to the patients who received IMI-CM for the 12 weeks alone. When IMI was continued for one year, relapse occurred at 32%, higher than the CBT patients. However, mean time to relapse, 17.3 months, was similar. Roth and Fonagy (1996) argue that this study provides good supporting evidence of the lasting value of CBT even when offered in brief treatment lengths. Care should be used when generalizing these results, due to the large initial attrition rate and small sample size at the two-year follow-up.

THE UNIVERSITY OF PITTSBURGH STUDY OF LONG-TERM MAINTENANCE THERAPY

Due to the substantial relapse rates that have been reported in all studies of depression, research that focuses on maintaining treatment gains is an area of obvious importance. The University of Pittsburgh Study was designed to examine these relapse rates by examining patients who had been successfully treated for an MDD episode (Frank, Kupfer, & Perel, 1989; Kupfer et al., 1992). In the study, 230 patients were randomized among five treatment conditions: medication clinic and imipramine (MC-IMI), interpersonal therapy and imipramine (IPT-IMI), medication clinic and a placebo pill (MC-PLA), interpersonal therapy alone (IPT), and interpersonal therapy with a placebo pill (IPT-PLA). It should be noted that patients were selected based on a history of recurrent depression, experiencing at least three previous episodes of MDD. As stated above, this is important because the natural history of depression has shown that patients with three or more episodes have a much poorer prognosis.

Treatment was provided once a week for 12 sessions. Patients were then treated two times weekly for eight weeks and finally were seen on a monthly basis. The Hamilton Rating Scale of Depression (HRSD) and the Raskin Depression Scale (RDS) were used to measure outcome. Once subjects had reached remission of symptoms, treatment was continued for 17 more weeks. If a subject's HRSD and RDS scores remained stable during this period, he or she was then randomized to one of the five maintenance treatments for three years or until relapse occurred. It should be noted that while IPT was prescribed at what would be considered a maintenance dose, imipramine continued to be prescribed at levels that are considered high for a maintenance condition, a mean of 207 mg daily (Roth & Fonagy, 1996). Results showed an average rate of recurrence of 22.6% for subjects treated in the two IMI conditions, IMI-MC and IMI-IPT. This was lower than the 78.2% rate reported for the PLA only condition. Patients in the IPT only and IPT-PLA conditions had an average 44.2% rate of recurrence. Patients in the IPT-IMI condition had the longest mean time to recurrence, that of 131 weeks, with a standard deviation of plus or minus 10 weeks. This should be contrasted with the MC-PLA condition, in which the mean time to recurrence was 45 weeks, with a standard deviation of 11 weeks. IPT, when offered by itself, had a mean relapse time of 82 weeks, plus or minus 13 weeks.

It should be noted that Frank, Kupfer, Wagner, McEachran, and Cornes (1991) reported that patients who received the highest quality of treatment in the IPT condition had recurrence rates equal to those of imipramine. Quality of treatment was determined by applying rating scales of therapy adherence to video tapes of selected sessions. This result is especially impressive considering that the median time to recurrence of patients who received high-quality IPT was close to 24 months, while subjects who received low-quality IPT had a median time to recurrence of only five months.

Kupfer et al. (1992) have reported on a further two-year follow-up of those patients who had been randomized in the imipramine conditions. These patients were further randomized into an additional trial of imipramine versus a placebo pill. Only 20 patients were selected for this trial, and, therefore, generalizability of results remains questionable. Of these 20, however, 13 continued to receive maintenance IPT and were evenly distributed among the IMI and PLA conditions. Once again, mean time to recurrence was statistically greater for patients receiving IMI with 99.4 weeks to recurrence, with a standard deviation of 4.4 weeks. In the placebo condition, mean time to recurrence was 54.0 weeks with a standard deviation of 14.6 weeks. It is important to note that only 11% of subjects who received neither medication nor IPT survived this period without an additional episode of MDD.

Psychotherapy offered in combination with pharmacotherapy appears to have impressive results in light of the University of Pittsburgh Study findings. These results are not only statistically but clinically significant. Further, the results reported for high-quality versus low-quality therapy implementation have significance for therapist training issues and merit further study.

Summary of Randomized Controlled Studies

In this chapter, four individual studies have been examined. These studies have been scientifically rigorous and appear to be some of the best the field has to offer. They employed randomized clinical trials and manualized treatments. Results have demonstrated the effectiveness of interpersonal therapy and cognitive behavioral therapy in treating MDD. The effectiveness of IPT and CBT have also been established when compared to imipramine, considered a standard reference pharmacological treatment for MDD. Patients have achieved results that are clinically significant and lasting, even when offered treatment for only a brief period of time. At the same time, these studies show that even when offered the best treatment available, many patients will relapse and approximately one in 12 patients will remain chronically depressed. Relapse rates, however, can be significantly reduced through effective maintenance treatments.

META-ANALYTIC REVIEWS

Two meta-analytical reviews, which will be discussed here, have been noted as standing out from others in the literature due to their thoroughness (Roth & Fonagy, 1996). Because they are based on much larger pools of subjects, and diverse methodology, meta-analytic reviews allow for more confidence in the conclusions than individual studies. A review of 39 studies stating psychotherapy is effective in treating depression represents a much surer foundation than one study. However, the studies that are compared in a review must be carefully selected to avoid applying statistical procedures to dissimilar patients and treatments.

Agency for Health Care Policy and Research Review

The United States Government Agency for Health Care Policy and Research (AHCPR) has published depression treatment guidelines based on a meta-analytic review published in 1993. This review analyzed 29 studies: 10 using behavioral therapy, 6 using brief dynamic therapy, 12 using cognitive therapy, and 1 using interpersonal therapy. Standard statistical practice for meta-analytic reviews involves computing effect sizes in order to establish treatment effectiveness. The AHCPR study, however, employed statistical techniques based on Bayesian models, titled the Confidence Profile Method (CPM). It has been argued that these methods, when used for meta-analytic reviews, increase sensitivity. While an account of the CPM is out of the scope of this chapter, the reader is referred to Eddy, Hasselbad, and Schacter (1990). Overall, results for the therapies reviewed showed behavioral therapy effective with 55.3%; brief dynamic therapy with 34.8%; cognitive therapy with 46.6%; and interpersonal therapy with 52.3%. The pooled effectiveness of all therapies was an even 50%. This issue can be compared with that arriving from the study of wait-list controls who had a 26% lower chance of achieving remission and placebo controls who had a 15.7% lower chance of achieving a remission. While the AHCPR review supports once again the effectiveness of psychotherapy against depression as compared to placebo or no treatment, the differential rates found between the therapies have been challenged. Roth and Fonagy (1996) argue that while CPM techniques are more sensitive than standard procedures, this method can also lead to misleading results. "Few clinicians would accept that behavior therapy alone was the most effective treatment for depression," (p. 82) as the AHCPR study reported. AHCPR researchers believe that a further extension of the data base is necessary before it will be sufficiently large to allow specific therapies to be accurately contrasted with one another.

Robinson et al. Review

The second meta-analytic review covered in this chapter was published by Robinson et al. in 1990. This review covered 58 studies ending in 1986, only 11 of which are covered by the AHCPR review. The studies appeared to be have less rigorous methodologies, including a notable absence of follow-up data. Overall results showed behavioral, cognitive, and cognitive-behavioral therapies to be moderately effective. Verbal therapies such as interpersonal therapy or brief dynamic therapy resulted in a more modest effect. It should be noted that, once again, investigator allegiance to a specific therapy was highly correlated with better results for that therapy. Evidence of differential effectiveness with specific patient characteristics and treatment outcome was not found.

Summary of Meta-Analytic Reviews

Meta-analytic reviews add further support for the effectiveness of structured psychotherapies in treating MDD. While the results of studies such as these should be viewed cautiously due to the ease with which misleading conclusions can be reached, meta-analytic reviews appear to bolster the evidence supporting the viability of psychotherapy as a treatment for depression. These same reviews have also supported the previous evidence of similar rates of remission for competing psychotherapies.

LESS STUDIED TREATMENTS

The variants of psychotherapy have proliferated to such a degree that one reviewer made reference to over four hundred types (Kazdin, 1986). Many of these therapies are derivatives of the most studied therapies reviewed above. However, a number of widely used therapeutic approaches have escaped rigorous examination. Experiential therapies comprise perhaps the largest of these approaches. These include client-centered, Gestalt, existential, and transpersonal therapy. In a review of the research on these treatments, Greenberg, Elliott, and Lietaer (1994) gathered information on all studies for which it was possible to calculate an effect size. Two of these studies were of depressed subjects and employed supportive/self-directive, Gestalt group and process-experiential therapies, respectively. The authors concluded that experiential therapies are clearly effective when compared to no treatment or placebo treatment. However, in comparison with cognitive and behavioral treatments, experiential therapies are slightly less effective. This finding did not hold for all varieties of experiential treatments reviewed and should be viewed with caution due to a wide range of subjects, designs, and outcome measures.

Beckham (1990) reported that while there has been no specific package developed for depression by analytic therapists, there have been six outcome studies that have included short-term analytically based treatments. Good results were obtained in five of the six with equal effectiveness to cognitive behavioral treatments found in those studies comparing the two treatments. Social skills training and self-control therapy, both components of some behavioral therapies, have been used as the main treatment in several studies which reported marked improvement and similar results to the comparison treatment—tricyclic antidepressants (Hersen, Bellack, Himmelhoch, & Thase, 1984; Roth, Bielski, Jones, Parker, & Osborn, 1982).

With few exceptions the research presented thus far has focused on therapy offered in a traditional manner, i.e., an identified patient meeting alone with a mental health expert. Other formats have for the most part received scant attention. Two alternative approaches that have been examined have shown positive results. The outcome literature on marital treatment formats has been reviewed by Jacobson, Holtzworth-Monroe, and Schamling (1989) and Beach, Fincham, and Katz (1998). Both groups report marital treatment as an effective approach to major depression with efficacy equal to CBT and IPT. This literature has also found relatively greater improvement in the marital relationship when expanding treatment to include the marital dyad.

Bibliotherapies also appear to be beneficial for some patients with depressive symptoms. A recent meta-analysis of bibliotherapy (Cuijpers, 1997) concluded that a variety of written material appeared effective, although the results were confounded by the small numbers of subjects and wide ranging types of bibliotherapy employed. Replication of these results under stricter methodology would have interesting implications since many variants of bibliotherapy involve no development of the therapeutic alliance, a common factor among treatments that is commonly accepted as a necessary ingredient in any successful outcome.

PSYCHOTHERAPY AND PHARMACOTHERAPY

As previously stated, Elkin (1994), reporting on the TDCRP study, found better results for antidepressants over psychotherapy in clients with more severe symptoms. This finding has been challenged by recent research (DeRubeis, Gelfand, Tang, & Simmons, 1999). Using similar cutoff scores on similar measures on a preexisting data set of an equal number of subjects as the TDCRP, McLean and Taylor (1992) found no evidence for better response rates among severe clients when treated with pharmacological interventions. Others have taken issue with the guidelines that emanated from the AHCPR review (1993) recommending antidepressant treatment as the first-line treatment. For patients receiving interventions in primary care settings at the University of Pittsburgh School of Medicine, no significant differences were found between antidepressant therapy (nortriptyline) and interpersonal personal therapy (Schulberg, Pilkonis, & Houck, 1998)—a finding that has additional importance in light of surveys showing psychological treatments are much more accepted by the public, and particularly IPT (Priest, Vize, Roberts, Roberts, & Tylee, 1996; Wilson, 1992). Further, the degree to which a client accepts the treatment has been presented as an important predictor of outcome (Ilardi & Craighead, 1994).

In a review of the evidence for the superiority of pharmacologic treatments, Antonuccio, Danton, and DeNelsky (1995) examined the literature from single studies and meta-analytic reviews comparing antidepressant medication and a range of psychotherapies including CBT, IPT, behavioral treatments, and social skills training. The authors concluded that psychotherapy treatment is equal to medication. While antidepressants alleviated symptoms more quickly than psychotherapy, pharmacologic treatments faired less well during follow-up. Specifically, CBT patients have less depression and IPT patients have better social functioning than medication patients in post-treatment periods (see also Beckham, 1990 and Fava, Grandi, Zielezny, Rafanelli, & Canestrari, 1996). Additionally, psychotherapeutic treatments were effective for vegetative symptoms. In contrast to Antonuccio, Danton, and DeNelsky's work, a recent study of combined treatment using IPT and nortriptyline as a maintenance therapy for elderly depressed patients found combination treatment superior to either therapy alone (Reynolds et al., 1999).

The research on the differential effectiveness between psychological and pharmacological interventions to date has involved tricyclic antidepressants (TCA). Newer antidepressants, specifically selective serotonin re-uptake inhibitors (SSRI) have not been studied. However, a recent report prepared for the AHCPR (1999) which reviewed the literature comparing the relative effectiveness of TCA's to SSRI's concluded the two drug classes have similar efficacy and only difference of 1% drop-out rate due to side effects with the results favoring SSRI's (see also Sheldon et al., 1993). Assuming that the same relationship holds for SSRI's and psychotherapy as TCA's and psychotherapy, it is possible to argue that psychotherapy is as effective as SSRI's. However, only a direct comparison between the two treatments would ensure the correctness of this reasoning.

If depression can be alleviated equally well with either psychotherapeutic or pharmacologic interventions, what effects does combining the two approaches have? While it might appear to be logically sensible that a package of psychotherapy and medication would contain additive properties leading to better outcomes, especially in light of findings that medication acts faster and psychotherapy has prophylactic effects after treatment has concluded, the research on this area has produced contradictory findings. Past research in support of combined treatment has been supported through a number of articles by Weissman and Klerman (see Weissman, 1979) who concluded that combined treatment appeared to be more effective than either treatment alone, albeit not at a statistically significant level. Antonuccio, Danton, and DeNelsky in the same review cited above take issue with Weissman and Klerman's findings due to methodological problems and the weakness of the reported differences among treatments. After conducting a further review of more recent literature, these researchers concluded that the available evidence does not support significant advantages of drug-psychotherapy combination treatments.

Common Factors

From the above discussion it is apparent that many theoretically disparate therapies have been shown to be effective in treating major depression, yet none has clearly risen above the rest as the treatment of choice. Not only does the type of therapy a person receives fail to predict outcome, studies have even reported a large proportion of the total amount of change occurs before therapy-specific techniques are introduced. For example, in a review of CBT studies, Ilardi and Craighead (1994) found the majority of patient change occurred prior to the introduction of cognitive-therapy-specific techniques. Lambert (1990) has stated "factors common across therapies seem to make up a significant portion, if not the bulk, of what is therapeutic in the psychotherapies" (p. 6). The factors comprising the largest amount of variance are attributable to characteristics the patient brings to therapy, the therapist, and the relationship that develops between the patient and therapist (Henry, 1998). Zuroff, Blatt, Sotsky, et al. (1999) have studied the interaction of the patient's perfectionistic tendencies and the alliance over the course of treatment. More perfectionistic patients have poorer outcomes and they seem to be impeded, in part, by their failure to develop stronger alliances. While a complete review of these common factors among therapies is out of the scope of our discussion, we will present several findings relevant to major depression treatment briefly. For a more complete exploration of these topics, we refer the reader to Garfield (1994) and Beutler, Machado, and Neufeldt (1994).

In an analysis of patient characteristics related to final status in the TDCRP study, Sotsky et al. (1991) reported six patient variables related to outcome regardless of therapy type: social dysfunction, cognitive dysfunction, expectation of improvement, endogenous depression, double depression, and episode duration. Initial severity was also predictive, however, as reported above this finding has not been replicated. Patient characteristics related to outcome in specific treatment modalities were as follows: Low social impairment was associated with better response to IPT, low cognitive impairment was associated with better response in CBT and IMI-CM, and high work-related impairment was associated with better response to IMI-CM. Results from the Second Sheffield Psychotherapy Project have also been analyzed using patient characteristics (Hardy, Shapiro, Stiles, & Barkham, 1998). Clients in the interpersonal/dynamic condition had worse outcomes if they had a co-morbid disorder and a low preference for psychological treatments. The cognitive/behavioral condition appeared to be less effected by similar clients characteristics.

As stated above, the degree to which a patient agrees with the treatment rationale is predictive of outcome (Ilardi & Craighead, 1994).

Others have also found clients perceived reasons for their depression to be predictive of differential response (Addis & Jacobson, 1996). Clients focusing on existential reasons for their depression faired better with cognitive therapy than behavioral. Interpersonally focused clients had poor outcomes in cognitive therapy. As these researchers and others have pointed out, random assignment to treatment condition destroys the potentially better outcomes that could occur with clients matched to treatments based on a best-fit basis.

The TDCRP data has been used to examine therapist-specific contributions to treatment outcomes. More effective therapists were found to be more psychologically oriented, to use fewer biological treatments, and to believe that successful treatment would take a longer period of time than less successful therapists (Blatt, Sanislow, Zuroff, & Pilkonis, 1996). Clinicians who created a strong alliance with the patient were also more successful. The role of therapist-patient gender match or mismatch has been evaluated in a separate analysis of the TDCRP study. No significant effects were found for gender of therapist, therapist-patient gender similarity or dissimilarity, or patient beliefs concerning which gender would be more helpful (Zlotnick, Elkin, & Shea, 1998).

CHAPTER SUMMARY

Major depression appears to affect approximately three percent of the population at any one time. Persons affected with this disorder are a major public health concern. Major depression is a disorder that affects not only the patient but also those involved in the patient's life, including family members, friends, employers, and treatment providers. Depression left untreated for the majority of cases is depression that can become chronic and debilitating. Implementation of effective treatments is urgently needed. As others (Beckham, 1990) have stated, due to the inherent complexity of evaluating psychological treatments, the power of psychotherapy cannot rest on a few studies alone. A substantial body of outcome research now exists which supports the effectiveness of psychotherapy as a first-line treatment for depression. Research using naturalistic designs, randomized controlled trials, and meta-analytic reviews show that patients treated by psychotherapeutic means achieve symptom amelioration at a clinically significant level. These results are impressive given the natural history of the disorder as reoccurring throughout the lifespan. Psychotherapy can achieve results comparable to medication, especially when treatment quality is high. This finding is of special importance to those who either can't or won't take antidepressants. Furthermore, research points to the possible prophylactic effects of particular therapies, particularly CBT.

Relapse and recurrence, however, continue among a substantial number of patients who have successfully completed treatment. Given that the majority of studies reported on here and in the literature involve a relatively short number of sessions, future studies should examine the relationship between treatment length and future depressive episodes. Continued research on maintenance treatments needs to be furthered, including cost-offset studies designed to show whether booster treatments are able to save money over the course of the disorder. These studies should include long-term follow-up periods.

Large multi-site undertakings such as the TDCRP study are not only possible, but represent some of the best research the field has to offer. Funding should be sought to continue such endeavors. Alternative, promising approaches need further attention in order to prevent these treatments from becoming relegated to an inactive status simply because we are lacking information on their effectiveness. Psychotherapy researchers also need to examine interventions for a wider range of subjects and formats, in order to increase the scope and viability of psychological treatments.

If the strongest change agents in psychotherapy are found within the patient, therapist and their subsequent relationship, efforts to understand these areas in relationship to depressive disorders need to be under taken. This research should be theory driven so that a confusing mass of variables are not left uninterpretable.

Nezu, Nezu, Trunzo, and McClure (1998) have made recommendations for both research and practice from the perspective of depression as a recurrent condition. Their suggestions are important to inpatient in future research and provide clinicians with a list of factors to consider as they consume research on depression and its outcomes. Research has consistently shown that psychotherapy works. Psychotherapists working with depressed persons can be confident that research supports the effectiveness of their interventions.

REFERENCES

Addis, M. E., & Jacobson, N. S. (1996). Reasons for depression and the process and outcome of cognitive-behavioral psychotherapies. *Journal of Consulting and Clinical Psychology, 64,* 1417–1424.

Agency for Health Care Policy and Research (1993). *Depression in primary care: Treatment of major depression* (AHCPR Publication No. 93-0551). Rockville, MD: U.S. Government Printing Office.

Agency for Health Care Policy and Research (1999). *Treatment of depression— Newer pharmacotherapies.* Summary, Evidence report/technology, Assessment 7, March 1999. Rockville, MD: Author. Available at *http:// www.ahcpr.gov/clinic/deprsumm.htm.*

American Psychiatric Association. (1994). *Diagnostic and statistical manual* (4th ed.). Washington, DC: Author.

Antonuccio, D. O., Danton, W. G., & DeNelsky, G. Y. (1995). Psychotherapy versus medication for depression: Challenging the conventional wisdom with data. *Professional Psychology: Research and Practice, 26,* 574–585.

Beach, S. R. H., Fincham, F. D., & Katz, J. (1998). Marital therapy in the treatment of depression: Toward a third generation of therapy and research. *Clinical Psychology Review, 18,* 635–661.

Beckham, E. E. (1990). Psychotherapy of depression research at a crossroads: Directions for the 1990s. *Clinical Psychology Review, 10,* 207–228.

Beutler, L. E., Machado, P. P. P., & Neufeldt, S. A. (1994). Therapist variables. In A. E. Bergin & S. L. Garfield (Eds.), *Handbook of Psychotherapy and Behavior Change* (4th ed.). New York: Wiley.

Bland, R. C. (1997). Epidemiology of affective disorders. *Canadian Journal of Psychiatry, 42,* 367–376.

Blatt, S. J., Sanislow, C. A., Zuroff, D. C., & Pilkonis, P. A. (1996). Characteristics of effective therapists: Further analyses of data from the national institute of mental health treatment of depression collaborative research program. *Journal of Consulting and Clinical Psychology, 64,* 1285–1289.

Blazer, D. G., Kessler, R. C., McGonagle, K. A., & Swartz, M. S. (1994). The prevalence and distribution of major depression in a national community sample: The national comorbidity survey. *American Journal of Psychiatry, 151,* 979–986.

Burke, K. C., Burke, J. D., Rae, D. S., & Regier, D. A. (1991). Comparing age at onset of major depression and other psychiatric disorders by birth cohorts in five U.S. community populations. *Archives of General Psychiatry, 48,* 789–795.

Cicchetti, D. K., & Toth, S. L. (1998). The development of depression in children and adolescents. *American Psychologist, 53,* 221–241.

Cross-National Collaborative Group. (1992). The changing rates of major depression: Cross-national comparisons. *Journal of the American Medical Association, 268,* 3098–3105.

Cuijpers, P. (1997). Bibliotherapy in unipolar depression: A meta-analysis. *Journal of Behavior Therapy and Experimental Psychiatry, 28,* 139–147.

DeRubeis, R. J., Gelfand, L. A., Tang, T. Z., & Simmons, A. D. (1999). Medications versus cognitive behavior therapy for severely depressed outpatients: Meta-analysis of four randomized comparisons. *American Journal of Psychiatry, 156,* 1007–1013.

Eddy, D. M., Hasselbad, V., & Schacter, R. (1990). A Bayesian method for synthesizing evidence: The confidence profile method. *International Journal of Technology Assessment in Health Care, 6,* 31–55.

Elkin, I. (1994). The NIMH treatment of depression collaborative research program: Where we began and where we are. In A. E. Bergin & S. L. Garfield (Eds.), *Handbook of Psychotherapy and Behavior Change* (4th ed.). New York: Wiley.

Ernst, C., & Angst, J. (1991). The Zurich Study, XII: Sex differences in depression: Evidence from longitudinal epidemiological data. *European Archives of Psychiatry and Clinical Neuroscience, 241,* 222–230.

Eysenck, H. J. (1952). The effects of psychotherapy: An evaluation. *Journal of Consulting Psychology, 16,* 319–324.

Fleming, J., & Offord, D. (1990). Epidemiology of childhood depressive disorders: A critical review. *Journal of the American Academy of Child and Adolescent Psychiatry, 29,* 571–580.

Frank, E., Kupfer, D. J., & Perel, J. M. (1989). Early recurrence in unipolar depression. *Archives of General Psychiatry, 46,* 397–400.

Frank, E., Kupfer, D. J., Wagner, E. F., McEachran, A. B., & Cornes, C. (1991). Efficacy of interpersonal therapy as a maintenance treatment of recurrent depression. *Archives of General Psychiatry, 48,* 1053–1059.

Garfield, S. (1994). Research on client variables in psychotherapy. In A. E. Bergin & S. L. Garfield (Eds.), *Handbook of Psychotherapy and Behavior Change* (4th ed.). New York: Wiley

Greenberg, L., Elliott, R., & Lietaer, G. (1994). Research on experiential psychotherapies. In S. L. Garfield & A. E. Bergin (Eds.), *Handbook of Psychotherapy and Behavior Change* (4th ed., pp. 509–539). New York: Wiley.

Hardy, G. E., Shapiro, D. A., Stiles, W. B., & Barkham, M. (1998). When and why does cognitive-behavioral treatment appear more effective than psychodynamic-interpersonal treatment? Discussion of the findings from the Second Sheffield Psychotherapy Project. *Journal of Mental Health, 7,* 179–190.

Harrington, R., Rutter, M., & Fombonne, E. (1996). Developmental pathways in depression: Multiple meanings, antecedents, and end points. *Development and Psychopathology, 8,* 601–616.

Henry, W. P. (1998). Science, politics, and the politics of science: The use and misuse of empirically validated treatment research. *Psychotherapy Research, 8,* 126–140.

Hersen, M., Bellack, A. S., Himmelhoch, J. M., & Thase, M. E. (1984). Effects of social skill training, amitriptyline, and psychotherapy in unipolar depressed women. *Behavior Therapy, 15,* 21–40.

Howard, K. I., Krause, M. S., & Orlinsky, D. E. (1986). The dose-effect relationship in psychotherapy. *America Psychologist, 41,* 159–164.

Ilardi, S. S., & Craighead, W. E. (1994). The role of nonspecific factors in cognitive-behavior therapy for depression. *Clinical Psychology: Science and Practice: Science and Practice, 1,* 138–154.

Imber, S. D., Pilkonis, P. A., Sotsky, S. M., Elkin, I., Watkins, J. T., Collins, J. F., Shea, M. T., Leber, W. R., & Glass, D. R. (1990). Mode-specific effects among three treatments for depression. *Journal of Consulting and Clinical Psychology, 58,* 352–359.

Jacobson, N. S., Holtzworth-Munroe, A., & Schmaling, K. B. (1989). Marital therapy and spouse involvement in the treatment of depression, agoraphobia and alcoholism. *Journal of Consulting and Clinical Psychology, 57,* 5–10.

Kazdin, A. E. (1986). Comparative outcome studies of psychotherapy: Methodological issues and strategies. *Journal of Consulting and Clinical Psychology, 54,* 95–105.

Kupfer, D. F., Frank, E., Perel, J. M., Cornes, C., Mallinger, A. G., Thase, M. E., McEachran, A. B., & Grochocinsky, C. J. (1992). Five year outcome for maintenance therapies in recurrent depression. *Archives of General Psychiatry, 49,* 769–773.

Lambert, M. J. (1990) Introduction to psychotherapy research. In L. E. Beutler & M. Crago (Eds.), *Psychotherapy research: An international review of programmatic studies* (pp. 1–11). Washington, DC: The American Psychological Association.

Lambert, M. J., & Bergin, A. E. (1994). The effectiveness of psychotherapy. In S. L. Garfield & A. E. Bergin (Eds.), *Handbook of Psychotherapy and Behavior Change* (4th ed., pp. 143–189). New York: Wiley.

Lewinsohn, P., Clarke, G., Seeley, J., & Rohde, P. (1994). Major depression in community adolescents: Age at onset, episode duration, and time to recurrence. *Journal of the American Academy of Child and Adolescent Psychiatry, 33,* 809–818.

Luborsky, L., Singer, B., & Luborsky, L. (1975). Comparative studies of psychotherapy. *Archives of General Psychiatry, 32,* 995–1008.

McLean, P., & Taylor, S. (1992). Severity of unipolar depression and choice of treatment. *Behavior Research and Therapy, 30,* 443–451.

Mirowsky, J. (1996). Age and the gender gap in depression. *Journal of Health and Social Behavior, 37,* 362–380.

Murray, C. J. L., & Lopez, A. D. (1997). Global mortality, disability, and the contribution of risk factors. *Lancet, 439,* 1436–1442.

Nezu, A. M., Nezu, C. M., Trunzo, J. J., & McClure, K. S. (1998). Treatment maintenance for unipolar depression: Relevant issues, literature review, and recommendations for research and practice. *Clinical Psychology: Science and Practice, 5,* 496–512.

Piccinelli, M., & Wilkinson, G. (1994). Outcome of depression in psychiatric settings. *British Journal of Psychiatry, 164,* 297–304.

Priest, R. G., Vize, C., Roberts, A., Roberts, M., & Tylee, A. (1996). Lay people's attitudes to treatment of depression: Results of opinion poll for defeat depression campaign just before its launch. *British Medical Journal, 313,* 858–857.

Reynolds, C. F., Frank, E., Perel, J. M., Imber, S. D., Comes, C., Miller, M. D., Mazumdar, S., Houck, P. R., Dew, M. A., Stack, J. A., Pollock, B. G., & Kupfer, D. J. (1999). Nortriptyline and interpersonal psychotherapy as maintenance therapies for recurrent major depression: A randomized controlled trial in patients older than 59 years. *Journal of the American Medical Association, 28,* 39–45.

Robins, L. N., & Regier, D. A. (Eds.) (1991). *Psychiatric disorders in America: The Epidemiologic Catchment Area Study.* New York: Free Press.

Robinson, L. A., Berman, J. S., & Neimeyer, R. A. (1990). Psychotherapy for the treatment of depression: A comprehensive review of controlled outcome research. *Psychological Bulletin, 108,* 30–49.

Romanski, A. J., Folstein, M. F., Nestadt, G., Chahal, R., Merchant, A., Brown, C. H., et al. (1992). The epidemiology of psychiatrist-ascertained depression and DSM-III depressive disorders: Results from the Eastern Baltimore Mental Health Survey clinical reappraisal. *Psychological Methodology, 22,* 629–655.

Roth, A., & Fonagy, P. (1996). *What works for whom?* New York: Guilford Press.

Roth, D., Bielski, R., Jones, M., Parker, W., & Osborn, G. (1982). A comparison of self-control therapy and combined self-control therapy and antidepressant medication in the treatment of depression. *Behavior Therapy, 13,* 133–144.

Schulberg, H. C., Pilkonis, P. A., & Houck, P. (1998). The severity of major depression and choice of treatment in primary care practice. *Journal of Consulting and Clinical Psychology, 66,* 932–938.

Segger, L. B., Lambert, M. J., & Hansen, N. B. (in press). Assessing clinical significance: Application to the Beck Depression Inventory. *Behavior Therapy.*

Shapiro, D. A., Rees, A., Barkham, M., Hardy, G., Reynolds, S., & Startup, M. (1995). Effects of treatment duration and severity of depression on the maintenance of gains following cognitive behavioral and psychodynamic interpersonal psychotherapy. *Journal of Consulting and Clinical Psychology, 63,* 378–387.

Shea, M. T., Elkin, I., Imber, S. D., Sotsky, S. M., Watkins, J. T., Collins, J. F., Pilkonis, P. A., Beckham, E., Glass, D. R., Dolan, R. T., & Parloff, M. B. (1992). Course of depressive symptoms over follow-up: Findings from the National Institute of Mental Health Treatment of Depression Collaborative Research Program. *Archives of General Psychiatry, 49,* 782–787.

Sheldon, T. A., Freemantle, N., House, A., Adams, C. E., Mason, J. M., Song, F., Long, P., & Watson, P. (1993). Examining the effectiveness of treatments for depression in general practice. *Journal of Mental Health, 2,* 141–156.

Sotsky, S. M., Glass, D. R., Shea, M. T., Pilkonis, P. A., Collins, J. F., Elkin, I., Watkins, J. T., Imber, S. D., Leber, W. R., Moyer, J., & Oliveri, M. E. (1991). Patient predictors of response to psychotherapy and pharmacotherapy: Findings in the NIMH treatment of depression collaborative research program. *American Journal of Psychiatry, 148,* 997–1008.

Spitzer, R., Koenke, K., & Linzer, M. (1995). Health-related quality of life in primary care patients with mental disorders. *Journal of the American Medical Association, 274,* 1511–1517.

Sprock, J., & Yoder, C. Y. (1997). Women and depression: An update on the report of the APA task force. *Sex Roles, 36,* 269–297.

Surtees, P. G., & Barklay, C. (1994). Future imperfect: The longterm outcome of depression. *British Journal of Psychiatry, 164,* 327–341.

Weissman, M. M. (1979). The psychological treatment of depression: Evidence for the efficacy of psychotherapy alone, in comparison with and in combination with pharmacotherapy. *Archives of General Psychiatry, 36,* 1261–1269.

Weissman, M. M., Bland, R. C., Canino, G., Faravelli, C., Greenwald, S., Hwu, H. G., et al. (1996). Cross-national epidemiology of major depression and bipolar disorder. *Journal of the American Medical Association, 276,* 293–299.

Wilson, G. L. (1992). Alternative models of treatment for depression: Validation of coping therapy. *Psychotherapy in Private Practice, 11,* 29–48.

Zlotnick, C., Elkin, I., & Shea, M. T. (1998). Does the gender of a patient or the gender of a therapist affect the treatment of patients with major depression? *Journal of Consulting and Clinical Psychology, 66,* 655–659.

Zuroff, D. C., Blatt, S. J., Sotsky, S. M., Krupnick, J. L., Martin, D. J., Sanislow, C. A., & Simmens, S. (1999). Relation of therapeutic alliance and perfectionism to outcome in brief outpatient treatment of depression. *Journal of Consulting and Clinical Psychology, 67.*

3

Cultural Considerations for Understanding, Assessing, and Treating Depressive Experience and Disorder

Anthony J. Marsella and Aaron Kaplan

INTRODUCTION

The Importance of Cultural Considerations in Depressive Experience and Disorder

Within the last decade, depressive experience and disorder has emerged as one of the world's major health and social problems (e.g., Bebbington, 1993; DesJarlais, Eisenberg, Good, & Kleinman, 1995). This fact can be attributed to a spectrum of *biological* (e.g., longevity, chronic diseases, toxin exposure, malnutrition, medications), *psychological* (e.g., identity confusion and conflict, loss of meaning, learned helplessness, powerlessness), and *sociocultural and environmental* (e.g., role confusion and conflict, uprooting due to war and natural disasters, urbanization, rapid social change, cultural disintegration and collapse, and racism and sexism) factors associated with the etiology, exacerbation, and maintenance of depressive experience and disorder. As a result of the increased worldwide risk and burden of depressive experience and disorders (Murray & Lopez, 1996), it is essential researchers and professionals improve their understanding of the complex cultural knowledge, issues, and concerns related to this problem.

This chapter reviews some of the important cultural knowledge, issues and concerns associated with the understanding, assessment, and treatment of depressive experience and disorders. These issues and concerns have now become an essential part of general mental health knowledge and also various academic and professional specialties such as transcultural psychiatry, psychiatric anthropology, culture and psychopathology, and cross-cultural counseling and psychotherapy (e.g., Marsella, 1993). These specialties, whose roots can be traced to the early 1900s, now occupy respected positions in the mental health field, and they developed an increased following. Ironically, it was Emil Kraepelin (1904), the father of modern psychiatry's classification system, who when confronted with diagnostic difficulties in Southeast Asia, first proposed the creation of a new psychiatric specialty—*Vergleichende Psychiatrie* or Comparative Psychiatry. Kraepelin suggested that cultural comparisons could help illuminate the problem of mental illness. Kraepelin wrote:

> The characteristics of a people should find expression in the frequency as well as the shaping of the manifestations of mental illness in general; so that comparative psychiatry shall make it possible to gain valuable insights into the psyche of nations and shall in turn also be able to contribute to the understanding of pathological psychic processes. (1904, p. 9)

It is now widely accepted that cultural factors influence our understanding, assessment, and treatment of depressive experience and disorder. Failure to accept this reality can lead to serious errors in clinical judgment and practice that could harm to the patient. In addition, failure to accept this reality can lead to violation in emerging professional and scientific guidelines and ethics, and this could result in legal action and professional censure (e.g., American Psychological Association, 1993; Casas, Ponterotto, & Gutierrez, 1986; Comas-Diaz & Griffith, 1988; Sue, Arredondo, & McDAir, 1992; Tapp, Kelman, Triandis, Wrightman, & Coelho, 1973). Thus, clinicians and researchers must develop an appreciation and awareness of this important topic.

Assessment and treatment of homogenous populations in Western cultures are complicated processes that are subject to considerable error because of reliability and validity issues. When ethnocultural considerations are introduced into research and clinical practice, these activities assume greater complexity and consequence. This is because cultural variations in the nature and meaning of depressive experience and disorder have critical implications for assessment, diagnosis/classification, and treatment. Cultural variations imply cultural relativism regarding notions of epistemology, personhood, self, body, health and disorder, normality, and the spectrum of social and interactive behaviors (e.g., Fabrega, 1989; Marsella & Yamada, in press). In brief, to the extent cultures differ in their constructions of reality, their meaning systems, and their socialization patterns, differences will emerge in psychopathology including depressive experience and disorder.

THE CONCEPT OF DEPRESSIVE EXPERIENCE AND DISORDER

Western Historical Perspectives

Depressive experience and disorder have long been a source of concern in Western cultural traditions. Hippocrates (330–399 BCE) included melancholia within his tripartite classification of disorders (i.e., mania, melancholia, phrenitis). He considered its cause to be a function of excessive black bile. Stanley Jackson (1986), in his scholarly book on the topic, *Melancholy and Depression: From Hippocratic Times to the Present*, points out that the term "melancholy" was first used in ancient Greece to describe a disorder characterized by fear, nervous conduct, and sorrow. By the fourth century AD, the Christian Church had begun to shape the concept of melancholy with its use of the term *acedia* to designate a cluster of feelings and behaviors associated with "dejection" (Jackson, 1986). The condition was often associated with religious fervor among monks and others that practiced isolation and self-denial. It came to mean sluggishness, lassitude, torpor, and non-caring, as well as those emotions associated with *tristitia* (i.e., sadness) and *desperatio* (i.e., despair) (see Jackson, 1986, pp. 65–70).

In the 13th century, David of Augsburg wrote the following commentary on *acedia*:

> The vice of acedia has three kinds. The first is a certain bitterness of the mind which cannot be pleased by anything cheerful or wholesome. It feeds

upon disgust and it loathes human intercourse. . . . The second kind is a certain indolent torpor which loves sleep and all the comforts of the body, abhors hardship, . . . and takes its delight in idleness. . . . The third kind is a weariness in such things only as belong to God. (see Jackson, 1986, p. 72)

"Melancholy" was used extensively in Europe until the 17th century when the term "depression" began to acquire currency. The promotion of "melancholy" as a major mood disorder, dysfunction, and problematic characterological orientation was assisted by the publication of Robert Burton's tome, *The Anatomy of Melancholia,* published in 1652. This book gained immediate and widespread popularity and remained a vital source of clinical insight and acumen on mood problems for subsequent centuries because of its encyclopedic coverage of the topic. Burton (1652/1998) wrote:

I'll change my state with any wretch,
Thou canst from gaol or dunghill fetch:
My pain's past cure, another hell,
I may not in this torment dwell!
Now desperate I hate my life,
Lend me a halter or a knife;
All my griefs to this are jolly,
Naught so damn'd as melancholy (1652/1998, XX)

"Depression," according to Jackson is derived from the Latin word *deprimere* meaning "to press down." With the passage of time, "depression" gained increasing currency in English, French, and German medical treatises. Initially, it was used as a subset of "melancholy," then as a synonym, and later as a replacement for the term. Kraepelin's use of the classic term "manic-depression" in his classification of the psychoses helped legitimize and promote the term "depression" within psychiatry, gradually elevating it to its present position of importance and concern. It is noteworthy, that "melancholy" has re-emerged in DSM IV as a major sub-type of depression characterized by symptoms associated with the previous concept of "endogenous depression" (e.g., APA, 1994; Jackson, 1986).

The continuous presence of the terms "melancholy" and "depression" through the past centuries of Western European and North American history—indeed its literal dominance of psychiatric thought and practice—suggests a massive and widespread cultural pre-occupation with the topic. This is especially true because of Judeo-Christian religious concerns with guilt, sin, sloth, despair, and worthlessness. But, the longevity and pervasiveness of this pre-occupation has not necessarily increased our understanding of the topic, especially with regard to its etiology, assessment, and treatment. Theories and classification systems abound today, as do a multiplicity of approaches to measurement and diagnosis/classification (e.g., APA, 1994). Controversy and debate continue as professionals and researchers seek to disentangle the complex web of biological, psychological, and social determinants, and the historical overlays that have shaped our understanding.

Problems in Psychiatric Diagnosis and Classification

Within Western psychiatry, biological and psychological perspectives have dominated thinking, and little attention has been directed to ethnocultural variations in depressive experience and disorder, and the significance these variations could have for rethinking current views. Clearly, ethnocultural variations in depressive experience and disorder demand that Western psychiatry and psychology—now exported throughout the world as universally applicable and relevant—revise many of their assumptions and practices. In a strong statement, Thakker and Ward (1998) noted that the implicit assumption of universality of DSM-IV primary syndromes limits its utility and validity. Good (1992) and Mezzich, Kleinman, Fabrega, and Parron (1995) point out the serious consequences of misdiagnosis and bias for minority populations.

Changing DSM-IV to accommodate to these criticisms is an unwelcome alternative for Western psychiatry. Yet, transcultural psychiatrists are mounting increasing pressure. For example, Kirmayer (1998), the editor-in-chief of the journal *Transcultural Psychiatry*, devoted an entire issue to the transcultural problems of DSM-IV. Kirmayer wrote:

> While cultural psychiatry aims to understand problems in context, diagnosis is essentializing: referring to decontextualized entities whose characteristics can be studied independently of the particulars of a person's life and social circumstances. The entities of the DSM implicitly situate human problems within the brain or the psychology of the individual, while many human problems brought to psychiatrists are located in patterns of interaction in families, communities, or wider social spheres. Ultimately, whatever the extent to which we can universalize the categories of the DSM by choosing suitable level of abstraction, diagnosis remains a social practice that must be studied, critiqued, and clarified by cultural analysis (1998, p. 342).

It is the current opinion of many clinicians and scholars that this is precisely what is demanded. Cross-cultural research in anthropology, psychiatry, psychology and other professionals and disciplines has been uniform in its conclusion that there are substantial variations in depressive experience and disorder (e.g., Kleinman & Good, 1986; Manson & Kleinman, 1998). Continued efforts to disregard or dismiss this fact can only result in problems for both patients and practitioners. Different historical and cultural traditions frame depressive experience and disorders within different contexts, thereby promoting and/or limiting particular symptoms, and shaping different understandings and meanings.

The Vagaries of the Term

A major problem facing clinicians and researchers is the semantic confusion surrounding the term "depression." "Depression" denotes a mood, a symptom, and various syndromes of disorder and disease, and simultaneously connotes a broad spectrum of affective experiences and social consequences. In many instances, the three terms—mood, symptom, and syndrome—are discussed apart from the many different life contexts in which they are shaped, experienced, communicated, and responded to by others. That is to say, they are decontextualized. This is a serious problem because decontextualization permits the researcher or clinician to assign their ethnocentric meanings and interpretations to the problems.

In addition, it is important to recognize that within Western (Northern European, North American) psychiatry, the moods, symptoms, and syndromes associated with depressive experience and disorder have been attributed and linked to varying pathologies, etiologies, onset patterns, manifestations, associated disabilities, courses/outcomes, and treatment responsivities. In brief, quite apart from the complexities introduced by cultural considerations, there is extensive disagreement within Western psychiatry itself about the nature of depressive experience and disorders. The clinical and research data indicate that there is no single nor uniform depressive experience or disorder. Rather, there are numerous patterns, subtypes, and aggregations of causes and clinical parameters (see Table 3.1) that indicate that depressive experience and disorder constitute a broad spectrum of distressful, dysfunctional, and disordered states and conditions.

Efforts to accommodate these variations within simplistic conceptual systems such as DSM-IV have proven unsuccessful because they also

TABLE 3.1 Examples of Pathologies, Etiologies, Symptoms, Onsets, and Treatment Responsivities Associated with Depression Experience and Disorder in Western Psychopathology

Biological Pathologies:
  Neural synapse
  Axonal Transport (K, Na, Ca, Cl)
  Thyroid
  Adrenals
  Hormones
  Pineal Body

Etiologies:
 Biological:
  Genetics
  Toxins
  Viruses (e.g., Borna, Epstein-
    Barre)
  Neural Injury
  Trauma Stress (Sudden,
    Kindling)
  Light Cycles
  Birth Injury (anoxia, drug and/or
    medication induced)
  Secondary to illness
  Secondary to medication
 Psychosocial
  Cognitive Styles and Beliefs
  Self Systems
  Personality Types
  Temperament
 Socio-Environmental and Cultural
  Stressors
  Urbanization
  Social Change
  Minority Status

Onset Patterns:
  Sudden and Precipatous (within 24
    hours)
  Acute (within a week)
  Slow (period of weeks or months)
  Life Style (always been that way)

Diagnostic Patterns/Type
  Major depression
  Dysthymic
  Melancholia
  Bipolar
  Atypical
  Grief Reaction
  Secondary to Medication
  Secondary to Illness
  Agitated
  Anxious
  Angry
  Endogenous/Exogenous

Therapeutic Responsivity
  Medications (e.g., tricyclics)
  Cognitive Therapy
  Psychodynamic Therapy
  Humanistic Therapy

Courses and Outcomes
  Continuous
  Complete Recovery
  Partial Recovery
  Cyclical
  Permanent
  Suicide

have failed to capture the multitude of combinations and permutations and the multitude of cultural factors that exist. This failure has finally begun to be addressed by conventional Western psychiatry. The American Psychiatric Association yielded to the pressures from ethnic minority mental health professionals and others who had studied depressive experience and disorder across cultures and agreed to include cultural commentaries on depression in the section on major depressive disorders. The DSM-IV (1994), in part, modestly states:

> Culture can influence the experience and communication of symptoms of depression. Underdiagnosis or misdiagnosis can be reduced by being alert to ethnic and cultural specificity in the presenting complaints of a Major Depression Episode. For example, in some cultures, depression may be experienced largely in somatic terms rather than with sadness or guilt. Complaints of nerves and headaches (in Latino and Mediterranean cultures), of weakness, tiredness, or imbalance (in Chinese and Asian cultures), of problems of the "heart" (in Middle Eastern cultures), or of being "heartbroken" (among the Hopi) may express depressive experiences (1994, 324).

It is also notable that DSM-IV provides a lengthy list culture-bound disorders (e.g., *latah, koro, susto*) and it does note that these should be considered. But, it stops short of providing specific diagnostic procedures for assessing culture-bound disorders, and for warning diagnosticians of the risks of using DSM-IV categories for non-Western patients.

CULTURAL SENSITIVITY IN DIAGNOSIS AND CLASSIFICATION

On a more positive note, DSM-IV (1994) does provide guidelines for the cultural formulation of a case. These guidelines have not yet resulted in a standardized interview schedule (e.g., SCIDS). However, this is only a matter of time. More than two decades ago, Leininger (1984) called for culturological interviewing and assessment. It is now clear that patients should have a medical interview, a psychiatric interview, a psychological interview, and a culturological interview. It is the latter that will provide the patient's life context and perceptual meanings—information that is essential for proper care. The DSM-IV (1994, pp. 843–844) guidelines suggest five major areas be addressed:

1. *Cultural identity of the individual* [e.g., ethnocultural identity, language abilities and preferences];

2. *Cultural explanations of the individual's illness* [e.g., idioms of distress, meaning and perceived severity, any local illness categories used, perceived causes or explanatory models, current preferences for care];

3. *Cultural factors related to psychosocial environment and levels of functioning* [e.g., interpretations of social stressors, available social supports, levels of functioning and disability];

4. *Cultural elements of the relationship between the individual and the clinician* [e.g., note differences in culture and status of patient and clinician and possible problems these differences may present including problems regarding perceived normality, symptom expression, communication];

5. *Overall cultural assessment for diagnosis and care* [e.g., how does the cultural formulation impact diagnosis and care].

It is noteworthy that increasing numbers of non-Western psychiatrists and psychologists throughout the world are beginning to question and to challenge conventional Western mental health assumptions and conclusions. For example, Chakraborty (1991), an Asian Indian psychiatrist, writes:

> Even where studies were sensitive, and the aim was to show relative differences caused by culture, the ideas and tools were still derived from a circumscribed area of European thought. This difficulty still continues and, despite, modifications, mainstream psychiatry remains rooted in Kraepelin's classic 19th century classification, the essence of which is the description of the two major "mental diseases" seen in mental hospitals in his time—schizophrenia and manic depression. Research is constrained by this view of psychiatry. A central pattern of (western) disorders is identified and taken as the standard by which other (local) patterns are seen as minor variations. Such a construct implies some inadequacy on the part of those patients who fail to reach "standard." Though few people would agree with such statements, there is evidence of biased, value-based, and often racist undercurrents in psychiatry. . . . Psychiatrists in the developing world . . . have accepted a diagnostic framework developed by western medicine, but which does not seem to take into account the diversity of behavioral patterns they encounter. (p. 1204)

Marsella (1998a) notes that it is time for Western mental health professionals and scientists to reconsider their assumptions, methods, and conclusions within the culturally pluralistic context of our world. The current world population is approaching six billion people. Of this number, only one billion are of white European and North American ancestry. However, because their nations are the dominant economic and political powers, their cultural tradition—their world view—exercises a disproportionate influence on our approaches to mental health theory and practices. Marsella (1998) points out that Western mental health professionals and scientists have been guided by two assumptions: (1) problems reside in individual brains and minds, and thus, individual brains and minds should be locus of treatment and prevention; (2) the world in which we live can be understood objectively through the use of quantitative and empirical data.

Both of these assumptions stand in direct opposition to the post-modernist views that currently characterize and inform the study of culture and mental health relationships. These views emphasize the importance of the sociocultural context of psychological problems (i.e., powerlessness, poverty, underprivileging marginalization, inequality) in understanding the etiology and expression of psychopathology, and in understanding its assessment, diagnosis and treatment. In brief, problems of depressive experience and disorder must be understood within the cultural context that socializes, interprets, and responds to them. This requires that we proceed from different values, perspectives, and practices, especially those that emphasize context, ecology, and qualitative and naturalistic methods (e.g., Marsella, Purcell, & Carr, in press).

CULTURE AND DEPRESSIVE EXPERIENCE AND DISORDER

The Concept of Culture

Ethnocentrism

Ethnocentrism refers to the natural tendency or inclination among all people to view reality from their own cultural experience and perspective. In the course of doing so, the traditions, behaviors and practices of people from other cultures are often considered inferior, strange, abnormal, and/or deviant. Ethnocentrism becomes a problem in the field of mental health when certain realities regarding the nature and treatment of mental health are imposed on people by those in power without concern for possible bias (Marsella, in press a).

Culture

The authors will define culture as:

> Shared learned meanings and behaviors that are transmitted within social activity contexts for purposes of promoting individual/societal adjustment, growth, and development. Culture has both *external* (i.e., artifacts, roles, activity contexts, institutions) and *internal* (i.e., values, beliefs, attitudes, activity contexts, patterns of consciousness, personality styles, epistemology) representations. The shared meanings and behaviors are subject to continuous change and modification in response to changing internal and external circumstances.

This definition acknowledges that the meanings and behaviors shaped by culture, in both its external and internal representations, are dynamic and subject to continuous modification and change. While the impulse is generally toward adaptation and adjustment, it should be noted that cultures can frequently become pathogenic (e.g., Leighton, 1959; Edgerton, 1992) because of the values and cultural constructions of reality they impart. Culture is the lens or template we use in constructing, defining, and interpreting reality. This definition suggests that people from different cultural contexts and traditions will define and experience reality in very different ways. Thus, even mental disorders must vary across cultures because they cannot be separated from cultural experience. Marsella (1982) stated:

> We cannot separate our experience of an event from our sensory and linguistic mediation of it. If these differ, so must the experience differ across cultures. If we define who we are in different ways (i.e., self as object), if we process reality in different ways (i.e., self as process), if we define the very nature of what is real, and what is acceptable, and even what is right and wrong, how can we then expect similarities in something as complex as madness (1982, p. 363).

Ethnocultural Identity

Ethnocultural identity refers to the extent to which an individual endorses and manifests the cultural traditions and practices of a particular group. Clearly, what is important is not a person's ethnicity, but rather, the extent to which they actually are identified with and practice the lifestyle of that group. In groups undergoing acculturation, there can be considerable variation in the extent of ethnocultural identity with a particular cultural tradition. Thus, it is important to determine both a person's ethnicity and their degree of identification with their ethnocultural heritage. While some individuals may be bicultural, others may be fully acculturated, and still others may maintain a traditional identification.

Ethnocultural identity has emerged as one of the most popular new areas of inquiry in cross-cultural research. It is the "new" independent variable in cross-cultural research, replacing the simple comparison of different ethnic groups. Today, ethnocultural identity is being assessed by a variety of methods including the measurement of similarities in attitudes, values, and behaviors of different groups (e.g., Yamada, Marsella, & Yamada, 1998) as well as the extent of acculturation (e.g., Paniagua, 1994; Ramirez, 1999, see page 171). In studying cultural aspects of mental disorder, it is important that patients be evaluated for their degree of ethnocultural identification and acculturation. For example, if we are studying mental illness in Hispanic-Americans, we should first determine the extent of the patients' identification with Hispanic culture. If we use Western standards for assessment and diagnosis, we may create many problems. Yamada, Marsella, and Yamada (1998) and others (see special issue of Asian-American and Pacific Islander Journal of Health, 1998, Volume 6, #1) have developed a valid and reliable behavioral scales for the assessment of ethnocultural identification across ethnic groups. Ramirez (1999) discusses acculturation scales. As noted previously, the DSM-IV (APA, 1994) guidelines for the cultural formulation of a case list the cultural identity of the individual as the first criteria to be assessed when conducting a cultural formulation (see page 843).

LITERATURE REVIEW ARTICLES ON CULTURE AND DEPRESSIVE EXPERIENCE AND DISORDER

By the 1980s, a sizeable number of literature reviews on cross-cultural studies of depression had been published (e.g., Marsella, 1980; Marsella, Sartorius, Jablensky, & Fenton, 1986; Prince, 1968; Pfeiffer, 1968; Singer, 1975; Weiss & Kleinman, 1988). These reviews culminated in the most important book on the topic, Kleinman and Good's (1986) *Culture and Depression*. This edited volume provided a spectrum of theoretical and empirical chapters that uniformly suggested the cultural decontextualization of depression had resulted in inaccurate clinical and research conclusions. These early publications reached the following conclusions:

1. There is no universal conceptualization of depressive disorders;
2. The experience, meaning, expression of depressive experience varies as a function of the cultural context in which it occurs;
3. Somatic signs, symptoms, and complaints often dominate the presentation of depressive experiences in non-Western cultural contexts;
4. Guilt, self-deprecation, suicidal ideation and gestures, and existential complaints vary across cultures and especially tend to be rarer within non-Western cultures;
5. Standard personality correlates of depression in Western societies (e.g., low self-esteem) may not be present across cultures;
6. There is a need to study idioms of distress specific to across cultures.

In the last decade, a number of other review papers have been published sustaining the conclusions of the Kleinman and Good (1986) volume and the previous literature reviews (e.g., Bebbington, 1993; Jenkins, Kleinman, & Good, 1990; Manson, 1995). These reviews, both recent and past, provide a summary and overview of the extensive literature on cultural aspects of depressive experience and disorder, and the interested reader should consult them for details about studies and conclusions. It is now clear, however, that cultural variations exist in the following areas: meaning, onset, epidemiology, symptom expression, course and outcome. These variations have important implications for understanding clinical activities including conceptualization, assessment, and therapy.

HOW DOES CULTURE INFLUENCE DEPRESSIVE EXPERIENCE AND DISORDER

Some Cultural Determinants

Culture can influence depressive experience and disorder via a number of different cultural mechanisms and forces. These mechanisms and forces are listed in Table 3.2 as part of a brief self-evaluation that professionals and researchers can conduct regarding the extent of their patient's or subject's participation in cultural traditions or life styles that vary from those assumed in conventional western psychiatry and psychology. Table 3.2 is not a measure of ethnic identity, but rather a quick way for appraising cultural factors that can influence depressive experience and disorder.

One of the major cultural influences of depressive experience and disorder is the concept of personhood or selfhood held by a particular cultural tradition. More than two decades ago, Marsella (1980) noted that cultures that tend to socialize unindividuated self structures (i.e., sociocentric, collectivistic) in combination with strong metaphorical languages and imagistic mediations of reality promote "subjective" (context-based) epistemological orientations that encourage people to remain attached and bonded to others. This mitigates the isolation, loneliness, narcissism, and perceived helpless associated with depressive experience and disorder in Western cultural traditions. Other researchers have reported support for the personhood concept (e.g., Kleinman & Good, 1986; Koenig, 1997; Manson, 1995; Shweder, 1991). In one of the classic statements on personhood in non-Western cultures, Geertz (1973), an American cultural anthropologist, wrote:

> The Western conception of the person as a bounded, unique, more or less integrated motivational and cognitive universe, a dynamic center of awareness, emotion, judgment, and action, organized into a distinctive whole and set contrastively—both against other such wholes and against social and natural background—is however incorrigible it may seem to us, a rather peculiar idea within the context of the world's cultures. (Geertz, 1973, p. 34)

Marsella (1980, 1985) noted that depressive experience and disorder in non-Western cultures is often expressed without the associated existential problems found in the West because the non-western collective or sociocentric identity encourages the construction and experience of the disorder in somatic or interpersonal domains. The result is that complaints of personal meaninglessness, worthlessness, helplessness, guilt, and suicidal thoughts are reduced or absent. But, within Western cultures, the long historical pre-occupation with "acedia" and "melancholia" frames depressive experience and disorders within personal responsibility for "sin" and sin's related behaviors sloth, self-indulgence, suicide, worthlessness, guilt, and despair. Thus, for so much of Western history, depressive experience and disorder have been associated with

TABLE 3.2 A Checklist of Some of Cultural Determinants of Depressive Experience and Disorder

How much does your patient identify with ethnocultural traditions, life styles, behavior patterns, and world views in which there are cultural variations in the following:

Very Much (4)	Somewhat (3)	A Little (2)	Not At All (1)	Don't Know (0)

_____ 1. Cultural variations in the concepts of personhood, selfhood, and self-structure.

_____ 2. Cultural variations in concepts regarding the nature and causes of abnormality and normality, health, and wellbeing, and social deviancy and conventionality.

_____ 3. Cultural variations in concepts and practices regarding attitudes toward illness and disease.

_____ 4. Cultural variations in concepts and practices regarding breeding patterns and high-risk genetic lineages.

_____ 5. Cultural variations in concepts regarding pre-natal care, birth practices, and post-natal care, especially in such areas as nutrition and disease exposure.

_____ 6. Cultural variations in concepts and practices regarding socialization, especially regarding the importance of family, community, and religious institutions.

_____ 7. Cultural variations concepts and practices regarding medical and health care, especially with regard to the number and types of healers, doctors, sick-role statuses, etc.

_____ 8. Cultural variations in stressors such as sociotechnical change, sociocultural disintegration, family disintegration, migration, economic development, industrialization, and urbanization.

_____ 9. Culturally-related variations patterns of deviance and dysfunction including participation in alternative economies and social structures.

_____ 10. Cultural variations in stressors related to the clarity, conflicts, deprivations, denigrations, and discrepancies associated with particular needs, roles, values, statuses, and identities.

_____ 11. Cultural variations in stressors related to sociopolitical factors such as racism, sexism, and ageism and the accompanying marginalization, segmentalization, and underprivileging.

_____ 12. Cultural variations resources and coping patterns including institutional supports, social networks, social supports, and religious beliefs and practices.

If your evaluation earns more than 24 points, use of conventional Western psychiatry and psychology can result in potential errors and risks. If you assign numerous "don't know" ratings, it would be appropriate for you to conduct additional interviews and assessments prior to developing and initiating a therapeutic program. These figures have not been validated in studies but represent useful clinical guidelines that have developed out of the authors clinical and research experiences with ethnocultural minority and non-Western patients.

individual will power and strength of character. Depressive experience and disorder has been framed within a "moral" context. The phrases are well known: "It's up to you!" "You have got to pull yourself out of it." "It is your choice." Western cultural thinking managed to turn dysfunctions of multiple origins and expressions into a battleground within the individual between "good" and "evil." Personal responsibility for depressive experience and disorder became the norm, and guilt, worthlessness, and failure became hallmarks of immoral character associated with depressive experience and disorder—it was a deficit, a lack, an inadequacy, a fault in personal determination. Furnham and Malik (1994) provide an interesting discussion of cultural variations in beliefs about depression in which they point out the cultural variations in ideas about etiology, expression, and consequence.

Culture-Bound Disorders

Yet another approach for understanding cultural influences on depressive experience and disorders involves the concept of culture-bound disorders. Culture bound disorders represent a major area of concern and debate in the study of culture and mental health because their existence raises questions about the cultural foundations on which Western psychiatry is based. The DSM-IV (American Psychiatric Association, 1994) states the following about culture bound disorders.

> Culture-bound syndromes are generally limited to specific societies or culture areas and are localized, folk, diagnostic categories that frame coherent meanings for certain repetitive, patterned, and troubling sets of experiences and observations. There is seldom a one-to-one equivalence of any culture-bound syndrome with a DSM diagnostic entity. (APA, *DSM-IV*, 1994, p. 844)

But, if culture bound syndromes are limited to specific societies or culture areas, who defines what are the criteria for mental illness— American or European psychiatrists? Is it not possible that Western disorders also constitute culture bound syndromes since they are found primarily in Western cultures? Consider the current views on "anorexia" and "bulimia." Marsella (in press), noted that there are many questions that are still being debated regarding culture bound disorders including: (1) Should these disorders be considered variants of disorders considered to be "universal" by Western scientists and professionals (e.g., Is *susto* [soul loss] merely a variant of depression?)? (2) Are all disorders "culture-bound" disorders since no disorder can escape cultural encoding, shaping, and presentation (e.g., schizophrenia, depression, anxiety disorders)? In the case of depressive experience and disorder, a number of culture bound disorders (e.g., APA, 1994) have been reported to be associated with "depressive" functioning including *brain fag* (West Africa), *dhat* (Indian subcontinent), *shenjing shairuo* (Chinese), *susto* (Latino-Hispanic), *tawatl ye sni* (Sioux Indian).

The universal human capacity for sadness, grief, and remorse does not mean that depression, as a psychiatric construct, is universal. In the West, depression and melancholia have been considered a dysfunction for more than 2000 years. This historical and cultural embeddedness brings with it a set of meanings and implications for both the patient and the societal response to them. Today, many different kinds and patterns of depression are used (e.g., despair, helplessness, major depression, melancholia, atypical, agitated, dysthymic). These constructions of depression reflect not only medical knowledge, but also ideas about religion, social relationships, morality, related emotions such as aggression/hostility and anxiety/fear, and responses to life activity contexts (e.g., marriage, child rearing, work, stress situations). They also reflect Western notions about the essential nature and purpose of the person.

When depressive experience and disorder is considered within a historical and cultural framework, the potential for cultural variations in meaning and consequence become more apparent. The following set of questions may be useful:

1. What are the range of expressions for depressive experience and disorder?
2. What functions does having depressive experience disorder serve?
3. What situations does depressive experience and disorder occur?
4. What is the social response to depressive experience and disorders?
5. What are the range of causes of depressive experience and disorders
6. What are the range of treatments for depressive experience and disorder?

CULTURAL CONSIDERATIONS IN THE ETIOLOGY OF DEPRESSIVE EXPERIENCE AND DISORDER

Conventional psychiatry and psychology often proceeds from assumptions that depressive experience arise from dysfunctions or disorders in biological (e.g., genetics, neurotransmitter deficits, anatomical disorders [e.g., thyroid deficiency, adrenal dysfunction], medical illnesses, and medication side effects) and/or psychological (e.g., poor self esteem, faulty cognitions, personality styles). Yet to treat these problems without consideration of the problems that cultural roles, institutions, and social structures may play in generating and sustaining them cannot truly solve the problem. In brief, by confining attention to biological and psychological variables, there is a failure to acknowledge the interaction and interdependencies of different strata or levels of variables. While neurotransmitter deficits in serotonin or norepinephrine may be dysfunctional, a full understanding of the etiology of depressive experience and disorder requires attention be given to ascending levels of variables at the microsocial (e.g., family, community, workplace), macrosocial (e.g., social change, class structure, poverty, war). Neurochemistry responds to both genetic and microsocial/macrosocial variables. This is a standard systems perspective (e.g., Marsella, 1998b).

Mental health professionals cannot be content to treat pained and disordered psyches with medications and therapies, they must respond to the social and cultural milieu that the biology of the synapses and psyches come to represent, including the problems of rapid sociotechnical change, racism, poverty, inequality, and acculturation. It is out of these milieus that spring hopelessness, helplessness, marginalization, fear, anger, and powerlessness. Thus, biological and psychological variables are shaped and constructed within the larger cultural context of the macrosocial world via internal cognitive and affective representations. The world in which we live can be a source of comfort or of madness (e.g., Edgerton, 1992; Marsella & Yamada, in press; Sloan, 1996; Wilbur, 1998).

Within the larger context of contemporary life, cultures around the world are being faced with critical challenges that are linked to depressive experience and disorder including the following:

1. Socio-Environmental (e.g., crowding, pollution, noise, slums, unemployment, poverty, crime, homelessness, violence, industrialization, community decay);
2. Psychosocial (e.g., racism, sexism, inequality, cultural disintegration, social drift, social stress, social change);
3. Psychological and Spiritual (e.g., hopelessness, helplessness, powerlessness, alienation, anomie, fear, anxiety, isolation, loneliness, rootlessness, low quality of life, marginalization);

4. Biopsychological (e.g., malnutrition, toxins, immune reactions, stress-related collapse with its attendant changes in neurotransmitters and hormones).

In brief, depressive experience and disorder cannot be treated solely as dysfunctions of individuals. Their roots, precipitating circumstances, exacerbating, and maintaining conditions reside at multiple levels, and these too must be addressed if the problem is to be understood and solved. For example, is the worldwide increase in depressive experience and disorder related to the upheavals of social change including the collapse of traditional cultures and the subsequent alienation, powerlessness and confusion that this brings? Lastly, even as we look at etiological factors, we must consider the presence of cultural resources and protective factors through the presence of mourning rituals, nutritional patterns, religious rituals, and family supports.

CULTURAL CONSIDERATIONS FACTORS IN ASSESSMENT OF DEPRESSIVE EXPERIENCE AND DISORDER

Assessment of depressive experience and disorder has been conducted with self-report (e.g., Beck Depression Scale, Zung Depression Scale), interviewer rating scales (e.g., Hamilton Rating Scale, SCID, WHO Rating Scale), and in more recent decades, non-clinical family, attitude, and social cognition scales (see Marsella, Hirschfeld, & Katz, 1987). While these scales have been used as standards for depressive experience across ethnic and cultural groups, their validity remains in question. These self-report and interviewer rating scales are based on symptom criteria that are developed with Western patients. As a result, use with non-Western patients may result in faulty diagnoses because they do not sample culturally relevant symptoms and idioms of distress (e.g., Bertschy, Viel, & Ahyi, 1992; Ebert & Martus, 1994; Ebigno, 1982; Fugita & Crittenden, 1990; Griffith & Baker, 1993; Hamdi, Amin, & Abou-Saleh, 1997; Takeuchi, Kuo, Kim, & Leaf, 1989; Thornicroft & Sartorius, 1993; Zheng & Lin, 1991). These problems are associated with linguistic, conceptual, scale, and normative equivalence (e.g., Marsella, Dubanoski, Hamada, & Morse, in press). Equivalence refers to the "comparability" of the scale. Quite simply, is it equivalent, is it the same?

Linguistic equivalence refers to the similarity of the language used in the assessment instrument. This term acknowledges the importance of administering tests in the language preferences of the subjects under study. Linguistic equivalence is mainly concerned with translation. Accurate translation is best achieved when back translation methods are used. *Conceptual equivalence* refers to the similarity in the nature and meaning of a concept. For example, in the United States, the word "dependency" is associated with immaturity, childishness, helplessness, and many other derogatory terms. Contrast this view with Japanese culture in which children are socialized to be interdependent and to be an integral part of the family. *Scale equivalence* refers to the cultural comparability of the scales that are used in the assessment instrument. For example, the MMPI uses a true-false scale format. However, in many non-Western cultures, answering questions as simply "true" or "false" is extremely difficult because situational factors rather than over-riding principles determine the appropriate action or behavior. In addition to "true–false" scales, many non-Western cultural groups are unfamiliar with Likert and Thurstone scales. *Normative equivalence* is probably the form of equivalence that will be most familiar and understandable to professional psychologists. Normative equivalence requires that norms be available for the group being studied. If the norms for a particular personality test are based on Western college students and you use them with Vietnamese immigrants, your conclusions are likely to be questionable (e.g., Marsella, Dubanoski, Hamada, & Morse, in press; Marsella & Leong, 1993).

Constructs like depressive experience and disorder that are developed and used in Western psychiatry and psychology do not have the same connotative meanings in non-Western cultures. Thus, before beginning comparative studies, it is necessary to use ethnosemantic procedures (e.g., Marsella, 1987) to identify similarity in meanings and behavior patterns. These procedures provide a foundation for testing and/or establishing cultural equivalence. Ethnosemantic procedures involve (1) eliciting the universe of terms in a particular domain (e.g., the emotions), (2) ordering the terms according to various dimensions (e.g., good-bad, strong-weak), (3) assessing their meaning through word association and antecedent-consequence methods, and (4) mapping their behavioral or action components through observation or behavior intention scales. The result is an "emic" perspective of the construct one chooses to study or at least a better understanding of the biases associated with using construct.

Since many depression studies are based on self-report replies, there is a risk of bias because of cultural variations in response style and perceived demand characteristics of the instruments. While definitive research on cultural variations is still needed, there are studies indicating some cultural groups have difficulty with five and seven point Likert scale items and tend to endorse the middle positions (e.g., Marin, Gamba, & Marin, 1992; Watkins & Cheung, 1995). Marsella, Dubanoski, Hamada, and Morse (in press) stated:

> The simple fact of the matter is that asking self-report questions is a complex task. This is made even more complex when psychologists move across cultural boundaries to ask questions of people whose perceptions of the task and whose motivations to participate differ from those on whom the scale was constructed. These perceptual and motivational differences include (1) desire to conform socially, (2) fear of possible persecution, (3) concern for giving the "right" answer rather than an accurate answer, (4) desire to please authorities, (5) limited self awareness and insights, (6) confusion with the perceived meaning and implication of terms and words used in the questions, and (7) variations in the construction of personhood and personality (in press).

Assessment of depressive experience and disorder across cultures must consider the following factors: (1) appropriate items and questions, including the use of idioms of distress; (2) opportunities to index frequency, severity, and duration of symptoms since groups vary in their reporting within certain modes; (3) establishment of culturally relevant baselines in symptom parameters; (4) sensitivity to the mode and context of response (i.e., self-report, interview, translator present); (5) awareness of normal behavior patterns; (6) symptom scales should be normed and factor analyzed for specific cultural groups. Dana (1993) and Paniagua (1994) provide some of the most thorough and detailed discussions of the risks associated with culturally biased measuring instruments. In addition to listing risks and preferred procedures for assessment, Paniagua (1994) provides a self-evaluation instrument for clinicians to assess their possible biases and prejudices. It is clear that the measurement of depressive experience is a complex task. Crossing cultural boundaries introduces yet new problems in validity and reliability because of variations in the nature, meaning, and consequences of signs and symptoms, and the variations in measurement procedures and approaches.

CULTURAL CONSIDERATIONS IN THE TREATMENT OF DEPRESSIVE DISORDER AND EXPERIENCE

Patient and Therapist are Cultural Members

The treatment of depressive experience and disorders across cultures introduces yet other challenges for Western mental health professionals and researchers (e.g., Marsella & Westermeyer, 1995; Paniagua, 1994). As the products of cultural histories, traditions, and activities, both the therapist (healer) and the patient bring assumptions, expectations, and practices to the therapeutic encounter. To the extent that these are shared, there is some degree of convergence, across values, communication content and styles, interpersonal styles, cognitive styles, and motivations, and while this convergence may not guarantee cure, it does reduce some of the many risks associated with assessment, diagnosis, and treatment. In contrast, the growing likelihood that the therapist (healer) and patient may differ in their cultural histories, traditions, and activities because of increasing cultural pluralism (e.g., Russian immigrant doctor treating a Haitian refugee) brings with it a new set of challenges. This is especially true for depressive experience and disorder because of the cultural variations in the definition, expression, and consequences associated with emotions and their dysfunctions. Indeed, even the use of psychoactive medications for depression across cultural and racial boundaries has been shown to be problematic because of variations in dosage levels, brain receptor responsivity (i.e., pharmacodynamics), side effects, circulating blood plasma level concentrations, and metabolism (e.g., Lin, Poland, Chang, & Chang, 1995; Lin, Poland, & Nakasaki, 1993). Thus, the challenge is to develop and apply techniques for behavior change that are relevant and meaningful to the patient, and this means to the patient's cultural history and traditions.

Patient Has Unique Bio-Psycho-Social Identity

Each patient is unique. This should be forgotten or minimized. Each patient must be considered with regard to their specific needs, concerns, styles, abilities, perceptions, and expectations. Just as it is wrong to treat patients from different cultural groups as if they were all the same, so is it wrong to treat a patient stereotypically as a member of a particular cultural, racial, gender, age, religious, or occupational social identity. This means that it is incumbent upon the therapist to consider and assess each of these factors at the beginning of therapy. This can be done informally by therapist appraisal or formally via various identification scales. The product of this appraisal is a portrait of the patient's embeddedness and attachment to the various identities. In addition, of course, the patient also has a unique biological history and existence. Kluckholm and Murray (1948) suggested that all people are like all other people, some other people, and no other person. This is important to remember in every therapy session with every therapy patient as there is a natural human inclination for both the therapist and patient to think categorically. It is only with time and skill that both parties may come to understand and accept the other's uniqueness. Knowing and understanding the patient's cultural history and identity is important because it can provide a set of general guidelines for understanding the patient. Indeed, it becomes as important to know whether the patient accepts or denies their cultural heritage and whether they choose to live within or apart from it.

Culture Is Omnipresent in Therapy

Marsella (1993), using the example of Japanese-Americans, suggested that therapists must consider a cultural group's values, communication styles, and models of disorder and health. He outlines specific considerations and practices that will minimize errors and conflicts. Others, such as Paniagua (1994), Ramirez (1999), and Tseng, Qui-Lun, and Yin (1995) also offer specific recommendations for improving the success of therapy across and within cultures. For example, Paniagua (1994), in his excellent practical guide to working with diverse clients, addresses such issues as language, opening remarks, therapeutic relationship, communication styles, value emphases, family involvement, patient's models of health and illness, and use of alternative therapies.

Although efforts have been made to use cognitive-behavioral therapy (CBT)—arguably the most popular therapy being taught in university psychology training programs—to treat depression across cultures (e.g., Organista, Munoz, & Gonsalez, 1994), methodological problems common to cross-cultural therapy research abound (e.g., acculturation level, outcome criteria) that leave this approach open to question. While the time-limited, directive, and problem-focus of CBT have certain attractions, the failure to consider the many complexities of cross-cultural therapy and counseling cited previously make it an option to be used with care, rather than an automatic response from therapists who may be unskilled in cultural sensitivities and competencies. It should be remembered that in dealing with depressive experience and disorder, the reliance of CBT on the rational, verbal, cognitive domain of functioning may be at odds with the patient's skills and abilities. Many cultural groups do not place a high value on rationality but may favor intuition, impulse, and affective cues and solutions. More research is needed on the utility and value of CBT and cultural diversity.

Indigenous Therapies

It is essential that therapists understand that each culture has both its conceptions of disorder and its therapeutic and healing systems. Thus, the therapist may wish to consider using them as either an adjunct or primary therapy. Sample non-Western therapies are presented in Table 3.3. As Table 3.3 indicates, reliance on Western psychotherapies or medications may not be essential for healing (see Jilek, 1993). There are increasing opportunities to work in conjunction with indigenous healers (e.g., Adler & Mukherji, 1995). While this thought may provoke some consternation in a Western therapist, the therapist would do well to imagine how alien their particular methods and approaches may be for the patient. If imagining this is difficult, perhaps the therapist could imagine that they are now a patient in an Ethiopian village, and they are compelled to use a Zar cult healer to cure their illness. Lastly, if the indignation is still high, the therapist might consider the fact that "middle-class Americans" are now using alternative and non-Western therapies with increased frequency and satisfaction (e.g., Zatzick & Johnson, 1997).

A CONCLUDING THOUGHT

In a challenge to Western psychology, Marsella (1998) proposed the development of a new psychology for the 21st century—global-community psychology. This psychology repositions Western psychology as one of many psychologies throughout the world rather than the only psychol-

TABLE 3.3 Examples of Non-Western Alternative Therapy and Healing Systems

Acupuncture (Oriental)
Ayurvedic Medicine (Hindu)
Brujos (a) (Latino "Witch" Doctor)
Charismatic Healing (Universal)
Curandero (a) (Latino Healer)
Dukhun (Indonesian Healer)
Hallucinogenic Cults (e.g., Peyote in American Indians)
Herbolarios (Latino/Filipino)
Ho'oponopono (Hawaiian Family and Group Therapy)
I-Ching (Chinese Taoistic Therapy)
Massage (Shiatsu: Japanese; Lomi-Lomi: Hawaiian)
Morita (Japanese Psychotherapy)
Moxibustion (Oriental)
Mudang (Korean Trance Therapy)
Naikan (Japanese Psychotherapy)
New Age Healing (American Folk, Natural, and Holistic Healing)
Prayer/Meditation/Propitiation (Universal)
Santerias (Latino)
Shamans (Universal)
Spirit Guide (American Indian)
Spiritualist Healers and Healing Cults (Universal)
Sweat Lodge (American Plains Indian)
Tai Chi Chuan (Chinese Taoistic)
Trance States (Universal)
Voudou (Carribean)
Yoga (Hindu Mind-Body Therapy)
Zen (Japanese Buddhist Psychotherapy)

ogy. Marsella pointed out that the dominance of Western psychology was less a matter of its accuracy than a matter of social, economic, and political power. Psychologist throughout the world are increasingly resisting the imposition of Western psychology. For example, Misra (1996) an Asian Indian psychologist, writes:

> The current Western thinking of the science of psychology in its prototypical form, despite being local and indigenous, assumes a global relevance and is treated as a universal mode of generating knowledge. Its dominant voice subscribes to a decontextualized vision with an extraordinary emphasis on individualism, mechanism, and objectivity. This peculiarly Western mode of thinking is fabricated, projected, and institutionalized through representation

technologies and scientific rituals and transported on a large scale to the non-Western societies under political-economic domination. As a result, Western psychology tends to maintain an independent stance at cost of ignoring other substantive possibilities from disparate cultural traditions. Mapping reality through Western constructs has offered a pseudounderstanding of the people of alien cultures and has had debilitating effects in terms of misconstruing the special realities of other people and exoticizing or disregarding psychologies that are non-Western. Consequently, when people from other cultures are exposed to Western psychology, they find their identities placed in question and their conceptual repertoires rendered obsolete (pp. 497–498).

This is the reality of our contemporary world. The empowerment of non-Western psychologies will bring with it a new and more critical response to widespread and indiscriminate use of Western psychology. The new psychology will need to be more responsive to the multitude of forces present in our world. The new psychology will need to be multisectoral, multidisciplinary, and multicultural. It will need to understand and accept the problems of ethnocentricity and the importance of cultural determinants of human behavior.

Contemporary mental health professionals and researchers now acknowledge, accept, and seek to understand and use cultural factors in their studies of depressive experience and disorder. They understand the importance of preserving diversity, rather than destroying it through the adoption and use of culturally inappropriate and biased clinical practices. They understand that the world is culturally pluralistic and that accuracy requires an understanding of phenomena within its unique cultural context. None of this means that we must ignore or disregard all previous knowledge generated on depressive experience and disorder in the West, but rather that we must be aware of its possible limitations, and the especially the potential consequences of its use and application. If we, as professionals and researchers value diversity and all that it means for creating opportunity and choice for human beings everywhere, then we cannot ignore cultural variation.

This thought was eloquently stated by Octavio Paz (1978), the Nobel Prize winning Mexican poet and essayist, when he wrote:

What sets worlds in motion is the interplay of differences, their attractions and repulsions. Life is plurality, death is uniformity. By suppressing differences and peculiarities, by eliminating different civilizations and cultures, progress weakens life and favors death. The ideal of a single civilization for everyone, implicit in the cult of progress and technique, impoverishes and mutilates us. Every view of the world that becomes extinct, every culture that disappears, diminishes a possibility of life. (*The Labyrinth of Solitude*, 1967)

When we ignore cultural factors in understanding, assessing, and treating depressive experience and disorder, we are contributing to the homogenization of cultures and reducing the very cultural pluralism on which human survival may depend.

REFERENCES

Adler, L., & Mukherji, B. (Eds.). (1995). *Spirit versus scalpel: Traditional healing and modern psychotherapy.* Westport, CT: Bergin & Garvey.

American Psychiatric Association. (1994). *Diagnostic and statistical manual of mental disorders. Fourth Edition.* Washington, DC: American Psychiatric Press.

American Psychological Association. (1993). Guidelines for providers of psychological services to ethnic, linguistic, and culturally diverse populations. *American Psychologist, 48,* 45–48.

Bebbington, P. (1993). Transcultural aspects of affective disorders. *International Review of Psychiatry, 5,* 145–156.

Bertschy, G., Viel, J., & Ahyi, R. (1992). Depression in Benin. *Journal of Affective Disorders, 3,* 173–180.

Burton, R. (1652/1988). *The anatomy of melancholia.* Cheapside, London: Thomas Tegg (1988 Reproduction Edition–Birmingham, Alabama: Gryphon Editions)

Casas, J., Ponterotto, J., & Gutierrez, J. (1986). An ethical indictment of counseling research and training: The cross-cultural perspective. *Journal of Counseling and Development, 64,* 347–349.

Chakraborty, A. (1991). Culture, colonialism, and psychiatry. *The Lancet, 337,* 1204–1207.

Comas-Diaz, L., & Griffith, E. (1988). *Clinical guidelines in cross-cultural mental health.* New York: John Wiley.

Dana, R. (1993). *Multicultural assessment perspectives for professional psychology.* Boston, MA: Allyn & Bacon.

Desjarlais, D., Eisenberg, L., Good, B., & Kleinman, A. (1995). *World mental health: Problems and priorities in low-income countries.* New York: Oxford University Press.

Ebert, D., & Martus, P. (1994). Somatization as a core symptom of melancholic depression: Evidence form a cross-cultural study. *Journal of Affective Disorders, 4,* 253–256.

Ebigno, P. (1982). Development of a cultural specific (Nigeria) screening scale of somatic complaints indicating psychiatric disturbance. *Culture, Medicine, and Psychiatry, 6,* 29–43.

Edgerton, R. (1992). *Sick societies: Challenging the myth of primitive harmony.* New York: Free Press.

Fabrega, H. (1989). Cultural relativism and psychiatric illness. *Journal of Nervous and Mental Disease, 77,* 415–425.

Fabrega, H. (1992). A cultural analysis of human breakdown patterns: An approach to the ontology and epistemology of psychiatric phenomena. *Culture, Medicine, and Psychiatry, 17,* 99–132.

Fugita, S., & Crittenden, K. (1990). Toward culture and population specific norms for self-reported depressive symptomatology. *International Journal of Social Psychiatry, 36,* 83–92.

Furnham, A., & Malik, R. (1994). Cross-cultural beliefs about "depression." *International Journal of Social Psychiatry, 40,* 106–123.

Geertz, C. (1973). *The interpretation of cultures: Selected essays.* New York: Basic Books.

Good, B. (1992). Culture, diagnosis, and co-morbidity. *Culture, Medicine, and Psychiatry, 16,* 409–425.

Griffith, E., & Baker, F. (1993). Psychiatric care of African-Americans. In A. Gaw (Ed.), *Culture, ethnicity, and mental illness* (pp. 147–173). Washington, DC: American Psychiatric Press.

Hamdi, E., Amin, Y., & Abou-Saleh, M. (1997). Problems in validating endogenous depression in the Arab culture by contemporary diagnostic criteria. *Journal of Affective Disorders, 44,* 131–143.

Jackson, S. (1987). *Melancholia and depression: From Hippocratic times to modern times.* New Haven, CT: Yale University Press.

Jenkins, J., Kleinman, A., & Good, B. (1990). Cross-cultural studies of depression. In J. Becker & A. Kleinman, *Advances in mood disorders: Theory and research* (pp. 67–99). Los Angeles, CA: L. Erlbaum.

Jilek, W. (1993). Traditional medicine relevant to psychiatry. In N. Sartorius, G. DiGirolamo, G. Andrews, G. Allen German, & L. Eisenberg (Eds.), *Treatment of mental disorders: A review of effectiveness* (pp. 341–390). Washington, DC: American Psychiatric Press.

Kirmayer, L. (1998). Editorial: The fate of culture in DSM-IV. *Transcultural Psychiatry, 35,* 339–343.

Kleinman, A., & Good, B. (1985). *Culture and depression.* Berkeley, CA: University of California Press.

Kluckholm, C., & Murray, H. (1948). *Personality in nature, culture, and society.* New York: Basic Books.

Koenig, L. (1997). Depression and the cultural context of the self-serving bias. In U. Neissner & D. Jopling (Eds.), *The conceptual self in context: Culture, experience, and self-understanding.* New York: Cambridge University Press.

Kraepelin, E. (1904). Vergleichende psychaitrie. *Zentralblatt fur Nervenherlkande und Psychiatrie, 15*, 433–437.

Lee, C., & Armstrong, K. (1995). Indigenous models of mental health intervention: Lessons from traditional healers. In J. Ponterotto, J. Casas, L. Suzuki, & C. Alexander (Eds.), *Handbook of multicultural counseling* (pp. 441–456). Thousand Oaks, CA: Sage.

Leighton, A. (1959). *My name is legion.* New York: Basic Books.

Leininger, M. (1984). Transcultural interviewing and health assessment. In P. Pedersen, N. Sartorius, & A. J. Marsella (Eds.), *Mental health services: The cultural context* (pp. 135–174). Beverly Hills, CA: Sage.

Lin, K. M., Poland, R., & Nakasaki, G. (Eds.). (1993). *Psychopharmacology and the psychobiology of ethnicity.* Washington, DC: American Psychiatric Press.

Lin, K. M., Poland, R., Chang, S., & Chang, W. (1995). Psychopharamacology for the Chinese: Cross-ethnic perspective. In T. Lin, W. Tseng, & E. Yeh (Eds.), *Chinese societies and mental health* (pp. 308–314). Hong Kong: Oxford University Press.

Manson, S. (1995). Culture and major depression: Current challenges in the diagnosis of mood disorders. *Psychiatric Clinics of North America, 18*, 487–501.

Manson, S., & Kleinman, A. (1998). DSM-IV, culture, and mood disorders: A critical reflection on recent progress. *Transcultural Psychiatry, 35*, 377–386.

Marin, G., Gamba, R., & Marin, B. (1992). Extreme response style and response acquiescence among Hispanics. *Journal of Cross-Cultural Psychology, 23*, 498–509.

Marsella, A. J. (1980). Depressive experience and disorder across cultures. In H. Triandis & J. Draguns (Eds.), *Handbook of cross-cultural psychology: Volume 6 Mental health* (pp. 237–289). Boston, MA: Allyn & Bacon.

Marsella, A. J. (1982). Culture and mental health: An overview. In A. J. Marsella & G. White (Eds.), *Cultural conceptions of mental health and therapy* (pp. 359–388). Boston, MA: G. Reidel/Kluwer.

Marsella, A. J. (1985). Culture, self, and mental disorder. In A. J. Marsella, G. DeVos, & F. Hsu (Eds.), *Culture and self: Asian and Western perspectives* (pp. 281–308). London: Tavistock Press.

Marsella, A. J. (1987). The measurement of depressive experience and disorder across cultures. In A. J. Marsella, R. Hirschfeld, & M. Katz (Eds.), *The measurement of depression* (pp. 376–399). New York: Guilford.

Marsella, A. J. (1993). Sociocultural foundations of psychopathology: A pre-1970 historical overview. *Transcultural Psychiatric Research and Review, 30*, 97–142.

Marsella, A. J. (1998b). Toward a global-community psychology: Meeting the needs of changing world. *American Psychologist, 53*, 1282–1291.

Marsella, A. J. (1998b). Urbanization, mental health, and social deviancy: An overview of research findings. *American Psychologist, 53,* 624–634.

Marsella, A. J. (in press). Culture bound disorders. In A. Kazdin (Ed.), *The encyclopedia of psychology.* Washington, DC: American Psychological Association Press/Oxford University Press.

Marsella, A. J., & Leong, F. (1995). Cross-cultural assessment of personality and career decisions. *Journal of Career Assessment, 3,* 202–218.

Marsella, A. J., & Westermeyer, J. (1993). Cultural aspects of treatment: Conceptual, methodological, and clinical issues and directions. In N. Sartorius, G. DiGirolamo, G. Andrews, G. German, & L. Eisenberg (Eds.), *Treatment of mental disorders: A review of effectiveness* (pp. 391–418). Washington, DC: American Psychiatric Association.

Marsella, A. J., & Yamada, A. (in press). Culture and mental health: An introduction and overview of foundations, concepts, and issues. In I. Cuellar & F. Paniagua (Eds.), *The handbook of multicultural mental health: Assessment and treatment of diverse populations.* New York: Academic Press.

Marsella, A. J., Hirschfeld, R., & Katz, M. (1987). *The measurement of depression.* New York: Guilford.

Marsella, A. J., Purcell, I., & Carr, S. (in press). Qualitative and quantitative research methods in intercultural relations. *World Psychology.*

Marsella, A. J., Dubanoski, J., Hamada, W., & Morse, H. (in press). The measurement of culture and personality: Issues and directions. *American Behavioral Scientist.*

Marsella, A. J., Sartorius, N., Jablensky, A., & Fenton, R. (1986). Culture and depressive disorders. In A. Kleinman & B. Good (Eds.), *Culture and depression* (pp. 299–324). Berkeley, CA: University of California Press.

Mezzich, J., Kleinman, A., Fabrega, H., & Parron, D. (Eds.). (1996). *Culture and psychiatric diagnosis: A DSM-IV perspective.* Washington, DC: American Psychiatric Press.

Misra, G. (1996). Section in Gergen, K., Gulerce, A., Lock, A., & Misra, G. (1996). Psychological science in cultural context. *American Psychologist, 51,* 496–503.

Murray, C., & Lopez, A. (Eds.). (1996). *The global burden of disease.* Cambridge, MA: Harvard University Press/WHO.

Organista, K., Munoz, R., & Gonzalez, G. (1994). Cognitive-behavioral therapy for depression in low-income and minority medical outpatients: Description of a program and exploratory analyses. *Cognitive Therapy and Research, 18,* 241–259.

Paniagua, F. (1994). *Assessing and treating culturally diverse clients: A practical guide.* Thousand Oaks, CA: Sage.

Paz, O. (1967). *The labyrinth of solitude.* London, UK: Penguin Press.

Pfeiffer, W. (1968). The symptomatology of depression viewed transcultur-ally. *Transcultural Psychiatric Research Review, 5,* 102–142.

Prince, R. (1968). The changing picture of depressive syndromes in Africa: Is it fact or diagnostic fashion. *Canadian Journal of African Studies, 1,* 177–192.

Ramirez, M. (1999). *Multicultural therapy: An approach to individual and cultural differences.* Boston, MA: Allyn & Bacon.

Shweder, R. (1991). *Thinking through cultures: Expeditions in cultural psychology.* Cambridge, MA: Harvard University Press.

Singer, K. (1975). Depression disorders from a transcultural perspective. *Social Science and Medicine, 9,* 289–301.

Sloan, T. (1996). *Damaged life: The crisis of the modern psyche.* London, England: Routledge.

Sue, D., Arredondo, P., & McDairs, R. (1992). Multicultural counseling competencies and standards: A call to the profession. *Journal of Counseling and Development, 70,* 477–486.

Takeuchi, D., Kuo, H., Kim, K., & Leaf, P. (1989). Psychiatric symptom dimensions among Asian-Americans and Native Hawaiians: An analysis of a symptom checklist. *Journal of Community Psychology, 17,* 319–329.

Tapp, J., Kelman, H., Triandis, H., Wrightman, L., & Coelho, G. (1974). Advisory principles for ethical considerations in the conduct of cross-cultural research. *International Journal of Psychology, 9,* 240–249.

Thakker, J., & Ward, T. (1998). Culture and classification: The cross-cultural application of the DSM-IV. *Clinical Psychology Review, 1998, 18,* 501–529.

Thornicroft, G., & Sartorius, N. (1993). The course and outcome of depression in different cultures: Ten year follow-up of the WHO collaborative study on the assessment of depressive disorders. *Psychological Medicine, 23,* 1023–1032.

Tseng, W., Qiu-Yun, L., & Yin, P. (1995). Psychotherapy for the Chinese: Cultural considerations. In T. Lin, W. Tseng, & E. Yeh (Eds.), *Chinese societies and mental health* (pp. 281–294). Hong Kong: Oxford University Press.

Watkins, D., & Cheung, S. (1995). Culture, gender, and response bias. *Journal of Cross-Cultural Psychology, 26,* 490–504.

Weiss, M., & Kleinman, A. (1988). Depression in cross-cultural perspective: Developing a culturally-informed model. In P. Dasen, J. Berry, & N. Sartorius (Eds.), *Health and cross-cultural psychology* (pp. 336–350). Newbury Park, CA: Sage.

Wilbur, K. (1998). *The eye of the spirit: An integral vision for a world gone slightly mad.* Boston: MA: Shambhala.

Yamada, A., Marsella, A. J., & Yamada, S. (1998). The development of the Ethnocultural Identity Behavior Index: Psychometric properties and validation with Asian-American and Pacific Islanders. *Asian-American and Pacific Islander Journal of Health, 6,* 35–45.

Zatzick, D., & Johnson, F. (1997). Alternative psychotherapeutic practice among middle-class Americans: I. Case studies and follow-up. *Culture, Medicine, and Psychiatry, 21,* 53–88.

Zheng, Y., & Lin, K. (1991). Comparison of the Chinese Depression Inventory and the Chinese version of the Beck Depression Inventory. *Acta Psychiatrica Scandinavica, 6,* 531–536.

4

The Case of Nancy

Mark A. Reinecke, Michael R. Davison, and Bertram Cohler

Although numerous books have been published on the assessment and treatment of depression, few offer the clinician the opportunity to compare and contrast alternative approaches side-by-side and few provide the detailed richness of an extended case study. Clinical texts often provide technical guidelines for how to approach treatment. Rarely, however, do they provide us with a clear sense of how the clinician is thinking about the case, or what treatment looks like in practice. Case studies allow for a deeper understanding of the practical complexities of assessment and case formulation. Moreover, they permit us to see how a clinician's working model of change guides both the strategic focus and the technical aspects of treatment.

The following case study served as the focus of our contributors' chapters. Their task was to describe how they would evaluate the patient, develop a treatment plan, and approach her care. This patient was self-referred, and the information was collected over the course of a 2-hour intake session. This case is, in many ways representative of depressed patients seen through an outpatient clinic. As is so often the case, her clinical presentation is somewhat complex. Moreover, a range of biological, developmental, and social factors appear to be contributing to her distress. These complexities challenge us in our attempts to develop a parsimonious formulation and an effective treatment program.

PRESENTING CONCERNS

Nancy T. is a 32-year-old, married, Catholic, Caucasian female. She sought therapy due to recurrent, subjectively severe feelings of depression, anxiety, and confusion. She attributed these difficulties to her "dysfunctional childhood" and to her belief that she had "difficulty dealing with these issues." When asked to elaborate she noted that she has had increasingly severe marital problems for several years and that these difficulties have led her to "feel horrible and to question what she is doing with her life." She stated that she "feels overwhelmed" by her marital difficulties, financial problems, and by pressures at work. Nancy remarked that she is frustrated by her inability to make a decision about separating from her husband, and noted that she "can never trust herself or her decisions." She noted that she has been feeling "low, dissatisfied, and terribly unhappy" and that she has "no self-confidence at all." She stated that she gets "next to no pleasure out of life" and that she feels "bad about herself . . . I know it's not true, but sometimes I just think I f– up everything." Nancy remarked that she tends to "need someone to help her take care of herself . . . and most everything I have to do." Nancy stated, in sum, that she "feels really negative about herself and everything in the situation . . . my life has become a total waste."

Nancy described her feelings as "a downward spiral of sadness." She observed that she feels hopeless at these times, and that she "can't see a light for her future." These episodes are accompanied by "intolerable" feelings of frustration, guilt, anxiety, anger, fatigue, and resentment. Nancy noted that she fears she will be alone if she leaves her husband, Steve, and stated that she "doesn't know what to do . . . I can't see how I would handle it without him." Nancy acknowledged that she can be quite self-critical, and stated that she "beats herself up big time . . . I feel I'm inept . . . just incompetent." She reported that she often ruminates about "why I can't handle these things," and observed that she "was never taught how to solve problems when I was growing up . . . so I don't have the confidence to take a leap of faith." She feels that she "tends to focus on herself too much."

Nancy's depressive episodes are characterized by "jags of crying," impaired concentration and memory, a loss of libido, difficulty making decisions, anhedonia, increased appetite and weight, fatigue, and insomnia. She sleeps approximately 4–5 hours per night, and wakes frequently. Nancy noted that she tends to withdraw from others when she is depressed, and acknowledged becoming "really irritable when I'm under stress . . . my friends tell me I can be a bitch, and I know it's true." Nancy feels discouraged about her life, and acknowledged that she "feels I've failed with everything." Nancy reported experiencing occasional thoughts of suicide and death, and stated that she has developed a suicide plan. Although there is no history of suicidal gestures or attempts, she noted that she "could always just park the car in the garage and let it run."

Nancy stated that she "gets upset very easily" and that she often feels tense and unable to relax. She reported that she frequently feels agitated and afraid, unsteady, nervous, and dizzy. Her feelings of anxiety are accompanied by moderately severe tachycardia and heart palpitations. As she stated, "sometimes I get worried and afraid for no reason at all . . . and these feelings just stay with me."

Nancy's feelings of depression and anxiety reportedly are worse on weekends, when she visits her husband's athletic club, while visiting with friends who have children, and while visiting with her mother. She stated that she often "feels pressured and trapped" at these times, noting that "my husband wants a big, traditional family, but it's not me . . . it's depressing." Nancy's mood reportedly improves when she is working, relaxing, exercising, or talking with her sister or friends. She observed that she "gets a boost from what she's doing at work . . . I like it when I've accomplished something," and that she feels particularly good while backpacking by herself.

Nancy has been married for 8 years. Her husband, Steve (33) completed law school several years ago, but has been unable to pass the state bar exam. They have no children. Nancy's feelings of depression and anxiety were first apparent during her engagement to Steve. She recalled that she "doubted getting married" as he "was so controlling and he took my self-confidence away." These feelings have become progressively more severe during the past 18 months as Steve has pressed for them to have children. Nancy noted that she "has no maternal feelings" when she is with Steve, and that she "fears making the commitment to having a family with him." As she stated, "I feel I'd have to give up myself." Nancy noted, however, that she "could see having children with another person." Nancy feels her marital problems are "*very* severe" and has sought marital therapy. Although she has met with a marital counselor on several occasions, her husband refuses to attend. Nancy noted that she is "extremely unhappy" about her marriage, and commented that it "would be nice if it succeeded . . . but I can't see how." She feels that "there isn't much more I can do than I am to make it work." She noted that Steve is rarely affectionate toward her, they seldom have sex, and she frequently regrets having married him.

Social and Developmental History

Nancy was born in Milwaukee, Wisconsin and is the eldest of two children. Her parents immigrated to the United States from Poland several years before she was born. Nancy recalled having felt "a lack of stability" in her family during her childhood. Her parents returned to Poland when she was 2, and came back to the United States the following year. Nancy's mother was employed as a cleaning lady and a dental assistant during her childhood, and her father was a janitor and a part-time carpenter.

Nancy described her mother as "a very critical person . . . who never knew how to give a compliment." She characterized her as "nervous," "frightened," and "full of shame." On a positive note, she described her mother as "strong and responsible." Nancy's mother reportedly was self-critical and maintained very high standards. Nancy recalls that her mother was "full of self-doubt" and that she "never gave anyone any slack." Nancy feels that, as a result, she has tended to "look for the worst things" which "makes for self-fulfilling prophecies." She recalled that her mother frequently became angry and that she yelled at her and her sister. Her mother occasionally threw objects at her, and on one occasion locked her out of the house for several hours. Nancy was approximately 7 years old at the time, and recalled having been frightened as she cried on the back porch. She stated that her mother disciplined them in an unpredictable, punitive manner, and recalled that she "seemed to always be hitting us."

Nancy described her relationship with her mother as "horrific" during her childhood. As she stated, "I was her helper and her emotional aide . . . I was always her sounding board." She felt that her mother never permitted her to make decisions for herself during her childhood, remarking, "there was always a match of wills . . . that mom always won." Nancy recalled having wished that her mother would have been more supportive and less critical of her. She reported that she had "always hoped for something or someone else for her to focus her attention on besides me." Nancy stated that she continues to believe that her mother "is living through me" and that she "doesn't have a life of her own." She stated, for example, that she "doesn't have a sense of privacy when I'm with her . . . I have trouble demanding my rights and she never takes my feelings into account."

Nancy recalled that her father was "comforting" and "lenient" during her childhood. He suffered from chronic schizophrenia, however, and frequently hallucinated and became paranoid. Nancy recalled that he often "went violently out of control" toward her mother. Nancy noted that her father was quite overprotective and that he frequently voiced fears that "others" might try to hurt her. Nancy nonetheless felt that she and her father "had a reversal of roles." As she stated, "he couldn't do much on his own a lot of the time, and he was always fighting with mom, so I stepped in . . . I was the adult and he was the child." Nancy's father returned to Poland when she was 12 years old. She has had little contact with him since that time, and only speaks with him 3 or 4 times per year. Nancy stated that she "feels abandoned" by him.

Nancy described her parents' relationship as "violent" during her childhood. She stated that they frequently argued and recalled having "cried and tried to protect my mother" at these times. Nancy noted that, as a consequence, she has become "afraid of confrontation and of being alone." She noted that these feelings are "much stronger than they should be." Nancy recalled that her parents had two close friends, Robin and Jeff, while she was growing up, and recalled having "always wished they were our parents . . . that was my dream." Nancy's parents separated when she was 4 years old, and divorced when she was 5. She was very upset by this event, and stated that she consequently "doesn't want a divorce . . . I won't be like my parents." Nancy's mother remarried 8 years later, and divorced again when Nancy was 17. She recalls that there "wasn't a lot of laughter in my childhood . . . it wasn't happy at home, there was a lot of anxiety and stress." Nancy's current relationship with her mother is strained.

Nancy has a younger sister, Lisa (28). She characterized their current relationship as "good" and noted that she "always took care of her during her childhood." Nancy stated that they "are good friends to this day . . . and stay close." Nancy feels that her sister can be supportive and enjoys talking with her. Regrettably, Nancy speaks with her only once or twice a month.

When asked to describe her husband, Nancy remarked that he is a "lazy and extremely critical person." She quickly modified the comment, stating, "he can also be really kind and generous and attentive . . . he's more like a father to me." Nancy was able to identify several points of compatibility with her husband. She noted, for example, that they both have immigrant parents, both "like a lot of the comforts of life," both "really need attention and have insecurities," and both enjoy sports. She feels, however, that as a lawyer, her husband can be "stilted and . . . too much of a stuffed shirt." When asked to elaborate, she noted that he "hangs around with his lawyer friends and wants me to be a mom . . . with a big Polish family in the suburbs." She continued by stating that she would "like a life with more art in it." When asked to elaborate, she noted that she doesn't enjoy living in the suburbs, that it "is Wonder Bread there . . . it's not stimulating culturally . . . it's not my life."

When asked to describe herself, Nancy noted that she "always wants to please people" and that she "has difficulty saying no" to others. She acknowledged that she is a fearful person and that she often feels "vulnerable." She reported that she is fearful about financial security and that she believes that people will not be there to meet her needs. She remarked, in passing, that she often is "afraid for no real reason at all." Nancy reported that she feels she "lacks a true base of emotional support" and that she "has got to sacrifice what I need for others." She appears, as such, to manifest long-standing feelings of emotional deprivation, perfectionistic standards for her own performance, and a belief that she needs to sacrifice her goals and needs. Nancy stated that she often "feels inadequate and . . . unprepared" and acknowledged feeling that the "future seems dark and vague." She observed that she tends to keep to herself when she becomes depressed and that she "focuses on myself and complains." Nancy is self-conscious and feels she is unattractive. She noted that she feels she "doesn't measure up" and that "no matter what I do it's never enough . . . I feel very guilty when I let people down." Nancy stated that she "can only be happy when others around me are happy" and acknowledged feeling unnaturally uncomfortable if I do what I want." She remarked that she "has a lot of anger built up inside me that I don't express."

When asked to describe her positive qualities, Nancy noted that she can be friendly, helpful, forgiving, kind, warm-hearted, and good-natured. She continued, however, by stating that she often "puts up a front" and that she "has a hard time breaking off a relationship, even if it is making me unhappy." She noted that she "lets people take advantage of me" and that she is "very sensitive to criticism by others."

She believes she is "too apologetic" and that she "can't let people know when I'm angry at them." Nancy first experienced these feelings during her adolescence, and recalled having felt that "everyone was smarter, better, and more normal" than she. She recalled having feared that others would learn of her home life and her father's behavior. Nancy stated that she "felt like an alien" during her childhood, and that she desperately wanted to fit in with her classmates. Although she did reasonably well academically during her elementary and high school years, Nancy recalled having felt "fearful of school" much of the time. Nancy had numerous friends during her childhood, but nonetheless "felt like an outsider." Nancy began dating when she was 16 years old, and had one boyfriend during high school. They broke up when he developed a drinking problem. She met her husband during her junior year of college. When asked if there was a pattern in her relationships, Nancy remarked that she "tends to become totally absorbed by the other person . . . and I look for them to protect and take care of me."

Nancy reportedly has two or three close friends. Although she described them as supportive, and noted that she is comfortable confiding in them, she sees them only once or twice per month. Nancy stated that she "gets along with people," but that she has "tended to keep to herself . . . and complain" during recent months. She noted that she "feels guilty about this," and that she consequently "tries to put on a happy face."

Education and Occupational Functioning

Nancy received a bachelor's degree from Marquette University and completed several graduate courses in art and graphic design at the University of Wisconsin. She is currently employed as a graphic artist and serves as the art director of a large consumer manufacturing company. She is attending graduate school during the evening and looks forward to completing an MBA. She reports that the quality of her work has suffered due to her depression. Nancy stated that she experiences difficulty concentrating, and remarked that she is "very self-conscious" about her performance.

Medical History

Nancy reportedly is in good health. With the exceptions of a tonsillectomy at 2 years of age and an appendectomy when she was 20, her medical history is unremarkable. There is no history of serious illnesses or accidents. She denies any history of head injury, loss of consciousness, high or prolonged fever, headaches, or seizures. With the exception of occasional use of cannabis during college, there is no history of alcohol or substance abuse. Nancy received a prescription of Zoloft (50 mg/ day) approximately 4 weeks ago from her family physician. Although she reports the medication "seems to be working well" in alleviating her insomnia, it has not been helpful in reducing her feelings of depression or anxiety.

There is an extensive history of emotional problems among Nancy's immediate relatives. As noted, her father reportedly suffers from schizophrenia. In addition, her mother and sister have experienced recurrent, subjectively severe episodes of depression.

Objective rating scales

Measure	Score	Interpretation
Beck Depression Inventory (BDI)	33	Severe
Beck Anxiety Inventory (BAI)	29	Severe
Hopelessness Scale	14	Severe
Scale for Suicide Ideation (SSI)		
–Current	9	Mild
–Past Episode	27	Severe

SUMMARY

The case of Nancy is prototypic of many encountered in clinical practice. Her presentation is complex in that, in addition to feelings of dysphoria and pessimism, she also experiences feelings of anger, frustration, anxiety, loneliness, boredom, and emptiness. The origins of her difficulties extend back into her childhood and appear to be exacerbated and maintained by current life circumstances. Many advances during recent years concerning the characterization, course, assessment, and treatment of depression have come about as a result of the use of diagnostic criteria based on the DSM and ICD systems. These criteria have provided a shared framework for research and a common language for clinical practice. As the case of Nancy suggests, however, an overreliance on nosological systems of signs and symptoms of depression can limit our clinical effectiveness. Treating severe depression requires that equal attention be given to the broader context of an individual's life, the meanings they attach to their experiences, the understanding of recent developments in theory, the empirical literature, and the advances in clinical practice.

Over the past several years a number of important advances have provided the stimulus for a developmental approach to the study and treatment of depression. Based upon this work, a number of important, practical questions arise:

1) How can we understand the complex interplay of social, psychological, cultural, genetic, environmental, and physiological factors processes that have placed Nancy at risk for depression?

2) How does our understanding of these various factors inform our clinical practice? Although some writers have made claims for the primary role of specific factors or components in development and psychopathology (e.g., Kohut for narcissism; Beck for cognition; Klein for aggression; Bowlby for attachment experience), others have attempted to consider the broad array of factors associated with difficulties in adaptation and have worked to development integrative models which address the ways in which these processes are organized. With this in mind, which specific factors do we emphasize and attend to? Which do we deemphasize? Why? What is our rationale for adopting one conceptual scheme in preference to another?

3) How do our models of human adaptation, development, psychopathology, and treatment guide us in conceptualizing Nancy's difficulties?

4) What is the role of assessment in treatment planning? How do our models of psychopathology determine the ways in which we evaluate factors contributing to Nancy's distress and her progress over the course of treatment?

5) How do our conceptual models influence our understanding of such important issues and concepts as adaptation, development, ontogeny, vulnerability, resilience, relapse, recurrence, treatment failure, resistance, and prevention.

Nancy is a complex individual. The complexity of her life and her essential individuality challenge us as clinicians to offer care that is both effective and humane. She challenges us as scholars to examine the validity and usefulness of our models and the techniques of change that are based on them.

5

Individual Psychology of Depression

Mark H. Stone

THEORETICAL ORIENTATION

Individual psychology (IP)[1] and its view of depression is based on the work of Alfred Adler (1870–1937) which emphasizes the indivisible nature of the individual and the interrelatedness of all that constitutes mind and body. More recently, Damasio (1994, pp. xvi & p. 88) makes a similar claim, "Body and brain form an indissociable organism." IP provides a practical, yet comprehensive understanding of human behavior, a "menschenkenntnis," and offers a pragmatic, social psychology.[2] Its tenets are grounded in the person as one among all humans. In this regard, IP offers a normative criteria for mental health—fellowship with others—designated as community feeling or social interest, from the German "gemeinschaftsgefühl" (Ansbacher, 1968, 1980; Ansbacher & Ansbacher, 1956, 1978). In IP, cooperation with others is the hallmark of mental health and stands in contrast to its polarity—a retreat from this challenge. Involvement with fellow humans in productive activities defines positive adaptation. Avoiding productive endeavors by withdrawal, whether modest or extreme, results from feelings of inferiority.

The concept of the "inferiority complex" (Adler, 1912) plays a central role in the IP model of psychopathology. How does it develop? Adler

(1927) proposed that a child begins life as the most dependent among the species and that maturation is required to reach productive independence. During these formative years, small physical stature and developing mental maturity can be easily overwhelmed by life's demands. A sense of accomplishment gradually occurs fostered by good parenting and the assistance of friends and teachers. Meeting life's challenges becomes a possibility. The problems of growing up are addressed, and the child matures into an adult who in turn will foster development in others. But what if a sense of inadequacy (physical and/or mental, real and/or imagined) pervades? What if, instead of nurturing, a child suffers from continuing adversity or is not provided with needed guidance? If children are excused from developing independence and responsibility, life's challenges come to appear as insurmountable obstacles. A sense of inferiority comes to dominate behavior, and "distance"[3] is put between the challenges of life and the person. As a result, life's challenges become self-defeating and lead to a fear of failure.

CONCEPTUALIZING DEPRESSION

Whether the course of personal growth is enhancing or frustrating, one develops a distinctive pattern of looking at life—a subjective perspective or leitmotiv—producing a unique, apperceptive view of self and life (Adler, 1970). Adler opened his second book, *The Neurotic Constitution* (1926, p. v) with a quote from Seneca which says, in effect, "It is not what happens that afflicts the person, but it is the opinion about this thing which afflicts the person" (in Hadas, 1961, p. 89). This choice of quote indicates what Adler considers preeminent in behavior—one's personal, subjective view of life.

Organ inferiority and the development of compensatory coping play a prominent role in the psychopathology of depression (Adler, 1925). One might, for example, use or feign a disability to escape tasks. Everybody knows the advantages that accrue from not feeling well. You get to stay home, earn some extra attention, and are released from the day's obligations. When this behavior becomes fixated, however, it can lead to avoidance of other obligations as well.

This model is supported by research suggesting that the less an individual feels in control of important life events the more likely they are to develop cognitive and emotional deficits associated with depression (Garber & Seligman, 1980; Seligman, 1975). In a similar manner,

Beck (1967) and Beck, Rush, Shaw, and Emery (1979) have found that idiosyncratic, maladaptive beliefs characterize the thoughts of depressed individuals.

Sometimes we strive in spite of our limitations. Although limitations may be intractable, they can serve as an impetus for action. Pursuing the profession of teacher or writer when poor vision prevails is but one example. Although limitations can be overcome by striving and compensation, feelings of inferiority may nonetheless persist, sustained by fear of failure. The influence of such mental distortions can be illustrated by the inverse of the popular expression, "Better to have loved and lost, than never to have loved at all." The alternative belief is adopted, "Better not to risk loving, than to love and lose." In this vein, Adler made reference to Richard III and his oft-quoted remark, "And therefore since I cannot be a lover, I am determined to prove a villain." Recent studies (Goldberg & Bridges, 1988; Katon, Kleinman, & Rosen, 1982; Lloyd, 1986) support Adler's contention that depression and somatization may be related.

Cognitive Distortion in Depression

How we cope with perceptions of personal inferiority belie the central strategy guiding a person's behavior. When individuals with weak vision pursue a vocation requiring visual acuity, they risk something due to their difficulty, but they compensate and persist in their goal. Other persons never try because for them to do so is to court failure. One way of coping with a sense of inadequacy is to create self-delusions by which to assuage these feelings. Ingenious means are sometimes developed to avoid feeling overwhelmed by life's problems. These fabrications, denoted as "fictions,"[4] can be modest or extensive. Fictions become a part of the self-created "working orders" in an individuals approach to life. Taken together, they constitute the individual's "Life Style" or personality pattern, their unique way of looking at life and understanding their experience. As Adler (1926) remarked, "I readily follow the ingenious views of Vaihinger (1925) who maintains that historically ideas tend to grow from 'fictions' (unreal by practically useful constructs) to 'hypotheses' and later to 'dogmas' " (Adler, 1926, p. 169), and "This change of intensity differentiates in a general way the thinking of the normal individual (fiction as expedient), of the neurotic (attempt to realize the fiction), and of the psychotic (reification of the fiction)" (Ansbacher & Ansbacher, 1956, p. 247).

Fictions and Life-Lies in Depression

Fictions are created to guide a person's coping but may contribute to negative behavior. A person may, for example, adopt a view of people and society that is colored by misperceptions. Treated unfairly in the past, a person may incorrectly generalize from this experience. Henceforth, the person does not participate in social activities. This avoidant behavior is purposeful, and conveniently circumvents potentially uncomfortable situations. It is accepted as a distorted "motto" for guiding behavior, "Don't trust people; you can be hurt." Whereas past experiences can be a useful guide, we also fabricate our own distortions for personal use. These illusions are fictions, but come to powerfully direct our attitudes and behavior. As Immanuel Kant had written, "The only feature common to all mental disorders is the loss of "sensus communis" [common, communal sense] and the compensatory development of a "sensus privatus" [private sense] of reasoning" (Kant, 1964, p. 19).

The concept of "life-lies" evolved into "life style" in Adler's nomenclature as a term for this concept of private, idiopathic thinking (Ansbacher, 1967). One finds in his writings a number of terms—including life-lie, life falsehood, life line, guiding line, and life style—to convey an individual's apperception of life. All describe the private reasoning that embodies the "goal" of one's behavior.

Assessing Depression

Life style assessment[5] is an important diagnostic strategy in individual psychology. Its purpose is to identify the goals and dominant strategies employed by the individual in apperceiving life. Life style assessment forms the foundation for therapeutic treatment. The task of the therapist, as Adler (1930) expressed it, " . . . is to help the patient reconstruct his assumptions and goals in line with greater usefulness. The fault of construction is discovered and a reconstruction is accomplished" (Adler, 1930, p. 22).

The process is one of cognitive reorganization by correcting "the faulty picture of the world, and the unequivocal acceptance of a mature picture of the world" (Adler, 1930, p. 333). This notion, that an individual's perceptions guide their emotional and behavioral reactions, is shared with several other schools of thought, including cognitive therapy and rational-emotive therapy (Beck, 1967; Ellis, 1961; Ellis & Harper,

1975; Mahoney, 1980). Many concepts proposed by Adler anticipated work by later cognitive, behavioral, psychodynamic, and interpersonally-focused psychotherapists. There may, as a result, be conceptual and practical similarities between alternative forms of treatment.

Early Recollections

An important aspect of life style assessment is the collection and inter-pretation of early recollections. Early recollections (ERs) reveal the dominating mental images constructed about the self, others, and the world. To recollect is to take stock of one's memory, which is itself a construction of self-selected information from those elements chosen to be significant in our lives. Early recollections are indicators of how we perceive life and signify information used to guide our perceptions. Early memories have value in that they reflect the "working plans" of the individual. They signify what has been selected to focus, guide, and direct behavior. With this in mind, Ruth Munroe (1955, p. 428) characterized the assessment of early recollections as the "first projec-tive test."

The Fictive Goal in Depression

An important objective of life style assessment is to determine the goal that guides an individual's behavior. It is a tenet of IP that *all* behavior is goal directed. Often, however, these goals are not recognized by the individual. As Adler stated,

> The goal of mental life becomes its governing principle, its causa finalis. Here we have the root of the unity of the personality, of the individuality. It does not matter what the source of its energies may have been. Not their origin, but their end, their ultimate goal, constitutes their individual charac-ter. (Ansbacher & Ansbacher, 1956, p. 94)

Whereas we know our expressed wants and needs in life, our hidden goal may not be self-evident. They are often hidden as bringing them to conscious awareness can be painful. Hidden goals stem from feelings of inferiority. They remain hidden as they excuse action where failure might be possible. Although a hidden goal isolates these contingencies, it prevents one from enjoying the advantages accruing from more oppor-tunities. IP addresses these hidden goals and related apperceptions in treatment. As Adler (1926) stated, "We aim to remove such errors through conversation, explanations, words and thoughts, to change the person who has become asocial into a fellow man" (Adler, 1926, (1970), p. 11).

A Life Style assessment also includes assessing the influence of birth order, sibling attributes, family atmosphere, parental behavior, assets, dreams, basic mistakes, and the governing fiction in one's life. The subjective interpretations we make regarding our siblings and parents serve as the basis for how we derive impressions of ourselves, others, and the world. Life Style assessment is conducted through a systematic and comprehensive interview. The results are presented to the client to explain how these events and perceptions contribute to the major theme of one's life.

Empirical Support

Although IP has supported the development of a range of clinically useful constructs, it has not stimulated a significant amount of research. This is due to the case study method that dominates IP (Mosak, 1989). As noted, IP emphasizes the phenomenological and subjective (idiographic) aspects of the individual in contrast to the objective (nomothetic). As a result, IP lacks a strong research base for providing treatment in depression beyond the original conceptual framework proposed by Adler.

The relationship of birth order to the development of personality has received some empirical attention (see Ernst & Angst, 1983; Falbo & Polit, 1986; and Watkins, 1992), and research has been conducted addressing several components of the IP theory.[6] In addition, objective measures have been developed for basic IP concepts, such as social interest (Crandall, 1975; Greever, Tseng, & Friedland, 1973; Sulliman, 1973). Validation studies of this measure have been completed (Curlette, Wheeler, & Kern, 1993; Mozdzierz et al., 1986). Studies have also been completed examining the concept of life style (Elliot, Fankouri, & Hafner, 1993; Fakouri & Hafner, 1993). Controlled outcome studies examining the efficacy of IP and the process of therapeutic change in IP, however, are lacking.

CASE CONCEPTUALIZATION: NANCY'S DEPRESSION

The initial description of Nancy, the client, is as a "married, Catholic, Caucasian female." Adler identified the three main tasks of life to be

(1) Intimacy (i.e., establishing a sexual relationship with another, "the question of love"); (2) Friendship (i.e., cooperating with others in productive ways, "the social relationship"); and (3) Occupation (i.e., assuming a productive activity "the question of occupation") (1970, p. 8). The tasks of living for Nancy are encapsulated in these four words that introduce the case. We find in "married" all the many issues contained in marriage—building a relationship, expressing and receiving love, achieving sexual intimacy, deciding whether to raise children, and, if so, establishing a supportive relationship wherein children will receive support and nurturance. We find in the word "Catholic" all the demands of religious faith and practice. Her religion fosters belief and implies participation in a community of believers. Nancy may practice her religion strictly or casually. She may conform to or rebel from the tenets of her religion. In whatever manner Nancy chooses to act, she is, nevertheless, addressing important aspects of her family and culture. Lastly, we have in the words "Caucasian female" expectations for the modern woman, including roles within her career and as a mother. Whatever role she chooses, Nancy has much to consider. We find, then, in just the first sentence of the case description, many of the major decisions that anyone, including Nancy, must face.

Life Style Assessment of Her Dysfunction

Although we cannot complete an actual Life Style assessment with Nancy, we can infer some of what might be identified in a Life Style assessment from statements ascribed to her. I have used this information to simulate her responses to a Life Style assessment interview.[8]

We begin with Nancy's recollection of an early event in her life. She recalled that, on one occasion, her mother locked her out of the house for several hours. Nancy was "frightened and cried on the back porch." Nancy recalled that she was approximately age seven at the time. In this case, the organization or arrangement of the case material can be revealing. Clients frequently present information in a non-sequential order. Organizing the information systematically often aids interpretation. The Life Style assessment accomplishes this function and helps avoid faulty inferential leaps that can occur when interpretation is based on isolated pieces of information. Nancy's feelings can be brought to life by having her state them in the first person. This is an IP technique for "getting into the shoes" of the person, and can be useful in clarifying their fictional goal and private logic.

Fictional Goal of Nancy

If we were to interview Nancy and to discuss her memory of this event and more recent experiences, she might remark, "I can't show how really depressed I am because, if I did, I would risk being rejected by others. What would happen if nobody liked me? I couldn't bear the thought of that happening, so I work hard and do my best to like everyone. I try to be friendly and do what others want me to do. This way, I get friendship and support from others. It's unfair, though, because sometimes I like doing what I want." Her goal, of maintaining the support of others, as such, becomes apparent.

Nancy's Private Logic

Similar approaches may be used in clarifying her private logic. Based upon the case reports and Nancy's comments, it is possible that she may believe:

1. Everyone has to like me or something terrible may result.
2. Because my parents were immigrants, I lack the proper background to be truly successful.
3. If I didn't have such a poor upbringing, I wouldn't have these problems.
4. I wish I could do what I wanted, but what might happen if I did?
5. I am unattractive; fortunately, I have a husband.
6. I'm doomed to suffer as a result of all of this.

It appears from Nancy's comments that she attribute her difficulties to a "dysfunctional childhood." Is this her way of disowning her involvement in these matters? Is she making an effort to cope or is she avoiding the issues? It appears that she finds external reasons for many of her problems. As noted, depressed individuals often demonstrate a need to blame others or external circumstances for their difficulties. Nancy appears to blame her parents. Are they actually to blame or is this merely a way out of her dilemma? In her logic, they must be; otherwise she is responsible. In order to alleviate her anxiety, something or someone else must be at fault—in this case, her parents and childhood experiences. By attributing her difficulties to them Nancy can feel less responsible or guilty.

Nancy's depression is longstanding. Although her marriage has lasted eight years, there are no children. Her husband reportedly wants to begin raising a family, and decisions must have been made regarding children. It is unlikely, however, that productive discussions have occurred between Nancy and her husband about their marriage or beginning a family. Life seems merely to have gone on. Time has passed and we see only a long history of indecision.

"Hesitation" is a term in Individual Psychology to describe this condition. One imagines a litany of promises Nancy has made to herself to move ahead, only to be followed by a lack of sustained effort. The result is a step forward followed by another step backward. This behavior appears longstanding, but occurs with increasing intensity. She ponders, " . . . what she is doing with her life?" After only four introductory sentences, we grasp Nancy's view of the problems that, by her own account, have grown to enormous proportions. Having reached this "overwhelming" state, she indicates that she cannot make decisions. Lacking confidence, Nancy states that she needs "someone to help her take care of herself . . . and most everything I have to do." She discounts her decision-making ability. This is similar in manner, in many ways, to William Styron's account of his behavior while depressed. In his memoir, *Darkness Visible* (1990), he characterized his behavior as completely lacking rational thought.

Feeling overwhelmed, Nancy agonizes over whether to leave her husband. He, apparently, has been the decision-maker. Although Nancy does not want to be left out of the process, she seems not to want the responsibility that goes along with decision-making. But, we ask, has Nancy shown any history of making important decisions? She graduated from college and married. It would be useful to hear her describe college life and how her marriage came about. Her husband may have been seen as a good prospect by Nancy and her family. What we find after eight years of marriage, however, is a woman who is dissatisfied with her life and who may not make important decisions for herself.

Nancy appears to fit the classic pattern described earlier: Dependent as a child, "saved" from making her own decisions, never knowing success from personal efforts and never having had to persist in her own goals. As a consequence, she does not know how to recover from defeat and persevere. Nancy perceives her life as crumbling before her. She is not satisfied with her career or her marriage. Moreover, she cannot describe her personal goals. She fears life and can only relate her list of problems. Compare this state of affairs to the elements previously outlined in the Individual Psychology view of depression. They dovetail all too well.

Transference and Countertransference

Filled with remorse, Nancy sits before her therapist sad, forlorn and dejected. Eight years of marriage, and nothing has worked out. There is nothing to feel happy about in her life. Isn't this a sad situation? Wouldn't you want to help? What is going to be our stance? Remember the scenario and her mode of behaving. Deploring her childhood and her married life, she comes for help. I would be interested in knowing how she made the initial appointment. What did she say on the phone? She may have expressed her problem directly, but I doubt it. I would speculate that she did not directly ask for help because to do so would indicate she is taking charge of her life and rationally seeking alternatives from someone. Rather, she might have recounted her many problems, the effect of which might overwhelm a less seasoned therapist almost as much as it does Nancy. One wonders how she could continue under these conditions. Is she not unique? Does this not make her special, a worthy client for a master therapist? If you could help Nancy, it would mean something to you both.

Her strategy appears to be one of recounting of issues, not a mobilizing for action. How should we respond to this? Empathic listening, of course, is necessary. She needs support and friendship, but should the therapist "take charge?" Will this not be similar to how her husband behaved? Will she solicit help from her therapist? I suspect that she may try to do so. She says that she wants independence, but may, instead, seek support and guidance. She may become dependent on the therapist. How should a therapist respond to this overture? Has she chosen a male or female therapist or did selection occur by chance? Can Nancy relate her unsatisfying life to a female therapist whom she may see as competent? Might she expect the therapist to "lock her out of the house" the way her mother did? How will she present to a male therapist? Will it be as a needy woman playing to manly virtues and his need to help? As we reflect on Nancy's predicament, additional questions come to mind. Does she actually want to face the decisions in her life? Will her therapist discover that Nancy feels safer in the self-deluded role she has made for herself than in working on life's tasks? Does she feel more secure in maintaining her dependent style than in risking change?

Let me speak to my own questions concerning these issues. First, IP does not specifically use the terms transference and countertransference. As Adler (1969) remarked,

> What the Freudians call transference (so far as we can discuss it apart from sexual implications) is social feeling. The patient's social feeling, which is always present in some degree, finds its best possible expression in the relation with the psychologist. (Adler, 1969, p. 247)

In IP, a bond is established with the patient to facilitate improvement. It is a bond characterized by a spirit of cooperation and facilitation. IP acknowledges that therapists who are unable to foster sufficient positive attributes in others may have encountered difficulty with these issues in their own lives. As Dreikurs (1970) wrote, "The proper therapeutic relationship, as we understand it, does not require transference, but a relationship of mutual trust and respect." With this in mind, the IP therapist may be challenged to gain a better understanding of his or her own life style. A therapeutic impasse is often the sign of a breakdown in the treatment relationship and cannot be blamed solely on the client.

Nancy exemplifies many characteristics of an exogenously depressed person. She appears to have come from a family that fostered dependency, not independence. Perhaps her parents fostered this dependency as the proper behavior for a woman. Perhaps Nancy and her parents believed her role in life was to marry and have children. Nancy's mother was aggressive in having her way, whereas her father was passive. Nancy appears to have married someone different from her father; somebody who took charge and made decisions. In this relationship, he viewed his choices as more important than hers. She has endured this situation, but isn't happy. Although she may have wanted something more, she was not prepared for making decisions. This is something that independence requires, and so she abdicated her own wishes to those of her husband.

Eight years of marital dependency and frustration have passed. At times, she may have tried to take charge and become more independent. Lacking experience in being independent, however, her efforts were ineffective. She lacks "stamina" and does not persist. Each new failure adds to her frustration. Lacking a supportive and understanding spouse, Nancy comes to feel more at fault. We see why she believes she must either blame herself or place the blame elsewhere. As noted earlier, Nancy sees only two alternatives, inferiority or superiority. To thwart the feelings of self-blame there has to be a culprit—childhood, husband, circumstances.

With this in mind, Nancy requires a supportive therapist who will balance personal support with encouragement for action. Nancy's own assessment of her assets quickly turned into a litany of negative attributes. It is worth noting that although she tenaciously clings to many mistaken beliefs, there appears to be a spunk and tenacity underneath. The task in therapy is to bring these assets into focus and support Nancy in achieving her goals. Her inclination will be to worry about larger problems—her depression, marriage and occupation. Although these are important matters, Nancy needs to begin by focusing on making small gains which will be beneficial in the long run. Before she can make big decisions, she has to learn to make a series of small ones.

Therapists can be perplexed by how depressed individuals accept their condition, and may become frustrated with such an attitude. These feelings can result from a failure to appreciate how depression serves a purpose. Depression cannot be alleviated until this is addressed and the client sees that something positive can happen.

Beginning and Framing Treatment

Life Style assessment guides IP case conceptualization and treatment. Ansbacher (1947) described four phases of treatment: (1) establishing a good relationship with the patient; (2) gathering data to understand him, to have source material for interpretation, and for conceptualizing his life style; (3) interpreting the data; and (4) provoking therapeutic movement. Depression, like other difficulties in life, is seen as a problem of relating to others. As Adler (1956) stated, "Psychotherapy is an exercise in cooperation and a test of cooperation. The first rule is to win the patient; the second is never to worry about your success" (in Ansbacher & Ansbacher, 1956, pp. 340–341).

This is an important principle. It illustrates the social emphasis of IP and the need to approach the patient with warmth and respect.

Psychotherapy Is a Cooperative Task

Symptoms of guilt, doubt, inadequacy, and self-reproach are seen as stemming from underlying "inferiority feelings." As noted, depression serves a function or purpose. This goal has two components: (1) the protection of the individual's sense of self-esteem; and (2) disparagement of the environment and/or others. Where feelings of inferiority are extreme, so also will be feelings of superiority. As Ansbacher and Ansbacher (1964) observed, "We soon perceive a greater or lesser degree of the feeling of inferiority in everyone, together with compensatory striving towards a goal of superiority" (p. 2). This is exacerbated by a tendency to dichotomize—to mistakenly believe that only two choices are available. Beck (1967), Beck et al. (1979), and Ellis (1961) have also commented on this pattern of thinking. Problems are seen as stemming from within or without. In this case, Nancy assigns responsibility to an external cause—a protective fiction that serves to bolster her self-esteem. Mower (1969) also believed that the distorted neurotic ambition that characterizes the thinking of depressed persons could be addressed by cultivating social feeling. It is important to keep in mind, however, that we are discussing the psychodynamics of depression; we are not advocating an expression of blame to the client. Nor does this imply that such a revelation to the client would serve a useful clinical purpose.

Depressed persons are often raised in a family where dependency is fostered. When they move beyond this dependent situation, a more threatening atmosphere is seen, a world that is not as supportive or helpful. As a consequence, they become upset by how people differ from their family and by how much more others expect of them. Lacking prerequisite experience in achieving goals, they also lack the satisfaction that comes from completing tasks. Instead of meeting life face-to-face, they fear the outcome from the moment they begin to contemplate a task. They often lose interest in projects once they start, and their interest diminishes if goals are not easily achieved. Avoiding tasks or abandoning them altogether becomes an accepted solution. Adler called this process a "disablement grant." Individuals come to offer themselves reprieves from obligations.

Depressed persons may also seek to garner blame. To do so makes them special, lets them stand out and elicits attention. This behavior often attracts the interest of others, especially that of those seeking to provide help. A "successful" depression, as such, can release one from many of life's obligations. The commonly observed tendency of depressed individuals to ruminate about the "cause" of their predicament can contribute to the "hesitating" condition.

I must add a caution lest the reader imply from this explication that the burden of depression must be placed upon client. This is not my

purpose. Rather, my goal is to illustrate how each behavior of a depressed person serves a larger purpose. Adler called these behaviors
"safeguarding devices." Other psychologies identify them as defense
mechanisms. The function or goal of these behaviors is to escape a
dilemma—in this case, how to face the tasks of life, yet keep secret the
feelings of inferiority.

What we observe about the strategies used by depressed persons is
not what will be initially conveyed to the client. Rather, for someone
with strong feelings of inferiority, support and encouragement should
be given. IP begins by helping the person mobilize existing resources
and move from a felt "under" position to one of facing life's challenges.
The major goal of therapy, according to Adler, is to enable the person
" . . . to realize what he is doing, and to transfer his egocentric interest
to social life and useful activity" (Ansbacher & Ansbacher, 1964, p. 40).

The early stages of treatment encompass a number of tasks. These
include:

(1)   Providing support and encouragement by building a relationship with the client. The goal of this step is to bring the client back
into the mainstream of productive interaction. In developing a relationship with the client, we encourage them to work cooperatively and seek
to mobilize existing resources. This notion is similar, in many ways, to
Rogers' (1957) suggestion that unconditional positive regard may serve
as a necessary and sufficient condition for therapeutic change.

(2)   By capitalizing upon existing assets and resources, we anchor
the client more securely to the mainstream of human activity. We need
to identify even minuscule examples of self-initiative and achievement
that can be used to prime the pump of action. These can be used by
the therapist to mobilize further client action. Even in situations where
things appear hopeless, one can find examples of human initiative. The
therapist must be alert in identifying these examples and skillfully use
them to facilitate additional productive action.

Subsequent stages of treatment focus upon educating the client about
his or her basic mistakes in perception. The goal is to diminish a
unique apperception of one's inferiority and reduce exaggerated goals.
Information is taken from the Life Style assessment to provide data.
This can be a long, slow process, and progress depends upon the degree
to which earlier stages have been adequately achieved. Unless we have
established a good working relationship with the client, we cannot

properly address this activity. In order for a person to hear interpretations, there must first be a spirit of cooperation. This activity requires a working relationship so that previous life style material can be incorporated into treatment activities.

Near the end of treatment a systematic review of life style is made. This can be prophylactic in that it provides the person with a better understanding of "self" and insulates them from negative intrusions of past modes of thought. The "fictive goal" of the client is brought to conscious awareness and the circumventing strategies are identified. Modest attempts by the client at more productive action are encouraged. Likewise, treatment continues to foster greater contact with others and more honest attempts at addressing the three main tasks of life—building lasting friendships, addressing an occupation, and participating in a loving relationship.

There are additional activities that might be included in Nancy's treatment. We might, for example, ask her to:

1. Write down her personal assets and determine how she can apply them in her life.
2. Establish a problem-solving approach. She might, for example, list those things she is dissatisfied with in her life, prioritize them, and determine possible solutions for each. She should evaluate alternative solutions before taking action, and should avoid taking premature steps to solve problems.
3. Renew contacts with her friends. Nancy needs additional support and, therefore, needs to take the initiative and reestablish her support system.
4. Keep in contact with her sister.
5. Encourage Nancy not to allow her graduate studies to deteriorate. Perhaps she should consider taking a leave from school. Steps should be taken to support her finishing graduate school.
6. Discuss her dissatisfaction with her husband. She might learn how to listen to his views, and how to express her own point of view about matters in the marriage.
7. Learn how to express her ideas to others without becoming fearful about what others may think.
8. Avoid major decisions for the time being. Develop the habit of making plans for small matters and implementing them successfully before moving to larger issues. A guidebook describing these and other IP strategies can be found in Mosak and Maniacci (1998).

Maintaining an active depression takes effort. This is something that often goes unrecognized and can be important in that it suggests the availability of a resource that can be used therapeutically. Although it is a power that has been mobilized in a negative direction, it is, nevertheless, a power that exists and one that can be used in more productive ways. Lacking any history of perseverance and saddled with a misguided goal, Nancy's efforts often amount to little more than a series of fits and starts that only add to her frustration. When all is said and done, she is left wondering why her good intentions don't bring the success that is sought. It is not uncommon to find depressed persons perplexed by their unsuccessful attempts to overcome their condition. It is a short step from here to the generalized fiction that it is their lot in life to suffer while others get to enjoy the advantages in life. This often explains why much agony is accepted and suffering is tolerated. But unlike the suffering Job in his Biblical tale of woe, the depressed individual believes that their condition is somehow justified. Job's friends offered varying advice for why his adversities occurred, but Job persevered in his belief that he had not caused the calamities that had befallen him. Nancy needs to contemplate Job's problems and how he resolved to deal with them. As Adler (1956) wrote,

> I expect from the patient again and again the same attitude which he has shown in accordance with his life-plan toward the persons of his former environment, and still earlier toward his family. At the moment of the introduction to the physician and often even earlier, the patient has the same feelings toward him as toward important persons in general. (in Ansbacher & Ansbacher, 1956, p. 336)

We must, as such, be prepared to face Nancy's resistance throughout the course of treatment.

Integration of Psychotherapy With Medication

For a client presenting with chronic or severe depression, there is often a need for immediate action. Hospitalization, medication, or ECT may be warranted. These conditions do not obviate the value of an IP approach to treating depression. IP acknowledges the importance of biological factors and is consistent with contemporary bio-psycho-social approaches to treatment. It also is consistent with the view that analytic and behavioral approaches can be combined (Wachtel, 1977).

When Nancy is at risk for suicide, more comprehensive treatment and hospitalization may be necessary. However, such an approach requires us to consider that the client may view it as "certifying the illness," which may reinforce their misguided interpretations. Such a misinterpretation of facts may only strengthen the "sickness" in the mind of the client, although the goal in treatment is to stabilize their condition. As a consequence, hospitalization or the initiation of a medication trial require "enhancement" with psychotherapy. In IP, no biochemical approach, ECT or hospitalization is sufficient in itself for treating depression. A personal relationship with a psychotherapist is required for any substantive improvement to occur, even in cases for which medication can be useful.

The problem with adopting a solely pharmacological approach is that when initial improvement is experienced, the major issues underlying the depression are pushed aside by the client. Because medication compliance can be a problem, a seemingly quick improvement in depression can suddenly change when the client begins to manipulate the dosage or discontinue it altogether. A well-established relationship with a therapist can help address these potential problems.

Relapse Prevention

Nancy has a long history of defeat and will most likely require much support for any action she undertakes. As she may easily fall back into old ways of operating, her actions must be in small steps in order to construct a new history of positive change. Change for Nancy may be more frightening than difficult. Bugental and Bugental (1984) described the fear of change as "a fate worse than death." With this in mind, Nancy should be seen for regular appointments. As failure is ego-syntonic for Nancy, attempts should be made to counter her tendency to avoid problems when difficulty arises. Treatment goals are a cooperative endeavor undertaken with the guidance of her therapist. As such, the therapist must be careful to support Nancy without "solving" her problems for her and becoming yet another "directive" person in her life. Although medications appear to have brought some relief, Nancy doesn't think they have solved her problems. She needs to be encouraged to follow the advice of her physician because she may "give up" on medication, as she has with other potential solutions.

Nancy appears less at risk for suicide now than at the time of her earlier episode. We don't, however, know her responses to critical items on the BDI. Careful monitoring is required, and a contract appears recommended so that any potential crisis will have been pre-planned regarding client and therapist actions. IP recommends insuring against suicide by making it ego-alien to the client (K. Adler, 1980). This can be accomplished by stressing that such action is not worthwhile, does not benefit others, can't bring about one's goals, and does not bring relief. Although confrontational strategies are not usually recommended, fortifying the client against self-destructive behavior is important.

CONCLUSION

Adler sometimes added a fourth task—creative endeavor (schopferische Gertaltung)—to the three life tasks already mentioned (Adler, 1970). Creative energy is manifested by the constructive activity of the mind. It can be mobilized productively for the useful benefit of others or it can be personalized to create self-delusions and "life-lies." Whereas the latter approach is self-defeating and nonproductive, creative energy can be focused upon the challenge facing all humans to forge their own destinies. It is this constructive activity of the mind that demonstrates the inherent optimism of IP. Snyder (1995) has discussed the role of hope in treatment, but cautioned that hope which is self-serving is counterproductive; it must be hope that fosters living and working together. We have the capacity to make what we will of this world. Adler said that such action can be on the "useful side" or the "useless side" of living. However we choose, it must be said that humans have the capacity to create new lives, and this is the optimism that must be conveyed to Nancy. In spite of all of her difficulties, she retains the capacity to grow and change, as do we all.

NOTES

1. Adlerian Psychology is the more commonly used term for describing Adler's psychology. Inasmuch as Adler chose individual psychology to emphasize the integrated view of a person, it being the central idea of his psychology, I have chosen to use "individual psychology" rather than "Adlerian Psychology" as the best designation for his position. The journal also uses this name.

2. Practice and Theory is the name of an early collection of Adler's papers (1925) dating from 1908 to 1920. Practice-before-theory summarizes Adler's approach. He was known as a superb diagnostician and therapist. His written work is largely distilled from talks. Practice before theory aptly categorizes the state of affairs in individual psychology. We do not have a standard set of Adler's writings as we do for Freud and Jung, although one is in early stages of development.

3. Distance connotes some purposeful "separation" inserted between the self and an anticipated act or decision. The intensity of this separation can range from modest discomfort to immobilization.

4. Adler derived the foundation and support for this concept from the German philosopher Hans Vaihinger who in his work, The Philosophy of As-If, (1925) and sub-titled "The theoretical, practical and religious fictions of mankind," documented many ingenious mental constructions used to cope in life. Not all of these mental creations are deleterious, but they are fictions nevertheless.

5. Life Style assessment is explained further in the works of Eckstein, Baruth, & Mahrer, 1975; Morris, 1978; Mosak & Shulman, 1971; Mosak, Schneider & Mosak, 1980.

6. Additional supportive studies of individual psychology include the following: Reliability: Colker & Slaymaker, 1984; Ferguson, 1964; Hedvig, 1963; Magner-Harris, Riordan, Kern, & Curlette, 1979. Validity: Mosak, 1969; Taylor, 1975; Bruhn & Davidow, 1983; Friedman & Schiffman, 1962; Hafner, Fakouri, Ollendick, & Corotto, 1979; Jackson & Sechrest, 1962; Mullis, Kern, & Curlette, 1987; O'Phelan, 1977; West & Bubenzer, 1978; Wheeler, Kern, & Curlette, 1986; Driscoll & Eckstein, 1982. Empirical validation of Adler's theories can be found in Ansbacher (1947), Ansbacher & Ansbacher (1964), Ferguson (1968), Faberow and Shneidman (1961), Taft (1958), Teichman & Foa (1972), and Maddi (1968).

7. A short reader's guide to individual psychology is as follows:

    1. Ellenberger, E. (1970), *Alfred Adler and Individual Psychology*, Chapter 8;

    2. Ansbacher, H. & Ansbacher, R. *Individual Psychology of Alfred Adler*, 1956; *Superiority and Social Interest*, 1964; and *Cooperation Between the Sexes*, 1978.

    3. Hoffman, E. (1994), *The Drive for Self: Alfred Adler and the Founding of Individual Psychology*.

8. One of the accounts in Nancy's history is suggestive of an early recollection. It is given here as an illustration and not as an example of a true recollection.

REFERENCES

Adler, A. (1912). *Uber den nervosen Character.* Wiesbaden: Bergmann. (Reprinted 1926 as *The neurotic constitution.* Salem, NH: Ayer.)

Adler, A. (1925). *The practice and theory of Individual Psychology.* Paterson, NJ: Littlefield, Adams.

Adler, A. (1926). *The neurotic constitution.* Salem, NH: Ayer.

Adler, A. (1927). Individual psychology. *Journal of Abnormal and Social Psychology, 22,* 116–122.

Adler, A. (1930). *The education of children.* Chicago: Henry Regnery.

Adler, A. (1969). *The science of living.* New York: Doubleday (Originally published 1929).

Adler, A. (1970). Fundamentals of Individual Psychology. *Journal of Individual Psychology, 26,* 36–49 (Originally published 1926).

Adler, K. (1980). Depression in the light of Individual Psychology. *Journal of Individual Psychology, 17*(1), 56–67.

Ansbacher, H. L. (1947). Alfred Adler's place in psychology today. *International Zeitschrift fur Individualpsychologie, 16,* 96–111.

Ansbacher, H., & Ansbacher, R. (1956). *The individual psychology of Alfred Adler.* New York: Basic Books.

Ansbacher, H. (1967). Life Style: A historical and systematic review. *Journal of Individual Psychology, 23,* 191–212.

Ansbacher, H. (1968). The concept of social interest. *Journal of Individual Psychology, 24,* 131–149.

Ansbacher, H. (1980). On the origin of "social interest" in Adler's writings. *Journal of Individual Psychology, 36,* 117–118.

Ansbacher, H., & Ansbacher, R. (1964). *Superiority and social interest.* New York: Viking Press.

Ansbacher, H., & Ansbacher, R. (1978). *Cooperation between the sexes.* New York: Norton.

Beck, A. T. (1967). *Depression: Clinical, experimental and theoretical aspects.* New York: Harper & Row.

Bruhn, R., & Davidow, S. (1983). Earliest memories and dynamics of delinquency. *Journal of Personality Assessment, 47,* 476–403.

Bugental, J. F. T., & Bugental, E. K. (1984). A fate worse than death: The fear of changing. *Psychotherapy, 21*(4), 535–549.

Colker, J., & Slaymaker, F. (1984). Reliability of ideographic interpretations of early recollections and their nomothetic validation with drug abusers. *Journal of Individual Psychology, 40,* 36–44.

Crandall, J. (1975). A scale of social interest. *Journal of Individual Psychology, 31,* 187–195.

Curlette, W., Wheeler, M., & Kern, R. (1993). *BASIS-A Inventory: Technical Manual.* Highlands, NC: TRT Associates.

Damasio, A. (1994). *Descartes' error.* New York: Avon.

Dreikurs, R. (1967). *Psychodynamics, psychotherapy and counseling.* Chicago: Adler.

Driscoll, R., & Eckstein, D. (1982). Empirical studies of the relationship between birth order and personality. In D. Eckstein, L. Baruth, & D. Mahrer, *Lifestyle: What it is and how to do it* (pp. 51–57). Dubuque, IA: Kendall/Hunt.

Elliott, W., Fankouri, M., & Hafner, J. (1993). Early recollection of criminal offenders. *Journal of Individual Psychology, 49,* 68–75.

Ellis, A. (1961). *A guide to rational living.* New York: Harper.

Ellis, A., & Harper, R. (1975). *A new guide to rational living.* Englewood Cliffs, NJ: Wilshire.

Ernst, C., & Angst, J. (1983). *Birth order: Its influence on personality.* Berlin: Springer.

Falbo, T., & Polit, D. (1986). Quantitative review of the only child literature. Research evidence and theory development. *Psychological Bulletin, 100,* 176–189.

Farberow, N. L., & Shneidman, E. S. (Eds.). (1961). *The cry for help.* New York: McGraw-Hill.

Ferguson, E. (1964). The use of early recollections for assessing life style and diagnosing psychopathology. *Journal of Projective Techniques, 28,* 403–412.

Ferguson, E. (1968). Adlerian concepts in contemporary psychology: The changing scene. *Journal of Individual Psychology, 24,* 150–156.

Friedman, J., & Schiffman, H. (1962). Early recollections of schizophrenic and depressed patients. *Journal of Individual Psychology, 18,* 57–61.

Goldberg, D., & Bridges, K. (1988). Somatic presentations of psychiatric illness in primary care settings. *Journal of Psychosomatic Research, 32,* 137–144.

Greever, K., Tseng, M., & Friedland, B. (1973). Development of the social interest index. *Journal of Consulting and Clinical Psychology, 41,* 454–458.

Hadas, M. (Ed.). (1961). *Essential works of Stoicism.* New York: Bantam Books.

Hafner, J., Fakouri, M., Ollendick, T., & Corrotto, L. (1979). First memories of "normal" and schizophrenic, paranoid-type individuals. *Journal of Clinical Psychology, 35,* 731–733.

Hedvig, E. (1963). Stability of early recollections and thematic apperception stories. *Journal of Individual Psychology, 19,* 49–54.

Jackson, M., & Sechrest, L. (1962). Early recollections in four neurotic diagnostic categories. *Journal of Individual Psychology, 18,* 52–56.

Kant, I. (1964). *The classification of mental disorders.* Doylestown, PA: The Doylestown Foundation.

Katen, W., Kleinman, A., & Rosen, G. (1982). Depression and somatization: A review. Part I. *The American Journal of Medicine, 72,* 241–247.

Lloyd, G. (1986). Psychiatric syndromes with a somatic presentation. *Journal of Psychosomatic Research, 30,* 113–120.

Maddi, S. R. (1968). *Personality theories: A comparative analysis.* Homewood, IL: Dorsey Press.

Magner-Harris, J., Riordan, R., Kern, R., & Curlette, W. (1979). Reliability of life style interpretations. *Journal of Individual Psychology, 35,* 196–201.

Mahoney, M. J. (1980). *Psychotherapy process.* New York: Plenum Press.

Morris, P. (1978). *LSA: Life style assessment process.* Arnold, MD: Adlerian Counseling Services.

Mosak, H. (1969). Early recollections: Evaluation of some current research. *Journal of Individual Psychology, 25,* 56–63.

Mosak, H. (1989). Adlerian psychotherapy. In R. J. Corsini & D. Wedding (Eds.), *Current psychotherapies* (4th ed., pp. 65–116). Itasca, IL: Peacock.

Mosak, H., & Maniacci, M. (1998). *Tactics in counseling and psychotherapy.* Itasca, IL: Peacock.

Mosak, H., Schneider, S., & Mosak, L. (1980). *Life style: A workbook.* Chicago: Adler.

Mosak, H., & Shulman, B. (1971). *Life style inventory.* Chicago: Adler.

Mower, O. H. (1969). New directions in the understanding and management of depression. In C. F. Frederick (Ed.), *The future of psychotherapy.* Boston: Little, Brown & Co.

Mullis, F., Kern, R., & Curlette, W. (1987). Life-style themes and social interest: A further factor analytic study. *Journal of Individual Psychology, 43,* 339–352.

Munroe, R. (1955). *Schools of psychoanalytic thought.* New York: Dryden Press.

O'Phelan, M. (1977). Statistical evaluation of attributes in Adlerian life style forms. *Journal of Individual Psychology, 33,* 203–212.

Rogers, C. R. (1957). The necessary and sufficient conditions of therapeutic personality change. *Journal of Consulting Psychology, 21,* 95–103.

Snyder, C. R. (1995). Conceptualizing, Measuring, and Nurturing Hope. *Journal of Counseling & Development, 73,* 355–370.

Styron, W. (1990). *Darkness visible: A memoir of madness.* New York: Random House.

Sulliman, J. (1973). The development of a scale for the measurement of social interest. Unpublished doctoral dissertation, Florida State University, Tallahassee, FL.

Taft, R. (1958). A cluster analysis for Hall and Lindzey. *Contemporary Psychology, 3,* 143–144.

Taylor, J. (1975). Early recollections as a projective technique: A review of some validation studies. *Journal of Individual Psychology, 14,* 46–53.

Teichman, M., & Foa, U. G. (1972). Depreciation and accusation tendencies: Empirical support. *Journal of Individual Psychology, 26,* 135–143.

Wachtel, P. L. (1977). *Psychoanalysis and behavior therapy.* New York: Basic Books.

West, J., & Bubenzer, D. (1978). A factor analytic consideration of life style data. *Journal of Individual Psychology, 34,* 48–55.

Wheeler, M., Kern, R., & Curlette, W. (1986). Factor analytic scales designed to measure Adlerian life style themes. *Journal of Individual Psychology, 42,* 1–16.

RECOMMENDED READINGS

Adler, A. (1989). *Health book of the tailoring trade.* Berlin: C. Heymanns.

Adler, A. (1914). Life-lie and responsibility in neurosis and psychosis. In *The practice and theory of Individual Psychology* (pp. 235–245). Paterson, NJ: Littlefield, Adams.

Adler, A. Melancholia and paranoia (1914). In *The practice and theory of Individual Psychology* (pp. 246–262). Paterson, NJ: Littlefield, Adams, 1959.

Adler, A. (1929). *The science of living.* London: Allen & Unwin.

Adler, A. (1932). *What life should mean to you.* London: Allen & Unwin.

Beck, A. T., Rush, J. A., Shaw, B. F., & Emery, G. (1979). *Cognitive therapy of depression.* New York: Guilford Press.

Bottome, P. (1957). *Alfred Adler: A portrait from life.* New York: Vangard.

Ekstein, D., Baruth, L., & Mahrer, D. (1982). *Life Style: What it is and how to do it.* Hendersonville, NC: Mother Earth News.

Ellenberger, H. (1970). *The discovery of the unconscious.* New York: Basic Books.

Ellis, A. (1970). Tributes to Alfred Adler on his 100th birthday. *Journal of Individual Psychology, 26,* 36–42.

Fakouri & Hafner (1993). Early recollections of criminal offenders. *Individual Psychology, 49,* 68–75.

Fenichel, O. (1945). *The psychoanalytic theory of neurosis.* New York: Norton.

Fiebart (1997). In and out of Freud's shadow: A chronology of Adler's relationship with Freud. *Journal of Individual Psychology, 53*(3), 241–269.

Garber, J., & Seligman, M. (Eds.). (1980). *Human helplessness: Theory and applications.* New York: Academic Press

Janet, P. (1920). *Major symptoms of hysteria.* New York: Macmillan.

Hoffman, E. (1994). *The drive for self: Alfred Adler and the founding of Individual Psychology.* New York: Addison Wesley.

Mairet, P. (1969). Hamlet as a study in Individual Psychology. *Journal of Individual Psychology, 25,* 71–88.

Maslow, A. (1962). Was Adler a disciple of Freud? *Journal of Individual Psychology, 18,* 125.

May, R. (1970). Tributes to Alfred Adler. *Journal of Individual Psychology, 26,* 39.

McGuire, W. (Ed.). (1988). *The Freud/Jung letters.* Translated by Ralph Manheim & R. E. C. Hull. Cambridge, MA: Harvard University Press.

Mosak, H. (1989). Adlerian psychotherapy. In R. J. Corsini & D. Wedding (Eds.), *Current psychotherapies* (4th ed., 65–116). Itasca, IL: Peacock.

Mozdzierz, G., Greenblatt, R., & Murphy, T. (1986). Social interest: The validity of two scales. *Journal of Individual Psychology, 42,* 35–43.

Nunberg, H., & Federn, E. (1967). (Eds.) *Minutes of the Vienna Psychoanalytic Society—1910.* New York: International University Press.

Shulman, B. (1973). *Contributions to Individual Psychology.* Chicago: Adler.

Shulman, B., & Mosak, H. (1988). *Manual for life style assessment.* Muncie, IN: Accelerated Development.

Stone, M. (1997). Ibsen's life-Lie and Adler's Lifestyle. *Journal of Adlerian Theory, Research and Practice, 53*(3), 322–330.

Vaihinger, H. (1925). *The philosophy of As-If.* London: Routledge & Kagan Paul.

Watkins, C. (1983). Some characteristics of research on Adlerian theory, 1970–1981. *Journal of Individual Psychology, 39,* 99–110.

6

An Object Relations View of Depression

Frank Summers

I. THE OBJECT RELATIONS MODEL

The object relations model of psychoanalytic therapy is founded on the principle that the child's development is impossible without others. This need for the other cannot be reduced to the reduction of biological tensions states (the view of classical psychoanalysis) nor learned behavior. The findings of developmental research overwhelmingly support the position that the child's attachment to early figures is autonomously motivated. Three relevant lines of research evidence support the view that the infant is inherently programmed to make contact with its caretaker rather than discharge tension. First, the findings from experimental research show that the neonate turns to the source of human sounds, differentiates human from nonhuman sounds, reacts with distress if the sound source is disengaged from the view of the speaker's mouth, recognizes the human face, and behaves differently to human and nonhuman objects (Lichtenberg, 1983; Stern, 1985). In the first few weeks of life, the infant's feeding behavior becomes regulated to the particular behavior of its caretaker. It seems that infants are programmed for human contact and are preadapted to form a relationship with the caretaker. According to Stern (1985), the infant has an active "social" life from birth. Evidence against the view of infants as tension-reducing comes from the fact that infants will pursue objects visually from the beginning weeks of life and even interrupt feeding to look at visually presented objects (White, 1963). The findings that infants actually seek stimuli and make active choices for preferred stimuli with no reduction in tension is strong evidence against the concept of the infant as a discharge-seeking organism (Stern, 1985; White, 1963). Infants will react aversively to noxious stimuli only. The view that emerges from the experimental data is of an infant programmed almost from birth to form a synchronous interaction with its caretaker and to regulate stimuli both by increasing and decreasing it (Lichtenberg, 1983).

The second primary source of evidence for the object relational view of motivation comes from naturalistic observation and experimental work with animals. John Bowlby (1969) marshaled an impressive array of ethological evidence demonstrating the existence of a powerful need for attachment among nonhuman primates. Newborn guinea pigs, lambs, and dogs will attach to physical objects or animals of other species if those are the only possibilities for contact without association to other sources of gratification. Indeed, puppies isolated for three weeks and punished upon their only contact with a human will become attached to that figure more intensely than puppies receiving reward or punishment. Equally compelling are Harlow's experiments with rhesus monkeys which showed that baby monkeys attach to cloth model mothers and not wire models even when the wire surrogate mother provided bottle feeding (Harlow & Zimmermann, 1959). Further, when a rhesus monkey is raised by a nonfeeding cloth mother surrogate, it will attach to the model mother and cling to it when alarmed or in a strange setting (Harlow, 1961). However, when the baby monkey is raised by a wire model which provides bottle feeding, it does not use the surrogate for comfort despite strange or dangerous conditions. Like lambs and puppies, monkeys cling more intensely to the cloth "mother" in the face of danger and punishment, even if the danger is from the surrogate mother itself. Bowlby's evidence shows that nonhuman primates have an autonomous need for attachment irrespective of gratification of biological needs and that this attachment endures.

Bowlby (1969) also summarizes the third line of evidence. He points to naturalistic data on human children showing that they will attach to figures who do not meet their physiological needs. Children in concentration camps reared without the opportunity to attach to a benign adult will form strong bonds with each other. A study of Scottish children

showed that about one-fifth attached to adult figures who did not participate in their physiological care. Furthermore, Bowlby points out that
there is as yet no evidence that human babies attach to adult figures
because of their association with the meeting of biological needs. Bowlby
(1969) summarizes the evidence this way: " . . . such evidence as there
is strongly supports the view that attachment behavior in humans can
develop, as it can in other species, without the traditional rewards of
food and warmth" (p. 218). This work supports the extension of the
autonomous need for attachment to humans.

The ethological and child research evidence provide solid support
for the object relational view that there is an autonomous human need
to attach to significant figures very early and that this attachment tends
to endure. These findings indicate that the infant is inherently object-
seeking rather than pleasure-seeking in psychoanalytic terms. According
to the experimental data, infants are preadapted to seek object contact
and, if it is available, will form an interactional synchrony with the care
giver. The object relational view adds to the experimental data that the
human, being a symbolic animal, will give meaning to these attachments
and use them to develop a sense of who she is, a sense of self. According
to this object relational model, the structure of the self is formed from
the meaning the child gives to these early attachment relationships. In
this way, these early object relationships not only endure, but define
the sense of self and influence later relationships with others.

Each object relational theory has a different way of understanding
the process by which early object contact forms the sense of self. Given
this diversity, it is not justifiable to speak of a single object relational
theory. However, each variant of this theoretical viewpoint is based on
the principle that autonomously motivated attachments to early figures
form the building blocks of the self which then motors development.

Although this need for relating to an early caretaker is one primary
motivation of early childhood, it does not subsume all the child's inborn
needs. We now know that the neonate possesses a variety of affective
states (Tomkins, 1962, 1963), is inherently active, and is born with an
impressive array of competencies that tend toward development (Demos, 1991, 1994). Close observation of neonates shows that from the
first days of life they spend at least some time in quiet, alert states and
playful exploration, the duration of which increases to about six hours
by one year of age. Neonates seek stimuli within the first few days,
actively tracking visual phenomena, even interrupting feeding to do so
(Stern, 1985; White, 1963). In addition, the neonate has the ability

to recognize stimulus patterns, invariance in patterns, contingencies between action and the environment, the difference between internal and external, perceptual differences, and light/dark contrasts (Demos, 1992, 1994). To give one example of the capabilities of the neonate, in an experiment by DeCasper and Carstens (1981), infants learned to increase their sucking pauses in order to turn on a female voice recording. When the contingency was removed, the infants showed visible signs of upset. This single experiment demonstrates that newborns can detect contingencies, show emotion, as evidenced by interest in the stimulus, plan, as shown by their ability to repeat the event, have the capacity for both voluntary motor control and memory, and possess the ability to coordinate all these activities. In brief, infants are not passive; they can and do actively influence what happens to them.

There is impressive evidence that the child has a need to realize these inborn capacities. The child prefers to do for herself, learning to do voluntarily what she does involuntarily (for example, Hendrick, 1942, 1943; White, 1963; Tomkins, 1978). Much of what appears to be random infantile movement is actually organized effort to reach and grasp objects that is unsuccessful due to muscle weakness (for example, Bower, 1977). Tomkins (1978) points out that infants from the first days of life will replace the involuntary sucking response with voluntary sucking when there is no biological need to do so, implying an attitude of "I would rather do it myself!" The infant quickly turns these capacities into intentions to achieve expected results suggesting that the creative utilization of inborn capacities to become a self appears to exist from birth. It should be emphasized that this infant research leads naturally to the conclusion that the infant is born not only with considerable cognitive and emotional capabilities, but also with the organizational and creative motivation and ability to make use of these inborn capacities to form a self. Tomkins' (1978) concludes that the development of the child's self represents an "extraordinary creative invention . . . amplified by excitement in the possibility of improving a good actual scene by doing something oneself. . . . we have evolved to be born as a human being who will, with a very high probability, very early attempt and succeed in becoming a person" (p. 215).

Developmental research has shed considerable light on the nature of the relationship between the child's development and the role of the other. For example, for the infant to develop a sense of agency, the caretaker must perform two key functions (Demos, 1992, 1994). First, interventions must be timed properly. If the infant is disturbed and the caretaker moves too quickly to comfort the child, he is given a solution before awareness of a problem. If, on the other hand, the caretaker is unresponsive, the child will become overwhelmed with distress, the affect becomes punishing, and the infant, unable to prevent the increased pain and intensity by himself, will feel helpless and eventually shut down. In the latter case, the infant experiences the problem, but without the belief he can do anything about it. There appears to be an "optimal zone of affective experience . . . that allows the infant enough psychological space to feel an internal need, to become an active participant in trying to address the need, and therefore to be able to relate subsequent events . . . both to the internal need state and to the plans and efforts to remedy it" (Demos, 1992, p. 220).

From this viewpoint, any view that the child becomes who she is by a simplistic internalization, or "taking in," of the caretaker is an oversimplification of the relationship between the developing child and her caretaker. The child creates meaning from the early interactions, meaning derived from her experience and ways she can find to relate to those on whom she depends. The outcome of this process is the creation of patterned ways of being and relating, patterns that form the structure of the self. In some cases, the created patterns may be strikingly similar to the caretaker's patterns; in other instances, the child's creation may not bear any obvious resemblance to the caretaker's relational style.

One implication of this view is that the child encodes not just ways of relating to the caretaker, but both sides of relationship between self and object, that is to say, an object relationship. Consequently, the child will relate both as she related to the caretaker *and* as the caretaker related to her, a process referred to as "reversal of roles." These object relationships form the self structure.

So, the developing child has two fundamental needs: for self realization and for attachment to the other. That these two basic motivations define the human condition is the basis of some of the most influential personality theories. Bakan (1966), Angyal (1951), Rank (1929), and Balint (1959) have all identified needs for attaching and relating to others along with the need for self development and definition as the dual pillars on which the human motivational system is built. Additionally, substantial research evidence supports these two primary needs. McClelland and his colleagues, using projective instruments, have found the needs for affiliation or attachment and the need for achievement or efficacy as primary human motivational motors (for example, McClelland, 1986; McClelland, Atkinson, Clark, & Lowell, 1953; Winter, 1973). McAdams (1985), using a narrational method, has also found the needs for intimacy and control over one's life to be the central dimensions of human personality.

In ideal circumstances the caretaking figures facilitate an attachment based on the child's spontaneous affects and her need to become herself. However, one or more early caretakers may require the sacrifice of aspects of the child's developing self to secure the formation of the needed bond. Because the relationship to the object is so important, the child will do what she needs to maintain the connection in whatever way possible. Under these circumstances, the child's development, rather than spurred by inborn potential and spontaneously occurring affects, becomes anxiety-motivated, and authentic aspects of the self are buried in favor of a defensive adaptation designed to avoid object loss. Self-development is then crippled and relating to the world becomes disconnected from authentic experience. However, the indomitable bid for self expression will not be denied. Direct protest against the burial of authenticity being threatening to critical attachments, the true self will be manifested in symptomatic form. From this viewpoint, psychopathology is always a disguised expression of buried authenticity. In effect, the symptoms are an unconscious protest of the burial of the true self.

According to this model, psychopathology is rooted in early relationships requiring derailment of self development. Adult patients appearing for treatment, although typically separated physically from their early caretakers, maintain the patterns established in childhood well beyond the family circle. One must account, then, for the continuance of pathological patterns well past their origins in early caretaking relationships. These early relationships define the child's ways of being and relating that form the sense of self. It is this core feeling of who I am and how I relate to the world and others that the child maintains. Threats to this sense of self invite the anxiety of losing the very feeling of existence, a dread that may be called, borrowing a term from Melanie Klein, "annihilation anxiety." Without a sense of self one is lost, without a way to navigate the world and other people, the very sense of being an existing person may slip away. This feeling is so dreadful the patient sustains patterns, however painful and even destructive they may be, rather than risk loss of self. Thus, annihilation anxiety is the explanation for the patient's adherence to pathological patterns and the difficulties encountered in efforts to change them.

II. IMPLICATIONS FOR PSYCHOANALYTIC THERAPY

The manifestation of the patient's object relationships between patient and therapist is the transference. The patient forms the therapeutic relationship according to her characteristic ways of relating and attempts to induce the therapist to collude with her object relationships. In this way, the self structure appears in the therapeutic context and becomes repeated in the transference-countertransference interaction. The enactment of the patient's patterns being an inevitable aspect of the treatment, the crux of therapeutic action becomes the resolution of these object relations configurations.

The goal of psychoanalytic therapy, from this viewpoint, is to overcome the patient's defensive adaptation and resume the development arrested by the burial of the true self. A two-stage therapeutic process is required to achieve this aim. The relinquishing of the patient's self-protective maneuvering is largely an interpretive process. The analytic therapist makes conscious the patient's defensive protection against genuinely experienced affects. Once the patient becomes aware that she is not basing her relationship with the therapist on authentic experience, the therapeutic space begins to open to new avenues of experience. The therapist's role, in this phase, is to facilitate new ways of being and relating within the therapeutic relationship. This therapeutic strategy marks a decisive difference from the classical psychoanalytic model according to which the therapist's role is to confined to interpretation (for example, Brenner, 1976). In the object relations view, one cannot depend on interpretation alone for therapeutic change. Because the therapeutic action resides in the creation of new ways of being and relating, making the unconscious conscious cannot be relied upon to create the needed therapeutic shifts. Consciousness makes the patient aware of what she is doing and even her motivations, but such awareness of patterns does not necessarily change them. The transformation of pathological ways of relating requires a relationship in which new patterns can be created. In this model, interpretation, making conscious previously unconscious patterns, and a new relationship in which ways of relating are created combine to form a dual therapeutic strategy.

I define interpretation as the giving of meaning to previously unsymbolized psychological phenomena. In this model a critical distinction is made between two types of interpretation. One can articulate the patient's defenses and unconscious motives as "resistance," an attitude that although often clothed in empathy, is tantamount to an attack on the patient's lack of awareness. For example, the therapist may say, "You are agreeing because you are afraid of being attacked if you are open about your disagreement. This is what you feared from your mother." While such a statement may be accurate and can be conveyed in an empathic manner, it focuses on the patient's inadequacy; it is the language of deficit. Alternatively, the patient's unconscious renderings can be looked at as an adaptive response to a conflictual dilemma. In this case, the therapist would make the same point by saying, "You feel safest convincing yourself that you agree with me because that way you feel our relationship is secured. This is the way you relieved your anxiety that your mother would abandon you." Such a statement shows appreciation for the patient's struggle and recognizes that the patient's character style, however defensive, reflects an adaptation which served a needed purpose. This therapeutic focus is not on the patient's "flaws," but on her adaptive strategy and its cost in terms of life goals. Therapy then becomes a process of understanding the patient's mode of adaptation and the price exacted by her defensive/adaptive strategy.

There is no decisive distinction here between the "pathological" and the "normal." All character is to some degree an adaptive compromise; what we call "pathological" is an adaptive maneuver that interferes with the attainment of life goals. Symptoms, from this viewpoint, are not simply a product of some deficit in the patient but a compromise adaptation that originally helped ameliorate childhood anxieties, but continuing to be used in this way, now interferes with life goals. So, to continue with our example: the therapist would interpret that while the patient feels safer complying than confronting conflict, the cost of living an inauthentic life is a sense of emptiness that issues in depression, the feeling of hopelessness and helplessness in controlling one's own destiny. This type of interpretation emphasizes the adaptive value of what the patient has done.

From this viewpoint, the therapeutic setting is a psychological space constructed from the therapist's understanding of the patient and the latter's attribution of meaning to the therapist's offerings. This transitional space is open to the patient's meaning creation as much as possible within the limits of the therapist's reality. This conception of therapeutic space finds its analogue in the baby's use of the transitional object: the child makes use of the blanket, for example, by attributing powerful emotional meaning to it, while adjusting to the reality of the blanket. The therapist's task is to keep the therapeutic space as open as possible for the patient's creative use while staying firmly aware of herself as therapist and what she can be used for.

III. EVIDENCE FOR THE MODEL

Historically, there has been little quantitative research on the psychoanalytic process. Psychoanalytic therapists have tended to rely on case reports and the intensive investigation of individual lives for their data rather than formal research findings. While there is a philosophical and scientific basis for this approach in the fact that psychoanalytic therapy is a hermeneutic enterprise best understood by grasping individual meaning (for example, Ricouer, 1980), a growing body of research has attempted to examine psychoanalytic hypotheses by quantitative methods. In general, efficacy studies have shown that long-term psychodynamic psychotherapy is an effective method for the amelioration of emotional distress (for example, Consumer Reports Survey, 1995). However, such studies investigate the broad arena of psychoanalytic therapy that may include therapists of many different psychoanalytic persuasions. Contemporary psychoanalytic therapy is so diverse that therapists adhering to different psychoanalytic theories cannot be presumed to be practicing the same craft. We will examine briefly the research evidence that bears most directly on the model presented here.

Researchers have used the concepts of *schema* and *script* to investigate the concept of transference. A *schema* is an organized cluster of meaningfully associated experiences (Bartlett, 1932), and a *script* is a construct that organizes sequences of events and includes expectations about specific outcomes (Tomkins, 1979). Numerous experimental studies have shown that schemas provide selection criteria for organizing knowledge, providing focus for encoding information about the world (for example, Taylor & Crocker, 1981; Fiske & Taylor, 1984; Fiske & Linville, 1980). Schemas about people, or *person schemas*, are a primary way people organize their interpersonal perceptions (Horowitz, 1988, 1990). Person schemas include categorizations of self, others, and the relationship between self and others. Anderson and Cole (1990) have shown that schemas regarding "significant others" are far more influential in the organization of one's life than schemas about less important figures. Furthermore, there is research evidence that personal scripts influence and distort experience that is not part of the dominant script (Fiske & Taylor, 1984), a finding that indicates that scripts selectively organize interpersonal situations. Thus, the research on schemas, especially person schemas, provides experimental support for the general concept of transference and specifically for the object relations view of transference as the repetition of significant early self-other relationships (Horowitz, 1988, 1990).

Tomkins (1979), who developed the script concept, showed that positive and negative scripts grow differently. Whereas positive scripts magnify through experiences that resemble the original scene but differ from it in significant ways, negative scripts grow through identifying new experiences with the old. That is, negative scripts are not expansive, they bring the new experience back into the character of the old. These data fit the theoretical proposition that pathological transference patterns tend to be stubborn even in the face of conflicting evidence. In object relations theory, this process has been referred to as "psychic gravity" (Bollas, 1987). This "gravitational pull" of negative experience accounts for the stubbornness of negative transference and the difficulties in its treatment.

Even more poignantly, consistent research evidence indicates that self-referential scripts and schemas are biased toward positive affects, self-referencing of events, and the tenacity of schemas and scripts even when confronted with contradictory information (Salovey & Singer, 1989; Singer & Salovey, 1991). This evidence supports the concept of transference of early experience and ways of being and relating onto later similar situations and the resilience of these patterns to change. The motivational basis of transference from this experimental tradition is the human need to simplify and organize experience from the very beginning of life (Flavell, 1963; Piaget, 1926, 1962). Some researchers in this area have concluded that the needs for attachment and individuality must be added to the need for organization to form a complete view of the human motivational system (Singer & Singer, 1992).

With regard to studies of transference in the treatment situation, researchers have used the Core Conflictual Relationship Theme (CCRT), a measure of the most frequent relationship conflicts appearing in psychotherapy narratives (Crits-Cristoph, 1984). Investigations using the CCRT have shown that there is a parallel between the conflictual themes with the therapist and other people, that this pattern tends to involve wishes or expectations of others and feared responses, that this pattern tends to be consistent over time, and that accurate interpretations of the pattern results in treatment benefits (Luborsky & Crits-Christoph, 1990a). Other studies directly assessing the value of transference interpretations indicate that frequency of transference interpretations is related to positive treatment results (Malan, 1976; Marziali, 1984). Most importantly to the model presented here, more refined studies of transference interpretation have shown that when patients respond affectively to such interpretations the outcome tends to be better than when a nonaffective response ensues. One study found that response to transference interpretations is a function of the patient's object relations.

There is also evidence that interpretation of object relations is important to positive treatment outcome. The accuracy of the therapist's interpretation of the patient's wish plus response-from-other, as measured by the CCRT, correlates with good outcome, whereas accuracy on the response-of-self component did not show such a correlation (Crits-Cristoph, Cooper, & Luborsky, 1988). Buttressing this finding are the results of another study showing that patient's level of self-understanding of the CCRT about the therapist and others correlated with good treatment outcome, but self-understanding in general and in relation to parents did not (Crits-Christoph & Luborsky, 1990a). With regard to change in transference during psychotherapy, it has been found that patients' expectations of others' responses tend to be less negative during the course of treatment and reduction in the pervasiveness of CCRT correlates with reduction of distress and overall mental health improvement (Crits-Christoph & Luborsky, 1990b). That is to say, as perceptions of others become less anxiety-ridden, the patient's overall well-being tends to improve.

These findings provide research support for much of the object relations model of personality development and psychotherapy. People selectively organize their ways of relating via schemas and scripts and bring their conflictual aspects into their relations with others including the therapist. The evidence indicates that a therapeutic focus on these transference themes correlates with good psychotherapy outcome. Thus, research confirms the theoretical importance of object relationships and their amelioration by transference interpretation as crucial components of the therapeutic action of psychoanalytic psychotherapy.

IV. APPLICATION OF THE OBJECT RELATIONS MODEL TO DEPRESSION

From this viewpoint, depression is one of a variety of possible reactions to the burial of the self. When the child is required to restrict her spontaneously occurring affects to maintain early attachments, she does not believe her authentic experience will sustain relationships, and social adaptation becomes motivated largely by anxiety avoidance. A defensive structure is devised to navigate the social world at the cost of affective connection. It would divert us too far from our topic to delineate all the possible adaptive/defensive strategies that may be used for this purpose. Whatever the patient's mode of adaptation, its disconnection from lived experience means the patient can derive little gratification from it. However, because relinquishing the defensive posture would trigger the threat of abandonment, the patient feels helpless, fated to a life of emptiness and anxiety avoidance. For some people, the defensive stance becomes a stable pattern. For example, a grandiose posture that seeks continual approbation and admiration is a frequent adaptation to helplessness that forms the narcissistic character structure.

For those who are unable to sustain the illusion of a gratifying existence, the defensive strategy breaks down and issues in the psychic collapse commonly called "depression." Finding no meaning in life, the patient loses all interest in the world and often loses appetite, or, in a desperate effort to protect against awareness of helplessness, the patient may overeat, possibly becoming obese or bulimic. Similarly, the lack of investment in the world and avoidance of meaninglessness frequently results in difficulty getting out of bed, but if the helplessness becomes conscious, the ensuing anxiety can lead to insomnia. Whether any particular case of depression is manifested in lethargy or anxiety, the depressive symptoms reflect a sense that the patient's destiny feels hopelessly out of her control.

A variety of strategies may be used to achieve some degree of interpersonal satisfaction despite poverty of authentic self-experience. Inflated views of the self, use of substances, and the obsessive search for approbation through achievement, status, or beauty are among the most typical maneuvers to fill inner emptiness through external means. Perhaps the most common such strategy is to attach to another person whose connection completes the sense of self. An intense attachment to an idealized other can provide both a feeling of wholeness that masks the lack of ownership of one's states and the helplessness to control one's fate. However, once such an object relationship is disrupted, the patient is left with the sense of emptiness and collapses into a state of depression. This use of objects by the depressive-prone personality explains why a more traditionally-oriented psychoanalytic formulation emphasizes object loss as a key component of the depressive picture.

In Freud's (1917) account, mourning becomes melancholia when the lost object is internalized and attacked within. This way of conceptualizing depression is understandable given the fact that depressive states are frequently precipitated by loss of a loved one. However, for object loss to result in the self depletion that characterizes depression, the object must have served the function of completing the sense of self. When the object is necessary for the experience of self, its loss issues in hopelessness and helplessness, the psychic collapse that we refer to as "depression." That is to say, the severity of the grief reaction to object loss is understandable only if the object has functioned to complete an unrealized self. The root of the depression, then, is not the loss of the object, but the incompletely developed self that led to the clinging tie to the object.

From this object relations viewpoint, depression is not only a symptom, but a communication from the buried self seeking to become articulated in the world. Whatever the particular depressive symptom constellation, it is an index of a longing to live in accordance with genuine experience, a deeply buried desire that cannot otherwise be elaborated. Because overt expression of desires and needs evokes the anxiety of abandonment, depression is the only way the patient can communicate this need. From this viewpoint, the depressive symptoms, although painful, are not simply "pathological," but an expression of the true self, the only such expression the patient is capable of making.

This formulation of depression as the collapse of an inauthentic existence is illustrated in the case of Dick, a highly successful businessman. This patient, who had completed many complex deals, became depressed ostensibly over a routine deal while home sick with a case of the flu. Fearful that the deal would fail, he felt threatened to the point of obsessing over a catastrophic view of his future. Despite his fabulous string of professional successes, Dick feared that his career was on the brink of collapse. Although his depression interfered with his sleep, he did not want to get out of bed after his bout of flu was over. Having lost interest in doing anything except staying in bed, when his illness had run its course, he resumed his business activities but without any of his former emotional investment. He felt chronically sad and often cried. After returning to the office, Dick still felt hopeless, had difficulty sleeping, and his appetite was minimal. Although intellectually he knew that he would not be materially affected if the deal was unsuccessful, he could not escape the emotional conviction that such a "failure" would be the beginning of the end.

Dick entered treatment looking exhausted and wan as he related his catastrophic fears that the impending deal would fail. As we discussed Dick's catastrophic anxiety, he acknowledged that he had always feared failure privately and had never embarked upon a business negotiation without painful anxiety and insomnia. Through his associations to this fear of failure, it became clear that his business career had not been a choice. His father wanted him to be a real estate developer, and he had never given consideration to any other career path. Awareness of this overpowering need to comply with his father's expectations, in turn, led to a thematic focus on the importance his father held in his life and the family in general. Dick regarded his father as the "pillar of strength" in the family whose fabulous business and financial success were achieved by his ample resourcefulness, intelligence, and resilience. Greatly admiring his father's rise from modest origins, Dick competed for his father's affection and approval with his two older brothers. Dick's associations to his mother were to an ineffective, weak woman who was so easily disturbed by problems of any sort that she denied their existence or sought comfort in her children. For example, Dick suffered a series of serious injuries as a child, spending much time at home recuperating. His mother denied the seriousness of each injury, and rather than comforting Dick, she became so upset that she sought his solace. To this day, she denies that Dick was hurt "any more than any other child." Because his mother was so easily disrupted and required comforting herself, Dick did not respect her and formed a strong bond with his father, as did his brothers. Being the only attachment he felt he could rely on, Dick put his emotional investment in gaining his father's approval to secure the needed bond. His father, a highly successful businessman, was consumed with his career and coveted business achievement for his sons, all of whom knew their father valued no other career path and measured life success by material wealth. Dick spoke with his father daily, sought his counsel frequently, and took pride in feeling he was the "favored son."

The importance of succeeding in his father's eyes made clear that Dick's fear of failure was connected to his anxiety of losing the paternal attachment. Dick gained a large measure of relief when he recognized that he feared losing his father if even a single deal was not highly successful. At this point in the treatment, Dick acknowledged that his business career brought him no satisfaction. The only "positive" feeling he could identify was a sense of relief when a deal did not fail. His professional motivation was fueled by the avoiding the anxiety of incurring his father's disapproval, a goal he achieved with his material success. Not being able to "win," he could only "not lose." Each impending deal made him highly anxious because he feared that if he did not succeed his father would abandon him by withdrawing his "special" feeling.

Dick's bout of flu in the midst of business negotiations evoked the childhood helplessness of being home injured without being able to rely on his mother who was unable to provide him with support and reassurance. This childhood anxiety, in turn, triggered the overwhelming importance of the need to please his father and consequent fear that if his impending deal failed, he would lose the paternal connection on which he still depended. Home ill, Dick could not take active steps to work on the deal, and his anxiety grew until it became debilitating.

The fact that his life ambitions were motivated by anxiety avoidance became apparent in his near-paralyzing depression over the possible loss of a routine business deal. Dick's depressive episode, then, was an index of the depth of his need to maintain his status as the "preferred son" and the allied fact that his work had no other meaning to him. On one level, his anxiety could be explained by his fear of the deal "failing" and consequent dread of losing his most important attachment. On a deeper level, such a potential loss felt catastrophic because his sense of self was derived from it: "failing" his father meant loss of his sense of existence. Without the glow of his father's approval, Dick felt lost; and his life, purposeless. This possibility panicked him, his dread reflecting the fragility of his sense of self. His lack of authentic self experience now becoming manifest, early in therapy he acknowledged what he had never before admitted to himself: his work life, which had never given him satisfaction, felt empty and he had no genuine interest in it. His false self adaptation had spent its course.

Longing for a more authentic life, Dick felt helplessly trapped in the pursuit of his ambitions. Unable to conceive of a different life, he had never seriously contemplated alternatives; this imprisonment in a meaningless life issued in a desperate sense of futility. Feeling hopeless and helpless about ever being able to free himself from a life that offered only anxiety and temporary episodic relief resulted in depression. His lack of motivation to continue his former life, appearing as depression, was the overt expression of what he had always felt but denied to himself. Feeling that his very existence depended on a life that issued in agony, anxiety, and emptiness, Dick could only express his pain and craving for self expression through his depression. Lying in bed withdrawn from his life he was symbolically protesting a prison he did not know how to escape.

While his almost paralyzing depression was a shock to his friends and family, it made sense from the viewpoint of his psychological state. What had been an underlying emptiness in his life became manifest when he could no longer maintain the social adaptation that others had mistaken for his self experience. The depressive symptoms, then, reflected the fact that his life of avoiding the anxiety of displeasing his father was unacceptable to Dick. His presumed lack of motivation and investment in the world demonstrated both that he could no longer go on with a life that offered him inner emptiness and that he sought a life built on a more authentic foundation.

A more traditional psychoanalytic formulation of Dick's depression would emphasize aggression toward his father which, because it could not be expressed directly to its object, was turned toward the self. It is true that Dick's aggression was inhibited, but the source of this suppression of aggressive feelings was his anxiety of object loss. Fearing that others would not tolerate his negative affects, he avoided conflict and tended to comply with others' expectations. Further, his anger at his father was not "psychological rock bottom," but a reaction to suffocating expectations that provided no room for the pursuit of his desires. Thus, inhibited aggression was not the cause of the depression, but a symptom of arrested self realization.

As his feelings of emptiness and dissatisfaction were discussed in therapy, Dick gave voice for the first time in his life to a desire to lead a different life, a life not so much focused on a new profession, but a life built on values in which he believed. His work life had so consumed him he had little time for his three children and barely saw them. He wanted a more pastoral life in which his family would play a major role. This value system, buried under the need to avoid the anxiety of loss via material and professional achievement, reflected a deeply felt authenticity: a life oriented around his family felt like a representation of him. Dick expressed frustration in not being able to live a life in accordance with values he now realized he cherished.

Dick's depression began to abate when he resolved to leave the frenetic pace of his business life. Eventually, he changed the structure of his life from the drive of his urban-based business to a rural area where his work fit into a more relaxed lifestyle that was less successful in conventional terms, but fit better his sense of what he wanted by including ample time for children and recreation. Thus, Dick's depression was a symptom not so much of repressed feelings, but of a life lived without authenticity that he had felt helpless to change. Analysis of the meaning of Dick's anxiety, lack of motivation, and insomnia revealed authentic values that coveted articulation in the world. These symptoms bore the unconscious meaning that he found his life meaningless and longed to transform it, but felt helpless to do so. By listening to the meaning of the depressive symptoms, Dick and his therapist were able to find the path to his liberation. This case demonstrates the object relations view that depression is a psychic collapse that occurs when the patient feels hopelessly fated to live a life that does not articulate his genuine experience.

V. THE CASE OF NANCY

A. The Dynamic Formulation

My initial contacts with Nancy would be two or three interviews devoted to our becoming acquainted with each other. I would ask her about herself and pay special attention to the affects embedded in her responses. Rather than conducting tightly structured interviews, I would ask her questions as I saw indications of affective responses or found aspects of her narrative to be puzzling. My purpose in this dialogue would be to gain some initial impressions of the relationship between her life themes and symptoms. Based on the material that emerges, I would suggest possible connections, so that she could have a "taste" of the kind of work in which we would be engaged. In this way, she has some experience on which to base her decision about continuing with me. My offer of psychotherapy is not an abstract promise, but a proposal to continue the exploration we have begun. She would have the opportunity to ask me anything she might want to know to help her with her decision about continuing with me. After these sessions, we would discuss our views about working together. My impression from the case material is that I would be eager to treat her as Nancy appears to be an ideal case for psychoanalytic therapy: her symptoms reflect the affectively-based conflicts for which this type of therapy is best suited. My formulation of her based on the case material is as follows.

I view Nancy as a case typical of the dynamics of depression. Her motivational life from childhood has been characterized by attending to others to the exclusion of her own desires. The very fact that she has so many major objections to her husband and does not love him but cannot leave indicates the depth of her anxiety of being alone. The marital situation indicates that she is divorced from authentic self-expression out of fear that others will leave her, and, therefore, she is driven to compromise her desires, her very sense of self, in order to maintain attachments. Implied in this pattern is a lack of faith in her own resources to lead her life. Even though she finds her husband "controlling," damaging to her self-confidence, and pressing for a life she finds noxious, the marital relationship provides her with a sense of connection to the interpersonal world, a feeling that offers a sense of safety. The depressive symptoms are the price she pays for this motivation as opposed to living from "the inside out" (Winnicott, 1960).

The source of Nancy's willingness to deny her authenticity is not difficult to find in her family relationships. Her mother, critical, unpredictably angry and punishing, was needy to the point that she focused her attention on Nancy not as a separate person, but as a source of her own gratification, an archaic selfobject (Kohut, 1971, 1984). That is, Nancy's mother could not recognize Nancy as an independent self, a source of subjectivity. Being angry and chronically unhappy with her own life, Nancy's mother was either highly critical and abusive of Nancy or used her as a "sounding board." The only recognition she received from her mother being highly negative, Nancy was convinced that she has minimal or even nonexistent qualities that would be worthy of others' attention. Consequently, Nancy was unable to construct a belief in her own resources.

Nancy's father, being psychotic and paranoid, could provide no sense of recognition and, in fact, she was forced to assume a parental role with him in order to protect her mother. Constantly threatened by her mother's criticism and unpredictable anger, and her parents' chronic violent battling, Nancy could not be certain of the continuance of parental bonds. Her mode of adaptation was to comply and, even further, to take care of both parents, providing emotional solace and assuming a parental role in which they relied on her for comfort, rather than vice versa. This reversal of roles was Nancy's way of trying to maintain connections with both parents and sustain the family unit. Although finally abandoned by her father, she managed to keep the maternal relationship by being useful to her mother.

The upshot is that Nancy not only lacks belief in her own capacities, but also is convinced that others will stay with her only if she complies with their needs to the detriment of her own. She cannot "demand my rights" because to do so may result in abandonment. That is to say, Nancy has no faith in her ability to draw others to her and believes she has no space in a relationship to assert her self. The relationship is either for the other person, or it is threatened. Unable to pursue her own interests and desires, Nancy gets "next to no pleasure out of life." Living without any connection to her authentically experienced desires, her life has been a "waste" in a very real sense: it is not hers.

The parental pattern is repeated in her relationship with her husband. She married not only *despite* his controllingness, but partially *because* of it. Lacking belief in herself, she unconsciously sought a partner who would "take over" for her. Further, the only kind of relationship she understands and knows how to sustain is a bond in which she is subservient. Nancy sees her husband's "controllingness," but cannot fully see her own need for someone to assume ownership over her life. Having found such a partner, she now suffers the consequences of this anxiety-driven need. She is unable to leave because she does not know any other type of relationship, has no faith in her ability to function on her own, and does not believe that anyone else will want her. Being trapped in a suffocating relationship is an inevitable consequence of her lack of sense of self. It is also the primary cause of her depression. Her "downward spiral of sadness" reflects Nancy's suffocation and helplessness.

Nancy's anger and even rage at her husband for his control and lack of recognition of her is the source of the anger that appears in the depressive episodes, but Nancy is unable to direct this anger at its object for fear that her aggressive feelings will terminate the relationship. Her rage becomes redirected to herself in order to save the relationship she fears will be disturbed by her anger. The anxiety of damaging the relationship with her anger is most likely the primary source of the guilt that appears in the depressive episodes. Furthermore, Nancy "keeps" the maternal relationship by treating herself as her mother treated her (Bollas, 1987); by internalizing her mother's voice she maintains the maternal bond from within. As a result, she "hates herself" and believes she "fucks everything up." What Nancy does not see is that these chronic self-deprecating statements are the voice of her mother talking inside her, a voice she needs to sustain the maternal connection. Thus, Nancy's self-flagellation is related to her anxiety of being happy. If she were to feel fulfilled, Nancy would be separated from her mother, a loss she does not feel she can bear. Her guilt, which keeps her from accepting good experience and feeling happy, is another way of maintaining the maternal connection by insuring misery.

One might wonder why Nancy would endure hardship to maintain a relationship with a woman who inflicted pain upon her. One of Fairbairn's (1941, 1943) great contributions to object relations theory was to point out that the parental relationship is so crucial to the child that if it is unsatisfactory the child becomes anxious about the fragility of the tie and clings desperately to preserve the bond. This was Fairbairn's explanation for the conundrum that abused children form clinging ties to their abuser. Recent work on adult survivors of sexual abuse have found that this pattern in sexual victims is explainable in Fairbairn's terms (Meissler-Davies & Frawley, 1992). Although it seems counterintuitive, the clinical reality is that children with disturbed parental relationships tend to have a much more difficult time separating than children who have secure attachments to parental figures. Having suffered both physical and emotional abuse from her mother, Nancy feels anxious about the security of the bond, causing her to cling tightly out of desperation. She is terrified of psychological separation from her mother because the maternal bond having always been fragile, she did not develop the belief in her self required to cope with life on her own.

Nancy's collapse into depression is the overt expression of her longing for a life lived "from the inside out," that is to say, a life in which she could "demand her rights" and pursue a direction of her choosing. Her helplessness to do so is manifested in her hopelessness and "spiral of sadness." The life she has is not a life she leads; in a very real sense, it leads her. There is little motivation to continue with such a life because not feeling authentically one's own, it can only feel like a "waste." Consequently, Nancy does not feel like having sex, she eats in a desperate effort to fill the void in her life, and she is so preoccupied with her sense of emptiness and dissatisfaction that she can neither concentrate nor remember.

B. Psychotherapy With Nancy

The psychotherapy I would conduct with Nancy would be guided by the dynamic formulation outlined above. I do not believe she will overcome her depressive episodes until she lives a life based on her authentically experienced affects, beliefs, and values. Therefore, the primary goal would be the realization of her buried potential. It is not possible to predict the length of time such a personality transformation would require, but the process would undoubtedly be both intensive and lengthy. I would see Nancy as often as practical, but I would expect to work with her at least twice per week initially and continue the work until we both felt that she had transcended her acquiescent childhood self sufficiently that she would be capable of leading a life based on her long-buried potential. "Potential" is not meant in the narrow sense of using particular talents, but in the psychological sense of possible authentic ways of being and relating. I would have no preordained concept of her capabilities; my focus would be on facilitating a life that makes sense to her in the way that her current life does not. It is neither possible nor necessary to foresee the end result of this process. I would assess the success of the psychotherapy not by the achievement of any particular functional level, but by the degree to which Nancy's ways of being and relating fit her authentic experience.

At the point of entering treatment Nancy does not know what her authentic affects are because, not having had space in her family relationships for her genuine experience, she buried any potential desires of her own in order to accommodate parental needs. The first task of therapy is to make Nancy aware of her own desires and values in order to facilitate a reorientation from living according to the cues of others to a life based on her experience. The achievement of this aim requires that Nancy become aware of the gap in her sense of self. Therefore, interpretation is a key therapeutic strategy. Within this overall approach, transference interpretation has a central role because it is within the therapeutic relationship that one can most easily see and resolve Nancy's self-denying pattern. I would fully expect Nancy to relate to me as she does to others: her focus would be on acquiescing to my judgments and opinions while taking extreme care not to disturb or disrupt me in any way. Interpretation of this deferential style would focus on: (1) the repetition of her childhood pattern of taking care of her parents, and (2) her fear that aggression or conflict in our relationship would send her packing. Central to the interpretive themes would be her assumption that there is no space in our relationship for her subjectivity. The purpose of this strategy is to make Nancy aware that she is making assumptions about the restrictiveness of our relationship that fit her past but do not necessarily correspond with our relationship and, by implication, other relationships. Once she grasps *that* she is making such an assumption the therapeutic space opens to the question of what Nancy's own feelings and thoughts may be. In this way, interpretation is a crucial component of her growth because it opens the therapeutic relationship to her buried affects and beliefs.

Nonetheless, eliciting her authentic experience will be difficult because her awareness has been dominated all her life by the anxiety of displeasing others. Inevitably, Nancy will be fearful of the direct articulation of any negative or potentially conflicting feelings in our relationship. Even after she is aware of what she feels and desires, Nancy is likely to continue to be fearful that verbalizing disagreement or aggression will threaten our relationship. Consequently, once Nancy's affective awareness is enhanced, an inevitable interpretive theme will be her anxiety of losing the relationship if she expresses any feelings she regards as potentially disturbing to me. I would put special emphasis on the inhibition of aggression toward me because she regards the expression of aggressive feelings as the most potentially damaging. Most importantly, she will be watchful of my responses to her affective expressions, especially her negative feelings, to see if I can absorb them without damage to the relationship. Consequently, my accepting, understanding response to the articulation of her authentic affects will be crucial to the continued elaboration of her previously buried affective life. When she feels the therapist is not just another person with an agenda of his own that must be catered to, she will test the freedom of the therapeutic space with the expression of long-suppressed affects and desires, the first step toward the achievement of her sense of self.

In accordance with the model outlined above, I would not expect Nancy to be able to yield her inhibitions solely in response to interpretation because increased awareness does not *by itself* lead to new ways of being. Her sense of self having been defined by compliance, any other way of relating would evoke annihilation anxiety, threat to the sense of self. Paradoxically, her very sense of self is threatened by efforts to realize her authentic self potential. Consequently, I would expect her to feel lost and disorganized, even disoriented, each time she begins to insert her self into our interaction. As we see her patterns operating repeatedly and the difficulty she has in changing them, I would point out this threat to her sense of self and her consequent inability to consider seriously alternatives. The discovery of new ways of being and relating, in turn, depends on a sufficiently empathic response on my part that she feels authenticity, even if her feelings may be unpleasant for me to hear, will not jeopardize our relationship. The development of her self will take place, then, in the therapeutic space, a space that, although created initially by the interpretive process, must expand beyond the deciphering of meaning to include room for new possible ways of being. Here free association is crucial because only in the uninhibited flow of Nancy's spontaneity will her authentic desires become accessible. Patients are often surprised at the interests and desires that seem to appear as if "out of nowhere," but when they occur, seem to fit so well that they seem to have "always been there."

Because the creation of new ways of being and relating requires use of the therapeutic space, I would encourage Nancy to find other ways of relating to me based on the spontaneity of the free associational process. As she experiments with openness, uninhibited relating, and spontaneity of affect, she will begin to create ways of being and relating that will make possible the assumption of ownership over her life (Summers, 2001). We saw how this occurred in the treatment of Dick, for whom a pastoral, family-oriented life was more authentic than his anxiety-driven, lifelong pursuit of ambition. By creating a life based on the former value system, he followed his destiny. It is neither possible nor necessary at this point to foresee what an authentic life would be for Nancy. The only certainty is that she has not authored her own life, and to do so would require a reversal of her life view so that her own spontaneous experience would be the guide for her life.

This is not to say that the journey to authenticity will be smooth. I would expect that each movement forward toward more authentic and aggressive relating would be fraught with the anxiety of damaging the relationship and fears of retaliation. It would be my responsibility to be alert for signs of Nancy's inevitable tendency to return to compliance and submission to me. Each instance of such regressive movement would be pointed out while interpreting her anxiety that aggression and negative feelings are intolerable to me. Willingness to engage in overt conflict and disagreement with me, including the assertion of her demands in opposition, would be the most positive indicators of growing self-realization. My expectation would be that before Nancy could achieve this state of self-affirmation we would engage in a lengthy oscillating journey between moments of self-realization and regressive compliance.

Even more difficult for the therapist are likely to be the needs opened up by her access to untapped self potential. Having missed out on the use of a mother on whom she could rely, once Nancy's needs emerge, they may well include intense expectations and devouring demands that were never allowed to emerge with the parents. As Nancy begins to risk the direct communication of negative feelings to me, her need for reassurance is likely to be exacerbated. Initially, demands and expectations will increase rather than decrease, as Nancy expresses her suppressed longings. The problem for me, as her therapist, is to contain my responses to the intensity of her affects and expectations. This "containment" is the major countertransference strain likely to occur.

I am convinced that many psychotherapeutic treatments founder at this point as the therapist shifts from her previously empathic, understanding stance to a severe, even punishing posture in order to reduce the intensity of the patient's needs. I regard such a response as not only contraindicated, but also a countertransference acting out. As psychotherapists we encourage patients to communicate their affects; if, after they express previously inhibited affects and needs, we attempt to suppress their new openness with punishing responses, we are involved in a very serious contradiction, and the patient feels justifiably betrayed. Most importantly, we are rejecting the very true self that it is our job to help develop. The way we respond to newly emerging affective states and desires is a crucial part of the treatment. For the psychotherapy to be successful, the therapist must welcome, even nurture, the patient's emerging needs as the expression, however extreme, of the patient's long-buried true self. We must always keep in mind that the authentic self is buried precisely because the patient has always assumed her genuine experience to be intolerable to others. If the therapist rushes to quash the patient's behavior, she risks confirming the patient's worst fears.

In this way, my capacity for tolerating Nancy's spontaneously expressed affect is key to the therapeutic outcome (Summers, 1997). The more Nancy's previously suppressed affective expressions can be tolerated, the greater will be the chances for treatment success. This is not to say that limits cannot be set. As indicated above, the psychotherapeutic dyad is a transitional space, a space limited by the reality of the therapist's offerings and within which the patient must create meaning. When the therapist's limits are reached, she delimits a therapeutic boundary.

Equally crucial is the way limits are set. If I felt the need to restrict Nancy's behavior, I would be clear about what boundary is being violated as well as my motives for controlling her behavior. That is, if Nancy made demands I could not meet such as expecting continual availability, I would tell her that I cannot fulfill her requests rather than imply that the expectation is "inappropriate." To judge her demand is to imply that her needs are somehow invalid and, thereby, risk reenacting her early experience that her authenticity is somehow unacceptable. Careful to make the distinction between the validity of her needs and my inability to meet them, I would assume ownership for my limit-setting. Maintaining the therapeutic boundaries by taking ownership of my limitations achieves two purposes: (1) it provides a sorely needed role model for ownership, and (2) it defines the relationship boundary without rejecting Nancy's demands as somehow "wrong" or "invalid."

The ultimate achievement of self-realization, as occurred in Dick's treatment, engenders belief in one's own potential. When Nancy begins to assume control over her ways of being and relating, first in the analytic relationship and later more generally, she will begin to believe in herself. This faith that one's own affects and desires are a reliable resource and guide for a satisfying life builds self-confidence. The literal meaning of confidence is "with faith," faith in the self. As discussed above, this crucial self-experience is created by the parenting figures' recognition of the child, the gaze of belief and acceptance. However, Nancy, never having felt this recognition, does not believe in her self; she feels reliant on others' "superior" judgment. Such faith in herself can be constructed only on the basis of authentic self-expression. When the therapeutic space affords the unfolding of the previously buried self, the patient can experience the joys and value of her self-expression. At that point, faith in the self, or self-confidence, can be constructed. Progress at this point becomes synergistic: self-confidence facilitates greater articulation of self experience that, in turn, enhances belief in oneself. I do not believe any direct interpretation of her low self-esteem in itself will transform Nancy's negative feelings toward herself. She will believe in herself when she experiences effectiveness in relating from "the inside out." The belief that she can use her own resources to relate to people and navigate the world provides her with the sense of ownership of self that is the antidote to depression.

Foremost among the indicators of Nancy's authorship over her life and the overcoming of helplessness would be her ability to make a fundamental change in her marital situation. At the point of entry into treatment, the primary symptom of Nancy's lack of self-realization is inability to be a self in the relationship with her husband. While she complains that he is controlling, she is unable to assume active control over any component of the relationship out of fear that she may lose him and would be unable to cope with life without him. Staying with or leaving her husband per se is meaningless because her problem is not the relationship per se, but her inability to maintain a sense of self in a relationship. The point of her therapy is not to leave the relationship, but to achieve ownership over her life. Consequently, I would not encourage Nancy to continue nor end the marriage. For Nancy to comply with any suggestions of mine would be counterproductive to the goal of self-realization. To leave or stay in the marriage without the ability to live an authentic life would not afford her the sense of self she lacks. As she becomes the self that had been buried under anxiety of loss, the current marital relationship will become intolerable as it comes into direct conflict with her growth trajectory. I would expect that as therapy begins to foster Nancy's sense of self, she will inevitably push to find room for her self in relationship to her husband. At that point, she will come to realize that the only possibilities consistent with her newly emerging self-realization are to form a more equal partnership with her husband or end the relationship.

Ultimately, it is ownership over her own life, beginning with the expression of authentic affects and epitomized by her unwillingness to tolerate a controlling relationship that will be decisive in transcending the acquiescent self of her childhood (Summers, 1997, 1999, 2001). In the realization of her potential by becoming the self she was not allowed to be in childhood, Nancy will transcend her tendency to depression. Authorship of one's life means that one carries out one's destiny, a life lived by articulating the possibilities inherent in the self, rather than feeling fated by anxieties that must be avoided. A consistent therapeutic focus on the exercise of latent self potential can facilitate replacing the sense of helplessness with authorship.

When these goals are achieved, we would discuss termination. In accordance with the overriding aim of self-realization, I would leave the final decision to Nancy. When she felt ready to leave, we would set a date to end based on her feeling of what she needs to end the relationship. This endpoint would be modifiable based on how ready she continued to feel as the final session drew near. I see no reason to impose an artificial structure on the termination process; again, to do so would be counterproductive to the goals of the treatment.

VI. CONCLUSION

I believe that Nancy's depression can be treated by a purely psychotherapeutic approach that sees her symptoms as indicative of a lack of opportunity for self-realization, that is, a self derived from authentically experienced affects and values. Nancy's depression is most usefully conceptualized as the breakthrough of dissatisfaction with a life in which her true self is buried. In this sense, the depression, although painful, must be regarded as a welcome indicator of her frustrated desire for an authentic life. For this reason, I would oppose the use of medication unless suicide became a serious problem, a concern I do not foresee from the material presented. Medication or other biological interventions, although they may help Nancy feel better temporarily, would sedate her into accepting a life situation that affords no room for her self development and that she finds intolerable.

Most importantly, such temporary soothing of Nancy's depressed state muffles the only voice of authenticity she is capable of mustering. The depressive symptoms, precisely because they are painful, are the best indicator that Nancy is dissatisfied with her life of compliance. To suppress her depression is to stifle her only voice of opposition. Palliative, behavioral, "supportive," and sedating approaches all stifle Nancy's only way of protesting her helplessness and longing for an authentic life. To remove the symptoms without addressing her life is to consign her to a life of compliance. Medication does not help her develop the skills she needs to extricate herself from her enslaved life nor to live in a different, more authentic manner. In fact, medication would run the danger of suppressing the most authentic move Nancy has made: her depression. That is to say, Nancy's desperate unconscious signal to herself and others, her desperate pleas for help, would be silenced by anesthetizing her dissatisfaction, the voice of authentic feelings.

While I do not doubt that different therapeutic styles can be effective in ameliorating Nancy's hopelessness and helplessness, my conviction is that for any approach to be meaningful it would have to address directly her inability to live a life based on her genuinely experienced affects and values. Any technique that fails in this regard can only foster continued compliance and a life of chronic dissatisfaction. The therapeutic strategy outlined here is designed to ameliorate her depression by helping her realize her self potential. I do not believe that there is as yet any nonpsychoanalytic method that would help a patient like Nancy see the roots of her unsatisfying life and facilitate a new life, a life authentically hers.

I end where I began: I regard Nancy as a prototypical case of depression. A life that is not authored is the soil in which depression grows. Anyone unable to live authentically experienced affects has succumbed to overwhelming anxieties. Depression, in whatever nuances or different forms it may assume, always means that my life does not belong to me. No resolution of the resulting depression can be meaningful unless this anxiety is resolved so that the true self is realized. Nancy's compulsion to follow others, including submitting to a controlling husband, is one form of the common depressive dynamic: I have no destiny to follow, my life is fated. Although Dick was professionally and financially successful and his life circumstances were markedly different from Nancy's, he felt equally fated to live a life of others' choosing. The object relations therapeutic strategy described here was used to help Nancy see that her life of compliance led directly to the helplessnesses and hopelessness she called her "depression." Most importantly, it helped her to conceive a life of her own creation.

REFERENCES

Anderson, S., & Cole, S. W. (1990). "Do I know you?" The role of significant others in general social perception. *Journal of Personality and Social Psychology, 59*, 384–399.

Angyal, A. (1951). *Neuroses and treatment: a holistic theory.* New York: Wiley.

Bakan, D. (1966). *The duality of human existence.* Chicago: Rand McNally.

Balint, M. (1959). *Thrills and regressions.* Madison, CT: International Universities Press.

Bartlett, F. C. (1932). *Remembering.* Cambridge, England: Cambridge University Press.

Bollas, C. (1987). *The shadow of the object.* London: Free Associations.

Bower, T. (1977). *The perceptual world of the child.* Cambridge, MA: Harvard University Press.

Bowlby, J. (1969). *Attachment and loss,* Vol.1: *Attachment.* New York: Basic Books.

Brenner, C. (1976). *Psychoanalytic Technique and Psychic Conflict.* New York: International University Press.

Consumer Reports Survey (1995). Does Therapy Help? *Consumer Reports, 60*(11), 734–739.

Crits-Cristoph, P. (1984). The development of a measure of self-understanding of core relationship themes. Paper presented at the National Institute of Mental Health workshop on Methodological Challenges in Psychodynamic Research,Washington, DC.

Crits-Cristoph, P., Cooper, A., & Luborsky, L. (1988). The accuracy of therapists' interpretations and the outcome of dynamic psychotherapy. *Journal of Consulting and Clinical Psychology, 56*, 490–495.

Crits-Christoph, P., & Luborsky, L. (1990a). Changes in CCRT pervasiveness during psychotherapy. In L. Luborsky & P. Crits-Christoph (Eds.), *Understanding transference: The CCRT method* (pp. 133–146). New York: Basic Books.

Crits-Christoph, P., & Luborsky, L. (1990b). The measurement of self-understanding. In L. Luborsky & P. Crits-Christoph (Eds.), *Understanding transference: The CCRT method* (pp. 189–196). New York: Basic Books.

DeCasper, A., & Carstens, A. (1981). Contingencies of stimulation: Effects on learning and emotion in neonates. *Infant Behavior & Development, 4,* 19–35.

Demos, E. V. (1992). The early organization of the psyche. In J. Barron, M. Eagle, & D. Wolitzky (Eds.), *Interface of psychoanalysis and psychology* (pp. 200–233). Washington, DC: The American Psychological Association.

Demos, E. V. (1994). Links between mother-infant transactions and the infant's psychic organization. Paper presented to the Chicago Psychoanalytic Society, Chicago, IL, May, 1994.

Fairbairn, R. (1941). A revised psychopathology of the psychoses and psychoneuroses. In R. Fairbairn *Psychoanalytic studies of the personality* (pp. 28–58). London: Routledge.

Fairbairn, R. (1943). The repression and the return of bad objects (with special reference to the 'war neuroses'). In *Psychoanalytic studies of the personality* (pp. 59–81). London: Tavistock, 1952.

Fairbairn, W. R. (1944). Endopsychic structure considered in terms of object-relationships. *Psychoanalytic studies of the personality* (pp. 82–136). London: Tavistock.

Fiske, S., & Taylor, S. (1984). *Social cognition.* Reading, MA: Addison-Wesley.

Fiske, S., & Linville, P. (1980). What does the schema concept buy us? *Personality and Social Psychology Bulletin, 6,* 543–557.

Flavell, J. (1963). *The developmental psychology of Jean Piaget.* Princeton, NJ: Van Nostrand.

Freud, S. (1917). Mourning and melancholia. *Standard Edition, 14,* 239–260. London: Hogarth Press, 1966.

Harlow, H. (1961). The development of affectional patterns in infant monkeys. In B. Foss (Ed.), *Determinants of Infant Behavior, Vol. 1* (pp. 75–88). New York: Wiley.

Harlow, H., & Zimmerman, R. (1959). Affectional responses in the monkey. *Science, 130,* 421–432.

Hendrick, I. (1942). Instinct and the ego during infancy. *Psychoanalytic Quarterly, 11,* 33–58.

Hendrick, I. (1943). Work and the pleasure principle. *Psychoanalytic Quarterly, 12,* 311–329.

Horowitz, M. (1988). *Introduction to psychodynamics.* New York: Basic Books.

Horowitz, M. (1990). A model of mourning: Change in schemas of self and others. *Journal of the American Psychoanalytic Association, 38,* 297–324.

Kohut, H. (1971). *The analysis of the self.* Monograph Series of the Psychoanalytic Study of the Child, No. 4. New York: International Universities Press.

Kohut, H. (1984). *How does analysis cure?* Chicago: The University of Chicago Press.

Lichtenberg, J. (1983). *Psychoanalysis and infant research.* Hillsdale, NJ: The Analytic Press.

Malan, D. (1976). *Toward the validation of dynamic psychotherapy.* New York: Plenum Press.

Marziali, E. (1984). Prediction of outcome of brief psychotherapy from therapist interpretive interventions. *Archives of General Psychiatry, 41,* 301–304.

McAdams, D. (1985). *Power, intimacy, and the life story: Personological inquiries into identity.* Homewood, IL: Dorsey.

McClelland, D. (1986). Some reflections on the two psychologies of love. *Journal of Personality, 54,* 334–353.

McClelland, D., Atkinson, J., Clark, R., & Lowell, E. (1953). *The achievement motive.* New York: Appleton-Century-Crofts.

Meissler-Davies & Frawley, G. (1992). *Treating the adult survivor of sexual abuse.* New York: Basic Books.

Piaget, J. (1926/1962). *The language and thought of the child.* Cleveland, OH: Worth.

Piaget, J. (1952). *The origins of intelligence.* New York: International Universities Press.

Rank, O. (1929). *The trauma of birth.* New York: Harcourt, Brace.

Ricoeur, P. (1980). *Freud and philosophy: An essay in interpretation.* New Haven, CT: Yale University Press.

Salovey, P., & Singer, J. (1989). Mood congruency effects in childhood versus recent autobiographical memories. *Journal of Social Behavior and Personality, 4,* 99–120.

Singer, J., & Salovey, P. (1991). Organized knowledge structures and personality. In M. J. Horowitz (Ed.), *Person schemas and maladpative interpersonal patterns* (pp. 33–81). Chicago: University of Chicago Press.

Singer, J. A., & Singer, J. L. (1992). Transference in psychotherapy and daily life: Implications of current memory and social cognition research. In J. Barron, M. Eagle, & D. Wolitzky (Eds.), *Interface of psychoanalysis and psychology* (pp. 516–538). Washington: The American Psychological Association.

Stern, D. (1985). *The interpersonal world of the infant.* New York: Basic Books.

Summers, F. (1997). Transcending the self: An object relations model of the therapeutic action of psychoanalysis. *Contemporary Psychoanalysis, 33,* 411–428.

Summers, F. (1999). *Transcending the Self: An object relations model of psychoanalytic therapy.* Hillsdale, NJ: The Analytic Press.

Summers, F. (2001). "What I do with what you give me": Therapeutic action as the creation of meaning. *Psychoanalytic Psychology, 18,* 635–655.

Taylor, S., & Crocker, J. (1981). Schematic basis of social information processing. In E. T. Higgins, C. P. Herman, & M. P. Zanna (Eds.), *Social cognition: The Ontario Symposium on Personality and Social Psychology* (pp. 89–134). Hillsdale, NJ: Earlbaum.

Tomkins, S. (1962). *Affect, imagery, and consciousness: The positive affects.* New York: Springer.

Tomkins, S. (1963). *Affect, imagery, and consciousness: The negative affects.* New York: Springer.

Tomkins, S. (1978). Script theory: Differential magnification of affects. *Nebraska Symposium on Motivation, 26,* 201–263.

Tomkins, S. (1979). Script theory: Differential magnification of affects. In H. E. Howe, Jr., & M. M. Page (Eds.), *Nebraska Symposium on Motivation, 27,* 201–236.

White, R. (1963). Ego and reality in psychoanalytic theory. *Psychological Issues,* Monogr. 11, Vol. 3, No. 3. New York: International Universities Press.

Winnicott, D. (1960). Ego distortion in terms of true and false self. In *Maturational processes and the facilitating environment* (pp. 140–152). New York: International Universities Press, 1965.

Winter, D. (1973). *The power motive.* New York: Free Press.

SUGGESTED READINGS

Jacobson, E. (1954). Transference problems in the psychoanalytic treatment of severely depressed patients. *Journal of the American Psychoanalytic Association, 2,* 595–606.

Kernberg, O. (1988). Object relations theory in clinical practice. *Psychoanalytic Quarterly, 57,* 481–504.

Summers, F. (1994). *Object relations theories and psychopathology: A comprehensive text.* Hillsdale, NJ: The Analytic Press.

Sutherland, J. (1980). Object relations theorists: Balint, Winnicott, Fairbairn, Guntrip. *Journal of the American Psychoanalytic Association, 28,* 829–849.

Winnicott, D. (1965). *Maturational process and the facilitating environment.* New York: International Universities Press.

Winnicott, D. (1972). Fragment of an analysis. In P. Giovacchini (Ed.), *Tactics and techniques in psychoanalytic therapy* (pp. 455–694). New York: Science House.

7

A Self Psychology Approach for Depression

Robert M. Galatzer-Levy

In the attempt to understand and aid in the complexities of real people's lives and suffering, therapists usually select a central organizing focus for their work. Therapists who base their work in learning theories ask how a dysfunctional behavior was learned and how a more adaptive behavior can be learned. Biological psychiatrists assume that problematic behaviors and psychological states result from some form of neurotransmitter dysfunction and prescribe medications designed to relieve or compensate for these abnormalities. As psychoanalytic conceptualizations have evolved, opinions about the central psychological issues worthy of close attention have shifted within psychoanalysis (Sandler & Dreher, 1996).

THE CENTRAL ISSUE OF METHOD—EMPATHY

The first and perhaps most important of Kohut's contributions to psychotherapy was the recognition that empathy is the central and most useful way to understand other people's psychological lives. While other means, such a figuring out from clues what is occurring in the patient's psychology may provide valuable information, such approaches are likely to omit important dimensions of the patient's psychological life or lead to misplaced emphasis in understanding the patient. Generally when people feel accurately understood (including, incidentally, that having it understood that there are aspects of themselves that they need to keep private for the time being (Winnicott, 1963)) they feel more secure and more able to communicate about themselves. Thus well conducted empathic inquiry not only enriches the therapist's perception by using the powerful mode of understanding, it invites the patient to tell more than he would otherwise tell.

Humans generally have a capacity to understand the subjective world of other people. Everyday experience converges with empirical psychological observation, evolutionary theory and neuroscience study to show that in ordinary interaction people can reasonably accurately judge the psychological state of another and that aspects of this capacity, particularly the capacity to comprehend others' emotional states, emerge early in development and are basic human capacities. This understanding of others is largely experienced as empathy,[1] the formation of an idea of what it is like to be that person at that moment, or as Kohut called it "vicarious introspection" (Kohut, 1959).

Like other human conceptual capacities empathy has limits and may fail in a variety of circumstances. Awareness of these problems should not confuse us about the very high level of empathic comprehension that is generally available to well functioning individuals. An analogy may clarify this point. The fact that we cannot see in many wavelengths and that our visual acuity is limited, or that some people have no, or significantly impaired, vision, in no way diminishes the remarkable fact that most people can on an extremely high practical level and with good reason have confidence in what they "see with their own eyes." Similarly, awareness of the limitations of empathy should not lead us to doubt its existence as a general capacity.

Like other perceptual abilities empathy may be improved though training, reduction in interferences and longer exposure to the subject of empathy. Training in empathy largely takes the form of learning about the wide range of human possibility through such activities as reading about people whose lives differ from one's own, interviewing and observing people in various circumstances and supervised clinical work, in which a more experienced clinician aids the student in perceiving more about the patient. It also consists in learning about those methods of interviewing and observation that are most likely to give access to the subject's inner life. Because emotionally evocative, detailed descriptions of experience that spontaneously seems salient to the subject is most likely to lead to accurate empathy, interview techniques that interfere with such communication are unlikely to provide good grounds for empathic understanding. Under the pressure of time and in the wish to gather information pertinent to descriptive diagnostic categories, such as those embodied in the recent editions of The American Psychiatric Association's *Diagnostic and Statistical Manual* (American Psychiatric Association, 1974, 1987, 1994, 2000), practitioners increasingly use structured interview techniques intended to elicit information that differentiates between various psychiatric conditions. These techniques tend to limit the information that would evoke empathic comprehension in the interviewer.

Because empathy almost always involves the implicit recognition of the possibility that the therapist's internal life has similarities with that of the subject or imagining the sometimes frightening position of being in the subject's shoes, a variety of anxieties can easily interfere with empathy. These interferences can broadly be labeled "countertransference." Though an inevitable aspect of psychotherapy, which can even be employed to better understand the subject, countertransference reactions often interfere with empathy because the therapist is motivated not to understand and vicariously experience the patient's inner life. Countertransference is ordinarily dealt with through self-monitoring. Noting an unusual psychological state in himself when with the patient or thinking about him, the therapist should begin a process of self exploration to try to understand both what about the patient stimulates such a response and how the response may distort empathy with the patient. Because psychoanalysts recognized that countertransference interferences in empathy are both common and especially difficult for the individual with little training in self-inquiry to recognize, a personal psychoanalysis designed both to significantly loosen personal defenses that interfere in understanding others and to assist the analyst in training to more quickly and accurately recognize anxiety-motivated responses in himself, psychoanalytic training came to include a personal analysis (called a training analysis). Therapists who use empathy as a central tool in their work are well advised to provide themselves with a personal analysis or similar experience just as an astronomer would be wise to calibrate and keep track of the function of the telescope through which he makes observations.

The longer and more frequently a therapist can speak with a patient, the greater the therapist's empathic understanding. For many people the best expression of their internals states are embodied in stories about their lives and their world. The therapist who has the time to hear these stories and their variations will learn a great deal about how the patient experiences his life and organizes those experiences. Conversation with the patient about a range of topics will refine the therapist's understanding since the patient will directly or implicitly correct the therapist's expressed understanding of the patient. Most patients become more trusting of a therapist who is seen frequently and over time so that they feel freer to describe material which they feel they must trust their therapist in order to divulge. In terms of coming to understand the patient the psychoanalytic arrangement of nearly daily sessions extending over years continues to be an optimal arrangement.

Let us look at the information we are provided about Ms. T. in the context of empathic understanding. We immediately notice that in the interviewer's attempt to delineate certain aspects of Nancy's situation he has focused attention on issues like the presence and absence of certain symptoms and relatively objective aspects of Nancy's relations to others. We hear little about Nancy's view of her situation or the meanings she ascribes to them. The price paid for this focus is that we are left with little feel for the patient and our ability to enter her subjective world is distinctly limited. The decision to take a descriptive history from the patient and to use psychological measures designed to describe her illness along defined dimensions moves attention away from the patient's subjective experience and the data that might increase the therapist's empathic understanding. The process of collecting these data from the patient, of course, communicates to the patient what the therapist regards as important. While it seems likely that issues such as the nature of the patient's symptoms, her overall level of function, and the quality of her relationship to other people would be significant to her, interviews focused on these limited areas commonly suggest to patients that the rest of their lives are of little interest to the therapist. Thus a self psychologist would neither conduct an initial interview in the fashion suggested by the case report nor would organize what he learned from an open-ended interview in this fashion.[2] Instead, while not ignoring the descriptive psychiatric elements of the patient's condition and exploring questions that would insure that any urgent psychiatric diagnosis was not missed, he would attend more fully to the patient's subjective world and her understanding of it. He would willingly sacrifice the opportunity to ensure that a descriptive diagnosis had been pinned down for the chance to indicate to the patient through his manner of interviewing that what concerned him was what concerned the patient. He might do this through a very open-ended style in which his main intervention would be to indicate his comprehension of what Nancy had to say. When he really did not understand he would seek clarification. For example, rather than leaving Nancy's description that she "need(s) someone to help her take care of herself . . . and most everything I have to do" the analyst would want to hear enough stories about this state, in sufficient detail that he could empathically comprehend what the patient meant. Naturally, if Nancy continued to speak in a vague, generalized fashion the analyst would take this too to reflect the way she experienced her situation or the care with which she felt it necessary to approach the interview.[3]

THE CENTRAL SOURCE OF INFORMATION—TRANSFERENCE

People obviously must base their interpersonal perceptions and interactions on their experiences, wishes and needs. These, in turn, are likely to be to varying extents available to awareness. Passing a police officer on the street we may feel anxiety, relief or so little that we barely notice his presence. The degree to which the officer's presence is salient to our current state of mind will depend not only on how we have previously interacted with sources of interpersonal perceptions and actions can be brought into sharp focus. If, for example, in passing the police officer an individual, who has no reason to believe he is suspected of a crime and has had no personal interactions with the police or any knowledge that persons like himself have been arbitrarily stopped by the police, feels frightened that he is about to be arrested, we may reasonable conclude that some process outside of awareness is in operation. Exploration of the person's feelings, thoughts and associations are likely to lead to a clearer picture of the sources of this idea. We refer to the aspects of the individual's perceptions and actions with regard to others that result from that person's current internal state as transference. Arguably Freud's greatest discovery was the recognition of the centrality of transference in psychological life and his discovery of a systematic means for exploring it (Bergmann, 1982; Bleichmar, 1988; Cooper, 1987; Freud, 1912; Freud, 1915–1958; Gill, 1979; Hoffer, 1985; Lipton, 1977; Luborsky, 1990; Meissner, 1971; Reed, 1990; Renik, 1990; Sandler, 1983).

Freud designed the traditional psychoanalytic setup to promote the development and analysis of transference. Frequent private sessions both encouraged the development of strong feelings about the analyst and helped to provide a sense of safety that allowed analysands to experience the feelings more clearly. The analyst's request that the patient say whatever came to mind and his accepting, interested attitude encouraged the patient to give the transference the fullest verbal expression possible. The analyst attempts to remain neutral, i.e., not to endorse one or another side of issues about which the patient is in conflict. He maintains relative anonymity, i.e., not providing the patient with more information about himself than necessary. He is abstinent in the sense of avoiding directly satisfying patients' (or his own) nonanalytic desires and needs. All of this is designed to provide the clearest possible picture of the patient's transference and to encourage its expression and analysis. (Partly because in the heat of transference the pull to deviate from these arrangements can become so strong, some analytic thinkers recommended a technical approach dominated by efforts to avoid breaches in neutrality, anonymity and abstinence (Eissler, 1953). In practice, the result ran precisely contrary to the goal of developing clear, analyzable transferences. When patients responded with hurt, dismay or anger to what amounted to rudeness or even cruelty on the part of their analysts it revealed little about them beyond an ordinary human responsiveness.)

Since transference provides the fullest information about the patient's psychology, it constitutes the analyst's most powerful diagnostic tool. Returning to the question of what we would have liked to have known regarding Nancy in order to make a meaningful diagnosis from the viewpoint of self psychology, we now add that of a clear picture of the transference she forms in therapeutic interviews. For a patient who is taken into psychoanalysis the answer is clear, " . . . as always, there is only one foolproof way of going about making decisions. That is to leave the patient alone, to watch the transference and see how it gradually unfolds, and to see whether it veers toward self pathology or toward structural conflict."

However, if the therapist lacks the opportunity to allow the emergence of transference in this manner, transference will still become evident in the treatment from the very first. Often during the first session or two patients are more open than they will be until long into treatment so that their responses to the therapist may be particularly clear, especially if they are not blotted out by a rush to collect information. In the first minutes of the intake interview Nancy reveals a central fantasy about her difficulties and the therapist. She attributes her problems to a "dysfunctional childhood" and her "difficulty dealing with these issues." It is a small leap to conclude that what she believes herself to need from the therapist is a means to deal with them and that beneath this apparently straightforward statement lie fantasies of what happened to her and how it can be mended.[4]

Another way that the central transference that will emerge to the therapist can be anticipated is to examine the patient's interpersonal relations. Configurations evident in interpersonal relations are likely to recur in the transference. However, the examination of current interpersonal relations will not give a full picture of the likely emergent transferences for three reasons. First, because of the anxiety that results from direct recognition of various transferences it is likely that the patient will disguise the meaning of the transference to people in the environment from herself. The patient is thus likely to only describe those aspects of their transferences that can be readily tolerated. For example, Nancy readily describes the ways in which her husband disappoints her, but only the fact that she has stuck with the relationship points to the strong factors that bind her to him. Second, failures in function are much more visible than ordinary good functioning. As a result the underlying central normal functions of people in the environment are largely invisible and we can easily mistake the visible disruptions for the central configuration. An analogy to breathing makes this point more clear. When breathing is normal, it is absolutely vital but entirely out of awareness. But if oxygen is for some reason not available we becoming intensely aware of it. We would certainly not conclude that oxygen is unimportant when we have these data. Looking again at Nancy's limited description of her husband we realize that her clear disappointment is very likely accompanied by experience of this husband in which he functions well to meet psychological needs that Nancy has not articulated and which are probably only partly in her awareness. Finally, the complexity of interpersonal interaction makes it difficult to determine from which of the parties and in which combination the actual observed configuration emerges. In the psychoanalytic setup, though both analyst and patient contribute to the actual configuration, the simplified interpersonal situation with its clear boundaries and clear contract make it far easier to delineate the sources of the actual interpersonal configuration that emerges in the treatment than is possible in describing relationships outside of the treatment. Descriptions of interactions outside the consulting room are more challenging to interpret because the role and even actions of the parties often remain obscure and are likely to be distorted in the patient's report. Yet reports of extratherapeutic interpersonal relationships, especially when they involve recurring themes, may be highly suggestive with regard to transferences.[5]

If we examine Nancy's interpersonal relationships as she describes them we notice certain recurring themes. Nancy believes that she needs someone to help her take care of herself and, in particular, imagines that she could not "handle" things on her own. At the same time she feels that her individuality is lost in relationships where she is cared for and that she must comply with her caretaker's demands at the expense of her own wishes. This is most obvious in her relationship to her husband, Steve. Sometimes she feels cared for by him as by a kindly father. Yet she feels oppressed in her relationship with Steve, by the demands he places on her and his criticism of her. This feeling began early in her relationship with him; in fact, the onset of her depression occurred during their engagement. Nancy's relationship with Steve is part of a recurring pattern of feeling dependant on others for support but at the same time feeling that her self is lost in the process. In contrast, her mood is more positive when she is with her sister or friends. Her mother is described as strong but angry and critical of both herself and her children. Nancy's feelings toward her mother are similar to those toward her husband, in that in both relationships she feels it is not possible to be herself. Both mother and husband are themselves inadequate but highly critical of her. Her father is described as schizophrenic, embattled with her mother and using Nancy in a parental role. Nancy's feelings of depression are clearly linked to her relations with other people but the exact nature of this connection remains unclear.

TRANSFERENCE AND DISORDERS OF THE SELF

Kohut's second major contribution to the understanding and treatment of pathology of the self was to describe several of the transferences that could develop in the analyses of individuals with such pathology. Freud (Freud, 1911) had offered the opinion that significant pathology of the self (or narcissistic pathology as it was then called) was not subject to direct psychoanalytic investigation because transference requires a deep psychological interest in other people. By definition, when the main problem involves a disorder of the self such that the central focus of psychological life is oneself and issues involving oneself, there is not sufficient interest available to form strong responses to others, including the analyst. Thus, Freud anticipated that strong analyzable transferences would not occur in individuals with narcissistic pathology. This led to an unfortunate bit of circular reasoning—when individuals with manifestly narcissistic pathology were found to develop transferences and to be analyzable, the manifest narcissism was reinterpreted as a defense against object attachment, i.e., as a means of avoiding recognizing that the patient loved or hated another person. Thus many of the phenomena that Kohut was later to describe had been observed by earlier analysts but understood as representing means of avoiding awareness of object ties.

Kohut attempted to allow transferences to develop in their full force and avoided interfering in these developments with premature interpretations that might interfere with that development. For example, if the patient gave indications that he greatly admired the analyst, Kohut did not offer the traditional interpretation that behind this admiration lay an unconscious wish to depreciate the analyst (Fenichel, 1945), but instead allowed the material to emerge more fully.

Using this approach, Kohut discovered that there were several transference situations with the property that when the transference was uninterrupted the patient felt vigorous and coherent but that when the transference was interrupted, for example by the analyst's physical absence or lack of empathy, the patient either experienced some form of personal incoherence or lifelessness, or tried desperately to maintain coherence and vigor in ways that could be very problematic. Examples of such responses included dreams of being in a bombed-out empty city, conscious feelings of meaninglessness and banality (empty depressions), or frantic sexual activity or other "extreme" activities designed to produce a "thrill," a sense of being alive. Often these transferences emerged in the analysis of individuals with narcissistic personality disorders. Kohut referred to these transferences as *selfobject transference* because the experience of the analyst was not based on the association of attitudes toward an important unconscious object of desire or hate but on the function of the analyst in supporting the patient's sense of self.

Kohut attempted to systematically describe these transferences (Kohut, 1971) and to link them to early experiences. This systematic description has as its major advantage the provision of a map that allows analysts to better tolerate exploring selfobject transferences. The difficulty in exploring these transferences arises from at least two sources. First, being treated in a manner that apparently does not make sense is always confusing. The traditional descriptions of common transference configurations provide the analyst with an explanation of the puzzling phenomena encountered in analysis; however, they may limit analytic thinking so that new possibilities are not considered. The second difficulty is more particular to selfobject transferences. The patient basically uses the analyst as a needed function for the self and may be quite exacting about the ways in which the analyst is to be if the patient is to avoid great distress. Beyond serving this function the patient is often indifferent to the analyst. As a result, the analyst's sense of being an independent person, with his or her own will, is commonly challenged by selfobject transferences. This leads to characteristic countertransference response (Kohut, 1971), which includes a tendency to avoid recognizing the underlying transference configurations.

Kohut (1971) divided the selfobject transference into two main groups—the idealizing transferences and the mirror transferences. In the idealizing transferences the individual feels vigorous and cohesive because of a relationship to a powerful, greatly admired figure. The paradigmatic developmental situation of which this transference is reminiscent is that of the latency age boy in relationship to his greatly admired father. The boy's admiration of his father and sense of being his son creates a sense that the boy himself is a fine person.

The mirror transferences all involve an increased sense of self resulting from the responses or relationship with another. In merger transferences the patient and analyst are experienced as a single unit maintaining a sense of self. This sense of together forming a unit can be understood by thinking about the common experience of group membership in which the members of the group feel that they form an emotional unit whose power and vigor far exceeds that of the individual. Members of athletic teams, workers within a company, faculty and students of universities all have experiences of belonging to "something bigger," that has a life of its own, which invigorates individual members when things are going well.

Twinship transferences occur when the patient feels himself to have a partner who is like himself and hence feels more coherent and alive. Twinship relationships outside of the analytic setting occur in those friendships that include the fantasy of the friends being alike. In the clinical situation such a transference may first become apparent when the patient discovers that the analyst does not exactly share his views on everything and becomes disorganized or experiences an empty depression as a result.

The third mirror transference is the mirror transference proper. In this transference the person feels alive and coherent because of the appreciative response of the other.[6] A developmental analogy is the child's experience of the parent's approving enthusiasm which contributes to a sense of global well-being.

Nancy consciously wants a relationship with a powerful figure who can take care of her. In this sense she is clearly in search of an idealizing transference. Yet she is unsuccessful in finding appropriate figures for idealization and is chronically angry and disappointed in her relationship with her husband. One way of conceptualizing her situation in regard to her husband and mother is that she longs to idealize these figures but being unable to sustain the idealization falls into depressed states that include significant rage (see below). The analyst would not be surprised to find that Nancy formed a similar transfer were she to enter psychoanalysis or a psychodynamic psychotherapy.

Additional selfobject transferences have been described (Gehrie, 1996; Wolf, 1988). For example, many people thrive and feel whole when they have a "good enemy" and show symptoms of fragmentation or depletions when such an adversarial selfobject is absent. One must wonder whether, despite the manifest pain that her depression causes her, if Nancy's suffering and anger in relation to her husband does not serve, in itself, to invigorate her and, whether her husband does not serve as a "negative selfobject" who keeps this lively part of herself going.

In actual practice selfobject transferences rarely occur in pure forms. The four typical transferences described by Kohut often overlap and intermix. The major value of Kohut's classification is that it provides the analyst with an outline of possibilities that provides some orientation in what might otherwise be a too confusing situation. Unfortunately it may be tempting to use Kohut's clear outline to obscure the richness of actual transference configurations. Galatzer-Levy and Cohler (Galatzer-Levy & Cohler, 1993) have suggested that the selfobject phenomena described by Kohut are best understood as dimensions of more complex relations to others that involve not only selfobject functions but a wide range of other attitudes, feelings and functions, none of which can be fully understood independent of the other. Similarly, Bacal and Newman (Bacal & Newman, 1990) advocate an integration of object relations theory with self psychology in which attention is given to the interacting significances of other persons in an individual's psychology. In Nancy's case it seems clear that she feels it necessary to be in a relationship that she at the same time needs, fears and despises. It might be hypothesized that she models her relationship to her husband on her vision of her relationship to her mother and unconsciously attempts to arrange the type of situation she associates most closely with maternal care. It could also be argued that primary masochistic elements in her personality come to the fore in this relationship. Finally, following Chodorow's (Chodorow, 1978; Chodorow, 1989) formulations, it could be that guilt about the possibility of leading a better life than her mother's leads Nancy to reproduce her mother's painful existence and to struggle against doing so. Remember that Nancy's major fear with regard to her husband is that she will be forced to become the Polish mother of a large family whose existence centers on a constricted suburban world, that is, she will become a slightly updated version of her mother. The therapist who is alert to the multiple possible emerging transferences that involve important selfobject dimensions is most likely to consider them amidst the welter of complex clinical material that would almost certainly emerge as Nancy enters treatment.

The key to recognizing selfobject transference does not lie in noting their presence when they are functioning as the patient needs them but rather in recognizing that the disrupted states reported by the patient occur when these transferences are disturbed. As mentioned earlier, selfobject transferences are largely silent until disrupted because their presence promotes the individual's best functioning. Patients like Nancy are both acutely vulnerable to the therapist's failure to respond in the manner she needs and vulnerable to the consequences of her own resistance to forming workable selfobject relations. Nancy clearly associates getting the supports she needs with being engulfed by the individual providing the selfobject function so that we can anticipate that she will experience self-generated disruptions in these functions as she tries to protect herself from being overwhelmed. It cannot be too strongly emphasized that while we may usefully speculate about the transferences that will emerge in Nancy's treatment, our diagnostic question about her central psychological concerns will only be answered over time with the development and analysis of the transferences that actually occur.

RAGE AND THE SELF

The problem of aggression and hostility has plagued psychoanalytic theory. Freud's early conceptualization of aggression as simply a means toward reproductive success gave way to a view that there is a primary destructive force within the human psyche (Freud, 1920). Although some earlier analysts embraced Freud's ideas as conceptual constructions (Ferenczi, 1938), Kleinian analysts demonstrated the usefulness of Freud's concept of a primary destructive drive in clinical work (Klein, 1937; Klein, 1969; Klein, 1948; Klein, 1957). Contemporary Kleinians have succeeded in reducing the rather mystical quality of the concept by showing its close relationship to ordinary experience (Segal, 1977; Segal, 1983; Segal, 1973) but the concept continues to remain problematic for many analysts despite the obvious importance of aggression in human life.

Without formulating an underlying theory of aggression self psychologists have underlined the observation that intense destructiveness, narcissistic rage, emerges in response to actual and anticipated disruptions in the self experience (Galatzer-Levy, 1993; Kohut, 1972; Marohn, 1993; Ornstein, 1993). The rage that results from disruptions of the self experience may be acute or chronic. But, though sometimes disguised, it is intense and nonspecific in its direction. It is the sort of "blind rage" that has little object or aim. In part it serves a restorative function—many people report feeling most alive and focused when enraged. However, it appears to have other, as yet unclear, roots.

Nancy exhibits a chronic state of rage directed at her husband, her self, and her parents. Confronted particularly with hostility toward the self it is worth wondering to what extent it represents a form of narcissistic rage, a fury at one's own person for not functioning well enough to provide a sense of cohesion and vigor in living. That such an attitude is manifestly irrational and is even likely to contribute to the patient's distress is not an argument against the idea that Nancy's hostility toward herself is a manifestation of narcissistic rage. Narcissistic rage seems to bring out the most manifestly irrational elements in human function. Anyone who has felt the urge to smash an offending piece of machinery (such as a computer), kicked a piece of furniture that "got in the way" causing one to stub one's toe or felt like pounding on the dashboard when stuck in traffic knows from direct experience how deeply irrational the processes associated with narcissistic rage can be.

Classical theories of depression (Freud, 1917) and their development within object relations theory (see Summers, this volume) suggest that the attacks on oneself evident in depression are best understood as resulting from primary process presences (Schafer, 1968), the internalized experience of objects that attack the individual. Such explanations are certainly plausible in Nancy's case. However, an alternative explanation, that the attacks on herself represent states of narcissistic rage, the detailed expression of which may be influenced by the details of her history, is also plausible.[7] This distinction is of great importance. If the self-directed hostility arises from internalized hostile presences, its resolution will come through understanding and working through of the ways in which they operate and the motives for their retention. If they are a manifestation of narcissistic rage only some form of restoration of the self will bring them to an end.

THE THERAPY OF THE SELF

Confronted with patients like Nancy the clinician is appropriately puzzled by the range of possible interventions. It might be argued that she is in the midst of a major depressive episode and that the difficulties she describes result from seeing the world through the distorting lens of depression. The apparently psychologically rich sources of her suffering would dissolve, like the suffering itself, with adequate doses of appropriate medication. At the other extreme it might be argued that basic flaws in the very fabric of Nancy's experience of herself are manifest in the problems she brings to treatment and that only their exploration and resolution will result in her achieving the kind of psychological health she deserves. It could even be argued that the current crisis provides an opportunity to address issues that otherwise would remain inaccessible, while greatly constricting Nancy's psychological life.

Fortunately for the clinician's professional ease patients are very likely to self select with regard to therapy either through their choice of therapists or through clear indications of their preferences with regard to treatment. Like many patients, Nancy comes to the current episode of treatment with some experience as a patient. We are told that she had a brief experience with a low dose of antidepressant medication, taken for an insufficient period of time and was not satisfied with the result. Given the patient's level of sophistication it is reasonable to assume that her not further pursuing pharmacological intervention is based on a preference for finding other types of solutions to her problems.[8]

If we assume that Nancy's problems arise in large measure from a self that is enfeebled or at risk of fragmentation, the question naturally arises whether we have the means to increase the vigor and cohesiveness of the self. Possible therapeutic approaches from the point of view of self psychology might be divided into two kinds. One, emphasized by Kohut and his followers is directed at firming the self experience within the psychoanalytic situation.[9] Another focuses on the possibility of improving the self experience through shifts in the use of selfobjects in the environment.

Though agreeing that the self may be strengthened within the analytic setting, self psychologists have disagreed about how this occurs. In his earlier writings Kohut (Kohut, 1971; Kohut, 1977) held that because the patient felt supported by the analyst's accurate understanding of the difficulties that arose when selfobject transferences were disrupted, such disruptions while remaining painful and problematic, did not overwhelm the patient by producing traumatic states. As a result the patient could gradually develop new means to deal with the potentially traumatizing situation and develop new psychological structures (stable configurations of psychological function) to manage such disruptions. For example, it might happen in Nancy's treatment that at the point she felt misunderstood by her husband and on the verge of being thrown into a state of self-castigating despair, that having talked about similar situations with her analyst she would be able to affectively recall his understanding response, be able to tolerate the experience without being overwhelmed and to begin to find new solutions for it. Even more important, similar experiences would repeatedly occur within the analysis itself, with the result that Nancy would develop an increased capacity to sooth and organize herself. Kohut recognized that some patients were unlikely to develop through psychoanalysis in a manner similar to ordinary development. For example, an individual who lacked the internalized experience of being valued might, nonetheless, achieve a reasonable degree of self structure through a particularly well-developed sense of association with particularly valued ideals. These "compensatory structures" could provide a good, if not necessarily conventional life. It might be, for example, that the experience of caretaking and being cared for were so injured in Nancy's early relationship to her mother that the establishment of this capacity would be nearly impossible. Her less troubled relationship to work might, however, become the basis for a different focus for her development and a fulfilling sense of self.

In his later work Kohut (Kohut, 1984) proposed a more radical concept of the curative effects of psychoanalysis in disorders of the self. He suggested that the action of psychoanalysis with patients with self disorders extended beyond the effects of interpretation and that the analytic situation was in many ways equivalent to the milieu provided for the child by the parents. It has been suggested that an intersubjective approach (Stolorow, 1991; Stolorow, Brandchaft, & Atwood, 1987; Stolorow & Atwood, 1992) reminiscent of the expectable mutual influence of infant and parent (Benedek, 1959; Stern, 1985; Stern, 1977) provides an opportunity for the optimal development of the self within analysis.

As mentioned earlier, the self ordinarily exists and is supported within a milieu of essential others who provide selfobject function across the entire course of life (Galatzer-Levy & Cohler, 1993). An individual who manifests self pathology may be thought of as unable to find or use appropriate essential others. If therapy can begin a process of finding satisfactory essential others a self-perpetuating series of experiences may be initiated in which the self becomes stronger. In referring to finding satisfactory essential others I do not necessarily mean forming new interpersonal relationships. The term essential other refers to an intrapsychic experience. People already in the environment may come to serve better as essential others by virtue of a shift in the patient's experience. For example, it might well happen that in the course of treatment Nancy would come to appreciate the courageous elements in her mother's personality that allowed her mother to emigrate to this country and to end an abusive relationship. In so doing Nancy would be making for herself a new essential other, whose admirable qualities would enhance her sense of self.

Unfortunately, the capacity to engage with essential others in a satisfactory way is at its peak at precisely those times when the self is most stable. For an individual like Nancy temporary improvements in the experience of self may be of particular importance in that they allow the individual to find new essential others whose selfobject function may sustain the improved sense of self. Feeling understood and appreciated in the therapeutic situation enables some individuals to find new, more satisfactory, essential others outside of therapy and to sustain development beyond treatment (Offenkrantz & Tobin, 1974). Brief psychotherapies, based on self psychology, may work through this mechanism.

CONCLUSION

Self psychology provides a coherent theory of the normal and disturbed function of the self. It provides a means of understanding the symptoms of depression and a therapeutic approach to the problems that are manifested through them. A detailed description of the process of therapy for a particular patient cannot be provided based on preliminary knowledge of the patient or her symptoms because the treatment that grows from a self psychology understanding necessarily involves an emerging understanding of the patient and adjustment of therapeutic interventions to that understanding.

Because all people need to be provided with selfobject functions by essential others and in the absence of such provision the self is threatened with devitalization and incoherence, it is reasonable to look for failures in the environment of essential others to explain how self pathology has emerged and is sustained. Although current descriptions of interpersonal relations provide strong suggestions about the essential other milieu, only the careful exploration of the transference in the analytic situation provides convincing evidence about these issues. Understanding and explaining how selfobjects function or fail to function in the maintenance of the person's self is at the core of self psychology-oriented theories, although the mechanisms through which change occurs remain controversial in self psychology.

NOTES

1. In following Kohut's use of the term empathy in this context there is some risk of confusion between the use of the term to refer to a way of knowing about others' internal lives (as we do here) and the urge that sometimes arises from that comprehension to aid, forgive, or otherwise help the individual. The two are not the same. For example, confidence men are often extremely empathic, in the sense of understanding the greed and other motivations of their victims very well but are simultaneously profoundly indifferent to the victims' welfare.

2. It should also be mentioned that though it is laudable to attempt to study psychotherapy by comparing the approach of therapists with different viewpoint to the same subject, the very manner in which the subject is described, the extent to which various issues are given prominence in the initial case presentation, and the extent to which pertinent data are absent from the write up will inevitably impact the quality and specificity of the response that the therapists can give. In this chapter, I will try to partly remedy this problem

by being explicit about the additional information that I would have liked to have had to do this exercise better. This is not a criticism of the editors but an indication of an inherent methodological problem in the study of comparative psychotherapy.

3. Therapists are often uncomfortable with the recommendation that initial interviews be as open-ended as we are suggesting here. Often without examining the reasons for doing so they have adopted a medical approach to thinking about psychological distress (Goodwin & Guze, 1984) in which the first task to to make a correct descriptive diagnosis because doing so provides vital information about the nature, course and treatment of the patient's condition. Although the knowledge promised by the medical approach is, in fact, only delivered in the case of a few Axis I disorders, the medical model and its authoritative texts, the third and fourth editions of the *Diagnostic and Statistical Manual(s) of the American Psychiatric Association* currently dominate American approaches to thinking about psychological distress. Therapists are encouraged to reach descriptive diagnoses rapidly and fail to do so at peril of losing managed care coverage or even, if things go badly, malpractice litigation. Not surprisingly, this leads therapists increasingly to begin their interactions with patients in a manner that approximates a structured or semistructured interview designed to collect the information necessary to make an accurate DSM diagnosis.

   In addition to the prices paid for adopting an overly descriptive approach to initial interviews, mental health professional trained to approach patients in this tradition seldom have had the chance to see how very much can be learned from an open-ended approach focused on the patient's subjective experience. Not only does the interview provide a clearer picture of the meanings and operation of personal distress in the patient's psychological life, it also gives the interviewer far more opportunity to observe how the patient actually behaves. When Nancy reports, for example, that she has "no self-confidence at all" it would be extremely useful to know whether this self description is consonant with her manner in the interview and to observe how she spontaneously comes to have this experience around particular matters under discussion.

4. That the therapist may agree with the manifest content of the patient's ideas about therapy makes those ideas no less fantastic and no less in need of exploration. Vague terms like "dysfunctional childhood" and "dealing with" often mean quite different things to

the patient and the therapist. More important, they usually disguise more elaborate and primitive images of what happened and what is needed to make it right.

5. Reports about relationships to parents are sometimes misunderstood as representing the historical base from which transferences emerge. This is not correct. Like any story of interpersonal relationships the patient's description of the parent is a description of current, conscious perceptions (as shaped in the context of reporting them to the therapist). Thus descriptions of relationships with parents are no more or less transference-laden than descriptions of any interpersonal relationship.

6. Kohut is sometimes misunderstood as recommending active positive responses to the patient for the purpose of providing mirroring. This is a misunderstanding of Kohut's technical recommendation, which always focused on interpreting the phenomena that were observed in analysis. Kohut did advocate an ordinary human responsiveness to patients and recognized that the experience of being accurately understood provided a mirroring response to the patient. Kohut believed that the vigorous avoidance of ordinary responsiveness advocated by some of the American ego psychologists in the middle of the twentieth century (Eissler, 1953; Eissler, 1958a; Eissler, 1958b) created an environment that was actually depriving and distorted transferences in such a way that it was more difficult to ascertain the patient's spontaneous transference configurations. In this, Kohut was like several other analysts whose views otherwise strongly differed from his (Gill, 1979; Gill, 1992; Lipton, 1977; Lipton, 1979).

7. Critics of self psychology, including the author of this chapter, often observe that self psychologists ignore important specifics of psychological situations, preferring to focus on broad affective configurations. For example, in their extensive investigations of driven sexual activity the symbolically rich specifics of these activities are commonly little attended to by self psychologists, who focus instead on the idea that the entire activity results from an actual or threatened breakdown in the self experience. The shift in focus implied in considering narcissistic rage to be the primary mover of the self-directed hostility manifest in depressive states involves a similar deliberate inattention to the specific fantasies involved.

8. Even though patients indirectly choose the type of treatment they receive, I believe that it remains the clinician's responsibility to lay

out for the patient as clearly and objectively as possible the alternatives available for dealing with the patient's distress. This is not only consistent with an ethical approach to patients but also often helps to make the patient's goals, fantasies and expectations about treatment explicit.

9. Psychoanalysis, in this context, refers to a treatment in which the central activity is an attempt to understand and explain the patient's subjective experience. The traditional psychoanalytic setup (frequent sessions, use of the couch, free association, etc.) is for many patients the best arrangement for conducting psychoanalysis but it should not be equated with the core psychological events that differentiate psychoanalysis from other interventions.

REFERENCES

American Psychiatric Association. (1974). *Diagnostic and statistical manual of mental disorders* (3rd ed.). Washington: American Psychiatric Association.

American Psychiatric Association. (1987). *Diagnostic and statistical manual of mental disorders* (3rd Revised ed.). Washington: American Psychiatric Association.

American Psychiatric Association. (1994). *Diagnostic and statistical manual of mental disorders* (4th ed.). Washington, DC: American Psychiatric Press.

American Psychiatric Association. (2000). *Diagnostic and statistical manual of mental disorders* 4th (Text revision ed.). Washington, DC: American Psychiatric Press.

Bacal, H., & Newman, K. (1990). *Theories of object relations: Bridges to self psychology.* New York: Columbia University Press.

Benedek, T. (1959). Parenthood as a developmental phase. In T. Benedek (Ed.), *Psychoanalytic investigations* (pp. 378–401). New York: Quadragle.

Bergmann, M. (1982). Platonic love, transference love, and love in real life. *Journal of the American Psychoanalytic Association, 30*, 87–111.

Bleichmar, N. M. (1988). Transference love: On the analysis of the Oedipus complex at the beginning and at the end of treatment. *Journal of the Melanie Klein Society, 6*(1), 83–107.

Chodorow, N. (1978). *The reproduction of mothering.* Berkeley, CA: The University of California Press.

Chodorow, N. (1989). *Feminism and psychoanalytic theory.* New Haven: Yale University Press.

Cooper, A. M. (1987). Changes in psychoanalytic ideas: Transference interpretation. *Journal of the American Psychoanalytic Association, 35*(1), 77–98.

Eissler, K. (1953). Effect of the structure of the ego on psychoanalytic technique. *Journal of the American Psychoanalytic Association, 1*(1), 104–143.

Eissler, K. (1958a). Remarks on some variations in psychoanalytic technique. *International Journal of Psychoanalysis, 39,* 222–229.

Eissler, K. R. (1958b). Remarks on some variations in psychoanalytical technique. *International Journal of Psychoanalysis, 39,* 222–229.

Fenichel, O. (1945). *The psychoanalytic theory of neurosis.* New York: Norton.

Ferenczi, S. (1938). *Thalassa, a theory of Genitality.* Translated H. Bunker. New York: Norton.

Freud, S. (1911). Psycho-Analytic Notes on an Autobiographical Account of a Case of Paranoia (Dementia Paranoides). J. Strachey (ed. and trans.), *Standard edition of the complete psychological works of Sigmund Freud,* Vol. 12 (pp. 3–82). London: Hogarth Press and the Institute of Psycho-Analysis.

Freud, S. (1912). The dynamics of transference. J. Strachey (ed. and trans.), *The standard edition of the complete psychological works of Sigmund Freud,* Vol. 12 (pp. 99–108). London: Hogarth Press.

Freud, S. (1915–1958). Observations on transference-love: Further recommendations on the technique of psychoanalysis II. J. Strachey (ed. and trans.), *The standard edition of the complete psychological works of Sigmund Freud,* Vol. 12 (pp. 158–171). London: Hogarth Press.

Freud, S. (1917). Mourning and Melancholia. J. Strachey (ed. & trans.), *The standard edition of the complete psychological works of Sigmund Freud,* Vol. 14 (pp. 243–258). London: Hogarth Press.

Freud, S. (1920). Beyond the Pleasure Principle. J. Strachey (ed. & trans.), *The standard edition of the complete psychological works of Sigmund Freud.* London: Hogarth Press.

Galatzer-Levy, R. (1993). Adolescent Violence and the Adolescent Self. *Adolescent Psychiatry, 19,* 418–441.

Galatzer-Levy, R., & Cohler, B. (1993). *The essential other: A developmental psychology of the self.* New York: Basic Books.

Gehrie, M. (1996). Empathy in broader perspective: A technical approach to the consequences of the negative selfobject in early character formation. In A. Goldberg (Ed.), *Progress in self psychology. Basic ideas reconsidered* (Vol. 12, pp. 159–179). Hillsdale, NJ: The Analytic Press.

Gill, M. (1979). The analysis of the transference. *Journal of the American Psychoanalytic Association, 27*(Suppl.), 263–288.

Gill, M. (1992). Merton Gill speaks his mind. *International Journal of Communicative Psychoanalysis & Psychotherapy, 7*(1), 27–33.

Goodwin, D., & Guze, S. (1984). *Psychiatric diagnosis* (3rd ed.). New York: Oxford University Press.

Hoffer, A. (1985). Toward a definition of psychoanalytic neutrality. *Journal of the American Psychoanalytic Association 33*(4), 771–795.

Klein, M. (1937). Love, Guilt and Reparation. In M. Klein, *Love, guilt and reparation & other works 1927–1945* (pp. 344–369). New York: Delacorte Press/Seymour Lawrence.

Klein, M. (1948). *Contributions to psychoanalysis 1921–1945.* London: Hogarth Press.

Klein, M. (1957). *Envy and gratitude.* London: Tavistock.

Klein, M. (1969). *The Psychoanalysis of children.* Translated A. Strachey. London: Hogarth Press.

Kohut, H. (1959). Introspection, Empathy, and Psychoanalysis: An examination of the relationship between mode of observation and theory. In P. Ornstein (Ed.), *The Search for the Self* (Vol. 1, pp. 205–232). New York: International Universities Press.

Kohut, H. (1971). *The analysis of the self.* New York: International Universities Press.

Kohut, H. (1972). Thoughts on narcissism and narcissitic rage. *Psychoanalytic Study of the Child, 27,* 360–400.

Kohut, H. (1977). *The restoration of the self.* New York: International Universities Press.

Kohut, H. (1984). *How psychoanalysis cures.* Chicago: University of Chicago Press.

Lipton, J., Irell, P., Manella-O'Connor, M., Terry, C., & Bellamy, E. Neutral Job Titles and Occupational Stereotypes: When Legal and Psychological Realities Conflict. *The Journal of Psychology, 125*(2), 129–151.

Lipton, S. D. (1977). The advantages of Freud's technique as shown in his analysis of the Rat Man. *International Journal of Psychoanalysis, 58*(3), 255–273.

Lipton, S. D. (1979). An addendum to 'The Advantages of Freud's Technique As Shown in His Analysis of the Rat Man'. *International Journal of Psychoanalysis, 60*(2), 215–216.

Luborsky, L. (1990). The convergence of Freud's observations about transference in the CCRT evidence. In L. Luborsky & P. Crits-Christoph, *Understanding transference to CCRT method.* New York: Basic Books.

Marohn, R. (1993). Rage without content. In A. Goldberg (Ed.), *The widening scope of self psychology. Progress in self psychology* (Vol. 9, pp. 129–141). Hillsdale, NJ: Analytic Press.

Meissner, W. W. (1971). Freud's methodology. *Journal of the American Psychoanalytic Association, 19*(2), 265–309.

Offenkrantz, W., & Tobin, A. (1974). Psychoanalytic psychotherapy. *Archives of General Psychiatry, 30*(5), 593–606.

Ornstein, P. (1993). Chronic rage from underground: Reflections on its structure and treatment. In A. Goldberg (Ed.), *The widening scope of self psychology. Progress in self psychology* (Vol. 9, pp. 143–159). Hillsdale, NJ: Analytic Press.

Reed, G. (1990). The transference neurosis in Freud's writings. *Journal of the American Psychoanalytic Association, 38*(2), 423–450.

Renik, O. (1990). The concept of a transference neurosis and psychoanalytic methodology. *International Journal of Psychoanalysis, 71*(2), 197–204.

Sandler, J. (1983). Reflections on some relations between psychoanalytic concepts and psychoanalytic practice. *International Journal of Psychoanalysis, 64*(1), 35–46.

Sandler, J., & Dreher, A. (1996). *What do psychoanalysts want? The problem of aims in psychoanalytic therapy.* New York: Routledge.

Schafer, R. (1968). *Aspects of internalization.* New York: International University Press.

Segal, H. (1973). *An introduction to the work of Melanie Klein* (2nd ed.). London: Hogarth Press.

Segal, H. (1983). Some clinical implications of Melanie Klein's work. Emergence from narcissism. *International Journal of Psychoanalysis, 64,* 269–280.

Segal, H. M. (1977). Psychoanalytic dialogue: Kleinian theory today. *Journal of the American Psychoanalytic Association, 25*(2), 363–370.

Stern, D. (1977). *The first relationship of infant and mother.* Cambridge, MA: Harvard University Press.

Stern, D. (1985). *The interpersonal world of the infant.* New York: Basic Books.

Stolorow, R., & Atwood, G. (1992). *Contexts of being: The intersubjective foundations of psychological life.* Hillsdale, NJ: Analytic Press.

Stolorow, R., Brandchaft, B., & Atwood, G. (1987). *Psychoanalytic treatment: An intersubjective approach.* Hillsdale, NJ: The Analytic Press.

Stolorow, R. D. (1991). The Intersubjective Context of Intrapsychic Experience: A Decade of Psychoanalytic Injury. *Psychoanalytic Injury, 11*(1&2), 171–184.

Winnicott, D. (1963). Communicating and Not Communicating Leading to a Study of Certain Opposites. *The maturation processes and the facilitating environment.* New York: International Universities Press.

Wolf, E. (1988). *Treating the self: Elements of clinical self psychology.* New York: Guilford.

8

Supportive-Expressive Psychodynamic Therapy for Depression

Paul Crits-Christoph, David Mark, and Mary Beth Connolly Gibbons

OVERVIEW OF THE MODEL

The first treatment manual for supportive-expressive (SE) psychodynamic psychotherapy was put forth by Luborsky (1984). Supportive-expressive therapy is a general psychodynamically-oriented approach to psychotherapy that can be applied to a broad range of problems. For treatment of a specific disorder or problem, the general SE treatment manual is supplemented by an additional manual that tailors the treatment to the particular issues relevant to patients with that disorder or problem. Luborsky et al. (1995) have described the application of SE therapy to patients with a diagnosis of major depression.

The origins of the SE model have been traced by Luborsky (1984) and Luborsky and Mark (1991) to Freud's papers on technique (Freud, 1911/1958, 1912/1958a, 1912/1958b, 1913/1958, 1914/1958, 1915/1958). Other writers (e.g., Bibring, 1954; Fenichel, 1941; Stone, 1951) have also had an influence on the principles of treatment described in the SE manual. The label "supportive-expressive psychoanalytic psycho-therapy" was first used to describe the psychotherapy treatment imple-mented at the Menninger Foundation (Luborsky, Fabian, Hall, Ticho, & Ticho, 1958; Wallerstein, Robbins, Sargent, & Luborsky, 1956; Wal-lerstein, 1986).

Basic Concepts

On the "supportive" side of supportive-expressive psychotherapy, the key concept is the curative significance of the *patient-therapist relationship*. SE psychotherapy recognizes that the patient-therapist relationship can be directly curative. Its helpfulness is not based upon interpretation or insight. Rather, the emotional connection between patient and therapist can, in and of itself, be healing. It may provide comfort, encouragement, bolster self-esteem, steady a person during a crisis—in short, whatever one person can mean and be for another.

The significance of the therapeutic relationship has been increasingly acknowledged as psychoanalytic theory has developed. Freud was wary about assigning any curative significance to the therapeutic relationship because he wanted to differentiate psychoanalysis from hypnosis. In hypnosis, change was seen as a function of the therapist's suggestion and authority. Nevertheless, Freud did, however reluctantly and incon-sistently, allow for some directly curative component of the therapeutic relationship. His concept of the "unobjectionable positive transference" involved the "friendly and affectionate aspects of the transference which are admissible to consciousness and which are the vehicle of success" (Freud, 1912/1958b, p. 105). Zetzel's (1956) later introduction of the term "therapeutic alliance" to refer to the positive affectionate attach-ment to the therapist, and Greenson's (1965) discussion of the "working alliance" provided the background for Luborsky's (1976) "helping alli-ance" and the emphasis on this factor within SE treatment. One main difference between Freud's specification of these "friendly and affec-tionate" feelings of the patient toward the therapist and Luborsky's (1984) description of the "helping alliance" is that for Freud, this aspect of the treatment process set the stage for the role of interpretation, while Luborsky proposes that the alliance is a curative element in its own right. Furthermore, attempts by the therapist to bolster the alliance (i.e., the supportive component of treatment) are clearly at variance with a traditional "blank screen" therapist role within psychoanalysis.

As SE psychotherapy has developed, the directly curative role of the therapist-patient relationship has expanded beyond these descriptions which are limited to the rational and basically benign connection between patient and therapist.

The key concepts on the "expressive" side of supportive-expressive psychotherapy are the relationship episode (RE) and the core conflictual relationship theme (CCRT). People naturally construe the experiences of their lives narratively. The kinds of narratives that people tell represent the quality of contact with one's own experience. Regardless of a therapist's intent, patients in psychotherapy or psychoanalysis talk about themselves by using narratives. Patients refer implicitly or explicitly to events, characters, scenes, actions, and reactions. Much of the psychotherapy session can be thought of as a series of narratives that the patient relates about his/her interactions with others. Luborsky (1984) refers to these narratives as relationship episodes (REs).

Luborsky's (1984) CCRT describes a patient's pattern of relationships across 3 categories: the wish, the response from other, and the response from self. Wishes include the wishes, needs or intentions that a patient has in relation to another person. Responses from other (RO) include the anticipated, imagined, or perceived responses from another person toward the patient. The response of self (RS) refers to the patient's reaction to the thwarting of the wish. The central purpose of both these key concepts, the RE and the CCRT, is to help organize the therapist's thinking in formulating interpretations.

Interpretations are the vehicle in SE therapy for achieving insight. Freud (1905/1953) highlighted the interpretation of transference themes in the patient-therapist relationship. Whereas the concept of interpretation in SE therapy is derived from Freud's writings, certain technical differences are also evident. One important difference is that SE therapy does not place central emphasis on the interpretation of themes in the relationship with the therapist. In contrast, SE therapy follows Lowenstein's (1951) recommendations more closely, with emphasis placed upon interpretation of themes in three domains (current relationships, past relationships, therapeutic relationships), and attention to the brevity and clarity of interpretations. The concept of accuracy of interpretation discussed by Fenichel (1945) is also of prime importance to SE therapy. SE therapists are taught to increase their accuracy by focusing interventions on a specific content (i.e., the patient's CCRT pattern).

Further differences between the SE model and Freudian psychoanalysis center on the time-limited nature of SE as applied in a research context. Another important difference between Freudian psychoanalysis and SE is the connection of recent versions of the SE model (e.g., Crits-Christoph, Crits-Christoph, Wolf-Palacio, Fichter, & Rudick, 1995) to the interpersonal school within the psychodynamic rubric. This is characterized by a movement away from drives and instinctual wishes, with greater emphasis placed on motivations arising from interpersonal transactions. In general, while some aspects of Freud's treatment model are contained in the SE approach, the theory of psychopathology is more closely aligned with recent psychodynamic theories.

Etiology of Depression

The SE model of depression is based on the development of maladaptive relationship themes in past relationships. Individuals enter interpersonal relationships with particular wishes and needs. Through past relationship experiences, patients develop stereotypic ways of perceiving responses of others. When these responses do not fulfill their wishes, patients develop maladaptive responses of self, including feelings of depression.

These CCRTs, although formed through past relationship experiences, can become activated in the patient's present life. The person may suffer some sort of loss or personal defeat. If the process stopped here, the person would experience only sadness or grief. These conditions are to be distinguished from depression, in that the former is primarily an affective response. Depression involves a second stage, the supervention of despair and hopelessness.

This second stage feeds into the third stage, which consists of a loss of availability of, and interest in, the external dimensions of experience. The severely depressed patient is often unable to report any significant events in his/her recent life, or will provide such a report in so sketchy and minimal a fashion that it is very difficult to generate any interest or feeling for either the patient or the therapist. The frequently observed inability to feel enjoyment from activities follows directly from this loss of availability and interest in the external dimensions of experience. A loss of the external dimensions of experience can be expected to affect the internal dimensions of experience. Thus, depressed patients often report feeling nothing or having no thoughts.

Maintaining Factors

In our view, the maintaining factors of depression cannot be conceptualized within one frame of reference. There is a biological aspect. When people are depressed for a certain length of time something happens at a neurological level; it's as if the biology takes on a life of its own. There is a social aspect. As a person becomes depressed, he or she inevitably has an effect on his/her personal world. A depressed person usually deadens and frustrates those around him/her. This, in turn, fails to nurture or enliven the depressed person. An angry, reproachful depressed person elicits withdrawal or retaliatory hostility from his or her interpersonal world, thereby confirming the depressed person's negative view of others. Finally, many psychological reactions characteristic of depression, such as hopelessness and helplessness, tend to gather their own downward momentum. That is, the more a person is hopeless, the less he or she attempts, the lower one's self-confidence and the less developed one's skills—all this merely exacerbates one's sense of hopelessness.

Mechanisms of Change

The three key curative factors in SE psychotherapy are: (1) the therapeutic relationship; (2) interpretation, insight, self-understanding; and (3) the deepening of experience. It is impossible to rank these factors in order of importance as every case and every therapy is different. We will return to this issue and the entire matter of curative factors throughout the text rather than discuss them at this point.

2. REVIEW OF EMPIRICAL EVIDENCE

Efficacy Studies

The manual for SE therapy of depression has been used in two uncontrolled pilot studies. In the first study, 25 patients with chronic depression received 20 sessions of SE psychotherapy. In the second investigation, 24 patients with major depression were treated with 16 sessions of SE therapy. The combined results of these investigations are reported by Luborsky et al. (1996). Patients in both the chronic depression and major depression groups demonstrated significant change across the acute treatment phase as measured by the Beck Depression Inventory and the Hamilton Rating Scale for Depression. Both groups maintained treatment gains across the follow-up period. In addition, the intake level of functioning and the presence of a comorbid Axis I disorder significantly predicted symptom change. These results suggest that SE therapy may be a useful treatment for depression. Controlled comparisons of SE therapy to other treatments for depression are necessary to fully evaluate the utility of SE psychotherapy in the treatment of depression.

Studies of Key Constructs in the Process of SE Therapy

Additional investigations have examined the potential mechanisms of change postulated in the SE model. Studies on the process of SE therapy conducted at the Center for Psychotherapy Research at the University of Pennsylvania have focused on two patient variables, the therapeutic alliance and the CCRT.

Studies of the Therapeutic Alliance

The role of the helping alliance in predicting the outcome of dynamically-oriented psychotherapy was evaluated for the 10 most improved and the 10 least improved patients from the Penn Psychotherapy Project (Luborsky et al., 1980). Morgan, Luborsky, Crits-Christoph, Curtis, and Solomon (1982) found that independent judges' ratings of the alliance significantly predicted treatment outcome. Using this same sample of patients, Luborsky, Crits-Christoph, Alexander, Margolis, and Cohen (1983) found that explicit signs of the alliance, scored from transcripts of sessions, also significantly discriminated the most improved patients compared to the least improved patients. Table 8.1 presents the items from the most recent version (Luborsky et al., 1996) of the Helping Alliance Questionnaire. These items provide a sense of what types of processes might be targeted with supportive techniques to improve the alliance in treatment (Table 8.1).

TABLE 8.1   Items from the Helping Alliance Questionnaire—Revised

1. I feel I can depend upon my therapist.
2. I feel my therapist understands me.
3. I feel my therapist wants me to achieve my goals.
4. At times I distrust my therapist's judgment.
5. I feel I am working together with my therapist in a joint effort.
6. I believe we have similar ideas about the nature of my problems.
7. I generally respect my therapist's views about me.
8. The procedures used in my therapy are *not* well suited to my needs.
9. I like my therapist as a person.
10. In most sessions, my therapist and I find a way to work on my problems together.
11. My therapist relates to me in ways that *slow up* the progress of the therapy.
12. A good relationship has formed with my therapist.
13. My therapist appears to be experienced in helping people.
14. I want very much to work out my problems.
15. My therapist and I have meaningful exchanges.
16. My therapist and I sometimes have *un*profitable exchanges.
17. From time to time, we both talk about the same important events in my past.
18. I believe my therapist likes me as a person.
19. At times my therapist seems distant.

Studies of the CCRT

Crits-Christoph and Luborsky (1990) evaluated the validity of the CCRT method by examining change in maladaptive relationship patterns across the course of dynamic psychotherapy. Negative responses of other and negative responses of self decreased significantly from early sessions to late sessions, while positive responses of other increased. In addition, changes on the wish and response of self components were significantly correlated with symptom change across treatment, suggesting that change in the CCRT mediates symptom change in dynamic therapy.

Studies indicate that CCRTs appear to be a function of what the patient brings to therapy, as opposed to the therapist's attempts to elicit patterns. Using a sample of patients with a diagnosis of major depression, Barber, Luborsky, Crits-Christoph, and Diguer (1995) found that CCRTs obtained from interviews before therapy were highly consistent with CCRTs derived from psychotherapy sessions. In addition, Eckert, Luborsky, Barber, and Crits-Christoph (1990) report that most patients diagnosed with major depression demonstrated the same CCRT pattern. In an investigation of self-understanding of CCRT patterns, Connolly et al. (1999) found greater change in self-understanding in SE as compared to a medication control condition; change in self-understanding, however, was not associated with change in symptoms.

Therapist Actions in SE Therapy

Accuracy of Addressing the CCRT

The accuracy of therapist's interpretations was examined by Crits-Christoph, Cooper, and Luborsky (1988) for a sample of 43 patients treated in moderate length dynamic psychotherapy. Although patients did not receive manual-guided SE therapy, Luborsky, Crits-Christoph, Mintz, and Auerbach (1988) demonstrated that the therapy was similar to SE. The CCRT method was used to identify patients' central relationship themes from the transcripts of 2 early therapy sessions. A separate set of independent judges extracted therapist statements from the session transcripts that met a definition of interpretation. The final accuracy judges rated each interpretation on a 4-point scale designed to assess the degree to which the therapist addressed each CCRT component. Accuracy on a composite measure of main wishes and responses from other was significantly related to outcome, controlling for the quality of the therapeutic alliance. However, accuracy in addressing the negative responses of self did not predict treatment outcome.

Crits-Christoph, Barber, and Kurcias (1993) further examined the relation between therapist accuracy and the development of the therapeutic alliance using data from the Penn Psychotherapy Project (Crits-Christoph et al., 1988). The Helping Alliance Counting Signs method (Luborsky et al., 1983) was scored on two early and two late psychotherapy sessions. A composite score representing accuracy on the wish and response from other components of the CCRT significantly predicted change in the alliance from early to late in treatment, controlling for psychological health-sickness. These results suggest that the alliance is not only a function of what the patient (and therapist) bring to therapy but also is influenced by the technical interventions made by the therapist.

Therapist Adherence/Competence in Delivering SE

The relation between adherence/competence in delivering SE therapy and treatment outcome was examined by Barber, Crits-Christoph, and

Luborsky (1996). The Penn adherence-competence scale for SE therapy (Barber & Crits-Christoph, 1996) was rated by 2 doctoral level clinicians on the audiotapes of session 3 for each of 29 patients treated with 16 sessions of SE psychotherapy for major depression. Competence on expressive techniques at session 3 was significantly associated with treatment outcome (r = .53, p < .01), even after controlling for the amount of improvement prior to session 3, initial health-sickness, and the quality of the therapeutic alliance. Thus, the quality of the therapist's interpretive work also appears important in predicting reduction in depression over the course of brief SE treatment.

3. CASE CONCEPTUALIZATION

SE psychotherapy provides a psychodynamic framework within which to understand people and their relationships with others. Therefore, our conceptualization of the sample case (Nancy), including key repetitive affective states, cognitions, and behaviors will be described through the categories provided by the CCRT method. To reiterate, The CCRT consists of three components: (1) a "core" or central wish; (2) an anticipated, feared, or perceived response from others to that core wish; and (3) a central action or response from the self, i.e., the emotional, cognitive, and behavioral reactions to the other person's response to one's core wish. The *conflict* in the core *conflictual* relationship theme involves either two conflicting core wishes, or a conflict between one's core wish and one's anticipated, feared, or perceived response from others to that core wish. On the basis of the clinical case presentation, what appears to be Nancy's "core" conflict?

Nancy describes a chaotic, violent, traumatic childhood in which she felt she both played the parental role with each parent and yet felt abandoned by each of them. The sense of abandonment is explicit with her father, while with her mother the incident of being locked out of the house is representative of a harsh, punitive abandonment. Furthermore, when her parents did play the parental role, they did so in an excessive and crazy way. Her mother is described as overcontrolling and critical, while her father was overprotective to the point of being, at least vaguely, paranoid that Nancy would be hurt by others. Given these conditions of under- and over-parenting, we would expect her to have particularly intense conflicts around the desire to be taken care of, to be protected, to have someone be "*her* [Nancy's and not her mother's] helper and *her* emotional aide." Indeed, this appears to be the case. Nancy's own conceptualization of her relationship pattern spontaneously includes the core wish: "I look for them to protect and take care of me."

Yet, we suggest that this core wish is anxiety-provoking for Nancy. Her wish to be taken care of conflicts with the wish to take care of herself so that she need not rely upon anyone else. To express the same point another way, the core wish to be taken care of conflicts with the core anticipated, feared, and perceived response from others of criticism, abandonment, and chaotic over- and under-parenting.

The data from the case presentation consistent with our formulations concerning Nancy's core conflicts are her descriptions of her husband as "really kind and generous and attentive . . . he's more like a father to me [the implication being a *good* father]." Yet, Nancy also reports that she "doubted getting married" as he "was so controlling and he took my self-confidence away." We are not suggesting that her perceptions of her husband are merely her distortions or fantasies—that, for example, she unfairly sees her husband as her controlling mother. Indeed, one of our therapeutic goals for Nancy might well be for her to gain an appreciation of the ways she helps "create" by her own behaviors (related to her indecisiveness, panic, and neediness) her husband's controllingness.

4. BEGINNING AND FRAMING TREATMENT

Brief SE treatment is delivered in once per week sessions for 16 weeks. The first step in treatment, after an evaluation, is the setting of goals. In SE psychotherapy goal setting is regarded as one of the key "supportive techniques" because simply asking the patient what her goals for therapy are tends to generate some hope and a collaborative relationship. Of course, the goals the patient states may need to be shaped by the therapist so that they are reasonably specific. For example, if Nancy merely replied "My goal is to feel better" we would need considerable elaboration. In addition, the patient's goals need to be within the realm of the therapist's competence. If Nancy stated that she wanted to decide about whether or not she ought to get divorced, we might well wish to redefine this goal. In part, we might wish to do so because we sense that Nancy would both hopefully and fearfully place too much responsibility on the therapist for crucial life decisions. By redefining a goal about deciding on divorce in therapy to one of, say, learning more about herself in intimate relationships, we are framing not only the treatment, but also the limits of who and what we are to Nancy. Goal setting occurs throughout treatment, not merely once in the first session; the goals are continuously defined and refined over the course of treatment.

SE therapy as practiced clinically does not involve the use of question-naires or other instruments. In a research context, however, we have used the Beck Depression Inventory (BDI) to assess session by session changes in depression. Therapists are free to review and use the informa-tion obtained on the BDI to assist in the clinical work. In particular, therapists can attend to deterioration in symptoms and evidence for suicidal thinking. Clinical observation and assessment throughout treat-ment is important in SE therapy, as it is in any psychotherapy. The primary clinical observations relate to obtaining relationship episodes and formulating a CCRT, as described below.

5. TREATMENT

While we think the CCRT framework can usefully organize the data contained in Nancy's case presentation, the above case conceptualiza-tion may give a misleading impression of how SE therapy is conducted. Therapy does *not* proceed by applying the CCRT template to the kind of data contained in this case. The data in the case presentation consist of a traditional psychiatric description of history and symptoms. This data differs from the sort of data we as SE therapists attempt to generate in at least three ways.

In a traditional psychiatric account, such as Nancy's case presentation, the patient's views are presented in the relative absence of concrete, sensory data. The following is typical: "Nancy stated that she continues to believe that her mother 'is living through me' and that she 'doesn't have a life of her own.' She stated, for example, that she 'doesn't have a sense of privacy when I'm with her . . . I have trouble demanding my rights and she never really takes my feelings taken [sic] into account.' " Here we are provided with a version of Nancy's beliefs or ideas about her mother and her mother's impact upon her. The data is not perceptual in the way it would be, for example, if Nancy told of something mother did or said during which Nancy felt her feelings weren't taken into account. We believe such perceptual data is more emotionally activating, and our interventions in SE psychotherapy are largely devoted to obtaining such data. In Sullivan's terms, this process is referred to as the *detailed inquiry*.

The second difference concerns the duration or time scale of the narrative framework within which clinical data is situated. As is invariably the case in a traditional psychiatric case history, the narrative framework within which Nancy's views are presented is extended in time. For example, the description Nancy offered about her mother presumably is based upon innumerable individual events, or *relationship episodes*. In SE psychotherapy, by contrast, we attempt to develop single-event relationship episodes. Rather than making interpretations on the basis of such data as, "there was *always* a match of wills . . . that mom *always* won [italics ours]" we would try to draw out some specific instance with Nancy. Thus, we might begin by asking her if she has a recent or relatively fresh example in which there was a clash of wills with her mother. The development of relatively concrete relationship episodes, we believe, has the capacity to directly deepen a patient's experience— even apart from any explicit therapist interpretation. This is not only because more concrete material is more affectively engaging, but also because important inner and outer details of experience which have previously been *selectively inattended* are brought into the center of the patient's attention. This deepening of experience is one of the important "curative" or therapeutic factors in the SE model of depression.

SPECIFIC INTERVENTIONS

Supportive Techniques

The SE model contains both supportive and expressive interventions. Two supportive techniques are included in the SE model and are summarized below.

Understanding the Patient From the Patient's Point of View

A certain kind of listening stance, a stance which can never be consistently maintained (indeed, useful information is provided when the therapist is unable to maintain such a stance) is recommended. This stance could be described as an effort to understand the patient from the patient's point of view. This, in essence, is a discipline on the part of the therapist to avoid premature closure on an experience the patient is describing. Premature closure is manifested when the therapist forms a judgment or offers an interpretation before the patient's experienced perspective is elucidated. The therapist is advised to ask him or herself, "Might this mean something other than what I assume it means?" The recommended listening stance tends to build a therapeutic alliance for most patients. Many patients have developed entrenched beliefs about themselves (e.g., "I'm too needy" or "too sensitive") that tend to cut short exploration of their experiences. Furthermore, they have come by these beliefs honestly in two senses, i.e., others, often parents, have labeled the patient in precisely this way, and, such a label tends to create a reality—the therapist will therefore be very tempted to draw exactly such a conclusion. Under such circumstances, it may be an enlivening, hopeful (and relationship building) experience for the patient to have a therapist less interested in coming to a judgment about the patient or adjudicating distortions than in their experienced perspective.

Maintenance of a Collaborative Relationship

The reader is advised to consult Luborsky (1984) for several examples of building a collaborative relationship. The point to be emphasized is that the patient defines what is collaborative, not the therapist. Many depressed patients anticipate glib optimism from others (i.e., what the therapist says is experienced as another person in the patient's life trivializing their experience, saying or implying "It's not so bad"). Others, feeling withdrawn and cutoff from society, are apt to regard therapist remarks that imply a shared experience as false, threatening, or suffocating. In such cases, "collaborative techniques" are far from it; rather they separate patient from therapist.

Expressive Techniques

The expressive techniques of SE therapy include both techniques to deepen the patient's contact with the external dimensions of experience and interpretations. Two techniques are suggested to help patients deepen their experiencing.

The Development of Relatively Complete and Coherent REs

Luborsky (1984) and others (e.g., Labov & Fanschel, 1977) have noted that much of a therapy session can be thought of as a series of narratives or relationship episodes that the patient tells the therapist. Patients' defenses operate to obliterate or obscure these relationship episodes. Such defensive operations result in REs that are incomplete, incoherent, or relatively barren of meaning. Because depressed patients have lost considerable interest in the external dimensions of experience, this is an especially severe problem. In SE therapy with depressed patients, many therapist interventions are aimed at generating more complete, and therefore more meaningful, REs. The clinical phenomena of transference, resistance, and anxiety, typically emerge during this process of elaborating REs.

It is a basic principle of SE that the therapist cannot make effective interpretations on the basis of generalities; specific contexts are needed. More concrete, complete, and coherent narratives provide the therapist with more adequate data for formulating interpretations and tend to be more affectively engaging for both patient and therapist. It takes a great deal of skill by the therapist to know when and how to intervene with questions and comments that help develop the patient's narratives. This requires supervision, where therapist and supervisor can listen to tapes of sessions together to hear, evaluate, and discuss how to develop narratives. However, within the context of this manual, we can suggest certain questions that can be helpful for the therapist to ask him/herself:

(1) Does the narrative have a graphic, vivid quality (Zucker, 1967)? Can the therapist picture what is being narrated? Are aspects missing from the picture that one might expect to be included?
(2) Is the narrative relatively coherent, with an intelligible experience, or is it fragmented?
(3) Does the narrative appear to engage the patient, concern the patient, or matter to the patient in some way? Does the narrative raise a question for the patient, either about what the patient or another person in his or her life, felt, thought, or did? Does the narrative have the quality of search (Zucker, 1967)?

Extending Enactments

Clinicians working with depressed patients will often sense that emotional exchanges between themselves and the patient evaporate in the mists of the patient's apathy and withdrawal. For example, a quick flash of irritability on the part of the patient will seem to disappear, with nothing but a slight increase in futility conveyed in the patient's vocal tones remaining. In such cases, interpreting the transference is premature; it hasn't survived long enough for the patient to apprehend it. One of the therapeutic methods used to prolong or deepen an experience between patient and therapist can be referred to as extending enactments. Enactments are behaviorally expressed events between patient and therapist. Along with patient narratives about events, enactments are the data from which the CCRT formulations are made. With depressed patients who have withdrawn their interest from the external dimensions of experience, it is important for the therapist to extend enactments so that they gain affective charge and their cognitive meanings become palpable.

Interpretations

What kinds of interpretations are recommended in SE? It is important to realize that the SE treatment of depression does not offer a specific narrative that will invariably characterize the disorder. Instead, SE offers a framework for conceptualizing interpretations (this is provided by the CCRT), and it offers areas where the clinician should look which are important in the development of depression, without suggesting what the clinician will find in those areas. To review, the framework of the CCRT involves three components: the wish, the response from the other, and the response of the self. Within the CCRT scheme, interpretations can be classified into two levels of generality:

The first type of interpretation includes interpretation of the patient's wish, response from other, and/or response of the self on the basis of a single relationship episode. Such interventions would be the most frequently occurring interpretations. Elsewhere in the psychodynamic literature, interpretations at this level of generality, i.e., on the basis of a single RE, are referred to as "interpretations of awareness" (Menninger & Holzman, 1958) or "interpretations of awareness of the transference" (Gill, 1982). Interpretations may involve a single component or several components of the CCRT. Interpretations may be directed at the content of the patient's narrated RE, interpretations may be directed to the process, i.e., what seems to be happening between patient and therapist during the patient's narration, or interpretations may be directed at the relationship between content and process.

Interpretations directed at the content of the patient's narrated RE are reasonably straightforward. They are either based on the patient's explicit formulations (i.e., their conscious material) or based on the more concrete aspects of the patient's narrative (i.e., their unformulated, selectively unattended or preconscious material). The latter require a certain clinical imagination and inferential skill, and because the material is not too far from consciousness, it is usually a good technique to ask the patient what he or she makes of the material. Thus, a collaborative relationship is built in the joint search for meanings.

Interpretations directed at the process are more difficult to teach and describe than are interpretations of content. What can be offered in the way of help are three orienting questions the therapist should ask him/herself (and when appropriate, ask the patient!). The reader can easily gather that the following orienting questions are based upon the categories of the CCRT. (1) Why is the patient telling me this narrative? What does the patient hope to get from me by telling me this RE? (2) Who is the patient telling this RE to? Does the therapist sense he or she is being used as the father who gives comfort, the mother who criticizes, the adolescent macho buddy? (3) What is the patient's experience in relation to me during this narration? Again, the possibilities are endless. Is the patient dutiful, but uninvolved? Is the patient ashamed, expectant, frightened?

Interpretations can also address the patient's wish, response from other, or response of the self across several relationship episodes. The therapist skills required to offer effective interpretations of awareness differ in emphasis from those skills required to offer interpretations based on more than one RE. The former emphasize careful listening, and the psychological senses of empathy, imagination, and intuition, whereas the latter interpretations put more emphasis on the intellectual ability of pattern detection, concept formation, the capacity to abstract similar themes across more than one RE. They are directed at such questions as: What is this patient's central goal or wish? What gives life meaning for this person? Such questions address the patient's central wish. What has the patient come to expect from others? What does the patient tend to elicit from others? Such questions address the patient's central response from the other. How does the patient tend to regard him or herself in a variety of contexts? How does the patient act to impede the realization of his or her basic wishes? How do the patient's actions tend to perpetuate the negative reactions from others he or she has come to anticipate? Such questions address the patient's central response of the self. These interpretations differ from "interpretations of content" (Menninger & Holzman, 1958) or from Gill's (1982) "interpretations of the resolution of the transference" in that the latter interpretations have the implicit form "You do, think, experience this *because of that.*" Interpretations of the CCRT involving several REs have no such causal implications.

The final part of this "techniques" section of the chapter will be devoted to describing certain areas the therapist should routinely explore in formulating CCRT interpretations in the treatment of depression. The SE model of depression, in which some sort of personal defeat is followed by a sense of despair, which is sufficiently intense and prolonged that the patient loses a certain contact with the external dimensions of experience, suggests several lines of inquiry.

(1)   What is the personal defeat that has brought the patient to treatment this time? For example, for one sample patient, the personal defeat consisted of his quitting a more challenging job after only two weeks in the position and returning to his former job.

(2)   What is the significance of the personal defeat to the patient? For the above patient, such quitting was another in a series of acts he considered cowardly. Furthermore, he felt humiliated by his wife and by his co-workers at the job to which he returned. Other actions were discovered that he also considered cowardly. All of this provided the nodal point around which the CCRT was formulated.

(3)   Why does the patient despair so? Here, the clinician needs to try to understand why failure seems inevitable to the patient. Since we assume depressed patients might manifest rather serious personality disorders, it is suggested that the therapist attempt to identify patterns of interaction that represent something of a vicious cycle. For the sample patient, he could see easily enough that this new job was doomed to failure from the outset. However, he considered it cowardly not to take the job. One can appreciate the vicious cycle as he confirmed his sense of cowardliness by quitting the job shortly thereafter.

Phases of Treatment

Early Phase

In the early phase of treatment, the therapist initially sets goals. Within a 16-session brief SE therapy, the early phase can be generally specified as sessions 1 to 5. The most important task of the therapist during this early phase is to build a positive therapeutic alliance.

The second major task during the early phase is to begin to formulate and interpret a preliminary CCRT. Adequate quality and quantity of relationship episodes need to be elicited during this early phase to serve as the basis for the preliminary CCRT. If negative transferential issues begin to emerge during this early phase, the therapist should empathize with the patient's feelings as much as possible in order to continue to build the alliance. Patients with an additional Axis II diagnosis in particular commonly display negative transference reactions in the early phase of treatment. The therapist's goal is to manage the Axis II issues so as to keep the patient engaged in treatment, but as much as possible return to working on the depression. Axis II defenses should be addressed in an empathetic way although always maintaining the goal of being in touch with the CCRT feelings and issues. Severe Axis II patients (e.g., borderline) are generally not accepted in a brief SE treatment.

Middle Phase

The middle phase of treatment can be generally defined as sessions 6 to 11. During this phase, the therapist refines the CCRT formulation using information from further relationship episodes. It is during this phase that the patient feels safer in treatment, defenses have lowered somewhat, and more memories and experiences are recalled and discussed. Thus, the therapist now has the opportunity to relate the CCRT pattern to earlier relationships and to illustrate to the patient the degree to which the same patterns are appearing in a variety of relationships in the patient's life, including potentially the relationship with the therapist.

Sometimes a therapist feels uncertain about which direction to go in if a patient brings up very serious issues in the middle of a 16-session treatment. For example, a patient might disclose an incident of abuse or other trauma halfway through the treatment. We have found that in most cases the incident can be talked about in therapy and used for understanding the patient's symptoms, defenses, and interpersonal conflicts. Thus, our view is unlike the view of some within the psychoanalytic camp who believe it is inherently countertherapeutic to get into such material in a brief treatment. If necessary, of course, the patient can be referred for additional treatment—if the patient begins to deteriorate once very traumatic experiences are brought up.

Termination Phase

The termination phase, approximately sessions 12 to 16, is of central importance in our brief SE treatment for depression. Although our treatment does not go quite as far as Mann's (1973) brief therapy that focuses on termination issues for almost the entire length of treatment, we nonetheless believe that the termination phase is critical. As Luborsky (1984) indicates, the termination phase is often characterized by a resurgence of symptoms in the context of an activation of the patient's CCRT in anticipation of the loss of the therapist. The loss of the therapist is meaningful not only in terms of the realistic loss of an important person in the patient's life, but also in terms of anticipation of not obtaining the CCRT wish in relationships (e.g., wishes for support, nurturance, love, closeness, acceptance, etc.). The therapist needs to interpret the upcoming termination in terms of the link to the CCRT pattern. The therapist must begin work on the termination issues no later than session 14 and preferably as early as session 12, whether or not the patient is making any explicit references to termination. Not uncommonly, a therapist will collude with a patient to not discuss the upcoming termination because other topics seem more pressing, when in fact both participants are having difficulty facing the feelings related to termination. If not discussed, the termination issues often explode in the last or next to last session, with both participants feeling there is not enough time to deal with the feelings and issues that have come up. With supervision, however, therapists learn after one or two training cases to address termination issues early enough and to be less apprehensive about the termination feelings that arise.

Booster Phase

Often brief SE treatment has been implemented with an additional booster phase. This phase was designed on an experimental basis as part of our research projects. However, our experience thus far in the use of booster sessions has been positive and we can now recommend their use as part of our clinical treatment package. The booster sessions are scheduled at a rate of one per month over three months. The therapist's task during the booster phase is to monitor and reinforce the improvements the patient has made, encourage and support internalization of the treatment and the therapist (i.e., the patient doing the work of therapy on his or her own), and if necessary interpreting relapse in terms of the CCRT and the loss of the therapist. The goal is to help prevent recurrences and relapses. If, however, during the booster phase, a serious setback or relapse occurs, the patient is of course referred for more regular treatment.

6. THERAPEUTIC RELATIONSHIP

Another potentially misleading aspect of simply applying the CCRT template to the material in Nancy's case presentation involves the issue of transference and countertransference. The case presentation is written from the perspective of an "omniscient narrator." The psychiatric interviewer is outside of the data-gathering and organizing process. In Sullivan's terms, the narrator of a traditional case history is an *observer* and not, as is inevitably the case in psychotherapy, a *participant observer.* It is in the process of obtaining sensory data organized in specific relationship episodes that transference and countertransference naturally emerge. In the first place, any question the therapist chooses to ask must reveal something about the mind of the therapist. Furthermore, the effort to expand the data, i.e., the therapist's effort to make more concrete and specific the patient's spontaneously reported narrative, inevitably generates anxiety for the patient. This anxiety mobilizes defenses or resistance as well as transference. Since one of the key "mechanisms of change" or therapeutic factors of SE therapy involves the working through of central transference-countertransference patterns, such mobilization of transference and countertransference is not only inevitable, it is necessary. A hypothetical example may help make all this more clear.

In the case presentation, the interviewer states that Nancy "feels that her sister can be supportive and enjoys talking with her. Regrettably, Nancy speaks with her only once or twice a month." Let's assume the SE therapist hears this and wonders "why 'regrettably?' " The therapist might begin to open this up by asking why Nancy speaks with her sister only once or twice a month. Note that while it is far from unambiguous, already something of the therapist is revealed by the question. Perhaps, something about the therapist's expectations about family. Or perhaps there's a hint in the therapist's question that Nancy ought to speak with her sister more than she does. Does this, in turn, reflect the therapist's irritation with the patient portraying herself as a victim? Or, does the therapist's question carry a suspicion that Nancy's sister isn't all that supportive of her? Does this reflect something of the therapist's experience? Like a skepticism about sibling supportiveness? As we have said, it's far from clear what is revealed about the therapist, but the very fact that the therapist chose to inquire here, rather than somewhere else, indicates the therapist is *in* the process; the therapist is inevitably a *participant*-observer. Furthermore, on some level, whether it is spoken about or not, the patient knows this. In fact, recalling Nancy's experience of her mother, we would suspect that a likely transference reaction would be that Nancy would feel criticized and forced to bend to the therapist's will. So we might expect her to experience the therapist's question as to why she speaks to her sister only once or twice a month as a covert criticism and instruction to contact her more frequently. To further complicate the matter, the therapist must be affected by Nancy—who herself can be quite a critical person! Perhaps the therapist will be critical in just the way Nancy fears, if for no other reason than to preempt, or to respond to, Nancy's—probably implicit—criticism of the therapist. Of course, all this is terribly hypothetical, and in fact the whole process is unpredictable, involving the collision of two complex personalities. But, as events are progressively drawn out (we have only been discussing the opening therapist intervention), the participant's meanings and feelings become progressively more unambiguous. Unfortunately, it isn't quite that simple. The interaction between patient and therapist becomes less ambiguous only if the therapist is willing and able to be relatively straightforward. A therapist who tries to hide his or her reactions, or obscure or mystify them, does not contribute to the development of progressively less ambiguous interactions. Thus, a relative lack of defensiveness on the part of the therapist is one of the attributes we would consider most essential to conducting SE therapy effectively.

Another important therapeutic attribute is the ability to listen, and more specifically, the ability to listen to both the content—what is being said—and the process—what is being done—simultaneously. Other skills include the capacity to imagine what is missing in patient's spontaneously delivered relationship episodes; this presupposes a certain knowledge of cultural expectancies—a knowledge of what tends to happen in certain situations.

Let us return to the issue of transference-countertransference. Would our presumed *core conflict*, that between the wish to be taken care of and the wish to not rely upon another, emerge in the transference? For example, would Nancy alternately experience the therapist as supportive and a good "sounding board" at some moments, and then as abandoning, or as someone with whom she "doesn't have a sense of privacy" at other times? If so, the termination would certainly involve these issues of abandonment and self-(or pseudo-self) sufficiency. Our experience in short-term therapy, however, is that core issues are not necessarily repeated in the transference. This is not necessarily a bad thing. In some therapies (we suspect when the patient is less psychologically sophisticated) the cognitive aspects of therapy, e.g., an understanding of the core conflictual relationship theme, is the most important curative factor. For others, a more intense involvement with the therapist is required.

One traditional "curative factor" of any "supportive" psychotherapy has been the supportive aspect of the therapeutic relationship. The therapist's consistency, interest in the patient and his/her goals, empathy, nonjudgmental listening, and recognition of the patient's strengths, all contribute to the patient's improved functioning and self-esteem. One could imagine that this might occur in SE psychotherapy with Nancy. Given her proneness to panic-like reactions, the therapist's steady, calm presence might alone be helpful. While Nancy reports she suffers from chronically low self-esteem, she appears to be a person with some strengths. For example, she has a responsible job in a large company. It is unclear from the case presentation what specific abilities have enabled her to rise to the position of art director, but the therapist might be able to identify her strengths. The therapist's recognition of these strengths might improve Nancy's self-esteem. Some of those strengths might even be relied upon in therapy (e.g., a sense of responsibility and integrity can be especially useful during stormy periods of therapy). Furthermore, the therapist's basic attempt to understand the patient's point of view might alone be therapeutic to someone such as Nancy who apparently has come to expect a high degree of criticalness from others. To repeat, all of these factors—the therapist's consistency and steadiness, the therapist's recognition of the patient's strengths, and a basic listening stance in which the therapist attempts to understand the patient's point of view—represent the supportive components of the therapeutic relationship.

Nevertheless, *supportiveness* does not adequately describe the therapist's role. After all, as Nancy tells it, she already has a supportive relationship with two friends and her sister (not to mention her husband, a more complicated case to be sure, but still described as "kind and generous and attentive"). If all that would be needed was supportiveness, she's already got that. What might be worked through with the therapist are Nancy's fears regarding these relationships. For example, it sounds as if Nancy suggested to the interviewer that she was guilty about complaining too much with her friends. Certainly, this is a common fear with depressed patients. They worry they turn off others with their negativity and self-absorption. One has the impression Nancy has withdrawn from, or at least severely limited, relationships with her sister and friends due to these fears. In order for the therapy to be deeply meaningful, the therapist may have to get turned off by Nancy's negativity and self-absorption. After all, how involved could the therapist be if she [the therapist] is not brought down by Nancy's negativity? Or chilled by her self-absorption? Or stung by her criticism? What would seem to be required in the face of such experiences is not supportiveness, but honesty. If Nancy learns that others may experience such things as being deadened, stung, or chilled by her, but that a relationship can survive these sorts of experiences, she may well have learned a very valuable lesson. Thus, the therapist's role extends beyond the merely supportive, and the therapeutic relationship encompasses such a degree of openness and honesty that each participant may share what it is like to be with the other.

A final issue involving the therapeutic relationship concerns the question of limits, boundaries, and limit-setting. Given her history, specifically the absence of a variety of self-destructive behaviors such as substance abuse, we would not anticipate a lot of attention to limit-setting. One area, however, might require intervention. We would like to hear much more about her "suicide plan." How long has she had such a plan? When pushed about it, is the idea of the plan itself something that provides relief (i.e., does the suicidal plan provide a comfort or reminder of escape but she would never enact it?). Or, does she sound more determined to act out the plan? How hopeless is she? Specifically, is there any response to her relationship with the therapist? If her plan really concerned us, we would hope to set some sort of limits around it. Certainly, we would like to get an agreement that if she feels suicidal she reaches us before acting! Because she doesn't have an obvious "hook" (like staying alive for children), we are likely to have to rely more upon the therapeutic relationship itself to hold her to some agreements (or limits) regarding her suicidal plans.

7. INTEGRATION OF PSYCHOTHERAPY WITH MEDICATION

It appears to us that on the basis of several criteria, Nancy ought to be given antidepressant medication. Her history and description of symptoms indicate a diagnosis of recurrent Major Depression. Her questionnaire test results are consistent with that diagnosis. Finally, she has already been started on a low dose of Zoloft, and her response, while mild, appears to be in the direction of symptom alleviation. Not only is she depressed, she has many of the psychological and somatic symptoms of anxiety (probably another Axis 1 Disorder). Many other factors would incline us to medicate sooner, rather than later. Her suicidal ideation, a concern in and of itself, contributes to the impression that her depression is becoming more serious. Her history of trauma, and her anxiety make her suicidal ideation more of a concern. Our hope would be that antidepressant medication would turn down the symptom volume enough that meaningful psychotherapy can take place.

8. RELAPSE PREVENTION

Relapse prevention is addressed in a number of ways in SE therapy. First, adequate working through of the CCRT issues throughout treatment serves to provide both insight and self-exploration skills that help the patient cope with difficult events and feelings after therapy, thereby potentially preventing a downward spiral into depression. Secondly, the process of internalizing the therapist ("what would my therapist say about this") helps the patient continue the work of treatment after it has ended, thereby preventing recurrences and relapses. Thirdly, working through of issues that arise at termination is often crucial for preventing relapses. Finally, the use of booster sessions can be an additional way to maintain improvements and prevent relapses.

9. SUMMARY AND DISCUSSION

SE therapy is a flexible treatment that has broad applicability in clinical practice. It's usefulness in the treatment of patients with major depressive disorder has not been established in controlled, clinical trials. However, promising uncontrolled data, as well as extensive research on the key process concepts of the model, suggest that there is ample justification for pursuing controlled outcome research on the role of SE treatment for depression. Moreover, SE therapy was developed as a codification of standard, once-per-week interpersonally-oriented dynamic psychotherapy. To the extent that such treatment resembles the relatively common practice of dynamic therapy in the community, controlled studies of SE therapy are also of interest in terms of evaluating whether there is a role for continuing to treat depressed patients with dynamically-oriented psychotherapy. Finally, with its primary focus on the core conflictual relationship theme concept, SE therapy is fundamentally an interpersonal approach. The developing literature on interpersonal factors in depression (Joiner & Coyne, 1999) provides another impetus for exploring treatment modalities that attempt to address interpersonal issues in therapy.

Because SE therapy relies primarily on observations of relationship narratives as told during psychotherapy sessions, we are able to only provide some initial speculation about the conceptualization of the sample case, Nancy. From statements about her parents, we expect that Nancy would have had particularly intense conflicts around the desire to be taken care of and protected and the wish to take care of herself so that she need not rely upon anyone else. The core wish to be taken care of conflicts with the core anticipated, feared, and perceived response from others of criticism, abandonment, and chaotic over- and under-parenting. This preliminary formulation would need to be confirmed during the early phase of treatment, with the therapist attending to the development of relationship narratives. Our further speculation is that treatment might have a supportive emphasis with Nancy, and that she may benefit from this component, provided that it is combined with an experience (and insight) in therapy that decreases her fear of supportive relationships.

REFERENCES

Barber, J. P., & Crits-Christoph, P. (1996). Development of a therapist adherence/competence rating scale for Supportive-Expressive Dynamic Psychotherapy: A preliminary report. *Psychotherapy Research, 6*, 81–94.

Barber, J. P., Crits-Christoph, P., & Luborsky, L. (1996). Therapist competence and treatment outcome in dynamic therapy. *Journal of Consulting and Clinical Psychology, 64*, 619–622.

Barber, J. P., Luborsky, L., Crits-Christoph, P., & Diguer, L. (1995). A comparison of core conflictual relationship themes before psychotherapy and during early sessions. *Journal of Consulting and Clinical Psychology, 63*, 145–148.

Bibring, E. (1954). Psychoanalysis and the dynamic psychotherapies. *Journal of the American Psychoanalytic Association, 2*, 745–770.

Connolly, M. B., Crits-Christoph, P., Shelton, R. C., Hollon, S., Kurtz, J., Barber, J. P., Butler, S. F., Baker, S., & Thase, M. E. (1999). The reliability and validity of a measure of self-understanding of interpersonal patterns. *Journal of Counseling Psychology, 46,* 472–482.

Crits-Christoph, P., Barber, J., & Kurcias, J. (1993). The accuracy of therapists' interpretations and the development of the therapeutic alliance. *Psychotherapy Research, 3,* 25–35.

Crits-Christoph, P., Cooper, A., Luborsky, L. (1988). The accuracy of therapists' interpretations and the outcome of dynamic psychotherapy. *Journal of Consulting and Clinical Psychology, 56,* 490–495.

Crits-Christoph, P., Crits-Christoph, K., Wolf-Palacio, D., Fichter, M., & Rudick, D. (1995). Supportive-expressive dynamic psychotherapy for generalized anxiety disorder. In J. P. Barber & P. Crits-Christoph (Eds.), *Dynamic therapies for psychiatric disorders: Axis I.* New York: Basic Books.

Crits-Christoph, P., & Luborsky, L. (1990). The changes in CCRT pervasiveness during psychotherapy. In L. Luborsky & P. Crits-Christoph, *Understanding transference: The core conflictual relationship theme method.* New York: Basic Books.

Ekert, R., Luborsky, L., Crits-Christoph, P., & Barber, J. (1990). The CCRTs of patients with a DSM-III R diagnosis of major depression. In L. Luborsky & P. Crits-Christoph, *Understanding transference: The core conflictual relationship theme method.* New York: Basic Books.

Fenichel, O. (1941). Problems of psychoanalytic technique. Albany, NY: *The Psychoanalytic Quarterly.*

Fenichel, O. (1945). *The psychoanalytic theory of neurosis.* New York: Norton.

Freud, S. (1953). Fragment of an analysis of a case of hysteria. In J. Strachey (Ed. and Trans.), *The standard edition of the complete psychological works of Sigmund Freud* (Vol. 7). London: Hogarth Press. (Original work published 1901 to 1905).

Freud, S. (1958a/1912). The dynamic of transference. In J. Strachey (Ed. & Trans.), *The standard edition of the complete psychological works of Sigmund Freud* (Vol. 12, pp. 97–108). London: Hogarth Press.

Freud, S. (1958b/1912). Recommendations to physicians practicing psychoanalysis. In J. Strachey (Ed. & Trans.), *The standard edition of the complete psychological works of Sigmund Freud* (Vol. 12, pp. 109–120). London: Hogarth Press.

Freud, S. (1958/1911). The handling of dream interpretation in psychoanalysis. In J. Strachey (Ed. & Trans.), *The standard edition of the complete psychological works of Sigmund Freud* (Vol. 12, pp. 89–96). London: Hogarth Press.

Freud, S. (1958/1913). On beginning the treatment: Further recommendations on the technique of psychoanalysis. In J. Strachey (Ed. & Trans.), *The standard edition of the complete psychological works of Sigmund Freud* (Vol. 12, pp. 212–244). London: Hogarth Press.

Freud, S. (1958/1914). Remembering, repeating and working through: Further recommendations on the technique of psychoanalysis. In J. Strachey (Ed. & Trans.), *The standard edition of the complete psychological works of Sigmund Freud* (Vol. 12, pp. 145–156). London: Hogarth Press.

Freud, S. (1958/1915). Observations on transference-love: Further recommendations on the technique of psychoanalysis. In J. Strachey (Ed. & Trans.), *The standard edition of the complete psychological works of Sigmund Freud* (Vol. 12, pp. 157–171). London: Hogarth Press.

Gill, M. (1982). *Analysis of transference.* New York: International Universities Press.

Greenson, R. (1965). The working alliance and transference neurosis. *Psychoanalytic Quarterly, 34,* 158–181.

Joiner, T., & Coyne, J. C. (1999). *The interactional nature of depression: Advances in interpersonal approaches.* Washington, DC: American Psychological Association.

Labov, W., & Fanschel, D. (1977). *Therapeutic discourse: Psychotherapy as conversation.* New York: Academic Press.

Lowenstein, R. M. (1951). The problem of interpretation. *Psychoanalytic Quarterly, 20,* 1–14.

Luborsky, L. (1976). Helping alliance in psychotherapy. In J. Claghorn (Ed.), *Successful psychotherapy* (pp. 92–116). New York: Brunner-Mazel.

Luborsky, L. (1984). *Principles of psychoanalytic psychotherapy: A manual for supportive-expressive treatment.* New York: Basic Books.

Luborsky, L., Crits-Christoph, P., Alexander, L., Margolis, M., & Cohen, M. (1983). Two helping alliance methods for predicting outcomes of psychotherapy. *Journal of Nervous and Mental Disease, 171,* 480–492.

Luborsky, L., Crits-Christoph, P., Mintz, J., & Auerbach, A. (1988). *Who will benefit from psychotherapy? Predicting therapeutic outcomes.* New York: Basic Books.

Luborsky, L., Diguer, L., Cacciola, J., Barber, J. P., Moras, K., Schmidt, K., & DeRubeis, R. J. (1996). Factors in outcome of short-term dynamic psychotherapy for chronic vs. nonchronic major depression. *Journal of Psychotherapy Practice & Research, 5,* 152–159.

Luborsky, L., Fabian, M., Hall, B. H., Ticho, E., & Ticho, G. (1958). Treatment variables. *Bulletin of the Menninger Clinic, 22,* 126–147.

Luborsky, L., & Mark, D. (1991). Short-term supportive-expressive psychoanalytic psychotherapy. In P. Crits-Christoph & J. P. Barber (Eds.), *Handbook of short-term dynamic psychotherapy.* New York: Basic Books.

Luborsky, L., Mark, D., Hole, A. V., Popp, C., Goldsmith, B., & Cacciola, J. (1995). Supportive-expressive dynamic psychotherapy of depression: A time-limited version. In J. P. Barber & P. Crits-Christoph (Eds.), *Dynamic therapies for psychiatric disorders (Axis I)* (pp. 13–42). New York: Basic Books.

Luborsky, L., Mintz, J., Auerbach, A., Christoph, P., Bachrach, H., Todd, T., Johnson, M., Cohen, M., & O'Brien, C. (1980). Predicting the outcome of psychotherapy: Findings of the Penn Psychotherapy Project. *Archives of General Psychiatry, 37*, 471–481.

Mann, J. (1973). *Time-limited psychotherapy.* Cambridge, MA: Harvard University Press.

Menninger, K., & Holzman, P. (1958). *Theory of psychoanalytic technique.* New York: Basic Books.

Morgan, R., Luborsky, L., Crits-Christoph, P., Curtis, H., & Solomon, J. (1982). Predicting the outcomes of psychotherapy by the Penn Helping Alliance Rating Method. *Archives of General Psychiatry, 39*, 397–402.

Stone, L. (1951). Psychoanalysis and brief psychotherapy. *Psychoanalytic Quarterly, 20*, 215–236.

Wallerstein, R. S. (1986). *Forty-two lives in treatment: A study of psychoanalysis and psychotherapy.* New York: Guilford Press.

Wallerstein, R. S., Robbins, L., Sargent, H., & Luborsky, L. (1956). The psychotherapy research project of the Menninger Foundation. Rationale, method, and sample use. *Bulletin of the Menninger Clinic, 20*, 221–280.

Zetzel, E. (1956). Current concepts of transference. *International Journal of Psychoanalysis, 37*, 369–375.

Zucker, H. (1967). *Problems in psychotherapy.* New York: Free Press.

SUGGESTED READINGS

Barber, J. P., & Crits-Christoph, P. (1993). Advances in measures of psychodynamic formulations. *Journal of Consulting and Clinical Psychology, 61*, 574–585.

Crits-Christoph, P., & Barber, J. (1991). *Handbook of short-term dynamic therapy.* New York: Basic Books.

Crits-Christoph, P., Crits-Christoph, K., Wolf-Palacio, D., Fichter, M., & Rudick, D. (1995). Supportive-expressive dynamic psychotherapy for generalized anxiety disorder. In J. P. Barber & P. Crits-Christoph (Eds.), *Dynamic therapies for psychiatric disorders: Axis I.* New York: Basic Books.

Crits-Christoph, P., & Connolly, M. B. (1998). Empirical basis of supportive-expressive psychodynamic psychotherapy. In R. F. Bornstein & J. M. Masling (Eds.), *Empirical studies of the therapeutic hour.* Washington, DC: APA Press.

Luborsky, L., Mark, D., Hole, A. V., Popp, C., Goldsmith, B., & Cacciola, J. (1995). Supportive-Expressive dynamic psychotherapy of depression: A time-limited version. In J. P. Barber & P. Crits-Christoph (Eds.), *Dynamic therapies for psychiatric disorders: Axis I.* New York: Basic Books.

Luborsky, L. (1984). *Principles of psychoanalytic psychotherapy: A manual for supportive-expressive treatment.* New York: Basic Books.

Luborsky, L., & Crits-Christoph, P. (1998). *Understanding transference: The core conflictual relationship theme method.* Washington, DC: American Psychological Association Press.

9

Behavioral Therapy
of Depression

E. Thomas Dowd

I. THE TREATMENT MODEL

Central to the behavioral approach to the treatment of depression is the assumption that there is a lack of response-contingent positive reinforcement of nondepressive behaviors as well as the often unintentional reinforcement of depressive behaviors. That is, the depressed individual does not obtain sufficient reinforcement from other people in his or her environment for exhibiting nondepressive behavior while often receiving reinforcement for depressive behavior, sometimes from the same people.

There are several ways in which the lack of positive reinforcement for nondepressed behaviors may occur. First, depression may result from a lowered overall rate of reinforcement for all behavior in general (Ferster, 1973). In this view, a generalized process of extinction takes place whereby the individual emits fewer responses and consequently receives less reinforcement. Significant losses in life, for example, may result in less reinforcement in general because there are fewer reinforcing individuals or situations to provide this reinforcement. Such losses might be interpersonal, as in the death of close friends, or environmental, as in the loss of gainful employment with little hope of a replacement.

Second, depression may result from a selective loss of positive reinforcers for nondepressive behavior (Lewinsohn, Biglan, & Zeiss, 1976). In this view, the individual no longer receives reinforcement for positive nondepressed responses; thus there is such a "thin" (i.e., highly intermittent) schedule of reinforcement that those behaviors can no longer be maintained, resulting in dysphoria and a reduced activity level. This can happen for two reasons. In the first case, there is a lowered *rate* of reinforcement; the reinforcing activities do not exist to the same degree in the individual's environment, illustrated, for example, by a divorce and the consequent loss of an important source of interpersonal reinforcement. In the second case, there is a loss of reinforcer *effectiveness*; although the reinforcers still exist in the individual's environment, he or she no longer finds them reinforcing. This is illustrated by the loss of interest in sexual expression, or what has been called *clinical anhedonia*. Chronic anxiety may also prevent an individual from making use of those reinforcers which do exist in the environment, illustrated by a shy person who is afraid to approach other people for dates or other social interactions.

Third, depression may result from a lack in the individual's behavioral repertoire of skills that would elicit positive responses from others, resulting in inadequate social reinforcement. In this view, the individual cannot obtain the necessary reinforcement for positive activities because he or she lacks the necessary social skills to elicit this reinforcement from significant others. Thus, an interacting cycle is fostered and maintained whereby a lack of social skills leads to impoverished reinforcement from others which in turn leads to a lack of opportunity to learn these skills. This situation may be responsible for much chronic, long-term dysphoria. In particular, lack of appropriate assertive responses seems to be implicated. Nonassertive individuals either cannot express themselves interpersonally in an assertive manner or else oscillate between a passive submission and an overly aggressive confrontation (Seligman, Klein, & Miller, 1976). Bellack and Morrison (1982) report data indicating a significant negative correlation between assertiveness and depression. Other important social skills include overcoming shyness (Joiner, 1997), seeking less reassurance from others (Joiner, 1994; Potthoff, Holahan, & Joiner, 1995), initiating positive interactions (Coyne, 1976a), less negative feedback-seeking (Joiner, Alfano, & Metalsky, 1993), and exhibiting a greater activity level.

Not only might nondepressed behaviors fail to be reinforced, the depressed behaviors themselves can reduce the positive interactions and social support available from others. Depressed individuals often elicit expressions of concern and offers of assistance from others in the short run, thus providing him or her with interpersonal gratification and reinforcement of those behaviors. This is known as *secondary gain.* However, depressed people are difficult to be around on a long-term basis and these reinforcing expressions will eventually extinguish if there is no change in the level of depression. Joiner, Alfano, and Metalsky (1993), for example, found that depressed students engaged in more reassurance-seeking and more negative feedback-seeking than nondepressed students which resulted in more negative evaluations by their roommates. Coyne (1976a) proposed a model of depression in which negative behaviors exhibited by the depressed person effectively drive significant others away and thereby reduce the level of social support available. Coyne (1976b) found that, following a phone conversation, individuals who had spoken to depressed individuals were themselves likely to be more depressed, anxious, hostile, and rejecting. Depression, in other words, can be catching and can lead to rejection by others, thus validating the depressed person's initial assumptions. However, the depressed person, knowing no other way of meeting his or her interpersonal needs, often has no choice but to redouble past efforts, thus further alienating others and resulting in fewer opportunities for reinforcement of positive nondepressed behavior in the future. A vicious cycle is thereby set up, where attempts to obtain reinforcement result in less reinforcement being obtained. Behavioral theory predicts that proximal (short-term) reinforcers will have more power than distal (long-term) reinforcers, so that behaviors that once resulted in short term reinforcers tend to persist, even though they do not result in reinforcement in the long run.

According to this model, dysphoric feelings are the results of lack of reinforcement and behavioral impoverishment, not the causes. People initially feel depressed because they do not or cannot obtain sufficient reinforcement from their environment; they do not obtain little reinforcement because they are depressed. However, once the depression has begun, others may in fact avoid them, thus beginning a circular process that is difficult to reverse.

The major treatment approach that follows from the behavioral model is an increase in level of activity and the provision for greater reinforcement of nondepressed behaviors and lack of reinforcement of depressed behaviors. Because Lewinsohn et al. (1976) proposed several causes of a loss or lack of reinforcement, it was initially thought that it would be important to match type of treatment to the type of primary deficit. However, subsequent research indicated that the interpersonal, cognitive, and activity-increase modules were all equally helpful in reducing depression, regardless of the particular skill deficit demonstrated. Later an interpersonal skills training module and a desensitization module were added to clients who exhibited social skill deficits and anxiety, respectively (Lewinsohn, Antonnucio, Breckenridge, & Teri, 1987). Skill deficits in problem-solving ability have also been implicated in depression (e.g., Miner & Dowd, 1996).

Thus, a comprehensive behavior treatment package for depression should include at the least increasing pleasurable activity levels, providing for increased reinforcement for these activities, and providing for additional sources of reinforcement. For individuals who show deficits in social skills and/or problem-solving capabilities, additional training in these areas should be provided as well. Anxiety is also often coincidental with depression and may prevent some depressed individuals from actually conducting activities they know how to perform. Therefore, anxiety management may be useful in some instances.

In general, research has supported the behavioral theory of depression (Carson & Adams, 1981; Rehm & Tyndall, 1993). For example, Lewinsohn and his colleagues (Carson & Adams, 1981; Rehm & Tyndall, 1993) found that depressed individuals emitted substantially fewer social behaviors and reciprocated fewer social behaviors than nondepressed. Depressed individuals have lower activity levels and report less overall pleasure from positive activities than nondepressed. Contingency management procedures and increased activity levels have been shown to successfully modify depressive behaviors (Carson & Adams, 1981). Although Lewinsohn et al.'s (1976) model initially postulated that interpersonal, cognitive, and activity-increase targeted interventions would differentially reduce depression in those specific areas of deficit, later investigations showed that, regardless of the type of treatment, clients improved in all three areas (Zeiss, Lewinsohn, & Munoz, 1979). Turner, Ward, and Turner (1979), in a dismantling study to investigate the active ingredients in Lewinsohn's behavioral treatment for depression, found that an increase in level of activities was more efficacious in overcoming depression than an expectancy-control group, a self-monitoring control group, and an attention-control group. A recent meta-analysis (Cuijpers, 1998) found that Lewinsohn's *Coping with Depression* course (Lewinsohn et al., 1987) was an effective treatment modality for depression and may be a means of reaching people who would not otherwise seek treatment. Although this meta-analysis did not directly compare this course with other treatments, comparison with another comprehensive meta-analysis of various treatments for depression (Robinson, Berman, & Neimeyer, 1990) reflected favorably on the Lewinsohn course. In a review of the literature, Turner and Wehl (1984) reported that concrete and highly structured behavioral treatment was superior to cognitive techniques in treating depression in problem drinkers, perhaps because cognitive deficits are common in this population. Lichtenberg, Kimbarow, Morris, and Vangel (1996) found that behavioral treatment for depression in urban African-American older adults was more effective than a no-treatment group. In a major comparative study, Jacobson et al. (1996) compared three groups for the treatment of depression: (1) a behavioral activation (BA) treatment group; (2) a combination of BA and a program to teach modification of automatic thoughts (AT); and (3) a full cognitive therapy package incorporating core schema modification as well as BA and AT interventions. There were no significant differences among the three treatments either post-treatment or at follow-up, indicating that the less costly behavioral treatment was just as effective as the more costly full cognitive therapy treatment. However, an earlier study by Shaw (1977) found a cognitive therapy treatment package to be more effective than a behavior modification treatment package and a nondirective treatment. The behavioral and nondirective treatments produced equivalent results.

While not directly involving the treatment of depression only, two other landmark studies can provide comparative data. The well-known and well-designed study comparing psychoanalytically oriented psychotherapy with behavior therapy (Sloane, Staples, Cristol, Yorkston, & Whipple, 1975) initially seemed to demonstrate no differences between the two conditions. However, Giles (1983), reassessing the Sloane et al. data, noted that only one statistically significant difference favored psychodynamic therapy while eight favored behavior therapy. In addition, at 12-month follow-up, only the behaviorally treated clients were rated as significantly more improved than the controls and were significantly better in work adjustment. Similarly, the original meta-analysis comparing behavior therapy with psychoanalytically oriented brief therapy (Smith & Glass, 1977) appeared initially to demonstrate equivalence. However, Andrews and Harvey (1981) reanalyzed these data, restricting their analyses only to those individuals who would normally seek psychotherapy, and found consistent and significant effect sizes in favor of behavior therapy.

It has been noted that some earlier investigations have largely relied on correlational analyses and therefore the assumption that a low rate of reinforcement *causes* depression, rather than simply being associated with it, has not been adequately tested (Carson & Adams, 1981). In addition, a number of the studies compared behavioral treatment with a no-treatment control condition rather than with other treatments. It has been demonstrated extensively in all aspects of psychotherapy research that doing something is generally better than doing nothing. Furthermore, different techniques do not appear to be differentially effective with different depressive skill deficits; an increase in behavioral activation appears to be the key technique. It is still a relatively open question whether behavioral activation is as effective as other, more comprehensive, treatment packages although the Jacobson et al. (1996) study would suggest that perhaps it is.

Research investigations of the efficacy of strictly behavioral approaches in treating depression appear to have fallen off dramatically since the heady days of the 1970s and early 1980s. A search of the outcome literature turned up very few investigations of behavioral techniques since 1984—and some of those were with special populations. It appears that the strictly behavioral treatment of depression has been replaced by a cognitive-behavioral hybrid or a strictly cognitive approach. Nevertheless, the Jacobson et al. (1996) study may forecast an increasing interest in the behavioral treatment of depression.

II. ESSENTIAL CLINICAL SKILLS AND ATTRIBUTES

Despite the reputation of behavior therapy as mechanistic and technique-driven, good therapist clinical and interpersonal skills are very important. Indeed, the importance of the interpersonal working alliance in treating depression has been stressed on a number of occasions (e.g., Blatt, Zuroff, Quinlan, & Pilkonis, 1996). Behavior therapists use *General Contingent Reinforcement*, in which the therapist reinforces client behavior which is necessary for therapy to occur at all, such as returning for subsequent sessions or working on problems (Follette, Naugle, & Callaghan, 1996). In other words, behavior therapists, like therapists of other orientations, make use of the core facilitative conditions, such as accurate empathy, unconditional positive regard, and interpersonal warmth.

However, behavior therapists make use of a number of important clinical skills beyond the basic interpersonal attributes. First among these is structuring and goal orientation (Wolpe, 1990). Behavior therapists argue that specific therapeutic goals must be set so that both the client and the therapist know and agree on what they are working toward and how they will know when they get there. Tightly structuring each session as well as the overall course of therapy increases therapeutic efficiency and enables clients to reach their goals in a minimum amount of time. Structuring also helps both client and therapist to feel that "something is happening," which can provide significant reinforcement for continued activity, therapeutic and otherwise. Therefore, a common behavior therapist question is, "Where are we going?"

Second is a consistent focus on the client's *behavior,* as opposed to the client's thoughts or feelings (Spiegler & Guevremont, 1993). This is not to say that behavior therapists ignore thoughts and feelings and consider them to be unimportant or nonexistent. But thoughts and feelings are considered to be secondary to behavior as a focus of treatment. *Specific Contingent Reinforcement,* or the therapist differential reinforcement of specific client behavior leading to the achievement of client goals (Follette et al., 1996). The focus on client behavior derives from two considerations. First, behavior change *precedes* cognitive or affective change, so that if we obtain the first, the others will follow (Hobbs, 1962). Second, only overt behavior is observable so it is the only psychological attribute about which demonstrable progress can be noted. Although clients may report thinking differently and feeling better, it is only in the realm of behavior change that progress can be noted by an independent observer. For these reasons, homework outside of the therapy session is often prescribed. A focus on behavior allows both client and therapist to measure and monitor therapeutic progress over time so that interventions may be modified if necessary. Therapist-observed behavior change can be mentioned to the client (who often will not notice or will discount such things), thus providing an important source of reinforcement for continued therapeutic activity. Therefore, another common question is, "What are you doing (differently)?"

Third is an emphasis on the active therapist direction of the therapeutic process. Although behavior therapy is collaborative in nature (Spiegler & Guevremont, 1993), the therapist is ultimately responsible for setting the overall direction and course of therapy. Therefore, behavior therapists must be skilled in and comfortable with directing without appearing to be controlling or lacking in empathy or caring. A common behavior therapist statement might be, "Let's come back to . . . " or "It might be helpful to focus on . . . "

Fourth is a skill at detecting the reinforcing and maintaining environmental contingencies in the client's environment (Wolpe, 1990). Ferreting these out takes real therapist skill, as they are often quite removed (distal) from the client's everyday life. For example, depression may have been partially maintained by increased attention from a spouse whenever it has occurred over many years. Or, depression may partially result from progressive interpersonal losses over the years and the lack of social skills needed to meet new people. Detection of vicious circles of behavioral, social, and emotional processes is also important. Although behavior therapists do not normally investigate past events, there are occasions when it is important in order to identify past environmental reinforcers so that new ones can be developed. A common behavior therapist question might be, "What do you think is causing (or maintaining) that?" or, "Where do you think that came from?"

Fifth, behavior therapists are skilled at conducting a functional analysis of the problem behavior and developing specific techniques for specific problems (Wolpe, 1990). The former refers to a behavioral assessment of client resources, client deficits, and maintaining environmental contingencies. The latter refer to interventions. While most psychological problems respond somewhat to basic therapeutic interventions, targeted interventions can provide additional benefits. For example, social skills training or anxiety management training may be useful for a certain subset of clients but may provide no additional benefit for most. An astute behavior therapist will know when to use what interventions, based on research findings and clinical intuition. For example, Nezu and Nezu (1995) present a decision-making model for selecting appropriate interventions, based on their problem-solving model. They suggest using all five steps in problem-solving for each clinical decision to be made. In (1), Problem orientation, the therapist may conduct a literature search that leads to information concerning issues to address later in the problem-solving approach. It is important here to minimize potential therapist bias and rely on external information. In (2), Problem definition and formulation, the therapist collects information from the client concerning current and historic functioning and identifies blocks to increased functioning. Essentially, a functional analysis of the problem behavior is undertaken. In (3), the therapist generates a comprehensive list of treatment alternatives and then evaluates these alternatives in light of their possible effects. In (4), the treatment plan selected is carried out, with provision always for appropriate modifications. In (5), Solution verification, the therapist collects data to indicate whether the treatment was effective. This data collection should begin shortly after the implementation (4) step. In essence, the behavioral approach emphasizes the collection of data (e.g., literature, outcome) to inform the clinical decision-making and treatment process in order to reduce the effects of shorthand heuristics on decision-making (Kahnemann & Tversky, 1973). These heuristics can bias the decision-making process because we tend to see what we expect to see and find what we expect to find (Dowd & Courchaine, 1996) unless we specifically look for (disconfirming) data. These targeted interventions may not only be at the individual level but also at the group, couple, or family level.

In general, the type of questions asked by behavior therapists tend to be "What" questions (e.g., "What are you doing?") and "When" questions (e.g., "When did you do that?") rather than "How" questions (e.g., "How does that make you feel") or "Why" questions (e.g., "Why did you do that?"). The latter two are considered to be speculative and therefore therapeutically nonproductive.

III. THE CASE OF "NANCY:" 15 CLINICAL QUESTIONS

(1) *What would be your therapeutic goals for this patient? What are the primary goals and the secondary goals?*

The primary goal is reducing Nancy's depression, specifically assessed as reduced scores on the BDI and HS into the low-moderate range. It is interesting to note that her "feelings of depression and anxiety were first apparent during her engagement to Steve." Thus, while they undoubtedly are rooted in her family of origin, they appear to have been caused primarily by her impending and actual marriage. It is interesting to note that her depression is worse during the weekends, deriving apparently from contacts with her husband's friends, friends with children, and her mother. These areas of Nancy's life seem to be providing the maintaining forces behind her depression. It would appear that Nancy functions best in occupational activities. It is difficult to understand if certain reinforcers have lost their reinforcing power for Nancy (sex might have) or if her environment never was particularly reinforcing, but I suspect from her family history that she never received much reinforcement for prosocial or other activities. Thus, her entire life may be characterized as "reinforcer impoverished." It is also interesting to note in Nancy the common co-occurrence of depression and anxiety.

The next, somewhat less primary, goal is improving Nancy's marital functioning, defined as a better description of her relationship with her husband and more sexual and social activities. More positive approach behaviors toward Steve would be another behavioral marker of goal progress. This is more difficult, as Steve refuses to come for couples' therapy, so that the focus for now will have to be individual work with Nancy.

The third goal, related to (and apparently entangled with) the second, is helping Nancy to make a decision about children, at least with Steve. It appears that Nancy's innate maternal feelings have been extinguished by conflicts and lack of positive relations in her family of origin and later by the same sort of relation with Steve. It's interesting to note in this context that Steve resembles her father in some ways and she seems to view him as such. Behavioral consistencies are often seen across generations and across individuals' different relationships. The environmental reinforcing consequences are often similar and behavior that is expected in another tends to be subtly reinforced and thereby exhibited, in a reciprocal, interactive fashion (Bandura, 1978).

A secondary goal for Nancy would be the exhibition of more assertive behavior. In general, she appears to be a passive dependent person who allows "people to take advantage of me" and "can't let people know when I'm angry at them." Her life has been filled with critical and judgmental people with whom she has had difficulty setting limits. Assertiveness training may help Nancy to begin to stand up for herself, pay attention to and communicate her wishes, and in the process perhaps overcome some of the helplessness that is associated with depression.

Another secondary goal would include the provision of a more reinforcing social and familial environment. Although Nancy is described as having "two or three close friends," she does not see them often so they cannot provide much reinforcement for her. In general, other people do not seem to provide her with reinforcing consequences for positive behaviors, only punishment for them. Her parents were critical, cold and distant and her husband appears to be similar. While behavior therapy with Nancy cannot change these people, if she can learn more and better social interaction skills, she may elicit different reactions from them that can then be reinforced. In turn, their different reactions to her may reinforce her new behavior, thus resulting in an adaptive spiral rather than a maladaptive one. It is possible that, as previous goals are worked on, this may happen naturally.

(2)   *What further information would you want to have to assist you in structuring this patient's treatment? Are there specific assessment tools you would use (i.e., data to be collected)? What would be the rationale for using those tools?*

As mentioned above, I would like to know if there is any area of her life in which she is not depressed (or much less depressed). With this information, I can assess the functional differences between situations in which she is and is not depressed and perhaps build in activities in the former situations which are found in the latter. It may also help me to understand more fully the precipitating and maintaining causes of the depression.

I would also like to know if she has had any past therapy (other than the brief marital sessions) and, if so what the presenting problems were and what the outcome was. In general, though, I would like to know about any previous therapy so I can: (1) learn what was addressed and accomplished, and (2) avoid mistakes of past therapists.

I would also like to know how strong her Catholicism is. In general, Catholics have more difficulty with divorce than adherents to some other religions, which might account in part for her distressed feelings about her marriage and ambivalent feelings about her husband. Although we recognize that not all Catholics are the same (there is substantial within-group variance), nevertheless there is enough between-group variance to justify an exploration of this topic. In order to practice culturally sensitive therapy it is necessary to inquire into and functionally assess the client's cultural and social background (Tanaka-Matsumi, Seiden, & Lam, 1996). This includes religion. I'd also like to know about any history of substance abuse in her family (the medical report only mentions her own), especially in view of her description of her parents' relationship as "violent." Substance abuse is often a factor in poor family relationships.

I would also like to know more about the precipitating and maintaining causes of her anxiety, as well as the anxiety-related cognitions around a theme of personal danger. Anxiety and depression often coexist and treatment of one may have an effect on the other. Treatment of both may result in more rapid improvement.

I would also like to know more about her husband and especially from an independent source. I say this for two reasons. First, I would like to be able to assess the potentiality for him to become a significant source of social support and reinforcement for her. Second, I would like to be able to assess the possibility that they can form a functional relationship in the future. To assess these, I need to know more about his behavioral flexibility, personality structure, and view of their relationship. In order to assess her relationship with her husband (since improving it is a primary goal), I might use specific assessment instruments such as the Marital Satisfaction Questionnaire (Lazarus, 1985) or the Dyadic Adjustment Scale (Spanier, 1976). These are among the best of the standardized instruments. I might also conduct a functional behavioral analysis of Nancy's marital relationship by asking her and her husband to conduct a problem-solving and an intimate interaction behind a one-way mirror to be observed and coded.

Finally, I would like a more detailed assessment of her global functioning, as called for in Axis V of the DSM IV.

(3)   *What is your conceptualization of this patient's personality, behavior, affective state, and cognitions?*

On the DSM IV, Axis I, it appears that Nancy is suffering from Dysthymic Disorder (300.4). Apparently her depression and anxiety have been present for many years; thus, a diagnosis of Adjustment Disorder does not appear appropriate. Alternatively, a diagnosis of Major Depressive Disorder, Recurrent (296.3x) may be considered, since the case description refers to "depressive episodes." However, one obtains the distinct impression that at best Nancy does not function well. Her overall functioning, at least from the case description, seems to have been characterized for years as dysthymic and anxious. Not only the depressed mood, but also the feelings of worthlessness, insomnia, inability to make decisions, weight gain, and fatigue all fit either diagnosis. If I were to diagnose her as Dysthymic Disorder, I might be inclined to focus more on the developmental antecedents of her depression and its current environmental maintaining conditions. If I were to diagnose her as Major Depressive Disorder, Recurrent, I might treat the current depression first by appropriate medication and behavioral activation methods and only later consider environmental maintaining factors.

Although Nancy may not have a true personality disorder (Axis II), there are definite stylistic features on Cluster C, primarily in Avoidant. She does not really have close friends and described herself as keeping to herself and an "alien" during her childhood. She feels inadequate and is excessively sensitive to criticism. There are also Dependent features, in that she "tends to become totally absorbed by the other person . . . and I look for them to protect and take care of me." On the other hand, she appears to be a caretaker in some situations, especially with her mother and younger sister. There are hints of Obsessive-Compulsive features in her perfectionism, perhaps useful in controlling her anxiety.

Nancy does not appear to have any medical conditions (Axis III). Her psychosocial and environmental functioning (Axis IV) appear to be adequate, although she reports some problems with her schoolwork. Since the issue appears to be quality, it may simply reflect her own perfectionism. She does not have a large social support network, apart from her mother, husband, or friends, perhaps due in part to her avoidant tendencies. Her global assessment of functioning (Axis V), appears to be rather poor.

Nancy's behavior may be characterized primarily as avoidant. She has avoided having children, avoided close relationships with her husband and others, and avoided facing her problems. Her affective state is, as described above, depressive, anxious, and hopeless. There are hints in the case description that she is unusually sophisticated about possible causes of her depression, e.g., attributing her difficulties to her "dysfunctional childhood," her analysis of her mother's and her own psychological states, and her belief that her relationship with her mother is in part the cause of her distress. Because there are personality styles (if not personality disorders) implicated in Nancy's presenting problems, I would emphasize building the client-therapist relationship and using therapist reactions to client behavior as an important source of heuristic data. I would also be aware that, although Nancy's depression may be reduced relatively quickly, the underlying schemas behind it may take considerably longer to be addressed. Because of Nancy's avoidant features, I would move slowly (so she wouldn't avoid me) and work initially on issues of trust. Small behavioral experiments would be helpful in assisting her to overcome her avoidant tendencies. Because of possible dependent features, however, it would be important for the therapist to reinforce her consistently for any movement towards independent activity and assist her in making internal attributions for the success of these activities.

(4)   *What potential pitfalls would you envision in this therapy? What would the difficulties be and what would you envision to be the source(s) of the difficulties?*

There are several difficulties inherent in conducting therapy with Nancy. The first is her long history of emotional deprivation and abuse, which has apparently affected her choice of a marriage partner and how she relates to him. Longstanding, entrenched problems become a life style and are much less amenable to change from any source as a result. Related to this is the history of mental instability in her family; schizophrenia in her father and depression in her mother and sister. Familial patterns are passed down through the generations by a complex interaction of biological/biochemical causes and environmental influences but, at the least, there may be significant genetic features to Nancy's depression that may lead to its management rather than its cure.

Second is the lack of a significant social support network for Nancy. The relationships with her mother, sister, and husband are, to a varying extent, not nurturing and she has few friends to call upon. Much research (e.g., Pengilly & Dowd, 1997) has shown the important role played by social support in buffering the effects of stress and life events on depression and she has few resources in this regard. One of the major social supports available to people, marriage, is not currently available to her; indeed, it's the source of her greatest stress. The difficulty of building a social support network for her is compounded by her avoidant personality structure.

Third is her level of hopelessness, although this is more modifiable than the first two. It is likely that her hopelessness has contributed to her depression and lack of motivation and then, in a circular fashion, been the cause of further depression. She does not see how things can improve for her, which is likely to act as a self-fulfilling prophecy. If her level of hopelessness can be changed, at least partially, it might act as a reinforcer for further changes. This is one reason for a further consideration of medication.

Fourth, her major potential social reinforcer (her husband) refuses to attend marital therapy (not an uncommon situation) and therefore that aspect of her problems cannot be addressed in an optimal fashion. It is also possible that if Nancy were to improve her current level of functioning regarding depression and anxiety her marriage might paradoxically deteriorate further. We all select mates consonant with our own level of functioning and comfort and significant changes by one partner can often result in relationship problems as the other partner attempts to restore the previous balance in the relationship.

(5)   *To what level of coping, adaptation, or function would you see this patient reaching as an immediate result of therapy? What result would be long-term subsequent to the ending of therapy (i.e., the prognosis for adaptive change)?*

As an immediate result of therapy, I would see Nancy reducing her level of depression sufficiently so she could function almost as well in the rest of her life as she does occupationally, perhaps to the high normal level on the BDI. Because she functions well occupationally, she has a coping model of successful performance that she and the therapist can use for other areas of her life.

Because of the difficulties discussed in the previous section, however, the long-term results may not be as optimistic. Perhaps the central difficulty is that her avoidant personality style in part prevents her from obtaining the social support necessary to mitigate the effects of stress on depression. Although I think it is possible for her to reduce her current level of depression to within the normal range within a relatively short period of time, I suspect she will always be a somewhat dysthymic and anxious person. Because of this, she may have a tendency to relapse. More problematical is the relationship improvement with her husband. It appears, at least from her description, that he recapitulates many of the characteristics she objects to in her mother (especially) and her father. In addition, he shares some of her problems (e.g., both "really need attention and have insecurities"). If Nancy begins to improve, it may threaten the relationship and her husband may not provide the support for these changes. Indeed, he may attempt to sabotage them.

Thus, I would see a realistic prognosis for long-term adaptive change as reducing the level of depression to a high normal and anxiety to mildly anxious. I would see one or two friends with whom she interacts on a regular level (perhaps through a women's support group) as important as well. The ultimate success of the marriage and children is more problematical and her goals in these areas may not be met.

(6)   *What would be your time line (duration) for therapy? What would be your frequency and duration of the sessions?*

Although behavior therapy has been historically noted for its relatively rapid treatment-response rate, this case may take considerably longer. Rapid treatment response is more likely in cases of acute, situationally-specific depression that have no other causal or maintaining factors than the initiating event. Nancy's depression, however, is chronic, rather than acute, and is maintained and exacerbated by a host of developmental and familial factors. Certainly 16 sessions may result in considerably less depression but I doubt that it will be below the clinical range at that time. I suspect that it will take approximately 30 sessions to reduce the depression to a subclinical range. Her anxiety can be addressed at the same time but would be likely to show less improvement both initially and at the end of therapy. During this time, the therapist should monitor Nancy's husband's response to her therapy as well as any changes in their marital relationship. I would recommend that the therapist initially see Nancy at least twice a week in order to provide support and initial encouragement for small changes. Once change has begun, therapy can be conducted once a week or even less, depending on progress.

Assuming sufficient improvement in her depression and the availability of more sessions, the therapist may wish to address Nancy's marital problems. But the likelihood of success will depend on her husband and his willingness to attend marital behavior therapy.

(7)   *Are there specific or special techniques that you would implement in the therapy? What would they be?*

The central technique to be used in the behavioral treatment of Nancy's depression would be behavioral activation so that she may obtain more reinforcement in the future than she has in the past. First, Nancy and the therapist should work together to develop additional sources of social reinforcement for pleasurable activities; communicating with her sister more frequently, seeing current friends more often, developing new friends, possibly joining a women's support group, and doing more activities with her husband. In addition, from the case description it appears that Nancy lacks certain social skills, especially around the area of assertion. If a behavioral analysis and case formulation determines that to be true, a structured assertiveness training program might be helpful to Nancy in learning how to appropriately state her needs and desires and avoid the negative thoughts and feelings associated with doing so in the past.

Behavioral marital therapy (e.g., Jacobson & Margolin, 1979) may be used later if Nancy and her husband decide this is one of their goals. This involves such activities as communication skill training, problem-solving skill training, and social exchange strategies.

(8)   *Are there special cautions to be observed in working with this patient (e.g., danger to self or others, transference, counter-transference)? Are there any particular resistances you would expect and how would you deal with them?*

In this context I would like to suggest that the therapist be a woman. First, a woman therapist may have more credibility in Nancy's eyes, especially when discussing marriage issues, as someone who may have experienced similar problems. Depression, for example, is much more common in women than in men. In addition, a woman therapist is less likely to elicit feelings and cognitions during therapy that may be more appropriately directed at Nancy's husband. Finally, a woman is less likely to be seen as a threat by Nancy's husband, as a possible alternative relationship. If Nancy's therapist *must* be a man, he should be alert for any difficulties deriving from his gender rather than his interventions and should, if at all possible, meet with her husband (with Nancy's knowledge and consent) to obtain his view of the situation.

Nancy does not appear to be a danger to others. There is some suicidal risk, given her score on the Hopelessness Scale, her occasional thoughts of suicide, and her plan. The therapist should develop a therapeutic contract with her regarding actions to be taken if suicidal thoughts continue.

Nancy's largest source of potential resistance is her hopelessness and her apparent view that things will not change for her. For example, she described her marriage problems as very severe, said she can't see how her marriage will succeed, and said that "the future seems dark and vague." These thoughts and feelings of hopelessness can become self-fulfilling in nature, undercut motivation, and act to prevent Nancy from working on overcoming her depression and anxiety. In addition, Nancy's negative cognitions are sufficiently entrenched and tacit that she will have difficulty articulating them and recognizing their relativistic nature. The human cognitive system is deeply conservative and acts to preserve meaning structures (Dowd & Courchaine, 1996).

From a behavioral point of view, the best way to deal with the resistance of hopelessness might be to reduce large behaviors that Nancy feels incapable of changing into smaller behaviors that she is more likely to be able to accomplish. For example, rather than attempting the global and vague task of "making her marriage better," Nancy might be encouraged to set aside one special evening to spend alone with her husband. Even smaller behaviors might be making a special dinner he likes or being especially affectionate on one evening. The therapist can then discuss the results of these small behaviors with Nancy and adjust them as needed. Generally, small successes in one area lead to a greater feeling of hopefulness and an enhanced view of self-efficacy, leading to a subsequent willingness to attempt further behavioral experiments.

(9) *Are there any areas that you would choose to avoid or not address with this patient? Why?*

I would not attempt marital or sex therapy with either Nancy or Nancy and Steve as a couple.

(10) *Is medication warranted for this patient? What effect would you hope or expect the medication to have?*

There is no hint in the case description that Nancy's depression is bipolar in nature, so medication may not be necessary. Certainly the Zoloft does not appear to be effective, at least not yet, and one of its possible side effects is loss of sexual interest. But four weeks may not be enough time for it to affect her depression. However, with a BDI score of 33 and an HS score of 15 (both in the severe range), additional medication may be helpful. Interestingly, in spite of the high HS score, the suicide ideation score (SSI) is "only" in the mild range and she has made no suicidal gestures although she apparently has a plan. For cautionary reasons, if nothing else, additional medication should be considered, perhaps an anti-anxiety drug. Medication may have the effect of increasing Nancy's activity level and reduce suicidal thoughts so that subsequent behavioral interventions might be more efficacious. The NIMH Collaborative Research Program for Depression (Elkin et al., 1989) showed that in general the psychosocial treatments were no more effective than imipramine for less severe depression and less effective than imipramine for more severe depression so perhaps medication might be differentially effective beyond that accounted for by behavior therapy. Since I am not an expert on medication, I would seek consultation from a psychiatrist.

(11)   *What are the strengths of the patient that can be used in therapy?*

Despite her problems, Nancy has several areas of strength (and I think as therapists we often tend to forget this area). First, despite her immigrant background, her family history, and her psychological problems, Nancy has achieved an impressive educational and occupational functioning. Not only has she earned a bachelor's degree but she is working on an MBA while working full-time. Furthermore, she apparently holds a responsible position as an art director in a large company. These accomplishments belie her feelings of incompetence and worthlessness and tend to make me think she is simply being unduly hard on herself when she reports that the quality of her schoolwork has suffered. I am also impressed that she has been able to continue these activities while depressed and I wonder if her depression score may be inflated. She may be self-conscious about her performance but it is nonetheless a good performance. Her behavior in this area is so much at variance with her view of herself that I'm surprised she has apparently been able to discount it.

Second, despite her psychological problems, she has been able to create and sustain an eight-year marriage to a professional man. This is more impressive than it may appear initially. About half of all marriages end in divorce, often within the first five years. Nancy does not want a divorce, which can be seen as reflective of strong values. In addition, women of low self-esteem often marry abusive men or men of lower social standing than themselves. Nancy appears to have married a man that, for all his faults, she describes as " . . . really kind and generous and attentive . . . " The more negative qualities she sees in him (e.g., he is "lazy and extremely critical . . . " and "stilted and . . . too much of a stuffed shirt") may either reflect her view of herself or represent relatively minor flaws that may be amenable to change or reframing. There is no hint that he is abusive or treats her badly in other ways. Her perfectionism may cause her to view an admittedly imperfect marriage too negatively. But all marriages are imperfect as are the people who inhabit them.

Third, Nancy has sought therapy on her own and appears motivated, despite her hopelessness. Motivation is a major variable affecting the process and outcome of psychotherapy. Therefore, as a result of this motivation Nancy would probably be a 'good client', adhering well to the suggestions of the therapist.

(12) *How would you address limits, boundaries, and limit setting with this patient?*

Because Nancy tends to be interpersonally dependent and has a very limited social network, it will be important for the therapist to immediately set the boundary conditions of the therapeutic situation. These should include, at a minimum, a regular schedule of appointments that should begin and end on time and not be changed except in a real emergency. The therapist should discourage (probably prohibit) Nancy from calling between sessions, either at the office or (especially) at home. Emergencies should be handled by standard office procedures for that purpose.

Sessions should ideally begin with a mood check and a (brief) recount of important events since the last session related to the therapy. Special care should be taken to see that Nancy does not become overly elaborate or extended in recounting these events, since they will detract from the therapeutic work. It is important initially that Nancy be given time to "tell her story," but this time should become less frequent as therapy progresses. The major therapeutic work should consist of behavioral assignments and discussion of and reflection upon these. I think it will be important to keep Nancy "on track" and focussed.

Nancy has a variety of concerns and may wish to talk about them all at one time. It will be important to help her prioritize and to work on those concerns that she and the therapist together identify as preeminent.

(13)   *Would you want to involve significant others in the treatment? Would you use out-of-session work (homework) with this patient? What homework would you use?*

It may be important to involve Nancy's husband in the therapy for several reasons. First, a major source of her distress is with her marriage. Second, he is in a position to sabotage the therapeutic work if he wishes to, so enlisting his support early on may be important. Third, it may be helpful for a thorough and complete case formulation to obtain the husband's view of the situation. All the case information so far is from Nancy and, since she is depressed, her perspective may be distorted.

Eventually, if marital therapy is to be pursued as a more distal goal, Nancy's husband will need to be involved. If he is included early on as a participant whose views are respected, it is possible that he may be a more willing partner in marital therapy later than he proved to be the first time. It is not possible to determine this from the case description, but it may be that he refused to participate earlier because he thought that he was seen as the source of Nancy's problems and would be made the scapegoat.

Homework would be important in Nancy's treatment. This should include participation in one or more current pleasurable activities as identified by Nancy and the therapist. An increase in the number of Nancy's social contacts should also be encouraged as homework. This initially should include more activities, initiated by Nancy, with her sister and also with current friends whom she now rarely sees. It should be broadened eventually to include provision for activities with new sources of social reinforcement. It may also be helpful for the therapist to foster more shared and pleasurable activities between Nancy and her husband between sessions. Later, encouragement for Nancy to join a social support group of women might be helpful. But following from the behavioral model, an increase of a variety of pleasurable activities between sessions is of paramount importance and is considered to be a major source of therapeutic gain. The sessions themselves are devoted to planning these activities and reflecting upon the meaning of those activities in which the client has already engaged.

(14)   *What would be the issues to be addressed in termination? How would termination and relapse prevention be structured?*

The behavioral model stressed a gradual phase-out of therapy as an aid to proper termination. Thus, the frequency of Nancy's sessions might move from two or three times weekly to once weekly to once every two weeks to once a month. In addition, termination should be discussed early in therapy in light of the goals agreed upon at first. Assuming that progress checks are made regularly (e.g., BDI scores each session), termination should happen naturally as the goals are reached. The major issue to be addressed in behavior therapy termination is attainment of the goals.

Relapse prevention is structured in general by this provision for attenuation of therapy coupled with subsequent "booster sessions" as needed. These sessions may be on an *ad hoc* basis to address issues that arise in the client's life that do not require continuous therapy. Indeed, provision for booster sessions may reduce or eliminate the necessity of continuous therapy. Relapse prevention for Nancy may be accomplished by the provision of greater social supports in her life. These can come from a variety of sources including more frequent contact with her current friends and her sister, regular contact with new friends, a social support group (some of these members may become new friends for Nancy), and her husband. It does not appear that she is likely to obtain more social support from her parents, since they appear to have actually fostered her depression. As noted earlier, social support is an important buffering agent between stress and depression. Pengilly and Dowd (1997) found that social support acted as a buffer between stress and depression. Those college students who had good social support did not become depressed if they were subjected to more stress whereas students who had poor social support did become depressed.

(15)   *What do you see as the hoped-for mechanisms of change for this patient, in order of importance?*

This is always a difficult issue to address because human psychological and behavioral change is interactional in nature, not linear. That is, behavior, cognition, affect, and the environment all interact together to cause change and it is difficult to determine which causes which. Nevertheless, I have argued elsewhere (Dowd, 1997) that, while all three human aspects (behavior, affect, cognition) influence each other in a reciprocal fashion, behavior change holds ultimate primacy. For if we change our behavior, we are more likely to reflect upon the meaning of this behavior change and subsequently change our thoughts and feelings. It is not that cognition cannot also be a first cause (though I doubt that emotion can); it is simply that it is ultimately less powerful. Behavior change is the most important mechanism for change followed by cognitive change. I view emotional, or affective, change as an epiphenomenon only; a combination of behavior and cognition (Schacter & Singer, 1962). Therefore, if Nancy's behavior changes, it is likely that her thoughts and feelings will too. Once the cycle has begun, however, each influences the other in an increasingly adaptive interactional cycle. Nancy's situation thus far has been characterized by the reverse; a maladaptive interactional cycle.

The role of the environment is important in fostering behavior change. For in the end, it is the environment that channels and constrains our behavior. Certainly Nancy's environment has influenced her behavior and therefore her thoughts and feelings. But the reverse is also true. Nancy's behavior has likely influenced her environment. For example, if she behaves in a negative way toward her significant others, she is likely to elicit as a result negative behavior from them—and ultimately perhaps distancing behavior in the form of a withdrawal from further contact (Coyne, 1976a). This is how the impoverishment of social reinforcement begins that is the hallmark of the behavioral analysis of depression. It is the task of the behavior therapist to enhance and deepen the supply of reinforcement and to insure its maintenance.

REFERENCES

Andrews, G., & Harvey, R. (1981). Does psychotherapy benefit neurotic patients? *Archives of General Psychiatry, 38,* 1203.

Bandura, A. (1978). The self-system in reciprocal determinism. *American Psychologist, 33,* 344–358.

Bellack, A. S., & Morrison, R. L. (1982). Interpersonal dysfunction. In A. S. Bellack, M. Hersen, & A. E. Kazdin (Eds.), *International handbook of behavior modification and therapy* (pp. 717–748). New York: Plenum.

Blatt, S. J., Zuroff, D. C., Quinlan, D. M., & Pilkonis, P. A. (1996). Interpersonal factors in brief treatment of depression: Further analyses of the National Institute of Mental Health Treatment of Depression collaborative research program. *Journal of Consulting and Clinical Psychology, 64,* 162–171.

Carson, T. P., & Adams, H. E. (1981). Affective disorders: Behavioral perspectives. In S. M. Turner, K. S. Calhoun, & H. E. Adams (Eds.), *Handbook of clinical behavior therapy* (pp. 125–161). New York: Wiley.

Coyne, J. C. (1976a). Toward an interactional theory of depression. *Psychiatry, 39,* 28–40.

Coyne, J. C. (1976b). Depression and the response of others. *Journal of Abnormal Psychology, 85,* 186–193.

Cuijpers, P. (1998). A psychoeducational approach to the treatment of depression: A meta-analysis of Lewinsohn's "Coping with depression" course. *Behavior Therapy, 29,* 521–533.

Dowd, E. T. (1997). *A cognitive reaction: Adlerian Psychology, Cognitive (Behavioral) Therapy, and Constructivistic Psychotherapy. Journal of Cognitive Psychotherapy: An International Quarterly, 11,* 215–219.

Dowd, E. T., & Courchaine, K. E. (1996). Implicit learning, tacit knowledge, and implications for stasis and change in cognitive psychotherapy. *Journal of Cognitive Psychotherapy: An International Quarterly, 10,* 163–180.

Elkin, I., Shea, M. T., Watkins, J. T., Imber, S. D., Sotsky, S. S., Collins, J. F., Glass, D. R., Pilkonis, P. A., Leber, W. R., Docherty, J. P., Fiester, S. J., & Parloff, M. B. (1989). National Institute of Mental Health treatment of depression collaborative research program: General effectiveness of treatments. *Archives of General Psychiatry, 46,* 971–982.

Ferster, C. B. (1973). A functional analysis of depression. *American Psychologist, 28,* 857–870.

Follette, W. C., Naugle, A. E., & Callaghan, G. M. (1996). A radical behavioral understanding of the therapeutic relationship in effecting change. *Behavior Therapy, 27,* 623–641.

Giles, T. R. (1983). Probable superiority of behavioral interventions: 2. Empirical status of the equivalence of therapies hypothesis. *Journal of Behavior Therapy and Experimental Psychiatry, 14,* 189.

Hobbs, N. (1962). Sources of gain in psychotherapy. *American Psychologist, 17,* 741–747.

Jacobson, N. S., & Margolin, G. (1979). *Marital therapy: Strategies based on social learning and behavior exchange principles.* New York: Brunner/Mazel.

Jacobson, N. S., Dobson, K. S., Truax, P. A., Addis, M. E., Koerner, K., Gollan, J. K., Gortner, E., & Prince, S. E. (1996). A component analysis of cognitive-behavioral treatment for depression. *Journal of Consulting and Clinical Psychology, 64,* 295–304.

Joiner, T. E. (1994). Contagious depression: Existence, specificity to depressed symptoms, and the role of reassurance seeking. *Journal of Personality and Social Psychology, 67,* 287–296.

Joiner, T. E. (1997). Shyness and low social support as interactive diatheses, with loneliness as mediator: Testing an interpersonal-personality view of vulnerability to depressive symptoms. *Journal of Abnormal Psychology, 106,* 386–394.

Joiner, T. E., Alfano, M. S., & Metalsky, G. I. (1992). When depression breeds contempt: Reassurance seeking, self-esteem, and rejection of depressed college students by their roommates. *Journal of Abnormal Psychology, 101,* 165–173.

Joiner, T. E., Alfano, M. S., & Metalsky, G. I. (1993). Caught in the crossfire: Depression, self-consistency, self-enhancement, and the response of others. *Journal of Social and Clinical Psychology, 12,* 113–134.

Kahnemann, D., & Tversky, A. (1973). On the psychology of prediction. *Psychological Review, 81,* 237–251.

Lazarus, A. A. (1985). *Marital myths.* San Luis Obispo, CA: Impact Publishers.

Lewinsohn, P. M., Biglan, A., & Zeiss, A. M. (1976). Behavioral treatment of depression. In P. O. Davidson (Ed.), *The behavioral management of anxiety, depression, and pain.* New York: Brunner/Mazel.

Lewinsohn, P. M., Antonuccio, D. O, Breckenridge, J., & Teri, L. (1987). *The coping with depression course: A psycho educational intervention for unipolar depression.* Eugene, OR: Castalia.

Lichtenberg, P. A., Kimbarow, M. L., Morris, P., & Vangel, S. J. (1996). Behavioral treatment of depression in predominantly African-American medical patients. *Clinical Gerontologist, 17,* 15–33.

Miner, R. C., & Dowd, E. T. (1996). An empirical test of the problem solving model of depression and its extension to the prediction of anxiety and anger. *Counselling Psychology Quarterly, 9,* 163–176.

Nezu, C. M., & Nezu, A. M. (1995). Clinical decision making in everyday practice: The science in the art. *Cognitive and Behavioral Practice, 2,* 5–25.

Pengilly, J. W., & Dowd, E. T. (1997). *Hardiness and social support as moderators of stress in college students.* Paper presented at the annual meeting of the Association for Advancement of Behavior Therapy, Miami Beach.

Potthoff, J. G., Holahan, C. J., & Joiner, T. E. (1995). Reassurance seeking, stress generation, and depressive symptoms: An integrative model. *Journal of Personality and Social Psychology, 68,* 664–670.

Rehm, L. P., & Tyndall, C. I. (1993). Mood disorders: Unipolar and bipolar. In P. B. Sutker & H. E. Adams (Eds.), *Handbook of psychopathology* (pp. 235–262). New York: Plenum.

Robinson, L. A., Berman, J. S., & Neimeyer, R. A. (1990). Psychotherapy for the treatment of depression: A comprehensive review of controlled outcome studies. *Psychological Bulletin, 108,* 30–49.

Schacter, S., & Singer, J. (1962). Cognitive, social, and physiological determinants of emotional state. *Psychological Review, 69,* 379–397.

Seligman, M. E. P., Klein, D. C., & Miller, W. R. (1976). Depression. In H. Leitenberg (Ed.), *Handbook of behavior modification and therapy* (pp. 168–210). Englewood Cliffs, NJ: Prentice-Hall.

Shaw, B. F. (1977). Comparison of cognitive therapy and behavior therapy in the treatment of depression. *Journal of Consulting and Clinical Psychology, 45,* 543–551.

Sloane, R. B., Staples, F. R., Cristol, A. H., Yorkston, N. J., & Whipple, K. (1975). *Psychotherapy versus behavior therapy.* Cambridge, MA: Harvard University Press.

Smith, M. L., & Glass, G. V. (1977). Meta-analysis of psychotherapy outcome studies. *American Psychologist, 32,* 752.

Spanier, G. B. (1976). Measuring dyadic adjustment: New scales for assessing the quality of marriage and similar dyads. *Journal of Marriage and the Family, 38,* 15–28.

Spiegler, M. D., & Guevremont, D. C. (1993). *Contemporary behavior therapy.* Pacific Grove, CA: Brooks/Cole.

Tanaka-Matsumi, J., Seiden, D. Y., & Lam, K. N. (1996). The culturally informed functional assessment (CIFA) interview: A strategy for cross-cultural behavioral practice. *Cognitive and Behavioral Practice, 3,* 215–233.

Turner, R., & Wehl, C. (1984). Treatment of unipolar depression in problem drinkers. *Advances in Behaviour Research & Therapy, 6,* 115–125.

Turner, R. W., Ward, M. F., & Turner, D. J. (1979). Behavioral treatment for depression: An evaluation of therapeutic components. *Journal of Clinical Psychology,* 166–175.

Wolpe, J. (1990). *The practice of behavior therapy* (4th ed.). New York: Pergamon.

Zeiss, A. M., Lewinsohn, P. M., & Munoz, R. (1979). Nonspecific improvement events in depression using interpersonal, cognitive, and pleasant events focused treatments. *Journal of Consulting and Clinical Psychology, 47,* 427–439.

10

Rational Emotive Behavior Therapy for Depression: Achieving Unconditional Self-Acceptance

Raymond DiGiuseppe, Kristene A. Doyle, and Raphael D. Rose

1. THEORETICAL ORIENTATION

Background of the Approach

In 1947 Albert Ellis began his career as a classically trained psychoanalyst. As a result of his dissatisfaction with the analytic approach due, among other reasons, to his interest in efficiency, Ellis adapted his therapeutic approach and became "one of the most active directive psychoanalytically oriented psychotherapists in the field" (Ellis, 1994, p. 5). What is called rational emotive behavior therapy (REBT) today began as rational therapy in the early 1950s. In 1955 Ellis formally combined principles of Greek and Roman Stoicism with behavior therapy and coined the term rational emotive therapy (RET). Whereas Ellis has always incorporated behavioral techniques into the practice of RET, the name was later changed to rational emotive behavior therapy

(REBT) to emphasize a formal acknowledgment of the use of behavioral procedures. Presently, REBT is practiced by cognitive-behavioral therapists throughout the world.

Basic Concepts of the Model

Rational emotive behavior therapy (REBT) postulates that humans have innate tendencies to be both rational or self-helping, and irrational or self-defeating. Furthermore, Ellis asserts that all humans learn both self-preserving and self-destructive thoughts, feelings, and behaviors. Illogical, absolutistic, falsely generalized thinking is associated with the development of self-defeating emotions; whereas logical, flexible, empirically-validated thinking generates self-enhancing emotions. REBT is based upon an assumption that thoughts, emotions, and behaviors are not independent entities, but function as an integrated, adaptive system (Ellis, 1994). REBT focuses on teaching clients strategies to control dysfunctional *emotions*, such as anger, depression, anxiety, and guilt. We outline and follow an "ABC" model of emotional disturbance during sessions in a structured format that clients learn to apply in their daily lives. Specifically, the REBT model proposes that **A**ctivating events elicit the client's **B**eliefs about those events and generate the emotional and behavioral **C**onsequences. Clients commonly believe that the Activating event (e.g., a delayed train, an insulting boss, or an obsessive thought) causes the disturbed emotional and behavioral Consequence. To correct this misconception, therapy begins by educating clients on the relationship between their **B** (beliefs) and **C** (emotional/behavioral consequences). The **A** (activating event) to **C** (emotional/behavioral consequences) connection is, as a result, dispelled.

The alleviation of Nancy's emotional disturbances will occur through (a) acknowledging that her emotions and behavior are dysfunctional, (b) identifying specific irrational beliefs, (c) recognizing that these irrational beliefs are illogical and maladaptive, and (d) replacing these dysfunctional cognitions with more adaptive, rational beliefs. Within the framework of the REBT model, clients first describe and acknowledge unhealthy negative feelings and self-defeating behaviors. An REBT therapist would socratically elicit Nancy's recognition that her depression and anxiety are dysfunctional in that they impede her from achieving her long-term goals. The therapist would also elicit from Nancy the recognition that "beating herself up" and isolating herself from others are self-defeating behaviors. The therapist would then ask Nancy to identify specific activating events that occurred before she experiences her feelings of depression.

REBT postulates that *demandingness* cognitions are the primary mediators of emotional disturbance. These include the "musts," "shoulds," "oughts," and "have to's" that commonly comprise our beliefs. Such beliefs are based upon dogmatic, rigidly held schema that the world *must* be how one *wants* it be. An REBT therapist would contrast these irrational beliefs with rational beliefs, such as *preferences*. Such beliefs acknowledge how one *wants* or *desires* the world to be, yet recognize that the universe has no obligation to comply with such desires. REBT postulates that other cognitions associated with psychopathology stem from these "demanding" beliefs. Other cognitions, including *global evaluations of human worth* involving the belief that oneself or others are worthless, also mediate emotional disturbance. The rational alternative belief maintains we can neither calculate nor equate human worth with one's global evaluation. It assumes that all people have equal worth, despite their desirable or undesirable behaviors. REBT teaches clients to achieve unconditional self-acceptance (USA), rather than hold the irrational belief that they are worthless for engaging in undesirable behaviors, failing at a task, or having an imperfection. USA maintains that one accept oneself despite having undesirable traits or behaviors. In a similar vein, *frustration intolerance* involves the belief that one does not have the endurance to suffer frustration and that one should not have to experience frustration. REBT postulates that most humans can tolerate more than they believe they can, and that one's level of frustration tolerance is self-defined. Related constructs include *awfulizing or catastrophizing*, which involve exaggerated negative evaluations of events. Awfulizing is associated with beliefs that events are entirely unacceptable or bad. REBT proposes that a goal for the therapist is to teach clients to actively challenge and replace their irrational beliefs with more rational alternatives, and to replace maladaptive behaviors with more adaptive ones.

Etiology of Depression

Ellis (1975) proposed that anxiety and depression are largely the result of absolutistic *must*urbation. According to this model, when individuals prefer, wish, or desire to accomplish particular goals (e.g., successful career, relationship, etc.) but fail to achieve such goals, such individuals will most likely experience sadness and regret, but *not* clinical depression. When individuals escalate their preferences into dogmatic demands, and convince themselves that they *absolutely should, must,* and *ought* (always) achieve their goals, they render themselves vulnerable to depression. This hypothesis is supported by research indicating relationships between severity of depression and the endorsement of irrational beliefs (Bernard, 1998; McDermut, Haaga, & Bilek, 1997; Solomon, Haaga, Brody, Kirk, & Friedman, 1998). Although it is possible that individuals may become depressed if they rigidly maintain strong preferences but do not manifest dogmatic demands, the likelihood of this occurring is believed to be small. Rather, such individuals are likely to experience feelings of disappointment and sadness (Ellis, 1987a).

Both Beck (1967, 1976) and Ellis (1962, 1971, 1973) assert that a principal element in clinical depression is self-criticism or feelings of worthlessness. Depressed individuals may believe, for example, that "I am not in control of my life the way I would like to be, and others around me are more in control of their lives." While unfortunate, this does not logically imply that "I *must* be more in control of my life." REBT proposes that unless depressed individuals challenge their unconditional *demand* that they be *must* be effective in controlling their lives, they will continue to conclude that they are worthless and experience feelings of depression. According to this model, it is when people assume that they must be perfect and in complete control of events that the "damnation of deeds and traits and themselves" occurs (Ellis, 1987a).

Negative thoughts about oneself, one's environment, and one's future result in feelings of sadness and disappointment. However, it is postulated that only when *absolutistic demands* that bad traits, an unpleasant environment, and a negative future *must not* exist will clinical depression ensue. Depression occurs when one "magically leaps" from describing one's reality as negative to refusing to acknowledge it and insisting that it be different. Ellis (1987a) postulates that individuals tend to draw conclusions based upon their beliefs. Individuals who dogmatically insist that (1) they be competent, comfortable, or safe, (2) others love them, or (3) that they are not achieving important goals and will not achieve such goals in the future, may be vulnerable to feelings of depression. They may conclude that: (1) "The poor results and discomforts I am experiencing (as I *must* not) are totally bad or more than bad (i.e., awful);" (2) "I cannot live with such horrible conditions (which *must* not exist) and be happy at all;" (3) "I am an undeserving, worthless person for not being (as I *must* be) able to do better and arrange more favorable living conditions;" (4) "I cannot control things (as I *should*) and be a worthwhile person who leads a happy life;" and (5) "I *should* not be as depressed and anxious as I am, and that proves that I am no good and that I cannot lead a satisfactory existence!" (Ellis, 1987a, p. 126).

Nancy appears to hold several dogmatic beliefs, including "others must approve of me, and if they do not, it is awful!" and "I feel I am inept . . . just incompetent (and I *should* be competent). Nancy also appears to believe that she *must* be perfect and that if she is not, it is *awful.* As a consequence, she is self-critical and views herself, in global terms, as a failure. Moreover, her view of her future is "dark and vague." By inference, Nancy may also believe that "her future should be better and that because it is not so, it is awful." A goal of therapy would be to develop Nancy's ability to unconditionally accept herself, *although* she may not be as competent in her relationships or her career as she would prefer.

In summary, REBT proposes that individuals will experience clinical depression when they endorse one or more of the following beliefs: (1) They view themselves negatively and believe that they *must* not have negative attributes and as such are *inadequate persons* when they do hold such attributes; (2) They hold a dark view of their environment and believe that it *must or should* be better and that it is *horrible* if it is not; (3) They predict an unfavorable future and believe that it *should* be more favorable and that they *cannot stand it* if it is not; (4) They give themselves low rates of self-reinforcement and high rates of self-punishment and believe that they *must* do better and *must* receive approval by significant others or else they do not deserve greater rewards and *should* repent for such inadequacies by greater self-punishment; (5) They continue to encounter a lack of pleasurable events and steadfastly believe that people and life *must* treat them better and it is *horrible* if they do not; (6) They anticipate negative things will happen, predict that they can do little to improve them, attribute this inability to themselves, believe that they *should* improve such conditions, and believe that they are *incompetent* when they fail to do so (Ellis, 1987a).

From this perspective, individuals who can accept events and attributes, no matter how negative, will experience natural feelings of disappointment and frustration, but will rarely manifest clinical depression. It is the process of not accepting oneself, and demanding that bad things not happen, that results in clinical depression. The REBT practitioner will encourage depressed clients to make a profound philosophic shift—from nonacceptance and demandingness to acceptance and preference. We emphasize an "anti-musturbatory" belief system. When clients relinquish the demands they place on themselves, others, and the world, change will occur. REBT attempts to teach clients to think more scientifically to prevent and remove the dogmatic, absolutistic thoughts that cause emotional disturbance.

Maintaining Factors

Many individuals with clinical depression "filter out" evidence that is inconsistent with their belief system, resulting in the maintenance of their disturbance. Consequently, Nancy may be selectively attending to incidents and evidence that support her beliefs that "I am a failure" and "I am inept . . . just incompetent." Furthermore, Nancy may be reinforced for her depression via attention from friends and family. An additional maintaining factor is Nancy's avoidance of events she once found pleasurable. By not engaging in pleasurable activities, Nancy's cognitive state of negativity is sustained. Finally, Nancy reports that her prescribed medication (Zoloft) has been unsuccessful in alleviating her feelings of depression. This may contribute to her believing that her dysphoria is untreatable, and so may contribute to the maintenance of her depression. We would suggest a pharmacological consultation to clarify the appropriateness of her medication and dosage.

Mechanisms of Change

Our first goal would be to assist Nancy to understand how her beliefs and thought processes influence her emotional and behavioral well-being, and that she has a *choice* of how she will feel. Nancy would develop rational thinking skills, including the ability to recognize the negative consequences of her demands for perfection and self-criticism, and to rationally evaluate and change these thoughts when in the presence of stimuli that elicit feelings of depression. In addition, Nancy would learn to generate adaptive solutions that will enable her to cope more effectively with emotionally upsetting situations. Social withdrawal and ruminative self-criticism would be discouraged. She would come to see how she perpetuates her depression by not engaging in pleasurable activities.

Finally, Nancy would learn to control upsetting situations by identifying her maladaptive beliefs and attitudes, challenging those beliefs and replacing them with more adaptive beliefs. Using the new skills in her everyday life would enable Nancy to internalize the range of rational beliefs so that they become a part of her general philosophy of life.

2. CRITICAL REVIEW OF EMPIRICAL EVIDENCE

REBT is a form of cognitive behavior therapy (CBT). As Ellis (1985) noted, "more than 200 controlled studies" support the use of REBT and CBT in treating a variety of emotional problems. Engels, Garnefski, and Diekstra (1993) report on REBT's effectiveness, and numerous studies support the efficacy of CBT for the treatment of depression (Beck, 1976; Blackburn & Bishop, 1979; Dobson, 1989; Rush, Beck, Kovacs, & Hollon, 1977). A careful review of REBT outcome studies, however, reveals a number of shortcomings. Few REBT dismantling studies have been completed, and research has not adequately tested the distinctive components of REBT. Rather, most outcome and process studies have used a heterogenous mix of cognitive and behavioral interventions (Gossette & O'Brien, 1992; Haaga & Davison, 1993). In essence, researchers who claim to be conducting REBT research may, in fact, not be; whereas others who do not mention REBT in their treatment protocols appear to be incorporating essential components of REBT (such as direct disputation of irrational or dysfunctional beliefs) in their treatment. These limitations in the outcome literature make it difficult to conclude, at this point, whether REBT offers distinct mechanisms of change as compared to other therapeutic approaches.

In an effort to examine the validity of the REBT model of depression, researchers have reported a connection between measures of depression and endorsement of irrational beliefs (Bernard, 1998; McDermut, Haaga, & Bilek, 1997; Solomon et al., 1998). In addition, numerous anecdotal reports and case studies have been published supporting the effectiveness of REBT for the acute treatment of depressed individuals (Ellis, 1987a, 1987b, 1987c; Young, 1984). In one of the few comparative studies conducted, Lipsky, Kassinove, and Miller (1980) found that REBT was more effective than relaxation training or a no contact control in reducing depressive symptoms in an outpatient population. More recently, Macaskill and Macaskill (1996) examined the effectiveness of medications with and without REBT in treating unipolar depressed adult outpatients. They reported the combined treatment to be significantly more effective than pharmacotherapy alone. Although these findings are promising, they highlight a significant weakness in the REBT literature, the dearth of comparative studies of REBT with other forms of psychotherapy. Although REBT is a form of CBT, and as such may be highly effective in the treatment of depression, future studies should compare it with other forms of therapy (including other forms of cognitive therapy) in order to identify REBT's distinct utility in the treatment of depression.

3. CASE CONCEPTUALIZATION

Nancy manifests both depression and anxiety. Furthermore, she is dependent on others and is quite sensitive to their reactions to her—she may, as a consequence, also meet criteria for dependent personality disorder. Nancy strongly desires social acceptance and attention. Although many people desire social affiliation, Nancy's needs may be excessive in that she becomes disturbed if she believes she is not receiving it. Moreover, she is emotionally labile—only minor hassles elicit strong emotions. In addition, Nancy appears to hold many irrational beliefs. She believes, for example, that she "must not" be alone, others "must" accept her, and she "must not" experience criticism from anyone. She appears to condemn herself for lack of approval by others.

According to Beck (1976), anger and depression are distinct emotions. He proposed that each emotion is elicited by separate and distinct cognitions, and that the thoughts and attitudes which are associated with feelings of depression, hopelessness, and worthlessness are different from those that trigger anger. As a result, we would address Nancy's depression and anger separately and not assume that the same beliefs and dynamics mediate both emotions. We would address her self-deprecation, criticism of others, hopelessness and omnipotent demands that others do as she wants as a means of alleviating her depression.

4. BEGINNING AND FRAMING TREATMENT

A primary goal for therapy is addressing Nancy's suicidal thoughts and plans. One way we would address this would be to develop a Suicide Prevention Agreement with her. Alternative behaviors to hurting oneself (e.g., taking a walk, calling a friend, writing in a journal), and phone numbers to call (e.g., family, friends, hospitals, suicide hotlines) are key components in this contract. We would make a copy for the thera-pist's file, and the original would be given to Nancy to keep. It is worth keeping in mind that although non-suicide agreements are regularly employed by mental health practitioners (Drew, 1999), there is little empirical support for their effectiveness in reducing suicidal behavior (Miller, Jacobs, & Gutheil, 1998).

After completing a Suicide Prevention Agreement, Nancy and her therapist would develop adaptive coping skills to prevent the reemer-gence of her suicidal thoughts. This entails developing alternative, ratio-nal self-statements that clients can rehearse if suicidal ideations reappear. Thoughts such as "I cannot stand this feeling of depression. It's unbearable. My life is hopeless and awful and I can't take it anymore. I'd be better off dead," for example, would be directly confronted. A more rational line of thinking might be: "Although this feeling of depression is uncomfortable, I can tolerate it. As bad as I think my life is now, it could be worse. It could, however, turn around and become better." The client is encouraged to recite this rational coping statement if thoughts of suicide reappear, and engage in the alternative incompati-ble behaviors listed in the Suicide Prevention Agreement.

After Nancy's suicidal thoughts have abated, we will turn our attention to identifying her core irrational beliefs. The identification and rational disputation of these beliefs is a primary goal of therapy. We would elicit these core beliefs through a variety of questions, such as "When you are feeling depressed, what thoughts go through your mind?" Nancy and her therapist would then formulate emotional, behavioral and interpersonal goals. These might include:

(a) Decrease Nancy's experience of depression.
   (1) Decrease social withdrawal and increase socialization.
   (2) Increase participation in pleasurable activities (backpack-ing, talking with her sister) (see Lewinsohn, & Amenson, 1978; Lewinsohn, Sullivan, & Grosscup, 1980).
   (3) Increase frustration tolerance and encourage acceptance of feelings of anxiety, depression, nervousness.
   (4) Encourage Nancy to relinquish demands for perfection.
   (5) Encourage unconditional self-acceptance (USA).
   (6) Improve the quality of Nancy's marital relationship by clari-fying and negotiating her goals for the relationship.

    (a) Become less upset by husband's criticism.

    (b) Negotiating aspects of her relationship with her husband to improve the quality of other interpersonal relationships so they are more rewarding.

(7) Identify and examine triggers for Nancy's anger so she can learn new responses to them. She may benefit from assertion training.

(8) Nancy experiences anxiety in social situations that causes a decrease in her enjoyment of these activities. We would identify the situations where she experiences anxiety, then train her in anxiety management skills.

The secondary goal of therapy involves Nancy replacing dysfunctional negative emotions such as depression, anxiety, and anger with appropriate and adaptive negative emotions, such as disappointment, sadness, and frustration. The inappropriate negative emotion of depression experienced by Nancy that stems from the irrational belief that "I *must* be in a relationship that makes me feel content" would be replaced with the appropriate emotion of disappointment, stemming from the more rational alternative of "I would prefer to be in a relationship that is satisfying, but if I am not, I can find satisfaction in other areas of my life."

Time Line for Therapy

REBT is a brief, problem-focused form of therapy. Based on two samples of more than 700 outpatients seen through the Albert Ellis Institute, we have found that patients receive an average of eleven sessions. Given the severity of Nancy's feelings of depression, anxiety, and worthlessness, and the relatively large number of problems targeted, we would anticipate that her course of treatment would be somewhat longer. We expect that at least 25 sessions with Nancy would be required to attain the goals mentioned above. A goal of therapy for Nancy is achieving unconditional self-acceptance (USA). Our experience suggests that achievement of USA is a difficult, though possible task that requires time and commitment in therapy.

As noted, our first goal would be to alleviate Nancy's suicidal thoughts. We would work to alleviate or significantly reduce her feelings of depression and anxiety through active disputation of irrational thoughts in conjunction with an increase in pleasurable events. Assisting Nancy in increasing her frustration tolerance for being alone would be an important step in therapy. Long-term change would require that Nancy learn active coping strategies to deal with the emotions elicited by being alone, rejected, and criticized. This would allow her to function more adaptively in the face of such circumstances, and would serve to prevent a relapse.

5. TREATMENT

To ensure that therapists include the essential components of the ABC model in an REBT session, Dryden and DiGiuseppe (1992) identified thirteen steps for therapists to follow. They recommend that novice REBT therapists employ the steps as outlined in Table 10.1 to avoid common mistakes. Step one of the treatment model involves asking clients what problems they wish to discuss during the session. Step two is agreement between the therapist and client regarding the session goal. Clients often come to therapy with a topic unrelated to the previous session, and choose that as the target problem for focus. However,

TABLE 10.1   The Thirteen Steps of REBT

Step 1:	Ask the client for the problem.
Step 2:	Define and agree upon the Goals of Therapy.
Step 3:	Assess the emotional and behavioral "C".
Step 4:	Assess the "A".
Step 5:	Assess the existence of any Secondary Emotional Problems.
Step 6:	Teach the B → C connection.
Step 7:	Assess the Irrational Beliefs.
Step 8:	Connect the Irrational Beliefs to the Disturbed Emotions and the Rational Beliefs to the Non-disturbed Emotion.
Step 9:	Dispute Irrational Beliefs: Circle all that you have done: logical, empirical, heuristic, design new rational alternative beliefs, didactic, Socratic, metaphorical, humorous.
Step 10:	Prepare your client to deepen his/her conviction in the Rational Belief.
Step 11:	Encourage your client to put new learning into practice with homework.
Step 12:	Check homework assignments.
Step 13:	Facilitate the working through process.

therapists may believe that continuing with ongoing topics before shifting to a new topic is preferable. It is important, as such, that client and therapist agree on the target problem before continuing. Arriving at a mutual understanding of the client's problem strengthens the therapeutic alliance. Clients often identify the goal as changing the "A" or activating event. However, REBT recommends that clients focus on overcoming their emotional difficulties, and as a result, therapists typically prefer to change the "C" or emotional consequences of some activating event.

Steps three, four, and five involve assessment of the "Cs," "As," and secondary emotional disturbances, respectively. Clients often present with secondary emotional disturbance about primary emotional problems. REBT posits that clients will improve more rapidly if the secondary disturbance is addressed first. To decide if Nancy does have secondary emotional disturbance about her depression, the therapist might ask, "How do you feel about feeling depressed?" Step six involves teaching clients the "B → C" connection. This involves the notion that one's emotional disturbance results from irrational beliefs or disordered ways of thinking about the activating event, rather than the activating event itself. Dryden and DiGiuseppe (1992) regard this step as crucial. If clients do not accept that their emotional upset results from their beliefs, they will not understand the purpose of your assessment of their beliefs during the treatment process.

Step seven requires therapists to assess clients' irrational beliefs. Walen, DiGiuseppe, and Dryden (1992) defined irrational beliefs as thoughts that are logically incorrect, inconsistent with empirical reality, or inconsistent with one's long-term goals. They involve tacit, unconscious, schematic cognitions. Although they are not experienced in one's stream of consciousness, they are potentially available to awareness. As a first step in assessing the client's irrational beliefs, many therapists will ask, "What were you thinking when you got upset?" However, this form of questioning elicits automatic thoughts, and does not elicit tacit irrational beliefs per se.

Automatic thoughts are inferences that individuals draw from the perceptions they make based upon the irrational beliefs they hold. DiGiuseppe (1991a) has suggested the strategy of "inference chaining" to reveal clients' irrational beliefs. By following the logic of the inferences, therapists can uncover the core irrational belief(s) of their clients. Essentially, inference chaining involves several follow-up questions to the automatic thoughts clients experience in emotionally upsetting situations. Therapists hypothetically posit the client's inference and then ask the client what it would mean if the inference were true. The therapist repeats this strategy until an irrational belief appears as a "must," (e.g., I must get what I want all the time), an "awfulizing" statement, (e.g., "If things do not go my way it would be *awful*"), and "I cannot stand it," (e.g., "I cannot stand the idea of my partner not loving me") or we uncover a global evaluation (e.g., "I am a loser") (Walen, DiGiuseppe, & Dryden, 1992). This process is similar, in some ways, to the "downward arrow" procedure used in Cognitive Therapy.

People do not store tacit, schematic cognitions in verbal memory. As a result, clients may have trouble expressing their irrational beliefs in language. In response to this, DiGiuseppe (1991a) suggested that therapists develop and offer hypotheses about their clients' irrational beliefs. To do this effectively and avoid one's own confirmatory bias, DiGiuseppe suggests that therapists: (a) state the hypothesis in suppositional language; (b) ask clients for thoughts about the correctness of hypotheses; (c) prepare to be wrong; and (d) revise the hypotheses based on negative feedback from the client.

ASSESSMENT

Further clarification of Nancy's anxiety and its effects on her experience of pleasure would be collected. Specifically, the therapist would address the question of whether or not anxiety inhibits the experience of pleasure. If this were the case, we would teach specific skills such as relaxation training and breathing exercises to reduce anxiety and help Nancy to experience pleasure. Further exploration of any family history of mental illness and Nancy's medical history would be useful in developing a treatment plan. Ruling out symptoms of endogenous depression would be a priority.

The most important information, however, would be the thoughts Nancy experiences *just before* her episodes of depression and anxiety. We would ask her what thoughts she was experiencing at these times and then would employ the inference chaining strategy mentioned above. If this technique failed, we would generate several hypotheses concerning what she was thinking based on the material presented, clinical experience, and the theory. The therapist might offer to Nancy the hypothesis that she experiences low frustration tolerance for negative emotions and believes that she cannot cope with intense negative emotions. Identification of Nancy's irrational beliefs would include her keeping a log of her thoughts during each emotional episode of depression and anxiety.

Instruments, Questionnaires, and Observations

As Nancy has a long history of depression, we would administer the MCMI-3 (Craig, 1994) or another objective measure for assessing the presence or absence of personality disorders. In addition to the measures reported in the case study, we might also ask Nancy to complete a self-report measure of irrational beliefs, such as the Irrational Beliefs Test (Jones, 1968) as an index of possible core irrational beliefs. An assertiveness scale, such as the Rathus Assertiveness Schedule (Rathus, 1973), would also be used. Finally, Nancy would be asked to complete an Idiosyncratic Schema Sheet (Linscott & DiGiuseppe, 1998) as a measure of her depressive and anxious episodes. This measure assesses activating events, irrational beliefs, emotions and behaviors, as well as new alternative rational belief(s) and the new desired emotions and behaviors. The idiosyncratic schema sheet contains ten Likert scales items for each scenario. Clients indicate their commitment to accompanying beliefs. Nancy would complete the scale at the beginning of each therapy session to monitor progress. Appendix 1 presents an example of a scenario based measure we would use to monitor changes in Nancy's beliefs.

SPECIFIC INTERVENTIONS

The next two steps involve linking the irrational beliefs with the client's emotional disturbance (step 8), and beginning to challenge the irrational beliefs (step 9). We regard step nine as the most difficult element of the REBT treatment model. One can dispute an irrational belief by challenging its logic (e.g., "Where is the logic?"), by testing its empirical accuracy (e.g., "Where is the evidence for your belief?"), and by evaluating its functional consequences (e.g., "How is your belief helping you? How is it hurting you?"). Therapists may also suggest alternative rational beliefs (RB) and challenge them with the same arguments to assess if the RB fares any better. DiGiuseppe (1991b) suggested that therapists vary their rhetorical style and use Socratic, didactic, metaphors, and humorous forms of disputation. REBT therapists prefer the use of the Socratic style of disputing. This involves asking questions regarding the illogical, inconsistent, and dysfunctional nature of the client's irrational beliefs. This form of disputing allows clients to evaluate the question for themselves. The didactic style involves giving clients explanations concerning why their irrational beliefs are self-defeating and how the rational alternatives are more productive. A humorous style can also prove effective in helping clients relinquish their irrational beliefs. Clients benefit most from humorous disputing when a good therapeutic relationship exists and they have displayed a sense of humor. It is important to keep in mind that humorous exaggeration should be directed toward the irrationality of the client's *belief* and not the *client* (Dryden & DiGiuseppe, 1990). Finally, therapists can employ metaphors as a disputation strategy (Muran & DiGiuseppe, 1990).

Kopec, Beal, and DiGiuseppe (1994) have created a grid with each cell representing a type of argument and a type of rhetorical style. They recommend that therapists identify an irrational belief and generate disputing statements for each cell in the grid before each therapy session. Their data suggest that this activity increased trainees' self-efficacy in disputing. Another important component of disputing is the use of imagery. Together, therapists and clients can construct scenes of the client approaching a particular activating event, rehearsing the new rational coping statement, experiencing adaptive emotions, and behaving appropriately.

Step ten involves deepening clients' convictions in their new rational beliefs. We accomplish this through continued disputation, defining how clients would behave differently if they held the new rational belief (step 11), and by agreeing to complete homework between sessions to achieve their goals (step 12). Dryden and DiGiuseppe (1992) regard homework assignments as an important element in REBT as they enable clients to put new learning into practice. REBT self-help homework sheets, for example, can aid clients in learning to dispute irrational beliefs. Finally, we may assign a behavioral activity, such as a "shame-attack." Shame-attack assignments teach clients that by doing a "dreaded" act in public, their world will not end and they need not denigrate themselves (Walen, DiGiuseppe, & Dryden, 1992). To increase homework compliance, therapist and client should negotiate the task together. In the final step (13), therapists review other examples of activating events clients have been upset about to promote generalization.

THE PATIENT'S STRENGTHS

We regard Nancy's self-referral for therapy as a strength. The fact that she initiated therapy without her husband or another family member's pressure suggests that she may be seeking treatment for her own discomfort, rather than to gain approval from significant others. Her self-referral suggests that she is in a "contemplative" stage of change. If and when progress is slow or resistance is encountered, the therapist can discuss Nancy's initiation of therapy. We would ask Nancy to recall the reasons she entered therapy, and would review with her the consequences of not continuing in treatment. Finally, her desire to please others and gain approval may lead Nancy to seek approval from her therapist. The therapist could use this "need" to influence Nancy to complete her homework assignments and follow through on predetermined treatment goals.

THERAPEUTIC TECHNIQUES

Preferential REBT strategies (philosophical changes) play a central role in REBT. Ellis (1994) identified preferential REBT as interventions focused at the core philosophical beliefs. An elegant solution to the client's problem involves replacing their demanding philosophy with a preferential one. That is, helping the client to recognize that the world does not have to give one what one prefers. This strategy entails helping Nancy to observe her own psychological disturbances and trace them back to their ideological, emotional and behavioral roots. In using this strategy, we would stress to Nancy that she is not "enslaved" or controlled by her biologically-based and learned dysfunctional thinking processes. This is important for Nancy as she strongly believes that she cannot handle events in her life and that she never learned problem-solving as a child. This strategy employs cognitive, emotive, and behavioral methods that the therapist vigorously applies. The forceful nature of REBT may be especially important in Nancy's case given her tendency to think that she is unable to control aspects of her life, including her emotions. In addition, we would employ a technique known as Cognitive-DIBS (Disputing Irrational Beliefs) (Ellis, 1974; Walen, DiGiuseppe, & Dryden, 1992, p. 159). This technique involves detecting irrational beliefs, debating irrational beliefs by asking for "proof" or "evidence," and discriminating between nonabsolute values and absolutistic values held by the client. Because preferential REBT techniques do not work for every client, Nancy may not achieve a philosophical change. If it becomes apparent to the therapist that a philosophical change will not occur, the therapist would employ other techniques used in CBT to challenge Nancy's inferential or automatic thoughts.

Nancy's husband Steve's apparent lack of interest in counseling suggests that he would not attend sessions in the beginning stages of therapy. Until Nancy's assertiveness skills are developed, inviting Steve into therapy may prove to be more of an obstacle than an advantage. However, as Nancy's irrational beliefs are replaced and her assertion skills improve, Steve's participation in therapy may be quite rewarding for Nancy. We may invite him to some sessions to discuss his perception of the marriage and to gauge his commitment to making the marriage work. Effective therapy requires an optimal level of arousal for the client. Involving her husband may provide an awareness of the destructive nature of her depression and its effects on others. This may serve to further increase her motivation for change.

Nancy would benefit from out-of-session homework assignments that serve to deepen her conviction in rational alternative beliefs. We would pursue bibliotherapy as a first course of action. Self-help books on depression would be recommended, including, *Overcoming Depression* (Hauck, 1976), *Feeling Good* (Burns, 1980), or *The Feeling Good Handbook* (Burns, 1999). It has been reported that homework compliance positively affects treatment outcome (see Ellis, 1973; Leung & Heimberg, 1996; Detweiler & Whisman, 1999). Rose, Terjesen, DiGiuseppe, and Ellis (1999) stated that clients' participation in formulating their homework increases their compliance with the assignment, and consequently, Nancy would play an active role in choosing weekly homework. An important byproduct of successful completion of homework is that Nancy will begin to generalize the gains she makes to other areas of her life that share the same underlying belief (e.g., I'm worthless).

Nancy would be taught how to use REBT self-help forms and asked to complete them after emotionally upsetting events. The use of forms helps clients gain practice in identifying and disputing irrational beliefs about upsetting events. Although clients new to REBT may have difficulty completing such forms, they can master them over time. We would also ask Nancy to engage in activities that she enjoys on a more regular basis, and would encourage her to practice rational-emotive imagery (REI) as homework. Because Nancy makes herself depressed by reflecting on her marital difficulties, we would develop imagery assignments using her marriage as an activating event. After constructing rational coping statements, we would ask Nancy to imagine events that provoke feelings of depression and anxiety while thinking of the coping statements. Nancy would be given a variety of assignments where she actively rehearsed more adaptive beliefs, and engaged in more desired overt behaviors (e.g., assertiveness). Taken together, these assignments will directly and indirectly promote cognitive restructuring by presenting her with new self-statements as well as evidence that will enhance more adaptive thinking. Finally, to deal with her fear of criticism, homework may involve having her talk to people who previously criticized her (i.e., her mother or her husband) and listen to their criticisms and then respond in an assertive manner.

POTENTIAL PITFALLS

Potential pitfalls to effective therapy include relationship obstacles, therapist obstacles, and client obstacles. The first pitfall, relationship obstacles, primarily stem from a poor match between therapist and client. An important first step for Nancy would be for her to find a therapist with whom she believes she can work effectively. Two types of therapist obstacles encountered are skill-oriented obstacles and disturbance obstacles. Skill-oriented obstacles include the following:

(a) failing to clarify one's role with the client;
(b) spending time dealing with "problems" that clients do not have but were identified by inaccurate assessment;
(c) failing to show clients the roots of their problems (i.e., ideological);
(d) expecting automatic change once the client identifies his/her irrational beliefs;
(e) working at an inappropriate pace; and
(f) working only on primary problems and ignoring a client's preoccupation with a secondary problem.

Disturbance-oriented obstacles include the therapists' irrational beliefs such as, "I have to be successful with my clients all of the time." The third obstacle to client progress involves the clients themselves. Client obstacles include the following:

(a) failing to dispute irrational beliefs *in vivo*;
(b) refusing to accept responsibility for unhealthy emotions;

(c) having low frustration tolerance about working toward change; and

(d) failing to do "homework" assignments.

In Nancy's case, her self-criticism and her belief that she is incompetent are of concern. Her need for approval may also prove to be an obstacle to change. Nancy may selectively attend to positive events, giving the impression that things are improving. Nancy's high need for approval presents a red flag in that she may try to please the therapist by doing homework assignments, yet may not make the philosophical change to acceptance. Moreover, Nancy may perceive the therapist as an authority figure that *must* approve of her. We would recommend using Socratic disputation to address this belief and to encourage Nancy to think for herself. Didactic methods might result in Nancy accepting and endorsing the therapist's perspective because of her need for approval.

As noted, Nancy's occasional thoughts of suicide and the development of a plan are a concern. As such, we would monitor compliance with the plan each session. Although her current SSI score is in the mild range, a past episode in the severe range coupled with a severe Hopelessness Scale (HS) score warrants consideration. In response to this concern, a Suicide Prevention Contract would be completed. In addition, Nancy would be encouraged to (1) reestablish relationships with individuals she has identified as supportive, (2) spend more time backpacking, and (3) engage in tasks that give her a sense of accomplishment.

As Nancy has a strong need for approval and reacts negatively to criticism, she may experience the disputing strategies of REBT as disapproval, which could negatively effect the therapeutic alliance. We would carefully challenge Nancy's dysfunctional thoughts to avoid any perception on her part that we were critical of her as a person. A review of the distinction between disputing Nancy's *beliefs* versus her as a *person* would occur during each therapy session. Nancy's family history of criticism, instability, and role-reversal suggests the possibility that she will point to these events as responsible for her current depression. With this in mind, she would learn to avoid "blaming" others for her depression or ruminating about the causes of her distress.

TERMINATION AND FOLLOW-UP

Before considering termination, Nancy's ability to use relapse-prevention skills to cope with future negative events would be evaluated, taught, and rehearsed. Relapse prevention strategies include teaching Nancy that everyone has setbacks and that if they occur, to accept them and not criticize herself for them. Nancy could learn to cope with setbacks by reminding herself to pinpoint the thoughts, feelings, and behaviors she has changed to cause her improvement. She could reflect on how she has used REBT to alleviate her depression in the past, and could rehearse rational coping statements, uncover and challenge irrational beliefs, and confront irrational fears.

Fading the frequency of the sessions would occur before termination. We might suggest weekly, biweekly, and monthly sessions. Additionally, the therapist and Nancy could anticipate future problems and imagine how she would successfully handle those problems using her newly learned REBT skills. Her ability to cope with feelings of loneliness, criticism and not being perfect, without becoming depressed would be rehearsed. Presenting Nancy with hypothetical situations similar to ones that upset her in the past would assess this skill. For each situation we would ask her how we would dispute the irrational beliefs, what new beliefs she could construct to cope with the situation, and how she would behave. During the final sessions, the therapist would highlight major issues that they had discussed and would schedule follow-up sessions to monitor Nancy's progress.

THE THERAPEUTIC RELATIONSHIP IN REBT

Ellis believes that an important therapist characteristic for effective treatment is the therapist's intelligence. As he remarked, "It is my impression that bright therapists get better results with difficult customers, including depressed individuals, because they have a better chance of talking them out of their fixed notions that they are worthless, cannot achieve anything, and cannot be happy at all" (personal communication, December 23, 1999). Therapist intelligence is often manifested in accurate problem formulation, the clarity of explanation of the REBT framework, maintaining problem focus, the use and timing of self-disclosure, the ability to interpret what the client is expressing, and the ease with which a therapist employs various cognitive, emotive and behavioral techniques during a session (Walen, DiGiuseppe, & Dryden, 1992).

In addition, Ellis regards empathy as an important quality of REBT therapists. The empathic REBT therapist lets clients know that he or she understands what clients are feeling *and* thinking. Therapists can express concern and care for clients through careful attention to clients' behaviors, the use of gentle humor, unconditional acceptance, and attempts to help clients solve difficult issues. Active confrontation that incorporates both genuineness and honesty is also considered crucial. REBT therapists are concrete, paying close attention to details of the client's experience. Moreover, therapists can confront clients on discrepancies between (a) what clients say and what they have said before, (b) what clients communicate verbally and nonverbally, and (c) how clients' view of their problems differs from the therapist's view.

Confrontation is among the most powerful tools of the REBT therapist (Walen, DiGiuseppe, & Dryden, 1992). Attending to their clients' emotions is preferable for therapists, as clients' emotions lead to the relevant irrational beliefs. Flexibility is an important attribute for therapists employing REBT. When necessary, therapists can replace a structured, active, directive approach with a less structured manner. Not evaluating their own self-worth by client outcomes is preferable for REBT therapists. Finally, as a multimodal, integrative form of therapy, REBT uses didactic, Socratic, imaginal, emotive and behavioral techniques to change dysfunctional thinking, emotions and behavior. REBT therapists should feel comfortable employing different treatment modalities when the need arises (Ellis & Dryden, 1997).

TRANSFERENCE AND COUNTER-TRANSFERENCE

Concepts such as transference and countertransference can be conceptualized in an REBT framework. Transference and countertransference are addressed in REBT by examining how clients' and therapists' beliefs are impeding progress. If the therapist found, for example, that Nancy was resistant to working toward agreed-upon goals, this would be addressed in session. Nancy might experience a "transferential" issue, of being unassertive with her therapist, as she was with her mother. Nancy's underlying belief of worthlessness and/or fear of confrontation would be challenged and Nancy would be encouraged to take an assertive stance with her therapist in session or as a homework assignment.

INTEGRATION OF PSYCHOTHERAPY
WITH MEDICATION

Medication alone would not be the course of action recommended for Nancy. Her prescription of Zoloft (50mg/day) has not effectively alleviated her depression or anxiety. Moreover, Nancy's belief system includes several core irrational beliefs that contribute to her depression. Her depression and anxiety will be reduced through identification of such beliefs, rigorous disputation, and eventual replacement with more rational alternatives. If, after eight to ten sessions of therapy no significant change occurs, we would recommend a referral for a different type of medication.

It should be noted however, that a different medication may help reduce Nancy's acute distress and, consequently, she may be better able to benefit from REBT. An important issue in REBT is that the therapist listen carefully to the client's experiences with a particular medication. It is necessary to maintain a stance of "collaborative empiricism" (Dryden & Golden, 1986, p. 74) between therapist and client when discussing medications (Bernard, 1991).

9. ADDITIONAL INFORMATION DESIRED

Additional information surrounding Nancy's family history of psychopathology may prove useful to help clarify biological contributions to her depression. A more detailed account of Nancy's academic and occupational functioning would be desired. Nancy apparently is successful in these areas. We would hypothesize that Nancy holds adaptive beliefs in work and school, and would attempt to help her generalize these to more problematic areas of her life (e.g., marriage and depression).

10. SUMMARY AND DISCUSSION

Rational Emotive Behavior Therapy (REBT) views human behavior, emotions, thinking and biology as overlapping entities, and proposes that humans have innate and learned tendencies to be both rational or self-helping, and irrational or self-defeating. It postulates that illogical, absolutistic, falsely generalized thinking generates self-defeating emotions; whereas logical, flexible, empirically-validated thinking generates self-enhancing emotions.

REBT therapists attempt to show clients that we can learn to think, act and feel in ways that will bring us closer to our desired goals. REBT teaches clients, among other things, that events in and of themselves do not lead to emotional upset or maladaptive behavior. Rather, it is our interpretations of those events that lead to emotional distress. Clients learn to distinguish between degrees of emotion, and come to understand that emotions such as concern, annoyance, and sadness are appropriate responses to certain events. Moreover, these reactions ultimately are more functional than all-consuming emotions such as rage, depression, and anxiety. Through a collaborative approach utilizing directive and active behavioral, cognitive, and emotive techniques, REBT therapists work with their clients to (1) alleviate individual distress, (2) increase daily functioning, (3) work toward desired goals, and (4) if possible achieve a philosophical change that will empower the client to successfully progress through life.

REBT focuses on the present—that is, on attitudes, beliefs, emotions, and maladaptive behaviors that are currently held by individuals. REBT acknowledges that individuals are often influenced by events and people from the past, and that current attitudes about oneself, others, and the world in the form of *beliefs* are often a result of such past experiences. While we cannot alter the past, we can address how we interpret the past and in turn let it influence us in the present and future. Therefore, REBT is ultimately an optimistic approach to addressing the quality of human functioning.

Our approach to addressing Nancy's concerns follows the approach outlined above by (a) recognizing that her emotions and behavior are dysfunctional, (b) identifying her irrational beliefs, (c) recognizing that these irrational beliefs are illogical, anti-empirical, and maladaptive, and (d) replacing her dysfunctional cognitions with more adaptive, rational beliefs as well as increasing and reinforcing more adaptive functioning and responding in her daily life. Nancy's primary presenting problem is that of depression. As noted, anxiety and depression are largely the result of absolutistic, dogmatic *must*urbation. If Nancy were to prefer, wish, or desire to accomplish particular goals (e.g., successful career, improved relationships, etc.) but fail to achieve such goals, she would most likely experience sadness and regret (and possibly strong feelings of each), but *not* depression. When Nancy escalates her preferences into dogmatic demands, and becomes convinced that she *absolutely should, must,* and *ought* (always) achieve her goals, she then is more likely to become depressed.

Nancy appears to hold several dogmatic beliefs, including "others must approve of me, and if I am not, it is awful!"; "I feel I am inept . . . just incompetent (and I *should* be competent). Nancy believes that she *must* be perfect and that because she is not, it is *awful*. A primary goal of therapy would be to develop Nancy's unconditional acceptance of herself, *although* she may not be as competent in her relationship, career, etc. as she would prefer. Ultimately if Nancy can accept events in her life and her own attributes as well as others, no matter how negative or unpleasant, she will experience disappointment and frustration, but will rarely make herself depressed.

The REBT practitioner would encourage Nancy to make a profound philosophic shift from one of nonacceptance and demandingness to acceptance and preferences. This philosophical shift is referred to as the "elegant solution" to Nancy's problems and is a distinctive component in REBT.

There is more to be learned about how CBT works and where REBT fits within that framework. We conclude with an old adage first attributed to Reinhold Neibuhr which nicely summarizes the REBT approach: "Grant me the courage to change the things I can change, the serenity to accept those that I cannot change and the wisdom to know the difference" (Pietsch, 1993).

REFERENCES

Beck, A. T. (1967). *Depression.* New York: Hoeber-Harper.

Beck, A. T. (1976). *Cognitive therapy and the emotional disorders.* New York: International Universities Press.

Bernard, M. E. (1991). *Using rational-emotive therapy effectively.* New York: Plenum Press.

Bernard, M. E. (1998). Validation of the General Attitude and Belief Scale. *Journal of Rational Emotive and Cognitive Behavior Therapy, 16*(3), 183–196.

Blackburn, I., & Bishop, S. (1979, July). *A comparison of cognitive therapy, pharmacotherapy, and their combination in depressed outpatients.* Paper presented at the annual meeting of the Society for Psychotherapy Research, Oxford, England.

Burns, D. D. (1980). *Feeling good: The new mood therapy.* New York: Avon Books.

Burns, D. D. (1999). *The feeling good handbook.* New York: Plume Books.

Craig, R. J. (1994). *Millon Clinical Multiaxial Inventory-III.* Odessa, FL: Psychological Assessment Resources, Inc.

Detweiler, J. B., & Whisman, M. A. (1999). The role of homework assignments in cognitive therapy for depression: Potential methods for enhancing adherence. *Clinical Psychology: Science and Practice, 6*(3), 267–282.

DiGiuseppe, R. (1991a). A rational-emotive model of assessment. In M. E. Bernard (Ed.), *Doing rational emotive therapy effectively*. New York: Plenum.

DiGiuseppe, R. (1991b). Comprehensive disputing in rational-emotive therapy. In M. E. Bernard (Ed.), *Doing rational emotive therapy effectively*. New York: Plenum.

Dobson, K. S. (1989). A meta-analysis of the efficacy of cognitive therapy for depression. *Journal of Consulting and Clinical Psychology, 57*(3), 414–419.

Drew, B. L. (1999). No suicide contracts to prevent suicidal behavior in in-patient psychiatric settings. *Journal of the American Psychiatric Nurses Association, 5*(1), 23–28.

Dryden, W., & DiGiuseppe, R. (1992). *A primer on rational emotive therapy*. Champaign, IL: Research Press.

Dryden, W., & Golden, W. L. (1986). *Cognitive-behavioral approaches to psychotherapy*. London: Harper & Row.

Ellis, A. (1962). *Reason and emotion in psychotherapy*. New York: Stuart.

Ellis, A. (1971). *Growth through reason*. North Hollywood, CA: Wilshire Books.

Ellis, A. (1973). *Humanistic psychotherapy: The rational-emotive approach*. New York: McGraw Hill.

Ellis, A. (1974). *Disputing irrational beliefs (DIBS)*. New York: Institute for Rational Living.

Ellis, A. (1975). *How to live with a neurotic*. New York: Crown.

Ellis, A. (1985). *Overcoming resistance: Rational emotive therapy with difficulty clients*. New York: Springer.

Ellis, A. (1987a). A sadly neglected cognitive element in depression. *Cognitive Therapy and Research, 11*(1), 121–146.

Ellis, A. (1987b). Treating the bored client with rational emotive therapy (RET). *Psychotherapy Patient, 3*(3–4), 75–86.

Ellis, A. (1987c). Integrative developments in rational emotive therapy (RET). *Journal of Integrative and Eclectic Psychotherapy, 6*(4), 470–479.

Ellis, A. (1987d). The impossibility of achieving consistently good mental health. *American Psychologist, 42*, 364–375.

Ellis, A. (1994). *Reason and emotional in psychotherapy: A comprehensive method of treating human disturbance—Revised and updated*. New York: Birch Lane Press.

Ellis, A., & Dryden, W. (1997). *The practice of rational emotive behavior therapy. Second edition*. New York: Springer.

Engels, G. I., Garnefski, N., & Diekstra, R. F. W. (1993). Efficacy of rational-emotive therapy: A quantitative analysis. *Journal of Consulting and Clinical Psychology, 61*, 1083–1090.

Gossette, R. L., & O'Brien, R. M. (1992). The efficacy of rational emotive therapy in adults: Clinical fact or psychometric artifact? *Journal of Behavior Therapy & Experimental Psychiatry, 23*, 924.

Haaga, D. A. F., & Davison, G. C. (1993). An appraisal of rational-emotive therapy. *Journal of Consulting and Clinical Psychology, 61*, 215–220.

Hauck, P. A. (1976). *Overcoming depression.* Westminster: John Knox Press.

Jones, R. G. (1968). A factored measure of Ellis' irrational belief system with personality and maladjustment correlates. *Dissertation Abstracts International, 29*, 4379–4380. (University Microfilms No. 69-6443).

Kopec, Beal, & DiGiuseppe (1994). Training in Rational Emotive Therapy: Disputation strategies. *Journal of Rational Emotive and Cognitive Behavior Therapies, 12*(2), 94–115.

Lachmund, E., & DiGiuseppe, R. (1997, Aug). Comorbidity of anger and depression: Implications for treatment. Paper presented as part of the symposium "Advances in the Diagnosis, Assessment, and Treatment of Angry Clients," at the Annual Convention of the American Psychological Association, Chicago.

Leung, A. W., & Heimberg, R. G. (1996). Homework compliance, perception of control, and outcome of cognitive-behavioral treatment of social phobia. *Behaviour Research and Therapy, 34*(5–6), 423–432.

Lewinsohn, P. M., & Amenson, C. S. (1978). Some relations between pleasant and unpleasant mood-related events and depression. *Journal of Abnormal Psychology, 87*(6), 644–654.

Lewinsohn, P. M., Sullivan, J. M., & Grosscup, S. J. (1980). Changing reinforcing events: An approach to the treatment of depression. *Psychotherapy, Research and Practice, 17*(3), 322–334.

Linscott, J., & DiGiuseppe, R. (1998). Cognitive assessment. In A. S. Bellack & M. Hersen (Eds.), *Behavioral assessment: A practical handbook.* Boston: Allyn and Bacon.

Lipsky, M. J., Kassinove, H., & Miller, N. J. (1980). Effects of rational emotive therapy, rational role reversal, and rational-emotive imagery on the emotional adjustment of community mental health center patients. *Journal of Consulting and Clinical Psychology, 48*(3), 366–374.

Macaskill, N. D., & Macaskill, A. (1996). Rational emotive therapy plus pharmacotherapy versus pharmacotherapy alone in the treatment of high cognitive dysfunction depression. *Cognitive Therapy and Research, 20*(6), 575–592.

McDermut, J. F., Haaga, D. A. F., & Bilek, L. A. (1997). Cognitive bias and irrational beliefs in major depression and dysphoria. *Cognitive Therapy and Research, 21*, 459–476.

Miller, M. C., Jacobs, D. G., & Gutheil, T. G. (1998). Talisman or taboo: The controversy of the suicide prevention contract. *Harvard Review of Psychiatry, 6*(2), 78–87.

Muran, C., & DiGiuseppe, R. (1990). Toward a cognitive formulation of metaphor use in Psychotherapy. *Clinical Psychology Review, 10*(1), 69–85.

Pietsch, W. V. (1993). *The serenity prayer.* San Francisco: Harper San Francisco.

Rathus, S. A. (1973). A 30-item schedule for assessing assertive behavior. *Behavior Therapy, 4*(3), 398–406.

Rose, R. D., Terjesen, M. D., DiGiuseppe, R., & Ellis, A. (1999, Aug). REBT group homework, content analysis, assignment generation, compliance and outcome. A poster presented at the 107th Annual Convention of the American Psychological Association, Boston.

Rush, A. J., Beck, A. T., Kovacs, M., & Hollon, S. (1977). Comparative efficacy of cognitive therapy and imipramine in the treatment of depressed outpatients. *Cognitive Therapy and Research, 1*, 17–37.

Solomon, A., Haaga, D. A. F., Brody, C., Kirk, L., & Friedman, D. G. (1998). Priming irrational beliefs in recovered depressed people. *Journal of Abnormal Psychology, 107*(3), 440–449.

Walen, S., DiGiuseppe, R., & Dryden, W. (1992). *The practitioner's guide to rational-emotive therapy* (2nd ed.). New York: Oxford.

Young, H. S. (1984). Practising RET with lower class clients. *British Journal of Cognitive Psychotherapy, 2*(2), 33–59.

SUGGESTED READINGS

Ellis, A. (1985). *Overcoming resistance: Rational emotive therapy with difficulty clients.* New York: Springer.

Ellis, A., & Dryden, W. (Eds.). (1990). *The essential Albert Ellis.* New York: Springer.

Lyons, L. C., & Woods, P. J. (1991). The efficacy of rational emotive therapy: A quantitative review of the outcome research. *Clinical Psychology Review, 11*, 357–369.

Oei, T. P. S., Hansen, J., & Miller, S. (1993). The empirical status of irrational beliefs in rational emotive therapy. *Australian Psychologist, 28*, 195–200.

Silverman, M. S., McCarthy, M., & McGovern, T. (1992). A review of outcome studies of rational emotive therapy from 1982–1989. *Journal of Rational Emotive & Cognitive Behavior Therapy, 10*, 111–175.

APPENDIX 1

Therapy Evaluation Form

Nancy

Date: _____

Session # _____

When I think about my present position in life, I think to myself, "I f–up everything. My life has truly become a waste." I also think that I am incompetent and need someone to help me take care of myself and everything I do. When I think this way, I feel depressed, anxious, angry, and hopeless. When I feel this way, I don't have the desire to do the things I once found pleasurable.

1. How often has such a scenario occurred recently?

1	2	3	4	5	6	7
not at all						extremely

2. How concerned have you been about this happening?

1	2	3	4	5	6	7
not at all						extremely

3. How easily can you imagine such a scenario?

1	2	3	4	5	6	7
not at all						extremely

4. How well does the scenario describe you and your relationship with others?

1	2	3	4	5	6	7
not at all						extremely

5. How far back in your life can you recall this scenario occurring?

1	2	3	4	5	6	7
not at all						extremely

6. How much do you think such beliefs help you or hurt you?

1	2	3	4	5	6	7
Helps me						Hurts me

7. How much do you think these beliefs are rational or correct, or
    are they irrational or incorrect?

1	2	3	4	5	6	7

    Rational &   Irrational &
    Correct   Incorrect

An alternative way to think, feel, and act about this situation would be
as follows:

When I think about my present position in life, I think to myself,
"Although I sometimes have difficulty with certain things, it does not
mean I mess up everything. I accept myself even when I don't do things
perfectly, as I know that it is not possible to be perfect. I am competent
in many areas of my life, and while it may be preferable at times to
have someone's help, I do not need it. When I think this way I feel less
depressed and anxious, more hopeful, and am more motivated to engage in pleasurable activities and pursue desired goals. I am also better
able to problem-solve about my marriage and future.

8. How easily can you imagine the alternatives ways for you to feel
    and think in this scene?

1	2	3	4	5	6	7

    not at all   extremely

9. How confident are you about your ability to act on these alterna-
    tives ways of thinking, feeling, and behaving?

1	2	3	4	5	6	7

    not at all   extremely

10. How often have you acted on these alternative ways of thinking,
    feeling, and behaving in such a scene recently?

1	2	3	4	5	6	7

    not at all   extremely

Thank You

11

Cognitive Therapies of Depression: A Modularized Treatment Approach

Mark A. Reinecke

Depression has been recognized for centuries as both a common and significant form of psychopathology. A number of factors appear to play a role in the onset and maintenance of the disorder (Shelton, Hollon, Purdon, & Loosen, 1991). Cognitive therapy has emerged over the past 25 years as an important model for understanding depression, and as an empirically-supported form of treatment. An impressive body of research attests to its utility for treating depressed adults (Dobson, 1989; Jarrett et al., 1999).

The purpose of this chapter is to summarize some of the major cognitive-behavioral models of depression. We will review research relating to these models, describe their clinical implications, and summarize treatment outcome studies. Given the breadth and depth of research related to cognition and mood, it is not possible to review this literature in detail. Our discussion, as such, is representative, not exhaustive. This will be followed by a discussion of the clinical case, and a description of how techniques derived from these models can be used in developing an integrated treatment plan.

COGNITIVE MODELS OF DEPRESSION

Over the years, investigators have drawn from numerous psychological perspectives in attempting to understand depression. In the early 1970s, the first primarily cognitive models were introduced. Since that time several cognitive-behavioral models of depression have been developed. These models propose that specific cognitive factors—including maladaptive beliefs, negativistic attributional style, self-focused attention, problem-solving deficits, ruminative style and social skills deficits—may be associated with risk for depression. Therapies based on these models have, in many cases, been published in the form of treatment manuals. They tend, as a group, to be problem-oriented, active, strategic, time-limited, and structured. They are psychoeducational in nature and offer the clinician a range of treatment strategies and techniques from which to chose. These programs have attracted empirical interest during recent years, and several are "empirically supported" (Chambless et al., 1998; Chambless & Hollon, 1998).

The term cognitive therapy is often associated with the seminal work of Aaron Beck, and is used to identify a short-term treatment for depression developed by him and his colleagues (Beck, Rush, Shaw, & Emery, 1979). It is worth noting, however, that there are a number of treatments for depression that are cognitive in nature. Although they vary in their goals and emphases, they share a number of assumptions about the nature of depression and its treatment. Cognitive therapy, as such, represents a family of therapies. As a family, the models are conceptually and technically similar. As individual models, they tend to overlap with one another—each emphasizing a somewhat different component of the depressive syndrome. All are mediational models—they assume that cognitive factors mediate (or moderate) human adaptation. In practice, all attempt to directly and efficiently change cognitive contents and processes as a means of enhancing behavioral and emotional adjustment. They assume that cognitive change will moderate behavioral and emotional improvement. An emphasis is placed on understanding the subjective world of the individual and the meanings they attach to their experiences. This is balanced by attempts to objectively assess cognitive, behavioral and emotional change.

Research in the field of cognitive therapy has had an important effect on the practice of psychotherapy. A number of cognitive models have been advanced and a veritable armamentarium of techniques have been added to the clinician's repertoire (McMullin, 1986). How can we make sense of this complex literature and use it to guide our practice? Inasmuch as a range of cognitive and social factors have been found to be associated with risk for depression, it seems sensible to examine how they interact to maintain a client's depressive episode. Clinically, patients tend not to demonstrate each and every cognitive deficit associated with depression. Rather, they demonstrate highly personal patterns of cognitive strength and weakness, and of adaptive coping and vulnerability. By adopting a broad view and systematically assessing patients' strengths and limitations in each of the areas to be discussed, clinicians will be able to develop a more individualized treatment program. This may be referred to as "modularized cognitive therapy" in that specific interventions or "modules" are introduced based upon the needs of the individual client.

The Assumptions of Cognitive Therapy

Cognitive models of depression all emphasize the central role of cognitive activity in the onset, course, and alleviation of depression. Each emphasizes the essential role of modifying thoughts, assumptions, and information-processing strategies for changing mood and behavior. As Dobson and Dozois (2001) note, each assumes that (a) cognitive activity affects behavior; (b) cognitive activity may be monitored and changed; and (c) that behavioral and emotional change may be affected through cognitive change. In addition, these models implicitly assume that (d) cognitive processes are ongoing, active, and adaptive; (e) affective, behavioral, and cognitive factors interact in a reciprocal manner over time; and (f) there is a relationship between cognitive contents (i.e., what a person thinks), cognitive processes (i.e., how they use this information) and the occurrence of specific symptoms (Freeman & Reinecke, 1995).

The foundation of cognitive therapy, then, is the belief or meaning system. An individual's knowledge base and ways of processing information are seen as organized and adaptive. The belief system develops from an early age and provides a lens through which the individual interprets experiences, as well as expectations and attributions that guide the development of plans and goals. The cognitive system is just that, a system, and coordinates the full range of processes involved in the assignment of meaning. These processes include attention, perception, interpretation, encoding and recall of memories, expectations and attributions, goal development, and executive function or planning. Cognitive processes, like behavioral skills and emotional responses, are assumed to be adaptive. They function together as an integrated system to guide our adaptation on a day-to-day basis. To paraphrase Ludwig Wittgenstein, the limits of our thoughts are the limits of our world. Thoughtful discussions of the assumptions of cognitive therapy are provided by Clark and Beck (1999) and Dobson and Dozois (2001). As noted, there are a number of cognitive-behavioral models of depression—each focusing upon a different component of clinical depression. We will now briefly discuss each and how they can inform our clinical practice.

Beck's Cognitive Therapy of Depression

Perhaps the best known of the cognitive models of depression is Beck's Cognitive Therapy (Beck et al., 1979). During the early 1960s Beck observed that the thoughts and dreams of clinically depressed adults were characterized by negative views of the self, the world, and the future (Beck, 1963, 1964). This constellation of negative beliefs was later labeled the cognitive triad. In addition, Beck noted that depressed patients demonstrated systematic cognitive distortions, including both perceptual and memory biases. According to this model, distorted or maladaptive thoughts and appraisals serve as a proximal cause for depression. Beck proposed that these beliefs and thought processes occur due to the activation of maladaptive schema. Schema are tacit beliefs and memory structures that serve to organize the processing of information. They develop from an early age and are consolidated by recent life events. Whereas the schema of nondepressed individuals are flexible and provide the individual with a sense of personal worth, efficacy, and control; the schema of depressed individuals are rigid and are characterized by perceptions of personal inadequacy and loss, the belief that others are unreliable or uncaring, that the future is bleak, and that they lack control over important outcomes in their life. Negativistic beliefs, such as these, are seen as placing individuals at risk for depression by leading to a maladaptive interpretation of life events. Although this processing of information typically is out of awareness (Kihlstrom, 1987), the contents of these beliefs can be consciously accessed and reviewed.

In an attempt to account for individual differences in vulnerability for depression, Beck proposed that two personality styles—Sociotropy and Autonomy—are associated with risk for depression, and that individuals become depressed when stressful life events "match" with their personal vulnerabilities. The sociotropic individual tends to base their sense of self-worth on the quality of their relationships with others. They value closeness and acceptance, and become depressed when they perceive an interpersonal loss, rejection or abandonment. The autonomous individuals, in contrast, tend to value independence, personal control, and achievement. Their sense of self-worth is based on productivity and personal accomplishment, and they become depressed when they perceive that they have failed or are not in control of important events in their life.

The goal of cognitive therapy is straightforward—to replace the patient's maladaptive perceptions with more adaptive beliefs. This is accomplished through the use of Socratic questioning, rational disputation, and behavioral experiments. Patients are taught to monitor their mood and the accompanying thoughts; to recognize relationships between events, thoughts, and emotions; to evaluate the validity of their thoughts; to develop behavioral skills; and to substitute more adaptive beliefs for their negativistic thoughts.

Beck's cognitive theory has received extensive empirical attention over the past 20 years (for reviews see Clark & Beck, 1999; Engel & DeRubeis, 1993; Haaga, Dyck, & Ernst, 1991; Hollon, Shelton, & Loosen, 1991; Moretti & Shaw, 1989). Drawing from these reviews and other research, a number of conclusions can be made. First, empirical support has been provided for descriptive components of the model, including the occurrence of negative beliefs among depressed individuals. Second, support for diathesis-stress and cognitive vulnerability components of the model have been positive but more limited. Although findings have been promising, methodological limitations have made it difficult to test these components of the model. Third, the hypothesis that depression may be distinguished from other disorders on the basis of specific cognitive contents and processes has received some support. Fourth, although there is little conclusive evidence that depressed individuals "distort" reality (i.e., that their perceptions conflict with "objective" measures of events), there is some evidence to suggest that depressed individuals are negatively biased (i.e., they tend to make negative judgments over time and across situations). Finally, outcome studies consistently indicate that cognitive therapy can be effective for reducing depressive symptoms. Studies typically find that cognitive therapy is as or more effective than other treatment methods in ameliorating

depressive symptoms, and that it may be more effective than pharmacotherapy in preventing the recurrence of depressive episodes. Moreover,
modified versions of Beck's Cognitive Therapy appear to be useful, in
combination with medications, in treating chronic depression (Keller
et al., 2000).

Helplessness/Hopelessness Theory of Depression

The original learned helplessness theory of depression was based on
observations made during animal learning experiments that dogs exposed to inescapable shock demonstrated motivational, learning, and
emotional deficits (Seligman & Maier, 1967). As these symptoms paral-
leled human depression, Seligman (1975) theorized that depression
may result from a perceived lack of contingency between important life
events and an individual's actions. In other words, individuals who
perceived themselves as helpless to control important outcomes subsequently become depressed.

Although the original learned helplessness theory garnered some
empirical support, it was soon criticized as conceptually incomplete. As
a more comprehensive theory was needed, Abramson, Seligman, and
Teasdale (1978) reformulated the model. The reformulation incorporated the concept of attribution of responsibility. As they stated,
" . . . when a person finds that he is helpless, he asks why he is helpless.
The causal attribution he makes then determines the generality and
chronicity of his helplessness deficits as well as his later self-esteem" (p.
50). The reformulated model proposed that when people are faced
with uncontrollable events, they make attributions about its cause along
three explanatory dimensions: internal or external (i.e., causes within
the person versus outside the person), stable or unstable (i.e., causes
that persist versus transient ones), and global or specific (i.e., causes
that affect many domains versus those that are more limited). Individuals who become depressed are viewed as having tendencies to attribute
negative, uncontrollable outcomes to internal, stable, and global causes.
The reformulated model has generated a considerable amount of research (e.g., Brewin, 1985; Sweeney, Anderson, & Bailey, 1986). Studies
generally support the notion that making internal, stable, and global
attributions for negative events contributes to feelings of depression.

More recently, Abramson, Metalsky, and Alloy (1989) revised the
reformulated helplessness model of depression into the "hopelessness

theory" of depression. They proposed a subtype of clinical depression, "hopelessness depression," and suggested that hopelessness may serve as a proximal and sufficient (though not a necessary) cause of depression. They define hopelessness as the expectation that desired outcomes will not occur or that aversive outcomes will occur but that one cannot control them. Hopelessness is seen as stemming from tendencies to (1) make stable, global causal attributions about negative events; (2) infer that negative life events will have negative consequences; and (3) draw negative inferences about the self. The theory predicts that hopelessness depression will occur when there is a match between a negative life event and an individual's depressogenic attributional style.

From this perspective, the focus of treatment is on restoring hope and a perception of control. Although no controlled outcome studies have been conducted to examine the effectiveness of interventions based on this model, a focus on instilling hope plays a central role in Beck's treatment for depression. Moreover, interventions designed to instill a more positive attributional style appear to be effective, at least in the short run, in preventing the onset of depression in at-risk youth (Gillham, Reivich, Jaycox, & Seligman, 1995).

Lewinsohn's Low Reinforcement Model of Depression

Although it was originally developed as a behavioral approach for treating depression, Lewinsohn's (1974) model has been elaborated into an integrated cognitive model of depression. Briefly, Lewinsohn postulated that depression is learned, and that it stems from extinction or "reinforcement strain." That is to say, individuals become depressed as they experience a loss of response-contingent positive reinforcement (see Dowd, this volume, chapter 9). This can occur due to losses or from a decrease in enjoyable or rewarding activities. A reinforcement loss is followed by a decrease in activity, leading to further losses of reinforcement. Symptoms of depression are seen as stemming from this loss of reinforcement.

Lewinsohn (1974) postulated that loss of reinforcement could come from several factors: (1) the environment may not provide sufficient reinforcement; (2) the person may not be socially skilled enough to receive positive reinforcement; or (3) reinforcers may be present, but the individual may not be able to appreciate them due to an interfering condition, such as social anxiety.

From this perspective, treatment focuses upon (1) increasing participation in rewarding, enjoyable activities; (2) improving social skills and
encouraging participation in social activities; and (3) alleviating anxiety
through relaxation training and systematic desensitization (Lewinsohn,
Sullivan, & Grosscup, 1980).

Self-Focused Attention and Depression

Ingram (1990) proposed that attentional processes play a role in the
development and maintenance of depression. He defined self-focused
attention as, "an awareness of self referent, internally generated information that stands in contrast to an awareness of externally generated
information derived through sensory receptors" (p. 156). Two cognitive-
behavioral theories of depression that emphasize self-focused attention
are a revision of Lewinsohn's loss of reinforcement approach and a
model proposed by Pyszczynski and Greenberg (1987). Recognizing
the limitations of his original behavioral model, Lewinsohn and his
colleagues proposed an integrated theory of depression that emphasized cognitive factors, including self-focused attention (Lewinsohn,
Hoberman, Teri, & Hautzinger, 1985). They proposed that depression
results when stressful life events activate depressogenic cognitive processes. Stressful life events tend to disrupt routine behavior patterns,
resulting in a negative emotional reaction. Combined with the continued effects of the stressful events, the negative emotional state leads to
an increased self-awareness, causing a sense of failure and producing
an ongoing cycle of cognitive, behavioral, and affective symptoms of
depression.

Along similar lines, Pyszczynski and Greenberg (1987) proposed a
self-regulatory perseveration theory of depression. They suggested that
depression results from the loss of a crucial source of worth, which
initiates a self-regulatory cycle. A central component of this cycle is
excessive self-focus regarding the loss. Because the loss is viewed as
essential to their sense of well-being, the patient is unable to lessen
their self-focus, which exacerbates the negative affect and promotes
self-criticism. The cycle continues, such that the self-focus, negative
affect, and self-criticism interfere with effective functioning in other
areas (e.g., social interactions), causing the individual to experience
recurrent self-blame. Moreover, the individual comes to overlook positive or reinforcing events. They tend, as a consequence, to focus upon

themselves when negative outcomes occur. The individual comes, over time, to adopt a "depressive self-focusing style" that reinforces their negative self-image.

Research has tended to support the notion that self-focused attention is associated with depression (Ingram, 1990; Pyszczynski & Greenberg, 1987). It is not clear, however, that self-focused attention serves as a vulnerability factor for the onset of depressive episodes, or that it is specific to clinical depression. Self-focused attention may, instead, be a characteristic of several forms of psychopathology. In practice, these theories suggest that dysphoric individuals should be discouraged from focusing upon recent losses. Rather, they should be encouraged to identify alternative sources of self-worth and to develop an "outward" or "socially-focused" perceptual style.

Nolen-Hoeksema's Ruminative Style Model of Depression

A substantial amount of evidence suggests that women are more likely to experience depression than men. Claiming that current models do not adequately explain this observation, Nolen-Hoeksema (1987, 1990) proposed a social learning model for the development of depression. She posits that all individuals experience mild to moderate feelings of sadness on occasion—this is a normal part of life. What differentiates those who become clinically depressed from those who do not is the way they have learned to cope with these "normative" depressed moods. Individuals who react to feelings of depression by engaging in activities are thought to be less prone to experience severe depression than are individuals who dwell on these events and their feelings. A "ruminative" response set amplifies the depression by interfering with instrumental behavior, increasing access to negative memories, and by increasing the likelihood that an individual will consider their depression a result of personal defects or flaws. As the astute reader will note, this model is similar in many ways to those of Beck et al. (1979), Lewinsohn et al. (1985), and Pyszczynski and Greenberg (1987). Although empirical support for the response-style explanation for depression is limited (few studies have been completed with clinical populations), a number of studies suggest that response style can affect mood and that men and women differ in predicted ways in their response styles (Nolen-Hoeksema, 1987). From this perspective, depressed individuals would be taught to distract themselves from negative moods, to actively develop solutions for their problems (rather than to unproductively ruminate about their distress), and to increase their activity level.

Self-Control Theory

Based upon Kanfer's (1970) work on self-regulation, Rehm (1977, 1984) proposed a model of depression that focuses on how individuals control their behavior in order to reach long-term goals. Rehm (1977) observed that depressed persons exhibit difficulties in several areas of self-control. Specifically, they manifest deficits in self-monitoring, self-evaluation, and self-reinforcement. According to Rehm, depressed individuals tend to: (1) selectively attend to negative events; (2) focus more on immediate than on delayed consequences of their actions; (3) maintain stringent standards and evaluate themselves in unrealistic, perfectionistic ways; (4) make more negative attributions for events; (5) not reward themselves for their successes; and (6) become self-critical and administer excessive amounts of self-punishment.

Research examining this model and treatments based on it have generally been positive (Rehm 1995). Interventions focus on remediating deficits in self-monitoring, self-evaluation, and self-reinforcement. Techniques include having the patients keep daily records for positive experiences, developing specific, attainable goals, and having them reward themselves when goals are met.

D'Zurilla & Nezu's Social Problem-Solving Model

D'Zurilla and Nezu (1982) proposed that clinical depression stems from deficits in rational problem-solving. They hypothesized that ineffective problem-solving is a causal factor in the onset and maintenance of depression and that developing effective problem-solving skills can be used to ameliorate the disorder (D'Zurilla & Nezu, 2001; Nezu, 1987; Nezu, Nezu, & Perri, 1989). They propose that reciprocal relationships exist between the occurrence of negative life events, the use of rational problem-solving skills, and depressive symptoms. A primary focus within Nezu's (1987) formulation is problem-solving coping, which consists of five components: problem orientation and problem-solving motivation, problem definition and formulation, generation of alternatives, decision making, and solution implementation and verification. Empirical support has come from studies indicating that relationships may exist between problem-solving and severity of depression (Haaga, Fine, Terrill, Stewart, & Beck, 1993; Marx, Williams, & Claridge, 1992).

A number of clinical protocols have been developed based upon this model, and several have been put to empirical test (Nezu, 1987; Nezu, Nezu, & Perri, 1989). Interventions focus on developing rational problem-solving skills and on improving problem-solving motivation. Patients are encouraged to approach problems optimistically, to think them through in a systematic, rational manner, to persist in the face of difficulty, and to inhibit impulsive attempts to resolve their difficulties.

Gotlib & Hammen's Cognitive-Interpersonal Model

Recognizing that cognitive, social and developmental factors interact in placing individuals at risk for depression, Gotlib and Hammen (1992) proposed a cognitive-interpersonal model of depression. They posited that adverse parent-child experiences (e.g., neglect, loss, unresponsive parenting, abuse) contribute to risk for depression by facilitating the development of negative cognitive representations and beliefs, depression-prone personality characteristics, and inadequate interpersonal behaviors. Individuals learn, in essence, to view themselves and their relationships with others in a negative manner, and fail to develop adaptive affect regulation and social skills. The onset of a depressive episode is thought to result from the interaction of these vulnerabilities and the occurrence of stressful life events. The emergence of depressive symptoms leads the individual to withdraw from others and to display a range of maladaptive social behaviors (e.g., poor eye contact, not smiling, excessive reassurance seeking, complaining). These behaviors ultimately elicit a negative response from others that, in conjunction with an increased self-focus and sensitivity to rejection, lead to the consolidation of patients' negative views of themselves and others. Although not developed as a treatment model, their theory has a number of clinical implications. Interventions based on this model focus on changing dysfunctional cognitions and interpersonal behavior, developing affect regulation skills, enhancing the quality of attachment relationships, and modifying the responses of significant others to the patient (Gotlib, 1990).

Teasdale's Interacting Cognitive Subsystems (ICS) Model of Depression

Drawing on research in experimental cognitive psychology, Teasdale (1983, 1988) developed an information processing model of depression.

Teasdale and Barnard's (1993) model borrows from node-network theory and parallel distributed processing models in suggesting that people store information about themselves and events in a series of associated cognitive networks. Like Nolen-Hoeksema, Teasdale (1988) begins with the observation that all individuals experience mild feelings of dysphoria from time to time. Although most individuals do not escalate from this mild depressive state to clinical depression, cognitively vulnerable individuals do. The escalation is hypothesized to result from the activation of a cycle of negative thinking and depression. Depressed affect is believed to increase the accessibility of negative memories and interpretative processes. Depressed mood and cognitive processing reinforce one other, establishing a cycle that maintains the depression. More recently, Teasdale and his colleagues have introduced the concepts of "kindling" and "sensitization" to explain how tacit knowledge structures can be activated by mild dysphoric moods. They note that, with continued reactivation, only minimal cues come to be needed to activate latent negative memories and perceptual processes. There is, in essence, a lowering of the threshold for the activation of depressogenic beliefs (Segal, Williams, Teasdale, & Gemar, 1996). Teasdale, Segal, and Williams (1995) argue that the risk for relapse and recurrence of depression will depend on the ease with which negative beliefs can be reactivated. This model is supported by research on mood-dependent memory suggesting that recovered depressives have greater access to dysfunctional attitudes during negative mood inductions than do never-depressed controls. Moreover, patients who demonstrate a greater accessibility to negative beliefs during negative mood induction demonstrate a greater risk of relapse than those who do not.

Clinically, these findings suggest that it may be important to attempt to change maladaptive schema, and to take steps to reduce the accessibility of those memories when the individual becomes mildly depressed. Attempts are made to develop the patient's ability to direct their attention away from cues that will activate depressogenic beliefs.

SUMMARY AND CLINICAL IMPLICATIONS

As we have seen, there are several alternative cognitive models of depression. All postulate that cognitive processes play a central role in the etiology and maintenance of depression. Moreover, all assume that these cognitive processes are accessible and amenable to change. All assume that cognitive, social, behavioral and environmental factors interact in contributing to vulnerability for depression, and all suggest that by actively addressing these factors the patient's depression can be alleviated. In practice, all forms of cognitive therapy are: (1) active, (2) problem-focused, (3) collaborative and supportive, (4) structured, (5) provide the patient with a clear rationale for understanding their depression, (6) offer the patient specific interventions they can use to alleviate their depression and, as a consequence, provide them with feelings of efficacy, control, and hope, (7) encourage self-monitoring and self-regulation, and (8) maintain a clear and consistent focus on changing cognitive structures and on developing adaptive skills. Modularized cognitive therapy for depression is individually tailored. It attempts to systematically assess and change the specific cognitive and behavioral deficits that are associated with depression for the individual patient.

CASE STUDY

The Initial Session

We begin our treatment of Nancy by attempting to get to know her and her concerns, and by developing a provisional case formulation. Although we would begin by asking Nancy to simply describe her concerns and what she would like to gain from treatment, the process of cognitive therapy is, from the outset, both organized and active. We might, for example, encourage her to share her feelings and to summarize her concerns as she is describing them. As she is doing this, we would want to more fully understand the meanings she is attaching to these experiences. What, for example, does she mean when she states that she "has difficulty dealing with issues," that she can "never trust herself or her decisions," and that she now "questions what she is doing with her life." We would want to know how long she has looked at herself and her life in this way, and what experiences she has had that led to these beliefs. What, specifically, does she mean when she uses the term "trust"? What of the word "issues"? As we work together to develop a list of her concerns, we would encourage her to describe them in behavioral, problem-focused terms. We would then ask her to list them hierarchically in order of severity. Given the phenomenological emphasis of cognitive therapy, we want to understand how Nancy is feeling at the times she is experiencing these difficulties, the situations in which these feelings are most severe, and the thoughts she experiences at those times. We would ask Nancy how she has attempted to cope with her difficulties, and to describe settings in which her mood is more positive.

As we develop a problem list, we will want to understand Nancy's understanding of her difficulties. That is to say, what attributions is she making about herself and her life? What does she see as the causes of her distress? Does she attribute her difficulties to internal, global and stable factors? Does she feel that she can control these events? These initial inquiries into the attributions that Nancy is making are important in that they will guide our initial interventions. When asked about the origins of her feelings of depression, for example, Nancy attributed them to her "dysfunctional childhood." It would be helpful to know what meanings she has attached to her childhood experiences. Does she believe, for example, that she wasn't afforded the opportunity to learn how to cope with day-to-day problems (something which, presumably, she could learn), or that she has been fundamentally and irrevocably scarred by these experiences (which may lead to the belief that she is incapable of change)? Inasmuch as depressed individuals often demonstrate negatively-biased perceptions and memories, the possibility exists that Nancy is selectively recalling negative events from her past, and is overlooking experiences which would provide her with a sense of competence and worth. Given her chaotic childhood, it would be interesting to know how it is that Nancy has come to function so capably in many areas of her life. Have her life experiences provided her with unrecognized skills, abilities and positive attributes?

A review of Nancy's responses on a battery of self-report questionnaires indicates that she is currently experiencing subjectively severe feelings of depression, anxiety, and hopelessness. Her responses on these scales would be reviewed with her, and we would inquire as to her feelings about the specific items she endorsed. It may be helpful, for example, to discuss which specific symptoms she feels are the most distressing, how severe they have been, the meanings she has attached to them, and how she has attempted to manage them. Our initial goal is threefold—to give us a clearer understanding of Nancy's specific concerns, to appreciate the subjective meanings she is attaching to them, and to help her to feel understood and supported. This is important in that feelings that "my therapist does not understand me" have been found to be a strong predictor of premature termination from treatment. With this in mind, careful attention would be given at the conclusion of each session to assure that Nancy has felt understood and supported during the hour.

Nancy appears, from the case example, to be able to develop a trusting relationship and to be comfortable describing her concerns. She has provided us with a great deal of information. Therapeutic process studies suggest that the ability to develop a trusting rapport, to identify specific, focal problems; to reflect upon one's thoughts, behaviors and feelings; to identify relationships between cognitions and emotions; and to evaluate the adaptiveness of one's beliefs are predictive of a positive response to cognitive therapy. Positive outcomes are also predicted by a lack of significant character psychopathology and by motivation to complete homework assignments between sessions. A goal during our initial sessions would be to informally assess each of these areas to determine if Nancy is an appropriate candidate for short-term cognitive therapy.

Case Formulation

As noted, the cognitive-behavioral models reviewed are not mutually exclusive or independent. Rather, they emphasize different facets of depression and can be viewed as complementary approaches. To illustrate how these models can be used in conceptualizing Nancy's difficulties, let's consider each in turn. Following Beck's model, it can be seen that Nancy demonstrates each of the features of the Cognitive Triad. She reports experiencing negative views of herself (e.g., "I'm inept . . . just incompetent"), the world (she reports experiencing stress at work, in her marriage, and financially) and her future (e.g., "I can't see a light for the future"). In addition, she appears to manifest a range of cognitive distortions, including magnification, perfectionistic thinking, and personalization of negative events. Nancy also appears to demonstrate "should" and "ought" statements. It is unclear from the case example, however, how often she experiences these thoughts, how pervasive and distressing they are, or how she copes with them. With this in mind, it may be helpful to ask her to note, on a daily basis, how often they occur, the situations that trigger them and how she feels at the time.

Nancy's early experiences appear to have contributed to the development of a range of maladaptive schema. She appears, for example, to believe that she is, in some ways, flawed, incapable and unlovable, that she has been emotionally deprived, that it is necessary to put other's needs before her own, and that people are uncaring, unreliable or rejecting. She appears, as well, to demonstrate unrelenting or perfectionistic standards for herself. Although we might speculate about the experiences she has had which have led her to view herself and her world in this way, this would be premature. Rather, it is often helpful to encourage individuals to describe their beliefs in detail, the meanings and associations they have to them, and the experiences they have had which support them. Only then can steps be taken to assist Nancy to look at these beliefs as hypotheses rather than as irrefutable facts.

Nancy appears, as well, to demonstrate characteristics of both sociotropic-dependent and autonomous personality styles. Sociotropy and autonomy are personality attributes that may place individuals at risk for depression. Sociotropy refers to a stable and ongoing tendency to base one's feelings of self worth on the acceptance and approval of others. The sociotropic person fears abandonment or social rejection, and is sensitive to cues that others may disapprove of them. They are sensitive to perceived disruptions in relationships, and tend to seek the reassurance, support, and appreciation of others. Nancy reported, for example, that she desires relationships and that she feels she "needs someone to take care of her." She also appears, however, to be achievement-oriented, and is quite accomplished in her career. Moreover, she reported that her mood tends to improve when she feels she has accomplished something at work. This may be suggestive of an autonomous style. It is important, however, not to over-interpret these statements. Automatic thoughts, which are best viewed as concomitants of depression, may or may not reflect the presence of stable personality factors which have contributed to the development of her depression. Further assessment of whether Nancy demonstrates a sociotropic-dependent or an autonomous personality style, and whether these traits predated the occurrence of her depressive episode, are needed. With these considerations in mind, her decision to pursue an MBA is interesting given her training in graphic design and her comment that she would "like a life with more art in it." Is this decision motivated by a desire for achievement, by concerns about their financial situation at home, by a desire to prepare herself for a possible separation, or by a loss of focus and direction in her career? Will completing an MBA be meaningful and enjoyable to her, or is it simply another task she feels compelled to complete? These possibilities are worthy of discussion. Although we might hypothesize that Nancy demonstrates a sociotropic style, further information about events that trigger her feelings of anxiety and depression will be necessary before we can know with confidence whether these personality characteristics play a role in her feelings of depression. It would be helpful to know, for example, what factors attracted Nancy to her husband and maintain their relationship. Despite their difficulties, their relationship has persisted. Why? What are her thoughts and feelings about separating from her husband? Does he possess characteristics she admires or values? Is their relationship, in some ways, adaptive for her?

Nancy's comments strongly suggest that she manifests a negative attributional style and that she feels both helpless and hopeless. She tends, for example, to attribute her negative life events to internal, global and stable aspects of her personality. She stated that she "feels inept" and that she "f— up everything." These attributions seem to be contributing to her feelings of hopelessness, as evidenced by her Hopelessness Scale score of 15 and by her thinking that the future "seems dark and vague." Although she attributes her difficulties to her "dysfunctional childhood," it appears that these experiences have led her to feel flawed, incapable, and vulnerable.

Lewinsohn's original model of depression postulates that depression stems, at least in part, from inadequate response contingent positive reinforcement and a consequent reduction in behavioral activity. This does, at first glance, appear to describe Nancy. Although she reported that she enjoys socializing with her friends and sister, she withdraws from her friends when she is depressed. Moreover, she talks with her sister only once or twice a month and noted that she behaves in ways that alienate others. She noted, as well that she often feels "tense and unable to relax." This statement is congruent with her responses on the BAI, a self-report measure of anxiety. Nancy's feelings of anxiety may interfere with her ability to enjoy positive events in her life. Although other people may potentially be available to support her, her tendency to withdraw and irritable demeanor may maintain her depressive episodes.

Nancy reported that she ruminates about her concerns when she is depressed. As she stated, "I tend to focus on myself too much." This self-focused attention and ruminative style may exacerbate her feelings of depression by directing her attention and memory away from positive events in her life, by preventing her from taking active steps to resolve her difficulties, by limiting her participation in enjoyable activities, and by leading her to perceive that her social and occupational performance does not meet the standards she has set for herself.

It is unclear from the case example if Nancy exhibits self-regulation deficits that often accompany feelings of depression. To be sure, Nancy sets stringent standards for herself and appears to be highly self-critical. She blames herself for her predicament and describes herself in pejorative terms. She appears, as such, to manifest several of the deficits described in Rehm's (1977) self-regulation model of depression. Nonetheless, she appears capable of identifying and pursuing important life goals (she is, after all, completing an MBA while she is employed full-time). It is not clear if she acknowledges her abilities and positive traits, rewards herself for her achievements, selectively attends to negative events, or excessively self-punishes. Although she reportedly enjoys backpacking, calling her sister, and exercising, it is not known how often she participates in these activities. Given Nancy's ruminative style, one suspects that she tends to focus upon negative aspects of her life. Further assessment will be necessary to clarify her self-regulation skills. This is important as not every cognitive vulnerability factor will be present in every case. Our goal is to direct our interventions toward ameliorating those which contribute to our patient's distress.

Nancy appears to be a bright, articulate woman, and has a history of academic and occupational accomplishment. This history of accomplishment suggests that her rational problem-solving skills are probably well-developed. It is likely that she is able to identify problems, develop and evaluate alternative solutions, and implement plans for solving problems. Despite these abilities, she appears to feel incapable of solving her problems. She appears, in short, to demonstrate a motivational deficit. This may be reflected in a "negative problem orientation" or "impulsive-careless problem solving style." Nancy doubts her ability to deal with life's problems and is unsure of her decision-making abilities. These beliefs appear to have been modeled and reinforced by her mother during her childhood, and may be exacerbated by her depressed mood. Nancy's belief that she is incapable of solving problems causes her to feel overwhelmed and inhibits her from attempting to actively address her concerns. This perception—that she is incapable and ineffective—may be an important target in therapy.

Gotlib and Hammen's (1992) cognitive-interpersonal model of depression may also prove useful in conceptualizing aspects of Nancy's depression. It is likely that events during Nancy's childhood placed her at an increased risk for depression. Based upon her family history, there may be biological or genetic contributions to her vulnerability for depression. Her early home environment appears to have been chaotic and stressful, and was characterized by violence, inconsistent nurturance, and major losses. It is plausible to assume that these experiences contributed to the development of an insecure attachment relationship between Nancy and her parents. Adaptive problem-solving and affect regulation skills were not modeled for her, and it is likely that she came to view important relationships as unstable, unpredictable, and unreliable. These beliefs may have been internalized in the form of maladaptive schema and a dependent interpersonal style. There may, as a consequence, be recurrent patterns in her relationships with family members, her husband, and her friends and colleagues. Maladaptive beliefs and interpersonal styles appear to play a role in the maintenance of Nancy's feelings of depression.

Teasdale (1988) postulated that maladaptive schema tend over time to be activated by increasingly mild dysphoric moods. In the absence of longitudinal data it is, of course, not possible to know if processes such as this are at play in this case. Nonetheless, it is reasonable to assume that, given the recurrent nature of her depression, Nancy's "representations of depressing experiences . . . [and] negative interpretative categories and constructs" have become more accessible. Negative attitudes and beliefs come to mind quite readily, and she tends to cast a negative spin on events in her life. Although we cannot know whether the specific processes described by Teasdale and his colleagues are occurring, their clinical recommendations—reduce life stress, develop problem-solving skills, reduce reflection upon negative affect, develop a sense that symptoms of depression are controllable—remain sensible. The cognitive and behavioral risk factors for depression are summarized in Table 11.1. These will serve as targets for our clinical interventions.

Beginning and Framing Treatment

When beginning therapy, one of our first tasks is to work with the patient to develop a list of specific problems and treatment goals (Persons, 1989). Developing a problem list can, in some situations, become complex. Consider, for example, the many potential problems and goals that Nancy may wish to address. She has reported experiencing strong feelings of depression, anxiety, irritability, resentment, hopelessness and dissatisfaction with life. She feels overwhelmed by events, troubled by childhood experiences, and is dissatisfied with her marriage. Nancy reports that she has withdrawn from others and that she does not feel

TABLE 11.1   Cognitive-Behavioral Factors Associated With Risk for Depression

Model	Author	Component	Case Example—Nancy
Cognitive Therapy	Beck	Cognitive Triad	Significant.
		Automatic Thoughts	Significant.
		Depressive Schema	High personal standards; Perfectionistic; Views self as emotionally deprived, flawed, vulnerable; Views others as unreliable, rejecting; Feels she must sacrifice own needs and goals for others.
		Cognitive Distortion	Possible magnification, selective attention, personalization.
		Sociotropy	Likely, may contribute to dysphoria.
		Autonomy	Possible.
Hopelessness	Seligman	Outcome independent of response	Possible, pessimistic and passive.
Helplessness	Alloy	Low efficacy	Significant.
Attributional Style	Abramson	Internal, stable global attributions	Significant, makes internal, global, stable attributions for negative events.
Inadequate Reinforcement	Lewinsohn	Low reinforcement	Likely.
		Social skills	Possible. Withdraws, irritable.
		Anxiety	Significant.
Self-focused Attention	Lewinsohn; Pyszczynski & Greenberg	Self-focused attention	Severe.
Ruminative Style	Nolen-Hoeksema	Ruminative response	Severe. Dwells, ruminates.

(continued)

TABLE 11.1 *(continued)*

Model	Author	Component	Case Example—Nancy
Self-Control	Rehm	Self-monitoring	Appears to selectively attend to negative events.
		Self-evaluation	Self-critical, maintains stringent performance standards.
		Self-reinforcement	Unclear.
Social Problem-Solving	D'Zurilla & Nezu	Rational problem-solving skills	Intact. Well-developed.
		Problem-solving motivation	Problematic. Patient is hopeless and pessimistic, feels incapable, low perceived personal efficacy.
Cognitive-Interpersonal	Gotlib & Hammen	Attachment style	Possible insecure attachment to parents, felt abandoned.
		Maladaptive schema	Significant.
		Social behavior	Irritable, withdraws, anticipates loss and rejection.
		Social reinforcement	Variable. Capable of developing close relationships, has several friends, close relationship with sister.
Interacting Cognitive Systems	Teasdale	Accessibility of Schema	Highly accessible, valent.

capable of overcoming her difficulties. She is experiencing a number of somatic symptoms of depression and reports a history of suicidal thoughts. It is an imposing list of concerns. Where do we begin? The multitude and complexity of her presenting problems requires that we prioritize her concerns and identify factors that may be maintaining them (Haynes, 1993).

In the case of Nancy, two issues appear to stand apart as important. Given the severity of her feelings of depression and hopelessness, as well as her history of suicidal ideations, our first goal will be to assess suicidal risk and to insure her safety. With this in mind, a comprehensive assessment of suicidal risk factors will be completed. A number of methods exist for assessing suicidal risk. These include structured and unstructured clinical interviews, gathering data from family members or friends, and the completion of objective measures designed to predict suicidality (for reviews, see Freeman & Reinecke, 1993; Reinecke, 2000; Rudd, Joiner, & Rajab, 2001).

After determining that Nancy is not at risk for making a suicide attempt, we will turn to our second therapeutic task, establishing a therapeutic rapport and developing Nancy's motivation for treatment. Nancy's high levels of depression and anxiety are quite distressing to her, and she appears to be motivated for treatment. Her feelings of pessimism and tendency to withdraw from others, however, are of concern as she may come to withdraw from her therapist as well. At least three beliefs have been found to predict premature termination—the belief that (1) my therapist doesn't really understand me, (2) change is not possible, and (3) change may be possible for others, but I can't do it. Given the risk of premature termination, we will directly address each of these possibilities. This is typically done through simple questioning. After discussing her concerns we might, for example, ask "Do you feel that I've understood your concerns, at least in broad brushstrokes, today? Is there anything important that you feel I don't understand? What am I missing? Do you feel that we are heading in the right direction . . . that the things we're coming up with may be helpful? Do you feel you can do it? Are there any things that may get in the way of trying these approaches out?" If Nancy responds to these questions in anything less than a fully positive way, we will explore her concerns and attempt to resolve them with her.

Time Line for Therapy

Although studies indicate that 60–70% of gains in cognitive therapy occur during the first month of treatment, it is difficult to know in advance how long a course of treatment will be for an individual patient. This is typically determined by a number of factors, including the patient's goals, the chronicity and severity of their difficulties, the presence of comorbid psychiatric disorders, the availability of supportive relationships, and the patient's psychological resources. Given the severity of Nancy's depression it initially may be useful to see her twice a week. It might also be helpful to suggest that she participate in a cognitive therapy group. This would provide her with additional support, and would serve to reinforce the skills she is developing in individual therapy. Our goal would be for Nancy to experience a meaningful decline in her depressive symptoms within 4 to 6 weeks. I would recommend that we assess her progress after 10 weeks of treatment, and refine our treatment goals at that time.

Assessment

Assessment of symptoms and mediating variables using a combination of objective and subjective approaches can be useful in developing a case formulation and for monitoring progress. Given the requirements of hospitals, insurance carriers, and health-care management organizations, it is important to develop an accurate diagnosis and to objectively evaluate patient progress.

The selection of measures is determined by our goals. Different measures are, of course, more appropriate for different tasks. Decisions must be made about whom we will turn to for information, their reliability, the methods of collection, and the psychometric properties of the instruments. Given Nancy's presenting concerns, we will want to focus on factors that may be maintaining her feelings of depression. It is important, given the phenomenological emphasis of cognitive therapy, to balance the use of objective measures with a clear understanding of the patient's subjective experience. Although rating scales and self-report questionnaires can provide us with an overview of Nancy's concerns, they do not speak to the meaning of those experiences for her. A sensitive discussion of her scores and responses to individual scale items can be quite helpful in this regard.

Instruments, Questionnaires, and Observations

The clinician has a range of choices for assessing the presence of a depressive disorder and its severity. Commonly used diagnostic interview schedules include the Schedule for Affective Disorders and Schizophrenia (SADS; Endicott & Spitzer, 1978) and the Structured Clinical Interview for DSM-IV Disorders (SCID; First, Spitzer, Gibbon, & Williams, 1995). The Hamilton Rating Scale for Depression (HRSD; Hamilton, 1967) can be completed by the clinician after a brief interview and provides a useful estimate of severity of depression. This can be augmented by a self-report measure of depression, such as the Beck Depression Inventory (BDI; Beck, Ward, Mendelson, Mock, & Erbaugh, 1961) or the Center for Epidemiological Studies Depression Scale (CES-D; Radloff 1977). As noted, Nancy also reports experiencing strong feelings of anxiety, irritability, pessimism and low self-concept. It may be useful, then, to assess the strength of these emotions and to explore events that contribute to them. Brief self-report measures, such as the Beck Anxiety Inventory (BAI; Beck, Epstein, Brown, & Steer, 1988), the Hopelessness Scale (HS; Beck, Weissman, Lester, & Trexler, 1974) and the Beck Self-Concept Test (BSCT; Beck, Steer, Epstein, & Brown, 1990) can be helpful in this regard.

The assessment of cognitive and social factors that may be contributing to Nancy's distress can be daunting given the large number of potentially relevant variables. Although it is possible to administer measures of each of the factors we have discussed, this would not be feasible in clinical practice. With this in mind, it can be helpful to select a set of measures that will be useful in developing a treatment plan. Inasmuch as each of the models discussed addresses a unique component of the depressive disorder, each may be relevant in developing a treatment plan. Measures commonly used to assess variables associated with depression include the Dysfunctional Attitudes Scale (DAS; Weissman & Beck, 1978), Automatic Thoughts Questionnaire (ATQ; Hollon & Kendall, 1980), Attributional Style Questionnaire (ASQ; Peterson, Semmel, von Baeyer, Abramson, Metalsky, & Seligman, 1982), Social Problem-Solving Inventory (D'Zurilla & Nezu, 1990), Personal Style Inventory (PSI; Robins et al., 1994), Pleasant Events Schedule (MacPhillamy & Lewinsohn, 1982), Unpleasant Events Schedule (Lewinsohn, Mermelstein, Alexander, & MacPhillamy, 1985) and the Interpersonal Events Schedule (Youngren & Lewinsohn, 1980).

Structure and Goals

Recent research suggests that the more effective forms of psychotherapy tend, as a group, to be active, problem-oriented and structured. Cognitive therapy meets these criteria. Each of the sessions is organized and includes a number of components. These are summarized in Table 11.2.

In beginning treatment we will want to develop a parsimonious formulation of Nancy's difficulties and share it with her. This will provide her with a constructive way of understanding her concerns, and will lead to a number of practical recommendations of things that might be done to alleviate her distress. Our goal is to allow her to see that her difficulties are neither inscrutable nor unpredictable, and to provide her with a sense of control over them. In presenting a case formulation it can be helpful to use simple, direct language. In reviewing the results of our initial assessment, we might, for example, state,

> Based upon what you've told me, it seems that your primary concern is the depression and that it's become quite severe. Right? You've noted that you tend to think very negatively about yourself and your life and the future, and that your mood tends to drop when you have these thoughts. It seems as though you've been dwelling on these problems a lot lately, but you haven't been able to come up with any solutions. They seem unsolvable. You've also noted that you tend to be quite self-critical and that you hold very high standards . . . you're a perfectionist. It sounds as though you may have learned this through your experiences growing up, and that the conflict at home may have led you to feel that you had to avoid confrontation and had to please others in order to keep them from leaving you. You've mentioned, as well, that you've tended to back away from others (which leads you to feel lonely and unsupported), and that you can get pretty irritable and "bitchy" at times. Right? I wonder if this is affecting your relationships with others. . . .

In simple terms, Nancy's depression appears to stem from a lack of rewarding social activities and relationships, in conjunction with

TABLE 11.2 Structure of the Cognitive Therapy Session

(1) Assess mood and review recent events
(2) Collaboratively set an agenda
(3) Review homework from the previous session
(4) Discuss issues on the agenda
(5) Introduce or review a specific skill to address these concerns
(6) Formulate a homework task, identify factors which may interfere with successful completion
(7) Help patient to summarize the main points and conclusions
(8) Discuss thoughts and feelings about the session

cognitive distortions, perfectionistic standards, self-criticism, a tendency to ruminate unproductively about her difficulties, and low perceptions of personal efficacy. These difficulties are based, at least in part, from the confluence of stressful life events and cognitive vulnerabilities stemming from early childhood experiences. In discussing this formulation with her, we highlight the ways in which social, environmental, cognitive, behavioral, and affective factors interact with one another in contributing to a "downward cycle" of depression. Inasmuch as these variables can influence one another, the formulation suggests points of intervention and ways in which this cycle can be reversed. Patients often find case formulations, such as this, to be quite helpful. The formulation provides them with a framework for understanding their distress and suggests specific actions that can be taken.

As noted, our models assume that cognitive activity affects behavior, and that emotional change may be brought about by changing an individual's belief system. We begin this process by encouraging Nancy to monitor her thoughts and moods. She might, for example, be asked to keep a diary of situations in which she feels upset, and to note her thoughts at those times. These would be reviewed in therapy, and both the reasonableness and adaptiveness of her beliefs, attitudes, attributions and thoughts would be explored. We would encourage her to look at her thoughts as objects or hypotheses, rather than as facts. For example, her thoughts that she has "f— up everything," she is "inept . . . just incompetent," and that she "always has to please others" may be worthy of discussion. Given the level of negative affect attached to these thoughts, Nancy may experience difficulty recalling contradictory evidence or developing alternative interpretations. Should this occur, it may be helpful to ask Nancy to discuss these experiences in the 3rd person. Nancy might, for example, be asked, "If a friend told you she felt "inept and incompetent" how would you help her?" Once Nancy has become able to monitor changes in her mood and to reflect upon her thoughts and feelings, we will be able to share a number of cognitive and behavioral techniques with her.

Specific Interventions and Techniques

A primary goal will be to provide Nancy with experiences that will serve to disconfirm and change her maladaptive beliefs. These experiences can take a number of forms. They may include behavioral experiments, rational examinations of the validity of her beliefs, a review of events that have occurred over the course of her life that supported the development of specific beliefs, an examination of how her beliefs affect her relationships with others, or an exploration of the ways in which the beliefs are expressed in the therapeutic relationship. Our objective throughout is to encourage Nancy to think critically about her beliefs and attitudes, and to approach her difficulties in an active, problem-oriented manner. Given Nancy's tendency to seek support and guidance from others, it may be helpful (at least initially) to offer her support and encouragement. Although her tendency to seek support can be used therapeutically to encourage her to complete homework assignments, one should be careful not to foster a sense of dependency upon the therapist. Rather, we will want to develop her problem-solving skills and will encourage her to pursue her goals and interests in a more autonomous manner.

Cognitive and behavioral strategies and techniques for alleviating Nancy's feelings of depression are presented in Table 11.3. Given the severity of her dysphoria, it may be helpful to begin with behavioral interventions, such as Mastery and Pleasure Scheduling. Patients are encouraged to record what they do on an hourly basis and to rate each activity as to how much of a sense of pleasure or enjoyment they derived from it, and how much of a sense of accomplishment or achievement it engendered. Monitoring of daily activities allows the therapist and the patient to evaluate the validity of thoughts such as "I didn't accomplish anything today" or "Nothing good ever happens in my life." Quite often such thoughts are incorrect. Negativistic perceptual and memory biases lead patients to overlook positive events that have occurred. In the event that they have, in fact, done little that might engender feelings of accomplishment or pleasure, activities which might provide her with a sense of accomplishment or fun can be identified and scheduled. Our goal will be to increase Nancy's activity level as well as the "reinforcement frequency" in her life. We wish to maximize her participation in activities that will provide her with a sense of pleasure, accomplishment and worth.

Given the role of social isolation in depression, it is important to reestablish Nancy's feelings of connectedness to others. Following Lewinsohn et al. (1980, 1985), we would assess the quality and nature of Nancy's social relationships. She might be encouraged to reestablish her relationships with her friends and to participate in a range of enjoyable social activities. This can, however, be a challenging task.

TABLE 11.3   Components of Cognitive Therapy for Depression

(1)   Describe concerns, objective assessment (i.e., affective, cognitive, behavioral social, environmental factors maintaining distress)

(2)   Develop problem list, goal-setting

(3)   Assess suicidality; address factors associated with premature termination

(4)   Develop case formulation

(5)   Share rationale with patient; socialization to the cognitive model

(6)   Mood monitoring

(7)   Behavioral activation
   (a)   Increase pleasant activities
   (b)   Increase mastery activities
   (c)   Increase social activities

(8)   Identify automatic thoughts and cognitive distortions (e.g., thought record, diary)

(9)   Rational responding; formulating adaptive alternatives

(10)   Address negative attributional style, maladaptive expectations

(11)   Social problem-solving
   (a)   Rational problem solving
   (b)   Problem-solving motivation

(12)   Relaxation training, systematic desensitization

(13)   Communication skills

(14)   Assertiveness training

(15)   Social engagement
   (a)   Identify recurrent maladaptive social patterns
   (b)   Identify specific social skills deficits

(16)   Address maladaptive schema
   (a)   Objective assessment (e.g., DAS, YBSQ)
   (b)   Downward arrow; developmental analysis
   (c)   Recurrent themes in relationships and the therapeutic transference

(17)   Relapse prevention
   (a)   Normalize recurrence of negative mood
   (b)   Change maladaptive schema
   (c)   Anticipate triggers and stressors
   (d)   Develop social supports
   (e)   Review and rehearse adaptive coping strategies
   (f)   Attentional control

(18)   Address feelings and thoughts regarding termination

Depressed individuals often behave in ways, both subtle and obvious, that alienate them from others. They frequently withdraw from others and believe that others will be critical or rejecting. Moreover, they frequently tend to avert eye contact, do not smile, seek reassurance, and dwell upon their own difficulties. We may, then, wish to begin with behavioral interventions—such as social skills work and activity scheduling. We will want to attend, as well, to cognitive factors that may interfere with her ability to enjoy social activities. It can be helpful, for example, to identify and change negative beliefs and expectations that can interfere with completion of behavioral homework assignments. Cognitive and behavioral interventions, then, are used in an integrated manner from the beginning of treatment.

Identifying, evaluating and changing maladaptive thoughts play a central role in cognitive therapy. Automatic thoughts are typically brief, involuntary, and automatic. They often seem reasonable to the individual. By definition they are accompanied by strong affect and are difficult to consciously control. As noted, maladaptive automatic thoughts often stem from biased or distorted thought processes. This is not to say, however, that all automatic thoughts are irrational. Individuals do, over the course of their lives, experience trauma, losses, setbacks, frustrations, and a range of overwhelming life events. Crises happen. The central question we ask as clinicians is not "Is this belief irrational?", but "Is this belief reasonable and adaptive in the current situation?".

With this in mind, Nancy might be encouraged to reflect upon her thoughts, the accompanying emotions, and the situations that trigger them in greater detail. A personal diary or a Dysfunctional Thought Record (DTR) can be quite helpful in this regard. She would first practice identifying automatic thoughts with her therapist, then would practice this skill at home. A sample of a DTR is presented in Table 11.4.

TABLE 11.4   Dysfunctional Thought Record (DTR)

Date/Time	Situation	Emotion	Automatic Thought
		(Severity)	
Sat. 2:30 pm	At the country club with my husband	Depressed 90%	I'm trapped . . . this is a show, it isn't me. He doesn't care what I'd like to do. This will never change.
		Frustrated 60%	It's *always* the same . . . I have to put on an act . . . there's nothing I can do.

Negative shifts in mood are typically accompanied by automatic thoughts. Changes in mood can be taken as a signal, then, that a cognitive process has been activated. With practice Nancy can learn to reflect on her negative moods and the thoughts that are maintaining them. Our next task is to test the validity, function and consequences of these thoughts, and to develop more adaptive ways of thinking about the events that triggered them. We begin by inquiring about the meanings Nancy attributes to her experiences. What does she mean when she states that she is "trapped"? What associations does she have to this term? Has she felt this way in the past? What has she learned about herself from these experiences? What are her thoughts and feelings when she remarks that he "doesn't care" about her? As we explore the meanings of her narrative, a range of emotions and memories will be activated. As these are activated, we can begin to use rational responding to evaluate their validity and adaptiveness. In its essential form, this involves asking a number of simple, direct questions—questions that challenge the validity of maladaptive beliefs. These questions are:

1. What is the evidence (both for and against this belief)?
2. Is there an alternative, more adaptive, way of looking at this? Are there other things that can be learned from this experience? Are alternative meanings and interpretations possible?
3. If not, so what? Is this a truly significant problem? What can I do to solve the problem?

In evaluating the evidence for an automatic thought it is worth noting that depressed individuals will be more likely to recall evidence that is supportive of their maladaptive beliefs. Both memory and perceptual processes are mood or state-dependent. Positive experiences and evidence, as such, are likely to be overlooked, forgotten or minimized; and negative evidence will be selectively perceived and remembered. With this in mind, care should be taken to attend to disconfirming events. Is it true, for example, that Nancy's husband doesn't care about her feelings and well-being? Has he ever shown affection or concern for her? Does he currently show affection or concern in ways she may not be aware of? Is it true that she *always* must put on an act for his friends and colleagues? What would happen if she did not? Might "putting on an act" in some ways be a reasonable thing to do? Are there opportunities for her to participate in activities she enjoys? How would she feel, and how would others react, if she were to politely decline to join him at the club for the afternoon? Has she been able to assert herself in the past? Why not in this situation? As should be apparent from these questions, cognitive therapy is, at its heart, a collaborative process of self-exploration.

As with a Socratic teacher, the questions continue. Our goal is not to simply disconfirm a negative automatic thought or belief, but to more deeply understand the meanings Nancy is attaching to her experiences and the narratives through which she understands herself and her life. The process of gently and persistently evaluating experiences and interpretations that support one's beliefs and attitudes, as well as the advantages and disadvantages of maintaining these views, are the foundation of cognitive therapy.

As Nancy reviews these thoughts, it is likely that larger themes and issues will become apparent. It is possible, for the sake of discussion, that Nancy will recognize that she maintains a tacit belief that "It is essential to have a stable family in order to feel secure" or that "Conflict should be avoided at all costs." Beliefs, such as these, would be reasonable given her experiences growing up, and may lead her to interact with her husband in an unassertive manner. These larger issues could be explored and their implications examined. More importantly, Nancy might be encouraged to develop a more flexible set of beliefs. Not all conflict, for example, is destructive or dangerous. Not all attempts to express one's desires and goals will be met with rejection and hostility. Given this knowledge, can we help Nancy to formulate a more adaptive way of approaching this situation? The specific ways in which she uses this new knowledge, however, are up to her. Might she be able to discuss her concerns with her husband? Could she engage in activities that will provide her with feelings of competence and pleasure (why not rent some space and paint on Saturday afternoons while your husband golfs with his friends)? What might be the consequences of acting in a more assertive manner? Are there things she might do to develop a closer, more intimate relationship with her husband and with others? What would be the implications of adopting a less perfectionistic, self-critical stance?

Similar approaches can be taken in addressing Nancy's negative attributional style and in developing her problem-solving skills. As in the case of automatic thoughts, the attributions that Nancy makes when a negative event occurs can be monitored and examined. The meanings she attaches to the belief can be explored, and the implications of understanding the event in that way can be evaluated. As in the case of negative automatic thoughts, there often is a more adaptive way of understanding the event. More adaptive ways of understanding events (incorporating external, unstable, and specific attributions) can be introduced.

Although Nancy's problem-solving skills appear to be reasonably well-developed, it may be helpful to assess these skills more directly. Is she able, for example, to effectively solve problems at home? At work? In her personal relationships? When strong emotions occur as part of the problem? Is she able to identify problems and their components? Can she effectively generate and evaluate alternative solutions? Does she implement the solution and persist if it is not immediately effective? If Nancy is not able to accomplish these tasks, it may be helpful to provide her with specific training in social problem-solving. Procedures for developing problem-solving skills, such as those described by Nezu, Nezu, and Perri (1989) and D'Zurilla and Nezu (2001) can be quite helpful in this regard.

The Therapeutic Relationship in Cognitive Therapy

Maintaining an empathic, trusting therapeutic relationship is critical for progress in cognitive therapy. Essential requirements for cognitive therapists include a capacity for accurate empathy, warmth, genuineness, patience, and responsivity. They must be able to take the patient's perspective and sensitively reflect this back to them, and also convey a caring concern and a sense of honest self-awareness. Although it is important to maintain a positive rapport, this is seen as necessary, but not sufficient, for therapeutic improvement. Warmth, sensitivity and therapeutic responsiveness are a foundation of progress, but do not guarantee that gains will be made. This view of the role of the therapeutic relationship is consistent with research indicating that progress in therapy is predicted by at least three sets of variables—the quality of the therapeutic alliance, technical factors, and patient variables.

Beck et al. (1979) used the term "collaborative" to characterize the optimal therapeutic stance in cognitive therapy. The term is interesting in that it implies that the therapist and the patient function as a team, with each sharing responsibility for therapeutic progress. In a collaborative relationship decisions are jointly made. This relationship is different in many ways from the passivity of traditional psychodynamic psychotherapy, and from the directiveness of contemporary behavior therapy.

Transference and Countertransference

Although the concepts of transference and countertransference do not play a central role in cognitive theories of therapeutic change, cognitive therapy does acknowledge the essential role of early experience in organizing human relationships and of the ways in which tacit beliefs may be reflected in the therapeutic relationship. Moreover, as Persons (1989) notes, the therapeutic relationship in cognitive therapy can be used both as a means of understanding the patient's thoughts and behaviors outside of the therapy session and as a tool for therapeutic change. The therapist's thoughts and feelings in response to the patient can yield important information about the patient's effects on others.

Cognitive theory and research acknowledge that relationships with significant others in one's past may have important effects on the nature and quality of current relationships. Although this notion—that past relationships may influence emotional and behavioral responses in current relationships—plays a central role in psychodynamic formulations of transference, the cognitive understanding of how these effects occur is quite different. Whereas transference is understood from a psychodynamic perspective as reflecting the expression of specific drives, conflicts, or the recapitulation of representations of subjective interactive experiences, cognitive models of psychotherapy conceptualize transference effects from a social learning perspective. As noted, cognitive therapy proposes that mental representations or schema develop from an early age. These representations incorporate tacit beliefs and expectations about the self, others, the physical world, the future, and relationships with others. These schema serve as templates to guide the processing of incoming information and the retrieval of relevant memories. From this perspective, mental representations of others and of past relationships are stored in memory and are activated with new individuals or social situations that are similar to those in the past. This conceptualization of schema and their relationship to transference is consistent with recent research on social cognition, relational scripts, and adult attachment style.

When presented with a new person or a novel or ambiguous social situation, people use past experiences with similar individuals to guide their reaction. Psychotherapy sessions can be both novel and ambiguous. It is not surprising, then, that preexisting schema, expectations, attributional tendencies, and perceptual biases might be activated. In therapy, as in day-to-day life, individuals tend to draw specific conclusions and to make inferences about new persons based upon past experiences with similar individuals. Transference, from a cognitive perspective, occurs not only in therapy but also in a wide range of social relationships. Inasmuch as relationships can be complex and require rapid assessment and evaluation of a great deal of nonverbal information, transference-based processing—using past experiences in similar situations to make sense of a novel social situation—can be both efficient and adaptive. When applied in a rigid or inappropriate manner, however, difficulties can arise. Not all males treat you like your father; not all females react like your mother. Interestingly, from a cognitive perspective, transference relationships are malleable—they can change in response to new experiences—particularly those that are accompanied by strong affect. Moreover, they are not limited to relationships with parents. Rather, they can be based upon experiences in any important relationship.

Relapse Prevention

Given the high rates of relapse and recurrence among adults with major depression, relapse prevention is an important part of the therapy process. Cognitive therapy approaches this issue in several ways. We begin by noting that shifts in mood—both positive and negative—are normal and adaptive. Having participated in cognitive therapy will not inoculate Nancy from experiencing feelings of sadness in the future. Rather, it can provide her with a rationale for understanding these moods and practical tools for managing them. With this in mind, it may be helpful to assist Nancy to distinguish normal lapses and shifts in her mood from a relapse. We wish for her to maintain a sense of hope in the face of adversity, and to recognize that feelings of sadness and anxiety *are*, in fact, normal reactions to many life events. A second approach is to identify and change maladaptive schema which serve as vulnerability factors for depression (see Young & Mattila, this volume, chapter 12), and to develop problem-solving and affect-regulation skills that Nancy can use in distressing situations. Having techniques, such as rational responding, rational problem-solving, and reattribution, available can be quite useful when faced with a loss, rejection or failure. Particular attention is directed toward combating feelings of hopelessness, perfectionism, and a loss of control that can occur in stressful situations. Given the role of the social environment in the maintenance of depression, we would encourage Nancy to note how she has made improvements in the quality of her relationships, and to develop a circle of friends she can turn to for support should her mood begin to worsen. It can be helpful to review specific skills that have been learned over the course of therapy, and to summarize what she has learned about herself and others. We want to understand, from Nancy's perspective, what has been helpful and to explore the meanings she attaches to her improvement. We are endeavoring, in essence, to consolidate her sense of herself as capable, positive, and desirable. Third, we may want to anticipate stressors that Nancy may encounter and work with her to develop a plan for coping with them. This might involve taking a "devil's advocate" position and attempting to refute her adaptive self-statements and coping strategies. In sum, relapse prevention in cognitive therapy is both active and focused. It attends to the full range of cognitive, behavioral, social and environmental factors that may have contributed to Nancy's initial distress.

As noted, recent work on the Interacting Cognitive Systems model of depression (Teasdale, 1983, 1988) suggests that repeated activation of negative belief systems can lead to an increased likelihood of them being reactivated by future periods of mild dysphoria. Moreover, generalization can occur as these belief systems come to be activated by a wider range of cues. Over time, depressed individuals become reactive to increasingly minor fluctuations in mood. These findings imply that, with time, stressful environmental events may come to play a progressively less important role in triggering of depressive episodes. Relapse can be viewed as a reactivation of depressogenic belief systems—a reactivation that becomes less and less dependent on environmental stress. This possibility is consistent with the view that factors associated with vulnerability for depression may differ from those associated with severity, maintenance and relapse. In practice, this suggests that attempts might be made during periods of positive mood to train individuals to redirect their attention and memory away from negative cues (Teasdale, Segal, & Williams, 1995). Nancy may be able to learn, then, to preempt the activation of a full depressive episode. In sum, there are four components of relapse prevention in cognitive therapy: (1) prepare for stressful events by rehearsing cognitive and behavioral coping skills; (2) develop social supports; (3) change maladaptive schema; and (4) develop control over attentional processes that serve to trigger depressive episodes in response to mild dysphoria.

SUMMARY AND DISCUSSION

Cognitive therapy for depression is based on social learning theory, and assumes that cognitive, behavioral social, and environmental factors interact over time to influence human adaptation. Cognitive therapies of depression emphasize the importance of developing behavioral skills and of changing maladaptive belief systems. As noted, a number of cognitive factors have been implicated in the etiology and maintenance of depression. These include negative automatic thoughts, cognitive biases and distortions, negative attributional style, negatively biased perceptions and memories, perfectionism, feelings of hopelessness and reduced personal efficacy, self-focused attention, impaired problem-solving, ruminative style, and maladaptive schema. Socially, depressed individuals tend to withdraw from others and manifest behaviors that may, over time, alienate others and lead to a loss of social reinforcement. They tend to engage in fewer activities that provide them with feelings of enjoyment, pleasure, belonging, mastery, or competence. A modularized cognitive therapy approach attempts to directly and systematically evaluate and address each of these factors in the context of a trusting, supportive therapeutic relationship.

In practice, we wish to provide Nancy with a framework for understanding her concerns and to develop her ability to monitor her moods. We want to assist her to reflect upon the adaptiveness of her beliefs and attitudes and to develop an alternative vision for herself and her life. In accomplishing this, we would encourage Nancy's participation in enjoyable, social activities and would work with her to improve the quality of her social interactions. We would endeavor to develop her problem-solving skills and affect regulation capacities. Finally, we wish to identify and modify maladaptive thoughts, attitudes, beliefs, expectations and attributions that may be contributing to her distress.

Is cognitive therapy effective? In many cases, yes. Controlled outcome studies completed over the past 30 years have been positive, and recent work suggests that cognitive therapy can be effective (in combination with medications) for treating even severe, chronic depression. We can, in short, have some confidence in the effectiveness of this approach. We must acknowledge, however, that other approaches are also effective and that there is much that we do not know about commonalities between alternative forms of treatment. Moreover, there are patients who do not benefit from cognitive therapy, and risk of relapse remains an important clinical and social concern. Our understanding of the development of maladaptive belief systems which place individuals at risk for depression is rudimentary, and we are only beginning to understand how cognitive models can be employed in preventing the onset of clinical depression. Finally, there is much that we do not know about the effectiveness of cognitive therapy when it is used in community settings, the effects of comorbidity on treatment response, and the mechanisms of therapeutic change.

Science is all about objective knowledge, and behavioral science is no exception. Cognitive-behavioral models of psychopathology and psychotherapy have developed at a seemingly exponential pace, and are continually tested by new findings and new theories. Perhaps the most striking thing about this period of rapid advance, however, is not how much we know but how little. As is so often the case, new research generates as many questions as answers. Cognitive therapy is not a field free from failure, confusion or contradiction. Important questions remain about the ways in which cognitive, social, environmental and biological factors interact over the course of normal development, and of how these factors function in placing individuals at risk for depression. These questions and issues represent an important challenge for future clinicians and researchers. Although cognitive therapy has emerged during the past 30 years as a promising and powerful treatment for clinical depression, much work remains to be done.

REFERENCES

Abramson, L., Metalsky, G., & Alloy, L. (1989). Hopelessness depression: A theory-based subtype of depression. *Psychological Review, 96,* 358–372.

Abramson, L., Seligman, M., & Teasdale, J. (1978). Learned helplessness in humans: Critique and reformulation. *Journal of Abnormal Psychology, 87,* 49–74.

Beck, A. (1963). Thinking and depression: I. Idiosyncratic content and cognitive distortions. *Archives of General Psychiatry, 9,* 324–333.

Beck, A. (1964). Thinking and depression: 2. Theory and therapy. *Archives of General Psychiatry, 10,* 561–571.

Beck, A., Epstein, N., Brown, G., & Steer, R. (1988). An inventory for measuring clinical anxiety: Psychometric properties. *Journal of Consulting and Clinical Psychology, 56,* 893–897.

Beck, A., Rush, A., Shaw, B., & Emery, G. (1979). *Cognitive therapy of depression.* New York: Guilford Press.

Beck, A., Steer, R., Epstein, N., & Brown, G. (1990). Beck Self-Concept Test. *Psychological Assessment: A Journal of Consulting and Clinical Psychology, 2,* 191–197.

Beck, A., Ward, C., Mendelson, M., Mock, J., & Erbaugh, J. (1961). An inventory for measuring depression. *Archives of General Psychiatry, 4,* 561–571.

Beck, A., Weissman, A., Lester, D., & Trexler, L. (1974). The measurement of pessimism: The hopelessness scale. *Journal of Consulting and Clinical Psychology, 42,* 861–865.

Brewin, C. (1985). Depression and causal attributions: What is their relation? *Psychological Bulletin, 98,* 297–309.

Chambless, D., Baker, M., Baucom, D., Beutler, L., Calhoun, K., Crits-Christoph, P., Daiuto, A., DeRubeis, R., Detweiler, J., Haaga, D., Johnson, S., McCurry, S., Mueser, K., Pope, K., Sanderson, W., Shoham, V., Stickle, T., Williams, D., & Woody, S. (1998). Update on empirically-validated therapies: II. *The Clinical Psychologist, 51,* 3–16.

Chambless, D., & Hollon, S. (1998). Defining empirically-supported therapies. *Journal of Consulting and Clinical Psychology, 66,* 7–18.

Clark, D. A., & Beck, A. (1999). *Scientific foundations of cognitive theory and therapy of depression.* New York: Wiley.

Dobson, K. (1989). A meta-analysis of the efficacy of cognitive therapy for depression. *Journal of Consulting and Clinical Psychology, 57,* 414–419.

Dobson, K., & Dozois, D. (2001). Historical and philosophical bases of the cognitive-behavioral therapies. In K. S. Dobson (Ed.), *Handbook of cognitive-behavioral therapies* (2nd ed.). New York: Guilford Press.

D'Zurilla, T., & Nezu, A. (1982). Social problem solving in adults. In P. C. Kendall (Ed.), *Advances in cognitive-behavioral research and therapy* (Vol. 1, pp. 201–274). New York: Academic Press.

D'Zurilla, T., & Nezu, A. (1990). Development and preliminary evaluation of the Social Problem-Solving Inventory (SPSI). *Psychological Assessment: A Journal of Consulting and Clinical Psychology, 2,* 156–163.

D'Zurilla, T., & Nezu, A. (1999). *Problem-solving therapy: A social competence approach to clinical intervention* (2nd ed.). New York: Springer Publishing Co.

D'Zurilla, T., & Nezu, A. (2001). Problem-solving therapies. In K. Dobson (Ed.), *Handbook of cognitive-behavioral therapies* (2nd ed.). New York: Guilford Press.

Endicott, J., & Spitzer, R. (1978). A diagnostic interview: The Schedule for Affective Disorders and Schizophrenia. *Archives of General Psychiatry, 35,* 837–844.

Engel, R., & DeRubeis, R. (1993). The role of cognition in depression. In K. Dobson & P. Kendall (Eds.), *Psychopathology and cognition* (pp. 83–119). San Diego: Academic Press.

First, M., Spitzer, L., Gibbon, M., & Williams, J. (1995). *Structured clinical interview for Axis I DSM-IV Disorders (SCID Version 2.0)*. Washington, DC: American Psychiatric Press.

Freeman, A., & Reinecke, M. (1993) *Cognitive therapy of suicidal behavior.* New York: Springer.

Freeman, A., & Reinecke, M. (1995). Cognitive therapy. In A. Gurman & S. Messer (Eds.), *Essential psychotherapies: Theory and practice* (pp. 182–225). New York: Guilford Press.

Gillham, J., Reivich, K., Jaycox, L., & Seligman, M. (1995). Prevention of depressive symptoms in schoolchildren: A two-year follow-up. *Psychological Science, 6,* 343–351.

Gotlib, I. (1990). An interpersonal systems approach to the conceptualization and treatment of depression. In R. Ingram (Ed.), *Contemporary psychological approaches to depression: Theory research, and treatment* (pp. 137–154). New York: Plenum Press.

Gotlib, I., & Hammen, C. (1992). *Psychological aspects of depression: Toward a cognitive-interpersonal integration.* New York: John Wiley.

Haaga, D., Dyck, M., & Ernst, D. (1991). Empirical status of cognitive theory of depression. *Psychological Bulletin, 110,* 215–236.

Haaga, D., Fine, J., Terrill, D., Stewart, B., & Beck, A. (1993). Social problem-solving deficits, dependency, and depressive symptoms. *Cognitive Therapy and Research, 19,* 147–158.

Hamilton, M. (1967). Development of a rating scale for primary depressive illness. *British Journal of Social and Clinical Psychology, 6,* 278–296.

Haynes, S. (1993). Treatment implications of psychological assessment. *Psychological Assessment, 5,* 251–253.

Hollon, S., & Kendall, P. (1980). Cognitive self-statements in depression: Development of an Automatic Thoughts Questionnaire. *Cognitive Therapy and Research, 4,* 383–395.

Hollon, S., Shelton, R., & Loosen, P. (1991). Cognitive therapy for depression: Conceptual issues and clinical efficacy. *Journal of Consulting and Clinical Psychology, 59,* 88–99.

Ingram, R. (1990). Self-focused attention in clinical disorders: Review and a conceptual model. *Psychological Bulletin, 107,* 156–176.

Jarrett, R., Schaffer, M., McIntire, D., Witt-Browder, A., Kraft, D., & Risser, R. (1999). Treatment of atypical depression with cognitive therapy or phenelzine. *Archives of General Psychiatry, 56,* 431–437.

Kanfer, F. (1970). Self-regulation: Research issues and speculations. In C. Neuringer & J. Michael (Eds.), *Behavior modification in clinical psychology.* New York: Appleton-Century-Crofts.

Keller, M., McCullough, J., Klein, D., Arnow, B., Dunner, D., Gelenberg, A., Markowitz, J., Nemeroff, C., Russell, J., Thase, M., Trivedi, M., &

Zajecka, J. (2000). A comparison of nefazodone, the cognitive-behavioral-analysis system of psychotherapy, and their combination for the treatment of chronic depression. *New England Journal of Medicine, 342*(20), 1462–1470.

Kihlstrom, J. (1987) The cognitive unconscious. *Science, 237,* 1445–1452.

Lewinsohn, P. (1974). A behavioral approach to depression. In R. Friedman & M. Katz (Eds.), *The psychology of depression: Contemporary theory and research* (pp. 157–185). New York: John Wiley.

Lewinsohn, P., Hoberman, H., Teri, L., & Hautzinger, M. (1985). An integrative theory of depression. In S. Reiss & R. Bootzin (Eds.), *Theoretical issues in behavior therapy.* Orlando: Academic Press.

Lewinsohn, P., Mermelstein, R., Alexander, C., & MacPhillamy, D. (1985). The Unpleasant Events Schedule: A scale for the measurement of aversive events. *Journal of Clinical Psychology, 41,* 483–498.

Lewinsohn, P., Sullivan, J., & Grosscup, S. (1980). Changing reinforcing events: An approach to the treatment of depression. *Psychotherapy: Theory, Research, and Practice, 47,* 322–334.

MacPhillamy, D., & Lewinsohn, P. (1982). The Pleasant Events Schedule: Studies on reliability, validity, and scale intercorrelations. *Journal of Consulting and Clinical Psychology, 50,* 363–380.

Marx, E., Williams, J., & Claridge, G. (1992). Depression and social problem solving. *Journal of Abnormal Psychology, 101,* 78–86.

McMullin, R. (1986) *Handbook of cognitive therapy techniques.* New York: Guilford Press.

Moretti, M., & Shaw, B. (1989). Automatic and dysfunctional cognitive processes m depression. In J. Uleman & J. Bargh (Eds.), *Unintended thought: The limits of awareness, intention, and control* (pp. 383–421). New York: Guilford Press.

Nezu, A. (1987). A problem-solving formulation of depression: A literature review and proposal of a pluralistic model. *Clinical Psychology Review, 7,* 121–144.

Nezu, A., Nezu, C., & Perri, M. (1989). *Problem-solving therapy for depression: Theory research. and clinical guidelines.* New York: John Wiley.

Nolen-Hoeksema, S. (1987). Sex differences in bipolar depression: Evidence and theory. *Psychological Bulletin, 101,* 259–282.

Nolen-Hoeksema, S. (1990). *Sex differences in depression.* Stanford, CA: Stanford University Press.

Persons, J. (1989). *Cognitive therapy in practice: A case formulation approach.* New York: Norton.

Peterson, C., Semmel, A., von Baeyer, C., Abramson, L., Metalsky, G., & Seligman, M. (1982). The Attributional Style Questionnaire. *Cognitive Therapy and Research, 6,* 287–300.

Pyszczynski, T., & Greenberg, J. (1987). Self-regulatory perseveration and the depressive self-focusing style: A self-awareness theory of reactive depression. *Psychological Bulletin, 102,* 122–138.

Radloff, L. (1977). The CES-D: A self-report depression scale for research in the general population. *Applied Psychological Measurement, 1,* 385–401.

Rehm, L. (1977). A self-control model of depression. *Behavior Therapy, 8,* 787–804.

Rehm, L. (1984). Self-management therapy for depression. *Advances in Behavior Therapy and Research, 6,* 83–98.

Rehm, L. (1995). Psychotherapies for depression. In K. Craig & K. Dobson (Eds.), *Anxiety and depression in adults and children* (pp. 183–208). Thousand Oaks, CA: Sage Publications.

Reinecke, M. (2000). Suicide and depression. In F. Dattilio & A. Freeman (Eds.), *Cognitive-behavioral strategies in crisis intervention* (2nd ed., pp. 84–125). New York: Guilford Press.

Robins, C., Ladd, J., Welkowitz, J., Blaney, P., Diaz, R., & Kutcher, G. (1994). The Personal Style Inventory: Preliminary validation studies of new measures of sociotropy and autonomy. *Journal of Psychopathology and Behavioral Assessment, 16,* 277–300.

Rudd, M., Joiner, T., & Rajab, M. (2001). *Treating suicidal behavior: An effective, time-limited approach.* New York: Guilford Press.

Segal, Z., Williams, J. M. G., Teasdale, J., & Gemar, M. (1996). A cognitive science perspective on kindling and episode sensitization in recurrent affective disorder. *Psychological Medicine, 26,* 371–380.

Seligman, M. (1975). *Helplessness: On depression development and death.* San Francisco: W. H. Freeman and Company.

Seligman, M., & Maier, S. (1967). Failure to escape traumatic shock. *Journal of Experimental Psychology, 74,* 1–9.

Shelton, R., Hollon, S., Purdon, S., & Loosen, P. (1991). Biological and psychological aspects of depression. *Behavior Therapy, 22,* 201–228.

Sweeney, P. D., Anderson, K., & Bailey, S. (1986). Attributional style in depression: A meta-analytic review. *Journal of Personality and Social Psychology, 50,* 974–991.

Teasdale, J. (1983). Negative thinking in depression: Cause, effect, or reciprocal relationship? *Advances in Behavior Research and Therapy, 5,* 3–25.

Teasdale, J. (1988). Cognitive vulnerability to persistent depression. *Cognition and Emotion, 2,* 247–274.

Teasdale, J., & Barnard, P. (1993). *Affect, cognition, and change: Re-Modelling depressive thought.* Hove, United Kingdom: Lawrence Erlbaum Associates.

Teasdale, J., Segal, Z., & Williams, J. M. G. (1995). How does cognitive therapy prevent relapse and why should attentional control (mindfulness) training help? *Behaviour Research and Therapy, 33,* 25–39.

Weissman, A., & Beck, A. (1978). Development and validation of the Dysfunctional Attitudes Scale. Paper presented at the annual convention of the Association for the Advancement of Behavior Therapy, Chicago.

Youngren, M., & Lewinsohn, P. (1980). The functional relation between depression and problematic interpersonal behavior. *Journal of Abnormal Psychology, 89,* 333–342.

SUGGESTED READINGS

Dobson, K. (Ed.) (2001). *Handbook of cognitive-behavioral therapies* (2nd ed.). New York: Guilford Press.

Beck, A., Rush, A., Shaw, B., & Emery, G. (1979). *Cognitive therapy of depression.* New York: Guilford Press.

Beck, J. (1995). *Cognitive therapy: Basics and beyond.* New York: Guilford Press.

Fennell, M. (1989). Depression. In K. Hawton, P. Salkovskis, J. Kirk, & D. Clark (Eds.), *Cognitive behaviour therapy for psychiatric problems: A practical guide.* Oxford: Oxford University Press.

Williams, J. M. G. (1992). *The psychological treatment of depression: A guide to the theory and practice of cognitive behavior therapy* (2nd ed.). London: Routledge.

12

Schema-Focused Therapy for Depression

Jeffrey E. Young and Daniel E. Mattila

OVERVIEW

Schema Therapy (ST) is an integrative model of psychotherapy developed by Jeffrey Young (Young, 1990/1999) that represents an expansion and revision of Aaron Beck's model of cognitive therapy for depression (Beck, Rush, Shaw, & Emery, 1979). Young (1990/1999) developed ST in an attempt to address limitations of early cognitive-behavioral models for conceptualizing and treating patients with chronic depression and personality disorders. Retaining the strengths of cognitive therapy, an explicit goal was to overcome theoretical and practical limitations of psychoanalysis, as well as the restrictive and reductionist nature of radical behaviorism (Dobson, 1988).

Many of the assumptions and values of CBT inform Schema Therapy. These include a recognition of the importance of the therapist-patient collaboration, active therapist involvement, behavior change, the examination of core beliefs, empiricism, and the efficient use of time. In addition, Young incorporated elements of constructivism, gestalt therapy, and object relations theory as a means of addressing broader and deeper patient themes.

BASIC CONCEPTS OF THE MODEL

Schema Therapy is based upon four main constructs: Early Maladaptive Schemas, schema domains, schema processes, and schema modes.[1] These constructs provide an integrative theory for both understanding clients' problems and guiding clinical interventions.

Early Maladaptive Schemas

The central concept in ST is the Early Maladaptive Schema (EMS). Beck (1967) described a schema as a "structure for screening, coding, and evaluating the stimuli that impinge on the organism. . . . On the basis of the matrix of schemas, the individual is able to orient himself in relation to time and space and to categorize and interpret experiences in a meaningful way" (p. 283). Schemas can be positive or negative, and can develop early or later in life. ST focuses primarily on those schemas that are maladaptive and that develop in childhood or adolescence. Throughout the chapter, the term "schema" will refer to Young's concept of Early Maladaptive Schema. A schema may be defined as a broad, pervasive theme that is developed during childhood or adolescence, elaborated throughout one's lifetime, and dysfunctional to a significant degree (Young, 1990/1999). Schemas develop as children try to make sense out of their experience, especially in the context of their relationships. For example, a child with a parent who is rarely available, or threatens to leave them, might develop an Abandonment schema. The development of such a schema does not stem from a child's faulty or inaccurate perception. Rather, the schema develops as an understandable conclusion based on painful realities. The schema becomes maladaptive when it becomes an entrenched or inflexible matrix for viewing relationships later in life, leading to faulty assumptions and thoughts that support the schema. Consistent with constructivist thought, the therapist views the individual's experiences (or constructions) of reality as the most relevant truth. A schema may exist in a "dormant" state—in which there are no observable manifestations—until life events trigger a schema "eruption." At this point, maladaptive thoughts, emotions, behaviors, or psychiatric symptoms emerge. In

---

[1]We will not be discussing schema modes in this chapter, as they are less relevant to the treatment of the typical depressed patient.

many cases, depression is seen as the result of schemas that have been activated in response to life events.

Young (1990/1999) postulated that 18 specific Early Maladaptive Schemas account for many core themes observed in long-term, characterological cases, including chronic depression and dysthymia. An objective self-report rating scale, the Young Schema Questionnaire (YSQ; Young & Brown, 1990/1999), was developed for assessing these beliefs. The psychometric properties of the YSQ have been examined in both clinical and nonclinical populations (Lee, Taylor, & Dunn, 1999; Reinecke & DuBois, 1994; Schmidt, Joiner, Young, & Telch, 1995).

Schema Domains

Based upon Bowlby's (1969) theory of attachment, object relations theory (Mahler, 1968), Erikson's (1950) stages of development, and clinical observations of patients with characterological issues, Young rationally grouped these 18 schemas into five broad developmental categories called schema domains. Each of the five domains corresponds to a basic need that children are postulated to need to meet to develop psychologically. The five domains are Disconnection and Rejection, Impaired Autonomy and Performance, Impaired Limits, Other-Directedness, and Overvigilance and Inhibition. When one of the needs is not met, an Early Maladaptive Schema may develop, which may block the patient from meeting that need later in life. We will briefly describe the five domains, with their associated schemas.

Disconnection and Rejection

Patients with schemas in this domain expect that their needs for security, nurturance, empathy, acceptance, and respect will not be met in a consistent or predictable manner. This domain is important in understanding depression as, based on clinical observation and research with depressed adolescents, patients with maladaptive schemas in this domain may be vulnerable to chronic depression. Schemas in this domain include Abandonment/Instability, Mistrust/Abuse, Emotional Deprivation, Defectiveness/Shame, and Social Isolation/Alienation. Typical origins of schemas in this domain are early experiences of caregivers who were detached, cold, rejecting, unempathic, critical, unpredictable, or abusive.

Impaired Autonomy and Performance

Patients with schemas in this domain have expectations about themselves and the environment that interfere with their perceived ability to separate, survive, function independently, or perform successfully. Schemas in this domain are Dependence/Incompetence, Vulnerability to Harm or Illness, Enmeshment/Undeveloped Self, and Failure. The typical family origin is enmeshed or controlling. These experiences undermine the development of the decision-making skills and contribute to the perception that they are not capable of functioning independently.

Impaired Limits

Patients with schemas in this domain have difficulty accepting responsibility, making commitments, or setting and meeting personal goals. Schemas included in this domain are Entitlement and Insufficient Self-Control/Self-Discipline. The typical family origin is characterized by permissiveness, indulgence, or lack of consequences, rather than appropriate guidance and limits in relation to taking responsibility, self-control, and self-discipline.

Other-Directedness

Patients with schemas in this domain focus excessively on the desires, feelings, and evaluations of others. Schemas in this domain include Subjugation, Self-Sacrifice, and Approval-Seeking/Recognition-Seeking. The typical family origin of the schemas in this domain is characterized by conditional acceptance and connection. Persons who develop in this environment learn to suppress their own needs and feelings in order to gain love and acceptance from others.

Overvigilance and Inhibition

Patients with schemas in this domain place an emphasis on controlling the expression of their feelings, impulses, and choices. This is usually done in order to avoid making mistakes, or to meet rigid, internalized rules and expectations about performance or ethical behavior. These behaviors are at the expense of the individual's happiness, self-expression, relaxation, close relationships, or health. Schemas in this domain include Emotional Inhibition, Punitiveness, Negativity/Pessimism, and Unrelenting Standards/Hypercriticalness. The typical family origins include an excessive focus on performance, duty, perfection, following rules, and avoiding mistakes.

The first two domains (Disconnection and Rejection, Impaired Autonomy and Performance) have emerged as higher order factors in recent validation studies of the YSQ (Schmidt et al., 1995; Lee et al., 1999). Longitudinal research with both clinical and nonclinical populations is needed to validate these domains and to clarify factors contributing to the development and maintenance of these schemas.

Schema Processes

Three processes—schema maintenance, schema avoidance, and schema compensation—serve to regulate the functioning of activated schemas. Consistent with constructivist models, Young (1990/1999) postulated that schema processes may have been adaptive in childhood but are no longer functional in adulthood. These coping styles involve three basic stances the individual can take when a schema is triggered: surrender to it (maintenance), avoid it, or fight back against it (compensation). Each of these processes can be expressed in any of three ways: behaviorally, cognitively, and affectively.

Schema Maintenance

Schema maintenance refers to processes by which individuals surrender to their schemas and thus perpetuate them. These processes include both cognitive distortions and self-defeating, repetitive behavior patterns. Schema maintenance is accomplished by selectively attending to information that confirms the schema, and by negating, minimizing, or denying information that is contradictory to the schema. Beck (1967) described many of these schema maintenance processes as cognitive distortions. Some of the most common distortions are magnification, minimization, selective abstraction, and overgeneralization. Individuals may also engage in behavioral schema maintenance. Patients with an Emotional Deprivation schema, for example, may repeatedly choose partners who are distant and detached. They choose partners who treat them in a manner that is congruent with their belief that others are emotionally unavailable.

Schema Avoidance

Avoidance includes both conscious and automatic processes that prevent either the triggering of schemas or the experiencing of affect associated with them. Individuals may, for example, use cognitive or behavioral strategies to avoid experiencing painful emotions associated with the activation of schemas. These processes ensure, however, that the schemas are not brought into the open and questioned. As a consequence, individuals who use schema avoidance miss opportunities to test and disprove the validity of their schemas.

Cognitive avoidance refers to conscious or automatic attempts to block *thoughts* or *images* that trigger a schema. Characteristic cognitive avoidance responses include patients who state, "I don't want to think about that," "I forgot," or "I don't think it was such a big deal," in response to the recollection of an event that triggers a schema. Cognitive avoidance maneuvers are similar in some ways to psychoanalytic defenses of repression and denial (McWilliams, 1994). Affective avoidance refers to processes, either conscious or automatic, that serve to block *feelings* that are triggered by schemas. Patients who use affective avoidance rarely experience strong feelings of anger, sadness, or anxiety. Rather, they report experiencing chronic, diffuse emotions and psychosomatic symptoms.

Patients may also avoid engaging in *behaviors* that might trigger painful schemas. In its more extreme forms, behavioral avoidance leads to social isolation, agoraphobia, or the refusal to attempt a productive career or to accept family responsibilities.

Schema Compensation

Schema compensation refers to processes of overcompensating for early maladaptive schemas. A patient who has experienced emotional deprivation as a child might, for example, develop a narcissistic style as an adult. In this case, an entitled, self-centered style emerges as a way of compensating for the underlying feelings of deprivation. In a similar manner, a patient with a Dependence/Incompetence schema may, in an attempt to regulate the expression of the schema, act in an overly self-reliant manner by refusing to accept help, feedback, or assistance from others. Unfortunately, schema-driven behaviors that overcompensate often infringe on the rights of others and ultimately may lead to damaging real-life consequences. Individuals who overcompensate for a

Subjugation schema, for example, may act in a defiant, uncompromising manner. This can have negative consequences for both intimate relationships and effective functioning in a career.

THE ETIOLOGY AND MAINTENANCE OF DEPRESSION

We hypothesize that most, but not all, cases of recurrent major depression and dysthymic disorder have a significant "schema-driven" component. According to this model, depression results from the interaction of three factors: schema eruption, life circumstances, and, often, a biological predisposition. Each individual has a "threshold" for schema eruption or activation. When life events trigger a schema eruption, dysfunctional cognitions, affect, and behaviors occur and symptoms of depression begin to appear. Schema maintenance may occur and the depression takes on "a life of its own"—it continues even though the events which triggered the episode have abated. Biological and schema processes are seen as interacting in maintaining the depressive episode. Biological vulnerabilities may influence both the threshold for schema eruption, and the likelihood that the depressive symptoms will continue.

According to this model, patients with "schema-driven" depression will continue to relapse unless one of the following occurs: the schemas are modified, life circumstances and behavior patterns are changed, or biological vulnerabilities are addressed with antidepressant medications.

Schematic and Environmental Maintaining Factors in Depression

We hypothesize that there are three primary mechanisms that perpetuate depression. Individuals strive to maintain a consistent view of the self and the world. By maintaining *cognitive consistency* (Abelson, Aronson, Newcomb, Rosenberg, & Tannenbaum, 1968), schemas are consolidated. This often is accomplished through the use of *cognitive distortions*—mental filters that patients use so that their perceptions of events are congruent with their core views of themselves and the world.

The second set of maintaining factors are schema avoidance and schema compensation. These processes do not allow patients to challenge their views of themselves or to obtain contradictory evidence, because the associated cognitions are not brought into awareness.

Finally, depression can be maintained by ongoing environmental events and dysfunctional behavior patterns. To be sure, some environmental realities (societal and systemic) may not be within the patient's control. However, many depressions result from circumstances that can be changed. Because depression stems, at least in part, from environmental influences (e.g., a bad relationship, a frustrating job), changing the environment becomes a high priority. Identifying schemas which may be blocking patients from making changes in their behavior and their environment becomes an important task.

SCHEMA THERAPY: THE CASE OF NANCY

Schema Therapy is divided into two phases: (a) Assessment and Education and (b) Change. We will look at the case of Nancy from the schema perspective to demonstrate its clinical application.

Phase One: Assessment and Education

There are three main goals in the assessment and education phase of ST. First, patients identify and are educated about their schemas. The relationships between schemas, presenting problems and life history are then noted. Finally, the therapist helps patients to experience the emotions surrounding their schemas. The components of this first phase include: the initial evaluation, symptom-reduction, pattern identification, schema identification, schema education, identification of schema origins, triggering schemas in-session through imagery and dialogues, observation of the therapy relationship dynamics and in-session behavior, and, finally, the case conceptualization.

Initial Evaluation and Symptom Reduction

During the first stage of ST the therapist identifies problems and symptoms. Nancy's depressive symptoms appear severe enough that it would be appropriate to begin by introducing symptom-reduction techniques. Since ST is not designed for acute symptom reduction, we would initiate traditional cognitive-behavior therapy, along with a reexamination of her medication regimen.

Once Nancy's acute depressive symptoms have improved, we would consider ST for relapse-prevention and for reduction of her remaining depressive symptoms. Nancy's suitability for ST would be assessed. Nancy appears to be a good candidate for ST for two reasons. First, her problems are chronic and appear to have developed during her childhood. They may, then, reflect "schema-level" issues. Second, she appears sufficiently stable to engage in more intensive work—there does not appear to be a serious risk of decompensation.

Identification of schemas begins during the evaluation sessions. During these sessions, the therapist identifies life problems and initial therapy goals. The therapist begins to draw out connections among emotions, life problems, and schemas. During this initial course of inquiry, *hypotheses* are developed about possible schemas.

Pattern-Identification

Pattern identification involves the linking together of patients' life history with their presenting concerns. We look for examples in the patient's adult life of dysfunctional behavioral and interpersonal patterns. Two main techniques are used for pattern identification. First, the therapist may ask the patient to complete the *Multimodal Life History Inventory* (Lazarus & Lazarus, 1991). This instrument asks patients about their past, family of origin, current relationships, images, beliefs, and other key issues. This information helps the therapist to refine hypotheses about schemas and their origins. Second, a focused life history interview is completed to clarify events in the patient's life that may be related thematically to their presenting problems. Hypotheses generated from the initial evaluation and from the *Multimodal Life History Inventory* provide a framework for the therapist's focused life history.

Nancy's life history suggests a number of patterns that may be linked to her present distress. Table 12.1 lists Nancy's presenting problems and links them to her life patterns, cognitions, and the associated schema domain.

During the pattern identification phase of therapy we are not yet using the language of schemas with patients. At this point we are only linking themes from her adult history to her current problems. We will not examine the childhood origins of her schemas until later.

Schema Identification

The next step is to identify specific schemas. One method for identifying schemas is the Young Schema Questionnaire (YSQ). This is a 205-

TABLE 12.1 Case of Nancy: Presenting Problems with Associated Life Patterns, Schema Domains, and Supporting Cognitions

Presenting Problems	Dysfunctional Life Patterns	Supporting Cognitions	Schema Domains
Nancy feels disconnected from her husband, along with feelings of isolation and low self-esteem.	Nancy has had relationships that are distant; she has not involved herself in social connections; and she has continued to put herself in situations where she feels criticized.	Nancy feels she "lacks a true base of emotional support." Nancy describes herself as "very sensitive to criticism."	Disconnection and Rejection
Nancy experiences significant dependence, marked by an inability to trust herself to make choices and a sense of not knowing her true "self."	Nancy has deferred decision-making to others throughout her life and becomes absorbed by those close to her.	Nancy says she can never trust herself or her decisions. Nancy says that she needs someone to help her take care of herself. Nancy says, regarding her husband "I can't see how I could handle it without him."	Impaired Autonomy and Performance
Nancy does not assert her needs and rights and is always caring for others' needs.	Nancy has continued to be in "caretaker" roles through much of her life and has not asserted herself when appropriate.	Nancy says that she "always wants to please people." Nancy admits that she has "difficulty saying no" and "has got to "sacrifice what I need for others." Nancy feels "pressured and trapped" in her life.	Other-Directedness
Nancy has very high standards for herself, tends to be self-punitive, and has trouble showing emotion.	Nancy has had long-standing perfectionism regarding her own performance and has been critical of herself.	Nancy says, "I just think I f– up everything." Nancy says that she has "a lot of anger built up inside me that I don't express." Nancy says she "beats herself up big time" when she makes a mistake.	Overvigilance and Inhibition

item self-report inventory that consists of self-statements related to each schema. The YSQ yields a score for each schema, which are plotted on a Schema Grid. This grid provides a graphical representation of the strength of the patient's schemas. In the case of Nancy, we will make predictions about her schemas based on the case report. These predictions are presented in Table 12.2, and will form the basis for the remainder of the chapter.

Schema Education

Before presenting the results of the YSQ to Nancy, the therapist educates her about schemas. The therapist explains that a schema is a strong and pervasive theme with considerable emotional strength regarding oneself and others, that they may have been learned at a young age,

TABLE 12.2   Case of Nancy: Presenting Problems with Hypothesized Associated Schemas

Hypothesized Schemas	Nancy's Presenting Problems
Abandonment/ Instability	Fearfulness and anxiety about being alone and her husband leaving
Emotional Deprivation	Feels that there is no emotional base for support or empathy; sense of loneliness
Defectiveness/ Shame	Severe low self-esteem and self-confidence
Social Isolation/ Alienation	Feelings of not fitting in with others and perceiving self as different
Dependence/ Incompetence	Feelings of not being able to make a decision, and insecurity about ability to function autonomously
Enmeshment/ Undeveloped Self	Lack of a sense of "self," and has experiences of being absorbed by other people
Subjugation	Inability to confront people, show anger, or assert her own needs
Self-Sacrifice	Belief that others' needs are more important
Unrelenting Standards/ Hypercriticalness	Pervasive perfectionism and hypercriticism toward self

and that they can be maladaptive. We explain that, since schemas have been with the patient since childhood, they are central to one's self image and view of the world. As a result, schemas are often difficult to change. There is often comfort in the familiarity of a schema, regardless of its negative consequences. Changing schemas inevitably involves changing one's basic views of oneself and others.

Schema education prepares patients for the process of change. We note that they will continue to distort information and engage in dysfunctional patterns in order to maintain their schemas, even when they intellectually recognize that they are maladaptive. To consolidate their understanding of the model, patients are asked to read *Reinventing Your Life* (Young & Klosko, 1994), a self-help book based on the schema approach. Patients are also given *A Client's Guide to Schema-Focused Therapy* (Bricker & Young, 1994), a short overview of Schema Therapy. This process allows the patient and therapist to develop a shared understanding of the patient's problems and core issues.

As Nancy comes to understand the schema model, the links observed in Table 12.2 would be shared with her. It appears, for example, that the Emotional Deprivation schema is activated in her intimate relationships. Nancy selects partners who are unable to connect to her emotionally. This began when she was 16 years old and developed a relationship with a boy who had a drinking problem, and it appears to have been repeated with her husband, from whom she feels distant emotionally. Nancy would come to see that the Emotional Deprivation schema leads her to seek out partners who are detached, as this is congruent with her schema. In a similar manner, it can be pointed out that her Dependence schema inhibits her from confronting her husband, as she doubts her ability to function without him.

Schema Origins

The origins of schemas are explored in the next phase of the assessment. We have found that many patients benefit from understanding how they developed their schemas and thus why they repeat self-defeating patterns. This knowledge can help patients gain a sense of distance from their schemas and to critically examine them. Through clinical discussion and use of the Young Parenting Inventory (YPI; Young, 1994a), an understanding of the patient's childhood and adolescence is constructed. The YPI taps the origins of schemas by asking patients to rate their mother and father separately on behaviors hypothesized to serve as origins for each of the schemas. Discussing scores on the YPI can be an important way of exploring the childhood origins of their schemas.

Nancy appears to be able to recall events during her childhood, which should make the identification of the origins of her schemas somewhat easier. The hypothesized origins of Nancy's schemas are presented in Table 12.3.

Triggering Schemas

Up to this point, the identification process has been rational. Our next step is to trigger affect associated with the schemas, both inside and outside of therapy sessions. This serves two purposes. First, it allows us to test whether the schemas have been accurately identified. A high level of affect often indicates that a schema has been triggered. Second, schema activation can be important for treating patients who display high levels of avoidance. Activating schemas enables avoidant patients to tolerate painful emotions in a supportive setting. This lays a foundation for later phases of treatment.

Guided imagery techniques are used to elicit affect associated with schemas. Patients are asked to close their eyes and to relax. The therapist then asks them to imagine a safe place in their current life, and to describe it in detail. Patients are then asked to "fade" out the safe image and to describe their most upsetting early memory with their mother. Patients are instructed to describe the image in the present tense, noting physical details. The therapist prompts the patient with questions such as: "What are you thinking?" "What are you feeling?" "What is your mother thinking and feeling?" "Tell your mother what you need and how you would like her to change" and "What happens next?" The patient is then told to switch to an image of a current life situation that feels the same. The patient describes this image in the present tense, noting details and associated emotions.

This process is repeated with the father. Depending on the patient's response, other relevant childhood experiences may be probed for images, such as incidents with peers. After each imagery exercise, the therapist instructs the patient to return to the safe place image. The patient and therapist then "debrief" by discussing the images and the schemas that were activated. This process of linking early childhood images to current life situations that feel the same can be useful in demonstrating to patients the pervasiveness and strength of their sche-

TABLE 12.3 Case of Nancy: Hypothesized Schema Origins

Hypothesized Schemas	Hypothesized Schema Origins	
Abandonment/ Instability	1.	Father's instability and departure when Nancy was 12 years old
	2.	Mother's unpredictable outbursts
	3.	Parents' separation and divorce
	4.	Violent fighting between parents
Emotional Deprivation	1.	Mother's inability to take Nancy's emotional needs into account
	2.	Father's schizophrenia compromised his ability to care for and protect Nancy
Defectiveness/ Shame	1.	Mother's extreme criticalness
	2.	No compliments from mother
Social Isolation/ Alienation	1.	Felt like an "alien" in school
	2.	Potential cultural conflicts as first child of immigrant parents made her feel different
Dependence/ Incompetence	1.	Mother's overprotectiveness
	2.	No reinforcement for independence
	3.	Never taught how to solve problems when growing up
Enmeshment/ Undeveloped Self	1.	No sense of privacy
	2.	Felt that mother lived through her
Subjugation	1.	Nancy never asserted negative feelings for fear of consequences (mother's temper, father's unpredictable outbursts)
Self-Sacrifice	1.	Was father's caretaker
	2.	Was mother's emotional aide
	3.	Took care of sister in childhood
Unrelenting Standards/ Hypercriticalness	1.	Mother's extremely high standards

mas. The process also demonstrates to the patient that some reactions to life situations may be schema-driven responses. In describing how guided imagery could be used with Nancy, we will have to hypothesize what she might say during such an exercise, since the case vignette does not provide this information.

The therapist would first prepare Nancy for the exercise by explaining the rationale and procedure. Nancy would then be asked to close her eyes, relax, and describe a "safe place." Nancy might answer, "I picture myself backpacking in the woods. I am sitting down, taking a break. It's a perfect autumn day. I feel peaceful and secure." The therapist would then instruct Nancy to let that image fade and to recall an upsetting childhood image with her mother. Nancy might recall the event of being locked out of the house. Describing the image in the present tense, she might say, "I am sitting on the back porch of the house crying. I keep knocking at the door but Mom won't let me in." The therapist would prompt Nancy by asking her what she is thinking and feeling. Nancy might reply, "I feel scared. What did I do wrong? Mom won't let me in the house, even though I'm crying and yelling for her to let me in. It goes on for so long. And I know Mom is in there! Why won't she let me in? I'm thinking that my mom doesn't want me or love me."

At this point, Nancy would probably be experiencing intense affect. The therapist would then prompt Nancy to tell her mother how she would like her mother to change. Nancy might say, "Mommy, I want you to open the door and give me a hug. I'm scared. I want you to tell me that you love me." Nancy is then asked by the therapist, "What happens next?" Nancy might reply, "My mom tells me to be quiet. She says that I'm always wanting too much from her and that she needs a break. She yells at me for crying." The therapist would then ask Nancy to hold on to the emotion of the childhood image and to picture a current life situation that feels the same. Nancy might say, "It feels like when Steve shuts me out. I ask him to hold me, and he says that he is too busy. It makes me feel so alone and scared." In another session, the therapist would conduct a similar imagery exercise regarding her father. At the end of the session, the therapist would discuss the meaning of the images with Nancy. In the image just described, we would note the presence of Abandonment, Emotional Deprivation, Defectiveness, and Subjugation schemas. The imagery exercise would confirm the primacy of these schemas for Nancy, and help her connect them to her presenting problems.

The Therapeutic Relationship and Assessment

How Nancy relates to the therapist is a final source of information about possible schemas. Although the therapeutic relationship is not explicitly used at this point to bring about change, it can be a useful source of information about schema activation. Nancy might, for example, "play out" several of her schemas in the therapy relationship. Her

Abandonment schema, for example, may be reflected in an oversensitivity to periods when the therapist is gone on vacation. Similarly, her Self-Sacrifice schema may become evident in her overconcern for the therapist's needs—she might be too willing to adjust to the therapist's schedule for appointments, even if it is inconvenient. The therapist would note these patterns as they arise in the therapy.

Case Conceptualization

The final step in this first phase of ST is case conceptualization. The therapist identifies relationships between schemas, emotions, triggering events, the therapy relationship, and childhood experiences. The therapist summarizes this formulation for the patient and asks for feedback. It is fine-tuned until the patient and therapist agree that the formulation is reasonably accurate. The therapist then attempts to distinguish between primary, linked, and secondary schemas. Primary schemas are almost always connected to the most distressing and enduring life problems experienced by the patient. These core schemas serve as the initial targets for the change procedures in phase two. After identifying the primary schemas, the therapist looks for linked and secondary schemas. These are schemas that can be best explained by reference to a primary schema or that are relatively independent of the primary schema.

In Nancy's case, her marital difficulties seem to be the most important presenting problem. They appear to be activating Defectiveness and Abandonment schemas. Thus, the change component of the therapy would first address these primary schemas.

Phase Two: Change

Four types of interventions are used in the change component of Schema Therapy: cognitive techniques, experiential methods, the therapeutic relationship, and behavioral pattern-breaking. The goals of the *cognitive* techniques are to restructure thinking related to schemas and to create "distance" from them. *Experiential techniques* are used to elicit emotions associated with schemas. The therapy relationship has two main functions. The first task of the *therapy relationship* is to provide "limited reparenting." That is, the therapist determines which early needs of the child were not met, and then attempts to meet them to a reasonable degree, within the accepted boundaries of a therapy relationship. A second, related goal involves confronting schema processes as they are activated within the relationship. Finally, the goal of *behavioral pattern-breaking* is to assign and rehearse new behavioral and interpersonal patterns as a means of changing lifelong, schema-driven patterns.

Throughout the change phase, the basic stance of the therapist toward the patient is one of "empathic confrontation." This involves empathizing with patients, while simultaneously challenging them to change their dysfunctional thoughts, feelings, and behaviors.

Cognitive Techniques

Cognitive techniques are used to change distorted views of the self and others that stem from schemas by presenting objective evidence to refute them. Cognitive exercises change habitual ways of processing information, thereby creating more accurate perceptions. Three cognitive techniques are commonly used in ST: the life review, schema dialogues, and schema flashcards.

The *life review* is an exercise in which the patient systematically examines evidence that supports and contradicts their schemas. This can help patients to recognize how their schemas can distort their perceptions and feelings, and allows them to gain a sense of distance from these beliefs. Empathic confrontation is used when reviewing evidence. This involves the validation of the patient's feelings while, at the same time, gently and persistently providing contradictory evidence. Maintaining a balanced empathic position is important. If the therapist is too confrontational, the patient will ignore the counterarguments on the grounds that the therapist does not truly understand how they feel. If the therapist is too empathic, the schema will not change.

There are four steps in the life review. First, the therapist and patient identify experiences, accumulated over a lifetime, that the patient uses to support the validity of his or her schemas. Second, this evidence is critically examined and, when possible, discredited. Third, patients are asked to provide data that contradict the schema. Finally, the therapist demonstrates to the patient how they discount the evidence that is inconsistent with the schema. The life review with Nancy might unfold in the following manner. Nancy would be asked to identify all of the evidence that supports her Defectiveness schema. In her list of evidence, Nancy might say, "According to my mother, nothing I ever did was right." The therapist would then help Nancy to critically examine this statement, and might comment on how she was assigned a role in her family and how her parent's difficulties affected her. For example, we might show Nancy how her father's schizophrenia created instability and forced her into a caretaker role. She could see that her mother's criticisms stemmed from difficulties at home, and may not be proof of her inherent defectiveness. The therapist would provide counterarguments, whenever possible, for each piece of evidence that Nancy uses to support the validity of her Defectiveness schema.

Nancy would then be asked to provide evidence contradicting the Defectiveness schema. Nancy might, for example, note that, "People say that I'm a likeable person . . . but they're just being nice." The therapist would point out how Nancy tends to overlook or discredit evidence that is inconsistent with her schema, and ask if this is reasonable or adaptive. This process would continue for each piece of evidence on the list.

In a *schema dialogue*, patients learn to confront negative emotions elicited by a schema. In this procedure, patients are asked to go back and forth between two chairs. While in one chair, they play the "voice" of the schema (i.e., thoughts consistent with their schema). In the other chair, they respond to this "voice" by presenting contradictory, "healthy" evidence. Patients typically are able to play the voice of their schema with ease as these thoughts are congruent with their self-concept. The "healthy side" often requires coaching by the therapist. This procedure helps patients to view their schemas as refutable and demonstrates to them how schemas are associated with negative feelings. With practice, patients learn to assume the role of the healthy voice.

Let's see how this approach might be used with Nancy in addressing her Subjugation schema. The following is an abbreviated example of what might happen in a schema dialogue regarding her relationship with her husband (T = Therapist, SS = Nancy as "Schema Side," and HS = Nancy as "Healthy Side").

T: Nancy, can you begin by saying something from your "schema side?"

SS: Just be quiet, don't get angry. Don't tell Steve how unhappy you are . . . he'll leave. Just make the best of it, don't rock the boat.

T: Okay, now respond from your "healthy side."

HS: I should tell Steve what makes me unhappy and angry.

T: Good! What does your "schema side" say to that?

SS: Steve doesn't want to hear it. Nobody wants to hear it. He'll leave and I'll end up alone.

T: And your healthy side says . . .

HS: Whether he wants to hear it or not, I need to tell him.

T: (simply pointing to other chair)

SS: He'll leave you if you do that.

T: And what does your healthy side say? (Nancy is quiet.) Maybe your healthy side can say something like, "I can't live the rest of my life worrying that my feelings will cause Steve to leave me."

HS: Yeah . . . I don't need a husband who doesn't care about what I think or what I need.

T: Keep going . . .

HS: My needs and feelings are important and he needs to hear them!

With practice, Nancy would be encouraged to continue these dialogues as homework. She could write down dialogues between each of her schemas and her "healthy side" in a journal.

An effective technique for changing EMS's is to repeat healthy responses when a schema is being activated. The *schema flashcard* (Young, 1996) can be used to facilitate this outside of the therapy session. Flashcards are index cards, developed by the therapist and the client, summarizing the most powerful evidence and counterarguments against specific schemas. Patients carry these cards with them and review them when a schema is triggered. Several flashcards could be made for Nancy. A flashcard for her Dependence schema, for example, might include the following:

> I often feel scared because I don't think I can make decisions on my own. This is probably due to my Dependence schema that I learned in childhood through constantly being made to doubt my own judgment and defer to my mother. This leads me to doubt my abilities. The reality is that I *can* make decisions. Evidence shows that I've made good decisions at work and about my career. Even though I feel like letting my husband make the decisions . . . I will try to make them myself.

The Therapy Relationship As a Treatment Tool

One of the most powerful methods for changing schemas is through the therapeutic relationship itself. The therapeutic relationship provides a real-life, in-the-moment context for activating and confronting schemas. In addition, it offers an opportunity for "limited reparenting" to counteract the effects of maladaptive schemas. With this in mind, the therapist is alert for indications that patients' schemas are being activated during therapy. This may be reflected in overreactions, misinterpretations, and nonverbal cues by the patient. When this occurs, the therapist links the patients' cognitions and emotions to their schemas. The therapist and patient explore associations and links to related memories or current events. The therapist then empathically examines the patient's emotional reaction and asks if there was "a kernel of truth" combined with the schema-driven misperception. It is important that the therapist be empathic and nondefensive. After all, a patient's reaction might be partially or wholly valid. In challenging schema-driven responses, the therapist may need to use self-disclosure. It can be helpful to share personal reactions to correct the patient's misperception of the therapist's thoughts and feelings.

Nancy's schema might be activated during therapy sessions in numerous ways. Her Defectiveness schema, for example, might make her sensitive to therapist statements she could misperceive as criticism. Similarly, her Dependence schema may lead her to feel unsure of her choices. These schemas might be activated if the therapist asked her: "Nancy, you are so interested in art. What prompted you to go back to school to study business?" If Nancy became withdrawn, defensive, or apologetic, the therapist would want to probe to see whether a schema had been activated. The therapist might say, "Nancy, you seem upset. Did I say something that hurt you?" If a Subjugation schema has been activated, Nancy might be reluctant to respond. The therapist would gently persist and would ask Nancy to share her thoughts and feelings. Nancy might respond, "You think I don't know what I'm doing. Maybe I don't . . . it seems I never do." This response may indicate the activation of a schema. The therapist would ask how she feels, leading Nancy to respond, "I feel incompetent . . . like I don't know what I'm doing or what I should do." The therapist, at this point, might comment that it appears that her Dependence schema has been activated, noting, "It must feel bad that you believe I think those things. I don't. But before discussing that, does your feeling right now remind you of anything else in your past?" Nancy might respond, "Yeah, it feels like when my mother criticized me for every choice I made . . . and like things with Steve . . . he criticizes me . . . I always worry about making the wrong decision."

The therapist would follow this by testing the veracity of her perceptions. The therapist might, for example, say, "I can see how you might have interpreted my question that way. I suppose it sounded like I was questioning your decision. I'm sorry about that. I didn't mean to imply any criticism of your decision. In fact, I find your decision to study business interesting in light of your career in art. I was curious how you decided that." Nancy would then be guided to see how her reaction was at least partially schema-driven, and how schema-driven responses can lead to misperceptions outside of the session.

The therapy relationship can also be used to counteract the effects of childhood experiences that may have caused the schema. Through *limited reparenting* the therapist tailors her or his therapy style as an antidote to patients' specific schemas and early life experiences. The therapist does not attempt to become a parent, to regress the patient, or to encourage dependency. Rather, the goal is to create an emotional experience that the patient can internalize to counteract the schema.

The therapist's limited reparenting role with Nancy would focus on providing her with experiences that are inconsistent with her primary schema. The therapist might, for example, invite Nancy to discuss her opinions and preferences. This would provide an experience that is inconsistent with her Enmeshment schema by encouraging her "real self" to emerge and have a voice.

Experiential Techniques

Experiential techniques are used extensively in ST and can be more effective than cognitive techniques alone. Research findings suggest, for example, that cognition is more amenable to change in the presence of strong affect (Safran & Segal, 1990). Experiential techniques enable the patient to experience affective arousal associated with the schema, which facilitates their modification. The main experiential techniques used are dialogues in imagery and letter-writing.

Dialogues in imagery are a powerful technique for changing schemas. In this procedure, patients are asked to visualize a disturbing scene from their childhood or current life as vividly as possible. They then respond to this image from the empowered, healthy part of themselves. Patients accomplish this by engaging in dialogues with parents and significant others within the image, expressing emotions and asserting their needs. This process allows patients to distance themselves from their schemas and to change their perception of their childhood and their current environment. Through this process, patients can understand the role of their parents in forming their beliefs and of people in their lives who reinforce their schemas. By "talking back" to their parents and significant others, schemas begin to weaken.

Nancy and her therapist might, for example, conduct an imagery dialogue with a memory of her parents fighting. The therapist would begin by asking Nancy to close her eyes and relax. As in the other imagery exercises, Nancy would first describe her "safe place." The therapist would ask Nancy to let this image fade and to recall an image of her parents fighting. Nancy would describe the scene in as much detail as possible. She might say, "I'm about five years old. It's a Saturday evening because I remember the television show that was on. It's winter—I can see the pajamas I was wearing. My mother is reading a book and I'm lying on the floor watching television. My father comes into the living room; he's acting weird. He goes up to my mother and throws the book out of her hand and starts accusing her of having an affair. He's yelling and screaming horrible words." The therapist might interject, "What are you feeling?" Nancy might respond, "I'm afraid. I'm really scared. My father goes crazy sometimes. My mother tries to get up and he pushes her back onto the couch. I start to cry." The therapist might ask, "What do your parents do when you're crying?" Nancy might say, "Nothing . . . they ignore me. I start to cry harder but they just keep fighting."

The therapist might now instruct Nancy to express her own needs to her parents. She would be encouraged to enter the image as an adult to speak on behalf of the child in the image. The therapist would coach Nancy to say to the parents, "Stop it! Dad, don't you see how afraid she is? What's wrong with you? She's a little girl crying . . . shaking in fear that you'll hurt Mom. Don't you care how she feels? She is only five years old. She has a right to feel secure in her home. How is she supposed to figure out what is going on? She needs someone to comfort her and make her feel safe." The therapist would then lead Nancy into an imagery exercise where she links this childhood image with a current life situation that involves the same schemas and emotions. Nancy might, for example, continue by asserting her needs with her husband, asking him to pay attention to her, show her affection, and empathize with her feelings. In this abbreviated example, Nancy has empowered herself to assert her feelings and her needs. This exercise would help counteract her Emotional Deprivation and Subjugation schemas by allowing her to identify her needs and rights, and then to assert herself in an appropriate manner in her current life.

Nancy might also be asked to *write letters* to both her mother and her father. In these letters, Nancy would express her feelings and her rights. In the letter to her mother, for example, Nancy might address her mother's criticalness and lack of nurturance. In the letter to her father, Nancy might address her father's unpredictability, departure from her life, and violent temper.

Behavioral Pattern-Breaking

Behavioral techniques are used in ST to modify self-defeating patterns of behavioral avoidance, schema maintenance, and compensation. There are five steps in this process. The first step is to assess the patient's coping style. Two instruments are helpful in this regard, the Young Compensation Inventory (YCI; Young, 1994b) and the Young-Rygh Avoidance Inventory (YRAI; Young & Rygh, 1994). The YCI assesses schema compensation strategies a patient may use, whereas the YRAI measures schema avoidance. The second step, after assessing coping styles, is to identify problematic behaviors and to link these to underlying schemas. Alternative coping behaviors are then rehearsed in the session. ST incorporates, when appropriate, many well-established techniques of cognitive-behavioral therapy—including social skills education, assertiveness training, and systematic exposure—to change behaviors that perpetuate schemas.

The third step is to prioritize the life problems and to develop behavioral homework assignments. The fourth step is to identify and overcome obstacles in making behavioral changes. The therapist may use flashcards, imagery, and contingency management to assist this process. Finally, if appropriate, couples or family sessions may be used to change the patient's interpersonal environment.

In applying these five steps with Nancy, we would first assess her coping style. It appears that Nancy maintains her schema behaviorally. There is little or no evidence of schema avoidance or compensation. Nancy seems to be aware of her feelings and does not try to escape from them. Rather she maintains her schemas by remaining in a depriving marriage, not asserting herself, deferring to others, and isolating herself socially.

The second step would be to identify primary problem areas in Nancy's life and link them to her schemas. We might discuss, for example, how patterns in her marriage may serve to perpetuate schemas of Abandonment, Emotional Deprivation, and Defectiveness. Nancy would then develop and rehearse alternate coping behaviors. Nancy might explore ways of actively addressing issues with her husband. She might learn to respond to his critical comments by responding to them assertively and setting appropriate limits.

The third step would be to put these alternative behaviors into practice. This would involve graduated homework assignments. Behavioral tasks—such as making simple decisions, expressing her feelings to her husband, and responding to his critical comments—would be broken into simple steps which could be practiced in session and then attempted at home. Behavioral assignments could also be used to overcome her social isolation and to develop a sense of fulfillment in her career.

Careful attention would be paid to anticipating obstacles that Nancy may encounter as she attempts to make these behavioral changes. Flashcards, imaginal rehearsal, and role-playing might be used to identify and overcome obstacles. We may encourage her husband to attend sessions with Nancy, and work with him to break dysfunctional patterns in their relationship.

Our goal throughout is to help Nancy achieve satisfaction and contentment in her intimate relationship, her career, and her social life. This may involve major life changes (such as divorce or a change in her career). In terms of her social circle, we would hope to see Nancy find a community (e.g., religious institution, social organization, club) that she could join. This would allow her to make new friends and to feel more connected to the larger social environment. In each area of her life, our goal is for Nancy to be able to move forward, unencumbered by the legacy of maladaptive schemas and behavior patterns.

CONCLUSION

Schema Therapy is a promising, integrative model for treating chronic and treatment-resistant depression. Schema Therapy adapts techniques used in traditional cognitive therapy, but goes beyond this approach by integrating it with interpersonal and experiential techniques. The concept of the Early Maladaptive Schema serves as the unifying element. ST should prove of greatest benefit to depressed patients who show a lifelong pattern of dysfunctional cognitions and behaviors that are difficult to change with conventional CBT.

REFERENCES

Abelson, R. P., Aronson, E., Newcomb, T. M., Rosenberg, M. J., & Tannenbaum, P. H. (Eds.) (1968). *Theories of cognitive consistency: A sourcebook.* Chicago: Rand McNally.

Beck, A. T. (1967). *Depression: Clinical, experimental and theoretical aspects.* New York: Harper & Row.

Beck, A. T., Rush, A. J., Shaw, B. F., & Emery, G. (1979). *Cognitive therapy of depression.* New York: Guilford.

Bowlby, J. (1969). *Attachment and loss: Vol. I. Attachment.* New York: Basic Books.

Bricker, D. C., & Young, J. E. (1994/1999). A client's guide to schema-focused therapy. In J. E. Young, *Cognitive therapy for personality disorders: A schema-focused approach* (3rd ed., pp. 71–80). Sarasota, FL: Professional Resource Press.

Dobson, K. S. (1988). *Handbook of cognitive behavioral therapies.* New York: Guilford.

Erikson, E. H. (1950). *Childhood and society.* New York: Norton.

Lazarus, A. A., & Lazarus, C. N. (1991). *Multimodal life history inventory.* Champaign, IL: Research Press.

Lee, C. W., Taylor, G., & Dunn, J. (1999). Factor structure of the schema questionnaire in a large clinical sample. *Cognitive Therapy and Research, 23*(4), 441–451.

Mahler, M. S. (1968). *On human symbiosis and the vicissitudes of individuation.* New York: International Universities Press.

McWilliams, N. (1994). *Psychoanalytic diagnosis.* New York: Guilford.

Reinecke, M., & DuBois, D. (1994). "Life events, schemata and suicide in adolescence." Paper presentation, 27th Annual Conference of the American Association of Suicidology, New York.

Safran, J. D., & Segal, Z. V. (1990). *Interpersonal processes in cognitive therapy.* New York: Basic Books.

Schmidt, N. B., Joiner, T. E., Young, J. E., & Telch, M. J. (1995). The Schema Questionnaire: Investigation of psychometric properties and the hierarchical structure of a measure of maladaptive schemata. *Cognitive Therapy and Research, 19*(3), 295–321.

Young, J. E. (1994a). *Young Parenting Inventory.* (Unpublished manuscript. Available from the Cognitive Therapy Center of New York, 120 E. 56th St., Suite 530, New York, NY 10022.)

Young, J. E. (1994b). *Young Compensation Inventory.* (Unpublished manuscript. Available from the Cognitive Therapy Center of New York, 120 E. 56th St., Suite 530, New York, NY 10022.)

Young, J. E. (1996). *Schema Flashcard.* (Available from the Cognitive Therapy Center of New York, 120 E. 56th St., Suite 530, New York, NY 10022.)

Young, J. E., & Brown, G. (1990/1999). Young schema questionnaire (2nd ed.). In J. E. Young, *Cognitive therapy for personality disorders: A schema-focused approach* (3rd ed., pp. 59–68). Sarasota, FL: Professional Resource Press.

Young, J. E., & Rygh, J. (1994). *Young-Rygh Avoidance Inventory.* (Unpublished manuscript. Available from the Cognitive Therapy Center of New York, 120 E. 56th St., Suite 530, New York, NY 10022.)

SUGGESTED READINGS

Young, J. E. (1990/1999). *Cognitive therapy for personality disorders: A schema-focused approach* (3rd ed.). Sarasota, FL: Professional Resource Press.

Young, J. E., & Klosko, J. (1994). *Reinventing your life.* New York: Plume.

13

Interpersonal Psychotherapy

Scott Stuart and Michael W. O'Hara

Interpersonal psychotherapy (IPT) (Klerman et al., 1984) is a time-limited, manual-based, and empirically supported psychotherapy which is designed to treat the symptoms of depression. IPT specifically focuses on "here and now" interpersonal problems that the patient may be experiencing. Reducing these interpersonal stresses leads in turn to an alleviation of the patient's depression.

There are three characteristics which define IPT as a unique therapy. First, IPT specifically focuses on interpersonal relationships. IPT is designed to renegotiate problematic interpersonal relationships or to modify the patient's expectations about those relationships in the service of symptom relief. Depression is hypothesized to occur in patients with a biological diathesis who are confronted with disrupted interpersonal relationships or a loss of social support.

Second, IPT is nontransferential in approach—i.e., it focuses almost exclusively on extra-therapy relationships rather than on the patient-therapist relationship as a means to bring about change. The transference which develops during the course of treatment is an important source of information for the therapist—it allows hypotheses to be drawn by the therapist regarding the patient's relationships outside of therapy. However, in IPT, this information does not become material for discussion between the patient and therapist. Rather, the therapist consistently directs the patient to work on his or her relationships

outside of therapy, and typically does not make any transference interpretations nor overtly discusses the therapeutic relationship.

Third, IPT is time-limited. Typical courses of therapy last for 12
to 16 weeks. This brief format requires that the therapy be primarily
symptom-focused, and also requires that the therapist be active and
directive during the therapy. It also necessitates that care be used in
selecting patients who are likely to benefit from short-term treatment.

REVIEW OF EMPIRICAL EVIDENCE SUPPORTING INTERPERSONAL PSYCHOTHERAPY

IPT was initially described in 1979 by Klerman, Weissman, et al. (1979),
and was found to be superior to non-scheduled treatment for patients
diagnosed with major depression (Weissman et al., 1981). IPT was
also found to be equivalent to amitriptyline in the treatment of major
depression (Weissman et al., 1979). Interestingly, this study demonstrated that IPT and amitriptyline had differential symptom effects. In
other words, amitriptyline appeared to be somewhat more effective in
treating physiological symptoms of depression such as sleep disruption,
appetite disruption, and poor energy, while IPT was more effective in
treating "psychological" symptoms such as low self-esteem, hopelessness,
and feelings of guilt (DiMascio et al., 1979). A comparison of treatment
with IPT or amitriptyline and treatment in which patients were receiving
both IPT and amitriptyline demonstrated that the combination of psychotherapy and medication was superior to either alone (Weissman et
al., 1981). Patients reported that the combination treatment was more
acceptable and better tolerated. This finding, however, has not been
replicated to date, nor has the finding of differential treatment effects.

IPT, along with cognitive behavioral psychotherapy (Beck et al., 1979)
(CBT), was chosen as a comparative psychotherapeutic treatment in
the National Institute of Mental Health Treatment of Depression Collaborate Research Program (Elkin et al., 1985) (NIMH-TDCRP). Both
psychotherapies were compared to treatment with imipramine and with
placebo. IPT was found to be superior to treatment with placebo, and
was equal to imipramine and CBT for mild to moderate depression
(Elkin et al., 1989). There was some evidence that IPT was more effective
than CBT for severe depression (though this has been disputed by some
CBT proponents), but neither psychosocial treatment was shown to be
as effective as imipramine. The consensus from the NIMH-TDCRP study

is that IPT and CBT are effective for mild to moderate depression, but antidepressant medication remains the gold standard for treatment of patients with severe depression.[1]

In the NIMH-TDCRP, 43% of patients who entered IPT achieved remission of depression; 55% of patients who completed a full course of IPT achieved remission (patients were treated with 16 sessions of IPT in the study). Twenty-three percent of patients terminated prematurely, and early terminators were, on average, more severely depressed at intake. Finally, 33% of the patients who remitted when treated with IPT relapsed within 18 months after treatment was concluded. This relapse rate was equivalent to that of patients who achieved remission with CBT or imipramine.

In addition to these general results, several other interesting findings were reported. In contrast to expectations, no long-term preventive effects were found for either IPT or CBT. Researchers had initially hypothesized that treatment with psychotherapy would reduce relapse rates as compared to treatment with medication, since psychotherapy would presumably teach patients new coping skills. However, relapse rates were equivalent for all patients who recovered, irrespective of the treatment they received, when they were evaluated at 6, 12, and 18 months after treatment was concluded (Shea et al., 1992). The NIMH collaborative study also demonstrated that there were no "mode specific" effects for any of the active treatments (Imber et al., 1990). In other words, recovered patients who were treated with IPT, CBT, or imipramine had similar changes in psychological and neurovegetative symptoms. This finding contrasts with the differential effects which were reported in the original IPT study by Weissman et al. (1981).

Further analysis of the NIMH data indicated that a positive response to treatment with IPT was predicted by several factors (Sotsky et al., 1991). These included a low level of social dysfunction at intake, as well as a high degree of interpersonal sensitivity. Patients who reported greater satisfaction with their relationships at intake were also more likely to benefit from IPT as compared to the other treatments. Additionally, patients with acute onset of depression and endogenous depression were more likely to respond to IPT, as well as the other two active treatments. The NIMH-TDCRP results can be summarized by stating that those patients with a relatively good social support system and an awareness of the way in which they communicate in interpersonal relationships typically fare well with IPT.

Another major study evaluating IPT involved maintenance treatment of patients with recurrent depression (Frank, 1991; Kupfer, 1992).

Acutely depressed patients who had suffered at least three prior episodes of depression were treated during an index episode of major depression with a combination of imipramine and IPT over 16 weeks. Those patients who recovered following this acute treatment were then assigned to one of five maintenance treatment cells: (1) imipramine alone; (2) imipramine plus monthly IPT; (3) monthly IPT alone; (4) monthly IPT plus placebo; and (5) placebo alone. The patients were then followed for a period of three years.

Mean depression-free survival time was significantly longer for those patients who received imipramine alone or imipramine plus IPT (Frank, 1990; Frank, 1991). Over the three-year period, the mean survival time before relapse of depression was about 120–130 weeks for patients who received imipramine with or without IPT as an adjunct. The patients who received IPT alone or IPT plus placebo had a mean survival time of about 75–80 weeks. Though significantly better than the mean survival experienced by patient who received only placebo (roughly 40 weeks), treatment with IPT without medication clearly was not as beneficial as treatment with maintenance antidepressant medication. The current consensus of experts is that recurrent depression should be treated with maintenance antidepressant medication (Kupfer, 1992), with IPT a viable alternative for patients who do not want or who cannot tolerate medication.

Though well designed, this study has been criticized because the dosages of imipramine and IPT were not equivalent. During the maintenance phase of the project, patients receiving IPT were treated once monthly. In contrast, patients receiving medication took it on a daily basis at the same dosage that they required to achieve remission from their acute episode of depression. It is not clear from the study whether increasing the frequency of IPT sessions would result in a higher survival rate from recurrence of depression in this particular population.

IPT has been demonstrated to be efficacious with a number of other depressed populations and with other psychiatric disorders as well, including depressed geriatric patients (Reynolds, 1992, 1996, 1997), depressed adolescents (Mufson, 1993, 1994, 1996), depressed patients who are HIV positive (Markowitz, 1992, 1993, 1995), and patients with dysthymic disorder (Mason, 1993; Markowitz, 1993, 1997). In addition, it has been tested with patients in the depressed phase of bipolar disorder (Frank, 1990) and with eating disorders (Fairburn, 1991, 1993, 1995). IPT has also been used for perinatal depression, including postpartum (Stuart, 1995; O'Hara, 1999) and antenatal depression (Spinelli, 1997;

Stuart, in press). Current research is underway testing IPT with depression associated with cardiac disease (Stuart, 1996), social phobia (Stuart, 1997), and somatization disorder (Stuart, 1998) as well. Finally, the use of IPT has been described with groups (Klerman, 1993), with couples (Foley, 1989), and in a family practice setting (Schulberg, 1993, 1996; Brown, 1996).

The research on IPT clearly demonstrates its efficacy as a time-limited treatment for acute depression, and as an effective alternative to medication for patients with recurrent depression. Further, there are numerous studies which suggest that IPT may be efficacious for patients with a variety of DSM-IV (1994) axis I disorders. Although there is evidence that IPT is effective in treating the depressive symptoms of patients with personality disorders who are acutely depressed, there is no evidence that it is effective in treating personality pathology.

As is true of all psychotherapies, there are few data regarding the optimum length of a course of treatment, the optimum length of individual sessions, and the optimum frequency of sessions. IPT is no exception to the rule that non-empirically-based traditional convention, such as conducting one-hour sessions, or meeting weekly with patients, is the basis for most of these decisions.[2] Additionally, IPT (and other therapies as well) lack data regarding effectiveness—though there is compelling data regarding the use of IPT in tightly controlled research settings, there is virtually no information regarding its use in non-controlled clinical settings. As a result, the reader is advised to remember that the IPT, CBT, and other programmatic psychotherapies are based on manuals which should guide treatment rather than dictate it—they are manuals, not therapeutic commandments inscribed in stone.

THEORETICAL ORIENTATION

IPT is grounded in both attachment and interpersonal theory. Attachment theory, as described by Bowlby (1969, 1977) among others, rests on the premise that people have a biological drive to attach to one another—i.e., to form meaningful relationships in which they receive and provide care. This drive to form and maintain relationships is a primary instinctual drive and is reciprocal in human relationships. Within each relationship, people negotiate the degree of closeness, autonomy, and dependency, and tend to develop a system in which these aspects of the relationship become fixed or stable. Further, within certain limits, people tend to maintain an emotional proximity to their attachment figures which allows them to feel emotionally secure.

This maintenance of proximity is best exemplified by small children, who typically maintain a distance from their parents which is far enough to allow them a sense of independence, but which is close enough that they can readily check to make sure their parents are still available if a threat is perceived. According to Bowlby, adults behave similarly, although more technologically sophisticated means such as phone and e-mail are used to maintain emotional bonds as the need for actual physical proximity lessens with maturation.

When crises occur, however, adults still attempt to gain closer proximity to their primary attachment figures, seeking care from those important to them. If not on a physical level, this care-seeking behavior is at least manifested on an emotional level by initiating and maintaining closer contact with people who may provide care. When such interpersonal support is insufficient or lacking during times of stress, individuals are less able to deal with crises and are more prone to become depressed.

According to attachment theorists, the hallmark of mental health is the capacity to form flexible attachments. Flexible attachments are those which allow people both to ask for care when it is appropriate to do so, and to provide care to others when asked to do so as well. Mental health is compromised when people are locked into a fixed attachment style in which they are persistently requesting care from others while unable to provide it to others when it is asked of them, or when they consistently provide care and are unable to ask for help from others during crises.

Bowlby has described three different types of attachment styles (1969) which drive interpersonal behavior in humans. *Secure attachment,* as the name implies, is an interpersonal style in which individuals are able to both give and receive care and are relatively secure that care will be provided when it is necessary. These individuals typically are the product of an early childhood environment in which their needs in general were met and "good enough mothering" was provided to them.

Anxious ambivalent attachment, in contrast, is an attachment style in which individuals behave as if they are never quite sure that their attachment needs will be met. The classic paradigm in which this type of attachment style develops is the situation in which the individual's mother may have been depressed during his or her childhood. At times when the mother was doing well, she was quite responsive and able to meet the individual's needs, but at times during which she was depressed, she might have been unavailable and emotionally unresponsive. As a result, the individual quickly discovers that in order to get his or her attachment, physical, and emotional needs met, care must be constantly demanded. Moreover, when these demands are not met, the urgency of the demands must be escalated in order to ensure that care is provided. Anxious ambivalent individuals are never quite certain that care will be provided and as a consequence are very insecure in most relationships, with dependent interpersonal behavior typically being manifest. Additionally, these individuals typically lack the capacity to care for others when asked to do so, since their concern about getting their own attachment needs met outweighs all other concerns.

The third attachment style described by Bowlby is *anxious avoidant attachment.* Individuals with this type of attachment style typically believe that care will not be provided by others in any circumstances. As a result, they avoid intimacy in relationships and avoid becoming close to others. An individual with this type of attachment style may have had an early childhood experience in which care was never adequately provided. Such individuals develop credos such as, "pull yourself up by your own boot straps," "if you want something done right, you have to do it yourself," and especially, "don't trust anyone." Avoidant, schizoid, and antisocial interpersonal behaviors are common among individuals who are avoidantly attached.

Attachment theory also states that these patterns of attachment typically develop in childhood, and while they tend to persist, they are not fixed. (The fact that they are not permanently set bodes well for the therapist, who would otherwise be collecting large fees for work that was futile. Theoretically, improving the patient's interpersonal relationships should have some effect on their attachment behavior and communication style.) Attachment theorists also hypothesize that patterns of attachment tend to persist within relationships. In other words, once a relationship (such as a marital relationship) is formed, the attachment styles manifested by an individual tend to be persistent during the course of that relationship. Patterns of attachment persist across relationships as well. In other words, individuals tend to relate to other individuals using consistent interpersonal attachment behavior. An anxiously attached individual will form new relationships with the same kind of anxious attachment style which is manifested in his or her other relationships.

In essence, attachment theory states that those individuals with less secure attachments are more prone to depression during times of stress.

A persistent belief that care must be constantly demanded from others, or that care will not be provided by others under any circumstances, typically leads insecurely attached individuals to have more difficulty in generating social support during times of crisis, leading to an increased vulnerability to mood disruption. In addition, even individuals with secure attachments who face disruption of important attachment relationships, such as death of a significant other, will have an increased vulnerability to depression.

Researchers such as George Brown (1978, 1989, 1994) have also stressed the importance of interpersonal relationships and disruption in those relationships in the genesis of depression. Loss either through death, divorce, or emotional disengagement especially during early childhood, may have a substantial impact on the attachment style which develops in individuals during adulthood.

IPT is also based on communication theory as described by Kiesler (1989) and others. According to this model, individuals communicate their needs to others in such a way that they invite complementary responses. An individual who asks for help, for instance, draws or elicits a caregiving response from others. While many securely attached individuals are able to communicate their needs effectively, those more insecurely attached communicate in ways which are indirect or even counterproductive. Rather than eliciting a caregiving response, their unclear or ambivalent requests for help may instead elicit a neutral response or even hostility. The persistent care-seeking behavior and communication of an anxiously attached individual, for instance, though initially drawing a caregiving response from others, will, over time, tend to exhaust the care provider and ultimately lead to rejection. This in turn further solidifies the insecurely attached individual's belief that adequate care will not be provided, leading to an escalation of demands and further rejection. The problem is compounded by the fact that the insecurely attached individual often does not understand his or her communication pattern, nor the consequences that it has on others.

Utilizing IPT to help an individual to recognize his or her communication patterns, and to make modifications in them, has a twofold effect. First, it has the immediate result of improving the patient's relationships—communicating in a way to which others can more readily respond will more effectively meet the patient's attachment needs. Second, over a longer period (which may include time after therapy is concluded), the improvement in communication may begin to help the patient to reconceptualize their internal working model of relation-ships. As changes in attachment style occur, the patient develops a sense that others can be depended on, and that his or her attachment needs are more likely to get met. The patient may move from a more ambiva-lent or avoidant attachment style to one that is more secure.

In sum, IPT hypothesizes that depression results from a combination of interpersonal and biological factors. Individuals with a genetic predis-position or biological diathesis to become depressed will be more likely to do so when stressed interpersonally. Conversely, individuals without this heritable predisposition may be protected from depression even when their interpersonal relationships falter. Of course, those individu-als with a family history of depression are likely to have the unfortunate combination of genetic risk and maladaptive attachment style which result from a poorly supportive childhood environment.

IPT is therefore designed to treat psychiatric symptoms by focusing specifically on patients' primary interpersonal relationships, particularly in the problem areas of *grief, interpersonal disputes, role transitions,* and *interpersonal sensitivity.* Although fundamental change in either personal-ity or attachment style is unlikely during short-term treatment, symptom resolution is made possible when patients are assisted in repairing their disrupted interpersonal relationships and when they learn new ways to communicate their need for emotional support.

CASE CONCEPTUALIZATION

Based on the interpersonal and attachment theories described above, the conceptualization for the patient (Nancy) described in the clinical case begins with her social and developmental history. As Nancy de-scribes it, she had a great deal of instability in her family due not only to the fact that both of her parents were immigrants, but also because her father was schizophrenic. By her description, her father was unavail-able for the long period of time during which he was psychotic. Of interest is that she describes him in somewhat dichotomous terms, initially describing him as being comforting and lenient and apparently providing some support, and at other times when he was severely ill, as being violent and out of control.

In a similar fashion, Nancy also describes a very conflicted relation-ship with her mother. Her mother is portrayed in a somewhat dichoto-mous fashion, on occasion being strong and responsible, but at other times being very critical. She describes her mother as very withholding, and also noted that she tended to discipline Nancy and her sister in very unpredictable ways. As with her father, Nancy notes that her mother became angry quite suddenly and occasionally became physically violent as well.

Nancy further describes both her father and mother as being quite overprotective at times. She states that this has made it very difficult for her to make decisions as an adult. At other times, however, she describes feeling as if she served as an auxiliary ego for both of her parents, stating that she was an emotional aide and helper to both of them. Within her family she was also put in the position of having to negotiate conflicts between her parents. The insecurity and inconsistency in these relationships appears to have led to ambivalent relationships with both parents.

The IPT therapist would hypothesize that, as a result of these early childhood experiences, Nancy developed an anxious ambivalent attachment style. In essence, Nancy experienced that her parents were available on some occasions for emotional support, but at other times found that they were completely unavailable or even physically violent. These unpredictable parental responses to her care-seeking behavior continue to drive her anxious ambivalent attachment style (which has persisted into adulthood).

As noted above, attachment styles, which develop in early childhood, tend to be persistent in adulthood although they are fortunately not absolutely fixed. They are also typically persistent across relationships. It appears that Nancy has developed a relationship with her husband which mirrors very closely her relationship with her parents. In particular, the ambivalence she feels towards her husband is a manifestation of the attachment style she developed with her parents. She describes, at one point, wanting to separate from her husband and is quite critical of him, but at other times, states she, "fears she will be alone if she leaves her husband." Her anxious ambivalent attachment style appears to be driving a need for her to continue the relationship for fear that she will be completely abandoned, while at the same time, she feels quite angry at the fact that she is dependent on her husband in this fashion. The hostile-dependent relationship she developed with her mother is also reflected in her ambivalence about making decisions about her relationship with her husband. She describes her husband as, "so controlling that he took away her self-confidence," but also states her husband is, "really kind, generous, and attentive; and is more like a father to me."

Nancy's anxious ambivalent attachment style is also evident in her relationship with friends and with colleagues at work. Nancy describes herself as a person who always wants to please people, and notes that she has difficulty saying no to others. The conceptualization of this dynamic is that Nancy's desire to please others is driven by her fear of abandonment, and fear that her attachment needs will not be met. She states that she feels like she, "lacks a true base of emotional support" and has to put on a pleasing facade in order to cultivate (and placate) others so that she can maintain what little support she does get. She notes that she typically tends to put up a front in order to continue a relationship, and that she has a hard time breaking off a relationship even if it is not particularly productive. Her interpersonal style and interpersonal behavior are essentially manifestations of her belief that her "attachment glass" is perpetually half empty, and that she needs to do whatever she can to attempt to fill it, so that she feels safe and secure.

Nancy's affective state appears to be driven by the attachment difficulties that she is experiencing. As her relationship with her husband deteriorates, the little support she gets from him is at greater risk. As a result, it is understandable that, faced with the threat of this loss, she is feeling depressed and anxious. Her feelings of depression and anxiety stem directly from her belief that she is not deserving of care and that care will never appropriately be provided. This particular belief is certainly justifiable from her point of view, given her early life experiences with her own parents. In essence, Nancy is fearful that she will be abandoned—she persistently makes attempts to obtain care from others, since her early life experiences have taught her that she can never fully depend on others to meet her needs. The anxiety that she is experiencing derives directly from her belief that her attachment needs will not be met in any of the relationships in which she is engaged.

Attachment theory hypothesizes that individuals develop "working models" of relationships. These working models are essentially internal conceptualizations or maps about what relationships are like. These models are derived in large part from early life experiences, and drive the kind of attachment behavior that the individual displays. A patient with an anxious ambivalent attachment style, for example, typically has a working model of relationships which state that he or she can never completely depend on others, and that he or she has to be extremely demanding or placating in order to get any needs met. This working model is imposed on both current and new relationships.

Nancy's working model of relationships is very clearly one in which she feels she cannot completely trust other people to care for her. Her interpersonal working model also includes elements, however, that she cannot survive without other people providing some care for her. The working model would also include some elements of fear of abandonment particularly based on her relationship with her father (who in reality did essentially abandon her during her childhood), as well as elements of needing to be dependent on others since she does not believe herself capable of making decisions on her own.

TREATMENT MODEL

The interventions used in IPT, and the framework of the therapy itself, are directly linked to attachment and interpersonal theory. The IPT therapist focuses on the depressed patient's interpersonal relationships, particularly the way in which the patient's attachment styles are manifest in these relationships. The therapist is also concerned with the communication style that the patient uses in both initiating, maintaining, and disengaging from relationships.

As noted above, IPT is also characterized by its time-limited format. IPT is time-limited for several reasons. First, the empirical evidence regarding IPT clearly supports its efficacy in alleviating depression when used in a short-term format. There is no evidence at present that a longer course of IPT is of additional benefit as an acute treatment, though as noted above, it is an effective maintenance intervention.

Second, longer-term treatment will eventually result in a need to address transferential issues in the therapy. As described by the attachment model, individuals will, given enough time, eventually establish relationships with new people which mirror those they have already established with their primary attachment figures. This is the theoretical basis for the transference phenomena—i.e., a patient will, given enough time, relate to the therapist in a way which reflects the way in which he or she attaches to primary caregivers. Over time, the attachment behavior which is directed toward the therapist will begin to become the primary focus of therapy, detracting from the primary goal of symptom relief.

The time-limited nature and treatment goals of IPT require that the therapist focus primarily on "here and now" interpersonal problems rather than working on issues from the patient's past. Change in current interpersonal relationships or expectations about those relationships should result in symptom relief. While fundamental personality change is unlikely in IPT because of the short-term nature of the treatment, there certainly may be cases in which a patient's attachment style, attachment behavior, or personality traits may be modified during the course of therapy. It is much more typical, however, that patients experience symptom resolution. Both the limitations and benefits of this therapeutic approach should be appreciated: IPT is very effective at alleviating depression, but may not be indicated for patients with severe personality pathology. Similarly, though IPT appears to be effective for patients with dysthymia (Markowitz, 1997), it is not indicated for patients with psychotic depression. Like a hammer, a therapeutic tool such as IPT doesn't work well if it is applied indiscriminantly—not every patient is a nail!

Beginning and Framing Treatment

Consistent with the objectives of IPT, the primary treatment goal for Nancy would be the alleviation of her depressive symptoms, with the conjoint goal of reducing her anxiety symptoms as well. Interpersonally, the goal of treatment is to assist Nancy to recognize that the ways in which she is communicating her needs are contributing to her interpersonal problems—they are actually pushing people away, with the result that she is less likely to get her needs met. Though a fundamental change in either her personality or her basic attachment style is unlikely in time-limited IPT, it is entirely possible that she will learn to communicate what she needs more effectively, and may begin to modify her attachment style as her expectations about being cared for are changed as well.

Consider, for example, Nancy's statement to her husband that she, "wants to leave the relationship." While this may be literally true to some degree, it is likely that what she is really wishing to communicate to him is that she feels lonely, misunderstood, or angry, and that she wants to leave the relationship *"if she continues to feel that her needs are not met."* The latter part of her communication in this example, however, is not being made verbally—it is being made implicitly, and is probably not even recognized by her husband. Her requests for care from her husband and for him to meet her attachment needs are phrased as threats. Not surprisingly, her husband's response to her verbal provocation is likely to be increasing frustration, and a sense of hopelessness about doing anything to improve or even salvage the relationship.

The goal of the therapist would be to help Nancy to recognize the unspoken elements of her communication, appreciate the fact that her husband can respond only to her spoken words, and to get her to be specific and direct in communicating what it is she wants from her husband. Something like, "I feel like leaving the relationship when my needs are not met, and I would like you (husband) to do . . . " would be ideal.

It should be noted that salvaging her marital and other family relationships is not a goal of IPT. The IPT therapist takes a neutral position on these issues, and leaves it to the patient to determine which relationships appear to be worth maintaining. The therapist's goals in this respect are to assist the patient to make the best informed choice possible—to help the patient make a conscious and rational choice about what to do, rather than feeling as if they have no control.

As IPT has been empirically validated as a short-term psychotherapy, the treatment duration for Nancy would be on the order of 16 weeks.[3] This length of treatment has been shown to be adequate even for dysthymic patients (Markowitz, 1997). IPT is also short-term by design. The reason for this is that IPT makes a specific point of not focusing on the transference relationship in therapy, unless it becomes problematic. The therapist will typically attempt to foster a positive transference with the patient in which the therapist is accorded some expertise and power in the relationship with some moderate dependence on the part of the patient, but the therapist does not interpret or work with the transference therapeutically. (IPT will, of course, be much more successful if the patient's attribution of expertise to the therapist is reality-based.) If therapy continues much beyond the time limit, however, it is frequently the case that transferential issues loom larger, and inevitably they must be dealt with in therapy. That is not to say that they may not be relevant, nor that long-term treatment is not beneficial; rather the transferential focus which is inevitable in longer treatment is not consistent with IPT.

The prognosis for Nancy in IPT is good with respect to symptom relief. She can be reasonably expected to recover from her depression and experience relief from her anxiety symptoms. Her social and occupational functioning should also improve. Further, her ability to communicate more effectively should also be enhanced. While she may ultimately choose to end her marital relationship, the therapy would aim to have her actively choose to do so after examining this and other alternatives carefully. The improvement in communicating her attachment needs should be general, and should be reflected across all of her relationships.

Nancy's long-term prognosis is not so clear, however. In a time-limited treatment such as IPT, personality change is unlikely. Though Nancy may be more able to communicate her needs more effectively, it is likely that she will continue to manifest an interpersonal style which reflects her underlying dependency and her ambivalent attachment style. Hopefully, as she is able to get her needs met more effectively and reliably, her working model of relationships will change and reflect more of a sense of security. This will depend in large part upon the quality of relationships she is able to develop after therapy concludes.

Her long-term prognosis is also uncertain because she has an extensive family history of psychiatric illness. Even if she is able to make changes in her communication style, and even if her attachment style is modified, her genetic predisposition may still lead her to become depressed again during times of stress. Strong consideration should be given to some type of maintenance treatment to prevent recurrence of depression.

Assessment

The purpose of conducting an assessment is, of course, to determine when IPT should be used, and to whom it should be applied. The therapist should be guided by several factors, including the available empirical evidence of efficacy, the attachment style of the patient, an analysis of the patient's communication style, and such factors as the patient's motivation and insight. Assessment of DSM-IV (1994) diagnoses should occur during the intake process. Particular attention should be paid to suicidal ideation, substance use, and the presence of medical problems which may require intervention. The patient should also be evaluated for the possible use of antidepressant medication.

In addition to the affective disorder diagnoses for which it has been empirically tested, IPT appears to be well-suited to patients with anxiety disorders. Special attention should be paid to patients diagnosed with personality disorders—those with cluster A disorders including paranoid, schizoid, and schizotypal personality disorders may be unable to form effective alliances with their therapists in short-term therapy, while those with cluster B disorders such as narcissistic, histrionic, borderline and antisocial personality disorders may require more intensive therapy than can be provided in an IPT format. However, many patients with depression superimposed upon a personality disorder may benefit a great deal from short-term therapy which restricts its focus to the treatment of depression.

An assessment of the patient's patterns of attachment should be conducted. This assessment should consist both of information about the patient's perception of his or her style of relating to others, and an evaluation of the patient's past and current relationships. Questions regarding what the patient does when stressed, ill, or otherwise in need of care are particularly helpful. The patient should also be queried about his or her typical responses when asked to assist others. The therapist is essentially developing hypotheses regarding the patient's world view about relationships—i.e., whether the patient tends to see the world as full of people who can generally be trusted, who need to be avoided, or who are needed but tend to be unreliable.

The patient's attachment style has direct implications regarding his or her ability to develop a therapeutic alliance with the therapist and the likelihood that treatment will be beneficial. Unfortunately, in IPT as in other psychotherapies, the old saw about the "rich getting richer" holds true. Those patients with relatively secure attachment styles are usually able to form a working relationship with the therapist, and because of their relatively healthy relationships outside of therapy, are also more likely to be able to renegotiate their relationships in a way that will be productive. Individuals with more anxious ambivalent attachments can usually quickly form relationships with their clinicians, but often have a great deal of difficulty with termination—a particular problem in time-limited therapy. Those with anxious avoidant styles of attachment may have difficulty trusting or relating to the therapist, and often require treatments of less intensity. These patients will often opt for medication management alone when they finally decide to seek treatment.

In addition to evaluating therapeutic suitability, the therapist should use the assessment to forecast and plan for problems which may arise during the course of therapy. For example, since patients with anxious ambivalent attachment styles have difficulty in ending relationships, the astute therapist may modify his or her approach by emphasizing the time-limited nature of the treatment, discussing termination during the middle phases of therapy, and by beginning the termination process earlier. Significant others may also be included in sessions more frequently to ensure that dependency on the therapist does not become problematic. When working with avoidant patients, the therapist should plan to spend several sessions completing an assessment, taking great care to convey a sense of understanding and empathy to the client. Soliciting feedback from the patient about the frequency of meetings is another tactic which may improve the therapeutic alliance with these individuals.

The therapist should also conduct an assessment of the patient's communication style. As is the case with attachment, the way in which the patient communicates his or her needs to others has profound implications for the therapeutic process, as well as for the likelihood that the patient will improve with therapy. The therapist should directly ask the patient for examples or vignettes in which a conflict with a significant other occurred. Patients who are able to relate a coherent and detailed story are likely to be able to provide the narrative information necessary to work productively in therapy. Insight can also be judged by noting the way in which the patient describes an interaction, and the degree to which he or she presents a balanced picture, particularly with regard to being able to accurately represent the other person's point of view.

Finally, the therapist should conduct an assessment of the match between him or herself and the patient. The old adage to "know thyself" cannot be overemphasized, for therapists, like patients, also have idiosyncratic styles of attachment and communication. Therapists who tend to be overly directive may have difficulty with avoidant patients, for example. Therapists who find it difficult to terminate may encounter problems with patients with dependent attachment styles.

In this particular case, it is clear that Nancy manifests an anxious ambivalent attachment style. Many dependent characteristics are evident. Nancy sees herself as needing other people, and as a result, goes to great lengths to maintain relationships. She is even willing to sacrifice some of her own needs to maintain them. Her ambivalence, however, is reflected in the resentment she seems to feel toward others, and toward herself, for needing other people and for staying in relationships in which she must sacrifice her own needs, and for staying in relationships in which she feels taken for granted.

It is not clear from the information provided in the case report what types of communication issues are present. The IPT therapist should collect specific examples of interactions between Nancy and the significant others with whom she is in conflict. These data will provide information to the therapist regarding her insight, interpersonal awareness, and communication style.

Consider, for example, the issue mentioned in the case report regarding the refusal of Nancy's husband to attend marital counseling sessions. Rather than take this at face value, the IPT therapist should ask specifically about when the request was made and how it was phrased. The impact and meaning of such a request made during a pleasant dinner conversation would be profoundly different than Nancy "trumping" her husband at the end of a fight by screaming, "you need to go to therapy" as she stormed away.

The importance of communication and context is perhaps best exemplified by a vignette presented by an IPT trainee several years ago. The student's female patient reported that her husband was not willing to come to therapy. Seeing her as a very pleasant and soft-spoken woman, the student assumed that the patient's interpretation of her husband's refusal was correct, and did not pursue any further details about the interaction. When goaded by his supervisor to pursue the specific dialogue further, the patient revealed to the therapist that she had asked her husband to attend therapy after one of their very infrequent sexual encounters. While she saw this as an opportune moment of communion and intimacy, her husband responded by saying that he would, "never go to some shrink to talk about my sexual problems!"

The IPT therapist must direct the patient to reproduce dialogues. The more precise and detailed the conversations the better, as this allows for more accurate diagnosis of communication problems. Nancy should be asked to relate a number of interactions between herself and her husband, mother, and co-workers.

Because of her dependent attachment style, Nancy is likely to be able to develop a good working relationship with the therapist in short order. While no specific mention was made about her biases regarding therapy or motivation for treatment (psychotherapy in particular), it is quite likely that, given her more dependent attachment style, she is willing to seek help from others initially. It is also likely that early in therapy, she will idealize the therapist to some degree, and see her therapist as being able to solve her problems for her.

Early in IPT, this type of positive transference is not to be discouraged. In fact, a relationship in which there is some idealization of the therapist and some attribution of expertise and authority can help to create an environment in which change is more likely. If she sees her therapist as a potential helper and invests him or her with authority, Nancy is more likely to be compliant with therapy (and medications if prescribed).

Given enough time, however, it is a certainty that Nancy will create the same kind of relationship with her therapist that she has with all of her significant others. In other words, given enough time (and it would probably be a relatively short time with Nancy given the pervasiveness of her attachment style), the therapy relationship will reflect her other extra-therapy relationships. This is a great development for a psychodynamic psychotherapist, but a very bad one for an IPT therapist. The latter is true because the intensity of the transference will obscure the ability of the therapist to direct Nancy to work on her extra-therapy relationships. Her feelings of dependency and anger at the therapist for being withholding and not caring for her enough will become the focal point of therapy. There may be much merit in this if Nancy is willing to engage in a long-term therapy (and if her insurance will pay for it!), but it is not consistent with IPT. Instead, the IPT therapist should literally "get in and get out" before the patient-therapist relationship becomes the primary issue in therapy. In order to keep the focus on the extra-therapy relationships, IPT must be time-limited.

Questionnaires and Other Assessment Instruments

Outside of research settings, questionnaires are typically not used during the IPT assessment process nor during the treatment itself. In large part, this is because IPT is less concerned with "objective" data reported by the patient than with the subjective way in which the symptoms are reported to others. It is the meaning of the symptoms and the way in which they are communicated which are at issue. In contrast to CBT, in which the questionnaires are used as a means to modify the patient's internal cognitions, IPT is concerned with the way in which the patient reports his or her symptoms to others and the way in which others respond. The way in which the patient conveys the symptoms to others as a means of eliciting a response from them is crucial.

This being the case, formal assessment instruments are a therapeutic hindrance in IPT. Divorcing the report of symptoms from an interpersonal context, as is done with rating scales and the like, detracts from the therapeutic goals of IPT. It discourages the patient from meaningful interpersonal communication. Rather than saying, "I have a BDI score of 32," the therapist's goal is to help the patient to describe his or her experiences in detail, to appreciate the way in which they are communicated, and to become aware of the responses he or she may be eliciting from others.

In a research setting, of course, empirically validated measurement is a necessity—both to assess efficacy and to obtain grant funding.

Historically, the traditional instruments to measure depression symptoms have been used in IPT research, such as the Beck Depression Inventory (Beck, 1961) and the Hamilton Rating Scale for Depression (Hamilton, 1967). The Social Adjustment Scale (Sullivan, 1953) was developed specifically to measure the changes in social functioning which are the focus of IPT.

TREATMENT

IPT can be succinctly divided into initial sessions, intermediate sessions, and termination. During each phase, the clinician has a well-defined set of tasks to accomplish, each of which is designed to foster the therapeutic goals of the patient. Undergirding the therapeutic tasks and techniques is the stance taken by the therapist. Clinicians must be active during the course of IPT, maintaining the focus of therapy and keeping the patient on task. The therapist should also be supportive—the "blank screen" approach should be abandoned in favor of a stance that is empathic and strongly encouraging—and should make every effort to convey a sense of hope to the patient and to reinforce his or her gains.

During the initial sessions (usually the first one or two meetings) the therapist has five specific tasks. The first is to complete a thorough diagnostic and interpersonal assessment as described above. The assessment should be conducted in such a way that the stage is set for the interpersonal approach that follows. For example, the therapist should inquire about symptoms of depression, and if they are acknowledged by the patient, should ask about how those symptoms have impacted the patient's interpersonal relationships. In discussing the patient's sense of hopelessness, the therapist might ask how that feeling has been communicated to the patient's significant other, how he or she has responded to it, and the degree to which the patient is feeling understood.

The therapist should also begin an interpersonal inventory. The inventory consists of a brief description of the important people in the patient's life, and for each individual includes information about the amount and quality of contact, problems in the relationship, and the expectations that the patient has about the relationship. These descriptions are not intended to be exhaustive—the relationships that are noted to be problematic and become treatment foci will be revisited in detail later. The purpose of the inventory is to help the patient (and therapist) determine which relationships are appropriate to work on, and to gather information regarding the patient's attachment and communication patterns.

Once the inventory is complete, the patient and clinician should mutually identify one or two problem relationships upon which to focus. Four problem areas are defined in IPT: grief or loss, interpersonal disputes, role transitions, and interpersonal sensitivity.[4] The therapist should frame the patient's problem as interpersonal, and should give specific examples of the way in which the problem fits into one of these areas.

The therapist should also explain the rationale for IPT in concrete terms. Attention should be drawn to the interpersonal orientation of the therapy, and the patient should be instructed that he or she will be expected to discuss interpersonal relationships. Further, the patient should be explicitly told that the goal of therapy is to modify communication patterns and/or expectations about relationships, and that as these changes occur, symptomatic relief is expected to occur as well. The more information the better—the patient cannot be too well informed about the rationale for IPT nor the theory of change which interpersonal theory espouses. Additionally, a thorough description of the rationale for IPT should increase the patient's hope for change and his or her investment in the therapeutic process as IPT is presented as a credible therapy.

During the intermediate sessions of IPT, the patient and therapist work together to address the interpersonal problems identified during the assessment. In general, work on these issues proceeds in the following order: (1) identification of a specific interpersonal problem; (2) a detailed exploration of the patient's perception of the problem, including communication patterns in the relationship and expectations about the relationship; (3) collaborative brainstorming with the therapist to identify possible solutions to the problem, or to identify ways in which the patient may be able to change his or her communication with the significant other; (4) implementation of the proposed solution (typically between sessions); and (5) reviewing the patient's attempted solution, with positive encouragement of the changes made and discussion of refinements in the solution to be carried out by the patient. The expression, "Give a man a fish and he eats for a day, teach a man to fish and he eats for a lifetime," is a useful reminder for the therapist, who should work diligently to help the patient develop the ability to be introspective about his or her relationships and to creatively change them.

During the intermediate sessions, the patient's interpersonal issues should be framed in one of the four problem areas which characterize IPT. The first, interpersonal disputes, is relatively self-explanatory, and includes relationships in which a conflict between the patient and a significant other is occurring. Role transition is a second area, and includes changes which may disrupt important relationships. These may include not only situations which are usually considered adverse, such as the loss of a job or a divorce, but may also include natural life-transitions, such as graduation, the birth of a child, or declining health during one's later years.

Grief is the third problem area, and encompasses not only those situations in which a significant other dies, but also includes other types of losses which may be perceived by the patient as grief issues.[5] For example, loss of functioning following a stroke or heart attack may be characterized as a grief issue by the patient (Stuart, 1996). Similarly, divorce or loss of a job may also be viewed by the patient as a grief issue. There is clearly overlap in all of these areas; divorce or declining health could also be conceptualized as role transitions. However, as a general rule, it is always best to place the interpersonal problem in the area which fits best with the patient's understanding—nothing but therapeutic alienation is gained when the therapist vainly and rigidly insists that the patient's issue is one of role transition while the patient understands the problem as a matter of grief.

The last problem area is interpersonal sensitivity. Patients who have difficulty in establishing or maintaining relationships may fall into this category; such patients may be less likely to seek therapy because of their desire to avoid intimacy. Interpersonal sensitivity describes an attachment style in which the patient is overly sensitive to interpersonal cues, constantly sensing or fearing rejection from others. The patient may also be lacking in the social skills needed to accurately recognize the social cues given by others. The therapist should appreciate the therapeutic value of describing the patient's problem as one of interpersonal sensitivity, rather than framing the problem as an interpersonal deficit.

In this case, Nancy's problems can probably best be categorized as interpersonal disputes in the case of her husband and mother, and as grief issues in the case of her father. As noted above, it is of little benefit for the clinician to artificially force patients to place their interpersonal problems in a certain area, and it is much better to be flexible and use the category which best fits the patient's conceptualization. At the end of the assessment (typically after one or two sessions), Nancy and her therapist should mutually determine one or two of these problem areas on which to focus.

Despite the severity of her symptoms, Nancy has many strengths which should help her in therapy. First and foremost, she appears able to articulate her problems. More difficult patients often describe their depression in vague terms with statements such as "I just feel bad" or, "I don't know what is wrong with me." Nancy, on the other hand, has pretty clearly identified her depression as stemming from several different interpersonal issues. A further strength is that she appears to have developed a somewhat balanced view of others with whom she interacts—she has insight into the fact that people are neither all good nor all bad, but are a combination of the two. For instance, in her description of her husband she notes that he, "is a lazy and extremely critical person," but later goes on to modify this, reporting some of his good qualities by stating that, "he can also be really kind and generous and attentive . . . "

Psychologically, she also appears to have already developed a fairly good understanding of the way in which she typically interacts with others. Statements such as, "(I have) a hard time breaking off a relationship, even if it is making me unhappy" and "(I) can't let people know when I'm angry at them" speak to her insight. It should be possible for the therapist to help her to appreciate that the way in which she communicates to others may have a profound impact on their responses to her.

Nancy also has several other strengths which will help her in therapy. She describes a fairly good social support network at work, and notes that her mood actually changes when working and spending time alone. She also appears to be a motivated individual—returning to school while working reflects her motivation as well as a capacity for delayed gratification.

TECHNIQUES AND THERAPEUTIC PROCESS

The distinguishing feature of IPT is its consistent interpersonal orientation in a time-limited format. Though there are several techniques (described below) which are unique to IPT, it is the focus on extra-therapeutic relationships rather than any particular intervention which characterizes the therapy. Not surprisingly, given its psychodynamic roots, IPT incorporates a number of "traditional" psychotherapeutic methods, such as exploration, clarification, and even some directive techniques—in fact, there are actually no techniques which are forbidden in IPT.[6] All of these are used, however, in the service of helping the patient to modify his or her interpersonal relationships.

In general, the middle phase of IPT consists of working with the patient to resolve one or two interpersonal issues. The therapist must be fairly directive—keeping the patient on task is important given the time-limit of IPT. The general format for the middle phase of treatment is: (1) identification of a specific interpersonal problem; (2) a detailed exploration of the patient's perception of the problem, including communication patterns in the relationship and expectations about the relationship; (3) collaborative brainstorming with the therapist to identify possible solutions to the problem, or to identify ways in which the patient may be able to change his or her communication with the significant other; (4) implementation of the proposed solution (typically between sessions); and (5) reviewing the patient's attempted solution, with positive encouragement of the changes made and discussion of refinements in the solution to be carried out by the patient.

Communication Analysis

The analysis of communication patterns is one of the primary techniques in IPT. The therapist's task is to assist the patient to describe more clearly what he or she wants from significant others, and to convey their needs more effectively. Patients often assume that their communication is clear, when in fact it may not be understood at all by the people to whom it is directed. IPT operates on the premise that modifying interpersonal communication patterns will assist patients to more effectively meet their attachment needs, and having elicited more appropriate social support, will reduce their psychiatric symptoms.

Communication analysis requires that the therapist elicit information from the patient about important interpersonal incidents. In psychotherapy, a typical patient will describe an interaction with a significant other in very general terms, leaving the therapist with very little information about the specific communication which occurred. For instance, a patient may say that her husband, "never listens to her." Taken at face value, the therapist and the patient are left with the dismaying "fact" that the patient's husband is a complete lout,[7] or at best, is very insensitive. If true, the only options left to the patient are to put up with the relationship and continue to be depressed, or to end the relationship.

General statements like these, though containing a grain of truth, almost always represent only one (very biased) side of the story. What is more likely is that while the patient's husband may indeed be insensitive, some of his non-responsiveness is due to the communication style of the patient. She may, though intending otherwise, come across as critical or uncaring, or may simply be trying to communicate at a time when it will not be well-received. She may also be unwittingly ignoring important communications from her husband.

Therefore, when eliciting interpersonal incidents, the therapist's goal is to have the patient recreate, in as much detail as possible, a typical interaction between herself and her husband. As this is not usually what patients spontaneously talk about, the therapist must direct the patient to produce this material. The goal is to use this "step-by-step" (or perhaps better put, "blow-by-blow") report to understand the way in which the patient conveys her attachment needs, acting on the hypothesis that she is communicating in such a way that she is being misunderstood and is therefore not being responded to as she would like.

The therapy proceeds from a general problem statement on the part of the patient to a specific recreation of the dialogue between the patient and her spouse. The therapist should ask not only about the verbal interactions that occur, but also the nonverbal communications that take place, such as using silence in a hostile fashion, slamming doors, leaving the situation in the middle of an interaction, and so forth. This should include a detailed description of what the patient said to begin the interaction, how her husband responded, what she understood him to say, how she responded in turn, and so forth until the end of the interaction. Special note should be made of the end of the interaction, as many conflicts may carry over to the next day, or may be brought up again in subsequent disagreements.

In this case, the therapist can direct Nancy by asking her to recall, in detail, a recent meaningful interaction with her husband. Once the specifics of the dialogue are obtained the therapist should actively direct Nancy to review the interaction, addressing what she was intending to communicate, and the kind of response she was hoping to receive. For instance, the therapist might ask her, "when you first asked your husband to talk with you about your marriage, how were you hoping he would respond?" Discussion of this issue would then be followed by an investigation of her views about what kinds of responses her statements to her husband were likely to elicit, e.g., anger from her husband, distancing behavior, silence. The therapist would then assist Nancy to recognize that the way in which she is communicating her needs does not appear to be productive. The possibility that she may be able to improve the situation by coming up with new ways to communicate more effectively is then introduced.

It is at this point that an explicit homework assignment might be valuable. After discussing these issues with Nancy, she may decide that she needs to plan some time to speak to her husband about her feelings. The goal would be to have Nancy attempt to incorporate new communication—to be more direct, and to avoid using threats to convey her feelings, for example. In order to foster this, the therapist may choose to "assign" Nancy this task, and tell her that she should be prepared to discuss the interaction with her husband in the next therapy session. When she returns the next week, the therapist can lead off the session by asking about the assignment, and can review the interaction with Nancy in detail, including again the entire interpersonal incident, i.e., the way in which the conversation started, what Nancy said, her husband's response, and the like. While certainly not a necessary part of IPT, the therapist should not shy away from requesting that patients do some work outside of therapy.

Work on communication can also be facilitated by including significant others in one or two sessions. Including Nancy's husband in a session, for instance, would allow the therapist to observe the in vivo interaction between Nancy and her husband, and would clarify the distortions in her reports about their communication. Including Nancy's husband also allows the therapist to provide some education to him regarding the nature of depression, Nancy's prognosis, and the plan for treatment.

Use of Affect

The more the patient is affectively involved in the issues being discussed in therapy, the more likely he or she will be motivated to change behavior or communication style. Consequently, one of the most important tasks for the IPT therapist is to attend to the patient's affective state during the course of therapy. Of particular importance are those moments in therapy in which the patient's observed affective state, and his or her subjectively reported affect, are incongruent. Examining this inconsistency in affect can often lead to breakthroughs in therapy.

Affect can be divided into that experienced during therapy (*process affect*) and that reported by the patient to have occurred at some time in the past (*content affect*). For example, when describing her relationship with her father, Nancy might describe that she was feeling completely depressed and overwhelmed when he left home, yet as she is relating this information in the session, she may be speaking with almost no affect as if she were reporting a story about someone else. Conversely, she might report that when her father left, she was the one that was responsible, took care of her other family members, and that she felt numb or felt nothing at all. Yet despite this reported absence of feelings, she may, as she is telling the story in session, appear extremely sad, tearful, or even be crying.

When met with this incongruence in affect, the therapist can focus directly on the discrepancy between content and process affect. In other words, when the report the patient gives about how he or she felt during an interpersonal event is different from the affect he or she is exhibiting during the session, it should be noted by the therapist and explored further.

Use of Transference

A common sticking point in IPT is that of transference—most therapists believe that transference is a universal occurrence in therapy, and wonder what to do with this information in IPT. Given the interpersonal and psychodynamic foundation upon which IPT rests, there is no doubt that transference can and does play an extremely important part in the therapy. However, in contrast to longer-term psychodynamically oriented therapies, information gleaned from the transference which develops during IPT, though an important source of data, is not typically a point of *intervention*.

By observing the developing transference, the therapist can begin to draw hypotheses about the way that the patient interacts with others outside of the therapeutic relationship. Sullivan (1953) coined the term "parataxic distortion" to describe this phenomena: the way in which a patient relates to the therapist in session is a reflection of the way in which he or she relates to others as well. Attachment theory also supports the idea that individuals tend to relate to others in a manner that is consistent both across relationships and within relationships. Thus the transference or parataxic distortion recognized in therapy by the clinician provides a means of understanding all of the other relationships in the patient's interpersonal sphere.

Using these data, the therapist can then begin to draw conclusions about the patient's attachment style, and about his or her problems in communicating to others. The developing conceptualization of the patient should direct the therapist to ask questions of the patient to confirm or disprove these hypotheses. For instance, if the therapist notes that the patient tends to be deferential in therapy, an assumption that the patient tends to be the same way in other relationships is reasonable. The therapist may want to ask about the experiences (or difficulties) that the patient has had in confronting others, or in dealing with rejection. Similarly, if the patient behaves in a dependent manner during therapy, the therapist may ask about the patient's perceptions about how he or she maintains relationships, or about experiences the patient has had in ending relationships.

The key difference between IPT and the more transference-based therapies is that the IPT therapist should avoid making transference comments, and particularly interpretations, about the therapeutic relationship. As long as a reasonably positive transference is maintained, ideally with the patient according the therapist some degree of expertise, therapy can proceed without the need to focus on the transference. In IPT, the trick, so to speak, is to "get in and get out" quickly. The therapist should focus on the here-and-now problems in the patient's extra-therapy interpersonal relationships. With well-selected patients, keeping the therapy short-term allows the therapist to assist the patient to solve his or her interpersonal problems before the transference becomes intense, and as a result, becomes the new focus of therapy.

Therapeutic Relationship

As a result of the time-limit on therapy, which is designed to prevent the transference from becoming the primary focus of therapy, the therapist need not be so concerned with avoiding interventions which have transference implications. In other words, in IPT it is not only permissible but helpful for the therapist to position him or herself as an advocate for the patient—there is no need to be a "blank screen" for the patient's projections. This may take the form of providing educational information to the patient, serving as an advocate for social services to which the patient may be entitled, and even assisting with financial arrangements to pay for therapy or arranging transportation to the sessions. It is not necessary to maintain a neutral position because the therapeutic focus is on extra-therapy relationships.

Successful IPT therapists are typically those with a solid grounding in psychodynamic psychotherapy. Though IPT, by virtue of its consistent interpersonal and non-transferential focus is not simply psychodynamic psychotherapy in a short-term format, the same principles are used in IPT as in psychodynamic psychotherapy, particularly regarding techniques and appreciation of the patient-therapist interactions which occur in therapy.

On occasion, therapeutic boundaries are threatened during the course of treatment. The IPT therapist should take a preventive approach to this problem, i.e., conducting a careful assessment so that only patients who are appropriate for time-limited treatment are selected for IPT. This implies that patients with severe personality disorders, and those in particular who are prone to violate therapeutic boundaries, such as borderline or antisocial patients, are not good candidates for IPT. Additionally, patients who would appear to require long-term psychotherapy should not be accepted as candidates for IPT. These would include patients with problems with marked dependency, or with personality disorders which would make it difficult for them to quickly establish a working alliance with the therapist. Finally, patients with substance abuse problems do not appear to be good candidates for treatment with IPT while their abuse is active.

In those instances in which the patient does cross therapeutic boundaries, the therapist should first attempt to address the issue without discussing the therapeutic relationship directly. For example, if a patient was late or missed several appointments, the therapist should respond by pointing out that the patient is not allowing him or herself to get the full benefit of therapy. Missing appointments is similar to missing doses of medication—taking half a dose, or skipping doses reduces the chances for recovery.

Other threats, such as suicidality or homicidality, can be dealt with in a similar direct fashion. Though melodramatic at first glance, the therapist can tell the patient that killing him or herself will have a deleterious effect on the treatment and will keep the patient from getting the full benefit from therapy; likewise, killing the therapist (or someone else) will also put a crimp in the proceedings. There is no benefit to the therapist in threatening to hospitalize a patient for suicidal statements—any patient worth his salt will quickly figure out that he should simply keep these thoughts to himself. The net result of this type of threatening intervention is to inhibit free and open communication with the patient.

Instead, the therapist should acknowledge that a determined patient can kill him or herself despite the therapist's intervention. Not only have patients been known to kill themselves on inpatient units, most patients are astute enough if they are truly serious about committing suicide to know they should simply avoid mentioning it to their therapist and follow through on their plans unhindered after the session. In IPT, the therapist should ask the patient to be open and honest, and to let the therapist know when hospitalization is necessary.

If these or similar interventions are not effective in refocusing the therapy and in alleviating the boundary problems, it is indicative that the patient is not a good IPT candidate. In such a case, the patient should be strongly considered for referral for longer-term transferentially based psychotherapy.

IPT AND MEDICATION

The use of antidepressant medication is perfectly compatible with IPT—in fact, the original studies of IPT demonstrated that combination treatment was more successful and better accepted by patients than either medication or psychotherapy alone (Weissman, 1979). Given the stress-diathesis model of depression which is inherent in IPT, in which interpersonal stress triggers depression in individuals with an underlying biological predisposition, the use of medication is theoretically defensible as well. While more empirical data are needed with regard to combined treatment (both for IPT and other therapies as well), it is common practice for IPT and medication to be used together to treat depression.

Nancy is currently on a dose of 50 mg of Zoloft. In addition to providing IPT, the therapist would be well-advised to either increase the dose of Zoloft or refer her to a psychiatrist who can do so. Barring side effects, there is no reason that the dose cannot and should not be increased. The goal of IPT is symptom relief, and it is indefensible to deny patients an effective psychopharmacologic treatment for depression simply so that the therapist can hold the theoretical high ground.

RELAPSE PREVENTION

Addressing the issue of relapse prevention assumes, of course, that the patient has actually recovered. While IPT is certainly an effective treatment, the wise clinician and reader should be skeptical that recovery actually occurs without exception. In fact, as has been repeatedly demonstrated in all studies of psychotherapeutic and psychopharmacologic treatments, the norm is that most patients experience improvement, but continue to have mild symptoms at the end of the treatment (Thase, 1999). Further, all longitudinal studies show that patients with depression are likely to have recurrent courses of depression, and many will need several courses of treatment during their lifetimes. To assume that "cure" will result from treatment is to do a disservice to the patient and to create unrealistic expectations for the therapist.

Relapse prevention and continuing treatment should be discussed at the outset of every treatment for depression. IPT is one of the few psychotherapies for which there is evidence that maintenance therapy is of benefit—once a month IPT has been shown to reduce rates of depression relapse as compared to no treatment (Frank, 1990). It is therefore necessary at the outset of treatment with IPT to discuss with the patient the possible plans for continued treatment. Treatment with IPT should be divided into two distinct phases—the acute treatment phase, during which the patient and therapist meet once a week for a specified number of sessions, and a maintenance phase, in which meetings once every month or two are arranged. The situation is analogous to a family practice model in which the physician may be treating an acute problem such as pneumonia. In this case, contact with the patient until the symptoms are resolved is frequent and treatment is aggressive. Once the symptoms are resolved, however, arrangements are made for continued contact and future treatment if needed, and preventive measures are stressed.

Nancy's therapist should discuss with her the likelihood that she may benefit from maintenance treatment following the acute sessions of IPT. A reasonable plan would be to meet with Nancy weekly for 12 to 16 weeks, and to contract at that point for monthly maintenance sessions of IPT.[8] As she is likely to continue on medication as well, these maintenance IPT sessions could be conducted conjointly with medication management.

TERMINATION

The completion of therapy holds special significance in IPT because of the focus on interpersonal relationships. The ending of the therapeutic relationship (or modification of it, if maintenance treatment is a component of treatment) is an important interpersonal event. Acknowledging feelings that the patient (and therapist) may have about the end of the relationship, such as a sense of loss, are important.

It is necessary to stick to the time-limit with IPT, even in cases in which the patient may not be fully recovered. The most compelling reason for this is that many patients continue to improve even after therapy is complete. Perhaps the best example of this phenomena is the gains that continued to be made by patients receiving short-term IPT for bulimia—these individuals continued to make substantial gains over the next year despite having completed therapy months before (Fairburn, 1995). Our experience with patients treated in a research setting, in which we have had the opportunity to conduct long-term follow-up, has been that most do continue to improve after the end of treatment. Termination with patients who have not fully recovered may also be made more difficult because of the therapist's desire to see him or herself as an essential ingredient for continued progress by the patient.

Second, failing to adhere to the contract and to complete therapy within the time frame agreed upon conveys several things to the patient. First, it may convey that the therapist has little confidence in the patient, and sees him or her as "hopeless" or unable to recover. Second, continuing beyond the time-limit will force a change in therapeutic focus—the longer the therapy, the more likely that transferential issues will interfere with progress and need to be addressed as primary treatment foci. Though it may be in the patient's best interest to address these issues in therapy, to do so shifts the therapy from the here-and-now problem focus of IPT to a psychodynamic format which is outside of the scope of IPT. In cases where continued psychotherapeutic treatment is absolutely necessary, or in which the patient may benefit from an open-ended psychodynamic approach to treatment, appropriate referrals may be made.

Finally, termination should also address the issue of maintenance treatment or the need for future treatment if another episode of depression should occur. This should come as no surprise to the patient, as maintenance treatment should have been mentioned in the initial phases of treatment. In those cases in which maintenance treatment is not deemed necessary, the IPT therapist can use the "family practice" model of treatment.

SUMMARY

IPT is characterized by its focus on interpersonal relationships, its non-transferential approach to therapy, and its time-limited format. It is grounded in both attachment and interpersonal theory, and rests on the premise that improvement in interpersonal relationships will lead to symptomatic improvement. IPT is specifically designed to treat psychiatric symptoms rather than modify personality—this is its strength as well as its limitation.

The short-term format requires that patients be wisely selected for treatment with IPT. Empirical data supports the use of IPT for both acute and maintenance treatment of depression, and research also support the use of IPT with bulimia. Concurrent use of medication is indicated and may actually be better received by patients. Additionally, IPT appears to be well-suited for anxiety disorders, and has shown promise for somatoform disorders as well. It does not, however, appear to be an appropriate treatment for patients with either severe personality pathology or active substance abuse.

According to attachment and interpersonal theory, Nancy is suffering from depressive and anxiety symptoms as a result of her anxious ambivalent attachment style. Based on her early childhood experiences with her parents, Nancy developed a working model of relationships which serves as a template for all of her relationships, including that with her husband. According to her model, she acts as if she believes that she can never completely depend on others—in order to get her attachment needs met, she must either placate others or insistently demand care. Her communication reflects this belief: she tends to be very deferential, to the point of feeling that she "loses herself" or is taken advantage of, or she tends to threaten to end relationships as a means of escalating her demands.

Communicating in this fashion, however, has the unfortunate effect of distancing herself even further from others. Her indirect style of communication renders others unable to understand what it is she wants, and may actually elicits hostility from those on whom she depends. Her psychiatric symptoms have come to a head as the little interpersonal support that she is receiving is now being threatened.

IPT appears to be well-suited for Nancy. Her depressive and anxiety symptoms should respond well to IPT. The therapist should be thinking about possible maintenance treatment, and should also encourage the use of medication along with IPT, as the goal of both treatments is symptom relief. Though it is unlikely that Nancy's attachment style will undergo significant change, she does appear to have insight into the interpersonal factors involved in her depression, and should be able to modify her communication patterns as a result. As her communication improves, she is likely to feel more secure in her relationships, particularly with her husband and her mother. With her attachment needs more closely met, she should experience improvement in her mood and overall functioning.

It is likely that an IPT therapist would accept Nancy for treatment, and be optimistic about her chances for recovery. Her substantial strengths of insight and motivation bode well for the treatment. During the first session the therapist would review her psychiatric symptoms, likely diagnose her with major depression with anxious features, and based on gut instinct (informed to some degree by empirical data) proceed with therapy along with increasing her dose of Zoloft. The therapist would also formulate a treatment plan with Nancy which would include a specified number of sessions (most likely 12–16 weeks of treatment) and discuss possible treatment options once acute treatment is completed.

The initial sessions would also include a discussion of the interpersonal problem areas which Nancy faces. Most likely the focus would be on Nancy's relationships with her husband and her mother, both of which could be identified as an interpersonal conflict. Beginning with one of these relationships, Nancy would be requested to begin discussing specific interactions in detail so that her communication style could be examined.

During the intermediate sessions, the therapist would collaborate with Nancy in discussing the specific interpersonal relationship, and in looking at ways in which her communication could be improved. The kinds of responses that her communication is eliciting would be explored, and alternative ways of meeting her attachment needs would be discussed. Nancy would be encouraged (or given an explicit assignment) to attempt to implement one of the alternative means of communicating with her husband or mother.

Nancy's somewhat dependent qualities would inform the therapist that termination should be discussed somewhat earlier in the treatment—mention might be made about midway through the treatment, and would be explicitly discussed with about 3–4 sessions remaining. The therapist might also invite Nancy's husband to reconsider his participation and to attend a session or two, giving the therapist an opportunity to observe the couple's communication in vivo and to enlist her husband in the treatment. While supporting Nancy's recovery, the therapist would take a neutral view about the relationship, aiming only to assist Nancy to make an informed and conscious choice about whether to continue her marriage or to end it.

Termination of acute treatment would occur after 16 sessions. Realistically, it is likely that Nancy may have a few residual symptoms, but she would also have noted a significant improvement in her sense of well-being and in her depressive and anxiety symptoms. She will need to be followed for medication management on a monthly basis for at least a year, and could either receive maintenance IPT from her psychiatrist at these appointments or from her counselor.

Nancy is a wonderful example of the type of patient that will do well with IPT. IPT is a very effective short-term treatment for depression, and while certainly not a panacea, is a treatment of choice for carefully selected patients.

NOTES

1. See DeRubeis et al. (1999) for a differing opinion regarding CBT.
2. Legend has it, for instance, that the real reason that psychotherapy sessions last an hour each is that an hour is the longest period of time Freud could hold his bladder.
3. It should be noted that while there is no research demonstrating whether 12, 16, 20, or even more sessions are optimal, clinical experience suggests that 12–16 weeks is long enough to bring about symptom resolution while being short enough to avoid the development of problematic transference.
4. It should be noted that the first description of Interpersonal Therapy in manualized form (Klerman et al., 1984) included interpersonal deficits as a problem area rather than interpersonal sensitivity.
5. It should be noted that the first description of Interpersonal Therapy in manualized form (Klerman et al., 1984) specifically states that the grief problem area includes only situations in which someone has died.

6. It should be noted that the first description of Interpersonal Psychotherapy in manualized form (Klerman et al., 1984) specifically prohibited explicit homework assignments. It has been the authors' experience, however, that explicit homework assignments may on occasion be very useful, particularly when dealing with communication problems in which the patient is to attempt or practice new communication patterns between sessions. The rational for the exclusion of homework in the Klerman et al. text is unclear, and may in part have been included to explicitly distinguish IPT from CBT in the NIMH Treatment of Depression Collaborative Research Program, in which the two treatments were compared. The NIMH-TDCRP was designed so that two clearly different therapies were being tested, thus excluding homework (which is an integral part of CBT) from the IPT treatment may have been a means of further differentiating the two treatments.

7. The patient's attempt to "blame" her husband in the face of his genetic deficiency (single X chromosome syndrome) may also be counterproductive.

8. It should be noted that the empirical efficacy data regarding the use of IPT as a maintenance treatment supports its use only for patients with *recurrent* depression (i.e., three or more episodes) (Frank, 1990). However, despite the fact that it has not been empirically tested for patients experiencing a single episode of depression, IPT is very likely an effective treatment in this situation as well.

REFERENCES

American Psychiatric Association. (1994). *Diagnostic and statistical manual of mental disorders* (4th ed.). Washington, DC: American Psychiatric Association.

Beck, A. T., Rush, A. J., Shaw, B. F., & Emery, G. (1979). *Cognitive therapy of depression.* New York: Guilford Press.

Beck, A. T., Ward, C. H., Mendelson, M., Mock, J., & Erbaugh, J. (1961). An inventory for measuring depression. *Archives of General Psychiatry, 4,* 561–571.

Bowlby, J. (1969). *Attachment.* New York: Basic Books.

Bowlby, J. (1977). The making and breaking of affectional bonds: Etiology and psychopathology in the light of attachment theory. *British Journal of Psychiatry, 130,* 201–210.

Bowlby, J. (1977). The making and breaking of affectional bonds, II: Some principles of psychotherapy. *British Journal of Psychiatry, 130*, 421–431.

Brown, C., Schulberg, H. C., & Madonia, M. J. (1996). Treatment outcomes for primary care patients with major depression and lifetime anxiety disorders. *American Journal of Psychiatry, 153*, 1293–1300.

Brown, G. W., & Harris, T. O. (1978). *Social origins of depression: A study of psychiatric disorders in women.* London: Tavistock.

Brown, G. W., & Harris, T. O. (1989). *Life events and illness.* New York: Guilford.

Brown, G. W., Harris, T. O., & Hepworth, C. (1994). Life events and endogenous depression. *Archives of General Psychiatry, 51*, 525–534.

DiMascio, A., Weissman, M. M., & Prusoff, B. A. (1979). Differential symptom reduction by drugs and psychotherapy in acute depression. *Archives of General Psychiatry, 36*, 1450–1456.

Elkin, I., Parloff, M. B., Hadley, S. W., & Autry, J. H. (1985). NIMH treatment of depression collaborative treatment program: Background and research plan. *Archives of General Psychiatry, 42*, 305–316.

Elkin, I., Shea, M. T., Watkins, J. T., et al. (1989). National Institute of Mental Health Treatment of Depression Collaborative Research Program: General effectiveness of treatments. *Archives of General Psychiatry, 46*, 971–982.

Fairburn, C. G., Jones, R., & Peveler, R. C. (1991). Three psychological treatments for bulimia nervosa: A comparative trial. *Archives of General Psychiatry, 48*, 463–469.

Fairburn, C. G., Jones, R., & Peveler, R. C. (1993). Psychotherapy and bulimia nervosa: The longer-term effects of interpersonal psychotherapy, behavioural psychotherapy, and cognitive behaviour therapy. *Archives of General Psychiatry, 50*, 419–428.

Fairburn, C. G., Norman, P. A., & Welch, S. L. (1995). A prospective study of the outcome in bulimia nervosa and the long-term effects of three psychological treatments. *Archives of General Psychiatry, 52*, 304–312.

Foley, S. H., Rounsaville, B. J., & Weissman, M. M. (1989). Individual versus conjoint interpersonal psychotherapy for depressed patients with marital disputes. *International Journal of Family Psychiatry, 10*, 29–42.

Frank, E. (1991). Interpersonal psychotherapy as a maintenance treatment for patients with recurrent depression. *Psychotherapy, 28*, 259–266.

Frank, E., Kupfer, D. J., & Cornes, C. (1990). Manual for the Adaptation of Interpersonal Psychotherapy to the Treatment of Bipolar Disorders. Pittsburgh, PA: University of Pittsburgh.

Frank, E., Kupfer, D. J., & Perel, J. M. (1990). Three-year outcomes for maintenance therapies in recurrent depression. *Archives of General Psychiatry, 47*, 1093–1099.

Frank, E., Kupfer, D. J., Wagner, E. F., McEachran, A. B., & Cornes, C. (1991). Efficacy of interpersonal psychotherapy as a maintenance treatment of recurrent depression. Contributing factors. *Archives of General Psychiatry, 48,* 1053–1059.

Hamilton, M. A. (1967). Development of a rating scale for primary depressive illness. *British Journal of Social and Clinical Psychology, 6,* 278–296.

Imber, S. D., Pilkonis, P. A., Sotsky, S. M., et al. (1990). Mode-specific effects among three treatments for depression. *Journal of Consulting and Clinical Psychology, 58,* 352–359.

Kiesler, D. J., & Watkins, L. M. (1989). Interpersonal complimentarity and the therapeutic alliance: A study of the relationship in psychotherapy. *Psychotherapy, 26,* 183–194.

Klerman, G. L., & Weissman, M. M. (1993). *New applications of interpersonal psychotherapy.* Washington, DC: American Psychiatric Press.

Klerman, G. L., Weissman, M. M., Rounsaville, B. J., & Chevron, E. S. (1984). *Interpersonal psychotherapy of depression.* New York: Basic Books.

Kupfer, D. J., Frank, E., & Perel, J. M. (1992). Five year outcomes for maintenance therapies in recurrent depression. *Archives of General Psychiatry, 49,* 769–773.

Markowitz, J. C. (1993). Psychotherapy of the post-dysthymic patient. *Journal of Psychotherapy Practice and Research, 2,* 157–163.

Markowitz, J. C. (1994). Psychotherapy of dysthymia. *American Journal of Psychiatry, 151,* 1114–1121.

Markowitz, J. (1997). *Interpersonal psychotherapy for dysthymic disorder.* Washington, DC: American Psychiatric Press.

Markowitz, J. M., Klerman, G. L., & Clougherty, K. F. (1995). Individual psychotherapies for depressed HIV-positive patients. *American Journal of Psychiatry, 152,* 1504–1509.

Markowitz, J. C., Klerman, G. L., & Perry, S. W. (1992). Interpersonal psychotherapy of depressed HIV-positive outpatients. *Hospital and Community Psychiatry, 43,* 885–890.

Markowitz, J. M., Klerman, G. L., & Perry, S. W. (1993). Interpersonal psychotherapy for depressed HIV-seropositive patients. In G. L. Klerman & M. M. Weissman (Eds.), *New applications of interpersonal psychotherapy* (pp. 199–224). Washington, DC: American Psychiatric Press.

Mason, B. J., Markowitz, J. C., & Klerman, G. L. (1993). Interpersonal psychotherapy for dysthymic disorders. In G. L. Klerman & M. M. Weissman (Eds.), *New applications of interpersonal psychotherapy* (pp. 225–264). Washington, DC: American Psychiatric Press.

Mufson, L., & Fairbanks, J. (1996). Interpersonal psychotherapy for depressed adolescents: A one-year naturalistic follow-up study. *Journal of the American Academy of Child and Adolescent Psychiatry, 35,* 1145–1155.

Mufson, L., Moreau, D., & Weissman, M. M. (1994). The modification of interpersonal psychotherapy with depressed adolescents (IPT-A): Phase I and phase II studies. *Journal of the American Academy of Child and Adolescent Psychiatry, 33,* 695–705.

Mufson, L., Moreau, D., Weissman, M. M., & Klerman, G. L. (1993). *Interpersonal psychotherapy for depressed adolescents.* New York: Guilford Press.

O'Hara, M. W., Stuart, S., Gorman, L., & Wenzel, A. (1999). Efficacy of interpersonal psychotherapy for postpartum depression. *Archives of General Psychiatry.*

Reynolds, C. F., Frank, E., Houck, P. R., et al. (1997). Which elderly patients with remitted depression remain well with continued interpersonal psychotherapy after discontinuation of antidepressant medication? *American Journal of Psychiatry, 154*(7), 958–962.

Reynolds, C. F., Frank, E., & Kupfer, D. J. (1996). Treatment outcome in recurrent major depression: A post hoc comparison of elderly ("young old") and midlife patients. *American Journal of Psychiatry, 153,* 1288–1292.

Reynolds, C. F., Frank, E., & Perel, J. M. (1992). Combined pharmacotherapy and psychotherapy in the acute and continuation treatment of elderly patients with recurrent major depression: A preliminary report. *American Journal of Psychiatry, 149,* 1687–1692.

Schulberg, H. C., Block, M. R., & Madonia, M. J. (1996). Treating major depression in primary care practice. *Archives of General Psychiatry, 53,* 913–919.

Schulberg, H. C., Scott, C. P., Madonia, M. J., & Imber, S. D. (1993). Applications of interpersonal psychotherapy to depression in primary care practice. In G. L. Klerman & M. M. Weissman (Eds.), *New applications of interpersonal psychotherapy.* Washington, DC: American Psychiatric Press.

Shea, M. T., Elkin, I., Imber, S. D., et al. (1992). Course of depressive symptoms over follow-up. Findings from the National Institute of Mental Health Treatment of Depression Collaborative Research Program. *Archives of General Psychiatry, 49,* 782–787.

Sotsky, S. M., Glass, D. R., Shea, M. T., et al. (1991). Patient predictors of response to psychotherapy and pharmacotherapy: Findings in the NIMH Treatment of Depression Collaborative Research Program. *American Journal of Psychiatry, 148,* 997–1008.

Spinelli, M. G., & Weissman, M. M. (1997). The clinical application of interpersonal psychotherapy for depression during pregnancy. *Primary Psychiatry, 4,* 50–57.

Stuart, S. (1997). *Use of interpersonal psychotherapy for other disorders. Directions in Mental Health Counseling* (pp. 4–16). New York: Hatherleigh Company.

Stuart, S., & Cole, V. (1996). Treatment of depression following myocardial infarction with interpersonal psychotherapy. *Annals of Clinical Psychiatry, 8,* 203–206.

Stuart, S., & O'Hara, M. W. (1995). Interpersonal psychotherapy for post-partum depression: A treatment program. *Journal of Psychotherapy Practice and Research, 4,* 18–29.

Stuart, S., & Noyes, R. (1998). *Attachment and interpersonal communication in somatization disorder.* Psychosomatics.

Stuart, S., & O'Hara, M. W. (in press). Psychosocial Treatments for Mood Disorders in Women. In M. Steiner, K. A. Yonkers, & E. Eriksson (Eds.), *Mood disorders in women.* London: Martin Dunitz, Ltd.

Sullivan, H. S. (1953). *The interpersonal theory of psychiatry.* New York: Norton.

Thase, M. E. (1999). How should efficacy be evaluated in randomized clinical trials of treatments for depression? *Journal of Clinical Psychiatry, 60*(Suppl. 4), 23–32.

Weissman, M. M., & Bothwell, S. (1976). Assessment of social adjustment by patient self-report. *Archives of General Psychiatry, 33,* 1111–1115.

Weissman, M. M., Klerman, G. L., Prusoff, B. A., Sholomskas, D., & Padian, N. (1981). Depressed outpatients: Results after one year of treatment with drugs and/or interpersonal psychotherapy. *Archives of General Psychiatry, 38,* 51–55.

Weissman, M. M., Prusoff, B. A., & DiMascio, A. (1979). The efficacy of drugs and psychotherapy in the treatment of acute depressive episodes. *American Journal of Psychiatry, 136,* 555–558.

SUGGESTED READINGS

Cornes, C. L. (1993). Interpersonal psychotherapy of depression (IPT): A case study. In R. Wells & V. Gianetti (Eds.), *Casebook of the brief psychotherapies* (pp. 53–64). New York: Plenum Press.

Elkin, I., Shea, M. T., Watkins, J. T., et al. (1989). National Institute of Mental Health Treatment of Depression Collaborative Research Program: General effectiveness of treatments. *Archives of General Psychiatry, 46,* 971–982.

Klerman, G. L., Weissman, M. M., Rounsaville, B. J., & Chevron, E. S. (1984). *Interpersonal psychotherapy of depression.* New York: Basic Books.

Kupfer, D. J., Frank, E., & Perel, J. M. (1992). Five year outcomes for maintenance therapies in recurrent depression. *Archives of General Psychiatry, 49,* 769–773.

Markowitz, J. C., & Schwartz, H. A. (1997). Case formulation in interpersonal psychotherapy of depression. In T. D. Eels (Ed.), *Handbook of psychotherapy case formulation* (pp. 192–222). New York: Guilford.

O'Hara, M. W., Stuart, S., Gorman, L., & Wenzel, A. (2000). Efficacy of interpersonal psychotherapy for postpartum depression. *Archives of General Psychiatry, 57,* 1039–1045.

Stuart, S., & Cole, V. (1996). Treatment of depression following myocardial infarction with interpersonal psychotherapy. *Annals of Clinical Psychiatry, 8,* 203–206.

Stuart, S., & Robertson, M. (2002). *Interpersonal psychotherapy: A clinician's guide.* London: Edward Arnold, Ltd.

Weissman, M. M., Markowitz, J. W., & Klerman, G. L. (2000). *Comprehensive guide to interpersonal psychotherapy.* New York: Basic Books.

14

Couple and Family Therapy

Norman Epstein

OVERVIEW OF THE MODEL

This chapter describes the application of a cognitive-behavioral approach to the assessment and treatment of depression within a relationship context. Although my theoretical orientation is primarily cognitive-behavioral, a variety of psychodynamic and family systems theoretical approaches offer valuable concepts and interventions regarding interpersonal processes in depression, and I commonly draw on them in clinical practice. Consequently, in discussing the conceptualization of Nancy's depression and its treatment with cognitive-behavioral couples therapy, I will illustrate the integration of other theoretical models.

BACKGROUND OF THE APPROACH

Theory, research, and clinical practice are reflecting a growing awareness that interpersonal factors can play significant roles in the etiology and maintenance of depression. Intrapsychic and biological models of depression are being supplemented by interpersonal conceptualizations of mood disorders, and it is now common for individual treatments to be integrated with couple or family therapy. An impetus toward the inclusion of a depressed individual's significant others in clinical assessment and treatment has been the high co-morbidity between depression and couple/family problems (Beach, Sandeen, & O'Leary, 1990; Gotlib & Beach, 1995; Halford & Bouma, 1997). On the one hand, Beach, Jouriles, and O'Leary (1985) report that 50% of couples seeking marital therapy include at least one clinically depressed spouse. Conversely, Weissman (1987) found that the risk for developing depression is 25 times higher among women who are maritally distressed than among those who are satisfied with their relationships. In addition, an increase in marital arguments and the occurrence of marital separation were the two life stressors most commonly identified by married women as preceding the onset of their depressive symptoms, and that best differentiated depressed from nondepressed individuals (Paykel et al., 1969). Events in family relationships (e.g., a family member's death, serious illness, or leaving home) were among the other major stressors linked to the onset of depression in Paykel et al.'s study. Furthermore, individually oriented treatments for depression tend to have minimal impact on clients' relationship problems (Beach & O'Leary, 1992; Halford & Bouma, 1997), and the presence of marital discord increases the probability of relapse following successful treatment with antidepressant medication (Hooley & Teasdale, 1989).

Given the overlap between relationship problems and depression, considerable attention has been given to identifying possible causal processes linking the two clinical disorders. Applying a cognitive-behavioral perspective, Epstein (1985) noted striking parallels between characteristics of depression and those of marital discord, such as hopelessness about the future, a tendency to "track" negative events and be highly critical, ineffective communication and problem-solving skills, and loss of pleasure in previously enjoyed activities. These similarities may reflect common risk factors and pathways to relationship distress and depression, but they do not clarify processes through which depression may precede and elicit relationship problems, or vice versa. Within a cognitive-behavioral model, two major processes linking depression and relationship problems have been considered.

BASIC CONCEPTS OF THE MODEL

One possibility is that an individual's depression may precede and elicit relationship distress through the effects of the negative cognitions (e.g., evaluating the self, world, and future with a negative bias) and mood states that are prominent components of the depression. Thus, the depressed individual's own negative cognitive set may lead him or her to experience the couple relationship negatively. Furthermore, Coyne (1976), in a systems-oriented interpersonal model, suggested that when an individual exhibits negative symptoms of depression over time, his or her significant others develop ambivalent feelings and behavioral responses. Spouses and other family members are likely to feel sympathetic regarding the depressed person's plight, and try to provide support. However, when the depressed person fails to respond favorably to others' supportive efforts, the family members may become frustrated and emotionally upset (i.e., depressed, angry). Reviews of empirical research (Beach et al., 1990; Beach, Smith, & Fincham, 1994; Gotlib & Beach, 1995) indicate some ambivalent responses by family members. Studies involving direct observation of family behavioral interactions indicate that an individual's depressive behavior tends to inhibit rather than elicit aggressive responses from family members. However, when depressed individuals exhibit hostility and aggression toward their family members, the family members tend to respond in kind, and couples with a depressed member commonly exhibit negative interactions typical of distressed couples. Beach et al. (1990) note that the negative feelings and communication of family members toward a depressed member seem to be based more on their perception of that individual as being dissimilar to them than on their experiencing a direct induction of depressed mood from the identified patient. In other words, the individual's depression does not appear to be "contagious," but its behavioral symptoms tend to alienate other family members, who eventually lose their ability to identify with the depressed person's experience.

Psychodynamic approaches to interpersonal processes in depression also focus on aspects of an individual's depression that lead to negative couple and family interactions. For example, emotionally-focused couple therapy (Johnson & Greenberg, 1995) is based on attachment theory concepts in which individuals with insecure "working models" behave in ways that create conflict rather than intimacy with their partners.

Traditionally, cognitive-behavioral theory and therapy have focused on *forms* of cognition (e.g., attributions, standards) that affect individuals' interactions with others, but there has been little attention to particular themes in the *content* of those cognitions. One exception is Pretzer, Epstein, and Fleming's (1991) assessment of marital partners' tendencies to attribute each other's negative behavior to malicious intent and a lack of love. Another exception is Baucom, Epstein, Rankin, and Burnett's (1996) development of a questionnaire that assesses individuals' personal standards for their couple relationships along dimensions of (a) the degree of boundaries between partners, (b) the balance of power in decision making, and (c) the degrees to which partners invest time and energy in their relationship. Psychodynamic models identify core interpersonal themes, such as insecure attachment and concern about being controlled by one's partner, that cognitive-behavioral couple and family therapists should assess in their clients' cognitions.

Systems theorists might view the above formulation as "linear thinking" in which one person's characteristics are viewed as the cause of a relationship problem. However, it is important to note that an individual's internal schemata such as an insecure attachment "working model" will have greater negative impact on the couple's relationship to the extent that the partners engage in a circular interaction pattern. Thus, the insecure individual's negative expression of his or her insecure schema elicits the other person's negative feelings and behavior toward the depressed person, which in turn increasingly confirms the insecure individual's schema, and so on.

The other major model of depression and relationship discord consistent with a cognitive-behavioral framework has been developed by Beach and his colleagues (Beach, 2001; Beach et al., 1990; Gotlib & Beach, 1995). Beach and his colleagues proposed that relationship discord constitutes a potentially severe life stressor that can elicit or exacerbate an individual's depression. Their marital/family discord model of depression posits that intimate relationships can serve as major sources of social support that protect (i.e., buffer) individuals from developing psychopathology in response to life stresses. Conversely, relationships characterized by discord and an absence of mutual emotional support can expose the members to major stress rather than providing a stress-buffering function. The model leaves room for cognitive and biological vulnerabilities in the development of depression (i.e., a stress-diathesis conceptualization), but focuses on the interpersonal processes that increase or decrease the risk for depression. Beach et al. (1990) note that their model is consistent with empirically supported stress, social support, and coping models of depression. For example, there is evidence that couples' discussions of conflictual topics elicit depressed behavior and that indices of marital discord predict future levels of depression in longitudinal studies (Beach et al., 1990). Furthermore, among individuals whose depression has remitted due to individual treatment, those who continue to experience marital and family discord are more likely to relapse (Hooley & Teasdale, 1989). Because individual psychotherapy for married depressed persons has minimal impact on the marital relationship, the continuation of marital problems can be a significant risk factor for relapse.

A variety of strategic and systemic approaches to family therapy have been based on the premise that problems develop due to a family's misguided attempts to cope with life difficulties. In other words, the family's attempted solution maintains or worsens the problem. For example, both members of a couple initially may have enjoyed it when one partner played the role of leader and caretaker for the other, because this pattern tended to meet each person's needs. However, when the more dependent partner subsequently developed greater self-confidence and a desire for more autonomy, the couple may have lacked adequate communication and problem-solving skills to change the "rules" in their relationship effectively. As both partners increasingly used a mix of direct coercive strategies (e.g., criticism) and withdrawal to attempt to influence each other, the aversive stalemate may increase the "one-down" partner's sense of hopelessness and elicit depression. That individual's depressive symptoms exacerbate the power differential between partners, which leads to more negative couple interaction, and so on. At times, strategic therapists have proposed that symptoms can serve a function in a relationship by maintaining the status quo and reducing the potential for stressful change. Strategic couple and family therapists use a variety of direct and paradoxical interventions to interrupt such dysfunctional solutions to relationship problems (see Nichols & Schwartz, 2001, for a review).

ETIOLOGY OF DEPRESSION

In a cognitive-behavioral couple and family therapy model, multiple factors are identified as possible contributors to the development of depression. These include (a) characteristics of the individual, (b) couple and family interactions, and (c) other environmental stressors beyond family relationships. As described in other chapters in this volume, characteristics of individuals can include biological vulnerabilities, past traumatic experiences, negative thinking styles, and deficits in social skills and problem-solving skills. Couple and family factors include both negative interactions (e.g., aversive exchanges) and deficits in mutual social support. Environmental stressors can be either normative developmental changes (e.g., the birth of a couple's first child) or non-normative events (e.g., unexpectedly losing a job; the premature death of a loved one). As multiple factors can operate in the etiology of depression, the cognitive-behavioral therapist must conduct a careful assessment of each area and plan interventions that address each relevant process.

In addition to focusing on current relationship problems that may be contributing to an individual's depression, couple and family therapists from a variety of theoretical orientations often consider family-of-origin experiences that have influenced the person's self-concept and ways of coping with life stressors. For example, those with an intergenerational focus (e.g., Bowen, 1978; Friedman, 1991) emphasize how family patterns of emotional and behavioral enmeshment (lack of "differentiation") tend to be extended from one generation to the next. Intergenerational family therapists propose that individuals who grow up in a family in which life problems elicit diffuse emotion (e.g., anxiety, depression) rather than cognitive problem-solving are likely to respond in similar ways in subsequent intimate relationships.

Cognitive-behavioral family therapists who operate from a social learning perspective (e.g., Dattilio, 1994; Epstein & Schlesinger, 1996; Epstein, Schlesinger, & Dryden, 1988; Falloon, 1991; Schwebel & Fine, 1994) describe how individuals develop behavioral, cognitive, and affective response patterns on the basis of their family-of-origin experiences. Through observing parental models and receiving reinforcement and punishment for their own responses, children learn particular constructive or problematic styles of communicating, such as verbal aggression, withdrawal, and unassertive submission. Based on how the individual is treated by other family members, he or she also forms particular self-schemata (e.g., "I'm incompetent and must depend on others.") and schemata about intimate relationships (e.g., "Open expression of conflict can only hurt a relationship."). Modeling and reinforcement processes within the family also can shape individuals' emotional responses and their beliefs about their emotions. For example, some families have a "culture" of emotional expressiveness, in which the members expect each other to voice their feelings in a relatively unbridled manner, and pay considerably more attention to each other when they express strong feelings. In contrast, children in some other families are exposed to models of people who either are relatively inexpressive or who find emotionality to be distressing. These children may grow up inhibiting their own emotional expression in relationships and experience fear of symptoms of their own emotional arousal.

MAINTAINING FACTORS

Couple and family therapists from a variety of theoretical backgrounds share an assumption that regardless of the initial etiology of an individual's depression, the depressive symptoms are likely to be maintained by interpersonal processes within the family. Circular causality is a key concept in which the responses of the depressed individual and his or her significant others mutually influence each other. For example, the depressed person behaves in ways that are aversive to other family members (e.g., frequent complaining), and the others respond with expressions of irritation. In turn, the depressed person views the others' irritation as further evidence that he or she is unlovable, which elicits more depressed feelings and behavior, and so on. Similarly, depressive symptoms that elicit overprotective responses from family members may confirm the depressed individual's negative self-concept ("My family thinks I'm incompetent") and produce more depressive symptoms of helplessness.

The concept that an individual's symptoms "serve a function" in the family system has been popular in the field of family therapy, and it generally has been taken to mean that the symptoms have the payoff of maintaining stability in the family. Within this view, if a couple or family is in danger of disintegrating due to significant conflict, a member's development of depression can keep the relationship together, as the others take care of the symptomatic individual. The family's stability is maintained by the depressed person's dependency and the other members' felt obligation to be supportive. However, a danger in this conceptualization, which has led to critiques of family systems theory (e.g., Luepnitz, 1988), is that it is sometimes taken to mean that the symptomatic individual intentionally develops problems in order to maintain homeostasis in the family. In this view, a depressed person is responsible for and contributes to the existence of his or her symptoms. Although cognitive-behavioral family therapists evaluate the possibility of "secondary gain," in which an individual's distressing symptoms elicit some reinforcement (e.g., attention) from significant others, they do not interpret such mutual influences as responsibility for the depression. Nevertheless, it is important to identify circular processes that may be contributing to the maintenance of an individual's depression and intervene to modify them.

MECHANISMS OF CHANGE IN COGNITIVE-BEHAVIORAL COUPLE AND FAMILY THERAPY FOR DEPRESSION

Marital and family interventions can influence depression in two major ways. First, the negative impact that an individual's depressive symptoms has on both that person and his or her family members can be reduced by increasing the entire family's abilities to cope with those symptoms whenever they occur. Marital and family therapists can provide education about common symptoms of depression (e.g., negative thinking, irritability, inertia, withdrawal) and shift the family members' attributions about them. For example, it is common for a depressed individual's pervasive fatigue and sense of hopelessness to interfere with his or her ability to respond favorably to family members' attempts to provide encouragement and motivation. The family members may become frustrated if they believe that the depressed person does not value their help or care about improving. Just as in individual cognitive therapy for depression, where the therapist educates the client about symptoms of depression and ways to counteract them, the marital and family therapist can help family members interpret symptoms in a less personal way and as responses that cannot easily be willed away.

In addition to cognitive restructuring, family members can be coached in developing personal strategies for reducing the emotional impact that the depressed person's behavior has on them. Thus, when a family member begins to feel frustrated and angered by the individual's inertia and negative talk, he or she can use relaxation techniques, or spend some time doing something that is personally enjoyable, in order to reduce the emotional arousal.

The therapist also can coach the depressed person and other family members in experimenting with alternative ways of interacting in order to cope with symptoms. For example, instead of trying to convince the depressed individual that his or her life "isn't so bad," the family members can be coached to acknowledge how bad their relative feels and to suggest a shift into a direct problem-solving approach. This approach might involve the depressed individual using cognitive restructuring techniques (Beck, Rush, Shaw, & Emery, 1979; J. Beck, 1995) to challenge his or her own negative thinking. Alternatively, it may involve family problem-solving discussions in which the depressed individual and other family members identify and plan to carry out potential solutions to problems that the depressed person views as hopeless.

All of these interventions are intended to alter negative effects that an individual's depression has on marital and family interactions. These interventions can reduce the other family members' own distress in response to the depression, and can also modify negative responses by the other members that maintain or exacerbate the individual's depression.

The second way that cognitive-behavioral marital and family interventions can affect an individual's depression follows from the research findings that conflict in significant relationships can contribute to the etiology and maintenance of depression. Marital therapy designed to resolve sources of relationship conflict and distress can reduce depression. Therefore, interventions that reduce aversive communication and other negative interactions will reduce some of the major life stressors associated with the development and maintenance of depression. In addition, interventions that increase positive marital and family characteristics such as cohesion and mutual emotional support will help the family serve as a resource that buffers the effects of other life stresses on its members' well-being.

To the extent that the depressed individual's cognitive, affective and behavioral responses in intimate relationships also may have been shaped by his or her family-of-origin experiences, it may be important to target these historical influences as well. For example, attempting to encourage an individual to behave in a more assertive manner with a spouse may have limited success if the person had long-term learning experiences in the family-of-origin, in which open expression of feelings was discouraged and punished. The individual may hold strong beliefs about dangers of expressing feelings, and modifying such cognitions may require helping the individual to understand their origin and to challenge their appropriateness in his or her adult life.

CRITICAL REVIEW OF EMPIRICAL EVIDENCE

There have been few well-controlled outcome studies evaluating the effects of couple and family therapy for depression, but the initial results have been encouraging. Two studies have compared the impacts of behavioral marital therapy and individual cognitive therapy in reducing depression. Beach and O'Leary (1992) randomly assigned women who reported both depression and marital distress to receive individual cognitive therapy (addressing negative thinking in general but not marital issues per se), conjoint behavioral marital therapy, or a waiting list control condition. Both individual cognitive therapy and behavioral marital therapy significantly reduced the wives' depression, in contrast to the control condition, and the two treatments were equally effective. However, behavioral marital therapy produced a significant improvement in the couples' marital distress, whereas cognitive therapy did not.

Jacobson, Dobson, Fruzetti, Schmaling, and Salusky (1991) provided individual cognitive therapy, conjoint behavioral marital therapy, or a combination of the two treatments to depressed married women who were not selected on the basis of marital distress. Jacobson et al. found that among the women in non-distressed marriages, cognitive therapy and the combined treatment produced greater improvement in depression than couple therapy alone, whereas among those in distressed marriages cognitive therapy and behavioral marital therapy were equally effective in reducing depression. As in the Beach and O'Leary (1992) study, behavioral marital therapy improved marital satisfaction, whereas individual cognitive therapy did not.

Foley, Rounsaville, Weissman, Sholomaskas, and Chevron (1989) randomly assigned depressed men and women to either individual interpersonal psychotherapy (focusing on relationship problems such as unresolved grief and role conflicts) or a conjoint couple version of interpersonal psychotherapy. Foley et al. found that the two treatments were equally effective in improving depressive symptoms, and the conjoint treatment produced modestly greater improvement in marital satisfaction than did the individual treatment. Reviews of marital and family therapy (Baucom, Shoham, Mueser, Daiuto, & Stickle, 1998; Beach, Fincham, & Katz, 1998; Prince & Jacobson, 1995) note a virtual absence of controlled outcome studies evaluating theoretical approaches to couple or family therapy for the treatment of depression other than behavioral interventions. There is a clear need for research on other approaches.

These research findings do not suggest that relationship problems are universal causal factors in depression or reduce the importance of treating psychological, life stress, and biological contributors to depression. Furthermore, Prince and Jacobson (1995) note that follow-up data from these studies indicated no better prevention of relapse in depression of individuals who received behavioral marital therapy. However, the studies do underscore the importance of assessing the quality of depressed individuals' significant relationships, and determining the need for relationship therapy as either the primary or an adjunctive treatment.

There has been increasing attention to including spouses in the treatment of individuals' anxiety disorders, such as the panic that Nancy experiences in this case example. These treatments have consisted primarily of "spouse-assisted" procedures, in which the non-anxious spouse participates in sessions and is taught to act as a coach as the anxious spouse engages in exposure exercises between sessions (Craske & Zoellner, 1995). However, Arnow, Taylor, Agras, and Telch (1985) found that treating the marital relationship itself through communication training contributes to improvement in the anxious partner's symptoms. Therefore, my approach to Nancy's presenting problems includes attention to relationship factors associated with both depression and anxiety.

CASE CONCEPTUALIZATION

Nancy reports many symptoms of depression, including dysphoria, ruminative self-criticism, hopelessness, suicidal ideation, crying, impaired concentration, fatigue, irritability, social withdrawal, loss of libido, a change in appetite, and insomnia. Her depressive thinking style involves catastrophic cognitions (e.g., she "can't see a light for her future") and overgeneralization (e.g., "I've failed with everything"). She also exhibits depressive attributions, viewing her life problems as due to unchangeable factors such as her "dysfunctional childhood" and personal "incompetence." Her sense of personal helplessness is associated with a belief that she must depend on others to take care of her.

Nancy also experiences symptoms of anxiety, such as tension, inability to relax, agitation, unsteadiness, nervousness, dizziness, tachycardia, and general fears (e.g., a general sense of vulnerability and a fear that she could not function on her own if she left her husband Steve). Her general anxiety appears to be associated with a basic schema that she cannot count on the support of others, and that she lacks the ability to cope with life without such support. It seems reasonable to hypothesize that the same insecurity she has about attachments to people in general inhibits her from being more assertive with her husband.

Concerning apparent family-of-origin influences, Nancy's mother modeled negative thinking, and her parenting of Nancy and her sister was unpredictable and at times abusive. Her mother placed her in an overly responsible role as her confidant, and she blocked opportunities for Nancy to develop autonomy (e.g., decision-making) and assertiveness skills. Furthermore, Nancy's schizophrenic father also was unpredictable, and as a child she took care of him as well. After experiencing her parents' divorce, and her mother's subsequent divorce from her second husband, Nancy is determined to avoid divorce herself. Nancy also reports that she took care of her younger sister during childhood, and in her description of her current relationships with her mother and husband, it appears that she has continued to place her own needs secondary to those of others in her life.

Nancy's negative self-schema seems to be inconsistent with some of the data we have about her educational, professional, and social background. She has been successful in school and in her career as a graphic artist, and she has been capable of sustaining friendships both as a child and as an adult. It appears that her own inhibition places some limitations on her adult friendships. Thus, I hypothesize that one component of Nancy's current depression and marital problems is the set of cognitions and interpersonal behavior patterns that she developed from childhood. Consequently, an important component of therapy involves modifying her cognitive and behavioral responses to her significant others. Conjoint couple therapy affords many *in vivo* opportunities to do so.

Unfortunately, the interactions between Nancy and Steve reinforce her negative self-schema and her unassertive behavior. According to Nancy, Steve often is critical of her, rejects her, and apparently attempts to dominate decisions about their lifestyle. Nancy traces the origin of her depression and anxiety to the time when she and Steve became engaged to be married, and she attributes her symptoms to distress about Steve's controlling, rejecting behavior. Nancy's report that she feels notably better when on her own or with her sister and friends suggests that her depression arises at least partly when the cognitive and interpersonal behavioral patterns that she brings from her personal history are activated by particular aversive interpersonal dynamics in her marriage. However, the situational variation in her depression also seems to be triggered in contexts beyond her marriage, such as visits with her mother. Similarly, her anxiety symptoms, perhaps components of panic disorder, occur in a manner that is unpredictable to Nancy.

An important area that I would pursue in further assessment with Nancy is greater specificity in information about the types of situations that elicit her depression and anxiety symptoms, as well as any cognitions that she is able to identify as occurring at such times.

BEGINNING AND FRAMING TREATMENT

A limitation of the data available from Nancy's self-reports is that they represent her subjective perceptions of the events in her relationship with Steve. Her statements that Steve is highly critical, "took my self-confidence away," and is rarely affectionate suggest that she views him as the primary cause of their troubled relationship, and herself as powerless to influence their interaction pattern. Family therapists often find that although individuals provide valuable information about their significant others, at times their perceptions can be biased. Therapists sometimes report being surprised when the significant others subsequently attend a therapy session and exhibit characteristics that are markedly different from those portrayed by the individual client.

Although such discrepancies do not necessarily indicate that the individual's reports about the family members were inaccurate representations of how they behave toward the individual at home, they do provide some evidence that the significant others are capable of behaving differently. In some cases, observation of the couple or family interaction in the therapist's office indicates that the individual client behaves in particular ways that elicit some of the others' negative behavior. There is evidence that members of distressed couples tend to blame each other for relationship problems and underestimate their own contributions to negative interactions (Baucom & Epstein, 1990). Consequently, the assessment of the patterns in Nancy's marriage must be considered tentative until the therapist can gather more direct information.

Nancy's statement that Steve has refused to attend marital counseling sessions in the past suggests that it may be difficult to gain his cooperation in the current assessment and treatment, but initially I would consider it to be one of my priorities to seek his participation. The manner in which Steve is asked to participate can make a difference in his cooperation, and it is unclear whether Nancy's approach contributed to his past refusal. The case description emphasizes Nancy's negativity, so it is possible that she described the need for marital counseling in a way that made Steve more defensive. Furthermore, Nancy reported that Steve has been unable to pass the state bar exam, and it is important to consider the possibility that he is experiencing low self-esteem, which may influence his receptivity to focusing on other problems in his life. These hypotheses point to the importance of gathering more information directly from Steve.

Thus, Nancy's depression and anxiety appear to be influenced by her personal characteristics, and it seems likely that she could benefit from individual therapy. In particular, her negative thinking about herself (as incompetent, helpless, a total failure) and her suicidal ideation are appropriate foci for individual cognitive therapy, and the fact that she has developed a suicide plan suggests some urgency in the need for intervention. Nevertheless, Nancy's depression and anxiety have been associated in a major way with her marital distress, and the previously cited research has indicated that individual therapy has limited impact on relationship problems. I am concerned that a treatment plan consisting only of individual therapy may alleviate Nancy's depression and anxiety symptoms in the short run but fail to alter the relationship stresses, and she would continue to be at risk for depression and anxiety.

Consistent with Bennun's (1997) reports of successful marital therapy with one spouse, I have found that some individual clients were able to shift relationship patterns sufficiently through their unilateral efforts. However, I also have observed many instances in which an individual practices new ways of relating to an absent partner during therapy sessions but reverts to old patterns of relating when he or she is once again faced with the partner's typical responses at home. Therefore, I would prefer to work directly with the couple to directly identify and modify interaction patterns that interfere with resolution of their conflicts. If all efforts to engage Steve in conjoint therapy were unsuccessful, I would discuss with Nancy whether she would like to set as a treatment goal unilateral change in how she relates to Steve, in the hope that such changes will induce changes she desires in him and their ways of interacting. I also recognize the possibility that as Nancy's sense of self-efficacy improves, through individual therapy with or without concurrent couple therapy, she may choose to end the marriage.

STRATEGIES FOR INVOLVING THE SPOUSE IN COUPLE THERAPY

If conjoint treatment is to be an option, it is important to work quickly toward inviting Steve to join Nancy in therapy, because extended individual work with one partner increases the possibility of an alliance forming between the therapist and that individual (Epstein & Baucom, 2002). Not only might the other partner feel uncomfortable about this preexisting relationship, but the partner who has had an individual relationship with the therapist may be upset about losing that special status. Consequently, during the phone call or an initial individual session with Nancy, I would discuss with her the two options for our continued work together. We could work together individually, developing her ability to interact with Steve in more satisfying ways, or we could focus on getting Steve involved in couple therapy as soon as possible.

First, I would ask Nancy to describe as best she can the events that occurred when Steve previously "refused" to attend marital counseling. Given her unassertiveness, general negativity, and self-blame, I would listen for evidence that she may have given him mixed messages about the importance of his joining the therapy. Nancy's descriptions of Steve in the case study suggest that he is unhappy in their relationship, but that he yearns for a "traditional family" with her, and he may not know any better ways of resolving their relationship problems. Although both partners have disengaged from each other in some ways, at this point I hypothesize that if they can learn more constructive ways to resolve conflicts and to reassure each other of their caring, their motivation to stay in the relationship may increase.

As Nancy describes her prior attempts to engage Steve in marital counseling, I would explore her concerns about what might occur in sessions if Steve were present. Some individuals anticipate that the partner will be so controlling and rejecting that it will be overwhelming for them, so they are ambivalent about couple treatment. I would attempt to counteract Nancy's fears in a number of ways. First, we would explore the available evidence that Steve still is invested in the marriage, and that his investment gives her more leverage than she typically perceives. Although I would not want Nancy to threaten divorce as a means of inducing Steve's participation, we would discuss various ways in which she could convey to him the positive consequences that couple sessions could produce for their marriage. She also could convey to him that his desire for a happy family life with her continues to be frustrated, and that the best hope for improving the relationship lies in working on it together.

Second, we would discuss how the likelihood of Steve behaving negatively in couple sessions may decrease if Nancy can communicate to him some empathy for his frustration with her chronic depression and anxiety, and tell him that his participation in therapy will increase the probability of improvement. If Nancy's description of Steve's prior refusal suggests that he does not want to be blamed or considered to be part of her problems, I would discuss with her how she might get the message across to him that the goal of couple therapy would be to achieve a more mutually satisfying life together. It is crucial that both members of the couple perceive the goal of therapy to be one of collaboration rather than blaming (Epstein & Baucom, 2002).

Third, we would identify the content of Nancy's thoughts and visual images of Steve behaving in a controlling or rejecting manner in sessions. In order to decrease the degree to which she is intimidated by either these cognitions or his actual behavior, we would explore exactly what danger she perceived in them, and in asserting herself with Steve. For example, if she anticipated that upsetting him would result in his leaving her, we would examine evidence that he tries to get his way but that he does not take steps toward dissolving their relationship. Concerning thoughts that Steve's controlling and critical responses would elicit her anxiety symptoms, which she finds intolerable, I would emphasize how this is an aspect of her avoidance that maintains her panic disorder. Just as *in vivo* exposure to other anxiety-eliciting situations is a key component of treatment for panic, repeated exposure to Steve's negative behaviors can help her learn to tolerate her anxiety symptoms. Thus, I would propose to Nancy that interactions with Steve will provide excellent opportunities to overcome her anxiety problems.

For the purpose of this chapter, I will assume that Nancy and Steve would work with me conjointly. In such a case, I would discuss with Nancy the option of a referral for concurrent individual therapy focused on her depression and anxiety. In order to maintain a balance in my relationships with the two spouses, I would avoid more than minimal individual work with either partner once the couple therapy began. I have found it possible to have occasional individual sessions with one or both members of a couple, in order to address individual issues, but when the concerns involve a person's partner, I believe that the most appropriate and effective forum for dealing with them is with both people present. The therapist then minimizes the chance of being pulled into a coalition with one spouse, and he or she also is able to observe and intervene directly with the couple's interactions surrounding the issues in their relationship.

TIMELINE AND ANTICIPATED OUTCOME

The major focus of couple therapy would be on the relationship between Nancy's individual functioning and the couple's functioning. My conjoint work with Nancy and Steve would be based primarily on the principles and procedures of cognitive-behavioral couples therapy (Baucom & Epstein, 1990; Epstein & Baucom, 1989, 2002). I anticipate that this therapy would consist of weekly one-hour sessions, for at least three or four months.

As Nancy can function well both socially and occupationally, there is good reason for optimism for her attaining a better level of coping and satisfaction as a result of individual therapy focused on her own cognitions, behavior, and affect. However, if the current level of stress in the marital relationship is not alleviated, I would be concerned about her well-being in the long run. Her mixed response to antidepressant medication also suggests that attention to the marital problems is greatly needed. The length and success of interventions designed to modify marital patterns will depend on both partners' willingness and ability to contribute to change.

TREATMENT

Assessment of Individual Dysfunction

The initial sessions would focus on assessing Nancy's current depression and anxiety symptoms, collecting information about the partners' personal and relationship histories, and observing their communication patterns (Epstein & Baucom, 2002). The assessment of depression and anxiety symptoms would include their frequency, intensity, situational variation, and associated cognitions. Nancy has indicated that the symptoms are worse in situations involving her husband and mother, but I would ask for greater detail about interactions between her and each of those individuals that trigger her symptoms. It also would be important to assess her suicidal risk, given that she has a specific plan and appears to feel fairly hopeless about her life. An initial treatment priority would be to reduce the level of suicidal risk by increasing her expectancy that she can take specific steps to improve her self-concept and her life. I would employ traditional behavioral and cognitive restructuring approaches (e.g., A. Beck et al., 1979; J. Beck, 1995) to achieve these goals.

Concerning Nancy's anxiety symptoms, the case description suggests the possibility of panic disorder, and a more systematic assessment of those symptoms is needed. During the conjoint session I initially would use a brief clinical interview, guided by DSM-IV criteria (American Psychiatric Association, 1994). If the initial assessment confirms that Nancy has panic disorder, I would likely schedule an individual session with her and conduct a more extensive assessment of her past and current symptoms, including agoraphobic avoidance, using a systematic format such as the Anxiety Disorders Interview Schedule (ADIS; Di Nardo, Brown, & Barlow, 1994).

It seems likely that Nancy will require a referral for some individual therapy sessions devoted to interventions specifically targeting her anxiety symptoms. Even if her panic symptoms initially were elicited by stress in her marriage, they likely are now triggered by a variety of situational cues, including her own thoughts of being trapped. Consequently, treatment of the marital distress may help her overall tension level, but the relatively autonomously functioning panic responses probably require additional treatment.

As noted, "spouse-assisted" treatments for panic disorder have been developed (Craske & Zoeller, 1995). Steve may find it less threatening to become involved in conjoint sessions if they are framed for him as means for helping Nancy with her anxiety, rather than as marital therapy. Perhaps as the therapist establishes a trusting relationship with both partners, Steve will be more open to examining areas of stress in the couple relationship.

Assessment of the Couple

Assessment of Nancy and Steve's relationship would focus on (a) each partner's cognitions that influence his or her affective and behavioral responses toward the other person; (b) each partner's affective responses that influence his or cognitive and behavioral responses within the relationship; and (c) the behavioral interaction patterns and skills exhibited by the couple, which influence each other's cognitions and affects. The advantage to conducting the assessment conjointly is that the therapist can make direct observations of cognitive, affective, and behavioral responses as they are occurring, rather than depending on each partner's self-reports that can be unreliable.

Conjoint Interview

During the first interview with the couple, I would ask each partner to describe briefly what his or her major concerns are about the relationship, and how he or she believes I might be of help to them as a couple. If Steve had reluctantly agreed to join Nancy in therapy, I would express my appreciation that he was taking the time to participate. My goal would be to learn how each person defines the problems in their relationship, and the attributions that each of them makes about the causes of the problems. For example, to what degrees do Nancy and Steve view Nancy's depression and anxiety as due to her internal personal characteristics, versus external factors such as stresses within their relationship? Similarly, when either partner describes a relationship problem (e.g., negative communication, infrequent expressions of affection, little sex), to what degree do the two of them agree that it is a problem, and what attributions do they express about its causes? The less they pay attention to relationship patterns, the more I will need to draw their attention to them during subsequent therapy sessions.

Because it is likely that Nancy and Steve initially will focus on negatives in their relationship, I would attempt to prevent the first session from becoming such an aversive experience for them that they might lose their motivation to continue in therapy. Consequently, I would ask each partner to rephrase each complaint as a request for positive change. For example, if Steve says that he is frustrated by Nancy's frequent negative talk about herself and their life, I would coach him in stating a goal of Nancy being able to think and talk about positive aspects of herself and their marriage more often. If Nancy complained that Steve rarely behaves affectionately toward her, I could guide her in stating that she enjoys hugs and kisses from Steve, and would like him to do those things more often. At this point, I am aware that there may be considerable negative sentiment between Nancy and Steve, and I do not want to give them the impression that I am glossing over the sources of their distress. However, I also want to convey the message that it is more palatable and effective to induce change in a relationship through positive means than through criticism and threats.

Specific to the marital context of Nancy's depression and anxiety, I would explore with her how such a pattern developed wherein she became intimidated by her husband's expressions of what he wants from their relationship (e.g., "a big, traditional family"). Because she noted that at times Steve can be kind, generous, and attentive, I would guide her in considering evidence that he has the potential to be flexible and responsive to her preferences. A benefit of discussing these patterns with Nancy in front of Steve is that it indirectly challenges him to prove her negative views of him to be wrong. Details about the interactions between them that Nancy viewed as Steve's "taking my self-confidence away" could be used to explore how much the intimidation was due to his behavior and how much to her own unassertiveness.

In a similar manner, I would interview Steve about his views concerning Nancy's depression and anxiety, as well as past and current patterns in their relationship. As with Nancy, I would emphasize that my goal was to learn about each person's perceptions of their relationship and concerns, and that I realize their views may differ. I would emphasize the importance of not interrupting each other, so that each could obtain a clear picture of the other's perceptions.

Relevant information in Nancy and Steve's personal histories would include family-of-origin experiences that have influenced their self-concepts and their schema and behavioral tendencies concerning close relationships. It also would be helpful to know about any significant couple relationships that each person had prior to getting involved with each other; in particular, any similarities or differences between the patterns in those relationships and the pattern in this marriage. For example, did Nancy perceive other partners as controlling, and to what extent was she able to voice her views openly? Was Nancy more relaxed and less depressed in previous relationships, and if so, what was different about them? Did Steve exhibit a similar pattern of avoiding direct conflict in previous relationships?

It also is important to gather information about the history of the current relationship from both partners, because their memories, perceptions, and feelings about past events may differ. Initially I would ask them to provide an overview of how they met, what attracted them to each other, how they each remember them progressing toward deeper involvement, and how they made the decision to get married. In addition, I would ask the couple for a brief chronology of events that seemed to influence their relationship in either positive or negative ways.

Questionnaires

Even though a systematic interview with a couple can reveal a wealth of information about the patterns in their relationship and each partner's subjective feelings about their interactions, it can be helpful to ask each person to complete a few questionnaires as part of the initial assessment. The following scales could be administered to Nancy and Steve. The therapist can select from among these and other measures, according to their apparent relevance for each couple's presenting problems and needs.

The Dyadic Adjustment Scale (DAS; Spanier, 1976) not only provides a global index of each person's feelings about the quality of the relationship, but also information about areas of conflict (e.g., finances, religion, friends, sex, decision-making). The last item on the DAS assesses the degree of commitment that the individual has toward working on the relationship. Nancy and Steve's responses to the DAS could help determine areas of conflict in their marriage, as well as the level of each person's marital distress.

The Communication Patterns Questionnaire (CPQ; Christensen, 1987) differs from other self-report communication scales by asking each partner to report dyadic interaction patterns. It includes subscales assessing mutual constructive communication, demand-withdraw, and mutual avoidance and withholding.

For therapists wishing to assess partners' responses to conflict in their relationship, the Conflict Tactics Scale—2 (CTS2; Straus, Hamby, Boney-McCoy, & Sugarman, 1996) and the Styles of Conflict Inventory (SCI; Metz, 1993) are two useful options. The CTS2 asks each person how often each member of the couple enacted each of 78 behaviors during the past year. The item content includes physical assault, psychological aggression, negotiation, and sexual coercion, with many items describing moderate to severe abuse. The SCI has subscales assessing each partner's cognitions, behavior, and perceptions of the other's behavior during relationship conflict. These subscales tap aspects of assertion, aggression, withdrawal, submission, and denial. Use of the CTS2 or the SCI can help the therapist identify possible abuse in Nancy and Steve's relationship, which may be related to Nancy's anxiety, feelings of intimidation, and depression. The SCI also can identify cognitions associated with Nancy's unassertive behavior.

Several questionnaires can be useful in eliciting partners' cognitions about their relationship, but I do not routinely use them in clinical practice. For example, the Relationship Belief Inventory (RBI; Eidelson & Epstein, 1982) and the Inventory of Specific Relationship Standards (ISRS; Baucom et al., 1996) both assess individuals' schemata about the characteristics that a relationship has or should have. The RBI includes subscales assessing beliefs that (a) open disagreement between partners is destructive; (b) partners should be able to mind-read each other's thoughts and feelings; (c) partners cannot change their relationship; (d) problems in relationships are due to innate gender differences; and (e) one should be a perfect sexual partner. The ISRS subscales assess the degree to which an individual believes that his or her relationship should be characterized by (a) minimal boundaries between partners (e.g., sharing of thoughts and feelings, activities), (b) investment of one's time and energy in the relationship, and (c) equitable decision-making and use of power. Although a clinical interview can uncover such beliefs, I have found that couples who are less introspective can benefit from having to think through questions about their standards for relationships. Partners also can gain insight into each other's beliefs by comparing their answers to specific questionnaire items. Additional discussion of self-report scales can be found in Baucom and Epstein (1990) and Epstein and Baucom (2002).

The decision whether to have the members of a couple share the information from their completed questionnaires with each other, at home or during a therapy session, centers on the issue of whether the therapist wants to be the potential holder of secrets. Either partner may reveal information on the forms but not during joint interviews. For example, a woman who is being physically abused by a male partner may make no mention of it during conjoint interviews, out of fear that the partner will retaliate later, yet may report the abuse on a questionnaire. Topics such as affairs, substance abuse, and lack of commitment to the relationship also may be reported differentially on questionnaires versus in joint interviews. The therapist needs to make an explicit agreement with the couple about confidentiality *before* they complete the questionnaires.

Observation of the Couple's Communication

Given the subjectivity of each partner's self-reports of couple communication, it is important that the therapist observe patterns in their interactions during conjoint sessions. Because couples commonly direct a large proportion of their comments to the therapist, the therapist must direct them to discuss some relationship topics with each other (Epstein & Baucom, 2002). Thus, I would ask Nancy and Steve to talk with each other about both positive topics (e.g., their memories of their first date) and conflictual issues. I would use caution in selecting problematic topics for them to discuss before we have worked together on constructive communication skills, so they do not have such an aversive experience during the session that they might avoid returning. For example, from their DAS responses I might identify a topic that both partners indicated was a source of moderate disagreement (e.g., use of leisure time) and ask them whether they would be willing to discuss it so that

I can get a sense of how they discuss issues. Major conflicts such as the decision about having children can be discussed later under more controlled conditions when I am coaching them in constructive communication.

As the couple discuss topics, I observe how much each person talks, who interrupts whom, what types of nonverbal messages are sent, how well each partner expresses his or her thoughts and feelings, how effectively each person listens to and communicates understanding of the other, and patterns such as demand-withdraw and reciprocal escalation of criticism. After collecting information about the couple's patterns, I would summarize my observations for them, noting strengths as well as behaviors that appear to increase their distress. Based on this feedback, I would attempt to engage the couple in setting goals to change their behavioral interactions (see Epstein and Baucom, 2002, for a detailed description of procedures for giving the couple assessment feedback).

Throughout therapy I monitor verbal and nonverbal cues to each partner's emotional states, particularly shifts in affect associated with specific behavioral interactions. When I notice such a shift, I inquire about the individual's emotion, associated cognitions, and the triggering event. For example, as Steve is saying that he finds it frustrating when Nancy talks negatively about herself, Nancy's facial expression and posture may suggest a depressive response. When I note that she seems to be reacting to Steve's statement, she may acknowledge feeling depressed and "hopeless that he sees me as a total loser."

As we shift into therapeutic intervention, I can use a variety of cognitive restructuring strategies (J. Beck, 1995) to help Nancy challenge her negative inference about Steve's attitude toward her. I also can use the opportunity to help both partners see how Nancy's moods are influenced by the events that occur between them, and that they both can experiment with alternative ways of communicating that will reduce her depressive responses. For example, during therapy sessions, Steve can practice prefacing statements about problems with statements about Nancy's characteristics that he values. Thus, he might say "I admire many of Nancy's qualities, such as her artistic talent and her loyalty to friends, so it is painful for me to hear her speaking negatively about herself. I'd like to hear her pay more attention to those positive qualities." This also is an opportunity to teach Steve about the automatic negative thinking that is commonly associated with depression. By decreasing his blaming of Nancy, some of the stressful interactions that contribute to her depression can be reduced.

Given the evidence that an individual's depression and anxiety symptoms can elicit distress in a partner, it also is important to monitor and address Steve's emotional states during therapy. When he exhibits affective shifts, the therapist can inquire about them, help him identify and challenge extreme or distorted cognitions associated with them, and coach the couple in experimenting with other ways of interacting. Thus, if Steve experiences irritation or sadness when Nancy speaks negatively about their relationship, he can be coached in identifying and modifying his associated cognitions (e.g., irritation associated with the thought, "She has no right to criticize me like that!"). From the case description, I am assuming that both partners are very distressed because they view themselves as helpless to change their negative interactions. Consequently, a goal of my interventions is to help them see that their patterns can be changed.

Assessment of affect also involves determining the degree to which the partners pay attention to their emotional states, and working to increase self-monitoring if necessary (Baucom & Epstein, 1990; Epstein & Baucom, 2002). Individual sessions may be necessary if either Nancy or Steve has such strong anger or other affective responses toward their partner that it interferes with their ability to interact constructively.

STRUCTURE AND GOALS OF THERAPY

The major goals of the couple sessions would be to (a) reduce negative interactions that contribute to marital distress and to Nancy's depression and anxiety, and (b) increase positive interactions associated with intimacy and mutual pleasure. The reduction of both marital distress and depression depends not only on eliminating the couple's aversive experiences, but also on building positive ones. Inducing such changes requires a combination of interventions focused on behaviors, cognitions, and emotional responses.

After identifying specific problematic behavioral patterns, I would spend portions of sessions coaching the couple in practicing constructive communication and problem-solving skills. In addition, we would identify specific behaviors that each partner believes he or she would enjoy receiving from the other, and we would devise informal agreements for each person to engage in some of those each week. In particular, we would focus on behaviors that address each person's basic needs, such as Nancy's need for more autonomy and self-efficacy. The couple could, for example, be guided in discussing ways in which Nancy could pursue her MBA degree and career, as well as being a wife and mother. The sessions also would reveal Steve's needs that have not been met adequately in the couple's relationship, and behavioral changes that could address these would be identified. Thus, my behavioral interventions would include efforts to restructure the couple's interactions such that they meet each partner's needs better (Epstein & Baucom, 2002).

As noted, I would elicit each partner's cognitions and emotional responses during sessions. I would balance the attention paid to assessing and modifying each individual's problematic cognitions, so neither person appears to be singled out as "the patient," even though Nancy initially was identified as such. Our sessions would address links between marital stress and depression, but the focus would be on developing a relationship that both spouses can enjoy.

SPECIFIC INTERVENTIONS

Communication and Problem-Solving Training

Although distressed couples commonly fail to use constructive communication and problem-solving due to deficits in their interpersonal skills, their problematic interactions often are influenced by cognitive and affective factors as well. For example, it would be important to identify any beliefs that Nancy may hold that focusing on and expressing one's own needs is always selfish and inappropriate. Given her historical role as a caretaker in her family of origin, such beliefs are likely to inhibit her from using communication skills to express her feelings and needs to Steve.

Cognitive interventions can be used to modify the partners' beliefs that interfere with effective communication. It appears, for example, that Nancy would benefit from discussions of how people have needs for both individual actualization and close connections with others (e.g., McClelland, 1987). Part of her marital distress, depression, and anxiety may result from the belief that she must sacrifice her individual needs in order to maintain her connections to others. It is important for her to see that it is possible to attend to both sets of needs in one's life. I often help each partner think about the differences in circumstances that existed earlier in his or her life, versus currently. For example, it would be important for Nancy to see that as a child she had little power to resist her parents' attempts to place her in a caretaking role, but in adult relationships with her husband, mother, and others, she has more power to set limits on that role.

I also would explore Steve's assumptions and standards about gender roles in marriage, as they may influence his communication and problem-solving efforts with Nancy. For example, if he believes that women cannot simultaneously fulfill individual and relationship needs, that may contribute to his controlling behavior, including his difficulty in listening empathically when Nancy describes her unease about having children. One purpose of these interventions is to open each person's pervasive negative view of the other to possible modification. Research on distressed couples indicates that partners who have global negative sentiment toward each other tend to overlook or discount positive actions by each other (Baucom & Epstein, 1990; Epstein & Baucom, 1993). Thus, if Steve can empathize with Nancy's lifelong personal experiences of self-sacrifice and Nancy can gain empathy for Steve's fear that she will be emotionally unavailable to him if she pursues her career, they may see each other less as adversaries.

I teach couples expressive and empathic listening skills in a fairly structured way (see Baucom & Epstein, 1990, and Epstein & Baucom, 2002, for details). This includes a didactic presentation (with handouts) of behavioral guidelines for the expresser and listener roles, based on Guerney's (1977) Relationship Enhancement approach. The guidelines for expressive skills include stating one's thoughts and emotions as subjective rather than as objective truth, including positive statements about the partner as well as negatives whenever possible, being as brief and specific as possible, and communicating empathy for the partner's feelings. The guidelines for empathic listening include nonverbally expressing acceptance of the partner's right to have his or her own feelings, working to take the other's perspective in order to understand his or her subjective feelings, and providing reflective summaries to the partner concerning the thoughts, feelings, and desires that he or she expressed. To be an effective listener and to facilitate the other's exploration and expression of feelings, the listener also is instructed to refrain from expressing his or her own views, making judgments, or offering solutions. Once the listener has provided reflective feedback to the expresser's satisfaction, the partners switch roles, and the listener is now the expresser. At that point reactions to the partner's statements can be expressed.

As the couple practices expressive and listening skills during therapy sessions, the therapist coaches them, providing corrective feedback and praising them for steps toward constructive communication. It is important to have a couple practice communication skills with relatively benign topics before taking on major conflicts, because the emotional upset associated with "hot" topics easily interferes with the mastery of expressive and listening skills (Baucom & Epstein, 1990). Thus, I would have Nancy and Steve begin their practice discussing topics involving life experiences that do not involve the other person directly (e.g., Steve's frustration with a co-worker). As the couple demonstrates effective communication, we would progress to relationship conflicts of increasing severity.

Problem-solving skills are taught to the couple in a similar manner to that used with expressive and listening skills (see Baucom & Epstein, 1990, and Epstein & Baucom, 2002, for details). The major steps involve jointly identifying a problem in behavioral terms, breaking a complex problem into a set of smaller problems to be approached one at a time, brainstorming a variety of possible solutions (without evaluating them), listing advantages and disadvantages of each potential solution, selecting a solution (or combination of solutions), and agreeing to try the solution during a specific period. If the couple subsequently reports problems in implementing the solution, the therapist and couple "go back to the drawing board," identifying what factors interfered with the solution and modifying the plan for their next attempt. For many couples, this approach reduces conflict and increases their confidence that they can work cooperatively. Given Nancy and Steve's ineffectiveness in resolving problems in daily life, practice in problem-solving would be an important intervention.

Cognitive Restructuring

Nancy and Steve can develop empathy for the other by listening while I conduct cognitive-restructuring interventions with the other person, and they also can provide important corrective feedback to challenge each other's cognitions. For example, it is possible that Steve's insistence that Nancy adopt a "traditional" family role is based at least in part on his impression that she has minimal interest in having children. I would encourage Nancy to let Steve know during a therapy session that her lack of interest in having children has been in response to feeling pressured by him, as well as by her concern that parenthood would commit her further to a relationship that she finds distressing. I then could guide Steve in shifting his attribution for the cause of Nancy's reluctance to have children. As he considers that she is reacting to pressure that she experiences from him, the three of us could devise behavioral experiments in which Steve will encourage Nancy's autonomous behavior and reduce his talk that she interprets as pressure. In a parallel manner, Steve may provide information about his preferences and intentions that can help challenge Nancy's pervasive negative views of him.

As noted, family therapists commonly assume that members of a relationship exert mutual, reciprocal influences on each other (Nichols & Schwartz, 2001). In other words, each partner's behavior is both a response to and an influence upon the other's behavior. Although this does not mean that either person is *responsible* for the other's actions (e.g., an abusive spouse is the only one responsible for that behavior), the concept of circular causality suggests that what each partner does will have some impact on the other. In the present case, I would propose to Nancy (with Steve present) that although she is not responsible for the choices that Steve makes, such as withdrawing affection and criticizing her, the ways that she responds to him may influence how he treats her. I would suggest that he has become accustomed to her thinking, feeling, and behaving in particular ways, but that he would be faced with adjusting his own responses if she modifies hers. Similarly, I would suggest to Steve that although he is not responsible for Nancy's depression or anxiety, the ways that be behaves toward her may influence her as well. She has become accustomed to his responding in particular ways and now assumes that he will continue to respond in those ways.

I then would encourage each to try some small "behavioral experiments," in which he or she behaves in atypical ways and observes the other's responses. In order to keep Nancy's anxiety at a manageable level, she and I would identify relatively small behavior changes that she could attempt initially. For example, I would point out to Nancy that she has described Steve as both "lazy" and "really kind and generous and attentive" during our conjoint sessions, and that this suggests some variation in his behavior. I would ask her to identify any apparent differences in the situations that elicit Steve's "lazy" versus "kind, generous, and attentive" behavior, and would coach her to generate some useful information about these conditions. I would ask Steve if he could offer any insights about circumstances that influence his behaviors that Nancy has identified as "lazy" and as "kind, generous, and attentive," without debating the validity of the labels she has attached to his behavior. Thus, Nancy may note that Steve has occasionally been kind, generous, and attentive by working on a household task when she has asked him to do so, but she also may say that he often declines or does not follow through when she makes such requests.

At this point I would ask both partners if they are aware of any situational conditions associated with Steve's greater versus lesser likelihood of complying when Nancy requests that he do household tasks. My goals are to (a) create an atmosphere of collaboration between partners as they both work to find a solution to this problem; (b) coach them in conducting a functional analysis, in which they identify situational variation in behavior; and (c) modify trait attributions such as Nancy's tendency to view Steve as a "lazy" person.

I would encourage Steve to provide information about the internal experiences associated with variations in his behavior. For example, he might report that he is less likely to comply with Nancy's requests when he feels she is interrupting something he is doing, when he has had a stressful day at work, or when she uses words or a voice tone that "show me she considers me obligated to do what she wants." I would encourage even more specific communication by asking Steve to tell Nancy more about each of these conditions. Thus, I would ask him to describe what kinds of words and tone give him the *impression* that Nancy considers him to be obligated to her. My emphasis on the subjectivity of his perceptions is intended to alert the couple to the importance of testing the validity of their cognitions about each other. Nancy may respond by telling Steve that she does not believe that he is obligated to help her but probably does express her frustration when she feels overburdened and would like him to share more of the workload at home.

Based on this type of exploration of the partners' internal experiences and behavioral interactions associated with household tasks, I would then shift the couple toward identifying conditions that could increase Steve's participation in household work. For example, Steve might state that he believes he would be more open to participating if Nancy prefaced requests with an inquiry about how his day had been and whether he was in the middle of something else. He also might suggest that she try to monitor how she expresses her requests. My role as therapist in this interaction is to facilitate constructive suggestions and block defensive responses by each partner as they work together to devise a plan to change their usual pattern.

We then would design at least two specific experiments to be carried out at home. Nancy would be asked to behave toward Steve in a manner that will be likely to elicit his helpful behavior, and Steve would focus on the positive qualities of Nancy's requests. Both partners would have the responsibility of observing his or her own behavior. It is important to conduct multiple experiments because extenuating circumstances (e.g., Steve was feeling physically ill) can lead to the failure of any single attempt. I would stress to the couple that these experiments are for the purpose of learning more about interactions that occur in their relationship, and that a negative result is only a signal that it is time to "go back to the drawing board" to think of other approaches. If carried out in a careful manner, such experiments will demonstrate to both partners that they have the capacity to produce variations in each other's responses by modifying their own behavior.

The major goal of this type of intervention is to challenge Nancy's pervasive belief that she is helpless to change the quality of the interactions between herself and Steve. However, it also can be conceptualized as a strategic intervention with a paradoxical quality, because it implicitly challenges Steve to show Nancy that he can behave in positive ways toward her.

In a similar manner, I would coach Steve in identifying variations in Nancy's behavior and in setting up "behavioral experiments" to test conditions that increase positive responses that he would like to see from Nancy. Because Steve may have developed generalized negative expectancies about Nancy's behavior and emotional availability to him, it will be important to conduct behavioral experiments that counteract his hopelessness about change.

This example illustrates some common cognitive-behavioral strategies for intervening with couples. They are relevant to work with depression, as couples with a depressed member tend to have negative interaction patterns, poor communication and problem-solving skills, and a mutual sense of hopelessness about improving their relationship. The interventions are designed to foster clear communication, collaborative problem-solving, the modification of negative views of each other, and positive expectancies concerning their ability to improve their relationship.

Over the course of therapy, I would assist the couple in applying behavioral and cognitive restructuring strategies to their presenting problems, including conflict concerning having children, Nancy's career, and emotional and sexual aspects of intimacy. Although Nancy's depression and anxiety likely will decrease as their relationship improves, it would be important for me to coordinate my efforts with her individual therapist's approaches to her treatment. In couple therapy sessions, we could discuss ways in which they can collaborate to maximize the effectiveness of Nancy's individual work on her depression and anxiety. Consistent with literature on spouse-assisted treatment cited earlier, we would explore ways that Steve can be helpful to Nancy (e.g., the best ways for him to respond when she is experiencing a panic attack).

TERMINATION AND FOLLOW-UP

Because I collaborated with the couple in setting goals for improving their relationship, the determination of when termination is appropriate would be based on discussions of their success in achieving those goals. I typically conduct a review of the couple's presenting problems and the degree of progress they and I perceive. As some couples are concerned that they will be unable to maintain their gains without my presence and monitoring, I commonly decrease the frequency of sessions gradually, allowing the couple to gain confidence in themselves. Similarly, I gradually decrease the degree to which I intervene actively in the couple's interactions during sessions, as their ability to monitor and control their interactions increases.

REFERRALS

As noted earlier, if initial efforts to engage Steve in conjoint therapy were ineffective, my work with Nancy would continue on an individual basis, although many of the interventions would be designed to influence the couple relationship. Once my individual therapeutic relationship with Nancy was established, it is possible that changes in her way of relating to Steve would increase his interest in couple therapy. My personal approach to this situation depends on my assessment of potential difficulties that may arise if we shift from individual to couple therapy. Most often the disadvantages to such a shift outweigh the advantages. For example, Nancy would lose a significant portion of her opportunity to practice changing her cognitive, affective, and behavioral responses to Steve in the safe setting of individual therapy. In addition, it may be difficult to build Steve's trust that the therapist will be equally supportive of him and Nancy, and his concern may be based in the reality that I may have become more supportive of Nancy's concerns. Nevertheless, it is possible to shift to couple therapy in some cases without decreasing the focus on improving the individual's functioning or siding with that partner. If the original client wants to make that change in modality and understands the implications, I will pursue it, unless I have serious reservations. In such situations, I will then refer the individual client to another therapist for continued individual therapy. In general, the longer that I have worked individually with one member of a couple, the less comfortable I would feel about shifting to couple therapy.

This chapter has focused on conjoint work with the couple, so the major referral that I would make would be to an individual therapist to treat aspects of Nancy's depression and anxiety that appear to have predated their relationship and affect other areas of her life. It would be important to stress to the couple that such a referral in no way singles out Nancy as "the problem" in their relationship, because there is ample evidence that they have developed problematic patterns between them that will be the focus of our work together.

THERAPEUTIC RELATIONSHIP

As illustrated in this chapter, the therapist is actively engaged in a collaborative relationship with the couple, assessing problems and planning interventions. The therapist's goal is to increase the partners' skills for assessing and modifying aspects of their behavioral, cognitive, and affective responses that contribute to conflict and distress. Consequently, the therapist gives the couple ongoing feedback about his or her observations and hypotheses concerning their relationship patterns, strengths, and problems. Although the therapist conveys expertise about relationships, it is crucial that he or she take an empirical approach to each couple's unique characteristics and goals. Rather than assuming that the therapist or either partner has absolute knowledge of what might work best for the couple, this approach focuses on setting up "experiments" to test the impact of specific changes. Although it can be easy to focus on "dysfunction" when the couple seeks help for their distress, it is important for the therapist to draw the partners' attention to their strengths and resources as well. As Epstein (1985) noted, distressed couples and depressed individuals share a sense of hopelessness, so building on existing positives can help counteract partners' global negative views of their relationship.

Because many of the partners' cognitive, affective, and behavioral responses to each other occur in a rapid, automatic manner, the therapist needs to structure sessions and intervene actively. Thus, the therapist models empathic listening skills but sets limits on partners' venting of anger. Although it is important that each partner feel understood, extended negative exchanges during sessions tend to increase their defensiveness and discouragement about their relationship.

TRANSFERENCE AND COUNTERTRANSFERENCE

The primary type of transference response likely to occur in couple therapy is between the partners. It also is common for each member of a couple to seek the approval of the therapist, as if the partners were siblings vying for favor from a parent. Therapists can shift back and forth between temporary alliances with each member of a couple, providing each with support for expressing thoughts and feelings. It is important to monitor one's balancing of such alliances, so the partners will experience the therapy as equitable. Despite the therapist's best efforts, however, some individuals will perceive him or her as siding with the partner. In such cases, the therapist can explore roots of such a perception, including the individual's experiences of inequity in their family of origin, or the partner's history of forming coalitions against the individual with family and friends. A hallmark of couple and family therapy is the discussion of such reactions when they occur during therapy sessions.

Therapists also must be aware of their own countertransference reactions to the dynamics they observe in couples. It is common for a therapist to identify more with one partner than the other, based on the therapist's personal relationship history. Nevertheless, a balanced treatment does not preclude the therapist from taking a strong stand concerning an abusive partner's responsibility for such behavior.

Couple therapists also need to develop skill in observing patterns in rapidly occurring interactions. However, therapists may sometimes have more difficulty focusing on interaction processes in addition to the content when a couple is arguing about a topic that has personal relevance to the therapist. Thus, if the therapist becomes aware that a couple's issue is similar to one that he or she has experienced as well, the therapist should make an extra effort to attend to the process by which this couple attempts to resolve the issue.

Couple therapists also must be able to tolerate both high levels of emotional expression and icy withdrawal between partners during therapy sessions. It is tempting to conclude that a vociferous couple are headed toward divorce, but their expression of strong emotion may reflect considerable investment in their relationship, which a therapist can help turn toward constructive change.

INTEGRATION OF PSYCHOTHERAPY WITH MEDICATION

Although it is likely that Nancy's depression and anxiety could be alleviated, at least somewhat, by medication, the continued stress from her marriage probably will contribute to chronic symptoms and risk of relapse. Nonetheless, medications may be helpful in preparing Nancy to cope with the stress of interacting with Steve during conjoint sessions. As Nancy most likely will be in individual therapy with another therapist, and perhaps a third professional will be prescribing her medications, it would be important to discuss with the other clinicians the possible effects that medication may have on Nancy and Steve's perceptions of their relationship and the role of couple therapy.

As the couple improve their interactions through more constructive communication and other behavioral and cognitive changes, it will be important that neither person attribute the progress to Nancy's being on medication. Consequently, I periodically review the couple's progress with them, ask them about the factors that they view as responsible for it, and review evidence that their personal efforts have played a role.

RELAPSE PREVENTION

Couple therapy is itself a means of reducing the chance that Nancy will experience a relapse of her depression and anxiety. In addition, the couple therapist must consider strategies for reducing relapse of the couple's negative behavioral interaction patterns, cognitions, and emotional responses to each other. The therapist can discuss how easily a couple can fall back into old patterns, but that the couple has developed skills for monitoring their own interactions. Rather than viewing setbacks as evidence that no progress was made, they can consider them to be warning signs that they need to practice the skills learned in therapy. I also discuss with couples the usefulness of "booster sessions" if they perceive a need for it.

It has been my experience that couples who present with a higher level of alienation and lower commitment to their relationships are less likely to make constructive changes that alleviate marital distress and depression. In addition, evidence that support and cohesion in relationships tend to buffer individuals from experiencing depression may have implications for prevention of relapse. Specifically, couples in which one or both partners are uncomfortable with intimacy and relatedness seem to have greater potential for relapse in depression. Similarly, individuals whose depression and anxiety predated their couple relationship and who exhibit broad patterns of intra- and interpersonal dysfunction may be more likely to have relapses of their symptoms following improvements in their relationships.

SUMMARY

This chapter describes the methods and process of couple therapy for Nancy's depression and anxiety. The goals of assessment and intervention were to reduce Nancy's vulnerability to stress from the marriage and to modify the distressing couple interactions themselves. The option of conducting individual therapy with Nancy if Steve declined to take part in treatment was discussed, although the advantages of conjoint couple therapy were stressed. Although both approaches have potential to alleviate Nancy's depression and anxiety, the depth and stability of change seem to depend on the degree to which the sources of stress in the marriage are resolved. It would be presumptuous to predict how successful therapy with the couple would be, particularly because so little is known about Steve's goals and his feelings for Nancy. Because Nancy's symptoms also occur in response to other life stresses, such as her relationship with her mother, the therapist can help her apply the coping skills that she develops in couple therapy more broadly in her life.

Couple therapy increasingly is seen as a key component of treatment for individuals who are in intimate relationships and experience significant depression or anxiety symptoms. There is great need for more controlled research investigating alternative theoretical approaches to couple and family therapy for depression and anxiety, particularly approaches other than behavioral. At a time when biological views of depression and anxiety have gained prominence, it is crucial that mental health professionals attend to the mounting evidence that intimate relationships play significant roles in the development, course, and treatment of these debilitating problems.

REFERENCES

American Psychiatric Association (1994). *Diagnostic and statistical manual of mental disorders* (4th ed.). Washington, DC: American Psychiatric Association.

Arnow, B. A., Taylor, C. B., Agras, W. S., & Telch, M. J. (1985). Enhancing agoraphobia treatment by changing couple communication patterns. *Behavior Therapy, 16,* 452–456.

Baucom, D. H., & Epstein, N. (1990). *Cognitive-behavioral marital therapy.* New York: Brunner/Mazel.

Baucom, D. H., Epstein, N., Rankin, L. A., & Burnett, C. K. (1996). Assessing relationship standards: The Inventory of Specific Relationship Standards. *Journal of Family Psychology, 10,* 72–88.

Baucom, D. H., Shoham, V., Mueser, K. T., Daiuto, A. D., & Stickle, T. R. (1998). Empirically supported couple and family interventions for marital distress and adult mental health problems. *Journal of Consulting and Clinical Psychology, 66,* 53–88.

Beach, S. R. H. (Ed.). (2001). *Marital and family processes in depression: A scientific foundation for clinical practice.* Washington, DC: American Psychological Association.

Beach, S. R. H., Fincham, F. D., & Katz, J. (1998). Marital therapy in the treatment of depression: Toward a third generation of therapy and research. *Clinical Psychology Review, 18,* 635–661.

Beach, S. R. H., Jouriles, E. N., & O'Leary, K. D. (1985). Extramarital sex: Impact on depression and commitment in couples seeking marital therapy. *Journal of Sex and Marital Therapy, 11,* 99–108.

Beach, S. R. H., & O'Leary, K. D. (1992). Treating depression in the context of marital discord: Outcome and predictors of response for marital therapy vs. cognitive therapy. *Behavior Therapy, 23,* 507–528.

Beach, S. R. H., Sandeen, E. E., & O'Leary, K. D. (1990). *Depression in marriage: A model for etiology and treatment.* New York: Guilford Press.

Beach, S. R. H., Smith, D. A., & Fincham, F. D. (1994). Marital interventions for depression: Empirical foundation and future prospects. *Applied & Preventive Psychology, 3,* 233–250.

Beck, A. T., Rush, A. J., Shaw, B. F., & Emery, G. (1979). *Cognitive therapy of depression.* New York: Guilford Press.

Beck, J. (1995). *Cognitive therapy: Basics and beyond.* New York: Guilford Press.

Bennun, I. (1997). Relationship interventions with one partner. In W. K. Halford & H. J. Markman (Eds.), *Clinical handbook of marriage and couples intervention* (pp. 451–470). Chichester, England: Wiley.

Bowen, M. (1978). *Family therapy in clinical practice.* New York: Jason Aronson.

Christensen, A. (1987). Detection of conflict patterns in couples. In K. Hahlweg & M. J. Goldstein (Eds.), *Understanding major mental disorder: The contribution of family interaction research* (pp. 250–265). New York: Family Process Press.

Coyne, J. C. (1976). Toward an interactional description of depression. *Psychiatry, 39,* 28–40.

Craske, M. G., & Zoellner, L. A. (1995). Anxiety disorders: The role of marital therapy. In N. S. Jacobson & A. S. Gurman (Eds.), *Clinical handbook of couple therapy* (pp. 394–410). New York: Guilford Press.

Dattilio, F. M. (1994). Families in crisis. In F. M. Dattilio & A. Freeman (Eds.), *Cognitive-behavioral strategies in crisis intervention* (pp. 278–301). New York: Guilford Press.

Di Nardo, P. A., Brown, T. A., & Barlow, D. H. (1994). *Anxiety Disorders Interview Schedule for DSM-IV: Lifetime.* Albany, NY: Graywind Publications.

Eidelson, R. J., & Epstein, N. (1982). Cognition and relationship maladjustment: Development of a measure of dysfunctional relationship beliefs. *Journal of Consulting and Clinical Psychology, 50,* 715–720.

Epstein, N. (1985). Depression and marital dysfunction: Cognitive and behavioral linkages. *International Journal of Mental Health, 13,* 86–104.

Epstein, N., & Baucom, D. H. (1989). Cognitive-behavioral marital therapy. In A. Freeman, K. M. Simon, L. E. Beutler, & H. Arkowitz (Eds.), *Comprehensive handbook of cognitive therapy* (pp. 491–513). New York: Plenum.

Epstein, N., & Baucom, D. H. (1993). Cognitive factors in marital disturbance. In K. S. Dobson & P. C. Kendall (Eds.), *Psychopathology and cognition* (pp. 351–385). San Diego: Academic Press.

Epstein, N. B., & Baucom, D. H. (2002). *Enhanced cognitive-behavioral therapy for couples: A contextual approach.* Washington, DC: American Psychological Association.

Epstein, N., & Schlesinger, S. E. (1996). Treatment of family problems. In M. A. Reinecke, F. M. Dattilio, & A. Freeman (Eds.), *Cognitive therapy with children and adolescents* (pp. 299–326). New York: Guilford Press.

Epstein, N., Schlesinger, S. E., & Dryden, W. (Eds.). (1988). *Cognitive-behavioral therapy with families.* New York: Brunner/Mazel.

Falloon, I. R. H. (1991). Behavioral family therapy. In A. S. Gurman & D. P. Kniskern (Eds.), *Handbook of family therapy* (Vol. II, pp. 65–95). New York: Brunner/Mazel.

Foley, S. H., Rounsaville, B. J., Weissman, M. M., Sholomaskas, D., & Chevron, E. (1989). Individual versus conjoint interpersonal therapy for depressed patients with marital disputes. *International Journal of Family Psychiatry, 10,* 29–42.

Friedman, E. H. (1991). Bowen theory and therapy. In A. S. Gurman & D. P. Kniskern (Eds.), *Handbook of family therapy, Vol. II* (pp. 134–170). New York: Brunner/Mazel.

Gotlib, I. H., & Beach, S. R. H. (1995). A marital/family discord model of depression: Implications for therapeutic intervention. In N. S. Jacobson & A. S. Gurman (Eds.), *Clinical handbook of couple therapy* (pp. 411–436). New York: Guilford Press.

Guerney, B. G., Jr. (1977). *Relationship enhancement.* San Francisco: Jossey-Bass.

Halford, W. K., & Bouma, R. (1997). Individual psychopathology and marital distress. In W. K. Halford & H. J. Markman (Eds.), *Clinical handbook of marriage and couples intervention* (pp. 291–321). Chichester, England: Wiley.

Hooley, J. M., & Teasdale, J. D. (1989). Predictors of relapse in unipolar depressives: Expressed emotion, marital distress, and perceived criticism. *Journal of Abnormal Psychology, 98,* 229–235.

Jacobson, N. S., Dobson, K., Fruzetti, A. E., Schmaling, D. B., & Salusky, S. (1991). Marital therapy as a treatment for depression. *Journal of Consulting and Clinical Psychology, 59,* 547–557.

Johnson, S. M., & Greenberg, L. S. (1995). The emotionally focused approach to problems in adult attachment. In N. S. Jacobson & A. S. Gurman (Eds.), *Clinical handbook of couple therapy* (pp. 121–141). New York: Guilford Press.

Luepnitz, D. A. (1988). *The family interpreted: Feminist theory in clinical practice.* New York: Basic Books.

McClelland, D. C. (1987). *Human motivation.* Cambridge, England: Cambridge University Press.

Metz, M. E. (1993). *The Styles of Conflict Inventory (SCI).* Palo Alto, CA: Consulting Psychologists Press.

Nichols, M. P., & Schwartz, R. C. (2001). *Family therapy: Concepts and methods* (5th ed.). Boston: Allyn & Bacon.

Paykel, E. S., Myers, J. K., Dienelt, M. N., Klerman, G. L., Lindenthal, J. J., & Pepper, M. P. (1969). Life events and depression: A controlled study. *Archives of General Psychiatry, 21,* 753–760.

Pretzer, J. L., Epstein, N., & Fleming, B. (1991). The Marital Attitude Survey: A measure of dysfunctional attributions and expectancies. *Journal of Cognitive Psychotherapy: An International Quarterly, 5,* 131–148.

Prince, S. E., & Jacobson, N. S. (1995). A review and evaluation of marital and family therapies for affective disorders. *Journal of Marital and Family Therapy, 21,* 377–401.

Schwebel, A. I., & Fine, M. A. (1994). *Understanding and helping families: A cognitive-behavioral approach.* Hillsdale, NJ: Erlbaum.

Spanier, G. (1976). Measuring dyadic adjustment: New scales for assessing the quality of marriage and similar dyads. *Journal of Marriage and the Family, 38,* 15–28.

Straus, M. A., Hamby, S. L., Boney-McCoy, S., & Sugarman, D. B. (1996). The revised Conflict Tactics Scales (CTS2). *Journal of Family Issues, 17,* 283–316.

Weissman, M. M. (1987). Advances in psychiatric epidemiology: Rates and risks for major depression. *American Journal of Public Health, 77,* 445–451.

SUGGESTED READINGS

Beach, S. R. H. (Ed.). (2001). *Marital and family processes in depression: A scientific foundation for clinical practice.* Washington, DC: American Psychological Association.

Beach, S. R. H., Sandeen, E. E., & O'Leary, K. D. (1990). *Depression in marriage: A model for etiology and treatment.* New York: Guilford Press.

Beach, S. R. H., Smith, D. A., & Fincham, F. D. (1994). Marital interventions for depression: Empirical foundation and future prospects. *Applied & Preventive Psychology, 3,* 233–250.

Craske, M. G., & Zoellner, L. A. (1995). Anxiety disorders: The role of marital therapy. In N. S. Jacobson & A. S. Gurman (Eds.), *Clinical handbook of couple therapy* (pp. 394–410). New York: Guilford Press.

Epstein, N., & Baucom, D. H. (1998). Cognitive-behavioral couple therapy. In F. M. Dattilio (Ed.), *Case studies in couple and family therapy: Systemic & cognitive perspectives* (pp. 37–61). New York: Guilford Press.

Epstein, N. B., & Baucom, D. H. (2002). *Enhanced cognitive-behavioral therapy for couples: A contextual approach.* Washington, DC: American Psychological Association.

Schwebel, A. I., & Fine, M. A. (1994). *Understanding and helping families: A cognitive-behavioral approach.* Hillsdale, NJ: Erlbaum.

15

Integrative Conceptualization and Treatment of Depression

John C. Norcross, Larry E. Beutler, and Roslyn Caldwell

OVERVIEW OF THE MODEL

As the field of psychotherapy has matured, the genesis of therapeutic change has been properly recognized as more complex and multifaceted than ever. The identical psychosocial treatment for all patients is now recognized as inappropriate and, in selected cases, even unethical (Norcross, 1991). The efficacy and applicability of psychotherapy will be enhanced by tailoring it to the unique needs of the client, not by imposing a conceptual Procrustean bed onto unwitting consumers of psychological services. Prescriptive matching is embodied in Gordon Paul's (1967) famous question: What treatment, by whom, is most effective for this individual with that specific problem, and under which set of circumstances?

An integrative model of treatment attempts to enhance the effectiveness, efficiency, and applicability of psychotherapy by tailoring it to the particular needs of clients, disorders, and situations (Norcross & Goldfried, 1992). This is done by identifying empirically informed principles that describe the conditions under which change will most likely occur. While some integrative models, particularly those identified with technical eclecticism, provide menus of specific techniques, the models to which we most identify are concerned with defining the principles for initiating change, leaving the selection of specific techniques that comply with these principles to the proclivities of the therapist. Accordingly, our integrative model is expressly designed to transcend the limited applicability of single-theory or "school-bound" psychotherapies. Put another way, integration—and our specific form of prescriptive eclecticism or systematic treatment selection—ascertains the treatment (and relationship) of choice for each individual patient, rather than restricting itself to a single view of psychopathology or mechanisms of change. It implicitly assumes that no theory is uniformly valid and no finite set of mechanisms of action are accurate for all individuals. Thus, the purpose of psychotherapy integration is not to create a single or unitary approach to treatment, but to select therapeutic interventions according to the responses of the patient and the goals of the treatment (Norcross, Beutler, & Clarkin, 1998).

The need to match patient and treatment has been recognized from the beginning of psychotherapy. As early as 1919, Freud introduced psychoanalytic psychotherapy as an alternative to classical analysis on the recognition that the more rarified approach lacked universal applicability and that many patients did not possess the requisite psychological-mindedness (Liff, 1992). He referred the majority of so-called "unanalyzable" patients for a psychotherapy based on direct suggestion. These and other early attempts at prescriptive matching, however, were largely serendipitous, theory-driven, and empirically untested.

Systematic and empirically generated prescriptive psychotherapy was probably inaugurated in the modern era by Frederick Thorne (1950, 1967), credited with being the grandfather of eclecticism in psychotherapy. Persuasively arguing that any skilled professional should come prepared with more than one tool, Thorne emphasized the need for clinicians to fill their toolboxes with procedures from many different theoretical models. He likened contemporary psychotherapy to a plumber who would use only a screwdriver in his work. Like such a plumber, inveterate psychotherapists applied the same treatment to all people regardless of individual differences and expected the patient to adapt to the therapist rather than vice versa.

Thorne's admonitions went largely ignored, but were followed more than a decade later by a similarly little noticed book by Goldstein and Stein (1976) that first identified "Prescriptive Psychotherapy." This book, far ahead of its time, outlined treatment programs for different people based on the nature of their problems and aspects of their living situations. Since the late 1960s, Arnold Lazarus (1967, 1989, 1997) has emerged as the most prominent and articulate spokesperson for "technical eclecticism." He was joined by ourselves and others soon thereafter (Beutler, 1983; Frances, Clarkin, & Perry, 1984; Norcross, 1986, 1987).

The recent evolution of health care delivery and the encroaching dominance of managed care have lent increased urgency to the task of tailoring psychological interventions to the client and his or her unique situation. Brief therapies demand integrative, explicit, and empirically-based models of treatment selection. Within 6 or 12 or 26 sessions (though some models focus on a single session), the practitioner is expected to diagnose psychosocial or mental disorders, select specific technical and interpersonal methods to remediate those disorders, apply those methods in sequences or stages over the course of treatment, and then rapidly terminate the efficacious treatment while preventing relapse (Barlow, 1994; Norcross & Beutler, 1997).

Our respective approaches to psychotherapy closely resemble each other in addressing these challenges, as expressed in their titles: *prescriptive eclectic therapy* (Norcross, 1994; Norcross, Beutler, & Clarkin, 1998), *systematic eclectic psychotherapy* (Beutler, 1983), and *systematic treatment selection* (Beutler & Clarkin, 1990). This form of integrative psychotherapy attempts to customize psychological treatments and therapeutic relationships to the specific and varied needs of individual patients. It does so by drawing on effective methods from across theoretical camps (eclecticism), by matching those methods to particular cases on the basis of empirically supported guidelines (prescriptionism), and by adhering to an explicit and orderly model of treatment selection (systematic). The result of such a systematic and prescriptive eclecticism is a more efficient and efficacious therapy that fits both the client and the clinician.

We maintain a core commitment to the central tenet of all eclectic and prescriptive models: Empirical knowledge and scientific research are the best arbitrators of theoretical differences (Lazarus, 1989; Lazarus, Beutler, & Norcross, 1992). We remain suspicious of global theories of psychotherapy that evolve from other theories, that may only reflect the strong opinions of their originators, and that consist of descriptions of psychopathology rather than mechanisms of change. We highly value the scientific method, not as an infallible guide to truth, but as the most reliable and valid method available by which to evaluate the value of any psychotherapy, integrative or otherwise.

On the face of it, virtually every psychotherapist endorses prescriptive matching; after all, who can seriously dispute the notion that psychological treatment should be tailored to fit the needs of the individual patient in order to improve the outcome of psychotherapy? However, systematic and prescriptive eclecticism goes beyond this simple acknowledgment in at least four ways. One: our basis of prescriptive matching is derived directly from outcome research, rather than from the typical theoretical basis. Two: we adopt an integrative or transtheoretical basis that acknowledges the potential contributions of multiple systems of psychotherapy, rather than working from within a single theory. Three: the guidelines for prescriptive matching are culled from multiple diagnostic and nondiagnostic client variables, in contrast to the typical reliance on the single, static variable of patient diagnosis. Four: our aim is the research-informed and practice-tested selection of technical interventions *and* interpersonal stances, whereas most previous prescriptive efforts focused narrowly on the selection of disembodied techniques (Norcross & Beutler, 1997).

In this chapter, we present our integrative model for selecting and sequencing the therapy formats, methods, and relationships of choice for unipolar depression, using the case of Ms. Nancy T. as an illustration. To begin, we trace the key principles, etiological conceptualization, and empirical evidence of our model. We then demonstrate our typical process of conceptualization, assessment, treatment selection, and therapeutic relationship, again illustrating these generic processes with the specific case of Nancy. We conclude by addressing relapse prevention, the integration of psychotherapy and pharmacotherapy, and several overarching matters regarding treatment selection.

ETIOLOGY OF DEPRESSION

Psychotherapy integration is a meta-model of psychotherapy. It is not a model of psychopathology, nor does it offer a specific view regarding the mechanisms through which psychotherapy works. Instead, it is superimposed over whatever specific model of psychopathology a therapist embraces.

Beginning with Freud, most theories of psychotherapy have also been theories of psychopathology. This is not true of our model nor most integrative models; the central focus is on the content and process of change. The integration is directly focused on the application of interventions and strategies, as opposed to theoretical constructs of how psychopathology develops.

We can illustrate the foregoing principles by comparing our prescriptive/integrative model with a traditional psychodynamic approach to the conceptualization of depression. A psychodynamic view holds that depression has its nucleus in psychic conflict. The nature of this conflict is frequently thought to derive from the suppression of hostile impulses and to the failure to establish stable attachments to parental figures. Either or both of these dynamics may leave the patient feeling helpless, defeated, and unworthy. In either case, the presumed mechanism of change is through achieving insight and understanding of one's unconscious needs for attachment and of one's methods of defending against these needs. It is assumed that the therapist's theory of how depression is developed and maintained is the principle guide to selecting treatment.

By contrast, a prescriptive conceptualization makes no specific assumption about how a given episode of depression may have occurred. Such a determination is relatively unimportant if one knows what types of interventions are likely to evoke a positive response in a specific patient. The intervention can be applied from the perspective of a wide number of theories or from no theoretical framework at all.

Neither does our prescriptive model assume that there is a single mechanism of change. The mechanism of action may be very different for different individuals, all of whom manifest similar symptoms of depression. To an individual who is impulsive and defensive, the mechanism may be through the benevolent, corrective modeling of trust and constraint offered by a kind therapist, but for an individual who is trusting and self-reflective, the mechanism of action may indeed be through insight and reconceptualization. Similarly, the change mechanism for helping a fearful and anxious patient may well be through exposure to feared events, supportive reassurance, and persuasion.

Especially important, prescriptive models make no assumptions that one's theory of psychopathology is a useful guide to developing interventions. If the latter assumption were true, then all therapists of a like theory would treat a given patient in the same manner. In fact, there are wide differences in how different therapists apply the theory and in the procedures used, and even the types of experiences on which they focus. The strength of prescriptive approaches is that they can be applied by individuals who have a variety of theoretical beliefs; they do not impose a single viewpoint on psychotherapists. The therapist's theory of the genesis and maintenance of psychotherapy is essentially a set of value statements that may be transmitted to patients to help them make sense of their condition. Having a viewpoint that makes sense may relieve guilt and provide reassurance. Beyond being a convenient explanation, however, the therapist's theory of psychopathology is independent of the empirically informed principles that direct the selection of interventions and relationships.

REVIEW OF EMPIRICAL EVIDENCE

The outcome research supporting our integrative model comes in two guises. First and most generally, the entire body of empirical research on psychotherapy informs our treatment decisions and key principles. This is the basis from which we have systematized our process of treatment selection. A genuine advantage of being integrative is the vast amount of research attesting to the efficacy of psychotherapy and pointing to its differential effectiveness with certain types of disorders and patients. Integration tries to incorporate state-of-the-art research findings into its open framework, in contrast to yet another "system" of psychotherapy.

In this regard, we should note that "integrative therapy," misconstrued as a distinct system of therapy, has not been subjected to controlled research for the treatment of clinical depression. There are no published studies comparing the efficacy of an "integrative therapy" with that of a "single theory" therapy for depression (Beutler, Clarkin, & Bongar, in press; Lambert, 1992; Norcross, 1993a). Nor, in our opinion, should this be a research priority in that we do not consider prescriptive eclecticism a distinct system of psychotherapy. This would largely and unproductively replicate the error of the ubiquitous horse-race designs that have stymied psychotherapy outcome research for the past decade. It is possible, of course, to compare single theory treatments to a prescriptive model in which each patient is treated by a different set of guidelines. Indeed, Beutler and associates are currently doing exactly this in a large study of patients with co-morbid depression and chemical abuse. Such demonstrations may help ensure the acceptability of an integrative approach, but the more important demonstration will be a series of prospective matching studies demonstrating the differential effectiveness of different therapies on the basis of specific client dimensions.

The second and more specific outcome research supporting our integrative model is ongoing programmatic research on systematic treatment planning according to client variables. Beutler, Clarkin, and Bongar (2000), for example, conducted an independent cross-validation of the principles of integrative psychotherapy among an archival and prospective sample of 289 depressed and chemically dependent patients. From this cross-validation, they extracted a series of ten basic principles and eight more selective and optimal principles that can guide the application of treatments. These principles can be applied independently of a specific theory of change and reflect indicators and contraindicators for applying different classes of intervention. In this chapter, we will present a sampling of the principles as we describe the treatment indicating patient qualities.

All the interrelationships among these patient qualities that predict differential treatment response have yet to be determined. The dimensions that have been identified as relevant for treatment planning comprise a dynamic list. However, the list of variables that we will describe here have been identified by an extensive review of contemporary literature (e.g., Beutler, Clarkin, & Bongar, 2000; Beutler, Goodrich, Fisher, & Williams, 1999). While this list is likely to change as research progresses, those variables currently identified have evolved from an extensive review of treatment literature. They are incorporated into our model of integrative/prescriptive therapy because they can be reliably identified and they have a substantial body of literature that supports their value for making differential treatment decisions. While a full review of research available on this topic is not possible here, aspects of it have been summarized elsewhere (Beutler & Clarkin, 1990; Beutler, Clarkin, & Bongar, in press; Beutler, Kim, Davison, Karno, & Fisher, 1996; Gaw & Beutler, 1995; Harwood et al., 1997; Lazarus, Beutler, & Norcross, 1992; Norcross, 1994; Norcross & Beutler, 1997; Prochaska, Norcross, & DiClemente, 1994).

- Patient diagnosis is one—and only one—marker to consider. Of the variables considered here, it is the one with the least evidence of differential treatment effects. But both because of its conventional use and because of its clinical utility in selecting pharmacological and some psychosocial interventions, it is included here. Although we cannot match with certainty, there are correlations to suggest that some marriages of disorder and treatment are differentially effective; for example, moderate depressions seem to be responsive to cognitive therapy, interpersonal therapy, and pharmacotherapy (Lambert & Bergin, 1992; Sotsky et al., 1991).

- Patient externalizing coping style is probably a differential predictor of responsivity to symptom-focused interventions and may contraindicate the use of insight interventions (Beutler, Engle, Mohr, et al., 1991; Beutler, Machado, Engle, & Mohr, 1993; Beutler, Mohr, Grawe, Engle, & MacDonald, 1991).
- The severity of symptoms or the degree of functional impairment is a probable predictor of response to medication and the length of treatment, and may even indicate the relative value of psychopharmacological versus psychological interventions (Beutler & Baker, 1998; Elkin, 1994; Elkin, Gibbons, Shea, & Shaw, 1996).
- Level of resistance is probably a specific indicator of using highly directive or nondirective, self-directed, and even paradoxical interventions (Beutler, Sandowicz, Fisher, & Albanese, 1996; Shoham-Salomon & Hannah, 1991).
- Level of patient arousal may interact with the use of procedures that heighten or directly reduce arousal and distress (Beutler, Kim, Davison, et al., 1996; Burgoon et al., 1993).
- The amount of patient social support and investment in social attachments may be predictive of the value of interpersonally focused and family therapies (Sotsky et al., 1991; Elkin et al., 1989).
- Patient readiness for change, as represented in the stages of change, is probably predictive of response to type of change processes and interpersonal stance (Prochaska, Norcross, & DiClemente, 1994; Prochaska, Rossi, & Wilcox, 1991; Prochaska, DiClemente, & Norcross, 1992). Specifically, clients in the contemplation stage respond best to awareness-inducing, self-reevaluation, and emotional processes and a therapist stance akin to a nurturing parent and a Socratic teacher. By contrast, clients in the action stage respond best to the change processes of contingency management, counterconditioning, and stimulus control and a therapist stance characterized as an experienced coach.
- Patient preferences and goals are frequently direct indicators of the type of therapeutic method and relationship for a patient. Decades of empirical evidence attest to the benefit of seriously considering, and at least beginning with, the specific preferences and treatment goals of the client (Duncan, Solovey, & Rusk, 1992).

All of this is to say that the science and art of psychotherapy have progressed to the point where clinically relevant and readily assessable patient characteristics can systematically inform specific treatment plans and thereby enhance the effectiveness and efficiency of our clinical work.

CASE CONCEPTUALIZATION

Integrative models of personality are predictably broad and inclusive. We are, functional and dysfunctional alike, the products of a complex interplay of our genetic endowment, social-learning history, and physical environment.

By the same token, we view psychological disturbances, including depression, as resulting from numerous influences. It is difficult to make a case that depressive disorders are distinctive conditions, with the possible exception of Bipolar Disorder. Indeed, non-bipolar depressions seem to be stress markers or common pathways that arise from confronting life changes and stressors (Beutler, Clarkin, & Bongar, in press; Gotlib, Lewinsohn, & Seeley, 1995; Gotlib & Robinson, 1982). The multifaceted nature of unipolar depression is usually more reflective of variations in severity rather than in qualitative type. Variations in vegetative signs reflect level of impairment and severity of dysfunction. Rather than being a set of different but related conditions, unipolar depression is a relatively continuous dimension largely reflected in dysphoria and secondarily by associated vegetative signs and level of social impairment.

Major depression is highly prevalent in society, affecting 8 to 18% of the general population with approximately twice as many women being affected as men (Clarkin et al., 1996). Depression can be a serious condition, associated with dysfunction in work and family roles, substance abuse, suicidality, increased use of social and medical services, and enormous financial costs for treatment (Nathan & Gorman, 1998). There is a wide range of symptoms associated with depression, such as sadness or melancholy, weight loss, negative self-attitudes, cognitive impairment, insomnia, bodily complaints, lack of energy, and loss of interest in pleasurable activities. While one patient will report all of the described symptoms, there is no one single way that depression is manifest (Nathan & Gorman, 1998).

In terms of the dimensions that we consider important, Ms. Nancy T. appears to present with an internalizing personality or coping style. She describes herself as being very self-critical, as beating herself up, as inept and incompetent, and as a pleaser who seeks to be taken care of by others. Indeed, she appears to face the world from a stance of fear and apprehension, seeing herself as vulnerable because of her own failures and inadequacies. On the positive side, this internalizing stance leads Nancy to seek help through self-understanding and to be motivated to engage in self-corrective activities. This coping style suggests that insight-oriented procedures may be helpful (Beutler, Engle, et al., 1991).

Her level of severity and functional impairment appears to be moderate. She feels quite dysfunctional, but continues to carry on her roles as student and employee. Yet, she has "jags of crying," experiences many sleepless nights, and is plagued by thoughts of death and suicide. Moreover, the pattern is longstanding, reflecting a recurrent and frequently problematic condition. These factors suggest that treatment intensity should be relatively high, though her current lack of suicidal intention argues against a restrictive environment. Ideal treatment might be long-term, even though the experience of depression is likely to resolve within six months to a year (Howard, Moras, Brill, Zoran, & Lutz, 1996; Kopta, Howard, Lowry, & Beutler, 1994), in order to reduce the probability of relapse and to alter dysfunctional personality styles.

It is difficult to assess Nancy's level of resistance. On one hand, she is likely to be very attentive and to attempt to engender the therapist's approval by compliance, as she does with many others. On the other hand, she also is an angry lady; together these patterns may be manifest as mild to moderate resistance in the form of passive-aggressive behaviors. If this proves to be true, nondirective and self-directed strategies are indicated (Beutler, Engle, et al., 1991).

This patient is clearly distressed. Her high scores on the BDI, BAI, and BHS all suggest, if one could not observe it in her own descriptions and presentation, that she is highly symptomatic and uncomfortable. This provides the basis for motivation for change and for working in a psychotherapy context. The fact that she also looks to herself as the one responsible for change further supports the level of motivation that she has (Mohr et al., 1990). Her heightened anxiety, however, suggests that the patient should be assisted in the development of skills for managing anxiety, for problem-solving, and for coping under high levels of distress.

Nancy has some friendships that provide a modicum of social support, though she seems to be ambivalent about these. On the other hand, she has no contact with her father, the relationship with her mother is erratic and apparently hostile, and we don't know what relationship she has with her sister. The relationship with her husband is problematic and does not appear to provide support or affirmation. Encouraging the development of friendships and sources of support is critical since it is implicated in both the long-term and short-term effectiveness of treatment (Beutler, Clarkin, & Bongar, 2000).

Nancy appears to be in the contemplative stage of readiness, confirming our speculations that her internalizing style of coping may serve as indicators for the use of awareness-inducing and insight-oriented interventions. These can serve as the basis for a personal reappraisal and self-evaluation and may foster a more realistic view of her role in her marital difficulties (Prochaska & Norcross, 1998).

We know little from what is provided about Nancy's preferences for therapy. We can speculate that the personal stance and interpersonal warmth of the therapist will be more important than his or her theoretical model given Nancy's general predilection to seek warmth and caring. Accordingly, the therapist should be mindful to enact behaviors that foster a sense of collaboration, support, and acceptance, even more than usual perhaps.

Our integrative model is principally concerned with the remediation of psychopathology, not with its explanation. Thus, the foregoing dimensions direct the therapist toward an integrative set of principles that foster change, but can be applied within any number of theoretical models of personality and psychopathology.

BEGINNING TREATMENT

Therapeutic Goals

The alleviation or elimination of a particular problem, in this case depression and anxiety, is the typical final goal of treatment. However, the mediating goals of treatment—those intermediate goals that must be reached in order to achieve the final goals—are not always so obvious. They are dictated by the model of the symptom picture/problem area or successive steps to health. These mediating goals will depend on the particular problem area, the theoretical orientation of the assessor, and current understanding of the particular diagnosis/problem area in question. The nature and extent of these mediating goals provides the indications for the various therapeutic settings, formats, strategies, relationships, and durations. Therefore, in the evaluation and treatment planning for any case, the clinician must be as precise as possible about the mediating goals of treatment.

The complexity of the patient's problem and the patient's readiness for change are the primary variables that go into selecting treatment goals and subgoals. Complexity is defined as the degree to which the problem represents an isolated or continuing problem. Complex problems are chronic, recurrent, affect many life functions, and usually reflect a recurrent interpersonal theme or pattern. Concomitantly, complex problems require a focus on more thematic and systemic goals than the symptomatic ones that are appropriate to a situational problem.

Usually an assessment of complexity begins with a determination of the problem for which the patient (or family) is seeking help and if it is identified as complex, then proceeds to a determination of what interpersonal pattern is present in their collective interactions. Changing this pattern is then included as a treatment objective, along with symptom amelioration and improved functioning. The information that is contained in the narrative about Nancy is incomplete for some of our purposes.

Even with only the information provided, it seems safe to assume that Nancy's problems are reasonably complex. They are recurrent, persistent, and pervasive. The next step is to identify the particular pattern on which work is needed. Here, the incomplete narrative description is a decided handicap.

Clinical Assessment

Clinical assessment in prescriptive eclecticism is relatively traditional with one large exception. The assessment interview(s) will entail collecting information on presenting problems, relevant histories, treatment expectations and goals, as well as building a working alliance. As psychologists, we also typically request or conduct psychological testing as a means of securing additional data and normative comparisons for Axis I and Axis II disorders. We recommend both symptomatic rating forms (e.g., Beck Depression Inventory, Symptom Checklist-90R) and a broader measure of pathology and personality (e.g., Minnesota Multiphasic Personality Inventory-II, Millon Clinical Multiaxial Inventory-III). The large exception to this traditional assessment process is that prescriptive eclecticism collects, from the outset, information on multiple patient dimensions that will guide treatment selection. Recently, we have also begun experimenting with a computer-assisted, clinician-based assessment procedure that is specifically committed to developing treatment plans within the prescriptive and eclectic approaches (Beutler, Clarkin, & Bongar, in press; Beutler & Williams, 1995).

One of the central challenges is the identification of productive patient dimensions that relate to treatment decisions. The complexity of this task can be grasped by enumerating the variety of potential combinations of patient, therapist, and treatment variables that may be included in a comprehensive model of psychotherapy. Even conservatively identifying the variables that are known to have an effect on psychotherapy, there are still millions of potential permutations and combinations that could contribute to relevant systematic treatment planning (Beutler, 1991). The very contemplation of such an extensive array of variables is daunting, made more so by managed health care systems that have historically eschewed the use of formal psychological testing. What is required is a new approach to psychological assessment, one that is highly focused and targeted on those dimensions of the patient and environment that are most predictive of differential treatment response (Beutler, Kim, Davison, et al., 1996; Harwood et al., 1997).

Within the large list of important patient variables, research has enabled us to select a smaller number that are most promising as prescriptive guidelines. In various combinations and with different amounts of emphasis, each of us has acknowledged the promising nature of multiple patient characteristics in treatment planning of which we will cover seven: (1) diagnosis/problem areas; (2) functional impairment; (3) coping style; (4) resistance potential; (5) stage of change; (6) severity of impairment; and (7) preferences for certain methods or relationships. The priority given to these different patient characteristics is still uncertain, as is their interaction and verification of their independence. Nonetheless, each of these client variables has been found to impact psychotherapy outcomes. In their most refined form, they are able to differentially predict the rate and magnitude of change accompanying different forms of treatment (see Beutler, Consoli, & Williams, 1995; Beutler, Clarkin, & Bongar, in press; Beutler, Kim, Davison, et al., 1996; Gaw & Beutler, 1995; Groth-Marnat, 1997; Beutler & Berren, 1995; Frances, Clarkin, & Perry, 1984; Prochaska, Norcross, & DiClemente, 1994).

A number of specific psychometric tests and clinical methods have been identified and used to assess these dimensions, along with methods of identifying the treatments for which each may be a prescriptive guideline (Groth-Marnat, 1997; Beutler & Clarkin, 1990; Beutler & Berren, 1995; Beutler & Harwood, 1995; Beutler, Clarkin, & Bongar, in press.) In contrast to traditional, broad-band evaluations which are not focused directly on treatment implications, our assessments attempt to derive a clinically focused, empirically supported, and relationship-based treatment plan. The assessment task, then, is to identify the most reliable predictors of differential treatment response.

The problems with this assessment tack have always been that the sheer number of variables are beyond the capacities of clinicians to use consistently, and that the way that these variables would be balanced and weighted has not been established empirically. However, the advent of the computer has introduced the capacity to manage large numbers of patient, therapist, and treatment variables and to identify predictive patterns that are objective and independent of the therapist's personal preferences. With available computers, it is now possible to rapidly extract relationships that will allow highly individualized and precise predictions of the effects of different therapists and different therapeutic procedures. Beutler and Williams (1995; Beutler, Clarkin, & Bongar, 2000; Beutler, Kim, Davison, et al., 1996) have introduced computer software that is designed to help clinicians summarize information gathered from numerous, individualized sources of data, into stable judgments that can then apply a number of patient, treatment, and therapist dimensions to reach empirically derived predictions of what procedures, therapists, and treatments will be most likely to yield positive effects.

Diagnosis

We organize our treatment planning in part around the disorders as described in DSM-IV. Although diagnosis alone is not sufficient for treatment planning, there are practical reasons why diagnosis is necessary. First of all, insurance companies demand a diagnosis, and utilization review is done in reference to diagnosis. Second of all, treatment research is usually organized around specific diagnostic groups and the major symptoms comprising a diagnosis make a suitable way of evaluating the effectiveness of treatment. In order to profit from this research, one must know the patient's diagnosis. Third of all, parallel with the accumulation of knowledge in some areas in which diagnosis has specific and limiting characteristics, specialized treatment procedures and empirically supported, manualized treatments have been developed.

The diagnoses are related to treatment planning by: (1) indicating the outcome criteria of treatment as directly related to altering dysfunctional behavior, e.g., reducing depression; (2) highlighting mediating goals indirectly related to reduction of the criterion, e.g., changing cognitions related to depressive affect; (3) suggesting mediating goals related to coping with the criteria; (4) suggesting mediating goals related to improving social skills that overcome isolation with the disorder, e.g., social skills training for schizophrenic patients; and (5) indicating mediating goals related to modifying the environment of the patient, e.g., lowering of family expressed emotion (EE) for the schizophrenic patient.

At the same time, there are many reasons why diagnosis *alone* is not sufficient for treatment planning (Beutler & Clarkin, 1990). The criteria sets for the disorders are multiple, ever changing, and select different groups of patients. Thus, we will emphasize the mediating goals of treatment that are somewhat unique in their combination for each individual patient. Axis I patients may also have comorbid Axis I disorders, in addition to one or more Axis II disorders. One formulates treatment planning for individuals, not for isolated disorders.

We focus on Axis I and Axis II disorders for treatment planning. However, the combination of all five axes—a large array of possibilities—must be taken into account in treatment planning for the individual. Given the multiaxial nature of DSM-IV, the diagnosis is not limited to just Axis I (symptoms) and Axis II (personality disorders) considerations, but also to environmental stress (Axis IV) and level of overall functioning (Axis V). This is why there should be no surprise that several patients with the same Axis I disorder could and should receive quite different treatments. The Axis V or GAF rating may be of particular importance in treatment planning, serving as a simple index of the patient's level of functional impairment.

Let us briefly utilize each treatment decision point in reference to Nancy T. Based on the case description, Nancy definitely meets the diagnostic criteria for major depression, unipolar, chronic. She may qualify for the diagnosis of double depression, Major Depressive Disorder and chronic Dysthymic Disorder, but insufficient information is available to make this any more than an educated hunch. Her subjective complaints and the results of her Beck Anxiety Inventory also reveal the presence of diffuse anxiety. Because anxiety and depression frequently co-exist, the existence of a more specific and definable anxiety disorder cannot be determined at this point.

The case description yields multiple indications for one or more of the Cluster C personality disorders (avoidant or dependent): indecision, seeking others to assume responsibility, fear of aloneness, fear of abandonment, self-condemnation, paucity of assertion skills, exaggerated fears of being unable to care for herself, self-defeating patterns of behavior, people pleasing, fearful and vulnerable, self-conscious, and hypersensitivity to criticism. In addition, she presents with a distressed marriage and vague "financial problems," suggesting some situational disturbances as well. Collectively, Nancy presents with the type of complexity and multiplicity of problems that are common in clinical practice but which frequently have been ignored in treatment research.

PLANNING TREATMENT

Treatment planning invariably involves five interrelated decisions: treatment setting; treatment format; strategies and techniques; treatment intensity; and somatic treatments. The latter shall be considered separately in a subsequent section of this chapter.

Treatment Setting

The therapeutic setting is where the treatment occurs—a psychotherapist's office, a psychiatric hospital, a halfway house, an outpatient clinic, a medical ward, and so on. The choice of setting depends primarily on the relative need for restricting and supporting the patient due to the severity of psychopathology and the level of support in the patient's environment.

Each treatment decision is related to the other treatment decisions, as well as to certain patient variables, which will be considered later in this chapter. The optimal treatment setting, for example, is partially effected by level of symptomatic impairment and partially reflects resistance level. Those clients who are most impaired and resistant have the greatest need for a restrictive environment. The optimal treatment format, for another patient, may be based primarily on less objective qualities, such as client preferences and adequacy of social support.

Ambulatory treatment is always preferred over a restrictive treatment setting. Hospitalization would be needed only if dysphoria and suicidal ideation become exacerbated. Otherwise, there are no other pressing indications in this case for a setting other than outpatient care.

Treatment Format

The therapeutic format describes who directly participates in the treatment. The format is the interpersonal context within which the treatment is conducted. Each of the typical treatment formats—individual, group, and family—are characterized by a set of treatment parameters, all determined largely by the number and identities of the participants.

Nancy's distress level is high, as is apparently the marital distress. We believe that a multi-person format is indicated if social support systems are low and if one or more of the major problems involve a specific other person. Here, Nancy may be considered a candidate for both individual therapy and for couple therapy, if her husband is willing. Because of the low level of general support, additional efforts may be directed to increase her level of social and interpersonal involvement in support and reference groups. Because of the high levels of depression and anxiety and because of the longstanding nature of the depression, we would give priority to individual therapy initially as a means of establishing some strength and understanding before initiating concomitant multi-person treatment. As her florid symptomatology abates, we would anticipate efforts to engage her husband in a few sessions, at least for evaluative and educational purposes, and perhaps invite him in with success. Further evaluation of the relationship between personal psychopathology (the psyche) and marital functioning (the system) is needed in order to predict the degree to which Nancy's disorders will be responsive to therapeutically induced changes in the marital environment.

As her depression remits, as her awareness of her dependent patterns deepens, and if she is unsuccessful in developing external support groups, we would consider the possibility of open-ended group therapy. In a heterogeneous group of other patients, Nancy may be able to observe interactions, practice new ways of interacting, and receive feedback from others.

Strategies and Techniques

The choice of psychotherapeutic strategies and techniques depends upon the mediating goals of treatment. Technique—what a clinician actually *does* with a patient—most closely reflects the clinician's view of the etiological and maintaining factors of mental disorders.

The selection of therapeutic techniques and strategies is the most controversial component of the prescriptive model. Proponents of disparate theories endorse decidedly different views of what appear to be the same techniques, and any given technique can be used in vastly different ways. Thus, rather than focusing on specific techniques per se, we have adopted the strategy of prescribing general principles of change. These principles can be implemented in a number of ways and with a diversity of specific techniques. By mixing and matching procedures from different therapeutic traditions, we attempt to tailor the treatment to the particular patient while distinguishing mediating goals and therapist roles.

We are conservative in our approach and emphasize only those classes of technique that are supported by at least a modicum of outcome research (such as behavioral, cognitive-behavioral, experiential, interpersonal, psychodynamic, and systems family techniques). In addition, we have tried to classify techniques with the goal of treatment planning specifically in mind. In this situation, the clinician must determine specific mediating goals for each particular patient, given his or her unique diagnosis, environmental situation, and personality assets and liabilities.

As we have noted, most therapists cannot keep in mind more than three or four matching dimensions at once. Rather than addressing each of the many dimensions that we have discussed, we will illustrate the selection of three treatment dimensions: Focus on symptomatic versus thematic objectives, use of abreactive versus emotional control interventions, and level of therapist directiveness.

Focus on Symptomatic versus Thematic Objectives

Nancy's internalized coping style indicates the advisability of work that is directed at insight, awareness, and thematic change. Nonetheless, research suggests that these objectives will be better served if preceded by a period of time during which the therapist focuses directly on facilitating symptomatic change (Beutler, Clarkin, & Bongar, 2000). Thus, we will recommend that the first 6–10 sessions be focused on changing depressive and anxiety symptoms, with a shift to her avoidant/dependent personality style to follow.

The symptoms of greatest concern involve suicidal thoughts and social withdrawal. Thus, we would construct homework assignments that request Nancy to monitor these patterns and to begin experimenting by becoming involved with various social groups. Social groups, rather than therapy groups, will be helpful at this point in establishing a stronger base of social support from which she can experiment with change.

We will also focus on vegetative signs, offering her structure and training in how to establish more consistent sleep patterns and with plans to reconnect with people from whom she has withdrawn. If appetite problems are present, these too will be addressed with plans to encourage both exercise and a healthy diet.

The long-term goals of Nancy's treatment are likely to be intimately involved with her pattern of dependency and her persistent need to sacrifice herself for the good opinion and love of others. The genesis of this pattern will be sought in the nature of the relationship she had with her parents. It is notable that her father is described as very caring, and her mother as being rather cold and erratic. But it was her father not her mother who abandoned her. The therapist may want to develop a general theme around these observations that seems to fit other relationships, including the relationship with her husband, and interventions may be directed to helping her see how her primitive fears and expectations color this latter relationship and exacerbate her sense of hopelessness, depression, and anxiety.

Use of Abreactive versus Emotional Control Interventions

The decision to intervene by increasing or decreasing Nancy's anxiety would classically be made on theoretical grounds. We prefer to make this decision on the basis of Nancy's presentation. Currently, she suffers from considerable subjective distress, probably too high to be consistently motivational. Thus, we will exert direct efforts to reduce her sense of vulnerability and fear by providing support, structure, and practice in coping with stress. It may well be that Nancy simply has not learned to tolerate high distress; if so, we would model and practice methods to do so, probably giving her related handouts on distress tolerance skills (Linehan, 1993).

As her distress gradually subsides, we will begin to apply interventions that will maintain it at a level where it motivates change. That is, we will not attempt to reduce it too far for fear that the motivation for change may dissipate as well. The therapist should carefully navigate between providing support and providing confrontation and ambiguity, in order to retain the motivation at an optimal point.

Level of Therapist Directiveness

High resistance indicates the need for nondirective, self-directed, or paradoxical interventions, while low resistance indicates the patient's accessibility to a wider range of interventions, including therapist-controlled ones (Beutler, Sandowicz, Fisher, & Albanese, 1996). Since reactant or resistant women tend to be more decisive and action-oriented than nonreactive women (Dowd, Wallbrown, & Sanders, 1994), the use of nondirective, supportive, self-directed interventions should be included in the treatment. If the client is low-resistant, treatment can be more directive and structured (Beutler et al., 1996), which can include cognitive restructuring, advice, and behavior contracting.

We do not know how resistant Nancy will be; as a consequence, we do not know how directive to be with our interventions. She may be overtly cooperative but have some difficulty following through with assignments, using passive-aggressive styles of avoidance. We can make this determination by reviewing Nancy's history of previous treatment (e.g., did she follow through on assignments, appointments, and agreements), but her report may not be accurate and this type of material is not usually reported in notes received from those who have provided prior treatment. Accordingly, we may elect to initiate a "reactance challenge," an assignment that is designed to test her response to directives. This assignment is likely to involve some emotional arousal, be focused on a difficult topic, and include some confrontation with other people. In other words, it will be challenging.

We will observe Nancy's response to this "challenge" and use this information to construct hypotheses about how cooperative or resistant she is. If she proves to be passively resistant, we will turn to more nondirective interventions. Bibliotherapy and other self-directed interventions have also been found to be useful among highly resistant individuals since these procedures allow the patient to set their own course and directions (Beutler, Engle, et al., 1991).

Treatment Intensity

The intensity of a psychosocial treatment is the product of the *duration* of the treatment episode, the *length* of a session, and the *frequency* of contact. It may also involve the use of multiple interventions, such as both group and individual therapy or the use of both psychopharmacological and psychosocial interventions. Treatment intensity should be assigned as a function of the multiplicity of goals of treatment, the functional impairment associated with the disorder, and the presence or absence of a personality disorder. Brief treatments are obviously not for everyone, and many patients need long-term treatment or lifetime care, but the clinical research attention to brief therapy has pushed differential treatment planning forward by clarifying which patient conditions can profit from planned treatments of relatively brief duration (Norcross, Beutler, & Clarkin, 1998).

The treatment duration is more multifaceted. The major reference is to the duration of the *treatment episode*, that is, the time from evaluation to termination of this particular treatment period. Alternatively, one could consider the duration of each aspect of the total treatment package. For example, the total treatment package for one episode of a disorder may include different treatment settings (inpatient followed by outpatient), treatment formats (individual and family therapy), medications of various durations, and different strategies. Finally, treatment can be lifetime, that is, involving many episodes of treatment throughout the lifetime of a patient who has a chronic psychiatric condition such as schizophrenia or bipolar disorder.

Nancy's major depression, anxiety, marital distress, and probable avoidant/dependent personality imply a chronic course, and it is predictable that she is presenting for another episode of care. We would recommend one or two sessions per week for an initial period of 10 to 16 weeks. If functional impairment were worse, we would recommend more frequent contact. However, the chronicity of the condition suggests that, while 16 sessions may be sufficient to ameliorate the depressive and anxiety-based symptoms, the prevention of relapse and maintenance of improvement would be enhanced if we can continue therapy beyond 16 sessions.

THERAPEUTIC RELATIONSHIP

The selection of psychotherapy methods occurs within the sensitive and curative soil of the psychotherapeutic relationship. We will address these relationship issues shortly. For the moment, we will assume that the therapist has spent initial time developing a working relationship with Nancy, has established a contract for the treatment within the context of this relationship, and has been able to overcome the initially expected distrust and fear by establishing herself as a caring and attentive person.

In this relationship-building phase, the goals of treatment are identified, both for the individual patient and, in the event that conjoint therapy is initiated, for the couple; the level of intervention is identified; and the therapeutic relationship is established.

The foregoing pages illustrate what is actually a more complicated process of selecting therapeutic strategies and determining the optimal course of treatment for Nancy. It would be a colossal misunderstanding, however, to view this process as a disembodied, technique-oriented model of psychotherapy. Prescriptive eclectics attempt to customize not only therapy techniques but also relationship stances to individual clients. One way to conceptualize the matter, paralleling the notion of "treatments of choice" in terms of techniques, is how clinicians determine "therapeutic relationships of choice" in terms of interpersonal stances (Norcross, 1993b, 2002).

In the case of Nancy, we would probably tailor the therapeutic relationship to her coping style, interpersonal preferences, and stage of change, among other things. The relational style of the therapist can vary from behavioral to insight and from individual to interpersonal, consistent with the coping style developed and used most dominantly in the family. Coping style varies from being externalized/impulsive to internalized/self-punitive, with intermediate expressions in the form of cyclic/unstable and avoidant. Research is increasingly suggesting that it is the level of externalization that drives the decision as to whether one will intervene at the level of behavior or insight. While insight-oriented therapies may do well for internalizing individuals, the presence of externalizing behaviors—those that move against people—mitigate this influence (Beutler, Engle, et al., 1991; Beutler, Mohr, Grawe, et al., 1991).

Nancy presents with what appears to be an internalizing coping style. Hence, the strategies for change would be those that foster insight and emotional awareness. The techniques used to apply these strategies would vary from therapist to therapist, but may include such interventions as interpretations of the parent-child linkage, analysis of transference and resistance, review of recurrent themes, and exercises to enhance awareness of positive and negative feelings, beyond those dictated by her depression.

When ethically and clinically appropriate, we prefer to accommodate a client's relational preferences—when to be warm, tepid, or cool, when to be active or passive, and so on. As is unfortunately the case in most clinical presentations, the information presented on Nancy does not indicate her relational preferences: what she would like from the therapist in terms of level of activity, formality, closeness, structure, and so forth.

As a contemplator, Nancy would probably respond best initially to a caring, Socratic teacher style of relating. As she steadily moves into the action stage, we would fully anticipate the therapist role would concomitantly evolve into more of an experienced coach—providing training, giving tips, monitoring practice, and continually supporting her valiant efforts against the depression, anxiety, and characterological patterns that have defeated her for years. Once into the maintenance stage, the therapist would adopt almost a consultant style to help Nancy consolidate her gains, rely increasingly on herself and her emerging social resources, and assist her with relapse prevention.

INTEGRATION OF PHARMACOTHERAPY AND PSYCHOTHERAPY

The treatment planner has two major questions to answer regarding pharmacotherapy: Is psychotropic medication indicated and, if so, how should it be prescribed—which drug in which dosage at which frequency and for how long? In Nancy's case, she has both sought and received a prescription for an antidepressant, one of the selective serotonin reuptake inhibitors. Although she reports that the Zoloft 50 mg has reduced the insomnia, her continuing sleep disturbance, anergia, anhedonia, and suicidal ideation (including a vague plan) suggest a need for a dosage reevaluation or a change in medication altogether.

Diagnostic symptoms may serve two purposes. They are most useful as indicators of change. Thus, a periodic review of them can serve as an index of treatment effectiveness. In addition, however, the sheer number of symptoms, particularly vegetative symptoms, are prognostic indicators for the effectiveness of pharmacotherapy. While psychotherapy appears to be equally effective among those with a wide variety of severity and symptom levels, medication effects are more selective, and medication is most useful if vegetative signs and symptoms are significant in the diagnostic picture (Beutler, Clarkin, & Bongar, in press). This is certainly the case with Nancy.

It seems likely that, in view of its recent effects and in the presence of vegetative signs, Nancy may be helped by medication. There are treatment guidelines for this condition and the psychoeducational packet about the disorder could be given to and shared with her support system (Frances, Docherty, & Kahn, 1996).

Unlike some systems of psychotherapy, the integrative model is perfectly congenial with integrating pharmacotherapy and psychotherapy when clinically indicated. This position, of course, is consistent with the pluralism underlying treatment selection and prescriptive eclecticism.

RELAPSE PREVENTION

Maintenance treatment is indicated when the problem is complex, associated with moderate or high levels of functional impairment, and when a personality disorder is present. All these conditions apply to Nancy's case. It may also be indicated when the course of treatment is erratic and when symptom resolution is not consistently obtained within a period of six months. Nancy will probably require psychotherapy beyond the point at which overt symptoms of depression and anxiety dissipate. These later sessions will combine both coping skills training and working through of insight and interpersonal themes.

One strategy in attempting to improve long-term effectiveness of treatment is to provide patients with some form of booster sessions or additional treatments. The booster sessions would be considered additional therapy sessions that occur at some point in time after the termination of the initial treatment program. Although this strategy has not been found to be of unqualified success in all cases of depression, booster sessions can be effective for these patients. Some strategies that may be helpful will be to incorporate anti-relapse sessions prior to termination of therapy in which specific skills designed to prevent relapse are introduced.

ADDITIONAL INFORMATION DESIRED

We congratulate the editors on producing a realistically complex and challenging case. Nancy's chief complaints, socio-developmental history, medical status, and psychometric results are clearly presented in a balanced and nonpejorative manner. All these provide considerable (and probably sufficient) data for an Axis I diagnosis. Further information on the chronological course and pattern of her complaints would have assisted with differential diagnoses.

At the same time, the case description fails to adequately convey nondiagnostic and interpersonal information upon which most of our treatment selection is based and which the accumulating outcome research suggests should be the basis for a comprehensive treatment plan. Most fundamentally, what are Nancy's goals for psychotherapy? Assuredly, she seeks relief, but what else? Symptom relief, improved marriage, character change? What are Nancy's preferences for treatment modality (psychotherapy, pharmacotherapy, both), therapy format (individual, group, marital), therapy strategy (directive, exploratory, supportive), and therapist characteristics (gender, formal, disclosing)? Finally, we have little reliable information on Nancy's personality style and readiness to change. The four rating scales, all yielding useful data on symptomatic distress, say nothing about her unique personality. What is her reactance level, her interpersonal strivings, her stage of change?

SUMMARY AND DISCUSSION

Although necessarily simplified and condensed, this chapter outlines our integrative model of the conceptualization and treatment of unipolar depression as applied to Ms. Nancy T. Our aim has been to demonstrate the process of systematic treatment selection, a process that applies knowledge from multiple theoretical orientations on both diagnostic and nondiagnostic variables to the optimal choice of technical and interpersonal methods. Such a model posits that many treatment methods and therapeutic stances have a valuable place in the repertoire of the contemporary psychotherapist. The particular and differential place they occupy can be determined by outcome research and seasoned experience which places individual client needs at the center of the clinical enterprise. In the future, psychotherapy will be enhanced by selecting among extant technical and interpersonal processes in specific circumstances. Herein may ultimately lie the promise of the scientific *and* human enterprise known as psychotherapy (Norcross, Beutler, & Clarkin, 1998).

REFERENCES

Barlow, D. H. (1994). Psychological interventions in the era of managed competition. *Clinical Psychology: Science and Practice, 1,* 109–122.

Beutler, L. E. (1983). *Eclectic psychotherapy: A systematic approach.* New York: Pergamon.

Beutler, L. E. (1991). Have all won and must all have prizes? Revisiting Luborsky, et. al.'s verdict. *Journal of Consulting and Clinical Psychology, 59,* 226–232.

Beutler, L. E., & Baker, M. (1998). The movement towards empirical validation: At what level should we analyze and who are the consumers? In K. S. Dobson & K. D. Craig (Eds.), *Best practice: Developing and promoting empirically validated interventions* (pp. 43–65). Newbury Park, CA: Sage.

Beutler, L. E., & Berren, M. (Eds.). (1995). *Integrative assessment of adult personality.* New York: Guilford.

Beutler, L. E., & Clarkin, J. (1990). *Systematic treatment selection: Toward targeted therapeutic interventions.* New York: Brunner/Mazel.

Beutler, L. E., Clarkin, J., & Bongar, B. (2000). *Guidelines for the systematic treatment of the depressed patient.* New York: Oxford University Press.

Beutler, L. E., Consoli, A. J., & Williams, R. E. (1995). Integrative and eclectic therapies in practice. In B. Bongar & L. E. Beulter (Eds.), *Comprehensive textbook of psychotherapy.* New York: Oxford University Press.

Beutler, L. E., Engle, D., Mohr, D., Daldrup, R. J., Bergan, J., Meredith, K., & Merry, W. (1991). Predictors of differential response to cognitive, experiential and self-directed psychotherapeutic procedures. *Journal of Consulting and Clinical Psychology, 59,* 333–340.

Beutler, L. E., Goodrich, G., Fisher, D., & Williams, O. B. (1999). Use of psychological tests/instruments for treatment planning. In M. E. Maruish (Ed.), *The use of psychological tests for treatment planning and outcome assessment* (2nd ed., pp. 81–113). Hillsdale, NJ: Lawrence Erlbaum.

Beutler, L. E., & Harwood, T. M. (1995). How to assess clients in pretreatment planning. In J. N. Butcher (Ed.), *Clinical personality assessment* (pp. 59–77). New York: Oxford University Press.

Beutler, L. E., Kim, E. J., Davison, E., Karno, M., & Fisher, D. (1996). Research contributions to improving managed health care outcomes. *Psychotherapy, 33,* 197–206.

Beutler, L. E., Machado, P. P. P., Engle, D., & Mohr, D. (1993). Differential patient x treatment maintenance among cognitive, experiential, and self-directed psychotherapies. *Journal of Psychotherapy Integration, 3,* 15–30.

Beutler, L. E., Mohr, D. C., Grawe, K., Engle, D., & MacDonald, R. (1991). Looking for differential effects: Cross-cultural predictors of differential psychotherapy efficacy. *Journal of Psychotherapy Integration, 1,* 121–142.

Beutler, L. E., Sandowicz, M., Fisher, D., & Albanese, A. L. (1996). Resistance in psychotherapy: What can be concluded from empirical research? *In Session: Psychotherapy in Practice.*

Beutler, L. E., & Williams, O. B. (1995, July/Aug.). Computer applications for the selection of optimal psychosocial therapeutic interventions. *Behavioral Healthcare Tomorrow,* 66–68.

Burgoon, J. K., Beutler, L. E., Le Poire, B. A., Engle, D., Bergan, J., Salvio, M. A., & Mohr, D. C. (1993). Nonverbal indices of arousal in group psychotherapy. *Psychotherapy, 30,* 635–645.

Clarkin, J. F., Pilkonis, P. A., & Magruder, K. M. (1996). Psychotherapy of depression: Implications for health care reform. *Archives of General Psychiatry, 53,* 717–723.

Dowd, E. T., Wallbrown, F., & Sanders, D. (1994). Psychological reactance and its relationship to normal personality variables. *Cognitive Therapy and Research, 18,* 601–613.

Duncan, B. L., Solovey, A. D., & Rusk, G. S. (1992). *Changing the rules: A client-directed approach to therapy.* New York: Guilford.

Elkin, I. (1994). The NIMH treatment of depression collaborative research program: Where we began and where we are. In A. E. Bergin & S. L. Garfield (Eds.), *Handbook of psychotherapy and behavior change* (4th ed., pp. 114–139). New York: Wiley.

Elkin, I., Gibbons, R. D., Shea, M. T., & Shaw, B. F. (1996). Science is not a trial (but it can sometimes be a tribulation). *Journal of Consulting and Clinical Psychology, 64,* 92–103.

Elkin, I. E., Shea, T., Watkins, J. T., Imber, S. D., Stotsky, S. M., Collins, J. F., Glass, D. R., Pilkonis, P. A., Leber, W. R., Docherty, J. P., Fiester, S. J., & Parloff, M. B. (1989). National Institute of Mental Health Treatment of Depression Collaborative Research Program: General effectiveness of treatment. *Archives of General Psychiatry, 46,* 974–982.

Frances, A., Clarkin, J., & Perry, S. (1984). *Differential therapeutics in psychiatry.* New York: Brunner/Mazel.

Frances, A., Docherty, J. P., & Kahn, D. A. (1996). The expert consensus guideline series: Treatment of bipolar disorder. *Journal of Clinical Psychiatry, 57*(12A), 5–88.

Gaw, K. F., & Beutler, L. E. (1995). Integrating treatment recommendations. In L. E. Beutler & M. R. Berren (Eds.), *Integrative assessment of adult personality* (pp. 280–319). New York: Guilford.

Goldstein, A. P., & Stein, N. (1976). *Prescriptive psychotherapies.* New York: Pergamon.

Gotlib, I. H., Lewinsohn, P. M., & Seeley, J. R. (1995). Symptoms versus a diagnosis of depression: Differences in psychosocial functioning. *Journal of Consulting and Clinical Psychology, 63,* 90–100.

Gotlib, I. H., & Robinson, L. A. (1982). Responses to depressed individuals: Discrepancies between self-report and observer-rated behavior. *Journal of Abnormal Psychology, 91,* 231–240.

Groth-Marnat, G. (1997). *Handbook of psychological assessment* (3rd ed.). New York: Wiley.

Harwood, T. M., Beutler, L. E., Fisher, D., Sandowicz, M., Albanese, A. L., & Baker, M. (1997). Clinical decision making in managed health care. In J. N. Butcher (Ed.), *Personality assessment in managed health care* (pp. 13–41). New York: Oxford University Press.

Howard, K. I., Moras, K., Brill, P. L., Zoran, M., & Lutz, W. (1996). Evaluation of psychotherapy: Efficacy, effectiveness, and patient progress. *American Psychologist, 51,* 1059–1064.

Kopta, S. M., Howard, K. I., Lowry, J. L., & Beutler, L. E. (1994). Patterns of symptomatic recovery in time-unlimited psychotherapy. *Journal of Consulting and Clinical Psychology, 62,* 1009–1016.

Lambert, M. J. (1992). Psychotherapy outcome research: Implications for integrative and eclectic therapists. In J. C. Norcross & M. R. Goldfried (Eds.), *Handbook of psychotherapy integration.* New York: Basic Books.

Lambert, M. J., & Bergin, A. E. (1992). Achievements and limitations of psychotherapy research. In D. K. Freedheim (Ed.), *History of psychotherapy.* Washington, DC: American Psychological Association.

Lazarus, A. A. (1967). In support of technical eclecticism. *Psychological Bulletin, 21,* 415–416.

Lazarus, A. A. (1989). *The practice of multimodal therapy.* Baltimore: The Johns Hopkins University Press. (Originally published in 1981 by McGraw-Hill)

Lazarus, A. A. (1997). *Brief but comprehensive psychotherapy: The multimodal way.* New York: Springer.

Lazarus, A. A., Beutler, L. E., & Norcross, J. C. (1992). The future of technical eclecticism. *Psychotherapy, 29,* 11–20.

Linehan, M. M. (1993). *Cognitive-behavioral treatment of borderline personality disorder.* New York: Guilford.

Mohr, D. C., Beutler, L. E., Engle, D., Shoham-Salomon, V., Bergan, J., Kaszniak, A. W., & Yost, E. (1990). Identification of patients at risk for non-response and negative outcome in psychotherapy. *Journal of Consulting and Clinical Psychology, 58,* 622–628.

Nathan, P. E., & Gorman, J. M. (Eds.). (1998). *A guide to treatments that work.* New York: Oxford University Press.

Norcross, J. C. (Ed.). (1986). *Handbook of eclectic psychotherapy.* New York: Brunner/Mazel.

Norcross, J. C. (Ed.). (1987). *Casebook of eclectic psychotherapy.* New York: Brunner/Mazel.

Norcross, J. C. (1991). Prescriptive matching in psychotherapy: An introduction. *Psychotherapy, 28,* 439–443.

Norcross, J. C. (Ed.). (1993a). Research directions for psychotherapy integration: A roundtable. *Journal of Psychotherapy Integration, 3,* 91–131.

Norcross, J. C. (1993b). The relationship of choice: Matching the therapist's stance to individual clients. *Psychotherapy, 30,* 402–403.

Norcross, J. C. (1994). *Prescriptive eclectic therapy.* Videotape in the APA Psychotherapy Videotape Series. Washington, DC: American Psychological Association.

Norcross, J. C., & Beutler, L. E. (1997). Determining the therapeutic relationship of choice in brief therapy. In J. N. Butcher (Ed.), *Objective psychological assessment in managed health care: A practitioner's guide.* New York: Oxford University Press.

Norcross, J. C., Beutler, L. E., & Clarkin, J. F. (1998). Prescriptive eclectic psychotherapy. In R. Dorfman (Ed.), *Paradigms of clinical social work.* New York: Brunner/Mazel.

Norcross, J. C., & Goldfried, M. R. (Eds.). (1992). *Handbook of psychotherapy integration.* New York: Basic.

Paul, G. L. (1967). Strategy of outcome research in psychotherapy. *Journal of Consulting Psychology, 31,* 109–119.

Prochaska, J. C., DiClemente, C. C., & Norcross, J. C. (1992). In search of how people change: Applications to addictive behaviors. *American Psychologist, 47,* 1102–1114.

Prochaska, J. O., & Norcross, J. C. (1998). *Systems of psychotherapy: A transtheoretical analysis* (fourth edition). Pacific Grove, CA: Brooks/Cole.

Prochaska, J. O., Norcross, J. C., & DiClemente, C. C. (1994). *Changing for good.* New York: William Morrow.

Prochaska, J. O., Rossi, J. S., & Wilcox, N. S. (1991). Change processes and psychotherapy outcome in integrative case research. *Journal of Psychotherapy Integration, 1,* 103–120.

Shoham-Salomon, V., & Hannah, M. T. (1991). Client-treatment interactions in the study of differential change processes. *Journal of Consulting and Clinical Psychology, 59,* 217–225.

Sotsky, S. M., Glass, D. R., Shea, T. M., Pilkonis, P. A., Collins, J. F., Elkin, I., Watkins, J. T., Imber, S. D., Leber, W. R., Moyer, J., & Oliveri, M. E. (1991). Patient predictors of response to psychotherapy and pharmacotherapy: Findings in the NIMH Treatment of Depression Collaborative Research Program. *American Journal of Psychiatry, 148,* 997–1008.

Thorne, F. C. (1950). *Principles of personality counseling.* Brandon, VT: Journal of Clinical Psychology.

Thorne, F. C. (1967). The structure of integrative psychology. *Journal of Clinical Psychology, 23,* 3–11.

SUGGESTED READINGS

Beutler, L. E., & Clarkin, J. (1990). *Systematic treatment selection: Toward targeted therapeutic interventions.* New York: Brunner/Mazel.

Beutler, L. E., Clarkin, J., & Bongar, B. (2000). *Guidelines for the systematic treatment of the depressed patient.* New York: Oxford University Press.

Norcross, J. C. (Ed.). (2002). *Psychotherapy relationships that work.* New York: Oxford University Press.

Norcross, J. C., & Beutler, L. E. (1997). Determining the therapeutic relationship of choice in brief therapy. In J. N. Butcher (Ed.), *Objective psychological assessment in managed health care: A practitioner's guide.* New York: Oxford University Press.

Norcross, J. C., & Goldfried, M. R. (Eds.). (1992). *Handbook of psychotherapy integration.* New York: Basic.

Prochaska, J. O., Norcross, J. C., & DiClemente, C. C. (1995). *Changing for good.* New York: Avon.

16

Psychopharmacology of Major Depression

Ilpo T. Kaariainen

The case of Nancy provides an excellent opportunity to discuss the psychopharmacologic approach to the treatment of depressive illnesses. Like many patients, she presents with a complicated mixture of depression and anxiety. The time course of her illness is vague at points, and she describes rapid and impressive fluctuations in symptoms. Numerous family and professional stresses have likely influenced how she has experienced her depression and may well have contributed etiologically. The complicated interweaving of factors make this story an ideal one for considering questions of if and how to address depressive symptoms with medications.

Textbook cases are found in textbooks. Although they provide useful guidelines for practice, they often leave clinicians wrestling with the complicated twists and wrinkles of "real life" patients. When evaluating patients for the appropriateness of a medication trial, it is best to begin with a balanced consideration of the nature of the complaints, symptom course, psychological and social factors that may be contributing to their distress, as well as the patient's personal values. Ignoring the unique life that is the context for the disorder, in favor of a "target symptom" approach, is simplistic and inadequate. An empathic interview focusing on the whole person and not merely the disease is more likely to foster a better therapeutic relationship. The importance of the quality of the doctor-patient relationship cannot be overstated. Often desperate patients in the midst of illness may derive hope from a healer who is also perceived as an advocate. Moreover, a trusting and supportive rapport can only help with medication compliance. Even patients of sophisticated practitioners, who accurately diagnose various depressive state disorders, will likely benefit from a more person-oriented practice of psychopharmacology.

In this chapter we will discuss evidence of biological contributions to unipolar depression and will review the general principles of medication management of this disorder. This will be followed by discussions of the case study and recent advances in psychopharmacology of depression.

THE BIOLOGY OF DEPRESSION

Important as considering the whole person is in the practice of modern psychiatry, psychopharmacology is firmly grounded in neurobiology. The basic belief is that depression is a medical illness with a biological substrate. Biological and environmental factors interact to produce a specific clinical scenario. Although competing hypotheses have been put forth, the "monoamine hypothesis of depression" has remained a seminal one for nearly four decades. The core concept is that an abnormality in one or more of three main central nervous system monoamine neurotransmitter systems, norepinephrine, serotonin and dopamine, underlies depression. Proposed mechanisms for the development of such abnormalities include both genetic predisposition and acquired central nervous system changes as a consequence of interactions with the psychosocial environment. The ongoing abnormality in the neurotransmitter system would maintain the state of depression, with clinical deterioration or improvement being related to dynamic changes of human physiology.

Although it has been known for some time that monoamine neurotransmitters may play a role in clinical depression, the specific mechanisms of this effect remain unclear. Recent work focuses on understanding neurobehavioral systems, neural circuits, and the role of regulatory mechanisms (Thase, 2000). A developing understanding of functional neuroanatomy (Panksepp, 2000) and the role of second messenger regulatory systems within nerve cells supplements our basic understanding of the importance of monoamine neurotransmitter abnormalities in depression. This is consistent with the observation that all effective medications for depression manipulate one or more of these systems. They appear to function by "correcting" or "reequilibrating" the putative biochemical aberrations in order to restore health. With regards to our patient, Nancy, it is postulated that by restoring a deficiency in one or more of these neurotransmitter systems, with the subsequent downstream changes in receptors and second messenger systems, the "state" depression could remit.

It is worth keeping in mind that discussions of a "cure" imply a sustained remission of symptoms with restoration of adaptive functioning. In this model, maintaining appropriate functioning of the relevant neurotransmitter systems would be required for optimal results. This might be achieved through ongoing medications, or by bringing about a more permanent central nervous system change. Looking ahead with the humility which must accompany speculation, one might envision stable central nervous system changes brought about through sustained medications. Further in the future, one might envision gene therapy for individuals with a significant genetic predisposition to develop a major affective disorder.

Clinical depression, as defined in the DSM-IV, is a stable, recurrent and reliably diagnosable clinical entity. We know that neurobiological factors play a role in etiology and maintenance of the disorder. It appears, for example, that relationships exist between structural brain lesions and mood (Robinson et al., 1984, 1995). Using computerized tomography, they observed associations between stroke-related lesions and the valence and severity of affective symptoms. Severity of post-stroke depression is related to the proximity of the lesion to the left frontal pole, and negatively related to proximity to the right frontal pole. These findings are consistent with evidence indicating that individual differences exist in the activation of the left and right frontal lobes and that these differences may be involved in the expression and experience of emotional states (Davidson, 1993, 1998). Davidson and his colleagues proposed a diathesis stress model in which hemispheric asymmetries in cortical activity become apparent when activated by an environmental stress or an affective challenge (Davidson, 1992). More recently, imaging studies have demonstrated diminished hippocampal (Steffens, 2000) and orbital frontal cortex volumes (Lai, 2000) in depressed geriatric patients. There also appear to be relationships between depression and neuroendocrine activity. Associations have been observed, for example, between depression and activity of the Hypothalamic-Pituitary-Adrenal,

Hypothalamic-Pituitary-Thyroid and Hypothalamic-Pituitary-Growth Hormone Axes (Musselman et al., 1998). Evidence exists, as well, of relationships between lateralized brain activation and mood. Baxter et al. (1985, 1989), for example, used functional imaging techniques, including PET and SPECT, to demonstrate diminished metabolism in the left lateral dorsal prefrontal cortex of depressed patients relative to control subjects.

Finally, there is provisional evidence of genetic contributions to vulnerability for depression. The results of twin studies, for example, suggest that genetic factors may contribute to the risk of developing unipolar depression (Kendler et al., 1992, 1993). In a meta-analysis of five studies, Sullivan et al. (2000) concluded that major depression is a familial disorder, and that it is primarily due to genetic influences. Although we do not yet have a full understanding of the neurobiology or neurogenetics of depression, or of the ways in which biological and psychosocial factors interact in contributing to risk, biological factors have clearly been implicated in the etiology and maintenance of certain depressive conditions.

In addition to medications, recent advances in the biological treatment of depression have included safer ECT, light therapy for seasonal affective disorder, and experimental work with repetitive Transcranial Magnetic Stimulation (Berman et al., 2000).

Progress in understanding the biological substrate of major affective disorders requires an understanding of the brain's functional organization. The mesolimbic system plays a central role in mood regulation. Serotonin, norepinephrine, and dopamine all are formed by a similar two-step modification of the amino acids L-Tryptophan and L-Tyrosine. Serotonin is formed by a hydroxylation reaction (addition of an OH group) of L-Tryptophan, followed by a decarboxylation reaction (removal of a CO_2 group). L-Tyrosine undergoes similar changes, albeit by different enzymes specific for that amino acid to form dopamine. When needed, a further hydroxylation reaction converts dopamine to norepinephrine (Montgomery, 1990). It is believed that antidepressant medications function by effecting the production, storage, release, and removal of these functionally active neurotransmitters.

EMPIRICAL EVIDENCE SUPPORTING THE APPROACH

The first effective antidepressant was an antitubercular medication, Iproniazid, which was observed to elevate mood (Loomer et al., 1957).

Although effective, the popularity of Monoamine Oxidase Inhibitors (MAOI), such as Iproniazid, declined, as side effects for these medications became known. Potentially catastrophic cardiovascular reactions can occur when MAOIs are mixed with foods containing tyramines (including many processed meats, cheeses and red wine). Although safer, more selective MAOI medications were developed, they never regained their status as first line treatment.

The ability of medications to relieve depression had, nonetheless, been demonstrated, and the search for increasingly more specific targets within the monoamine neurotransmitter system began. These included Tricyclic Antidepressants (TCA), followed by the Selective Serotonin Reuptake Inhibitors (SSRI) and atypical antidepressants, such as, Venlafaxine, Nefazodone, Trazodone, and Mirtazapine.

The first tricyclic antidepressant compound, Imipramine, was shown to be effective in elevating moods in depressed schizophrenic patients and subsequently in patients with unipolar depression (Kuhn, 1970). After Glowinski and Axelrod (1964) suggested a relationship between Imipramine's ability to inhibit the reuptake of both serotonin and norepinephrine and it's antidepressant properties, a number of related medications including Desipramine, Nortiptyline and Amitriptyline were developed. Anticholinergic side effects, including dry mouth, constipation, blurred vision, and orthostatic hypotension, however, are common with TCAs and can be a treatment limiting concern.

The first Selective Serotonin Reuptake Inhibitor developed for the treatment of depression was Fluoxetine (Beasley et al., 1991). The superior safety and side effect profile of this medication quickly made it a first line choice for the pharmacotherapy of depression. The fact that it was no longer necessary to conduct preliminary cardiac assessments or to regularly monitor blood levels contributed to the popularity of SSRIs and allowed primary care providers to begin treating depression with greater confidence.

The antidepressant properties of these medications are associated with their ability to raise central nervous system levels of serotonin. This is congruent with studies showing low CSF concentrations of 5-HIAA, the principal serotonin metabolite, in depressed patients (Asberg et al., 1976). Finally, after successful treatment of depression with SSRI antidepressants, restricting Tryptophan from diets, a known strategy for rapidly lowering central nervous system serotonin levels, has been associated with a relapse of depressive symptoms (Smith et al., 1997), suggesting that diminished serotonin production or transmission may be associated with depressive symptoms.

As Fluoxetine's efficacy became evident, several other SSRI medications, including Sertraline, Paroxetine, Fluvoxamine, and Citalopram were developed. All of these medications function by inhibiting the reuptake of serotonin from the interneuronal synapse, resulting in elevated synaptic serotonin levels. There is, as a consequence, a downregulation of beta receptors in the postsynaptic neuron and a reduction in the production of cAMP (Hollister, 1992). If and how these changes produce an antidepressant effect is not known. However, the consistent efficacy of medications with these properties suggest that these postsynaptic changes may be initial steps in the regulation of mood. More recently, Buproprion has been found to have antidepressant properties. Buproprion is an atypical antidepressant and has been found to have no affinity for dopamine D_2 or $5\text{-}HT_2$ receptors, and weak affinity for histamine H_1 and α_1-adrenoceptors. It has effects on serotonin and norepinephrine reuptake, and is a relatively selective dopamine reuptake inhibitor (Feighner et al., 1991), reconfirming the role of dopaminergic functioning in clinical depression.

Most modern atypical antidepressants target several strategic serotonergic or adrenergic receptors or combine the reuptake inhibition of several monoamine neurotransmitters. This serves to achieve better results and to reach subgroups of patients who may not have responded other strategies. Mirtazapine (Schatzberg, 2000), for example, targets $5\text{-}HT_2$, $5\text{-}HT_3$, and α_2 receptor sites. In a similar manner, Venlafaxine is both an SSRI and a norepinephrine reuptake inhibitor. It is available in both short and extended release preparations (Amsterdam, 1998). Nefazodone, another novel antidepressant (Feighner et al., 1998), and its cousin, Trazodone (Cusack et al., 1994), are postsynaptic serotonin receptor antagonists. Both demonstrate modest serotonin reputake inhibition properties. Trazodone is a relatively weak norepinephrine uptake blocker and primarily antagonizes post-synaptic $5\text{-}HT_2$ receptors. As it can be quite sedating, it is commonly used as a non-bezodiazepine hypnotic in clinical practice.

The evidence for the effectiveness of antidepressant medications, as a group, is strong. The improved safety and side effect profiles of newer antidepressant medications translate into very real quality of life benefits for patients. The overall efficacy of antidepressant medications is approximately 65% versus 30% for placebo for any given medication. Psychomotor retardation and anhedonia appear to be the best predictors of a favorable medication response, at least for Tricyclic Antidepressants (Downig & Rickels, 1973). In general, long durations of symptoms correlate with a negative treatment outcome (Keller et al., 1984).

Although studies comparing SSRIs with tricyclic antidepressants have shown similar efficacies between the two types of medications (Feighner et al., 1993; McGrath, 2000), data indicate that tricyclic antidepressants may be more effective than SSRI's for patients with melancholic depression (Roose et al., 1994). Although Monoamine Oxidase Inhibitors appear to be particularly effective for treating atypical depression (McGrath et al., 2000), and the tricyclic antidepressant, Nortriptyline, may be more effective than the SSRI, Fluoxetine, for post-stroke depression (Robinson et al., 2000), there is little consistent evidence to support the selection of one agent over another in most clinical situations. The initial choice of a medication involves a consideration of clinical circumstances, such as atypical symptoms, severe melancholia, or a post-stroke depression, and trying to optimize the "fit" between a given medication's known side effects with a given patient. For example, one may want to avoid anticholinergic agents, such as amitriptyline or paroxetine, in elderly male patients with benign prostate hypertrophy. A depressed patient who also suffers from irritable bowel syndrome, however, would not only benefit from the antidepressant properties of these same medications, but might also experience improvement of the bowel symptoms due to their anticholinergic properties.

Sequential trials with several agents improve the chances of achieving a positive outcome. Typically, one of the SSRI or atypical antidepressants are tried for four to eight weeks. If there is no response, and noncompliance is not suspected, a second SSRI or a different atypical is a reasonable next choice. Many clinicians will change classes of medications, for example an SSRI to an atypical or a tricyclic. The key is to make sure that an adequate trial is achieved, both in terms of dose and duration. If significant side effects persist, it may be necessary to change to a different medication to reduce the risk of non-compliance. It is worth acknowledging, however, that fully 10–30% of patients do not receive meaningful help from psychotropic medications (Nierenberger, 1991). Augmentation strategies may be helpful should this occur. These include the addition of complimentary antidepressants, Lithium, thyroid hormone, or stimulant medications such as Ritalin. A recent study provided encouraging results with chronically depressed patients receiving the atypical antidepressant, Nefazodone, and a variant of cognitive-behavioral therapy (Keller et al., 2000). This is a provocative and important finding, and is clearly in need of replication with a more heterogenous sample of chronically depressed adults.

CASE CONCEPTUALIZATION

There are three issues to consider when conceptualizing a case of depression for a medication trial. The first goal is to establish a clear diagnosis of a depressive state, as opposed to a nonspecific reactive disorder or trait related symptoms. The next priority is to clarify the history of the illness with regards to date of onset, chronicity, number of episodes, and severity of illness. One needs to evaluate suicide risk and assess the effect of the disorder on social and professional functioning, as well as to be aware of complicating factors. These include medical illnesses, the use of other medications or recreational drugs, and psychosocial issues which might influence compliance.

Nancy is a thirty-two year old professionally successful, unhappily married, Catholic, Caucasian female who presents for help with "recurrent subjective severe feelings of depression, anxiety, and confusion." She perceives her troubles as originating from a "dysfunctional childhood." Nancy states that she feels "overwhelmed" by her life and "really negative about herself and everything in the situation." By focusing on what the patient perceives as her main concerns and what she believes to be the causes of her depression, one can establish a strong doctor-patient alliance. The psychopharmacologist can help to reformulate the situation in a way that will allow the patient to accept medications as a reasonable strategy. For example, Nancy may be more likely to believe medications might be helpful if she can accept the possibility that biological factors may contribute to her depression, instead of focusing exclusively on her childhood and current marital problems.

Growing up, Nancy described "a lack of stability in her family." Her father suffered from a recurrent psychotic disorder, probably schizophrenia, and Nancy felt a role reversal, actually caring for him. She recalled that he was caring at times, but violent at others. He left the family to return to Poland when Nancy was twelve, and she distinctly remembers feeling "abandoned." The family history of depressive illness in both her mother and sister is important. The loss of a parenting figure and strong family history for psychiatric illness are both risk factors for depression. This supports the emerging impression of an individual who is suffering from clinical depression rather than an adjustment reaction. Nancy may, therefore, benefit from a medication trial.

After a childhood during which she felt unempowered to make many decisions, Nancy found herself in adult relationships where she "tends to become totally absorbed by the other person . . . and I look for them to protect and take care of me." Her self-doubts and poor self-esteem stand in contrast to her professional success. She received a bachelor's degree from a prestigious university, enrolled in graduate education, and works as the art director of a large manufacturing company. Her marriage, however, has not been a happy one. Consistent with her difficulty with decision making and her desire to be cared for, she has been unable to make a decision about leaving him and feels trapped in an unhappy marriage. Appreciating the dissatisfaction Nancy experiences in her relationships and her general unhappiness with life alerts the clinician to the importance of being realistic about what can be accomplished with medications. It will be important to discuss this with her.

We do not have much information about Nancy's mood during her childhood and adolescence, although she was clearly frustrated and unhappy at times. Unhappiness alone, of course, does not depression make. Her good academic performance and lack of social isolation or behavioral difficulties suggest an absence of mood disorders at that time. She may well have been suffering, however, from a lower amplitude or more chronic depressive disorder through those years.

In her early twenties Nancy begins to experience characteristic symptoms of depression. She recalls feeling depressed and anxious during her courtship. These feelings escalated over the next eighteen months. She recalled experiencing sadness, crying, impaired memory and concentration, anhedonia and an intensification of her difficulty with decision making. She also described an increase in appetite with accompanying weight gain, sleep disruption, fatigue and an increased interpersonal irritability. Although some palpitations accompanied her anxiety and depression, no panic attacks were described. This part of her story provides the valuable information for making a diagnosis of major depression. Given her longstanding dissatisfaction with many aspects of her life, the importance definitively making a diagnosis of an affective state disorder is of paramount importance before recommending medications.

The absence of alcohol or other substance abuse is also important. If present, a dual-diagnosis approach would be necessary. If Nancy's history had been complicated by substance use, one might recommend a trial of rehabilitation treatment to determine if sobriety would bring relief of her depressive symptoms before initiating a medication trial. Fortunately that is not the case.

Although Nancy was clearly suffering, to the point of developing a suicide plan, the degree to which this episode of depression affected her social and occupational functioning is not clear. No suicide attempts were reported and she went through a ten year period without treatment. What is important, but not known, is the course of her symptoms during this time. That is, did she proceed to recover to her baseline after some months, did she remain in this state of depression for the next ten years, or did she have a partial recovery with intermittent symptom exacerbations? Also important is the absence of any symptoms suggestive of mania or psychosis. This is important, given the powerful genetic load for schizophrenia in her family. A clinical impression of psychosis, however subtle, would broaden the differential diagnosis to include Depression with Psychotic features, Schizoaffective Disorder, Depressed Type, and mild Schizophrenia. Her level of functioning argues against the latter diagnoses, but the presence of such symptoms would alter the medication recommendations to include an antipsychotic medication.

Finally, the observation that her feelings of depression intensified predictably during the weekends and in certain social situations is noteworthy. This suggests that even though a mood disorder is present, the contribution of environmental factors must be considered. The possibility of personality traits contributing to her distress in these social situations is real. Although the potential benefits of a medication trial remain, this might suggest a less optimistic prognosis for complete symptom remission.

BEGINNING AND FRAMING TREATMENT

Based upon her report, Nancy appears to meet DSM-IV criteria for:

I.   Major Depressive Disorder, Moderate, Recurrent
      Rule Out Dysthymia (double depression)
II.   Dependent Personality Traits
III. None
IV.   Marriage stresses
V.   70

Medications are best at alleviating symptoms that are part of state disorders, including dysphoria, mania and psychosis. The effectiveness of antidepressant medications for resolving acute "state disorder" episodes of depression have been shown in several trials. Relevant to Nancy, tricyclic antidepressants and SSRI's have been shown to be effective in preventing recurrence of depressive symptoms in patients with multiple episodes of depression (Kupfer, 1992). As noted, an atypical antidepressant, Nefazodone, was shown to be effective, when combined with a form of cognitive therapy, in patients with chronic depression (Keller, 2000). This approach might be considered in Nancy's case if a chronic course was confirmed.

Although effective in treating depression, medications do not fix marriages, provide fulfillment in life, or make people happy. In spite of Nancy's professional success, she expresses considerable dissatisfaction with her marriage and her life in general. Her social concerns will not be remedied by any medication currently on the market. With this in mind, Nancy would likely benefit from either individual or group therapy.

Although Nancy's depressive symptoms may be helped with antidepressant medications, without psychotherapy she will likely remain dissatisfied with many aspects of her life. The realistic goals of a medication trial would be to alleviate her feelings of sadness, anxiety, and hopelessness, to normalize her sleep and appetite, and to resolve her suicidal ideations. One would expect a significant improvement in four to eight weeks and a return to full or near-full productive functioning over several months. Given her long history of depressive episodes without full recovery, and the possibility that this might represent a single refractory depression, she will also likely benefit from maintenance treatment. This would entail full treatment doses of whichever agent restored her mood to euthymia. Secondary goals would include optimizing her work performance and allowing her to work on issues related to her marriage.

TREATMENT

When performing a medication evaluation, the initial task of the psychopharmacologist is to insure a correct diagnosis. The next step is to assess symptom severity in order to determine the urgency of intervention and whether a outpatient plan can be devised. The goal is to implement a safe and effective plan with an eye toward health maintenance, once clinical improvement has occurred.

In Nancy's case, the working diagnosis is major depression and the initial priority is to insure her safety. Although the majority of patients with depression do not commit suicide, up to 15% of untreated or treatment resistant patients do (Bulik et al., 1990). The task of predicting suicide risk remains a difficult task. Until recently, clinicians were limited to weighing long-term suicide risk factors, including male gender, co-morbid alcohol or other substance abuse, age greater than 65, and the presence a chronic medical illness (Slaby, 1998). A recent prospective study identified six factors associated with suicide within one year, including panic attacks, severe psychic anxiety, global insomnia, poor concentration, active alcohol abuse and anhedonia (Fawcett et al., 1990). Although Nancy manifests symptoms of anxiety, anhedonia and diminished concentration; the absence of panic attacks, alcohol use, or global insomnia, as well as, the lack of prior suicide attempts, allows an outpatient plan to be initiated.

Having determined it safe to initiate treatment in the outpatient setting, it will be necessary to gauge the degree of social and professional dysfunction. This allows monitoring of treatment progress and provides another method for assessing severity of illness. Nancy's ability to maintain meaningful relations and an ongoing productive work schedule, in spite of her depression, are reassuring. In addition to focusing on the patient's functioning, one may also use objective rating scales, such as the HRSD (Hamilton, 1960) and the BDI (Beck, Steer, & Garbin, 1988), to assess severity and monitor progress.

The decision to treat depression with medications is justified by the presence of severe symptomatology, significant social and professional dysfunction, psychotic symptoms, or the presence of significant suicidal ideations. Although Cognitive Behavioral Therapy and Interpersonal Therapy are recognized as excellent alternatives for mild to moderate depression, with severely depressed patients, those with a prior response to medication, or anyone requesting a pharmacological approach, a medication trial may be justified. It is important to note that a recent "mega-analysis" suggested that CBT may also be effective in treating patients with severe Major Depression (DeRubeis et al., 1999). Two newer antidepressants, Fluoxetine and Bupropion, have also been found to be effective for treating chronically depressed patients (Thase et al., 2000). These data underscore the importance of an open-minded, but critical, review of new information, as one formulates a treatment plan in this rapidly changing field.

Nancy's suicidal ideations are intermittent and, although she developed a passive plan, she appears to have minimal intent. She is subjectively suffering, however, and has doubtlessly not been performing at her potential during much of the past decade. Before moving onto the choice of an antidepressant, it is worth reiterating the importance of probing for a history of mania or psychosis. In very depressed patients, somatic delusions may be difficult to detect. Even subtle signs of psychosis would require a revision of the diagnosis and would change the treatment plan to include an antipsychotic medication with the antidepressant or to consider ECT. A history of mania or hypomania would also change the diagnosis and would suggest the use of a mood stabilizer. As neither scenario is present in the case of Nancy, a course of antidepressant monotherapy is the most appropriate initial strategy.

There are currently over twenty different antidepressant medications available. Because of their safety and favorable side effect profiles, the initial choice of an SSRI medication has become the standard of care in the medication management of depression. The choice of Sertraline by Nancy's family doctor is reasonable and the starting dose of 50 mg is sensible. One might reasonably have chosen one of the other SSRIs, however. The novel antidepressants, including Nefazodone, Venlafaxine, and Mirtazapine are also gaining popularity as first line agents for many practitioners. Some practitioners also rely on family treatment history to guide the initial choice of medications. That is, one may select an agent known to be effective in treating the patient's parent or sibling.

Some anxious patients cannot tolerate the standard starting doses due to an initial serotonin activation syndrome. They may experience a paradoxical increase in anxiety for several days. Therefore, as with geriatric patients, it can be helpful to initiate treatment of the anxious depressed patient at half the standard starting dose. For some commonly used medications, this translates into 25 mg of Sertraline, 10 mg of Paroxetine, 5 or 10 mg of Fluoxetine, and 10 mg of Citalopram. If significant anxiety or panic symptoms are present, one may also initiate simultaneous benzodiazepine coverage to provide immediate anxiolysis for three to fourteen days, depending on the individual patient, with a goal of eventual antidepressant monotherapy.

During the initial visit it is important to screen for common medical causes of depression. These include thyroid and adrenal diseases, as well as chronic medical disorders or malignancies. A return visit is scheduled in three or four weeks to assess progress. If the patient is severely depressed, but not in need of admission, it is advisable to see them again in one to two weeks. A verbal contract for the patient to call or to present at the emergency room should difficulties arise provides a second layer of comfort, but is not a substitute for ongoing personal contact with the psychopharmacologist which communicates a caring attitude, and allows for ongoing assessment of progress.

Nancy's four week trial of 50 mg of Sertraline is reasonable. As she has demonstrated only a minimal response of improving sleep, it is advisable to raise the dose to 75 or 100 mg. We would reassess her progress in four weeks and again increase by 25–50 mg increments to a maximum dose of 200 mg over a total of 16 weeks of monitoring. If Nancy demonstrates a more robust response at a lower dose, such as 100 mg, or does not tolerate a higher dose due to side effects, it would be reasonable to monitor her longer at that dose—assuming ongoing improvement is occurring. Given the presence of atypical symptoms, including interpersonal reactivity and hyperphagia, Nancy might be a candidate for an MAO-I trial, if several other medications, fail to produce an adequate result (Liebowitz et al., 1988). One reasonable course would be to follow the Sertraline trial with a second SSRI agent, followed by one of the atypical antidepressants if the second trial was not successful. Alternatively, one might switch classes immediately and follow the Sertraline trial with one of the atypical antidepressants, including Mirtazapine, Nefazodone, and Venlafaxine. If she was still not responding, one might consider a different atypical agent or a Tricyclic antidepressant. Given a motivated and compliant patient, one might certainly try a MAO-I agent sooner, with an understanding that the improved likelihood of response would be at the expense of considerable dietary adjustments.

Once she is symptomatically in remission, and is not experiencing significant side effects, I would monitor her once every two to three months if she is also receiving psychotherapy. If she has declined therapy she should be seen more regularly.

THERAPEUTIC RELATIONSHIP

The relationship between a patient and the psychiatrist is a therapeutic one by definition. The interactions are intended to alleviate symptoms, prevent recurrences, and maximize functioning and satisfaction with life. When medications are employed for treatment, this relationship is affected by a number of practical issues. The first issue is the relative urgency for reaching a diagnosis in order to initiate a medication trial. As medications for depression take weeks to work and are frequently prescribed for "sicker" patients (i.e., suicidal, psychotic, catatonic, etc), the need to quickly initiate treatment often weighs heavily on the clinician's mind. This contrasts with the option of a longer diagnostic process when seeing less depressed patients or ones with clinical conditions not requiring medications. In the latter scenario the process of having the patient "tell their story" in a safe and confidential place can be an important part of the treatment.

The next consideration in forming a strong therapeutic alliance is the time constraints imposed by modern medical practice. Diagnostic evaluations are typically completed in one 45 to 90 minute session, followed by fifteen to twenty minute visits. Few payors permit weekly medication management visits, other than during crises or the initial stabilization period. Therefore, depressed patients receiving medications who are candidates for outpatient treatment will be seen for an initial diagnostic session followed by brief follow up appointments every three to four weeks initially, and then every two to three months.

Monitoring a medication trial requires us to assess not only the patient's progress and improvement, but also potential side effects and drug-drug interactions. This is especially true for medically ill patients, who comprise a significant portion of depressed patients. The need to regularly inquire about relatively technical and mundane matters, such as hours of sleep, bowel habits, dryness of mouth, and the like can make it difficult for the psychiatrist to maintain a positive therapeutic relationship during these brief visits. It is not surprising, then, that a striking percentage of patients prematurely discontinue their medications. Over 25% of patients discontinue treatment after the first month, and nearly 45% terminate care by the third month (Lin et al., 1995). A recent review of drug utilization studies revealed that medication discontinuation rates after 10 weeks ranged from 30%–48% (Linden et al., 2000). The reasons for patients discontinuing medications are many and certainly include side effects. Many of these practical problems could be overcome by a skilled psychopharmacologist if the quality of the relationship permits them to be addressed.

INTEGRATION OF PSYCHOTHERAPY WITH MEDICATION

Nancy, like other depressed patients with significant interpersonal issues, may benefit from psychotherapy. For severe depression with significant suicidal ideations, psychotic symptoms, or very significant interpersonal or professional dysfunction, therapy may serve the dual role of providing support and an opportunity to monitor progress. These are patients who may not be unstable enough to warrant inpatient treatment, but who may also be too sick to be safely monitored on a monthly basis.

Psychotherapy is also recommended for less depressed patients who report significant interpersonal problems, such as marital difficulties, parent or child conflicts, or past abuse. Even the most successful medication trial will not resolve these problems. Not addressing these issues amounts to ignoring important stressors that can negatively influence the patient's condition and may increase the risk of relapse or recurrence. There is ample room in biological of theories of depression to acknowledge, at a minimum, the aggravating effects of psychosocial issues on depressed patients. It is consistent, as well, with recent work suggesting that biological vulnerabilities and environmental stressors may interact in contributing to risk.

There has been discussion over the years about the advantages and disadvantages of dividing medication management and therapy between two individuals. The practical realities of our health care system dictate that the majority of depressed patients who are receiving both medication and therapy will have two mental health care providers: a psychiatrist or another physician prescribing and monitoring the medication trial and a non-physician therapist. Interdisciplinary collaboration, such as this, can be efficient and benefit patients (Keller et al., 2000).

RELAPSE PREVENTION

The importance of relapse prevention in the treatment of depression is well recognized. Over half of depressed patients will experience a recurrence of their depression (Angst, 1990). The risk of recurrence for patients with two episodes of depression is approximately 70% and after three episodes, this climbs to 90% (Kupfer, 1994). Given theses findings, it is reasonable to conceptualize depression as a chronic condition, or at least a recurrent one. This raises several questions. First, what can be done to predict and prevent relapse? Second, if prevention is possible, how can we identify appropriate candidates for maintenance treatment as a sizeable minority of patients do not experience a recurrence of symptoms after their initial episode of depression?

Until recently, little empirical evidence was available to answer the these questions. Two important studies speak to the efficacy of using maintenance medications to prevent the recurrence of depression. A three year prospective study of 128 patients with unipolar depression showed an impressive advantage for imipramine compared with placebo in preventing recurrences (Frank et al., 1990). A continuation of this study examined twenty patients who had remained free of depression in the imipramine arm of the study for three years, and randomized them to two more years of imipramine maintenance or placebo. Only one out of eleven patients on imipramine became depressed, whereas six out of nine patients in the placebo group relapsed (Kupfer et al., 1992). Although the overall number of patients in this study is relatively small, the data is statistically significant and the results make a powerful case for the usefulness of tricyclic antidepressants as an effective maintenance strategy. Shorter trials have yielded similarly encouraging results for four selective serotonin reuptake inhibitors as being effective in preventing recurrences of depression for one to two year periods. These include Fluoxetine (Montgomery et al., 1988), Sertraline (Doogan et al., 1992), Paroxetine (Montgomery & Dunbar, 1993), and Sertraline and Fluvoxamine (Franchini et al., 1997). Although additional studies are needed, these data suggest that using treatment doses of antidepressants for maintenance can be helpful in relapse prevention for major depression.

There is little research to guide us, however, in identifying appropriate candidates for maintenance treatment. With this in mind, a prudent clinical approach is to recommend indefinite maintenance treatment for all patients who have had three or more episodes of depression, or who have experienced a rapid return of symptoms when medications have been reduced or discontinued. Maintenance treatment is also recommended for patients who have had two or more episodes of depression where severe suicidal ideation has been present, or when a serious suicide attempt has occurred. Maintenance treatment after a single severe episode may be considered when the patient requests every possible advantage of not having to experience depression again, especially if there is a family history of affective illness.

ADDITIONAL INFORMATION DESIRED

Helpful additional information for treating Nancy would include an accurate time course of her psychiatric symptoms since adolescence, ideally from a collateral source. It would also be helpful to know if she experienced seasonal variations in her mood or a cyclicity of symptoms. A cycling of mood would be suggestive of a bipolar affective disorder. Information from her spouse or from other family members would be useful for assessing a history of hypomanic or manic symptoms, as she might recall a euphoric period as "normal" or simply a "good period" in her life if there were no negative personal or social consequences from it. Finally, given her family history of psychosis, it would be helpful to more carefully assess her lifetime history of psychotic symptoms. All of these areas of inquiry directly impact the best medication strategy and would assist in confirming the diagnosis and refining the treatment program.

SUMMARY AND DISCUSSION

The goal of this chapter has been to provide a practical discussion of the psychopharmacology of depression for mental health professionals. A "person oriented" approach to medication management integrating a rigorous syndromal diagnostic evaluation with careful attention to each individual's psychosocial circumstances and personal values is recommended. The importance of beginning with an assessment of risk, including an evaluation of depression, anxiety, pessimism, and suicidality is emphasized. The value of addressing symptoms of anxiety, panic, psychosis, mania, and active alcohol or drug abuse were discussed. The emergence of the selective serotonin reuptake inhibitors as an accepted first line choice of antidepressants was reviewed. The importance of maintaining a close and trusting therapeutic relationship was emphasized throughout, as were the special challenges this presents for the psychopharmacologist. Finally, the section on relapse prevention focused on the importance of conceptualizing depression as a chronic or recurring illness. As noted, there is a small but promising literature on the use of antidepressant medications as a prophylactic strategy.

There are several important issues which may effect the way in which we approach the treatment of depressed patients during the years ahead. These include an increasing appreciation of gender differences in the treatment of depression, the relationship between cardiovascular disease and depression, and the growing popularity of herbal treatments.

Gender differences in vulnerability for depression have been recognized for some time. The heightened prevalence of depressive disorders among women places a special burden on all professionals who care for women. The widely recognized post-partum vulnerability for affective disorders deserves special mention, as does the recognition of premenstrual dysphoric disorder (PMDD) as a legitimate condition (Endicott, 2000). It appears that selective serotonin reuptake inhibitors may be more effective than other classes of antidepressants in treating this disorder (Steiner et al., 2000). There may also be gender differences in the effectiveness of specific medications. An interesting prospective study comparing Sertraline with Imipramine, for example, suggested that chronically depressed women were more likely to respond favorably to a SSRI, whereas men showed a preferential response to a Tricyclic medication. When the women were subdivided by menopausal status, premenopausal women responded more strongly to Sertraline, whereas the postmenopausal had similar rates of response to both medications (Kornstein et al., 2000).

With the aging of our population and the resulting increase in the burden of cardiovascular disease in society, the emerging relationship between coronary artery disease and depression is an important new area of study. Several recent studies indicate that there is an increased risk of depression among patients who manifest an acute coronary syndrome. The risk of developing depression after a myocardial infarction is greater than 20% (Forrester et al., 1992). Moreover, the presence of clinical depression was found to be as an independent predictor of death in post myocardial infarction patients. The presence of depression quadrupled the risk of death among these patients and was found to be as powerful a negative prognostic indicator as left ventricular dysfunction, the accepted predictor of long term outcomes in cardiology (Frasure-Smith et al., 1993).

How can we account for the observed relationship between depression and cardiac death risk after noncompliance and suicide have been accounted for? The possibility exists that peripheral serotonin levels may be implicated in risk of clotting. One study found that an SSRI, Paroxetine, may exert an antithrombotic effect among depressed patients after a myocardial infarction (Pollock et al., 2000). Although additional studies are needed, these findings suggest that the serotonin reuptake inhibitors may emerge as the antidepressant of choice for depressed patients with coronary heart disease—they may benefit both the heart and the mind.

Finally, there has been a recent increase in the popularity of herbal treatments and other alternative remedies in health care. Several "natural" remedies are touted for the relief of various symptoms, including Kava-Kava for anxiety and St. John's Wort for depression (Wong et al., 1998). Although some of these treatments may be found to be effective, many will not. An ongoing NIMH sponsored prospective trial is comparing an SSRI with St. John's Wort for the treatment of depression. Regardless of efficacy, however, many of these treatments may have interactions with psychiatric medications and tomorrow's psychopharmacologist will need to be aware of what psychoactive agents their patients are consuming. One pointed example is the risk of a very dangerous serotonergic syndrome when SSRIs are combined with St. John's Wort. Whatever one's opinions about this minimally regulated industry, a growing familiarity with these agents and a willingness to discuss all treatment options is necessary to prescribe medications in a safe and responsible manner.

In summary, medications can be effective in alleviating emotional distress, including severe depression. They offer a means of assisting another human being afflicted with a debilitating illness and allow hope to return, after the dark cloud of depression has lifted.

REFERENCES

Angst, J. (1990). Natural history and epidemiology of depression. In J. Cobb & N. Goeting (Eds.), *Results of community studies in prediction and treatment of recurrent depression* (pp. 121–154). Southampton, England: Duphar Medical Relations.

Amsterdam, J. D., Hooper, M. B., & Amchin, J. (1998). Once-versus twice-daily venlafaxine therapy in major depression: A randomized, double-blind study. *Journal of Clinical Psychiatry, 59,* 236–240.

Asberg, M., Thoren, P., Traskman, L., Bertilsson, L., & Ringberger, V. (1976). "Serotonin depression"—A biochemical subgroup within the affective disorders? *Science, 191,* 478–483.

Baxter, L., Phelps, M., Mazziotta, J., Schwartz, J., Gerner, R., Selin, C., & Sumida, R. (1985). Cerebral metabolic rates for glucose in mood disorders studied with positron emission tomography (PET and (F-18)-fluoro-2-deoxyglucose (FDG). *Archives of General Psychiatry, 42,* 441–447.

Baxter, L., Schwartz, J., Phelps, M., Mazziotta, J., Guze, B., Selin, C., Gerner, R., & Sumida, R. (1989). Reduction of prefrontal cortex glucose metabolism common to three types of depression. *Archives of General Psychiatry, 46,* 243–250.

Beasley, C., Dornseif, B., Bosomworth, J., Sayler, M., Rampey, A., Heiligenstein, J., Thompson, V., Murphy, D., & Masica, D. (1991). Fluoxetine and suicide: A meta-analysis of controlled trials of treatment for depression. *British Medical Journal, 303*(6804), 685–692.

Beck, A., Steer, R., & Garbin, M. (1988). Psychometric properties of the Beck Depression Inventory: Twenty-five years of evaluation. *Clinical Psychology Review, 8*, 77–100.

Berman, R., Narasimhan, M., Sanacora, G., Miano, A., Hoffman, R., Hu, X., Charney, D., & Boutros, N. (2000). A randomized clinical trial of repetitive transcranial magnetic stimulation in the treatment of major depression. *Biological Psychiatry, 47*, 332–337.

Bertelson, A., Harvald, B., & Hauge, M. (1977). A Danish twin study of manic depressive disorders. *British Journal of Psychiatry, 130*, 330–351.

Bulik, C. M., Carpenter, L. L., & Kupfer, D. V. (1990). Features associated with suicide attempts in recurrent major depression. *Journal of Affective Disorders, 18*, 29–37.

Cade, J. (1949). Lithium salts in the treatment of psychotic excitement. *Medical Journal Aust, 36*, 349–352.

Crane, G. (1956). The psychiatric side-effect of Iproniazid. *American Journal of Psychiatry, 112*, 494–501.

Cuscak, B., Nelson, A., & Richelson, E. (1994). Binding of antidepressants to human brain receptors: Focus on newer generation compounds. *Psychopharmacology, 114*, 559–565.

Davidson, R. (1992). Anterior cerebral asymmetry and the nature of emotion. *Brain and Cognition, 20*, 125–151.

Davidson, R. (1993). Childhood temperament and cerebral asymmetry: A neurobiological substrate of behavioral inhibition. In K. Rubin & J. Asendorpf (Eds.), *Social withdrawal, inhibition, and shyness in children* (pp. 31–48). Hillsdale, NJ: Erlbaum.

Davidson, R. (1998). Affective style and affective disorders: Perspectives from affective neuroscience. *Cognition and Emotion, 12*, 307–330.

Davis, R., & Wilde, M. (1995). Mirtazapine: A review of its pharmacology and therapeutic potential in the management of major depression. *CNS Drugs, 5*, 389–402.

Delay, J., & Deniker, P. (1952). Trente-huit cas de psychoses traitees par la cure prolongee et continue de 4560 RP. Le Congres des Medicins Alienistes et Neurologistes de France, Vol 50. In Compte redu du Congres. Paris, Masson et Cie.

DeRubeis, R., Gelfand, L., Tang, T., & Simons, A. (1999). Medications versus cognitive behavior therapy for severely depressed outpatients: Mega-analysis of four randomized comparisons. *American Journal of Psychiatry, 156*, 1007–1013.

Doogan, D., & Caillard, V. (1992). Sertraline in the prevention of depression. *British Journal of Psychiatry, 160*, 217–222.

Downig, R. W., & Rickels, K. (1973). Predictors of response to amitriptyline and placebo in three outpatient treatment settings. *Journal of Nervous and Mental Disease, 156,* 109–129.

Endicott, J. (2000). History, evolution and diagnosis of Premenstrual Dysphoric Disorder. *Journal of Clinical Psychiatry, 61*(Suppl. 12), 5–8.

Fawcett, J., Scheftner, W. A., Fogg, L., Clark, D. C., Young, M. A., Hedeker, D., & Gibbons, R. (1990). Time related predictors of suicide in major affective disorder. *American Journal of Psychiatry, 147,* 1189–1194.

Feighner, J., Gardner, E. A., Johnson, J. A., Batey, S. R., Khayrallah, M. A., Ascher, J. A., & Lineberry, C. G. (1991). Double-blind comparison of bupropion and fluoxetine in depressed outpatients. *Journal of Clinical Psychiatry, 52,* 329–355.

Feighner, J. P., Cohn, J. B., Fabre, L. F., Jr., Fieve, R. R., Mendels, J., Shrivastava, R. K., & Dunbar, G. C. (1993). A study comparing paroxetine, placebo and imipramine in depressed patients. *Journal of Affective Disorders, 28,* 71–79.

Feighner, J., Targum, S. D., Bennett, M. E., Roberts, D. L., Kensler, T. T., Damico, M. F., & Hardy, S. A. (1998). A double-blind, placebo controlled trial of Nefazodone in the treatment of patients hospitalized for major depression. *Journal of Clinical Psychiatry, 59,* 246–253.

Forrester, A. W., Lipsey, J. R., Teitelbaum, M. L., DePaulo, J. R., Andrzejewski, P. L., & Robinson, R. G. (1992). Depression following myocardial infarction. *International Journal of Psychiatry and Medicine, 22,* 33–46.

Franchini, L., Gasperini, M., Perez, J., Smeraldi, E., & Zanardi, R. (1997). A double-blind study of long-term treatment with sertraline or fluvoxamine for prevention of highly recurrent unipolar depression. *Journal of Clinical Psychiatry, 58,* 104–107.

Frank, E., Kupfer, D. J., Perel, J. M., Cornes, C., Jarrett, D. B., Mallinger, A. G., Thase, M. E., McEachran, A. B., & Grochocinski, V. J. (1990). Three-year outcomes for maintenance therapies in recurrent depression. *Archives of General Psychiatry, 47,* 1093–1099.

Frasure-Smith, N., Lesperance, F., & Talajic, M. (1993). Depression following myocardial infarction. *Journal of the American Medical Association, 270,* 1819–1825.

Glowinski, J., & Axelrod, J. (1964). Inhibition of uptake of tritiated noradrenaline in the intact rat brain by imipramine and structurally related compounds. *Nature, 204,* 1318–1319.

Hamilton, M. (1960). A rating scale for depression. *Journal of Neurology, Neurosurgery, and Psychiatry, 23,* 56–62.

Hollister, L. E. (1992) Antidepressant agents. In B. G. Katzung (Ed.), *Basic and clinical pharmacology* (5th ed.). Norwalk, CT: Appleton & Lange.

Keller, M., Klerman, G., Lavori, P., Coryell, W., Endicott, J., & Taylor, J. (1984). Long-term outcome of episodes of major depression: Clinical and public health significance. *Journal of the American Medical Association, 252,* 788–792.

Keller, M. B., McCullough, J. P., Klein, D. N., Arnow, B., Dunner, D. L., Gelenberg, A. J., Markowitz, J. C., Nemeroff, C. B., Russell, J. M., Thase, M. E., Trivedi, M. H., & Zajecka, J. (2000). A comparison of Nefazodone, the cognitive behavioral-analysis system of psychotherapy, and their combination for the treatment of chronic depression. *New England Journal of Medicine, 342,* 1462–1470.

Kendler, K., Neale, M., Kessler, R., Heath, A., & Eaves, L. (1992). A population-based twin study of major depression in women. The impact of varying definitions of illness. *Archives of General Psychiatry, 49,* 257–266.

Kendler, K. S., Pedersen, N., Johnson, L., Neale, M. C., & Mathe, A. A. (1993). A pilot Swedish twin study of affective illness, including hospital- and population-ascertained subsamples. *Archives of General Psychiatry, 50,* 699–706.

Kornstein, S. G., Schatzberg, A. F., Thase, M. E., Yonkers, K. A., McCullough, J. P., Keitner, G. I., Gelenberg, A. J., Davis, S. M., Harrison, W. M., & Keller, M. B. (2000). Gender Differences in Treatment Response to Sertraline Versus Imipramine in Chronic Depression. *American Journal of Psychiatry, 157,* 1445–1452.

Kuhn, R. (1970). The imipramine story. In F. J. Ayd & B. Blackwell (Eds.), *Discoveries in biological psychiatry* (pp. 205–217). Philadelphia: J. B. Lippincott.

Kupfer, D. (1994). Recurrent depression: Prevention of a lifelong disorder. Depression. Special Report. pp. 29–35.

Kupfer, D. J., Frank, E., Perel, J. M., Cornes, C., Mallainger, A. G., Thase, M. E., McEachran, A. B., & Grochocinski, V. J. (1992). Five-year outcome for maintenance therapies in recurrent depression. *Archives of General Psychiatry, 49*(10), 769–773.

Lai, T., Payne, M., Byrum, C., Steffens, D., & Krishnan, K. (2000). Reduction of orbital frontal cortex volume in geriatric depression. *Biological Psychiatry, 48,* 971–975.

Lin, E., Von Korff, M., Katon, W., Bush, T., Simon, G., Walker, E., & Robinson, P. (1995). The role of the primary care physician in patient's adherence to antidepressant therapy. *Medical Care, 33,* 67–74.

Linden, M., Gothe, H., Dittmann, R. W., & Schaaf, B. (2000). Early termination of antidepressant drug treatment. *Journal of Clinical Psychopharmacology, 205,* 497–519.

Loomer, H., Saunders, J., & Kline, N. (1958). A clinical and pharmacodynamic evaluation of iproniazid as a psychic energizer (Psychiatric Research Report No. 8). Washington, DC: American Psychiatric Association, pp. 129–141.

McGrath, P. J., Stewart, J. W., Janal, M. N., Petkova, E., Quitkin, R. M., & Klein, D. F. (2000). A placebo-controlled study of fluoxetine versus imipramine in the acute treatment of atypical depression. *American Journal of Psychiatry, 157,* 344–350.

Mendlewicz, J. (1988). Genetics of depression and mania. In A. Georgotas & R. Cancro (Eds.), *Depression and mania.* New York: Elsevier.

Montgomery, S., Dufour, H., Brion, S., Gailledreau, J., Laqueille, X., Ferrey, G., Moron, P., Parant-Lucena, N., Singer, L., & Danion, J. (1988). The prophylactic efficacy of fluoxetine in unipolar depression. *British Journal of Psychiatry, 153*(Suppl. 3), 69–76.

Montgomery, S. A., & Dunbar, G. (1993). Paroxetine is better than placebo in relapse prevention and the prophylaxis of recurrent depression. *International Clinical Psychopharmacology, 8*(3), 189–195.

Musselman, D. L., Debattista, C., Nathan, K. I., Kilts, C. K., Schatzberg, A. F., & Nemeroff, C. B. (1998). Biology of mood disorders. In A. F. Schatzberg & C. B. Nemeroff (Eds.), *The American Psychiatric Press Textbook of Psychopharmacology* (2nd ed., pp. 549–588). The American Psychiatric Press, Inc.

Nierenberger, A. A., Keck, P. E., Jr., & Samson, J. (1991). Methodological considerations for the study of treatment-resistant depression. In J. D. Amsterdam (Ed.), *Advances in neuropsychiatry and psychopharmacology* (Vol. 2, pp. 1–12). Refractory Depression. New York: Raven.

Panksepp, J. (2000). Emotions as natural kinds within the mammalian brain. In M. Lewis & J. Haviland-Jones (Eds.), *Handbook of emotions* (2nd ed.). New York: Guilford.

Pollock, B. G., Laghrissi-Thode, F., & Wagner, W. R. (2000). Evaluation of platelet activation in depressed patients with ischemic heart disease after paroxetine and nortriptyline treatment. *Journal of Clinical Psychopharmacology, 20,* 137–140.

Robinson, R., Kubos, K., Starr, L., Rao, K., & Price, T. (1984). Mood disorders in stroke patients. *Brain, 107,* 81–93.

Robinson, R., & Downhill, J. (1995). Lateralization of psychopathology in response to focal brain injury. In R. Davidson & K. Hugdahl (Eds.), *Brain asymmetry* (pp. 693–711). Cambridge, MA: MIT Press.

Robinson, R., Schultz, S., Castilla, C., Kopel, T., Kosier, J., Newman, R., Curdue, K., Petracca, G., & Starkestein, S. (2000). Nortriptyline versus fluoxetine in the treatment of depression and in short-term recovery after stroke: A placebo controlled, double-blind study. *American Journal of Psychiatry, 157,* 351–359.

Roose, S., Glassman, A., Attia, E., & Woodring, S. (1994). Comparative efficacy of selective serotonin reuptake inhibitors and tricyclics in the treatment of melancholia. *American Journal of Psychiatry,* *151*(12), 1735–1739.

Schatzberg, A. (2000). Pharmacologic mechanisms of antidepressant action. In M. B. Keller, R. M. Pinder chairs. The Role of Mirtazapine in the Pharmacotherapy of Depression. *Journal of Clinical Psychiatry,* *61,* 609–616.

Slaby, A. (1998). Outpatient management of suicidal patients. In B. Bonger, A. Berman, R. Maris, M. Silverman, E. Harris, & W. Packman (Eds.), *Risk management with suicidal patients.* New York: Guilford Press.

Smith, K. A., Fairburn, C. G., & Cowen, P. J. (1997). Relapse of depression after rapid depletion of tryptophan. *Lancet, 349,* 915–919.

Steffens, D. C., Byrum, C. E., McQuoid, D. R., Greenberg, D. L., Payne, M. E., Blitchington, T. F., MacFall, J. R., & Krishnan, K. R. (2000). Hippocampal volume in geriatric depression. *Biological Psychiatry, 48,* 301–309.

Steiner, M., & Pearlstein, T. (2000). Premenstrual Dysphoria and the Serotonin System: Pathophysiology and treatment. *Journal of Clinical Psychiatry, 61*(Suppl. 12), 17–21.

Sullivan, P., Neale, M., & Kendler, K. (2000). Genetic epidemiology of major depression: Review and meta-analysis. *American Journal of Psychiatry, 157,* 1552–1562.

Thase, M. E. (2000). Mood disorders: Neurobiology. In B. J. Sadock & V. A. Sadock (Eds.), *Kaplan & Sadocks comprehensive textbook of psychiatry* (7th ed.). William & Wilkins.

Thase, M. E., Friedman, E. S., Fasiczka, A. L., Berman, S. R., Frank, E., Nofzinger, E. A., & Reynolds, C. F., 3rd. (2000). Treatment of men with major depression: A comparison of sequential cohorts treated with either cognitive-behavioral therapy or newer generation antidepressants. *Journal of Clinical Psychiatry, 61,* 466–472.

Weissman, M. M., Gershon, E. S., Kidd, K. K., Kidd, K. K., Prusoff, B. A., Leckman, J. F., Dibble, E., Hamovit, J., Thompson, W. D., Pauls, D. L., & Guroff, J. J. (1984). Psychiatric disorders in the relatives of probands with affective disorders: The Yale University-National Institute of Mental Health Collaborative Study. *Archives of General Psychiatry, 41,* 13–21.

Wong, A. H. C., Smith, M., & Boon, H. S. (1998). Herbal remedies in psychiatric practice. *Archives of General Psychiatry, 55,* 1033–1044.

SUGGESTED READINGS

Janicak, P. G., Davis, J. M., Preskorn, S. H., & Ayd, F. J. (Eds.). (1997). *Principles and practice of psychopharmacotherapy* (2nd ed.). Williams & Wilkins.

Kaplan & Sadock's Comprehensive Textbook of Psychiatry Sadock BJ, Sadock VA
    (2000) (Eds.) 7th ed. Lippincott Williams & Wilkins.
Kandel, E. (2000). Disorders of mood: Depression, mania and anxiety
    disorders (Chapter 61). In E. Kandel, J. Schwartz, & T. Jessell (Eds.),
    Principles of neural science (4th ed.). Elsevier Science Publishing Co.
Schulberg, H. C., Katon, W. J., Simon, G. E., & Rush, A. J. (1999). Best
    clinical practice: Guidelines for managing major depression in primary
    medical care. *Journal of Clinical Psychiatry, 60*(Suppl. 7), 19–26.

17

Comparative Treatments of Depression: Entering the Zen Garden

Mark A. Reinecke and Michael R. Davison

There stands, in Kyoto, a 16th century Buddhist temple. Behind the temple is a formal garden. Like many traditional Japanese gardens, it is at the same time simple and elegant in form. It contains several clusters of three to four stones, each surrounded by a raked sand bed. Given the size of the garden, however, it is not possible to view each of the clusters simultaneously. To take in all of the rocks one must move. One must take a number of vantage points. As you step through the garden, different perspectives become available. Moving, however, requires us to relinquish one perspective in order to gain another. So it is with our understanding of human development and adaptation. This volume represents an effort to explore human depression and its treatment. As the contributors to this volume ably demonstrate, a range of perspectives on depression and its treatment are available.

In reflecting upon these models we must acknowledge that any attempt to view them simultaneously entails both a challenge and a risk. There is a challenge inherent in attempting to grasp the conceptual and technical nuances of several perspectives simultaneously. It can be difficult to fully and deeply understand alternative perspectives without offering favor to one. It can also be challenging to appreciate the factors that guide and support a clinical theorist's commitment to a specific perspective. There is risk, as such, in any attempt to integrate or synthesize alternative models. Inasmuch as the assumptions made by alternative models vary greatly, attempts to integrate them may lead us to overlook essential components of one or more of the perspectives. At the same time, it is worth noting that an appreciation of one model can offer insight into another. Psychodynamic formulations of unconscious motivation, for example, can inform attempts by cognitive-behavioral and schema-focused psychotherapists who use metaphors derived from information-processing theory to understand nonconscious thought.

In order to make sense of these alternative models it may be helpful to impose a structure or framework upon them. As we have noted, there are a number of conceptual and technical differences between the models and these can be described along a series of dimensions. Taken together, these dimensions provide us with a typology for comparing and contrasting alternative perspectives, and may make our walk through the garden more meaningful.

As noted at the outset, psychotherapy may be defined as a trusting interpersonal relationship in which developmental, social, and intrapsychic factors associated with personal distress are explored. It is a process between two individuals leading to the examination of old meanings and the creation of new ones. Most clinicians would accept that positive outcomes stem from the additive effects of common or nonspecific factors and theory-specific interventions. As we have seen, forms of psychotherapy differ dramatically both in the ways in which they conceptualize depression and in the proposed technologies of change. How can we make sense of these differences? There are at least three dimensions along which alternative forms of treatment can vary. These include (1) the relative structure or organization of the therapy; (2) the emphasis placed upon intrapsychic versus environmental mediators; and (3) the emphasis placed on insight versus skill acquisition.

THE STRUCTURE OF THERAPY

Psychotherapy sessions vary from highly directive and didactic to nondirective and supportive. There is a great deal of variability in the degree to which therapists impose a structure or organization onto the therapeutic process. At one end of the continuum are highly structured forms of psychotherapy, such as behavioral therapy, cognitive therapy, and schema-focused psychotherapy. Sessions are typically organized, and attempt to follow a problem-focused agenda. At the other end of the spectrum are nondirective forms of psychotherapy, including person-centered and self-psychological approaches. An emphasis is placed, from these perspectives, on allowing the patient to determine the pace and focus of the materials discussed. It is worth acknowledging, however, that all forms of therapy recognize the importance of providing a supportive structure for maintaining the stability of depressed patients. All forms of therapy impose a structure upon the therapeutic interaction. Differences, then, center on how explicit the therapist is in his or her attempts to guide the treatment process, and in how flexible he or she is in response to a patient's attempts to redirect the therapy session. In practice, all forms of therapy are inherently flexible. Good therapists, regardless of orientation, are responsive to the needs of their patients— they attempt to provide structure, guidance and support in ways which facilitate the development of their client. Therapeutic flexibility and responsiveness—the ability to maintain a strategic focus while responding to the immediate needs of the patient—may, in fact, facilitate clinical improvement.

INTRAPSYCHIC VERSUS ENVIRONMENTAL CHANGE

A second dimension along which models of psychotherapy vary is the relative emphasis placed on the importance of intrapsychic versus environmental factors in understanding depression and its treatment. As we have seen, research indicates that a number of biological, developmental, social, environmental, cognitive, behavioral and intrapsychic variables are associated with risk for depression. Models differ in the relative emphasis given to each, and in the ways in which they account for their interaction. Several theories of depression postulate, for example, that maladjustment stems from distortions, deficiencies, delays, or compromises in the development or functioning of internal mediating processes. Object relations, self-psychology, supportive-expressive, interpersonal, and schema-focused psychotherapy all assume that therapeutic interventions function by modifying, remediating, reorganizing, or developing these internal processes. In simple terms, these models postulate that the problem is not simply that something has happened in the past, but that its effects persist and the patient continues to act upon its sequelae or the conclusions drawn from it. Attempts are made, both directly and indirectly, to modify these internal processes.

At the other end of the continuum are traditional behavioral models, which assume that depression is mediated by stressful life events, reinforcement schedules, and availability of social support. As these are nonmediational models, little importance is given to assessing or changing internal processes. Mixed models, including cognitive therapy, RET, integrative psychotherapy, and newer forms of behavioral therapy, acknowledge that both intrapsychic and environmental factors play a role in clinical depression and explicitly attend to both sets of variables.

INSIGHT VERSUS SKILL ACQUISITION

The models discussed vary in the emphasis placed on insight as a mechanism of therapeutic change. They also vary in the importance placed on the role of the therapeutic relationship as a motor of clinical improvement. Psychodynamically oriented psychotherapies tend, as a group, to place a relatively greater emphasis on these factors than do cognitive and behavioral therapies. Although the importance of therapeutic interpretation and insight has been debated during recent years, the possibility exists that forms of insight may play a role in several forms of psychotherapy. Recent work suggests, for example, that "behavioral enactments"—the provision of a new experience relating to a problem, accompanied by strong affect, and resulting in the disconfirmation of expectations about the self and others that mediate the problem—may function as a common pathway for change in behavioral, psychodynamic and cognitive-behavioral psychotherapy (Arkowitz & Hannah, 1988).

It is worth acknowledging that insight and "enactment" are not synonymous. Several forms of therapy, including RET and behavior therapy, do not view the development of insight as necessary or sufficient for behavioral or emotional change. Rather, they view depression as stemming from either cognitive or behavioral skill deficits. They endeavor, through modeling, practice, and reinforcement, to develop these skills. Not surprisingly, these forms of psychotherapy tend, as a group, to be structured and psychoeducational in nature. Moreover, they tend to focus on the ways in which these factors function in the here-and-now, rather than on explicating their developmental antecedents.

Along the same lines, therapeutic models vary in the extent to which they view abreaction—the open expression of emotion—as a prerequisite for therapeutic improvement. Psychoanalytic and supportive-expressive therapies, for example, encourage the free expression of negative affect. Cognitive and schema-focused psychotherapy, in contrast, view depression as stemming from the activation of maladaptive beliefs and from deficits in the development of affect regulation skills. From this perspective, the regular expression of negative affect may be contraindicated as it may lead to the lowering of thresholds for activation of depressogenic schema. Attempts are made, with this in mind, to develop patients' affect regulation skills and to encourage the redeployment of attention away from depressing events and thoughts.

TECHNICAL DIFFERENCES IN PSYCHOTHERAPY FOR DEPRESSION

There are differences between alternative models of treatment in the form and organization of the therapy itself. At its most basic level, models differ in the importance given to identifying and pursuing specific treatment goals. Problem-focused treatments, including behavior therapy, cognitive therapy, interpersonal psychotherapy, and schema-focused psychotherapy, for example, explicitly attempt to alleviate depressive symptomatology. Other approaches, including psychodynamic and psychoanalytically informed psychotherapy, however, focus upon the development of insight and an internal sense of coherence or authenticity. A positive outcome, for them, is not measured by depression inventories, clinician ratings or semistructured diagnostic interviews. There are, then, important differences in the dependent variables used to define the effectiveness of alternative models.

Not surprisingly, alternative models also differ with regard to the importance of objective diagnosis and the assessment of symptom severity. Once again, problem-focused forms of therapy emphasize the value of diagnosis and objective assessment, whereas psychodynamic, integrative, and person-centered approaches eschew the use of diagnostic instruments and formal assessment. An emphasis is placed, from their perspective, on developing a phenomenological understanding of the patient and their experiences. It is worth noting that cognitive-constructivist models of psychotherapy tend, as a group, to adopt a centrist stance (Neimeyer & Mahoney, 1995). While acknowledging the value of objective diagnosis and assessment, they recognize that there are no simple or accepted criteria for determining the validity of an individual's experience. They acknowledge the very personal nature of the individual's experiences and narratives, and the ways in which these are embedded in larger familial, social, and cultural frameworks.

A number of attempts have been made to identify patient characteristics that predict a positive response to treatment. Not surprisingly, many of the variables identified are theory-based. That is to say, the variables identified typically are congruent with the treatment approach being used. Patient variables found to be predictive of a positive outcome include (among other things) ego strength, neuroticism, verbal information-processing ability, ability to develop a trusting therapeutic alliance, positive response to trial interpretation or analysis, presence of a personality disorder, ability to identify and label emotions, ability to identify thoughts, reflective insight, IQ, SES, and the ability to identify a focal problem. It is a broad list and, at a minimum, suggests that response to treatment may be predicted by a range of patient, therapist, and environmental factors Interestingly, the possibility exists that different variables may predict response to different forms of treatment.

Alternative forms of treatment differ, as well, in the emphasis placed on case formulation for guiding the selection of specific interventions. As we have seen, cognitive, supportive-expressive, and interpersonal psychotherapies are highly prescriptive in that they attempt to identify specific cognitive, behavioral, social, and intrapsychic factors that may be contributing to an individual's distress, and then introduce interventions designed to ameliorate these deficits. Other forms of psychotherapy, including self-psychology and object relations approaches tend, in general, to be less prescriptive in their approach. Attempts are made to elicit affect, integrate current problems with past experiences, facilitate speech, point out defensive maneuvers, and identify recurrent interpersonal patterns as they occur in the transference relationship. In the broad sense, the technical approach to therapy does not vary depending upon the specific deficits of the patient.

THE EFFECTIVENESS OF TREATMENT

Given these differences between models, what can be said of their relative effectiveness? Research completed over the past 20 years indicates that psychotherapy and medications can be effective in alleviating clinical depression (Reid, Balis, & Sutton, 1997). Although a sizable percentage of clinicians believe that major forms of therapy are equally effective (Smith & Glass, 1977), this has not been supported by recent study (Nathan & Gorman, 1998). Rather, controlled outcome studies suggest that specific forms of treatment tend to be more effective for specific disorders. Although reassuring to patients who are seeking relief from their distress, these findings have not escaped criticism.

Research demonstrating the efficacy of specific interventions has led scholars, health care management organizations and public policy analysts to propose that "empirically supported treatments" should be accepted as a standard of care for clinically depressed patients. Cognitive therapy and interpersonal psychotherapy have fared well in controlled outcome studies, and research indicates that they may have enduring effects not found with other approaches. For mildly to moderately depressed outpatients, these forms of psychotherapy appear to be as effective as tricyclic and SSRI antidepressant medications in alleviating acute depressive symptoms. SSRI medications, cognitive therapy, and interpersonal psychotherapy appear to stand, at this time, as the treatments of choice for major depression among adults.

Although the results of controlled outcome studies have been reasonably clear and consistent, attempts to develop guidelines for the treatment of depression based upon the empirical literature has been vigorously debated (Addis, 1997; Chambless & Hollon, 1998; Fensterheim & Raw, 1996; Nathan, 1998; Silverman, 1996; Strosahl, 1998; Wilson, 1998). Inasmuch as empirically supported treatments have tended to place a greater emphasis on symptom reduction, rather than on the development of insight or a sense of personal coherence, an argument can be made that their success owes as much to the selection of the outcome variable as to the treatment itself. Concerns have also been raised that manual-based interventions are, by definition, inflexible and so may not meet patients' needs. These criticisms, however, are not entirely justified. If patients are seeking treatment for clinically significant depression, symptom reduction would seem to be a reasonable and appropriate objective. Moreover, there is no evidence that the use of empirically supported forms of psychotherapy compromise the quality of the therapeutic relationship or the ability of the therapist to tailor treatments to meet their patients' needs. To be sure, the relationship between therapeutic alliance and outcome is in need of further study, and treatment manuals should include a thorough discussion of the role of a positive therapeutic relationship and how it can be developed. It is important, as well, to avoid unnecessary distinctions between technical and nonspecific aspects of therapy—both appear to be related to treatment response.

This is not to say, however, that clinicians should focus only upon symptom reduction. John Maynard Keynes once noted that the goal of economics was to help mankind to "live wisely, agreeably, and well." He was suggesting that the science of economics should have a larger goal than maintaining economic stability and growth. It should attend to the general well-being of man as much as to specific economic markers. So it is with psychiatry and clinical psychology. Although symptom reduction *is* an important and appropriate therapeutic goal, it is not the only goal. General life functioning—the social, spiritual, and vocational adjustment of our patients—are affected by depression and are worthy of attention. Moreover, this should not imply that only those interventions which have been empirically validated are effective. The lack of empirical support for several widely used models of psychotherapy should serve as an impetus to refine these approaches and to document their usefulness.

Criticisms have rightly been made about the ecological validity of outcome studies supporting the efficacy of many forms of treatment. Given the highly selected samples used and the tightly controlled nature of clinical trials, it has been suggested that manualized treatment protocols may not be effective for treating patients seen in general outpatient settings. Comorbidity, compliance, patient acceptability, and the availability of these treatments remain important concerns. Although initial findings are promising (Persons, Bostrom, & Bertagnolli, 2000), the effectiveness of many forms of treatment in community settings has not yet been demonstrated. Further research on the ways in which these treatments can be used with a broader range of depressed individuals is clearly needed. Along similar lines, little is known about the long-term stability of treatment gains, or about the effectiveness of combined psychotherapy and pharmacotherapy for treating depression.

SUMMARY AND FUTURE DIRECTIONS

We began our summary in the Japanese garden. The garden's meaning is apparent in the contradiction of attempting to apprehend the whole and its parts at any one time. There are a limitless number of alternative perspectives possible for understanding human development and adaptation, and for conceptualizing and treating depression. The perspective one adopts, and the assumptions one implicitly makes, will influence one's understanding of depression and its treatment. Although these assumptions are accepted as fundamental givens or truths, the case can be made that they should be opened to explication, examination, and review.

Depression is an illness with a high prevalence and serious morbidity. Epidemiological evidence indicates that depression is the world's most common mental disorder, and that its incidence is increasing (World Health Organization, 1998, 1999). Studies indicate that depressive episodes tend to recur and that depressed individuals experience high levels of distress and disability during these episodes. Although various forms of psychotherapy and medication are effective in alleviating clinical depression, a number of concerns and difficulties remain. Existing treatments are not effective in all cases, and comorbidity, recurrence, and relapse remain important concerns. Our understanding of the etiology of depression is incomplete, and our ability to prevent its onset is limited. Given these concerns, additional study is clearly needed. A number of conceptual and strategic difficulties will need to be addressed, however, in order for progress to be made. Shortcomings in the literature include a relative lack of attention to (1) the effectiveness of pharmacological and psychotherapeutic interventions in community settings; (2) the ways in which biological and psychosocial factors interact over time in contributing to vulnerability for depression; (3) long-term stability of gains; (4) the prediction of relapse/recurrence, and the effects of interventions on "general life functioning"; (5) the mechanisms of change in pharmacotherapy and psychotherapy and the identification of common pathways; (6) the effects of specific interventions on specific symptoms; (7) the definition of constructs within models and their construct validity; (8) the prediction of treatment response; (9) the identification of protective factors and moderator variables; (10) resilience and the normative development of affect regulation capacities; and (11) the ways in which cultural factors inform our models and interventions.

This final point is worthy of further comment. As Marsella (this volume) notes, cultural values and standards strongly influence the ways in which mood is understood and disturbances of mood are addressed. Cultural assumptions thoroughly infuse the ways in which we conceptualize human adaptation and development and the means by which we attempt to alleviate suffering. Cultural and ethnic factors may be related to depression, however, through a number of more direct means as well. Cultural factors may, for example, effect the availability of social support provided to individuals who have suffered a loss and the ways in which they are encouraged to think about their distress. Associated factors, including cultural cohesion, minority status within a larger community, acculturation, socioeconomic status, and the availability of community resources may also play a role. The relationship of these factors to the onset of depression, the ways in which it is experienced by individuals and their families, and the effectiveness of various treatments has received little consideration. It is likely that cultural factors contribute to differences in the content, expression, and course of mood disorders. Moreover, vulnerability factors for depression may be influenced by the cultural context in which social, emotional, and cognitive development occurs. Finally, it is worth acknowledging that the relevance and usefulness of contemporary models and interventions for individuals from different cultural backgrounds have rarely been explored. The relationships between culture, adaptation, vulnerability and mood are, no doubt, quite complex. They are deserving of careful attention.

The contributors to this text have presented a range of perspectives on development, mood, adaptation, and the process of clinical change. The chapters provide a useful overview of the current literature along with recommendations for clinical practice. As the reader will note, we have come a long way from descriptive studies of depressive psychopathology and case-report or open-trial outcome research. We must now address more difficult questions regarding etiology, the prediction of clinical course, and the processes of therapeutic change. A developmental emphasis, with attention given to the ways in which risk and resilience factors (both biological and psychosocial) interact over time in contributing to vulnerability for depression is needed. These lines of inquiry may lead us to question the validity of current diagnostic schemes, classification systems, and our very understanding of mood and adaptation. We will want to more fully understand dimensional risk factors as they function among both normal and at-risk individuals, as well as social and cultural factors which influence human development. This will allow us to chart the origins of clinical depression and to develop effective prevention programs.

Although this was designed as a clinical book and offers the reader practical guidelines for treating depressed adults, our goal was, in fact, somewhat larger. We hope, by juxtaposing alternative models and interventions, to provide a framework for comparing and contrasting conceptual models and to encourage reflection upon their relative strengths and weaknesses. This will allow clinicians to make an informed choice about which interventions to use and how to use them. More importantly, we hope that this volume will stimulate further research and clinical innovation.

REFERENCES

Addis, M. (1997). Evaluating the treatment manual as a means of disseminating empirically validated psychotherapies. *Clinical Psychology: Science and Practice, 4,* 1–11.

Arkowitz, H., & Hannah, M. (1988). Cognitive, behavioral, and psychodynamic therapies: Converging or diverging pathways to change? In A. Freeman, K. Simon, L. Beutler, & H. Arkowitz (Eds.), *Comprehensive handbook of cognitive therapy.* New York: Plenum Press.

Chambless, D., & Hollon, S. (1998). Defining empirically supported therapies. *Journal of Consulting and Clinical Psychology, 66,* 7–18.

Fensterheim, H., & Raw, S. (1996). Psychotherapy research is not psychotherapy practice. *Clinical Psychology: Science and Practice, 3,* 168–171.

Nathan, P. (1998). Practice guidelines: Not yet ideal. *American Psychologist, 53,* 290–299.

Nathan, P., & Gorman, J. (Eds.) (1998). *A guide to treatments that work.* New York: Oxford University Press.

Neimeyer, R., & Mahoney, M. (Eds.) (1995). *Constructivism in psychotherapy.* Washington, DC: American Psychological Association.

Persons, J., Bostrom, A., & Bertagnolli, A. (1999). Results of randomized controlled trials of cognitive therapy for depression generalize to private practice. *Cognitive Therapy and Research, 23,* 535–548.

Reid, W., Balis, G., & Sutton, B. (1997). *The treatment of psychiatric disorders* (3rd ed.). Bristol, PA: Bruner-Mazel.

Silverman, W. (1996). Cookbooks, manuals, and paint-by-numbers: Psychotherapy in the 90's. *Psychotherapy, 33,* 207–215.

Smith, M., & Glass, G. (1977). Meta-analysis of psychotherapy outcome studies. *American Psychologist, 32,* 752–760.

Strosahl, K. (1998). The dissemination of manual-based psychotherapies in managed care: Promises, problems, and prospects. *Clinical Psychology: Science and Practice, 5,* 382–386.

Wilson, G. (1998). Manual-based treatment and clinical practice. *Clinical Psychology: Science and Practice, 5,* 363–375.

World Health Organization (1999). World Health Report, 1999. Making a difference. Geneva: WHO.

Appendix

SUMMARY OF MODEL

1. Individual Psychology

Based upon neo-analytic work by Adler, Dreikurs, and others, individual psychology proposes that persons function as an indivisible whole, and that there is a fundamental need for persons to function as part of a larger community. Depression, from this perspective, is seen as stemming from the adoption of a maladaptive "lifestyle" as a means of resolving longstanding feelings of inferiority. The thoughts of depressed individuals are characterized by criticism and distrust, in conjunction with a "hesitant" attitude toward others and a decrease in social interest.

2. Object Relations

Based on early work by Fairbairn, Klein, Thompson, Bowlby, Winnicott, and Stern, relational models of psychoanalysis focus upon mental representations of objects, the relationship of the self to the world of inner objects, and the reenactment of this inner world in interpersonal relationships and fantasies about relationships. Depression is seen as stemming from fundamental disturbances in early relationships leading to a "burial of the self" and the lack of an "authentic self experience." Clinical improvement stems not only from information provided by the therapist, but from the experience of a reparative therapeutic relationship.

3. Self-Psychology

Based upon work by Kohut, self-psychology proposes that maintaining a sense of a cohesive and authentic self is a primary aim of development and that depression stems from narcissistic rage that occurs in response to actual or anticipated disruptions in the self experience.

4. Supportive-Expressive Psychodynamic Therapy

Based upon work by Luborsky, supportive-expressive psychodynamic therapy proposes that individuals reenact core conflictual relationship themes and that clinical improvement occurs by providing the individual with an opportunity to understand and change these patterns in the context of a supportive, empathic therapeutic relationship.

5. Behavioral Therapy

Based upon operant and social learning theories, depression is viewed as stemming from a decrease in available reinforcement, a loss of response contingent reinforcement, or a decrease in the ability to perceive and appreciate available reinforcers.

6. Rational-Emotive Behavior Therapy

Based on work by Ellis, REBT postulates that depression stems from distortions in thinking, including the activation of specific cognitive biases, which lead to the development of a self-critical, judgmental cognitive set.

7. Cognitive Therapies

Based on work by Beck, Abramson, Lewinsohn, Rehm, Meichenbaum, Seligman, Gotlib, and others, cognitive therapy posits that depression stems from the interaction of learned cognitive vulnerabilities (e.g., maladaptive beliefs, cognitive distortions, negativistic schema, sociotropic personality style, attributional style, problem-solving deficits) and personally-relevant stressful life events. Perceptual and memory biases contribute to a consolidation of negative beliefs and attitudes about the self, others, and the future.

8. Schema-Focused Therapy

Based upon work by Young, schema-focused therapy proposes that depression stems from the activation of latent maladaptive early schema or tacit beliefs. Active attempts are made to provide patients with experiences that modify these beliefs.

9. Interpersonal Psychotherapy

IPT theory does not make strong statements about the etiology of depression. Based upon work by Klerman, Weissman, Moreau, Frank, Mufson, Markowitz, and others, IPT proposes that relationships exist between depression and difficulties in social relationships, and that depressed mood perpetuates and exacerbates these difficulties through a cycle of interpersonal friction and withdrawal. IPT endeavors to alleviate depression by clarifying relationship difficulties, educating patients about the effects of their mood and behavior on their relationships, developing more effective communication skills, and improving their ability to manage interpersonal problems.

10. Couple and Family Therapy

There are a number of distinct models of marital and family therapy, including psychodynamic, behavioral, functional, experiential, strategic, structural, systemic, intergenerational-contextual, family of origin, and cognitive-behavioral. They tend, as a group, to focus upon intrapsychic, developmental, and interpersonal dynamics as they are reflected in family relationships. They differ with regard to the relative emphasis placed on each of these factors. Depression, from a cognitive-behavioral family therapy perspective (as described in this volume), is seen as stemming from interpersonal conflict, deficits in effective communication, and reduced support.

11. Integrative Psychotherapy

Borrowing from several schools of thought, integrative psychotherapy proposes that depression is multiply determined, and that individuals may vary with regard to factors that underlie and maintain their distress. Attempts are made to select interventions based upon the needs of the individual patient, their readiness for change, and the severity of their difficulties.

12. Psychopharmacology

From this perspective, depression is viewed as a medical illness with a biological substrate. Biological and environmental factors interact to produce specific symptoms. The monoamine hypothesis of depression posits that abnormalities in the metabolism and utilization of norepinephrine, serotonin, and dopamine underlie depression, and that these difficulties stem from a combination of genetic and developmental factors. Contemporary genetic models explicitly acknowledge that gene activation may be mediated by psychosocial events.

THERAPIST SKILLS AND ATTRIBUTES

1. Individual Psychology

Adler remarked that the first rule of treatment is to win the full confidence of the patient, and that the second is to not worry about therapeutic success. The therapist serves, from this perspective, as an active co-participant in the treatment and provides patients with insights that will allow them to examine and change their mistaken style of life. The therapist acts to "reeducate" the patient in the "art of living."

2. Object Relations

The therapist attempts to maintain an analytic attitude, characterized by genuine interest in the patient and the creation of a secure, nonjudgmental therapeutic relationship. Therapists maintain an attitude of objective distance and are aware of both transferential and countertransferential reactions. Therapists frame the therapeutic interaction, identify patterns of relating as they occur, and determine their adaptive or defensive function. They should be self-aware and able to tolerate strong negative transferential reactions without losing judgment or objectivity.

3. Self-Psychology

Therapists encourage patients to acknowledge distressing thoughts, feelings, fantasies, and defensive maneuvers that have been out of conscious awareness. They listen attentively to what is said and unsaid, and interpret this in the context of the patient-therapist relationship. As is characteristic of other forms of psychodynamic psychotherapy, the therapist attempts to maintain an attitude of objective distance and is aware of both transferential and countertransferential reactions. They should be self-aware and able to tolerate strong negative transferential reactions without losing judgment or objectivity.

4. Supportive-Expressive Psychodynamic Therapy

The therapist listens attentively to what is said and unsaid, and comments upon recurrent patterns in important relationships. These may be interpreted in the context of the patient-therapist relationship as a means of identifying core conflictual relationship themes. As is characteristic of other forms of psychodynamic psychotherapy, the therapist maintains an attitude of objective distance and is aware of both transferential and countertransferential reactions. He or she should be self-aware and able to tolerate strong negative transferential reactions without losing judgment or objectivity.

5. Behavioral Therapy

The behavioral therapist adopts an active therapeutic stance and guides the patient in developing specific behavioral skills. The relationship is similar in many ways to that of a coach or mentor. This is balanced by the ability to maintain an empathic, supportive rapport.

6. Rational-Emotive Behavior Therapy

The rational-emotive behavior therapist adopts an active therapeutic stance and guides the patient in developing specific cognitive and behavioral skills. The relationship is similar in many ways to that of a coach or mentor, and can be quite directive. This is balanced by the ability to maintain an empathic, supportive rapport.

7. Cognitive Therapies

Nonspecific therapist factors (including warmth, accurate empathy, therapeutic responsiveness, and genuineness) appear to be associated with a positive response to CBT. It has been suggested, as well, that an understanding of philosophy of science and facility in Socratic questioning may be helpful. Studies have found an association between homework completion and improvement in CBT. With this in mind, cognitive therapists encourage the completion of homework between sessions. The ability to provide a parsimonious rationale for the treatment and to quickly address negative reactions toward the therapist that may interfere with compliance are essential. Psychological mindedness and interest in actively assisting patients are also associated with positive outcomes.

8. Schema-Focused Therapy

Little research has been completed on therapist factors associated with clinical improvement in schema therapy. Inasmuch as schema therapy and CBT are technically similar, it is reasonable to assume that therapist variables associated with improvement in CBT may also predict a positive response to schema therapy. With this in mind, warmth, empathy, and the ability to establish a trusting rapport, as well as the ability to provide a parsimonious rationale and active support for completing homework assignments may be helpful.

9. Interpersonal Psychotherapy

Attempts to empirically identify therapist characteristics that are associated with a positive patient response to IPT have not yielded replicable results. It has been suggested that the ability to quickly identify interpersonal patterns, as well as nonspecific therapist factors (including warmth, accurate empathy, and genuineness) can be helpful.

10. Couple and Family Therapy

Therapist characteristics and the nature of the therapeutic stance vary depending on the specific form of family or marital therapy being used. The psychodynamic marital therapist, for example, attempts to provide a supportive holding environment that will allow for re-parenting of the family. The systemic marital therapist, in contrast, adopts a technically "neutral" stance, and allows family members to assume responsibility for change. Structural family therapists typically adopt a more authoritative stance and actively attempt to subvert ongoing interaction patterns as a means of facilitating change. Finally, cognitive-behavioral marital therapists maintain a "collaborative" stance, and serve as a consultant or coach in the development of cognitive and behavioral skills.

11. Integrative Psychotherapy

As the therapist's stance will vary with the patient's stage of readiness for change, technical flexibility and a sensitivity to the nuances of patient's motivation are essential. Integrative psychotherapists recognize that it is neither possible nor desirable to be perfect role models for their patients. With this in mind, tolerance for ambiguity and patience with oneself are highly desirable. An understanding of processes of change and a practical knowledge of how one can assist clients to move from contemplation of change to action are critical.

12. Psychopharmacology

A sound understanding of psychopharmacology and the ability to establish a trusting therapeutic rapport are essential. As difficulties with medication noncompliance are not uncommon, an ability to engage patients and to encourage them to continue with their medication trials can be quite helpful.

ASSESSMENT

1. Individual Psychology

The primary method of assessment is the Life Style Assessment Interview. Objective self-report rating scales are not typically used and referrals for psychological testing are relatively uncommon. A lifestyle analysis examines family-of-origin issues, early recollections, early trauma or feelings of inferiority, and the influence of birth order.

2. Object Relations

The primary method of assessment is the clinical interview. Objective self-report rating scales are not used and referrals for psychological testing are relatively uncommon. Material presented during therapy sessions is used to elucidate etiological and dynamic factors that may be contributing to the patient's distress.

3. Self-Psychology

The primary method of assessment is the clinical interview. Objective self-report rating scales are not used and referrals for psychological testing are relatively uncommon. Material presented during therapy sessions is used to elucidate etiological and dynamic factors that may be contributing to the patient's distress.

4. Supportive-Expressive Psychodynamic Therapy

As in other forms of psychodynamic psychotherapy, the primary method of assessment is the clinical interview. Objective self-report rating scales are not typically used and referrals for psychological testing are relatively uncommon. Material presented during therapy sessions is used to elucidate etiological and dynamic factors that may be contributing to the patient's distress. Particular attention is paid to recurrent relationship themes.

5. Behavioral Therapy

Objective self-report and clinician ratings of mood are used in conjunction with observations of patient behavior in natural settings. Functional analyses of specific behaviors are completed.

6. Rational-Emotive Behavior Therapy

Objective self-report and clinician ratings of mood and cognitive processes are used in conjunction with observations of patient behavior in natural settings. Particular attention is paid to the assessment of cognitive distortions and negative thoughts.

7. Cognitive Therapies

Objective self-report and clinician ratings of mood and cognitive processes are used in conjunction with observations of patient behavior in natural settings. Whereas functional analyses of specific behaviors are completed, these often include a consideration of thoughts occurring before, during, and after distressing events. Particular attention is paid to the assessment of automatic thoughts, cognitive distortions, schema, attributional style, sociotropy and autonomy, and rational problem-solving skills. Objective measures of personal beliefs and information processing styles (e.g., DAS, YBSQ, CBQ, ATQ, SAS, PSI, ASQ) may be used. The use of objective rating scales is balanced by an assessment of subjective meanings attached to events in the individual's life.

8. Schema-Focused Therapy

As in cognitive therapy, objective self-report ratings of mood and cognitive processes are used. Particular attention is paid to the assessment of maladaptive early schema and schema processes. The use of objective rating scales, such as the Schema Questionnaire and the Dysfunctional Attitudes Scale, is balanced by careful attention to subjective meanings attached to events in the individual's life.

9. Interpersonal Psychotherapy

Clinical interviews are often used to make a diagnosis and to determine the level of psychosocial functioning. When available, information is sought from multiple informants. Objective self-report and clinician ratings of mood may be used. Particular attention is paid to reviewing significant relationships and life events associated with feelings of depression.

10. Couple and Family Therapy

As there are a number of schools of marital and family therapy, approaches to assessment tend to vary with the modality being used. Cognitive-behavioral family therapy (as described in this volume) uses objective and subjective assessment techniques to examine environmental, cognitive, and social contributions to the family's distress. The learning histories of family members are explored, and factors that may be maintaining maladaptive interaction patterns are examined. Particular attention is paid to understanding each family member's beliefs, attitudes, attributions, expectations, values, goals, and standards as they relate to conflict in the home.

11. Integrative Psychotherapy

The patient's diagnosis, symptom severity, coping style, level of resistance, level of arousal, social supports, and readiness for change are evaluated. A flexible approach to assessment—using clinical interviews, observations, and objective or subjective measures—is used depending upon the needs and resources of the individual patient.

12. Psychopharmacology

Given the importance of making an accurate and reliable diagnosis, clinical interviews are often used to make a diagnosis and to determine the level of psychosocial functioning. Semi-structured diagnostic instruments, such as the SCID or the DIGS, may be employed. A careful review of symptoms and medical history is completed. Objective self-report and clinician ratings of mood (e.g., BDI, CES-D, HRSD) may be used to determine symptom severity and to monitor progress.

GOALS

1. Individual Psychology

Symptom reduction is accomplished through the cultivation of feelings of social interest, confronting superiority strivings (and the underlying feelings of inferiority), relinquishing mistaken "lifestyle" or "life lie," and developing a more adaptive lifestyle.

2. Object Relations

Symptom reduction is not an explicit goal of treatment. Rather, an emphasis is placed upon developing insight and an authentic self-experience. Depression is viewed as both a symptom and an expression of a "buried self." Depression stems, as such, from the arrest of self-realization due to unconscious anxiety regarding possible abandonment by others. With this in mind, a primary goal is the realization of one's potential by acting upon authentically experienced emotions, beliefs, and values. Following Fairbairn, therapy serves to support the development of individuals from absolute dependence on others to a "mature dependence" characterized by a balance of intimacy and autonomy. It is helpful to assist the patient in achieving a deeper understanding of conscious and unconscious motivations, their self, their relationships with others, and recurrent patterns in their lives.

3. Self-Psychology

Symptom reduction is not an explicit goal of treatment. Rather, an emphasis is placed upon developing insight. Therapeutic improvement requires that dysfunctional intrapsychic structures be changed and that compensatory structures be developed.

4. Supportive-Expressive Psychodynamic Therapy

Develop insight into intrapsychic factors contributing to depression, including core conflictual relationship themes. Symptom reduction may or may not be an explicit goal of treatment.

5. Behavioral Therapy

Develop behavioral skills, including social skills and problem-solving; increase frequency of reinforcement. Rapid symptom reduction is an explicit goal.

6. Rational-Emotive Behavior Therapy

Alleviate cognitive distortions; encourage self-acceptance. Rapid symptom reduction is an explicit goal.

7. Cognitive Therapies

Reduce depression by alleviating cognitive distortions and maladaptive schema, improving social skills and social problem-solving abilities, decreasing self-focused attention and rumination, and encouraging participation in enjoyable and rewarding activities. Short-term goals include developing the patient's ability to monitor their mood on an ongoing basis, setting clear goals, identifying negative thoughts associated with depression, and addressing maladaptive expectations, attributions, and distortions. Rapid symptom reduction is an explicit goal.

8. Schema-Focused Therapy

Alleviate depression by changing maladaptive tacit beliefs about the self, relationships with others, and the world. Rapid symptom reduction is an explicit goal. Attempts are made to change core schemas and underlying beliefs as a means of reducing risk of relapse.

9. Interpersonal Psychotherapy

Alleviate depression by changing maladaptive patterns of social interaction. Rapid symptom reduction is an explicit goal.

10. Couple and Family Therapy

Alleviate depression by changing maladaptive patterns of interaction with family members. Direct attempts are made to reduce conflict and criticism, improve communication, and to develop a more supportive and affectionate relationship. Differences between family members with regard to goals, attributions, standards, expectations, values, and beliefs are discussed.

11. Integrative Psychotherapy

Rapid symptom reduction is an explicit goal.

12. Psychopharmacology

Alleviate depression by rectifying neurochemical or metabolic dysregulation. Rapid symptom reduction is an explicit goal.

TIMELINE FOR TREATMENT

1. Individual Psychology

The length of treatment in individual psychotherapy is variable, and depends on the motivation and resources of the patient. Symptomatic improvement is anticipated within 3 months.

2. Object Relations

Long-term.

3. Self-Psychology

Long-term.

4. Supportive-Expressive Psychodynamic Therapy

Moderate to long-term. Treatment is focused and time-limited.

5. Behavioral Therapy

Relatively brief.

6. Rational-Emotive Behavior Therapy

Relatively brief. Symptomatic improvement is typically achieved within 12–15 weeks.

7. Cognitive Therapies

Relatively brief. Symptomatic improvement is typically achieved within 12–15 weeks.

8. Schema-Focused Therapy

Brief to moderate in duration. Symptomatic improvement is typically achieved within 12–15 weeks. Schema-focused work may continue for several months after this point depending upon the needs of the individual patient.

9. Interpersonal Psychotherapy

Relatively brief. Symptomatic improvement is typically achieved within 12–15 weeks.

10. Couple and Family Therapy

Variable depending upon the needs of the family and the model of marital and family therapy used.

11. Integrative Psychotherapy

Although integrative psychotherapy is problem-focused and strategic, it is difficult to predict the duration of therapy in advance. Duration is determined by both the patient's readiness for change and the severity of the difficulties to be resolved.

12. Psychopharmacology

Relatively brief. Weekly to biweekly medication management sessions, becoming less frequent as symptoms remit. Maintenance medications are typically prescribed for a minimum of 6 to 12 months. A reduction of depressive symptoms typically occurs within 4–6 weeks.

THERAPEUTIC RELATIONSHIP

1. Individual Psychology

A hopeful, supportive, and professional stance is advocated. The therapist is active, interested, noncritical, reliable, and confident. The therapist accepts the clients' statements in a friendly manner, and focuses upon the exploration of the patient's lifestyle. Although therapists avoid offering advice prematurely, they are open and direct in addressing procedural questions. Whereas the therapist assiduously avoids comments that may lead the patient to feel inferior, an attitude of "assured disdain" is used to skillfully debase the patient's maladaptive lifestyle.

2. Object Relations

A neutral, nondirective analytic attitude is maintained. The development of transference reactions is encouraged as a means of providing the patient with insight into underlying motivations and defensive maneuvers. The therapist listens empathically by attempting to develop a transient, partial identification with the patient such that they are able to cognitively and affectively apprehend the patient's phenomenological experience.

3. Self-Psychology

A neutral, nondirective analytic attitude is maintained. The development of transference reactions is encouraged as a means of providing the patient with insight into underlying motivations and defensive maneuvers. The therapist listens empathically by attempting to develop a transient, partial identification with the patient such that he or she is able to cognitively and affectively apprehend the patient's phenomenological experience. An empathic failure occurs when a significant self-object, such as a parent or the therapist, does not respond in the affective way that the patient wished or needed. Both therapeutic resistance and negative transference reactions are viewed, from this perspective, as reflecting an empathic failure. Resistance stems from a lack of emotional attunement by the therapist; whereas a negative transference reflects the activation of empathic failures with early self-objects, such as parents.

4. Supportive-Expressive Psychodynamic Therapy

As in other forms of psychodynamic psychotherapy, a neutral, nondirective analytic attitude is maintained.

5. Behavioral Therapy

A relatively directive therapeutic rapport is maintained. Treatment is active, problem-focused, and psychoeducational. The therapist adopts the stance of a coach or mentor.

6. Rational-Emotive Behavior Therapy

A "collaborative" therapeutic rapport is maintained. Treatment is active, problem-focused, and psychoeducational. An empathic therapeutic rapport is viewed as necessary but not sufficient for behavioral and emotional change. The therapeutic relationship does not have a direct curative effect.

7. Cognitive Therapies

A "collaborative" rapport is maintained. Treatment is active, problem-focused, and psychoeducational. Transference issues are quickly identified and addressed as negative reactions within the therapy session that may interfere with the development of a collaborative rapport. An empathic therapeutic rapport is viewed as necessary but not sufficient for behavioral and emotional change. The therapeutic relationship may not have a direct curative effect.

8. Schema-Focused Therapy

A "collaborative" therapeutic rapport is maintained. Treatment is active, problem-focused, and psychoeducational. Transference issues are directly identified and addressed. The therapeutic relationship is used to provide "limited reparenting" as a means of modifying maladaptive tacit beliefs.

9. Interpersonal Psychotherapy

Interpersonal therapists attempt to maintain an honest, open, and trusting relationship. The relationship is directive, active, and psychoeducational. The therapist and client work collaboratively to support the patient's engagement in problem identification, formulation and clarifying feelings. The therapist's reactions to the patient are used to understand the patient's interpersonal difficulties. Negative transference issues are quickly addressed. Attempts are made to limit the development of a transference relationship with the therapist.

10. Couple and Family Therapy

The therapeutic stance adopted depends on the model of marital and family therapy used. In many cases, an active and supportive therapeutic rapport is maintained. Attempts are made to equitably and evenly attend to each member of the family.

11. Integrative Psychotherapy

The nature of the therapeutic relationship in integrative psychotherapy varies with the stage of treatment. With patients in the early "precontemplative stage" the therapist will be active, supportive, encouraging, and nurturant. They attempt to identify with the patient's ambivalence or defensiveness and to join with them in understanding their hesitancy about treatment. As the patient progresses into the "contemplative" stage, the therapist becomes somewhat more passive, nondirective, and Socratic. As treatment progresses, the therapist adopts the role of an experienced coach or mentor, helping patients to refine their approach to solving life problems. As termination approaches, the therapist serves as a consultant, providing the patient with an increasing amount of autonomy and latitude.

12. Psychopharmacology

An empathic and supportive doctor-patient relationship is maintained.

TECHNIQUES AND INTERVENTIONS

1. Individual Psychology

Therapeutic questions are used to develop insight and to encourage a rethinking of the patient's lifestyle. Social activity is encouraged. The therapist pursues three goals: (1) understanding events from the patient's perspective; (2) developing a formulation of the patient's difficulties; and (3) instructing the patient in the features of his or her lifestyle. Identifying key components of a mistaken lifestyle implies the alternative, corrective action. Through a process of "comparison," the therapist directly attempts to identify possible goals or functions of actions. Events, attitudes, and handicaps from the patient's past are then examined to understand the etiology of the lifestyle prototype. Early recollections are discussed and dreams (viewed as reflecting goals and frustrations) are examined. Specific techniques, referred to as "gamesmanship tactics," are used to encourage the development of social interest and to develop insight.

2. Object Relations

An emphasis is placed on understanding and interpreting projective and introjective identifications as they occur within the therapy session. Patterns of interaction with family members are identified and examined.

Interpretation of transference and countertransference reactions are the primary technique. As the focus is on the interaction between the therapist and the patient, it is difficult to prescribe specific techniques. An attempt is made to strike a balance between that which is comfortable and secure, and that which challenges the patient to a new understanding. Empathy, supportive statements, and mirroring, for example, may be used to join with the patient and to develop a supportive rapport. Questioning, challenging, reframing, and interpreting may be used to create an emotional distance or separation within the therapeutic relationship and to support the development of insight.

3. Self-Psychology

The development of empathy—an accurate cognitive and affective understanding of another's experience—is essential. This understanding must be communicated, then interpreted. As change occurs only in the context of a therapeutic relationship that is sufficiently supportive to sustain a selfobject transference, interpretations are not directed toward addressing distortions, misperceptions, or irrational beliefs. Rather, an emphasis is placed on understanding the context in which the emotion or behavior occurred. The therapist remains acceptant, tolerant, and empathically attuned to the patient throughout the process. Reorganization and building of intrapsychic structures occurs through a process of "transmuting internalization" such that the patient develops a more coherent and integrated sense of self.

4. Supportive-Expressive Psychodynamic Therapy

Identification and interpretation of core conflictual relationship themes (CCRT's) in "relationship episodes" (RE) are the primary techniques used. RE's have three components: a wish, a response from others, and a response from the self. These are interpreted in the context of (1) the patient's current relationships, (2) their past relationships, and (3) the therapeutic relationship. Relatively little emphasis is placed on the interpretation of drives, instinctual wishes, or defenses.

5. Behavioral Therapy

A functional analysis of cues and reinforcers of specific behaviors may be completed. Adaptive behaviors are modeled, practiced, and reinforced.

Problem-solving skills are taught, and direct attempts are made to increase the quality, number, and range of reinforcers in the patient's life.

6. Rational-Emotive Behavior Therapy

Cognitive and behavioral interventions, including rational disputation and behavioral homework assignments, are used to reduce perfectionism, alleviate self-critical beliefs, encourage social activity, and discourage rumination. An emphasis is placed on providing the patient with perceptions of efficacy or control over their emotions. Patients are encouraged to recognize their choice and responsibility for their emotional reactions to events.

7. Cognitive Therapies

A range of interventions designed to change thoughts and behaviors are introduced. These may include mood monitoring, pleasant activity scheduling, mastery and pleasure scheduling, dysfunctional thought record, rational responding, assertiveness training, adaptive self-statements, relaxation training, social skills training, and a developmental analysis of maladaptive schema.

8. Schema-Focused Therapy

Rational and experiential techniques are used to modify early maladaptive schemas. Specific techniques used include psychoeducational interventions (e.g., bibliotherapy), rational disputation, life review (a developmental examination of experiences that are inconsistent with tacit beliefs), schema dialogue, schema flashcards, guided imagery, behavioral pattern breaking, behavioral homework assignments, and an exploration of the ways that schemas are reflected in the therapeutic relationship.

9. Interpersonal Psychotherapy

Patients are explicitly encouraged to adopt a sick role. Psychoeducational approaches are introduced to teach patients about relationships between interpersonal processes and depression, and their role in treatment. A formulation is developed and shared with the patient as a treatment contract. Recurring relationship patterns are identified and direct attempts are made to develop more effective social behaviors. Specific social skills, for example, may be practiced, and patients are encouraged to discuss their expectations for their relationships. Nonreciprocal expectations and assumptions are identified and attempts are made to negotiate a resolution of them. Communication and affect regulation skills are practiced. Particular attention is paid to (1) role disputes, (2) role transitions, and (3) interpersonal deficits.

10. Couple and Family Therapy

Interventions vary depending upon the specific model of marital and family therapy used. Cognitive-behavioral family therapy (as described in this volume) endeavors to identify and change maladaptive behavioral, cognitive, and emotional response patterns that may be based upon family of origin experiences. Particular attention is paid to reciprocal negative interactions between family members. The therapist serves as a coach or mentor in modeling, practicing, and reinforcing new patterns of interacting. Depending upon the needs of family members, a focus may be placed on developing communications skills, affect regulation skills, and family problem-solving. The expression of support and affection is encouraged; whereas critical, demanding statements are discouraged. Cognitive restructuring techniques may be used to change maladaptive beliefs, attributions, expectations, and standards that are contributing to distress.

11. Integrative Psychotherapy

Techniques and interventions are selected based upon the patient's stage of readiness for change and the "level" of problem to be addressed (i.e., situational problem, specific symptoms, maladaptive beliefs or cognitions, interpersonal conflict, family or systems conflict, intrapsychic conflict). Initial interventions are typically at the symptom or situational level. Matching of the intervention to the patient's stage of readiness and level of problem is seen as essential for maintaining a therapeutic rapport.

12. Psychopharmacology

Selection of appropriate medication based upon the patient's symptom profile, medical history, and preferences. Side effects are monitored and medications are augmented with other agents as needed.

MECHANISMS OF CHANGE

1. Individual Psychology

Insight is the primary mechanism of change in IP. Social feelings are established through therapeutic insight and intellectual means. They are cultivated by conscious intellectual effort, and by direct attempts to meet and to develop a sincere interest in others. Therapy, as such, is viewed as a process of "re-education" in living. The therapist serves as a nurturant maternal figure, allowing the patient to develop an empathic bond that can be transferred to others. The therapeutic relationship per se is *not* viewed as a vehicle of change. Rather, insight is the primary mechanism of cure. Transference is seen as a form of social interest. In a reworking of traditional psychodynamic views of transference, the IP therapist does not focus upon negative transference reactions by the patient toward the therapist. Rather, the IP therapist attempts to transfer "healthy features" of the therapeutic relationship into the lifestyle of the patient.

2. Object Relations

The therapeutic relationship and insight are viewed as the primary mechanisms of change. The relative importance of insight and relationship factors may vary depending on the nature and severity of the patient's difficulties.

3. Self-Psychology

Kohut argued that the therapy relationship is therapeutic in its own right, and that interpretations facilitate change indirectly by supporting the development of a therapeutic bond between the therapist and the patient. Change occurs through a two-step process of understanding (empathy) and interpretation.

4. Supportive-Expressive Psychodynamic Therapy

Three factors are believed to serve as mechanisms of change in supportive expressive psychotherapy: (1) the therapeutic relationship; (2) interpretation and insight; and (3) a deepening of experience. As in self psychology, the therapeutic relationship is believed to have a directly curative function (independent of insight).

5. Behavioral Therapy

Change occurs through the development of behavioral skills, and through an increase in rates of social and environmental reinforcement.

6. Rational-Emotive Behavior Therapy

Change occurs through rational disputation of cognitive distortions and biases, and through the alleviation of self-critical and perfectionistic self-statements and beliefs.

7. Cognitive Therapies

Clinical improvement is mediated by changes in maladaptive cognitive contents and information-processing strategies. This may involve changes in automatic thoughts, assumptions, schemas, attributions, goals, expectations, standards, attentional processes or problem-solving skills. Clinical improvement is predicted by quality of the therapeutic relationship, the use of specific techniques and strategies, and completion of homework.

8. Schema-Focused Therapy

Clinical improvement is believed to be mediated by changes in maladaptive early schema. Little research has examined processes of change in schema therapy.

9. Interpersonal Psychotherapy

Little research has examined processes of change in IPT. Clinical improvement is believed to be mediated by an improvement in social functioning and a reduction in psychosocial stress.

10. Couple and Family Therapy

The putative mechanism of change varies depending on the model of marital and family therapy used. In cognitive-behavioral marital therapy, clinical improvement is mediated by changes in maladaptive cognitive contents and information-processing strategies. These, in turn, are associated with improvements in communication, a reduction of aversive interactions, and an increase in social support.

11. Integrative Psychotherapy

The model does not presume that there is a single mechanism of change. Mechanisms of change may differ for different patients with similar symptom profiles. The provision of support, modeling, insight, and cognitive reframing may all play a role.

12. Psychopharmacology

Clinical improvement is believed to be associated with a normalization of neurotransmitter function and brain metabolism.

TERMINATION AND RELAPSE PREVENTION

1. Individual Psychology

Regular booster sessions would be scheduled and approaches for managing external stressors would be discussed.

2. Object Relations

Follow-up or booster sessions are not typically recommended. A return to treatment is possible should relapse occur.

3. Self-Psychology

Follow-up or booster sessions are not typically recommended. A return to treatment is possible should relapse occur.

4. Supportive-Expressive Psychodynamic Therapy

SE treatment is often supplemented by a booster phase. Sessions are scheduled at a rate of 1 per month for 3 months. Therapists provide support and encouragement, reinforce gains, and support the internalization of insights.

5. Behavioral Therapy

Relapse prevention is an integral part of behavior therapy. Behavior therapists acknowledge that generalization and maintenance of treatment gains requires explicit planning. Patients are encouraged to anticipate that setbacks *will* occur. Situations which may precipitate a relapse are identified, and adaptive coping strategies are modeled and reinforced. An "inoculation" paradigm may be used to reinforce effective coping. Regular booster sessions are scheduled.

6. Rational-Emotive Behavior Therapy

Relapse prevention is an integral part of REBT. Patients are encouraged to anticipate that setbacks *will* occur and to prepare for them. Regular booster sessions are scheduled.

7. Cognitive Therapies

Relapse prevention is an integral part of cognitive therapy. Patients are encouraged to distinguish momentary lapses from a relapse of their depression, and to anticipate that setbacks *will* occur. As setbacks are a normal part of life, it is important to maintain a sense of hope and a perception of personal efficacy in the face of adversity. Clients practice techniques for alleviating maladaptive attributions that may be made about negative events. A systematic review of the client's presenting concerns is completed, and techniques that have been helpful in alleviating them are discussed. Attempts are made to anticipate stressful life events and to develop social supports. Regular booster sessions are scheduled.

8. Schema-Focused Therapy

The schema-focused therapist attempts to prevent relapse by identifying and changing maladaptive early schema that may be activated in stressful situations, and by developing more effective schema coping strategies. Patients are encouraged to return to treatment for further sessions as necessary.

9. Interpersonal Psychotherapy

Research indicates that maintenance IPT sessions may have a prophylactic value in preventing recurrence of major depression. The conclusion of treatment is framed as a formal termination and follow-up sessions may be scheduled.

10. Couple and Family Therapy

Little research has been completed on maintenance of therapeutic gains after couples or family therapy. Given the observed relationships between social factors and risk for depression, marital and family therapy may itself be viewed as a means of reducing risk of relapse or recurrence. Booster sessions may be offered depending on the needs of the patient and their family. Strategies for reducing relapse may include addressing negative interaction patterns, maladaptive cognitions, and emotional responses to each other. Risk of relapse can be discussed, and family members can be taught skills for monitoring their interaction patterns. Direct attempts are made to develop feelings of support, family cohesion, and intimacy as a means of moderating the effects of stressful life events on family members.

11. Integrative Psychotherapy

Maintenance sessions are recommended when the problem is complex, associated with moderate or high levels of functional impairment, when consistent improvement is not achieved, and when a personality disorder is present. Coping skills training, insight-based approaches, and interpersonal techniques may be used.

12. Psychopharmacology

Maintenance medications are typically recommended for 4 months after the remission of symptoms as a means of preventing relapse. Medications are continued indefinitely for patients with a history of recurrent major depression as a means of preventing recurrence.

Index